Praise for BOB SPITZ'S

Dearie

"It's a revelation."   —Lev Grossman, *Time*

"Those with a hunger for all things Julia have a substantial new biography by Bob Spitz to sink their teeth into. . . . Author and subject almost become one, as Spitz channels the spirit of Child in his own words."
                                                   —*The Washington Post*

"[Spitz] reveals how [Child] helped redefine domesticity in the media age, transforming the way we cook, eat and think about food. . . . The book makes a strong case for Child as a 'cultural guerrilla' on par with Andy Warhol, Bob Dylan and Helen Gurley Brown."   —*Newsday*

"[An] enthusiastic, heroically researched biography. . . . Spitz goes beyond mere history and provides a full, human portrait of Julia."
                                                          —*The Economist*

"[A] mammoth, inspiring biography."   —*The Washington Times*

"A comprehensive and compelling biography . . . that also functions effectively as a history of twentieth-century American culture on topics ranging from the evolution of the O.S.S. to the quirks of public television."   —*The Christian Science Monitor*

"The most engaging celebrity biography we've read in years. . . . Spitz manages to convey the vigor, curiosity, confidence and booming voice of a truly *remarkable* woman as if she is sitting at the kitchen table with you. . . . [He] is a fantastic writer."   —*LA Weekly*

Bob Spitz

Dearie

The Remarkable Life of JULIA CHILD

Bob Spitz is the award-winning author of *The Beatles,* a *New York Times* bestseller, as well as seven other nonfiction books and a screenplay. He has represented Bruce Springsteen and Elton John in several capacities. His articles appear regularly in magazines and newspapers, including *The New York Times Magazine; The Washington Post; Rolling Stone;* and *O, The Oprah Magazine,* among others. He can be reached at dearie@ bobspitz.com.

www.bobspitz.com

ALSO BY BOB SPITZ

The Saucier's Apprentice
The Beatles: The Biography
Shoot Out the Lights
Dylan: A Biography
Barefoot in Babylon
The Making of Superstars

Yeah! Yeah! Yeah! (young adult)
The Silent Victim (screenplay)

Dearie

Lopaus Point, Maine, July 1951

Dearie

The Remarkable Life of
JULIA CHILD

Bob Spitz

Vintage Books
A Division of Random House, Inc.
New York

FIRST VINTAGE BOOKS EDITION, APRIL 2013

Copyright © 2012 by Bob Spitz

All rights reserved. Published in the United States by Vintage Books,
a division of Random House, Inc., New York, and in Canada by
Random House of Canada Limited, Toronto. Originally published
in hardcover in the United States by Alfred A. Knopf, a division of
Random House, Inc., New York, in 2012.

Vintage and colophon are registered trademarks of Random House, Inc.

The Library of Congress has cataloged the Knopf edition as follows:
Spitz, Bob.
Dearie : the remarkable life of Julia Child / by Bob Spitz.
p. cm.
Includes bibliographical references and index.
1. Child, Julia. 2. Cooks—France—Biography.
3. Cooks—United States—Biography. 4. Cooking, French. I. Title.
TX649.C47s65 2012
641.5095—dc23
[B] 2012019632

Vintage ISBN: 978-0-307-47341-7

Author photograph © Elena Seibert
Book design by Cassandra J. Pappas

www.vintagebooks.com

Printed in the United States of America
10 9 8 7 6 5 4 3 2 1

For my mother,

one of the earliest *French Chef* groupies,

and

all the mothers who gave up their casseroles

to follow Julia's teachings

Contents

Dearie

Paul tends to the star, on the set of *The French Chef*

Prologue

Boston, Massachusetts—February 1962

N
ow, dearie, I will require a hot plate for my appearance on Professor Duhamel's program."

Russ Morash, who had answered the telephone in a makeshift office he shared with the volunteers at WGBH-TV, was momentarily startled, not so much by the odd request as by the odder voice. It had a quality he'd never heard before—tortured and asthmatic, with an undulating lyrical register that spanned two octaves. A woman's voice? Yes, he thought, like a cross between Tallulah Bankhead and a slide whistle.

With brusque Yankee economy, Morash tried to decode the caller's m.o. "You want—*what?*"

"A hot plate, dearie, so I can make an omelet."

Doesn't that beat all, he thought. A hot plate! An omelet! What kind of a stunt was this gal trying to pull? Morash had worked at the station for a little under four years, and in that time he had heard his share of doozies, but they were workaday doozies, what you'd expect to hear at "Boston's Educational Television Station." The principal clarinetist for the symphony orchestra needed an emergency reed replacement, a beaker broke during a *Science Reporter* rehearsal, those were the tribulations that befell such an operation. But—a hot plate . . . and an omelet . . .

"Well, from my experience that's a first," Morash told the caller, "but I'll be happy to pass it on to Miffy Goodhart, when she gets in."

The twenty-seven-year-old Morash knew that commercial television was in remarkable ascendance; since the end of World War II, it had catered to an enormous, entertainment-starved audience that was hungry for distraction, and creative minds were struggling to feed the greedy beast. But educational TV—and WGBH, in particular—was a different creature altogether. Educational TV was an anomaly, a broadcasting stepchild in its infancy, still in the crawling phase, with no real road map for meaningful development. "We were kind of making it up as we went along," Morash says of an experiment that was barely six years old. "There was tremendous freedom in what we could put on the air." Still, there was nothing exciting about the programs on WGBH. Audiences were as scarce as scintillating programming. A scattering of viewers tuned in to watch Eleanor Roosevelt spar with a panel of wonks; fewer tuned in Friday evenings when a local character, jazz priest Father Norman J. O'Connor, introduced musical figures from the Boston area. Otherwise there were no hits to speak of, nothing to attract people to the smorgasbord of brainy fare. The station was licensed through the Lowell Institute to the cultural institutions of Boston: the museum, the libraries, and eleven universities, including Harvard, MIT, Tufts, Boston College, Boston University, and Brandeis. The educational backdrop was a fantastic resource. Each member of the Institute provided support, financial and otherwise. If one of them said, "Hey, we've got a great professor. Let's broadcast his lecture," that was enough to launch a new show.

Such was the case with Albert Duhamel—make that P. Albert Duhamel—one of Boston College's most lionized teachers. Duhamel was a man who loved books and their authors. A suave, strapping academic with a penchant for Harris tweed, he was addicted to the intellectual interplay that came from talking to writers about their work. Al was an author himself—his steamy *Rhetoric: Principles and Usage* was a campus blockbuster—and his show, *I've Been Reading,* was the tent pole of WGBH's Thursday-night lineup.

I've Been Reading was the forerunner to shows like *Fresh Air* and *Charlie Rose,* but in those days, with a budget based primarily on the host's pocket change, books on loan from his personal library, and no such thing as an author tour sponsored by a publisher, it was television—*educational* television—at the most basic level. Because the dirt-poor station shied from appearance fees, let alone train fare, the authors who appeared came mostly from the Boston area, and to make attracting them easier, guests were usually college colleagues—a noted economist or quantum physicist. Thus, in the words of one WGBH crew member, "The shows were dry as toast," but plans were afoot to inject a little jam into the equation.

Morash, who was familiar with the show's static format, realized that *I've Been Reading,* however tedious, served the greater good. For one thing, it was the only book-review show in Boston—this was long before the days when "breakfast television" would trot out authors five mornings a week—so there were no other outlets for writers promoting their work. And his neighbors, the university crowd, loved to read. *They loved to read.* They formed the show's small, faithful audience, creating buzz about any book that happened to catch their fancy.

The guest who had telephoned, Morash imagined, might just throw this gang a curve.

Later that day, when he caught up with Miffy Goodhart, he told her, "Miffy, you've got a hot one here this week. Some dame named Julia Child called, and she wants a *hot plate,* thank you very much. She says she'll bring all the other ingredients for—get this!—an *omelet.*"

Miffy wasn't the least bit surprised by this last detail. As assistant producer of *I've Been Reading,* she had conspired for some time to bring about a makeover to the show. It needed pizzazz, something to appeal to a wider spectrum of viewers, *younger,* more engaged viewers who looked beyond academia for their jollies. Politics, science, and literature were fine . . . in moderation, she thought. "But I was trying to lighten the mood and make it completely different," she recalls.*

Goodhart had been hearing about Julia Child and her "super new cookbook" for some time. For several months, in fact, word had buzzed around Cambridge that this cookbook sensation, *Mastering the Art of French Cooking,* offered a remarkable new take on food, and once that crowd got it in their bonnets that something had cachet—well . . . *look out!* . . . there was no way to stop the groundswell. This Cambridge set—they were called *Cantabrigians,* of all things—saw themselves as an extremely enlightened circle, a clique of wellborn WASPs who were slightly bohemian and slightly rebellious. If there was someone in their midst who could entice their wary eye, you could be sure the Cantabrigians would take notice and respond.

---

* Quotes framed in the present tense (e.g., he says, she recalls) are taken from the author's interviews. All other quotations, with a few exceptions, are from print sources cited in the notes.

That's what Miffy Goodhart was banking on when she booked Julia Child for a segment of *I've Been Reading*. All that week, Miffy awaited the Thursday-night broadcast with an eagerness that bordered on impatience. There had been something in this woman's voice that promised to shake up the eggheads. She'd felt it from the start, when they'd first talked on the phone. There was an energy, a spark, that conveyed a broader characteristic. Miffy tried to put her finger on it. Spirit? Spunk? No, more than that—a *joie de vivre* laced with mischief. "Making an omelet on TV didn't seem to confound Julia one scrap," Miffy recalls.

"It'll be *fun,* dearie!" Julia warbled. "We'll teach the professor a thing or two. Just watch."

LITTLE DID MIFFY Goodhart realize how much *fun* figured into Julia Child's universe. The revolutionary idea of linking fun with food was a pivotal component in a groundswell of social change that would not only reshape the way Americans ate but the way they lived, as well. When Julia first appeared on television, as the insatiable 1960s unfolded, the marriage of fun and food were light-years apart. Most households remained devoted to Jell-O molds, frozen vegetables, and tuna-noodle casseroles. Barbarous meat-and-potatoes families roamed the earth; Swanson's TV dinners were flying off supermarket shelves. Nothing on the menu spoke of well-made food and fun. Understanding how these elements eventually intersected goes toward understanding why the nation, at a crucial crossroads in its fast-moving history, anointed Julia Child its culinary messiah and beloved cultural icon. She was every bit a sixties superstar as Jackie Onassis or Walter Cronkite, whose personalities magnified the contributions they made. But unlike other luminaries fixed in the public eye, Julia gamely thrust a sense of humor into the mix. Cooking was fun for her, it was the shadow ingredient in every recipe in her repertoire, and she wanted everyone to experience it that way, too. This spirit was striking even in her youth. "I was sort of a comic," Julia recalled of her storybook childhood, a natural cut-up, "just normally nutty." As a young coed at Smith College, a roommate reflected that Julia "was almost too much fun," due to a mischievous streak that competed with her studies. And in her diary, where she dished with only sketchy regularity, Julia confessed to a weakness for "an unconscious wicked devilish goodness." But it took years—half a lifetime, in fact—to harness that behavior into her own unique expression. To master the art of cooking, French or otherwise, you first had to demystify the process, to not be intimidated by it, to be fearless, to plunge right in. Technique was essential, of course, but you had to find the pleasure in it. Without pleasure there was no payoff. The irrepressible reality of Julia Child was a combination of spontaneity, candor, and wit, which is why her passion for cooking bore unparalleled results. She not only brought fun headfirst into the modern American kitchen, a place that housewives equated with lifelong drudgery, but used it to launch public television into the spotlight, big-time.

NO ONE, THAT day in 1962, suspected the impact that Julia Child would have on their lives, not Russ Morash, who, with his wife, Marian, would be inextricably linked with her for the next thirty-five years, nor the suits at WGBH, which would become, thanks to Julia, a media colossus, one of the most influential producers of highbrow TV in the world and the platform for Julia's rise to prominence. That day, you could sense the droning boredom inherent to educational television. The set was woefully spare: two leather Harvard chairs, a coffee table, and a fake philodendron, nothing more. The crew, uninspired, went about business with monotonous languor. It was hard to get it up for two scholars discussing a book.

There was some confusion in the studio leading up to airtime. The cameraman for *I've Been Reading* apparently misheard the assignment. It sounded like the director said there would be ... a live demonstration. *Impossible!* This show was a walk-through, practically a paid night off. There was no rehearsal to speak of and, therefore, little for him to do. It was the same thing, week in, week out: two heads talking for a scant half hour. Since no one ever moved, the cameraman merely set up the shot and took a seat. Nothing to it.

But someone had gone and thrown a monkey wrench into the works. The guest actually *was* going to do a demonstration. On a book show, of all things! No rehearsal necessary; they'd go into it straightaway. And the camera set-up promised to be tricky. It was obvious the minute the guest walked in the door.

Julia Child wasn't your basic Cambridge housewife. She was huge— Bill Russell huge—the kind of person who filled a room. And larger than life: her square footage, swimming in a loose-fitting blouse and pleated skirt, seemed to expand as she swung herself along as if nothing in the natural world could contain her. She was a fair, russet-haired woman, already fifty, going soft in her waist, yet well-aligned, with fine-toned arms that suggested constant physical use. Her body from the side provided a glimpse of the curse imposed on middle-aged women, with their expanding torsos and athletic legs, which threw their symmetry off balance. At six foot three that aspect verged on anarchy. Most women that size and build appeared lumbering, gently clumsy. But there was an aristocratic self-possession in the way Julia carried herself, something solid, yet graceful, that gave her presence an assertive, irrefutable quality. Her size seemed like a tool she could use, like a car salesman with a grin, though she resisted turning it into an unfair advantage.

Whatever anxieties weighed on the cameraman when he learned there would be a demonstration, he could not have been prepared for the spectacle Julia created. He was clearly awestruck by her, pop-eyed and openmouthed. This impression was punctuated by the paraphernalia cradled in her arms. Framed under a bank of overhead spots, she stood in the middle of the studio clutching a ring burner, a long-handled pan, and a distended bag of groceries: ready to roll. In the coming years, that very image—Julia Child, poised and prepared, in a TV kitchen—became the iconic image of cooking in America. But in 1962, this was quite an odd scene. Cooking, like sex, was practiced privately—and, some might say, without much enthusiasm—in the home. Few gave the process much of a second thought. Preparing a delicious meal on TV, with an elaborate array of ingredients and specialized equipment, was unheard of, to say nothing of harebrained. The notion of Julia lumbering about in front of the camera, juggling pots, pans, and who-knows-what-all, flanked by a baffled host who couldn't have cared less about cooking, much less her book, could not have escaped the cameraman's gaping eye. When Julia finally piped up and those vocal flourishes, the trills and flutters, began to shoot about like fireworks, the image turned almost comical.

Against the general tide of upheaval running through the studio, Miffy Goodhart attempted to reassure her guest. She knew that Julia had no experience in front of a TV camera. Nothing was more likely to flummox a novice performer than talking to a host while cooking a recipe. They were two dissimilar acts, like patting your head and rubbing your stomach. To make matters worse, the show was going out live, so, in effect, they were flying without a safety net. The chances for disaster were better than good. To distract Julia, Miffy filled the downtime with an explanation of their whereabouts, which had been cobbled together in appreciable haste.

Some months before, WGBH had occupied space in a reconverted

roller-skating rink on the MIT campus, a state-of-the-art television center with gorgeous hardwood floors. Everyone at the station—the production staff and crew—was notorious for "smoking their brains out" on the
job, leading to a horrific fire that burned the place to the ground. Everything was lost, except for the trusty mobile unit, an old Trailways bus
with about seven million miles on it. Thanks to that, they could broadcast from various borrowed facilities. One of them, in fact, was the studio they were prepping at the moment, the Boston University Catholic
Center, in which the Diocese of Boston produced the morning Mass.
Perfunctorily, the *I've Been Reading* stagehands pushed the religious objects
out of the way. A hawk-eyed viewer could still make out the center's
motto, *in hoc signo vinces,** etched into an exposed beam; otherwise, with
TV magic, the space resembled a cozy book nook. Julia wondered aloud
at all the clergy nosing about, but Miffy assured her they were harmless.
"Except for Cardinal Cushing," she warned, pulling a face. "Be careful.
He likes following one upstairs, if you know what I mean."

EVEN BEFORE HER improbable stardom, Julia could take care of herself. "She is unusually strong physically," her husband, Paul, had written his brother, in 1944, " . . . and appears not to be frightened easily and
is therefore emotionally steady rather than hysterical when things get
tough." In "nightmarish" situations, she would gather the durable threads
of her character until "I could literally feel myself knitting together," she
said, owing to the strong self-image she'd cultivated since childhood.
Jacques Pépin described her as the most generous person he'd ever met,
who "could be as tough as nails" when it came to protecting herself. "She
was like a boxer, you know, who puts up the gloves just-so, making it
impossible to land a punch."

    There was never any need, however, to go to the mat. For Julia, the
fight was never physical, but a visceral necessity. Conformity offended
her; it was behavior to reject, like a foul-smelling turnip, and she fought
all her life to transcend its strictures. She defied all the expectations
that had been laid out for her. Privilege intruded at the top of that list.
Julia Child grew up in a haven of Southern California, an exclusive
sun-drenched paradise where privilege was a birthright, like education or
fresh air. Pasadena in the 1920s doubled as a gorgeous Hollywood back-

* "In this sign you will conquer."

lot, a scenic resort of palatial mansions, lush orange groves, posh country clubs, and opportunity galore. Wealth was the ticket into this selectively upscale enclave, and Julia's family could afford the extravagant price. But prosperity and entitlement were not on Julia's agenda. The oldest of three children in a traditional Republican family with deep Yankee roots, she scuttled her destiny as a "dilettante" and "social butterfly," just as later, after graduating from Smith College, she foreswore the inevitable marriage track in search of something more meaningful. Relying on her self-esteem and a reservoir of optimism in an attempt to fashion a career, she succeeded beyond her—or anyone's—wildest dreams. Imagine the gumption it took, in 1942, for a thirty-year-old woman who'd never been farther east than New York, to go halfway around the world to join a spy network in Southeast Asia. And, afterward, to enroll in an all-male cooking class whose French martinets scorned a woman's touch.

Conformity: Julia refused to conform. There wasn't so much as a trace of it in her DNA. Unflinchingly, she pursued an area of expertise that had not been tackled before—or, at least, not in a way that resonated with the public. She was determined to teach French cooking to American housewives captivated by tuna casseroles and beef Stroganoff—"taking [it] out of cuckooland," as she put it, and making it accessible to all. It fazed her not one bit that a large, middle-aged, unpolished woman who lived out of the loop should take her campaign to the masses via television, at the time a vehicle for glamourpusses like Gale Storm and Loretta Young. To hell with conformity! Without design or forethought, she created an enormously appealing personality that was unlike anyone else's. Julia could seem at times gregarious, instantly chummy, like an eccentric aunt who comes to visit. Her personality left, in the course of a half-hour encounter, an individually personal impression, both because of its sweeping, informal power—she was capable of being gracious, entertaining, flustered, neighborly, ham-fisted, sly, and self-deprecating—and because the mechanism of that personality was unburdened by ideology. The world had never encountered such an embraceable character, but TV changed all that. "She had an animated way about her that was infectious," says Russ Morash. "She wasn't performing it; she actually felt that way." Detailed instructions, the cooking lessons, came packaged as an intimate get-together between old friends. When she ordered a box of pears over the telephone, she would say, "This is Julia, dearie, I need some pears, *and I bet you have some good ones.*" The friendliness—that *infectious* quality—came bursting across on camera. After her appearance on the scene, people began talking about food, not as sustenance but as a staple of pleasure. She sparked an interest and understanding of food that whet people's appetites for a different kind of culinary experience. It takes a real nonconformist to start a revolution, and Julia Child started a corker, one that was to affect the nation's behavior and change the way its people lived their daily lives.

NOTHING IN THE studio immediately augured those dramatic changes. Julia was nonchalant, all business, as she arranged her equipment on the coffee table. The way she went about it, her easy approach, seemed totally unrehearsed, even though there'd been plenty of practice. She'd spent all week anguishing over the set-up and the demo: several dry runs enacted in the kitchen of Anita Hubby, a classmate from Smith, who lived around the corner; more in her own kitchen under Paul's watchful eye. You had to concentrate, Julia discovered; the delivery wasn't easy. Ten or fifteen omelets took the guesswork out of the process, but one never knew when that camera began to roll.

　　Plus there were unforeseen hitches specific to the studio. The moment the cameraman laid eyes on Julia he cried out in exasperation, "How do you expect me to light this woman?" and he circled her dubiously like a livestock judge at the county fair. Ideally, in a conventional room, the camera rested at eye level. But if the person to be photographed was six foot two—or, in Julia's actual case, six foot three; she had a lifelong tendency for shaving inches off her height—and the ceiling was eight feet, with lights hanging eighteen inches from the top, well then, brother, you have to be a magician to keep the lights out of the shot. Tilt the camera up or down and something got cut from the frame; pull back, and the scene wasn't as interesting. For an instant, the cameraman contemplated sitting Julia down for the segment, but that seemed to defeat the purpose of a demo. "I take it you've never worked with *T. Rex*," she joked. She took the problem into her own hands, placing the burner on a stack of coffee-table books and raising the pan a few inches so that the field of action was condensed. The cameraman peered into the viewfinder and gave the crew the high sign.

　　Professor Duhamel, shunted to the side, looked lost in the process. Inviting this guest to the studio hadn't been his idea, that was for sure. *I've Been Reading* was a show about big ideas; theories and doctrines were its stock-in-trade. He wasn't the least bit interested in cooking, but the girls in the office had insisted. *They'd insisted.* It wasn't just his show, they'd reminded him. Cooking was a particular enthusiasm of theirs—and, by the way, while they had his attention, there'd be something in the future on sports, as well.

Al Duhamel, as it turned out, was the perfect host. He introduced Julia with a bouquet of adjectives befitting a movie star, held up a copy of *Mastering the Art of French Cooking,* and ceded the spotlight to this amiable creature. His cockeyed grin, however, betrayed a hint of concern: What in the world was this woman going to do?

The same question dogged Miffy Goodhart, the young assistant producer, who stood in the wings among a mostly female support staff, wealthy Cambridge housewives who volunteered at the station on a regular basis. They had more of a stake in this than anyone realized. Julia's appearance was something of a breakthrough, a counterforce to the clubby fraternal order that cinched the ranks of academia. Miffy could count on one hand the number of women who had appeared on the show: finchy types with degrees in stupefying disciplines. Julia Child was going to cook. *She was going to cook!* And on TV, imagine that. This promised to be one for the record books.

There was a brief, awkward moment as Julia unwound her giant frame from the precious leather chair. Producing a small copper bowl and a whisk, she looked directly into the camera with the intimacy of a lover, and said, "I thought it would be nice if we made an omelet . . . " To Professor Duhamel and other viewers, she might have said, "I thought it would be nice to create nuclear fission," the process was that unfathomable to their superior brains. "They're so *delicious* and so easy to make." She cracked two eggs into the bowl with a one-handed flourish and began to beat them with the fury of a half-crazed thug.

Next she introduced her sturdy black-rimmed omelet pan. *An omelet pan.* It was unreasonable to think you could find an omelet pan in any store in Boston, but Julia assured her audience it was exactly what they needed. And butter, rich, silky butter—not that artificial stuff they produced in a lab. An omelet had to be exciting in the mouth, she purred, making it sound like oral sex.

The cameraman crept forward, closing in on Julia's paw-like hands, but had it picked up Professor Duhamel you would have seen bewilderment crisscrossed on his face. "This is going to work on that little burner?" he wondered aloud.

"Oh, *yes!* And it's going to be *delicious,* just you wait."

The butter crackled and sputtered as a chunk hit the hot pan, followed by a hush, what musicians call *decrescendo,* as molten egg flowed across the bottom. "This all happens very fast," Julia said breathlessly, "in just thirty seconds or less."

By this time, everyone in the studio, host and crew alike, was transfixed.

In a sudden, sweeping motion, Julia grabbed the pan's long handle and began jerking it back and forth, as if some unseen force was trying to wrench it from her grip. The energy behind it convulsed her body in sharp spastic tremors. This vision of Julia Child, gyrating like a wind-up toy, would be an enduring, endearing image to millions of viewers for the next forty years, but that night, without warning, it set off alarms. In the wings, Miffy Goodhart held her breath, watching the unfolding action in horror.

"[Julia's] loose, white shirt was open at the collar," she recalls. "And as she made the omelet, her rather large boobs were going furiously. And *going!* And *going!* The energy with which she made this omelet while talking about her book and . . . staring into the camera and . . . laughing madly and . . . talking to Albert on the side and . . . whisking everything up and . . . turning it over and . . . looking triumphant *all at once*—I was absolutely sure those buttons were coming undone. And *what then?*"

What then, exactly. It was a function of live TV that nothing was foreordained. There were no contingencies in place for the unscripted faux pas or sudden expletive—or the unforeseen appearance of a locomotive breast. One did as Miffy Goodhart did: she held her breath and prayed. For just a moment, through the blinding skein of lights, Miffy glimpsed the entire future of WGBH resting on the breasts of Julia Child.

In the end, there was nothing to cause anyone more than a mild case of heart failure. Julia Child, going rogue, was nothing less than a revelation. Her omelet was perfect, intense and creamy, a masterpiece of eggdom. Despite the constraints of black-and-white TV, it was hard for those at home to keep from drooling. You could practically smell the buttery concoction through the cathode-ray screen. Even Al Duhamel had to admit it was exciting in the mouth. Reluctantly, at Julia's insistence, he'd taken a bite from her fork and had the kind of slow facial awakening akin to a child's tasting something chocolaty for the first time. He lit right up, mouth still full, while Julia beamed from above. "*Therrrre.* You *seeee,*" she cooed. "Just as I said: *delicious.*"

THE JUNGLE DRUMS started beating the next morning. Calls came into WGBH from viewers, wondering when that Julia Child woman would be back on the air. Not a lot of calls, but enough to get a producer's attention. For a TV station, it was still the Dark Ages when it came to gauging audience reaction. There was no method in place for collecting scientific data, no Neilsen ratings, no overnight numbers. Response was measured strictly by what executives heard on the golf course or from their close circle of friends. They multiplied the anecdotal information they got by any number they wanted. So if the station received twenty calls, which would have been a lot for *I've Been Reading,* they would say, "We've had an overwhelming response."

"We've had an overwhelming response," Miffy Goodhart told Russ Morash, when he checked in the next morning. She related in breathless detail the entire Julia Child saga. "I was just blown over by her energy and how good she was on telly," she says. Russ, for his part, wasn't immediately convinced. "I had absolutely no interest in a cooking show," he recalls. "I was twenty-seven years old, making $83 a week, and newly married, with a working wife whose party piece was a franks-and-beans casserole. Cooking was as relevant to me as Norse poetry read in the original Scandinavian tongue." Besides, he already had a full plate directing a show called *Science Reporter,* which showcased the greatest minds at MIT and required all his energy. But Miffy Goodhart was not to be denied. "Let's see if we can do something with her," she pleaded. "What do you say, Russ? What do you say?"

Before he could answer, she had Bob Larsen on the phone. Larsen, the program manager at WGBH, had missed Julia's performance, but he'd already heard how well it had gone. Miffy mentioned there was a tape of the show. "Really, you've got to watch it," she said. "For once you've got to watch the Duhamel show."

You had to admire Miffy's gumption. She was a firecracker when it came to pressing her case. Bob Larsen was only stage one in the offensive she was mounting; she also called Dave Davis, the station manager, and laid it on thick, as well as her husband's cousin, Henry Morgenthau III, who ran the entire operation. In a flash, she was knocking on Julia's front door, purportedly to thank her for the bang-up performance over a cup of coffee. But more groundwork was being laid. Miffy remembered Julia's excitement after the show. Her adrenaline had been palpable. "Julia was

elated, she'd really had fun," Miffy recalls. "I told her, 'As far as I'm concerned, we will be using you again.'"

By March, WGBH could no longer deny the inevitable—either to itself or to the whim of its demanding viewers. There was something more than intriguing about Julia Child. This woman bore a special quality that appealed to their audience, yet a lot of unanswered questions remained. Could she fill a half-hour week after week? Would she have the kind of impact, the charisma, that ignited her *I've Been Reading* appearance? Did anyone out there give a hoot about cooking? Would lightning strike twice? The answers to these and other relevant questions boiled down to one salient fact: the station was desperate for a hit. *Desperate!* Without a must-see show—without real growth of loyal viewership—there'd be no increase in donations at WGBH, no money to expand. It was unlikely anyone would pony up to watch a physics professor discuss string theory. Or an educator who led preschoolers in arts-and-crafts projects. But . . . cooking?

COOKING: IT WAS the axis on which Julia Child's world turned. The ingredients, the meals, the pursuit of pleasure and the sublime all dazzled her like nothing she had ever encountered, not as a scion of the Pasadena social scene nor as an operative of the CIA. Cooking signified her break from conformity. It was an expression of her freedom from a legacy of dead ends, but especially from taking the expected path of a mid-century homemaker. Julia was determined to stand at the center of her own world, to express herself without following timeworn rules. Being a housewife—that is, the ideal of a housewife—wasn't in the cards. The bounds of domesticity couldn't contain her. Through cooking Julia found real purpose in her life, and through that purpose a greater meaning.

The story of her emancipation and self-realization runs parallel—and it is no coincidence—to the struggle of the post-war modern-day American woman: the dearth of opportunity available to her, the lack of respect for her untapped talents, the frustrations of the educated housewife who felt bored and trapped by the traditional role that had been handed to her, by the tedium of housework, the demands of motherhood, being the perfect cheerleader, the perfect hostess, the perfect lover, perfect wife—responsibilities that for generations kept most women from pursuing other dreams and desires. The domestic life of that era was fraught with dissatisfaction. Many women wrestled with the dilemma that personal creative and intellectual challenges weren't being met. There was a discrepancy between what they wanted and what was expected of them. A shakeup was long overdue. The assumptions of what a woman's place was were about to be altered, and Julia Child, despite looking like everybody's Aunt Ethel, was one of the revolutionaries leading the charge to uproot the norm. It is no accident that Betty Friedan's game changer, *The Feminine Mystique,* was published only eight days after *Mastering the Art of French Cooking.* As journalist Laura Shapiro noted: "Homemakers read *The Feminine Mystique* for the same reason they watched *The French Chef.* They had been waiting for a long time, and they were hungry."

Julia's hunger was a well-known symptom. She was a woman with boundless appetites—for food, absolutely, but also for the tides of change. Nothing sustained her like a ripe idea, a fresh experience, a saucy challenge, the impossible. In that respect, her timing was impeccable, because Julia came into her own during the early 1960s, when not only the role of women, but also other cultural paradigms, were undergoing upheaval. The arts, politics, fashion, values were all breaking out of the narrow concept of everyday life. Julia, being an iconoclast herself, was eager to shake up the norms. She took up arms alongside the other cultural guerrillas who were busy knocking down walls: Andy Warhol, Lenny Bruce, Bob Dylan, Hugh Hefner, Philip Roth, Martin Luther King Jr., Helen Gurley Brown, Allen Ginsberg, the Beatles. The Kennedys: their sophistication and youthful exuberance gave all of this momentum, leading Americans to look beyond their own culture for inspiration. "With the Kennedys in the White House, people were very interested in [French cooking]," Julia said, "so I had the field to myself, which was just damn lucky."

Actually, Julia Child found herself the leading advocate of cooking in America for reasons that had nothing to do with luck. She achieved that position of prominence by the same means that had shaped her skills from the beginning. Aside from stanching her insatiable hunger, there was nothing in her upbringing to suggest an interest in food, even less that signaled a desire to cook. "As a girl I had zero interest in the stove," Julia recalled. She was "never encouraged to cook and just didn't see the point in it." Her foray into the culinary arts had less to do with pure talent than a desire to fully engage her passions. Throughout her long and distinguished career, she indulged in pleasure after pleasure, serving them up, without any stigma, to her loyal public to be sampled as one would a canapé or a sticky pudding. Her initial success, which most personalities might see as something not to tinker with, only gave her greater freedom to say and do as she pleased. "Out came whatever was on her mind," says Jacques Pépin, "no matter how controversial or what the repercussions. It was a breath of fresh air, and people loved her because she said what she felt."

Like with most insular families, however, in which competition simmered, feuds erupted, and jealousies raged, there were those in the food world who found Julia's straight talk all too threatening. Her outspokenness never failed to provoke new controversies, new challenges, often rooted in the fragile terrain on which her reputation rested: that she was an interloper, neither French nor a chef—at least not with the traditional provenance of a serious cook. She would eventually convince these skeptics, just as she convinced cooking novices everywhere, to take her seriously; to embrace her casual approach to a vital and substantive discipline; not just to laugh at her, but to respect her, to respect her research and techniques, and ultimately her cooking.

SOMETIME THAT SPRING, in April 1962, Russ Morash appeared on the doorstep of 103 Irving Street in Cambridge, one of the more unprepossessing houses on a street lined with splendid residences described in realtors' listings as estates. John Kenneth Galbraith lived a stone's throw down the block, as did Arthur Schlesinger, interspersed among other homes belonging to Harvard's leading minds. As he knocked at the half-open door, Morash must have marveled, as other outsiders had, at the naked privilege on display in the perfectly manicured neighborhood and the strange circumstances that brought him to this place. Clearly, he was out of his element. Raised in "a very modest family," Morash was blue-collar Boston—in his own words "a plain, driven guy"—armed with a strong work ethic that lacked any false sense of entitlement. Cambridge, to Morash, was uptown, Brahmin. One came here to see how the other half lived.

Ostensibly, Russ was here against his better wishes. His boss, Bob Larsen, had corralled him at the studio and mentioned that WGBH was considering doing something with Julia Child. "What do you think, Russ?" he asked. It was a loaded question. If Larsen was involved, then Morash knew something was already in the pipeline. There would have been others, influential friends, who'd already weighed in with enthusiastic opinions. "What do you think, Russ?" wasn't a question, it was a caress that needed a hug. In other circumstances, Morash might have given it a quick thumbs-down. A cooking show was absolutely of no interest to him. Food, as he knew it, was a necessity, nothing more: Sunday roasts cooked beyond well-done into gray shades, glutinous gravy, rubbery vegetables, and Italian Swiss Colony wine. And French cooking?— *ooh-la-la!* One of the more "ridiculous assignments" Russ had at WGBH was directing *En Français,* a program that attempted to teach French to elementary school children. Russ didn't have to remind Larson that "there was no student with less potential for learning classical French than" he. Put it all together, Russ Morash was the wrong guy for this job. He could have convinced Larsen of his inadequacy. Instead, he hemmed and hawed.

"We have no studio at the moment, so we'll have to do it in the field somewhere," Russ grumbled. "Plus, I need to know what kind of support we're going to have, what kind of resources you'll give me. And this person—Julia Child—I need to meet her and see what sort of a character she is."

Larsen arranged their introduction at 103 Irving, and over the next few months, Morash would return there again and again, drawn to the formidable character he encountered, a fearless, ambitious, supremely self-confident woman, a force of nature, "with this ebullient spirit, and her voice and her manner and her enthusiasm and her wit and her charm."

When push came to shove, her appeal was the one surefire way Julia Child could convert the skeptics who resisted French cooking. In the warm glow of personality, she could transfer her passion for good food to men and women everywhere, in kitchens in the loneliest corners of the country to galley nooks in teeming metropolitan sprawls, from farmhouses and suburban developments to Park Avenue and Beverly Hills—and everywhere in between. Ultimately, cooking was the way to unite these extremes, to nourish their spirit, and to make them feel loved.

Communicating was Julia's essence. Her brilliance rested in her capacity to articulate her experiences with food and relate them to anyone, no matter how little or great their desire to cook or eat. Less than twenty years after Russ Morash stepped into Julia Child's kitchen, his wife, Marian, the same woman whose franks-and-beans casseroles blighted the family menu, gained recognition as a masterful cook in her own right, with a television series and go-to cookbooks of her own, and a restaurant in Nantucket that showcased her innovative food. No woman had demonstrated less talent for cooking until Julia Child swept into her life. Countless others had a similar story—without the cookbooks, TV series, and restaurant, of course—discovering and realizing their own talents, with Julia as their personal mentor, instructing, cheerleading, encouraging, being blunt, genuine, and unaffected, as only she could be.

Americans were inspired and changed forever by Julia Child—even if they never saw it coming.

The McWilliams family, Pasadena, 1922

One

Paradise

There were days in Ceylon, Kunming, Cambridge, Paris, Oslo, really any outpost in her globe-trotting exploits, when Julia Child would close her eyes, inhale, and let the exquisiteness of home wash over her. With the instincts of a sorcerer, she would summon up ribbons of pastel light unspooled across powder-blue sky, peaks that seemed drawn with a finely sharpened pencil, Craftsman-style bungalows set among orchard lanes quaintly named for trees, blackbirds in evergreen oaks singing their unsteady melody, and roses, a riot of roses, stretched like a crimson carpet from yard to yard, street to street, across canyons and dry river bottoms that, for all their gentility, bore "a touch of wilderness." "It was paradise—just about the best place you could think of to grow up," she recalled, during a flashback while in Sicily, halfway around the world and sixty years later. The landscape, with its lush, radiant magnetism, energized the city, as though by accident it had been waiting for a chance to stake its claim on a paradise as versatile and as unspoiled as this valley, the pure dry air, its ancient hills, a gift of nature. Pasadena wasn't a typical California settlement established for fortune hunters and sun-worshippers, but a sumptuous cluster of missions and ranchos at the foot of the coastal range of the Sierras, whose ideal climate attracted the health-conscious wanting "to get where life was easy." The generosity of the land, with its cornucopia of natural resources—orchards, towering oak groves, alluvial streams, succulent vegetation, and cowboy vistas—offset a terraced,

urban beehive of dusty adobe and verdant parkland that showcased Pasadena as an oasis in the desert.

Julia often said that Pasadena was "California through and through,"
but that description couldn't be further off the mark. Unlike neighboring California cities, Pasadena did not develop from a gold mine, a train
stop, or a dune overlooking the beach. It was settled by a co-op of disgruntled Midwesterners, from Indianapolis of all places, who hoped to
abandon the snow-ridden Plains in favor of mild climes. Their scheme to
go west, as far west as possible, drew tremendous interest from friends;
over a hundred families joined this so-called Indiana Colony, which sent
an advance team to California in 1873, searching for fifty thousand acres
of arable land. The mission, at first, sounded like a boondoggle to the
frozen Hoosiers left holding down the fort. Anyone familiar with the
California land rush knew that the territory was "theirs for the picking."
The West was big, as big as their dreams. But after a month pushing
from valley to valley, the scouts grew discouraged. Santa Anita was too
expensive, San Diego too overrated, Anaheim too sandy, San Fernando
too arid, San Bernardino too hot, and Los Angeles too *too*. And their
dreams began to fade.

Julia's grandfather, John McWilliams, had suffered the same sensory letdown in 1846, when he went west in search of gold and a mother
lode of dreams. Landing in California, fresh from the Illinois prairie, he
became "pretty well down at the mouth" when the reality of the countryside set in. The canyons, nettles, mosquitoes, and dry gulch were enough
to try a man's soul. And the heat! Good Lord, one of the pale Indianans
groused, "Your face and nose get scalped with the sunshine and you need
a new hide about twice a week."

Fortunately, those in the Indiana contingent were thick-skinned.
These men, who had endured brutal snowbound winters on tundra cratered by frost and then had slogged up and down the sunbaked California
range of hills—"120 miles of villainous stage riding" and endless hikes that
stretched their backs to the breaking point—would not let their dreams
be denied. Trudging further north and then east, they crossed into the
San Gabriel Valley and entered one of the most picturesque settings in
Southern California, a place that, to their eyes, resembled the Garden of
Eden. They were, in fact, on a portion of the sprawling San Pasqual Valley Ranch, in the northwest corner of the old Mission lands. It was a sight
for sore eyes, that oasis in the desert, with rolling mountain vistas, purple
mesas, leafy shade trees and flora. The air was drier, warmer, and more

healthful than in Los Angeles, the sky clearer and deeper blue. There was no lack of wood—about five hundred acres of tall oak lined a canyon suitable for grazing. And plentiful water—"water delicious and cool leaping out of the rocks." And more water: a vast underground reservoir would provide well water galore. And still more: silver mountain streams that sluiced through whispery wooded slopes and escarpments had eroded centuries-old bedrock and carved out a great gorge, the Arroyo Seco, destined to irrigate the valley.

And where there was water, these Indianans knew, there was fertile soil. These men and the families of the co-op would be dependent on the land for their means of survival—and that was why the condition of the pastureland, the fabulously rich loam, was what captured their attention. They gazed out on a horizon that foretold ideal growing conditions and more. Each acre was an eye-opener, one could easily envision their yield—so much so, in fact, that only two years later, following the settlement of Pasadena, the collective would successfully have planted more than ten thousand orange and lemon trees, several thousand deciduous fruit trees, countless olive trees, and 150,000 grapevines. And nuts—nuts seemed to be exploding out of the soil: almonds, filberts, chestnuts, butternuts, pecans, walnuts, hickories, and beechnuts.

This was more than even they had envisioned. The goal had been to find a more comfortable place to live, a place where simple, humble farmers could plow their land and provide. Several churches, perhaps, and a school would serve to round out the settlement.

What they got instead was a filthy-rich paradise.

Pasadena grew faster than the national debt. Less than five years after its incorporation, in 1886, the city was transformed from a sleepy-eyed agricultural village into an action-packed resort. Tourists and speculators from across the country poured into a frontier town that was bulging at the seams. Houses sprung up—and not just California-style bungalows, but mansions the size of palaces, packed shoulder-to-shoulder along adjacent streets. Hotels opened for business—and not just inns or roadhouses, but showplaces, as grand and elegant as San Simeon or Xanadu. Railroads marked the spot—and not just as a whistle-stop on an otherwise meandering route, but a major destination of the Southern Pacific and Santa Fe lines. Property values soared—and not just gradual increases that reflected real estate prices across America, but in wild leaps on the order of an impressionist auction at Sotheby's. Land sold to members of the original Indiana Colony for $6 an acre reached a whopping

$1,000 an acre in 1876; according to town records, a tiny parcel sliced from a ten-acre lot sold for $36,000 that same year. Banks opened for business on practically every corner, an opera house thrived, trolley lines multiplied, a commercial district emerged, and not one newspaper, but *three* dailies, reported on the sweeping developments straining the city limits. That made it official: Pasadena was a boomtown.

And the boom brought boomers, America's wealthiest snowbirds who came to bask in the sunshine and build winter residences along Orange Grove Avenue. From St. Louis came beer mogul Adolphus Busch; from Minnesota, Hulett Merritt, the founder of U.S. Steel; from Chicago, publisher Andrew McNally of the Rand-McNally empire, followed by George Pullman, whose sleeping cars were world-renowned, and chewing-gum magnate William Wrigley, soon to found the Chicago Cubs; from New York, the piano Steinways, Lamon Vandenburg Harkness of Standard Oil, and John S. Cravens, whose wife oversaw the Liggett-Myers tobacco fortune. Before they'd even unpacked, Marshall Field arrived from Chicago, as well as the Rockefellers, both John D. and John D. Jr. And more: financiers and industrialists from all points of the country came west in successive waves to this former Indiana Colony, staying for three or four months, seldom longer, each year. By 1913, a reporter tallied the adjoining "boom mansions" of fifty-two plutocrats on Orange Grove Avenue, a few posh blocks known as Millionaire's Row. Overnight, little Pasadena, settled by a group of tubercular pioneers, had become a different sort of paradise: "the richest city in America."

When the McWilliams family arrived there in 1908, everything that glittered had turned to gold. The millionaires plowed their fortunes into civic projects that refaced the natural beauty of Pasadena with a sumptuous high-toned veneer. Thanks to the largesse of Andrew Carnegie and other philanthropists, in 1903 a solar observatory was established atop Mount Wilson, overlooking the city. By 1906, Busch Gardens—a grand arboreal fantasyland assembled on thirty sylvan acres—became a magnet for tourists to wander and gape. The City Beautiful concept whitewashed public buildings with elaborate Beaux Arts façades. Parks, pools, and open plazas flourished. Even an annual parade, the Tournament of Roses, took place to flaunt the city's fine bounty. The spirit of pioneering and comfort that had created Pasadena was being supplanted by the spirit of enterprise. Town guardians fixated on the credo of architect Willis Polk: "To make a city attractive is to make it prosperous." Indeed! High finance was already churning from a business district at Colorado and Pearl Streets. A Board of Trade was established to promote the city's economy. And a streetcar line, the big Red Car express, snaked along Lake Avenue to transport Pasadena's tycoons directly to the financial district in Los Angeles.

Pasadena's boom economy was catnip to a man like John McWilliams. Like the city's Indiana forefathers, he had been lured west, from Griggsville, Illinois, as early as 1849, lured by gold, of course, and the prospect of instant riches. Every sixteen-year-old, trapped on an isolated farm and laboring long hours in the fields, got the "going fever" that year. You couldn't help it, reading the daily newspaper accounts of each fresh gold strike. For young John McWilliams, there was no other recourse. He was either "going to California . . . or die," he told his father, James, a stern, determined lumberyardman reluctant to give his consent. Nevertheless, on April 9, 1849, John left town with two friends from school and his cousin, Abner. They packed a wagon with supplies—bacon, coffee, quinine, gold pans, guns with ammunition, and a butcher knife—and joined the greatest mass migration the young country had known, some eighty thousand men, Argonauts, as they were called, pioneers, dreamers, future settlers of the West.

John's father feared for his son—and with good reason. The boy had been left a semi-invalid thanks to a "hereditary consumption"—tuberculosis—that had killed his mother and brother. He was all skin and bones, a mere 122 pounds on a six-foot, one-inch frame, known as "legs-a-mighty" to the boys back home. Grown men twice his size died on that damned trip west. As it was, they hit "snow storms all the way to Missouri." Stampedes were common. Long marches without water disoriented them during interminably dry days. But strange things happen to determined young dreamers. By the time they reached California in October, six months later, John had put on twenty-eight pounds thanks, in part, to a diet of "fat bacon." He was in tip-top shape, ready to prospect, to mine his weight in gold.

What John McWilliams found in Old Shasta, where he joined a sludge-caked campsite on a ridge of the Sierra Nevada, echoed the words of Prentice Mulford, another teenage Forty-niner from back East, on the make: "Them stories about finding gold in Californy was all true."

That they was. Prospectors hit new veins of ore with staggering success, and young John McWilliams was no exception. A teacher from Griggsville trained him to work a rocker and a riddle, two handmade tools used for sifting the gritty dirt and, as John recalled, "on the first day we tried it we took out about a hundred dollars." The potential sites where gold lay buried stretched as far as the eye could see, up one side of the Sierras and down the other, endless rolling vistas north and south and west. A solitary prospector like John McWilliams could work that range forever, driven by his imagination—dreams of independence and the promise of riches. But it took courage, as well. There were no amenities. The conditions were brutal, barely civilized, the elements a scourge on the human soul: a lengthy wet season battered by winds and steady, sodden downpour, followed by fetid warm months, when "clouds of mosquitoes rendered sleep utterly out of the question." Packs of coyotes preyed on the campsites at night. Four years were all that John could take toiling on that infernal squalid slope, but he did relatively well, considering. Regular shipments of gold were sent by courier to family in Illinois, so much, in fact, that large nuggets were passed down to generations of the McWilliams clan.

But it wasn't enough for him to be welcomed upon his return.

In late January of 1852, John showed up in Dwight, a tiny farming community near Griggsville, where his younger brother, David, now flirted with success. David owned a mercantile, McWilliams and Judd, which provided equipment for crops and happened to have the only safe in town. Thus, when local farmers got paid and needed a secure place to deposit their cash, David parlayed his little safe into the Bank of Dwight. It became clear soon enough that there was no place in it for John. He stayed just long enough to marry his sweetheart, pretty Mary Dana, then enlisted in an Illinois volunteer infantry regiment and disappeared into the mist.

In due time, John was swept up in the War Between the States, commissioned as a quartermaster for Sherman on his march through Georgia. A modestly published memoir is filled with his exploits. "He was a fearless son-of-a-bitch," says Alex McWilliams, his great-grandnephew. "The gold rush and the war had toughened him hard as nails."

When he returned to Dwight, in 1865, the lay of the land only made John harder and tougher. McWilliams family lore maintains that David pretended not to recognize his brother, lest he demand a share of the family business. More determined than ever, John decamped to Odell, a mere eight miles from Dwight, where he homesteaded and opened his own bank, in competition with his brother. Odell was even tinier than Dwight, maybe seven or eight hundred people tops, but it was the largest grain-shipping area in Livingston County, and the Bank of Odell became its anchor, as much the social center of the community as it was a place of business. John McWilliams made loans to local businesses based on personal relationships, money that came out of his own pocket. Meanwhile, he began buying up farmland all around Odell, ground that, to this day, remains in the family portfolio.

"John was a very astute businessman," says Alex McWilliams, as was his brother, David. "They were serious people; their determination was fierce. They passed the ground on [to their heirs], very rarely selling it."

In time, the brothers developed "a familiarity with the land," something innate, so sound, like nature itself. John, especially practical, prized the value of the earth's minerals, based on his Eureka experiences out West. Land was something you could touch, sift through your fingers, and they banked on it almost exclusively, unlike their counterparts in Chicago who dealt in intangibles: credit and mortgages. In a quiet but persistent manner, John expanded his budding empire, acquiring land in a variety of disparate places: abundant rice fields east of DeWitt, Arkansas, on the White River, where he maintained a family farm; parcels in Arvin, near Bakersfield, on which they eventually found oil; seemingly worthless real estate in what is now Palm Springs; and underground chambers, which the government later contracted for storing fuel. He also played an unobtrusive role in the development of the Mississippi Valley and "is said to have made a fortune [there] during the Reconstruction period."

Through all these transactions, one constant prevailed: character. It was character that kept their empire from the vicissitudes of ill will. Ambition and savvy never tarnished the family name. The McWilliams brothers were "the epitome of gentlemen—straitlaced, taciturn, pillars of their respective communities," says a great-grandniece who still resides in Dwight. She recalls hearing an expression shared by the two communities that defined her family's profile: small-town royalty. The brothers were every inch the county's power elite, the "leading lights" of the area, its major bankers, major land barons, active in the Methodist church and community service, major contributors to local libraries and hospitals and schools.

The custom of service and character wasn't lost on John's son—also named John—who elected, by choice or simply destiny, to follow in his father's footsteps. John McWilliams II, Julia Child's father, was bred to be a gentleman, "a carbon-copy of the old man," to one observer's eyes, prudent and practical and disciplined to a fault.

John Jr. was born in 1880, and, based on physical characteristics, left no doubt from the get-go that he was "genuine McWilliams." He cut quite a figure in that flat, barren country. Tall, reed thin, spindly, but with the graceful unself-conscious gait of a natural athlete, decidedly handsome despite a generous chin that Julia would inherit, he had the McWilliams superiority and air of command. But the air of command didn't come naturally to young John; it was something he cultivated, something he earned, under the tutelage of his father. He spent his youth—and much of his manhood—at the elbow of John Sr., now a cold, hard-shelled man who showed his son little outward affection. The father-son alliance was a clear, calculated enterprise whose chief concern was to mine the family interests. "The obligation they felt was relentless," a relative recalls. "Don't let the family down. Maintain the status. There was no room for tenderness."

Demanding though he was, John's father recognized his son's need for independence. After all, he'd become his own man in California and Georgia. So in 1895, when John Jr. was fifteen—the age when most local boys spent their days at work in the fields—he was sent to the Lake Forest Academy, an all-boys prep school just north of Chicago. This was part of the blueprint his father had mapped out for him. He would attend Lake Forest for two years, then head to Princeton, to study some aspect of the humanities, before returning to the fold.

At Princeton, John McWilliams Jr. displayed the same discipline he'd developed in Odell. He was all business. His studies came first, a fairly general mix of classical history and contemporary politics, with a regimen of sports that included tennis and golf. Though no BMOC, he was elected vice president of his class and considered a campus leader. Still, John took school seriously, seeing it as a chance to round out his character so that he might bring a more informed dimension to his duties back home. One thing was for certain: there was no horsing around. He wasn't part of the go-go crowd that spent weekends at one of the many sister schools, where Princeton men hitched their wagons to a starlet, or prowled the New York social scene making contacts for future career moves. Unlike other classmates who sought to compete for the best firms, it wasn't urgent that John distinguish himself in college. His future was already spoken for. John had learned all he needed from his father, the one person who knew all the ropes. As far as the McWilliams family business was concerned, there was one sovereign authority, one way to do business, one way to conduct yourself in every aspect of life.

To say that John McWilliams was a scaled-down version of his father gave him too little credit for his later success, but there was a rigidity about him that was hard to mistake and a chilliness, an aloof side, taken directly from the family playbook. "He wasn't a warm man by any stretch of the imagination," his granddaughter, Patti McWilliams, says. "He had no sense of humor, no warmth of any kind."

Banking and finance suited his personality. It was practical, unsentimental. The process involved with making sound decisions required no emotional investment, just good dollars and cents, which was squarely within John's comfort zone. Otherwise there was no desperate urgency to making his mark. In 1901, following his graduation from Princeton, John was content to return to Odell and start from the ground up, as the assistant cashier in his father's bank. It wasn't a glamorous job, but it gave him visibility in the community, an opportunity to build recognition and trust.

Visibility, he knew, was money in the bank. So were trust and recognition, and by 1907 he had combined all three elements, becoming an alderman of Odell on the Prohibition ticket. He also made his first independent land purchase, buying 4,600 acres in Kern County, California, the southern part of the Central Valley, an area rich in agriculture and where work had already begun drilling wells that would eventually yield oil.

But Odell could compete with the pull of the West for only so long. The Midwest was solid and steady, but as far as growth went it was as flat as the Plains—and they were "flatter than a pancake," according to local wisdom—that stretched for hundreds of miles in every direction. To speculators like the McWilliamses, its potential was limited. They had taken their business there as far as it could go. By 1908, John Sr. had already returned to California, this time permanently, where his land investments were making him richer by the day. The old prospector had struck gold again—rich veins of real estate, from Bakersfield to Pasadena. He bought more land, and more, until by the time he settled in Pasadena he owned practically as many acres as the whole of Odell, Illinois. He formed the McWilliams Land Company in 1909, just as Pasadena was enjoying its most rapid growth.

Everyone assumed that John Jr. would follow suit, if not immediately, then as soon as he could get his affairs in order. "He was smitten with California the first time he saw it," recalls a woman who eventually became his daughter-in-law. Smitten and pulling down his own deals out

West. But his father put the brakes on any plans for a hasty exit. The McWilliams family had obligations to the people of Odell, and he had every intention of seeing them through. Meanwhile, John Jr. was promoted to president of the Bank of Odell and given additional commissions that included the rice fields in Arkansas.

Smitten as he was by the West, it was nothing compared to an enchantment back home. In 1903, while visiting his Princeton classmate, Alex Smith, in Chicago, John Jr. was introduced to two sisters, Julia and Dorothy Weston, both Smith College alumnae, both "free spirits" with a legacy of their own. Julia Carolyn Weston—called Caro—in particular, had caught his eye. A fair pink-faced redhead, with unruly hair often pulled back into a bun and braided like a challah, she was tall and striking, not in a loud, vulgar manner, but statuesque, drawing attention with elegance. She was more vigorous than her sister, livelier, captivating: a Cupid's-bow mouth just this side of voluptuous, eyes a startling pale blue, slightly crescent-shaped and tinged with sadness that belied an earthy wit. Neither sister was shy, but Caro was downright outgoing. She could engage and hold an audience in any crowded room. "Vivacious" was a word used often to describe her nature. So were "saucy" and "independent," the latter of which proved a nuisance to John McWilliams.

Caro and her sister, Dorothy, were constantly in motion. Since graduating from college, they had hopscotched across the country, ingratiating themselves in any number of settings that offered easy and open companionship. In New York, in Chicago, in El Paso and Denver and Santa Barbara, they joined the stratified social circles of their upbringing, given entrée on the strength of their names. Being a Weston opened doors wherever they went. Not with the small-town royalty distinction that pegged the McWilliamses, but an aristocratic birthright of national prominence.

The Westons were thoroughbreds, old money, with ties stretching back to the *Mayflower*—and beyond. Caro's mother, Julia Clark Mitchell, was a direct descendant of Priscilla Alden and Experience Mitchell, who settled the Plymouth Colony in 1623, and pruned an ancestral tree rife with notable branches: William Bradford, governor of the Plymouth Colony; poet William Cullen Bryant; Justice Oliver Wendell Holmes. No one had more blue blood running through her veins, though Caro's father, Byron Curtis Weston, brought his own respectable credentials.

Byron's roots also descended deep into the Plymouth Colony, which his great-uncle Edmund helped found. A nephew of Zenas Crane, who practically invented fine papermaking, Byron started a rival company right in the Cranes' backyard—Dalton, Massachusetts, on the Housatonic River—where he manufactured high-grade cotton-fiber books, ledgers, and tablets that gained worldwide renown. The Crane Paper Company and Byron Weston Paper competed for every major account, including printing dollar bills for the U.S. government, which the Cranes managed to snag. (The Westons made some Chinese money.) Descendants of both families say "the Cranes and Westons hated each other," but in truth they shared an uneasy détente. They struck up friendships and inter-married *on occasion,* but about as easily as the Capulets and Montagues. They even socialized *on occasion,* though each family lived on their own side of town—the Westons in the eastern section, known as the Center; the Cranes in the western or "Flat" neighborhood, called "Craneville." Their churches were separate; they buried their dead in different plots of the cemetery. "You couldn't attend a Crane function and be welcomed at the Westons'," says John Kittredge, himself a mixed-blood relative of the two rival clans. Both families possessed an unshakable belief in their own moral superiority. This was especially true among the elders, whose infighting affected all phases of local life. Byron Weston, especially, was spiteful. If one of his merchants defected to the Crane fief, he'd move an outsider into the vacant post to let the scoundrel know there was no chance of return.

Despite the petty rancor, Byron Weston was popular enough to be elected lieutenant governor of Massachusetts, and not just once but for three terms (the Cranes were quick to note they fielded governors), during which his wife gave birth to ten children, in rapid succession. Caro, the seventh, resembled her mother most. She had a stubborn streak, was smart as a whip, treasured her independence, displayed a wicked sense of humor, and courted adventure in a way that seemed, at times, extreme, if not reckless. She was the first woman in Berkshire County to get a driver's license, and she tooled around those dirt roads like they couldn't contain her. She was an outspoken feminist, or whatever term stood for individualism and self-reliance in her day. She was also quite the athlete, a formidable tennis player and scratch golfer, which appealed to John McWilliams; indeed, they'd both played basketball for their respective schools. John liked everything about this gutsy New England gal, every-thing except that she wasn't available.

About the time Caro began her sophomore year at Smith, growing restless and casting about for her own identity, her father, who suffered from high blood pressure, died suddenly of a stroke. Three years later, her mother, Julia, died of Bright's disease, or kidney failure, bequeathing to Caro the responsibility for raising her three younger siblings, Donald, Dorothy, and Philip. "We are all orphans," she noted with gravity in her diary, signifying the upheaval in their lives. In any case, this twist of fate handcuffed Caro to the family, waylaying any plans for an independent future, let alone something as superficial as romance. Her world, once boundless, was now confined to Dalton, Massachusetts, which she accepted with the grace of someone destined for nothing more. Still, her role as surrogate mother provided its own experiences and rewards. "She was a strong-willed woman who met challenges with a sense that she could walk through walls," recalls an admiring relative. But the family—Caro's kryptonite—stunted her ostensible superpowers.

In the summer of 1903, her sister Dorothy, who suffered from fatigue and a persistent cough, was diagnosed with galloping consumption, or what we now know as tuberculosis. Thus began Caro's eight-year-long search for a remedy to the disease, traveling from one spa to another in an attempt to revitalize Dorothy's lungs. Dry, clear air was essential to their quest, but it gave the sisters' lives a fractured itinerant quality. Seasonal changes meant packing up and moving on. This gypsy life might have had a disillusioning effect on anyone with less pluck, anyone less determined to battle illness or bet against the odds. Living out of trunks and steamers, however, never seemed to discomfit Caro. She may also have felt that she deserved more from life than what Dalton, Massachusetts, had to offer. Dalton was a company town, with a company mentality. Whether you were a Weston or a Crane, making paper—and more paper—was the focus of everyone's lives. While at college, Caro had learned something of the world beyond, and knew there was more to it than Dalton's myopia. "She was sick and tired of that scene," recalls her granddaughter, Phila, "and Dorothy's illness, sad to say, may have been her ticket out." Whatever its drawbacks, the travel proved favorable in advancing the Weston sisters' social status and, with their native New England beauty and cultivated charm, they became welcome fixtures on the Ivy League country-club circuit. In Santa Barbara and Colorado Springs—two places where the Weston sisters put down provisional roots—Caro infiltrated the close-knit social circles without breaking a sweat. She and Dorothy were in great demand at the various society balls and cotillions, to say nothing of the tennis and golf tournaments that always seemed to attract a certain crowd.

John McWilliams Jr. joined their exploits whenever possible, but it was exhausting keeping up—and personally frustrating. For seven long years he shadowed the Weston sisters, from Chicago and out through the west to Colorado, and then further south and west, spending his free time wherever they turned up next. Caro made it clear that Dorothy's health was her priority, and that nothing—neither romance nor marriage—would hinder her goal. She didn't discourage John, per se, so long as he knew where everything stood. Otherwise, they enjoyed a mutually exclusive, if rather arm's-length, relationship.

To John McWilliams Jr., this ritual of courtship seemed more like a war of attrition. Caro seemed disinclined to settle down anytime soon—or perhaps she was uninterested. Was Dorothy's health a raison d'être—or an excuse? He couldn't be sure. Either way, John's prospects offered him little in the way of comfort. As he approached his thirtieth birthday in 1910, he became increasingly restless. He was at an age when most of his friends were already married, starting families, but Caro Weston gave him nothing more than vague gestures of faith. And his desire to branch out on his own, ditching the small-town routine in Odell for a larger platform out West, was discouraged by his father.

A year later, an unforeseen event threw John's mounting despair a welcome lifeline. That summer, Caro's sister Dorothy became engaged to Wilber Hemming, a Yalie from a Texas banking family who was working in Colorado Springs. Despite an accelerating illness, she planned to marry him the next June. Practically on the spot, Caro, now thirty-three, decided the time was right for her to marry as well. John McWilliams Jr. was a primo catch and, like him, she wanted to live in "the Golden West," as far away from Dalton as one could get without a boat. They intended to "grow up with the country," as John quipped in the handbook of his tenth class reunion at Princeton.

In any case, Caro wasn't kidding about the timing. She and John married on January 21, 1911, just as soon as the ink was dry on Dorothy's engagement notice. It was a festive, jubilant ceremony on as grand a scale as the West had seen, considering Caro was a daughter from one of America's most prominent families. Guests traveled from Boston, New York, and Chicago to pack St. Stephen's Episcopal Church in Colorado Springs, where John and Caro were celebrated as "the golden couple" by their friends. One can imagine the splendid figure they cut when the newlyweds—both tall and choice, with quick grins and a gawky kind of energy that washed the starch from their Puritan trappings—sashayed

down the aisle to an explosion of cheers and hollers. Their union, someone said, was "one for the ages"—perhaps an offhand comment on the
couple's advancing years.

The old prospector—John McWilliams Sr.—didn't attend the wedding, but he sent a gift that was more precious than anything they'd
anticipated. It was an honorable discharge of sorts—his blessing for John
to leave Odell at long last and for the newlyweds to relocate to Pasadena,
where he lived. But while Caro would, in later years, retell this story with
a smile, the gift from "Father," as she called him, turned out to be a mixed
blessing at best. The elder McWilliams insisted that the couple live with
him, that John work alongside him, that they consult him on any decision
pertaining to future plans, all of which dealt Caro's independence a serious blow. Caro could manage John's traditional nature, but his father was
a tougher customer. The old man's stare, it was said, could turn your soul
into salt. When he was around, Caro took pains to mind her p's and q's.

In the relationship with her father-in-law, Caro was respectful to a
fault, but she always felt a binding tension between them. It seemed like
a competition—they were competing for his son's/her husband's attention. Even in small, unimportant matters like meals and attire a raised
eyebrow from McWilliams Sr. could hijack John's loyalty. Once, in fact,
Father ordered his son to change his shirt before leaving the house, even
though Caro had picked it out for John moments before. Other times
he dictated the details of dinners down to the amount of salt used in a
particular dish. There was little latitude for a new bride's touch. Father
and son huddled over land deals all day long, while Caro tended house in
a perfunctory fashion. In the evenings their dinners were stiff, plodding
affairs. She worked hard in order to fit into this routine, although, God
knows, it placed a strain on the couple's new marriage.

But John encouraged her, kept her chin up, promised better days
ahead. He was "a good egg," according to Julia, who heard stories about
how her father held that marriage together, stories that later would prove
despairing to her. John was a different man in those early days in Pasadena, when "growing up with the country" seemed like an ever-evolving
godsend. The city was custom-tailored to his deliberate Midwestern style,
a style whose Victorian passions and rigid philosophies stood in contrast
to the heathen Los Angeles, which was ten miles from Pasadena "as the
Rolls-Royces fly." The city had its practical side, too, none of the boisterous indulgence of L.A., none of the flash or the clangor. Fenced off from
those decadent forces, John and Caro found their kind of people in Pasa-

dena, a discriminating country-club set whose high-toned high jinks and ritualistic pastimes created a well-defined division between the Elite and the Otherwise. "It was quite a social place," recalls Julia's sister-in-law, Jo McWilliams, a Pasadena native. John and Caro took advantage of all the scene had to offer. They tapped into a circle of young, wealthy snowbirds from the East, and joined the exclusive Valley Hunt Club, whose Sunday-night suppers and annual theme balls, such as the Sheik's Frolic, gave them a place to ride, trapshoot, play tennis, and swim.

The Valley Hunt, as it was called, also gave them entry to an in-crowd that would advance their rising status as members-elect to what one knowledgeable observer called "the *crème de la crème* of California." These weren't your run-of-the-mill plutocrats. It was said that "rich people who move to southern California do not go to Pasadena to live unless they have had money for at least two decades." And rich Pasadenans didn't join the Valley Hunt unless they had money to burn. John had exactly what the guidelines called for—the right pedigree, an abiding moralism, a bulging portfolio, and a wife from patrician stock—and Caro already held sway with this crowd. There were plenty of familiar faces from back East, debs from Smith and Wellesley and New York's Social Register who had married well and prospered. The couples entertained each other with frequent well-staffed dinners and compared family notes, although John and Caro were childless.

That changed in August 1912, just as the McWilliams family, *père et fils,* were planning a move further west, to a recently built, much grander home on South Euclid Avenue, with gardens and palms and a huge view of the mountains. Caro thought she and John should live by themselves, perhaps closer to town, anywhere that gave her some privacy from her in-laws. The gregarious, fun-loving woman needed her space, space to run her own home, to express her opinions freely, to make her own mistakes, space to relax and to *breathe,* without the old prospector, Father, looking over her shoulder. Though Caro had raised all reasonable objections, John convinced her that the move would benefit his future—*their* future. It would be temporary, just until he was more established in the community.

So that was the plan: they would all move to South Euclid together, where John and Caro would enjoy their own en suite wing of the house, with a veranda off their bedroom, overlooking the camellias. It was a substantial three-story affair, but unlike any of the many popular Mission style or Swiss chalet style or French manor style or Gothic stone homes that neighbored the grounds. No, Father had commissioned his own *faux*-style mini-mansion to resemble the kind of solid Midwestern farmhouse of his childhood: a warren of bright, high-ceilinged rooms, a back staircase, the kind of wraparound porch that invited the family to pull up a rocking chair and sip iced tea on warm afternoons. At the last minute, he had added servants' quarters whose level differed by two steps from the main residence. It was a stunner as far as new houses went, and even Caro had to admit that the place suited their needs.

But the best-laid plans went awry when Caro discovered she was pregnant. It was a well-known fact that Father was allergic to children. "Seen but not heard" was a McWilliams family credo. A screaming baby just wouldn't do. Of course, Father never said as much, but he *suggested* that it might be to everyone's benefit if John and Caro kept the State Street house, at least for a while, until "everybody" got settled.

So that became the new plan: Father would move into the South Euclid house ahead of Caro's delivery, his son and daughter-in-law would remain behind *on their own,* and the entire clan would assemble on Sundays, precisely at six, for family dinner—a plan that secretly pleased everyone involved. The details necessary to revise that plan were never fully spelled out.

But one thing was certain: life in the John McWilliams Jr. household would never be settled again.

Two

"On Her Way"

It seems only right somehow that, a few days before Julia Child's birth, when all of Southern California was captivated by events surrounding the Los Angeles bribery trial of Clarence Darrow, a new column began running in the *Pasadena Evening Post*. With the title "Practical Meals for Pasadena Housewives," the city's young homemakers were encouraged to prepare three square meals a day, selecting from a menu that included such standard cupboard fare as farina, baked potatoes and eggs, broiled chops, and sliced tomato salad, along with a special recipe of the day. The premiere piece, written with the kind of instructive detail only a home ec teacher could love, might have been called "Mastering the Art of Cooking with Canned Goods."

"Open a can of salmon early in the morning, turn it out and flake the fish, discarding skin and bones," it began. Later the same day, after what one can only imagine has been hours during which the salmon festered in the Pasadena heat, various fillers are added, including "two teaspoons of baking powder and sufficient sifted flour to make a thick batter." This whole concoction is then dropped "into a kettle half-filled with smoking-hot fat . . . and cook[ed] like thick pancakes."

As Julia might have later deadpanned: "Indeed!"

Clearly America was waiting for someone to introduce better food. Julia Carolyn McWilliams arrived in the nick of time, following an ungodly stretch of labor at Pasadena Hospital. Her size at birth was noth-

Julia's student years at the
Katharine Branson School, 1928

ing out of the ordinary—seven pounds, eight ounces—no indication of her subsequent prodigious height. Nor was there any disagreement over what to name the baby. For a while, Caro toyed with naming her Dorothy Deane, after her ailing sister; however, she hewed to the original plan: after herself if it was a girl, otherwise there'd be another installment in the long line of John McWilliamses.

Her parents were thrilled with the baby. "She's the spitting image of her mother," John exclaimed, while handing out cigars on whose wrapper was stamped *It's a Girl!* to everyone he encountered. In fact, Julia's hair was light brown at first, not red like Caro's, nor did she have the supple Weston mouth. She had her mother's heart-shaped face and sensitive eyes, but her father's patrician features and stately chin. It would be several more years before her most identifiable attribute emerged: *the voice,* a high-pitched warble that descended directly from the Weston side. The family called it "hooting," the result of unusually long vocal cords, which gave the voice a kind of comical slide-whistle effect. Caro had *the voice,* and so did her siblings. With Julia, however, it would eventually be launched into an inimitable cultural brand, like the NBC chime or Bob Dylan's husky growl.

Only a few weeks after Julia's birth, a mammoth collection of new recipes was published that underscored "the progress of the last few years" taking place in the American kitchen. *A New Book of Cookery* would be Fannie Farmer's final contribution to her extraordinary cookbook canon, but it signaled a huge sea change away from the domestic science movement popular at the turn of the century—a trend that gave us processed cheese, sliced white bread, and instant mashed potatoes— and a return to the more traditional methods of food preparation. Miss Farmer's 860 new recipes relied on cooking instead of chemistry. Her approach was that the process be analytical and precise—both qualities related to science—but ultimately "delicious." Successful beyond her dreams and devoutly reform-minded, Farmer was inured to criticism that her sauces for this collection were too rich, too decadent, and already pushing beyond the typical bland fare to focus on recipes more creative and international in scope: Spanish Lamb Chops, Chicken Maroc, Eggs à la Russe, Bavarian Veal.

Eventually, Fannie Farmer's outlook would have a huge impact on Julia's life. At the time, however, and until she left for college, Julia's worldview was restricted by the insularity of Southern California. For a young girl, it was the paradise that she'd later extol—a spacious home set in a posh residential neighborhood, the natural playground of the Arroyo Seco, her family's seaside retreat in nearby San Malo, and all points in between—a paradise as delicious and satisfying as any culinary feast.

And no one's childhood was more satisfying than Julia's. There was a house full of love, a community full of promise, and for two years Caro and John doted on their infant daughter with the kind of dizzy devotion that a newborn gleans. Caro's attachment was especially moving. In a formal picture taken when Julia was six weeks old, Caro's gaze conveys a soft, affecting tenderness, while Julia, resting upon a lacy crocheted pillow, stares intently toward the camera, her tiny hands clasped across a white lace smock with pleated front and puff sleeves. On the other side of the picture, in a loopy scrawl, someone had written: "The Little Goddess." While Julia was still very young, her mother spent long lazy afternoons reading her stories. There was a small, wooden bookcase in the corner of Julia's bedroom crammed with well-thumbed volumes of children's favorites, among them: *Freckles* by E. Boyd Smith, *Mother Carey's Chickens* by Kate Douglas Wiggin, the Beatrix Potter classics, *Tales of Peter Rabbit* and *The Tale of Mr. Tod,* Alice Caldwell's *Mrs. Wiggs of the Cabbage Patch,* and, of course, the fairy tales of Hans Christian Andersen. Julia would curl up on the living room couch, listening raptly, while Caro delivered the narrative in a variety of stagy voices until, at some point each afternoon, the child would drift off to sleep.

It was idyllic in a formative sense, but Julia was an unusually high-spirited child. Her mother was constantly running through the house, frantically calling out for her daughter after Julia had inched off, exploring some new cluttered corner or wedging herself under a low-slung table. Because the wide French doors were left open most days, Caro was particularly fearful that Julia would wander off outside, making her way off the porch, through the garden, and into the deeply rutted street. "One of these days we'll have to put up a fence," she'd lament in exasperation, until eventually she did exactly that, cordoning off rooms with little accordion fences.

That may have contained Julia, but not enough to keep her out of trouble. "I locked myself in the bathroom and they got the fire department to get me out," Julia recalled. And as she became more ambulatory, her antics grew peskier.

Neighbors who lived several blocks away would come upon a tiny figure sitting on the curb outside their homes, attempting to throw stones at horse-drawn carriages. Or lob a ball into an open-hatched car. John's hard-assed father, hearing of his granddaughter's shenanigans, exhorted Caro to get on the girl's case, but Caro would throw up her hands and say, "She's a child, for goodness' sake," refusing to scold Julia with anything more than a sigh.

Life became eminently more complicated when the family expanded in size. A son, John III, was born in August 1914, during a family holiday in Santa Barbara. Like many Pasadena families, the McWilliamses summered on nearby beaches in order to escape the inland heat. They were staying with John's sister, Bessie, when Caro went into labor, and rather than scramble home over the hilly coastal roads, the delivery became a rather spontaneous affair.

With two children to raise, Caro and John moved into a larger house a few streets away, on Magnolia Avenue. Finally, a place of their own! Not that they were entirely free from John's despotic father. Conveniently—or not—he lived just around the block. In fact, Julia would often cut through backyards to visit, even though, as she later said, "He scared the living daylights out of me." Alas, it was not her grandfather's crusty manner that drew Julia to his door, but an ever-present plate of doughnuts that sat on the windowsill in the kitchen. They were like catnip to a girl who complained she was "always hungry"—dense circles of cake batter that had been deep-fried in oil and dusted in powdered sugar with the faintest whiff of nutmeg. They were delicious, one of her grandmother's Midwestern recipes that never failed to please. Julia would pick up a doughnut and hold it up to her nose, inhaling its sweet, exotic aroma before taking a first bite. God, they were things of beauty. And she was *always hungry*.

Even at such a young age, food was always on Julia's mind.

But—where to find it? Not on Magnolia Avenue, that was for sure. Caro hardly ever made dinner once they moved, and when she did it was Alka-Seltzer time. "All she knew how to cook was baking-powder biscuits and Welsh rarebit," Julia recalled. There was some genial nonsense about codfish balls, as well, deep-fried specimens as hard and deadly as one of Grandfather's mini-balls and drowned in a gluey white sauce that would clot on impact. They may have been "delicious" to some castaway stranded on a New England whaler, but were hardly enough to satisfy an interminably hungry child. Fortunately, Caro employed a cook to make most of the family dinners, a black woman from the valley who prepared acceptable meals—mostly standard meat-and-potatoes fare from *The Boston Cooking School Cookbook*.

But when push came to shove, Julia headed to her grandparents' house. Lo and behold, Grandmother McWilliams, whom Julia described as "a modest and retiring little woman with gray hair in a bun at the back of her neck," was, in her granddaughter's estimation, "a great cook." Growing up on the Plains, where the finest provisions lay right outside the front door, she learned cooking as a second language—farm-fresh omelets, succulent roasts, rustic stews, home-baked pies, hand-churned ice cream, all part and parcel of her seasonal repertoire. And *chicken*—the word alone made Julia's mouth water—"some of the best broiled chicken I ever ate," she declared, long after eating in the finest French bistros. Of course, Grandmother McWilliams had an ace up her sleeve: she was schooled at the elbow of her family's French cook. Imagine that: a French cook in the Midwest in the late 1800s, where dreaming of France was quite a feat. But having a French cook at your service—*oh-la-la!*

Still, one didn't acknowledge one's Frenchness around Julia's father. Somewhere along the way, John decided the French posed a threat. What kind of threat he never quite said, but he had a bill of particulars. The French were *intellectuals,* he said, making it sound about as unsavory as *escargot.* They were snooty and artsy. When you came right down to it, they were . . . well, *French.* That alone was enough to make his case. No, John didn't trust the French *one damn bit* (pardon his French). The only thing John hated more than snooty, artsy intellectuals were snooty, artsy French intellectuals. It was a favorite rant of his that often dominated the table talk.

Since moving west, John McWilliams Jr. had become a very opinionated man. He distrusted government, or at least any statesman with a progressive point of view. And anything foreign. And intellectuals. And Jews. Just for starters. "My grandfather was fairly outspoken when it came to his prejudices," Phila Cousins recalls. "He would make all these right-wing pronouncements that horrified Grandma Caro, but everyone knew better than to disagree with him."

Fortunately, his sympathies never rubbed off on young Julia. As a child, she was "completely disinterested" in her father's partisan views. Besides, when it came to politics, John never attempted to engage his children. Their role was to remain silent and listen—listen and learn. It was only much later, when Julia had formed her own opinions, that she distanced herself from his bias and intolerance. "The way I lived my life never sat well with Pop," Julia observed. "It was bad enough when I became *The French Chef.*"

Her politics, thankfully, were still a long way off. In any case, there was too much for Julia to discover beyond the front yard. She loved to roam the neighborhood, from the top of their street to the orchards on Orange Grove Avenue, where she picked up fallen fruit and gorged herself on their sticky-sweet juice. As soon as she was physically able, she pedaled a tricycle around the block, although the streets were fairly dangerous, shared by horse-drawn carriages, trolleys, and cars. It was easy to spot the young Julia McWilliams, who was unusually tall for her age. From her fourth birthday, she started shooting up into a gangly stalk of a girl, with extremely long arms and an untamable mess of hair. Julia was noticeably larger than the other kids her age—and her behavior around them became more striking.

In an era when young girls were expected to be demure and behave as princesses, Julia indulged in rambunctious behavior. She was "always the instigator," according to an entry in her mother's diary—the first one to suggest an adventure or a prank and the first one to lead the charge. Even more striking, considering Julia played mostly with older kids, girls and boys alike, all of whom bowed to her enthusiasms. It was easy to persuade them to go along with her schemes. *Always the instigator.* Yet more than that—more a case of speaking up. If a playground group put on a skit, Julia usually wangled the lead. If there was a dare on the table, Julia no doubt made it—and took it.

A few weeks later, Julia began going to school, and from that day on her independent spirit began to emerge. The proper age for enrollment was five years old, but her parents decided against a public school anyway; the choices available weren't up to their particular standards. The Garfield School, a few blocks away on California Street, catered to a diverse mix of students—children who grew up on Millionaire's Row as well as those whose parents were Mexican laborers—and the focus there was more disciplinary than instructive; the Arroyo Seco School, opened that year to serve strictly Anglo families, was still largely untested. Instead, Julia was sent to a nearby Montessori school that emphasized hands-on activities—seeing and feeling and doing—as opposed to the imaginative play of most kindergartens. Jukie, as she'd been nicknamed, mastered the school's physical drills intended to develop a youngster's hand–eye coordination: hammering round pegs into round holes, squares into squares; organizing containers so that they fit inside one another; rearranging alphabet blocks in their proper order. "I started doing handwork when I was three," Julia recalled. "We rang bells, learned the scale, put buttons on button frames." There were exercises that stressed graceful movement and good posture, handwriting prompts that sharpened sensory-motor skills. Precision and control, practice and dexterity: all prerequisites for chopping, dicing, and slicing. Although Julia marched to the beat of her own drum, she learned to follow the rules, to listen to instructions: all prerequisites for completing a recipe.

Of course, none of this was on Julia's mind at the time. By 1917, all of her attention had turned to the family, growing again with the coming of spring. Caro was pregnant—"For the last time!" she swore—and Julia devoted herself to praying for a sister. Her brother, John, was tolerable, as brothers went, but definitely on a different wavelength. He was an unusually dozy boy, adrift, almost withdrawn, which his parents made light of to mask their dismay, but privately they were saying that John was "slow." He had trouble concentrating on the simplest concepts; life, in general, seemed to confound him. He was a lovely boy, with an easy, exuberant smile, but "somewhere in the machinery a wire was crossed." Phrases often came out backward. He was clumsy, easily distracted. As a child, Julia just thought he acted goofy. It wasn't until much later, well into his adulthood, that John learned he was "severely dyslexic." "The boys in the family were all dyslexic," says his niece, Phila. "It was genetic—two chromosomes right next to each other." Caro should have recognized the symptoms. Her brother, Donald, was much the same way. But the less fuss made over John the better, she decided, especially with another baby on the way.

In any case, Julia got her wish. Caro gave birth to a girl on April 17, 1917, and there was no doubt whatsoever about her name. Two months earlier, Caro's twenty-three-year-old sister, Dorothy, collapsed in her husband's arms and died instantly, the demon tuberculosis finally catching up with her. It came as no surprise when the baby was named in her honor—Dorothy Deane McWilliams. The family never called her Dorothy, however. From that day on, she would always be Dort.

Despite the age difference, Julia seemed to take a special pride in her younger sister. Dort was the baby, and for that reason, it seems Julia went overboard feeling responsible for her, taking care of her so that she didn't get into trouble. She dragged Dort along on all of her escapades, up Fair Oaks Avenue, through the groves, even into the arroyo, where Julia was forbidden to play. Julia gave Dort the attention she craved. But the four-year difference between them would eventually take its toll.

A sibling rivalry developed almost as soon as the McWilliams family moved into a new, much larger house, at 1207 South Pasadena Avenue. The sprawling two-story structure occupied the best location on the street, a lush two-acre lot with a rolling lawn, fine gardens, a copse of orange and avocado trees, and a clay tennis court, where almost every morning, before the noonday sun made play unbearable, Caro would face off against her friends after their husbands left for work. Julia always "loved this house," describing it in detail, years later, as "a happy, warm, enfolding" place. With its attractive shingled façade, wide eaves, wrap-around porches, and a bay window overlooking the grounds, it was a house that represented the family's upward spiral in the community. In a relatively short time, John McWilliams Jr. had made his mark in a city of fabulously rich men. A series of lucrative investments and land deals placed him on the fringe of their golden circle, with enough respect and influence to function in their orbit. The house added to John's already prominent image. It was a place where he and Caro could entertain in style, although John's tightwad tendencies put a damper on those affairs.

The move, for Julia, was a dream come true. She had her own corner suite of rooms on the second floor, which was flooded by sunlight, and enough built-in shelves for a menagerie of stuffed animals. More important, she made instant friends with the Hall kids who lived across the street. Charlie Hall was in the same class as Julia, but his sister, Babe, who was one year younger, had a sparkle that appealed. Babe Hall was a wiry little firecracker, one of those girls for whom the rules were made to be broken. There was a persuasiveness about her even then, an irresist-ible rascally streak that lapsed into mischief, with her intriguing propos-als for unsupervised play. They could smoke or play pranks, even "take things" that didn't exactly belong to them but were nevertheless up for grabs, like fruit left unattended at the posh Raymond Hotel or plunder from one of the many construction sites nearby. In no time, Julia and Babe were inseparable. They formed the McHall gang, which featured a revolving-door cast, but usually included Charlie and John when the girls were feeling benevolent, and various playmates from up the street who adhered to their whims.

From 1918 until the summer of 1921, Julia and Babe Hall ran rough-shod through their neighborhood, flouting authority and raising as much hell as two girls could get away with. It was not unusual to see them tooling around on bicycles, their baskets overflowing with doo-dads to set some shenanigan in motion: spools of wire, safety matches, shears, nails—whatever they could get their hands on. Anyone who ran into them knew they were up to no good. Julia, especially, was developing quite a reputation. "She was always the leader, the center of things, the instigator," according to her friend, Gay Bradley. "All activities centered around Julia, who was a lively prankster."

Mostly, the pranks were acts of mischief. For instance, one afternoon, she and Babe climbed on the roof of a neighbor's garage and flung mud pies at cars as they sped along Fremont Avenue. They were wildly off-target; the road was littered with muddy clumps. Occasionally, however, they managed to land a few bull's-eyes. There'd be a loud splat, followed by the awful screech of tires, at which point the girls sprawled face-flat to avoid detection, while struggling to stifle their laughter. Julia thought it was a howl, just great fun—until one enraged driver doubled back and crept up behind them. Babe jumped off the roof and scrambled over a fence with Julia hot on her trail, but the driver got his hand around her ankle and threatened to call the police. Julia's tears must have served to distract her captor, because at some point she managed to shake free and escape.

Sometimes, the pranks were destructive. Like the time Julia and Babe dismantled a chandelier in a neighbor's abandoned house and buried the glass finials where the owner wouldn't find them. Or dropped rocks on cars of the Sante Fe trains as they sped beneath the Columbia Street overpass.

But too often her pranks courted danger. One time, while casing a vacant house, she and Babe decided to explore the rooms inside. The doors were padlocked, but that wasn't going to stop them. Earlier, they had spied an open window on the second floor and, rather painstakingly, shimmied along a metal gutter under the roof until they were close enough to swing their legs through to safety. All seemed to go according to plan, until Julia snagged her finger on a piece of sharp wire. She dangled there for some time, trying desperately to free herself, before jumping and ripping away the skin, from fingernail to knuckle. Another time, while prowling around a construction site, Julia wedged herself in the chimney of a new house, requiring a little spontaneous demolition in order to rescue her.

Her curiosity was insatiable—and fed her desire to break the rules. Wherever she wasn't supposed to be, whatever she wasn't supposed to do, were temptations too great for Julia McWilliams to ignore. No one is sure whose idea it was to buy a mail-order cartridge gun in the name of Charlie Hall, but Julia's fingerprints were all over that scheme. The same went for smoking, a favorite pastime of the girls. "I don't believe there was anything they didn't try to smoke," Babe's brother, Charlie, recalled. At first they used a pipe, which Julia kept in a cigar box hidden in the backyard. Later, they stole cigars from Babe's father. Julia's father also had cigars, which the girls smoked from their lookout high in an oak tree, but they much preferred the cigarettes from a music box in his study, slipping a piece of paper between the lid and a clasp to disable its sound.

Even on family vacations, Julia couldn't resist doing things her own way. The McWilliamses' annual getaway to the beach always stirred up some brouhaha or another. One particular squabble was over their dog, a high-strung Airedale by the name of Eric the Red, an ungovernable beast with a penchant for wreaking havoc. Her father forbid, absolutely *forbid,* Julia from taking the dog along on trips. No matter how she tried to change his mind, he wouldn't budge. The dog, he argued, was an unnecessary bother—which didn't stop Julia: she simply stashed Eric in a laundry basket in the backseat of the car and waited until they were twenty miles out of Los Angeles, at which point she produced the dog.

The beach came as something of a release for Julia. It was the place where she could channel her wild energy into more harmless diversions. As far as she was concerned, there was nothing as "magical" as a trip to the coast, where she could swim, climb the dunes, and walk barefoot along the sandy lanes. "I think Santa Barbara is the most beautiful place in the world," she said often of her childhood summers, after decades spent circling the globe. Each June, she and her family, along with the maid and Dort's nurse, joined a caravan of Pasadena families who made the annual pilgrimage north, bumping along sections of coastal highway that were nothing more than patchy dirt and logs. They steered their cars through what locals called the back country, miles of farmland that cut through Whittier and on out to the coast, over rocky ridges, climbing high into the hills, then dipping precariously toward wetlands on either side. The trip seemed endless, a hairy, dramatic journey just to get to Santa Barbara. Yet, to Julia, it ended at another locus of paradise.

It appeared like Oz, emerging from the rustic terrain, a sight to behold. The water in that horseshoe cove was such a brilliant blue, a blue the shade of the stalky irises that overran her mother's garden. Abutting that cove the drama of jagged rocks breaking the surface, barnacled and slippery, and the distant range of mountains whose peaks filtered through the sifting haze. The smell, that salty seaside musk that soothed the senses and seeped into every pore like an invigorating balm. And the beach, the incomparable beach with its velvety pink-tinged sand, a vast, inexhaustible playground where young imaginations ran wild. These were the impressions that stayed with Julia all her life.

For several summers, the McWilliamses stayed in lovely Montecito Park—"Little Pasadena"—a community of modest gray-shingled cottages surrounded by marshy bamboo thickets, where a splash of familiar faces from back home enlivened the scene. Most of Julia's friends from school showed up at one time or another. The weekends were especially exhilarating. There were family-oriented social gatherings on the beach, with daily picnics, spilling back into homes after nightfall. Meals were strictly informal. A smoky cloud from the cookouts, weenie roasts, hung over the enclave. "When we went out to eat there on Sunday noon, we ate at the Miramar Hotel, in a big circular dining room," Julia recalled. "I was fascinated by the fact they served sherbet in the middle of the meal." Formalities like that were few, however. The weeks were, for the most part, a confection of sun, surf, and sand. Caro took the kids swimming every day, dressed in mummy-mode, to ensure maximum protection from the sun. "Mother wore a black swimming costume and black stockings," Julia remembered. Otherwise, they spent afternoons at the big city pool, with a "Tot Lot" attached, where a young instructor led children in games and craft projects.

It was magical, all right, the perfect retreat—while it lasted. Julia adored the lazy, idyllic months, even when her parents packed her off, with a cousin, to nearby Rancho Asoleado for a few weeks each July. The camp was a more structured place than she was used to, where "the girls wore knee socks and elastic-bottomed pants above the knee." Julia, predictably, recalled only the food. "The camp," she said, "was owned by two women who were very good cooks. Every Sunday there was a pancake race to see how many we could eat." Smart money bet on the unusually tall girl from Pasadena. But in 1927, when plans were announced to raze Montecito Park to make way for the Biltmore Hotel, John and Caro decided to move farther along the coast.

Remarkably, they landed in an even more magical place. San Malo, a narrow slip of beach at the mouth of the Buena Vista Lagoon, was founded in 1928 by Pasadena architect Kenyon Keith as an ultraexclusive sanctuary. To an almost comic extent, it was modeled after an island fishing village off the Brittany coast, with identical oceanfront cottages built in a Disneyfied French-Norman motif, with slanted roofs and wood shingles, matching redbrick chimneys, and animal-shaped weathervanes.

Keith sold off the cottages to a group of select friends, all prominent captains of industry, all "old money" from L.A. and Pasadena, who eagerly signed covenants assuring a strict code of silence—what went on in San Malo stayed in San Malo—which exists to this day. Thus, barons like the Chandlers, the Doheneys, and the Sepulvedas could maintain an iron-fisted privacy in the midst of twenty-eight acres of pristine seaside and lush gardens; in its vast gingerbread clubhouse in which members played cards at linen-covered tables; on its cobbled terraces, the scene of endless cocktail parties stocked with unlabeled bottles of Prohibition-era hooch; passing through its well-guarded gatehouse each Friday evening, in a cavalcade of chauffeur-driven vehicles that deposited the weary husbands who'd been in L.A. all week tending their empires.

Julia's family lived just outside the gates, although they were considered adjunct members, welcome anywhere inside San Malo. "In those days, everybody knew everybody else," recalls Julia's girlfriend, Katie Nevins, a frequent visitor to the retreat. "The kids were on the beach all day long or sailed sailboats on the Slew," a basin filled with brackish water, which flowed inland to the sea. "We could wander anywhere, with one exception, the railroad tracks on the eastern end of the community, which went right by us toward Santa Barbara." It should come as no surprise—"Julia played on the tracks whenever she got the chance."

She also disappeared regularly into the Slew, hidden by the tall reeds, where she'd break off stems of bamboo and fashion them into makeshift pipes, in which she would stuff a pinch of tobacco or corn silk. "Many San Malo kids learned how to smoke courtesy of Julia McWilliams," Katie Nevins says.

What they *couldn't* learn from Julia, ironically, was how to cook. Several times each summer, Julia, Katie, and another friend aptly named Berry Baldwin would hijack the McWilliams kitchen, where they attempted to make jam from local strawberries. "Nobody had a damn idea how to do it," Katie remembers, "especially Julia, who was the ringleader of the bunch. It was always a real gooey mess. Nor did she know how to cook, though, God knows, she tried."

All types of experiments-gone-wrong emanated from that kitchen—casseroles with the density and destructive capability of a SCUD missile, sandwiches containing more sand than wich. Julia McWilliams was "a terror at the stove," lacking flair or any kind of technical know-how.

To her credit, however, she was a prodigious eater. Julia loved food—*loved food.* "She could pack it away," says a friend from the neighborhood, who recalls watching with awe and admiration as Julia wolfed down copious helpings at family meals. She ate with gusto, albeit with an indifference to the fare on her plate. Food—and more food—was essential to this ever-expanding girl's growth. By the age of nine, Julia was "already a head taller than her playmates," and edging into her teens she towered over everyone else. "I grew out of my clothing almost overnight," she recalled of those gawky years, when nothing off the rack seemed to fit her leggy frame. "I was always one size bigger than you could ever buy."

It was awkward, being the biggest kid in the class. And in school, for the most part, she stood out from the pack: one could always pick out Julia in the annual student photos. She was placed in the back row, usually among the boys, most of whose heads peaked at a point just below her earlobes. It was impossible for her to go unnoticed. Yet her size was never a source of ridicule or exclusion. At the Polytechnic School, where Julia spent her grammar-school years, she attracted a devoted group of friends who were impressed by her ability to throw a softball as hard as any boy or to shoot a basketball within fingertips of the rim. When it came to sports, she was a natural. Betty Parker, a Poly classmate, described Julia as a tomboy—"more boy than girl." But there was something deeper in Julia McWilliams's makeup, something strong and self-confident, that allowed her to swing easily between her feminine and tomboy identities. It was not unusual to see Julia sewing costumes for a skit or singing in a choir. Like most girls, she longed to play "the beautiful princess" parts in school productions, even though they eluded her. The girly girls, those who played with dolls and studied ballet, felt as close to Julia as they did to any of their like-minded friends.

But Julia wasn't a girly girl—not by any stretch of the imagination. Each morning before school, she'd head across the street, swinging by the Halls' back door to scoop up Charlie, after which they'd tear off on their bikes, slicing in and out of traffic on their way to Poly. Julia was a terror, hell on wheels, swooping along those busy streets like a dervish. It was a free-for-all in those days—no traffic lights, no regulations. Danger lurked at every corner. Although she could be physically awkward on her feet, Julia handled a bike with amazing dexterity, and her nerve often pushed her into madcap situations with it. Hooking rides was one such example. When the spirit moved them, Julia and Charlie would pedal up behind a bus or truck, grab hold of the fender, and glide along at breakneck speeds until they reached their destination, then simply let go. If they were daring enough, they'd hook from one truck to another, which meant flinging themselves through intersections with reckless disregard.

Her one nod to discipline was a weekly dancing class attended—via parental decree—by all the neighborhood kids, an exercise with all the mirth of a root canal that stretched from the fourth through the ninth grades. In a waxy lamplit ballroom at the Vista del Arroyo Hotel, two dozen boys and girls suffered the imperatives of old Mrs. Travis, who drilled them in the starchy protocols of Victorian etiquette. A dress code was carefully scrutinized: boys wore suits and ties, their hair slicked back with pomade, girls donned their Sunday finest, and everyone sported white gloves and black patent-leather shoes. The emphatic proviso was manners, manners, manners.

Julia was a quick study in the manners department. "She had a very proper side to her," says Katie Nevins. There was something innate in the way she handled herself, something almost aristocratic passed down from generations of Westons and McWilliamses. Julia curtseyed like a governess when asked to dance, kept a respectable arm's-length distance between her and her partner, and always thanked him for the pleasure. The same young girl who hooked home behind trucks, smoked cigars, and instigated any number of naughty schemes could "turn on the charm" when the situation arose. Surprisingly for a "giantess," Julia was also light on her feet. In no time, she'd managed a pretty mean box step, while the fox trot and the waltz took her more time to master. Julia could dance—in fact, she loved to dance—but few partners ever gave her a twirl. Most boys—those who were there against their will, to begin with—dreaded being coupled with the tallest girl in the class. They shied from catching Julia's eye; otherwise, stiff and unsmiling, they led her solemnly around the floor, eyes level with a spot somewhere below her collarbone. "She blocked out the light," complained a reluctant dance partner. One poor mutt even admitted to hiding out in the bathroom until it was time for him to go home.

That dance class was anathema to boys and girls alike. They lay awake nights, scheming of ways to get out of it. For the most part, however, the kids in Julia's circle led a decidedly charmed life. Adventure abounded in a neighborhood teeming with hideaways. They explored ravines and caves in the Arroyo Seco, where every childhood fantasy came to life. From one of its escarpments, called Devil's Gate, Julia could survey the whole San Gabriel Valley, all the way west to Los Angeles, where miles of fertile farmland were being developed like a spreading virus. Or she could watch the hard hats at a sandy outpost of the canyon work the jaws of a rapacious backhoe as it consumed tons of dirt from a basin where the Rose Bowl would eventually stand. Hot days—which nature delivers practically year-round in Pasadena—demanded a dip in one of the ubiquitous backyard swimming pools or at the Brookside Plunge, a public rec center, where "white women and girls were restricted to one day a week." There was fishing and trips up the funicular to the Mount Lowe Observatory and, once in a great while, outings with Caro to Los Angeles, which Julia found "so exciting in the twenties."

Excitement was L.A.'s unique allure, but for Julia, "Pasadena had it all." She could tick off any number of virtues that captivated her about the city, with one conspicuous exception: *food*—it wasn't part of her Pasadena zeitgeist. Although an enthusiast at the table when it came to meals, the food Julia ate was of little or no interest to her. "Our family had a series of hired cooks, and they'd produce heaping portions of typical American fare," she recalled. She consumed whatever was put in front of her, usually oversauced haunches of meat cooked, as Pop insisted, to a ghastly "medium gray."

Restaurant food was of little or no consequence. "Few Pasadena families went out to eat," according to Jo McWilliams. In fact, the restaurant scene in America had crumbled in a precipitous collapse, owing, in large part, to Prohibition, which made high-end cooking unsustainable throughout the 1920s. But Pasadena, in particular, was a gastronomic wasteland. Aside from the posh hotels, where upscale food was a mandatory staple, its most fashionable dining rooms were coffeeshops, automats, cafeterias, and luncheonettes, which reflected the convergence of economics and domestic-science cookery. "You could get a pretty good hot dog or a ham-and-cheese sandwich," Julia recalled, along with staples from the labs of national brands: Heinz ketchup, Coca-Cola, Campbell's soup, Borden's sweetened milk. The sole bastion of fine cuisine was François's French Restaurant, a small boîte on Colorado Street that was as dubiously fine as it was dubiously French. Its owner, François Giametti, was unmistakably Italian, and his menu, featuring a mixed bag of roasts and red-sauce spaghetti, claimed "our famous French dressing" as its link to a foreign heritage.

Still, that was enough to keep John McWilliams from its doors. For anything French—or anything continental, for that matter—Julia's father felt only contempt. But in October 1926, a few months after Julia's fourteenth birthday, John and Caro broke protocol by taking her out to eat in a foreign locale. Prohibition had driven them to drink . . . in Tijuana, just south of the Mexican border from San Diego, where the streets were filled with Anglos flouting the Eighteenth Amendment. Although a notorious seat of hedonism, where pleasures of every kind were available for fifty cents or less, the town had become a magnet for a coterie of Los Angeles nightcrawlers intent on making a new scene. It was party time in Tijuana, with bars and restaurants packed to the walls and liquor flowing like the Rio Grande.

At John's insistence, they avoided the casinos and honky-tonks and made a beeline for Caesar's Place on the dirt-caked Avenida Revolución. Two years earlier, during an unforeseen July Fourth run on the kitchen, chef Caesar Cardini had averted disaster by concocting a dinner salad—who ever heard of a *dinner salad*?—from what was left in the larder. In a stroke of genius, he assembled it tableside, with all the finesse of a close-up magician: a bouquet of tender hearts of romaine lettuce were fanned out on a plate and swaddled in a rich, creamy Parmesan dressing. A few tomato slices were added, some puréed garlic for pizzazz. And, by the way—it was meant to be eaten, leaf by leaf, with the fingers! It was an instant sensation that captivated his clientele and drew a surge of Hollywood celebrities clamoring for—what else?—a Caesar salad.

John and Caro "were wildly excited" that they should finally lunch at Caesar's restaurant. "My parents, of course, ordered the salad," Julia remembered. "Caesar himself rolled the big cart up to the table [and] tossed the romaine in a great wooden bowl." It was a sight to behold for a fourteen-year-old with a serious appetite. Fifty years later she could envision the artfully flamboyant process. "I can see him break two eggs over that romaine and roll them in, the greens going all creamy as the eggs flowed over them." What decadence! "Two eggs in a salad? And garlic-flavored croutons, and grated Parmesan cheese?" The way he conjured that dressing was an unforgettable performance. And yet the lingering memory for Julia was of her father *eating a salad*. "Before then," she said, "salads were considered rather exotic, definitely foreign, probably Bolshevist, and, anyway, food only for sissies."

If there was anything John McWilliams loathed more than exotica, foreigners, and Bolshevists, it was sissies. Frenchmen, of course, were unpardonable sissies. And *artists*! Artists of any kind had a chromosome in the wrong chamber. John suspected anyone who wasn't an upright, honest straight-shooter—someone like himself, that is—of deviant behavior.

Since moving to California, he had become gradually more right-wing and irritable, a hard-ass contrarian whose positions would turn more extreme—and uglier—with each year. He erupted in red-faced tirades when anyone challenged his views, and his views were expressed with clockwork regularity. John despised Woodrow Wilson and the League of Nations and lashed out at anyone expressing pro-union sentiments. "Reds," "pinks," and subversives threatened America's stability. Negroes and Mexicans: a drain on decent society; Jews were contemptible, beneath his respect. A man's man—someone like himself, that is—engaged in business, invested conservatively, drank bourbon, and voted Republican. All others—the foreigners and Bolshevists and Jews and *sissies*—be damned.

John's polemics bewildered his eldest daughter. Julia idolized her father; he held a heroic presence in her life. She admired her father's stature and success in the influential business community, his prestige, and his aristocratic bearing. Long and sinewy, with broad shoulders and ice-blue eyes, he dominated people with his tenacity as well as with his size. He was exceedingly effective at imposing his will. As an entrepreneur, John was shrewd and meticulous, given to calculated moves that disarmed his detractors. Everyone agrees that his charm was considerable. In the house, however, John was a despot: he demanded unqualified respect—attention to his utterings, silence when he was working. Obedience was sacred. And he was stern, hard on his children, especially when it came to Julia. She found it blindingly difficult to please him. "My father was too hard on Julia because she was the oldest," recalled Dort. "He could be very intimidating." Especially toward a daughter from whom he expected great modesty. During dinner table conversation, when Julia might be bubbling and fidgety, he could cut her off with a raised eyebrow in her direction. Or a dismissive cough. Or lethal silence. In those instances, Julia would have to shut down, to subvert her personality in order to please her father, and she learned to do so with crushing disappointment. It was a process that promised endless collisions.

Inevitably, Julia took her disappointment out on Dort. As the baby of the family, Dort enjoyed privileges that grated on Julia, building resentment that was manifest by cruelty and retribution. Dort "was an easy target," says her daughter, Phila. She had hair that stood on end—and had a personality that stood on end, too. "Even as a child, it was very easy to provoke her, which Julia would take advantage of whenever possible. Often, after [Dort] was done playing outside and tried to enter the house,

Julia would lock the front door. And when she finally let [Dort] in, Julia would pretend she didn't know her." Looming over her younger sister, Julia would demand: "Who are you? What do you want here?" As Dort, flummoxed, grew ever more upset, Julia would announce: "I'm calling the police." Eventually, Dort learned how to neutralize this prank, but Julia refined and expanded her strategy. One of her favorite ploys was to cast doubt on Dort's origin. "Julia told my mom that she was adopted," Phila says. It was an elaborate hoax that stretched over months. Of course, Julia thought it was hysterically funny, but Dort "would go nuts."

Of all Julia's mischief, nothing tormented Dort as much as their competition on the tennis court in the backyard. The girls would take turns drawing the chalk lines in the red clay dust, but no matter where Dort hit the ball, Julia called it out. A well-placed shot in the server's box—*"Out!"* A return dropped neatly inside the baseline—*"Out!"* Dort would kick and scream in her own defense, point like a detective at the evidence in the dirt, to which Julia would imperviously shrug. *"Out!"*

Caro wisely refused to take sides. Her practice was to let the girls work out their own differences. Raising three kids was a handful. Lord knows, she had enough trouble keeping their bodies in proper balance. There were so many aspects she had to watch over. Their noses, for one thing. Caro was convinced that rubbing a child's nose kept it supple and small. So every afternoon at a prescribed hour Julia, John, and Dort had their noses massaged. And their stomachs, for another—each child got a dreaded tablespoon of cod liver oil every day, "for regularity." Julia remembers taking it as one would "a shot of poison." She "held [her] breath, shuddered and tried not to gag."

And their lungs—fresh air was the elixir of life; the good citizens of Pasadena, in particular, were addicted to it. The papers were full of articles preaching what would come to be known as New Age advice, and those eager to hear the message strained for every word. Quacks as well as "a generous sprinkling of . . . fortunetellers, swamis, and purveyors of 'electronic vibrations' . . . were plentiful and popular in Pasadena," all of whom contributed to the general health craze. "Medical experts of the time advocated living, or at least sleeping, out-of-doors, for everyone, not just respiratory sufferers," wrote a local historian. So almost every house had a wraparound sleeping porch to accommodate a grouping of beds, and the McWilliamses were no exception. John insisted the children sleep outside, "rain or shine, 365 days a year."

Julia always claimed she never got enough rest. Perhaps the arrange-

ment on the porch intruded on her peace and quiet—or inflamed aller-
gies, any number of which she and her sister fought throughout their
childhoods. They fought among themselves, too. At night, with the
porch flaps rolled up and a view of the brilliant nightscape overhead, the
girls would start in on each other, needling, needling, until one of them,
usually Dort, was reduced to tears. It was a classic sibling rivalry. Julia,
older and brimming with self-confidence, bullied her younger sister any
chance she got, pushing Dort's buttons—though not to any extreme, not
in a way that did permanent damage. "There was plenty of love between
them," insists Dort's daughter, Phila. But, as she said, her mother was an
easy target—and Julia was expert when it came to hitting the bull's-eye.

TARGET PRACTICE ENDED abruptly when, in 1927, Julia's parents
decided to send her to boarding school. This was in no way intended as
punishment for her behavior toward Dort, nor did it reflect her evident
uninterest at Poly, whose curriculum ended anyway with the ninth grade.
As far as Caro and John could tell, Julia was as happy and focused as any
girl her age. A little more restless perhaps, but nothing that required an
extra measure of discipline. Rather, it followed a Weston family tradition.
Caro and her sisters, Nellie and Louise, attended Miss Capen's School in
Northampton, Massachusetts. Boarding school, the family believed, gave
a daughter's education a larger perspective, including the vital elements
of finishing and charm.

It seems illogical, therefore, that they chose the Katharine Branson
School. Located in Ross, California (fifteen miles north of San Francisco), a town not unlike Pasadena—bucolic, wealthy, and devoutly
conservative—there was every expectation that Julia would adapt. But
had they done their due diligence, Julia's parents would have discovered that KBS viewed finishing and charm as scornfully as they might
partying. The school, founded in 1920 and rooted in a grind of classical studies, "believed [in] a college education for all young people who
were endowed with sufficient gray matter." It wasn't a marriage mill,
like so many of the private boarding schools of the era. Students were
groomed to attend a prestigious university and assumed that KBS stood
for "knowledge before sex." But college preparation was not its sole purpose, according to the school's eponymous headmistress. "We wanted
the girls to learn not only to think independently," she wrote, "but to
exercise self-discipline, to cherish self-respect, to value things of the

spirit as well as things of the mind . . . and [to have] a high expectation of one's self and one's school."

In 1927, the year that Julia arrived, KBS wasn't yet much of a school. The Residence Hall—a creamy stucco Mission structure with dark wood interiors and big living rooms—could accommodate only eight boarders, and had been built on the steep rise of an old dairy farm so that anyone standing on its veranda overlooked a patchwork of woods and fields that seemed to isolate the campus from the outside world. But "the Res," as it was known, doubled as the dining hall and the library, with two other cottages—"Oaks" and "Stairways"—converted into cramped classrooms. A gym and pool were in various stages of construction; otherwise, there was little else in the way of functional buildings.

Still, "it was a marvelous, magical place," as Julia recalled, a place for privileged young women to grow and to blossom. There were tennis courts and a lake and a soccer field where students played a dazzling range of sports. A woodsy amphitheater—called "the glen"—served as a natural backdrop for dramatic productions. But, at the outset, many of these girls from the land of plenty suffered culture shock. They got a blow on registration day, when their parents finally left and, standing there alone, in unfamiliar surroundings with unfamiliar classmates, everyone in new dresses and hats, the boom was lowered. The Katharine Branson School wasn't a refuge for dilettantes; they weren't in business to pamper or indulge. The school had rigid rules and uniforms and demanding academic standards. No one would be given any special treatment. For many girls, it was the first time they'd encountered anything of the sort: being away from home and at the mercy of a no-nonsense headmistress. And for others, like Julia McWilliams, it was nothing to sweat.

Julia dealt with rules the way she later dealt with vegetarians: she pretended they didn't exist. She wasn't intimidated by the guidelines or the alien situation. She wasn't subdued. So comfortable was Julia with her new surroundings, moreover, that when rooms in the Res became unexpectedly overbooked, she volunteered to live apart in a quirky little cottage with her cousin Dana, who was enrolled in the same class. When it came to readjustment, Julia was one cool customer, owing, as one classmate observed, to "her complete lack of self-consciousness . . . feeling at home and at ease anywhere," and a natural rhythm for marching to her own drumbeat.

She rolled herself right into the social structure of KBS, although there were rules aplenty that invited much grumbling. The Bible, for one thing. It was mandatory that girls bring a Bible to school and carry it to services at St. John's Episcopal Church every Sunday morning. Even as a teenager, Julia was outspoken in her attitude toward religion. "She thought it was rot," says a family member familiar with her beliefs. Julia's parents were Presbyterians, "but only in a WASPy kind of way," abandoning regular church attendance by the time Julia was ten. And Julia made no bones about the school's fussy requirement. "I hated having to go to church," she complained, which extended to morning prayer, the saying of grace before meals, and the singing of vespers before bed.

Nor was there any love lost with respect to school uniforms—and there were compulsory outfits for myriad occasions. One thing was clear: the school's motto, "Truth is beauty and beauty is truth," did not extend to the uniforms. Miss Branson, no clotheshorse by any stretch of the imagination, was oblivious to fashion. Each year before the school term began, she went to Spaulding's in San Francisco and placed an order for two ensembles that the girls would rotate according to seasons. The summer uniform, befitting a waitress at Chock Full o'Nuts, was blue-and-white checked gingham, worn with Spaulding loafers or saddle shoes. In winter it was replaced by something known as "the lapis lazuli tweed." "It had a skirt which didn't do the most for any of us," recalled a 1926 alumna, "and a short little jacket with a round collar that came open in the front in a rather weird way." A blue or red sweater accompanied the get-up. Girls wore different dresses to dinner: short frocks with either white crêpe de chine pleated with cascading sleeves or the famous Katharine Branson blue—"French Blue" they called it—found in every decorative feature on campus. To complete the wardrobe, there were athletic uniforms for the school's intrasquad teams, the Blue Bonnets and the Tam o'Shanters, for which the girls wore cardigans with "floppy hats that were really awful," and for basketball games, long, baggy, black-satin bloomers and white middies with black cotton leggings that never failed to draw disapproving groans.

At least the dining rules didn't bother Julia. Girls were expected to eat everything on their plates, whether they liked it or not. And there was a lot not to like. The school cooking was mediocre, institutional—worse: indifferent. But food was nothing but fuel to Julia, who continued to grow off the charts. There wasn't anything she refused to eat. Gluey rice pudding, calf's liver, sardines—all fine by Julia. She never went through the contrivances that beset other girls, who would fill their cheeks with whatever food they dreaded and then bolt for the bathroom.

Julia, for the most part, was an exemplary KBS girl. She threw herself into that first year of school, jumping center for the basketball team, acting in a number of dramatic revues, attending current-events lectures and the occasional cultural outing to San Francisco, where the girls, in groups of two, spent time rummaging through shops. "On Saturdays, my friends and I would put on Prince Matchabelli cherry-red lipstick and go in to San Francisco and have artichokes and cinnamon toast," she told *The New York Times* in 1989. Nothing seemed to inhibit Julia—aside from her schoolwork.

"I wasn't anyone's idea of a model student," she admitted. The classes were demanding, an everyday mix of traditional subjects, with extra emphasis on both Latin and French. Julia "hated Latin," which was taught by the steely-eyed Katharine Branson herself, "who demanded perfection and generally got it." And French—one would assume it came naturally to Julia. *Mais non, non,* according to her teacher, Mademoiselle Bègue. She blamed it on Julia's "explosive consonants attributed to Scotch ancestry," but the reason was probably closer to lack of interest. "I was pretty well caught up in the social aspect of school," Julia recalled without a trace of remorse. "There were so many wonderful distractions. As far as the studies went, I did just enough to get by."

Julia's feeble report card didn't seem to bother her parents. Nothing extraordinary in the way of scholarship was expected of her; after all, a daughter's role was to become a good wife. During the Christmas break, at the end of her first semester, John and Caro treated Julia like a special guest. Average grades weren't about to spoil her homecoming. That, as it turned out, would take something completely unexpected.

The first sign of trouble came on the afternoon of December 8, 1927, when Caro took a frantic call from her friend, Betty Stevens. The Stevens and McWilliams families enjoyed a close and entangled relationship. Francis Stevens, who was vice-president of both the First National Bank of Pasadena and First Trust and Savings Bank, handled most of John's personal business in addition to being his longtime golfing partner and most trusted friend. Julia and their daughter, Carol, had played together since childhood, as had John Jr. and their youngest son, George. Many of their family celebrations were joyously intertwined. In fact, when John put the State Street house up for sale, it seemed right and proper when Francis bought it. They had their share of trying times, as well. When young George was expelled from school, Caro spent time comforting Betty without discussing the expulsion's actual cause, an incident of homosexuality. More comfort and encouragement had been needed a few months earlier, when Francis Jr., a star pupil at the University of Michigan, wrapped his car around a telephone pole, suffering a basal skull fracture that affected his mind.

This time, however, it was something much more serious. That morning, Francis Stevens went to work early, around eight, making small talk with the cashiers as they prepared their morning cash drawers. He seemed in a cheerful enough mood, even as he made certain that his will was in order. An hour later, he drove over to the Garfield School and picked up George. They sat in the car talking for several minutes before driving off—*where* no one knows, but it must have been to a secluded spot, because at 9:15 he put a pistol to George's temple and shot him dead. A few minutes later, he pulled up to Las Encinas, a posh sanitarium where his son Francis Jr. was recuperating in a private bungalow. They took a leisurely walk around the grounds until they came to the tennis courts in the rear, where Francis murdered his second son. Afterward, Stevens put the barrel of the gun into his own mouth and finished the job.

Julia's family was predictably distraught. No one had seen this coming, not even John, who had shared every intimacy with Francis Stevens. There was even a letter left for him the morning of the tragedy, a handwritten note addressed to John in the pages of the will, assuring all successors that the family's finances were in order. John was inconsolable—over the seemingly senseless deaths, over the loss of his dear friend. How did one put something so incomprehensible into perspective? How does one equate it to one's own family circumstances?

The murders' effect on Julia was also profound. The impact from the shock was complex, confusing. This was her first experience with tragedy of any kind, the first time her safe, perfect world was jolted by unpleasantness. The death of young George was especially disturbing. He was the same age as her brother, John, with similar traits—at least, as far as Julia knew. George was described as slow, odd, even "retarded," all euphemisms, of course, to mask his true nature. Homosexuality wasn't part of anyone's vocabulary, not in Pasadena, not among the cream of society. Nor would Julia have understood it had she heard the word used. But *slow, odd* . . . she'd overheard her parents say they had a son who was unnaturally slow, so slow, in fact, that they'd been discussing sending him to the Los Alamos Ranch School, a rigorous boot-camp type academy on an isolated plateau in the New Mexico wilds, where "difficult" boys got a "disciplined" education. The similarities were too troubling for Julia to process. Usually, she was so upbeat, so irrepressible, but throughout the holiday she lapsed into inscrutable silences, long, brooding reveries when that outlook seemed unreachable. Her parents grew more guarded. There was talk of keeping Julia at home with them, for the time being, instead of sending her back to boarding school. But Julia eventually shook herself out of it. She insisted on returning to KBS at the end of her vacation, joining her cousin on the trip back to school, a long, meandering journey by train, ferry, and limousine, during which her personality reemerged. Not a word was mentioned about the tragedy in Pasadena. Years later, Julia's closest friends would recall how she always managed to maintain a game face, how intimate questions were deflected with glancing expertise. There were places, personal places, she just refused to go. In an essay entitled "A True Confession" that appeared in her senior yearbook, Julia came as close as she ever would to questioning her "emotional machinery," when she wrote: "Bear in mind always that an X-ray would show my heart to be no softer than a rock!" Julia's deepest feelings were invariably off-limits, perhaps even to herself. She pushed them aside and went on.

None of her classmates at KBS saw anything more than the occasional silences.

Julia McWilliams became a standout at boarding school, the kind of student who, in those days, was recognized as BMOC. She was elected student council president, as well as captain of the basketball team. A blooming extrovert, she joined the Fantastics, a drama group made up of the resident girls, who put on two or three plays a year, including the annual performance of *A Midsummer Night's Dream* that was a legendary botch job. She was named president of the Vagabonds, a hiking club, whose ambitious climb to the top of Mount Tamalpais capped a year of grinding marches along dirt roads. And the first week of May, when all regular classes were canceled to launch a play on the front lawn, Julia usually snagged herself a plum part, not a lead—those were reserved for the ingénues, which wasn't Julia's style—but something that stole the spotlight and occasionally the show. "I was usually cast as a fish or something," she recalled, "never as the beautiful princess." Playing men also seemed to be her stock-in-trade—Michael, the Sword Eater was a particularly memorable role—and when her roué had to romance the heroine in *Pomander Walk,* the audience cracked up as Julia leaned in to plant a kiss.

There wasn't anything, short of prayer, that Julia wouldn't attempt. It was impossible to dispirit her. She had great reserves of spunk, which was what made her one of Katharine Branson's favorites. Despite Julia's "moderately good" grades—praise from the headmistress that was generous at best—she loved Julia's "joyousness of spirit . . . [her] refreshing naïveté." There was a lot to recommend Julia McWilliams. Though, had Miss Branson discovered that Julia and a day student who lived across from campus routinely broke into her uncle's liquor cabinet and made themselves martinis, it seems likely Julia's stock would have plummeted. Instead, on graduation day, in June 1930, at a ceremony on the lawn under an enormous cedar tree, Julia was awarded the vaunted school cup presented to the senior considered to be the School's First Citizen.

Julia McWilliams was "on her way," Katharine Branson announced to a gallery of beaming faces. She was a "practical, wholesome type of girl with superior intelligence." Nothing would stop her from attaining anything she wanted.

But what she wanted was a mystery to even Julia herself.

Three

Julia of the Almost Spring

Julia studied the Smith College registration form with a degree of unease. On the line below the space provided for course preferences, there was a question that threw her an unexpected curve. It was labeled "Vocational Choice," with room enough to write half a résumé. The many forms at orientation required only standard information, but this one was tricky. The girls on either side of her were scribbling away, compiling a wish list of impressive professions: pediatrician, nutritionist, interpreter, lawyer, choreographer, historian . . . Smithies were known to reach for the stars. There were so few colleges that encouraged women to excel, to compete for the same jobs as those open to men. Smith entertained no such limitations. Its goal, according to a mission statement, was "to develop fully as may be the powers of womanhood and furnish women with the means of usefulness, happiness and honor now withheld from them."

The young women striving toward that goal—toward breaking new ground and setting new standards—were determined women, for most of the students entering the class of 1934 had tenacious minds, scholarly minds, the minds of women trained to learn and grow. But the mind of Julia McWilliams was distracted. She wasn't goal-oriented, or particularly driven, or, for that matter, much of a student. Years later, Julia realized she was nothing more than "an utter adolescent" at the time she entered Smith; she was immature, totally unprepared for the col-

With Tom Johnston, the man who broke Julia's heart,
New York, 1936

lege experience. "Somebody like me should not have been accepted at a serious institution," she concluded. For Julia, academics were incidental to her real objective at Smith, which was having a nice environment in which to grow up.

Vocational choice? That was about as far from her mind as the start of freshman classes. She picked up her pen and filled in the blank: "No occupation decided; marriage preferable."

WHAT WAS JULIA doing here in the first place? All evidence suggests it was preordained. "There was never the slightest doubt in my mind that I would go to Smith," Julia said. Caro had studied there as a member of the class of 1900, when a woman's attending college "was rather a daring thing to do." Less than 2 percent of the female population went on to higher education. From then on, Caro embraced her college experience in the core of her identity; she would always be a Smithie. It was her dream that Julia would follow suit. "And the day I was born," according to Julia, "I was entered at Smith College."

Location was also a factor. Smith was back East, in Northampton, Massachusetts, a stone's throw from the Weston stronghold in Dalton. The family could keep an eye on Julia—and vice versa. Caro still had a financial stake in her father's paper business, now being run by her brother, Philip. But Philip lived in the shadow of his domineering wife, Julia's Aunt Theodora, whose tentacles extended deep into the ledgers of the Weston empire. Theodora was a scold, mercurial and belligerent, but mindful of the Family and its collective identity. Like it or not, Julia would be welcome at the Weston homestead during school holidays, when returning to Pasadena was inexpedient. She would be Caro's emissary, her eyes and ears, in the shifting politics at Byron Weston Paper.

If Julia's entrée to Smith was "my destiny," as she put it, her transition there was anything but smooth. There were several factors that left her feeling unsettled, insecure. Even though she had been to an exclusive boarding school in California and should have felt in sync with her surroundings, Smith presented an altogether different picture. At Katharine Branson, Julia admitted, she "was never a brilliant student." She "wasn't particularly politically aware, hardly read the newspaper." Her aptitude test scores were mediocre, at best. Now, arriving at Smith, she encountered women who were serious about their education—they were academically minded, worldly, what Julia saw as "real scholars"—and faculty she considered "really wonderful brains." How, after skating through KBS for four years, was she supposed to compete at this level? Would she stumble through her classes, fall behind, and get bounced for poor grades like a third of Smith's undergrads? Suddenly she was all the way across the country, by herself, with nobody to rely on, which made Julia feel frightened for the first time in her life.

Fortunately, Caro had contacted one of her Smith classmates who also had a daughter entering the class of '34 and suggested that the two girls room together for their freshman year. Mary Case was a dark-haired, serious-looking young woman whose pale complexion owed much to the fact that she'd kept her head buried in a textbook throughout high school. The admissions committee at Smith considered her a prize catch, an academic standout who was loaded with potential and fit the Smith profile. She was smart as a whip, disciplined, and extremely ambitious. In fact, everything about Mary ran counter to Julia's carefree approach. Even physically, they were an unlikely pair, as different as Mutt and Jeff. Mary, nicknamed Casey, was a squat, 160-pound dumpling who "had eaten too many hot fudge sundaes"; Julia, naturally slender, had grown so tall she was unable to fit on the standard-issue bed in the dorm. Despite the differences, said Julia, "We liked each other immediately."

What's more, Mary was at home in a world from which Julia felt excluded. She not only had the Smith mind-set, she had the Smith look: a Brooks Brothers crew-neck cable-knit sweater, a pastel tweed skirt and camel's hair coat from Best & Co., a strand of five-and-dime pearls, and brown-and-white Spaulding saddle shoes. "I didn't have anything like this," Julia said. "I was just an absolute mess." The façade of a Seven Sisters coed seemed unassailable, exposing Julia as a western girl who dressed like one, not chic, like the easterners, but in ginghams and lace. Julia was despondent, an outcast. More than anything, she longed to fit in. By late November, the role of outcast was killing her. "Finally Mother came east for Thanksgiving," Julia recalled, "and I wept upon her neck, and we went to New York and I came back with my Spaulding two-tone leather shoes, my sweater, my pearls. Then, I felt in." At last, "I was finally in."

In—but still indifferent. Nothing in Julia's classes managed to engage her, a standard freshman load that included English Comp., Hygiene, History, Zoology, French, and Italian. Sidetracked and distracted, she resorted to reading mysteries, carousing, doing just enough homework for a respectable grade. Meanwhile, Mary Case burned the midnight oil, splitting their corner suite at Hubbard House into two very different zones. But a virtual split proved by no means enough. Julia's antics never failed to crack Mary up. "I have never had a roommate who was so utterly fun to be with," she said. But with Julia around, it was becoming impossible to concentrate on her studies. The girls got "into such terrible giggle fests" that eventually they had to swipe the fire rope from the hall, stretch it across the room, and hang their bedspreads on it so they couldn't see each other.

While Mary hit the books, Julia immersed herself in a variety of extracurricular activities, jumping center for the Smith basketball team, on which her mother had starred, and acting in skits, most of them glib, lightweight burlesques written by one or another of the English majors planning a Broadway career. Julia loved the stage, loved the delicious theatrics involved, expressing herself eloquently, if a little over-the-top. She had a gift for it, always delivering her lines in that riveting fluttery voice. Her friends would laugh appreciatively as Julia loped across the stage, swallowing her lines with guttural abandon, never dreaming how, years later, they would become her signature shtick. To anyone observing her at the time, it seemed unlikely that Julia McWilliams would command any serious spotlight. She was outgoing and frisky, which made her popular at Smith, but never targeted for success. "A grand person generally but she does go berserk every once in awhile," the Hubbard housemother wrote in Julia's confidential file.

Behavior of this nature spelled uncertainty for a career-minded young woman—although the housemother might have altered her opinion slightly had she any inkling that two companies, RCA and Westinghouse, were in the throes of discussing a new medium that would someday thrive on grand and occasionally berserk personalities. They weren't yet sure what to do with it, but they were already calling it television.

JULIA HAD NO such eye on the future. She lived entirely in the present, larking across the Smith campus, doing the bare minimum of study to get by. "I was not going full steam," she recalled. "I did not have all the burners turned on." They were only turned to low, in fact—an output that earned a B-minus average her freshman year. The next year, her flame grew even dimmer, barely meriting Cs. Ostensibly, she was an undisciplined worker, and her work, haphazard. As far as flunking out went, she was right on the cusp, but that prospect apparently never worried her. "Julia did not really worry much about anything," said Mary Case, who by sophomore year no longer shared a dorm room with Julia. Mary's grades—and weight—had suffered at the hands of her erstwhile roommate. "I couldn't play all night and laugh with Julia and [hope to] stay in college."

Remarkably, Julia never gave serious thought to cutting her losses and dropping out of school, a fate not uncommon to young women at the time. Such a ruthless decision, as opposed to languishing at Smith, might have set her on a path of earlier accomplishment. Nevertheless, it almost surely would have landed her in the doghouse at home. Leaving college would have especially crushed her mother's spirits.

In fact, Caro's health was more than just an idle concern. Two years earlier, in 1929, Julia's mother had suffered a stroke while vacationing in Santa Barbara. She was only forty-nine years old and still as vigorous as any of her children, but an emotional, high-strung disposition had finally caught up to her. The Weston birthright had inflicted its share of injury. "Extreme inbreeding in Dalton," was one relative's hazy conclusion. Perhaps so, perhaps the Westons' trust in primogeniture had finally done them in. But there appeared to be mitigating factors. For generations, congenital high blood pressure had taken its toll—on Caro's parents certainly, both of whom died young, but also on her nine siblings, many of whom were sickly, weak—or dead. Caro had seemed fortunate; she seemed to have avoided a similar fate. She was fun-loving, ostensibly hearty, always running on a full tank of exuberance. Her son, John, considered her nothing short of a "dynamo." The last thing anyone suspected was a ticking medical time bomb. When Caro grew fatigued, as was often the way things stood, it was written off to a case of burnout— or hot flashes. This time, however, there were no such pretenses. The stroke had caused one side of her face to permanently sag. And there were other, less perceptible symptoms: occasional unsteadiness, tremulous reflexes, some minor disorientation. Those closest to Caro could tell "she'd kind of faded."

No, dropping out of Smith was never an option for Julia. She knew better. Caro couldn't have taken it. "It would have killed my mother," Julia insisted.

By her own admission, Julia accepted her role stoically, "doing just enough work to get by." In her junior year, her grades improved slightly, thanks to an undemanding major in history. But to even the most chance observer, Julia minored in partying. For most of the year, she immersed

herself in a smorgasbord of campus activities that sidetracked her studies and channeled her energies elsewhere. There were weekend socials
and recitals and committees that organized the socials and recitals. A
column in *The Tatler,* Smith's humor monthly, kept her gainfully preoccupied. Fellow students recall seeing Julia, along with Mary Case and other
pals, parading around campus as "grass cops," the so-called elite squad
of whistle-blowing enforcers who shooed people off the lawn. And she
continued playing basketball despite the nonstop complaints from oppo-
nents who, Julia said, "were awfully mad at me for being so big."

"There was so much going on at the college," Julia recalled. "And then
there was, of course, Amherst and Harvard and everything [else] right
near." You could strike out in any direction and get swept up in another
school's spirit. Dartmouth's carnival was a favorite that Julia never
missed. The same went for Princeton's foxy men, who raided the Smith
henhouse as if it were a private harem. Annually, Smith and Amherst
staged a joint musical sketch that collapsed into a drunken bacchanal.
"And if you went down to a game in New Haven," Julia recalled, "everybody just got terribly drunk."

"Julia had quite a taste for the spirits," recalls a classmate who wit-
nessed her drunken antics during the last two years of college. "Even during Prohibition, she had the knack for coming up with a bottle of gin."
Or she knew of a place to get it. There were several bootleggers, notoriously shady characters, who supplied the student market in and around
Northampton, and while they "scared the bejesus" out of most proper
students, Julia never felt intimidated. The same went for speakeasies,
which were famously wicked establishments. Once, she heard about such
a joint in nearby Holyoke and organized a field trip to scout out its potential. "It was up on the top floor of a warehouse," Julia recalled. "Everyone was very nice to us, and we all drank one of everything and drove
home and most of us were heartily sick—but it was terribly exciting." On
another occasion, following a night of enthusiastic drinking, Mary Case
encountered Julia, shitfaced, prowling the Hubbard Hall corridor on her
hands and knees.

Julia McWilliams could party with the best of them. She was a big
girl with a seemingly bottomless tank and the energy to push the limits of
authority as far as they could go. You could always count on Julia when it
came to raising a little hell. Her insatiable curiosity allowed for any kind
of experience. Without self-discipline, without any real goal in life, she
had nothing to lose.

Perhaps the only night of carousing in which Julia didn't partake was November 8, 1932, when Smith students celebrated FDR's landslide election. Progressivism had deep roots on campus, where liberal causes flourished and where Roosevelt was viewed as "the Second Coming of Christ." Despite a general complexion of rich, privileged women, the Smith student body was forward-thinking, broad-minded; there was a groundswell of support for FDR's dynamic social platform. Julia, how-ever, was a staunch Hoover girl, an old-style Republican from a house-hold where party loyalty—that is, Republican Party loyalty—was equated with patriotism. Julia's father "hated Roosevelt," according to any num-ber of friends and relatives. "He literally said Roosevelt was a traitor to his class." Worse, FDR was despised for being, of all things, *intellectual.* For John McWilliams, that was the most cunning kind of subversion. "In fact, intellectuality and communism went hand-in-hand," said Julia. "And if you were Phi Beta Kappa, you were certainly a pinko."

That was one epithet Julia wouldn't have to worry about. There was no Phi Beta Kappa in her future. And no being branded pinko—at least, not at Smith, not for the time being.

All things considered, Julia's college experience was unremarkable. She had set out, she always said, "to become a great woman novelist," but there was little evidence that she worked toward that goal. Despite the opportunity to study with Mary Ellen Chase, whose memoirs and nov-els were widely admired, Julia sabotaged any opportunity to develop her skills. "I purposely didn't take any writing classes," she said, owing to a fatuous "romantic" belief that one had to live before she could write. The closest she came to any creative writing was a lurid play based roughly on the Stevens murders in Pasadena. Otherwise, Julia did nothing to develop her literary ambitions at Smith.

She fulfilled the school's course requirements with as much gusto as she conformed to its rules. History intrigued Julia, but only insofar as it satisfied her need for a major. She took more courses in music, study-ing ear-training and harmony, as well as four years of piano lessons to broaden her character. Under guidelines that applied to all Smith stu-dents, the women were required to master two foreign languages, which would assist them later, should they ever pursue an international voca-tion. Many classmates contemplated careers in the foreign service, one of the few lines of work that employed smart women (in part because they would perform secretarial work as well as their more professional duties). From 1930 until 1933, Julia studied French and Italian, though she didn't achieve any degree of proficiency in either. Her French, especially, had fallen flatter than a crêpe. She seemed to fulfill her KBS teacher's prophecy that she had an "inability to detect shades of sound in French." And after years of conjugating Italian verbs, she was less *sciolta* than she was *frustrata.**

With graduation looming, most senior Smithies engaged in a mad scramble to solidify their futures. Many used contacts to schedule job interviews in New York (although a staggering number of women from Julia's class enrolled in Katharine Gibbs secretarial classes), while several others, many others, announced plans to marry their boyfriends. In the rush to destiny, Julia remained a bystander. By the end of midterms, less than six months before commencement, she grew increasingly anxious over her lack of initiative. "I only wish to god I were gifted in one line instead of having mediocre splashings in several directions," she lamented to her mother.

For all the promise of a Smith College education, for the intellectual atmosphere, the luminaries who taught there, and the academic freedom, Julia graduated in 1934 with little to show for it. She had failed to take advantage of the riches that Smith had to offer. "Looking back on it," she said almost forty years later, "I say, 'What a shame!' There it all was." But for one reason or another her interest was never awakened. She never felt challenged, never challenged herself. A classmate attributed it to "a stunning lack of maturity." And even Julia herself decried an "adolescent" point of view, noting that she had no expectations of using her education; it was for building character, not a career. Especially for a girl from her side of the tracks. Julia dismissed this thinking as "something of a class thing." Young women with her pedigree were not expected to work. "You were supposed to go back [home]," she said, "and live the social life."

Mrs. Gilchrist, the Hubbard House adviser, shared a similar outlook for Julia. Mingled with praise for Julia's energy and school spirit were reservations about the future. In an evaluation she filed just prior to graduation, Mrs. Gilchrist wrote, "She would do well in some organized charity or social service work." Nothing more substantial was predicted for her. In any case, she continued, Julia's family was "wealthy. She will not need 'a job' I do not believe."

----

* *Sciolta,* fluent; *frustrata,* frustrated.

DESPITE HAVING A diploma in hand from Smith College, Julia McWilliams was slated for a life of leisure. "She will return here after graduation," cited a column in the *Pasadena Star News,* "and will pass the summer with her family at the McWilliams beach home in San Malo." Beyond the sun and fun, no mention was made of Julia's immediate plans. She had come home to the lifestyle she was born to: that of a junior socialite. No one was ever more suited to the role or rose as high to the occasion. She threw more parties—"a whirl of parties," to quote her mother—than her family thought possible, including a black-and-white ball for forty that nearly rent the house asunder. Afternoons, she stormed the grounds of the posh Midwick Country Club in Alhambra, where her father served as a director and where Hollywood royalty gamboled on the polo fields, often playing competitive tennis after a round or two of golf. Otherwise, she bombed around town in a decrepit old Ford, which she'd nicknamed Eulalie and whose tailpipe let out rude bursts of gas that sent passersby running for cover.

Caro McWilliams, who functioned as her daughter's guardian angel during those dog days of summer, searched for distractions to occupy Julia's copious stretches of down-time. Over the months, she had tried various strategies designed to keep Julia out of trouble—by sending her to the movies, especially to the Strand, on Colorado Boulevard, where an all-lady orchestra still accompanied the features; by encouraging her to join the Junior League, whose do-good projects raised her presence in the community; and by increasing her allowance to $100 a month so she could attend premieres at the Pasadena Playhouse, where a repertory company of young actors, including Henry Fonda, Eleanor Parker, Dana Andrews, and William Holden, were launching their careers. With so much time on her hands, Julia drifted around Pasadena with no real purpose. She told the Smith alumnae bulletin that she "has been taking German and music this winter and also supervising youngsters at a clinic," but that was so much wishful thinking. Those months were strung together without a whiff of accomplishment, and by the fall of 1935, even Caro had run out of patience. In light of Julia's increasing restlessness—she bumped around the house for hours, playing the piano or reading mysteries—a different approach was in order. A trip abroad, perhaps, or a change of scenery.

At Caro's prompting, Julia accompanied her mother and sister on a cross-country drive, as part of a road trip intended to drop Dort off at college. A KBS graduate like Julia, she'd passed on Smith and enrolled at Bennington, in Vermont, a few hours from Dalton, where the women were headed after tucking Dort into her dorm. It had been agreed, after much protest, that Julia would remain back East, at Aunt Theodora's house in Massachusetts, and take a basic secretarial course at the Packard Commercial School in Pittsfield. One can only imagine the resentment this stirred in Julia. Julia was a spark plug, full of unharnessed energy. The last thing she desired was something so dull and unimaginative. The classes in the brochure sounded a leitmotif of boredom: filing, stenography, typing, clerical administration . . . Was this where four years of a Seven Sisters education had taken her?

Julia gave secretarial school a halfhearted shot, but a month at Packard was all she could withstand. The options it presented were too bleak to consider, the future without it—even bleaker. But in October, Julia finally caught a break. Thanks to the efforts of the Smith vocational guidance office, she landed an entry-level job at W. & J. Sloane, in New York City, as a girl Friday for the upscale home-furnishings company. In exchange for juggling a broad range of secretarial duties, writing press releases, scheduling photography shoots, and anything else they could offload on her, Julia was paid eighteen dollars a week—only a fraction of what it would cost her to live in the city. Nevertheless, she wasn't about to let money derail such a golden opportunity. The monthly allowance from home helped her to underwrite the expense. A young woman could live quite lavishly in New York during the Depression with $100 in her pocket. Necessities like food and lodging were ridiculously cheap. Finding suitable accommodations certainly presented no problem; the city was teeming with empty apartments, with more than a million New Yorkers living on government aid. Julia tapped into her trusty Smith resources, rooming with two recent grads who also worked in retailing in an $80-a-month brownstone at the corner of East Fifty-ninth Street and First Avenue, in the shadow of the Queensboro Bridge.

For Julia, whose only experience with a job of any kind had been chalking the lines on her mother's tennis court, the work at Sloane's was a revelation. Her boss, the company's advertising manager, kept her busy all day, cranking out reams of copy on the decorative arts, everything from antique case clocks to a Baker bedroom ensemble. It was an enjoyable routine, not a lot of pressure, but enough to keep her engaged. In between her advertising assignments, she helped to work the floor. "I am learning quite a bit about store management and interior decoration," she enthused in a letter to the Smith vocational office. "In fact, I couldn't be more pleased."

Meanwhile, Manhattan was an eye-opener to a girl from the West. "I just loved New York and everything it had to offer," she recalled, acknowledging the kid-in-the-candy-store effect the city had on her. The razzle-dazzle of it suited Julia perfectly, the crush of people in constant motion, going, doing, hustling. It was more than mere nourishment for her hungry soul. "While I was there, I tried to take advantage of as much of it as I could." At the outset, that meant wandering the streets, giddy with amazement, enjoying the simple luxury of blending in with the crowds. At Smith, Julia wasn't just the tallest woman at school; she towered over her classmates, a bit of a freak. But in New York her height wasn't anything unusual. Among the skyscrapers she "felt humbled" in contrast to their size.

The buildings helped to put things in perspective, and so did the multitudes that besieged her on the street. In a city known for its impersonal makeup, Julia had ready-made friends to draw on. "Most of my friends . . . went to New York for a job," she recalled, citing those who were self-respecting enough to work. College classmates had found their way into the retailing and advertising fields, and some were determined to see their names in lights. The Smith grapevine wrapped itself around new arrivals, making the transition to Manhattan a less overwhelming experience. There were plenty of companions with whom to take in the nightlife. Theater and the opera were among Julia's favorite pastimes, while dining, a New York specialty, failed to register on her action meter. Food, for Julia McWilliams, was more of a necessity than an indulgence. She wasn't drawn to the gastronomic auras of, say, Delmonico's or Lüchow's. There were plenty of restaurants in the mid-1930s where you could have a perfectly respectable meal for around a dollar, and Julia, more preoccupied with satisfying her hunger than refining—or even defining—it, haunted many of them. She could often be found at the counter of one of the chains, a Huyler's, a Chock Full o'Nuts, or ironically a Childs, all of which served classic, if indifferent, food. If she felt ambitious, Julia would walk the long blocks across Fifty-seventh Street to the Schrafft's, just west of Carnegie Hall, whose air-conditioned Columbus Room had a more fashionable appeal.

Food was less important to her than landing a more intriguing job. Julia had never given up the hope of writing serious novels, and she continued to bombard *The New Yorker* with writing samples—chatty "Talk of the Town" pieces and book reviews—as a way into a staff position. Unfortunately, they were riddled with clichés and rejected by form letter. Her applications to *Time* met with no greater success, and at *Newsweek,* which actually granted Julia an interview, she got no further than the typing test, which she failed.

At least her writing at Sloane's—mostly catalogue copy and press releases about new products—was free from outside critical response. Julia was no Thurber when it came to sparkly humor, but her prose, for the most part, was exuberant. "When you have put your all into a party, and struggled over making sandwiches that are chic and dashing as well as tastey [*sic*], it is terribly deflating to have their pretty figures ruined by guests who must peak [*sic*] inside each 'wich to see what it's made of," she wrote about a little gizmo called Sandwich Indicators—"wooden picks which you stick in the sandwich plate, nicely shaped and painted. There is 'Humpty Dumpty' for egg, a rat in a cage for cheese, a dog, boat, and pig for meat, fish, and ham. And it seems like a very sound idea." It was unlikely that such efforts would attract *The New Yorker,* but Julia was writing for a living nonetheless, developing a voice and a style that would eventually come in handy.

She was also beginning to develop an active social life in New York. There were parties and galas almost every weekend of the year, most of them a consequence of the go-go Ivy League circuit. Julia could usually count on an invitation to one bash or another, but it was no fun always going unattached. As she approached her twenty-third birthday, Julia anguished over her inexperience with the opposite sex. "Being very, very tall, I had difficulties from that point of view," she lamented, "so I did not go through some of those things that a short, pretty girl does." Boyfriends and romance were uncharted territory. There had been very few dates in college, none of them serious, fewer opportunities to be choosy about men. Many of her Smith classmates were in serious relationships or already married. Although she claims to have felt no peer pressure in that regard, men and intimacy were clearly on her mind.

Sometime in the fall of 1936, Dort spent a weekend visiting her sister, and Julia took her to a gala at the Waldorf-Astoria. The party turned out to be another Ivy League mixer, a gathering of the upper crust of the post-college-age society, familiar faces she'd seen at similar events. One face, in particular, had hijacked her attention. Julia knew Tom Johnston from a number of Smith parties, where he and his Princeton classmates invariably made hay. Johnston was a notorious "party animal," a big, strapping guy—as big and strapping as Julia—with an outsize personality, who'd played football and boxed on his college teams. Julia was attracted by his irrepressible charm and the confidence he exuded; she found him "very attractive, a free-thinker," and, at a deeper level, a fellow maverick. Johnston hoped to forge a career in high-stakes advertising and was kicking around the New York agencies with another Princetonian, Andy Hewitt, who would eventually launch his own firm, Hewitt, Ogilvy, Benson, and Mather.

At some point during the evening, after some energetic drinking, Julia and Dort coaxed Johnston onto a plank they'd found and paraded him around the ballroom like a Persian prince. It was the kind of hoopla, the kind of unembarrassed levity in which the McWilliams sisters excelled. Julia loved these happy-go-lucky scenes, and Dort, who was a theater major at Bennington, seemed to be a chip off the old block. "They were a couple of high-spirited gals," an acquaintance recalls, and Johnston apparently appreciated their moxie.

Soon Tom and Julia began bumping around the city together, showing up at dinner parties or browsing through the bookstores along lower Fifth Avenue. The figure they cut as a couple was unconventional, even by New York standards: twin towers with lofty personalities. And literary ambitions. Tom is "full of Melville," Julia confided in a diary entry, struck by his passion for the great books. His passion for fantasy was even greater, captivated as he was by stories of high-seas adventure and exotic locales. The intensity of their relationship isn't as clear, but evidence suggests it was lopsided. Julia, by all accounts, had fallen "profoundly" in love. Everything about Tom Johnston delighted her no end. Whether he felt as strongly about Julia or not, she perceived in his attentions, for the first time in her life, that romance had come her way—*at long last*! In any event, sex seemed likely; Julia was "in heat," she said, and eager to give it a whirl.

Before the momentous ritual could occur, however, the relationship ran out of steam. Julia mistakenly attributed it to the "financial stress" Tom seemed under all the time. "He wasn't a rich boy, like the other Princeton guys," says his son, Jim, "but he traveled in their fast lane and aspired to their lifestyle." Money was always a nagging issue. That might have affected him to some degree, perhaps a smidgen, but it wasn't the reason for his romantic malaise. In fact, unknown to Julia, Tom had been two-timing her for months, conducting a long-distance relationship with

Izzy McMullen, a Smith grad a few classes ahead of Julia, now living in Detroit. Eventually, as with all deceptions, the truth wanted out. On September 6, 1936, when a "Dear Julia" letter arrived in the post, Julia was blindsided, devastated. She never saw it coming. All the symptoms of heartbreak converged on her at once: she couldn't eat, couldn't get her breath, her stomach was in knots. Johnston hadn't even the decency to tell her face-to-face. He'd taken off for Detroit so that Julia couldn't reach him.

This "jilting," as she referred to it, dealt a serious blow to her self-esteem. Julia's height had always served as a cornerstone of her identity, but now she described herself as "big and unsophisticated." The impact of rejection had distorted her self-image. "I was always struggling to be a pretty person," she said, in a revisionist diary entry from that period. Nothing anyone said could relieve her wounded pride. For days, weeks, afterward, Julia lay prostrate on her couch, like Violetta in *La Traviata,* striking a pose of epic suffering, while being consoled by friends and family who took turns damning Tom Johnston to an unhappy fate.*

For a while at least, reading a series of books about detached existences and *la vie de bohème,* Julia forgot about heartbreak and Tom Johnston. Friends took her out to nightclubs, hoping to edge her back into circulation. A number of soulless dates were arranged, soullessly consummated. But Julia was unable to let go of Tom. Rashly, she dashed off a letter to him, professing her undying love. With newfound hope, she held out for some word of encouragement or a reconciliation. The hiatus provided a welcome lift for a while. Julia spent several weeks reconstructing her damaged self-image, redefining ideas about relationships, and especially marriage. Ideally, according to her diary, she sought a man who would stimulate her intellectually, someone levelheaded, who inspired confidence and contentment, but also able to provide "FUN and complete mutual understanding and respect." Though this was supposed to be a new, revised mission statement, it was clear that Julia had Tom Johnston in mind. He was the whole package. But when word from him finally arrived, in early 1937, it was the news of his marriage on New Year's Day.

Once again, Julia was distraught. It was almost as though he had broken her heart twice. Reeling from the news and seething with anger, she opened her diary and dashed off several drafts of a letter, accusing Tom of untold deceptions. His behavior had really touched a nerve. "Taken

---

* Tragically, his marriage did end in the worst possible way. Two years later, Tom's wife committed suicide.

in," "misled," "strung along," "pulled the wool over my eyes"—they all added up to the same thing: treachery. *Tomfoolery!* Julia had never been so mistreated before. Each draft took on a blacker cast. In the end, however, she wished the couple much success and happiness.

Her romantic life was an unqualified mess—and her professional life wasn't in much better shape. Though Julia had received a nice raise at Sloane's, to thirty dollars a week, and an employee evaluation that put her on a fast track for advancement, she was unhappy, deeply unhappy, in an otherwise unstimulating job. One thing was certain: she had no real passion for advertising. It didn't excite this young woman for whom excitement was life's nectar. There was nowhere to deploy her "great magnetism," as one friend defined it. She had a burning ambition to do something wonderful, something that turned her on, fascinated her. Though she suffered from a blow to her self-confidence, deep down Julia believed she was "like no one else," a young woman with "unique spiritual gifts" who was "meant for something" extraordinary. Her job at Sloane's, while agreeable, would never offer the extraordinary. By April 1937 that had finally sunk in, and Julia gave her notice.

"I do not want to be a business woman!" she declared. Julia still dreamed of the literary life, still hoped to crack *The New Yorker*'s exclusive editorial staff, but the dreams and hopes seemed ever beyond her grasp. A charitable assignment from her cousin, reviewing Sherwood Anderson's *Puzzled America,* for the *Saturday Review,* went uncompleted, which just about dashed her chances for a freelance career. No, a job in publishing wasn't in the cards. And as for a New York makeover, she "just didn't have the stamina."

As early as March—two months after Tom Johnston's marriage was formally announced and a few weeks before the job at Sloane's ended—Julia was restless to go home to Pasadena. She'd become "bored with nightclubs," she said, and the hustle of New York, tired of the grind, wanting something else, something more. It was too dispiriting. She couldn't keep up, couldn't compete. In May, she was due to be in California for a friend's wedding. That would be the end, she thought. She wouldn't return to New York. "Julia of the almost spring," she noted in her diary. She was still awaiting her time to bloom.

Four

Only a Butterfly

For a few weeks after her return, Julia unwound in the hot California sun, hopscotching between San Malo, where her father had built a new Tudor-style cottage on a cliff above the beach, and the family house, in Pasadena. She was thrilled to be home, relieved to be back West. "Life there seemed so much less complicated," she said. Julia never outgrew her attachment to Pasadena. She loved the sleepy, laid-back lifestyle, the clear, dry air, and, no less, the privileges of the leisure class.

Her hometown was every bit the paradise she remembered. Sitting in her rickety jalopy, Eulalie, on one of the veiny roads that traversed Mount Wilson, Julia often stopped to enjoy a panoramic view of the growing city that stretched all the way to the Los Angeles basin. Progress, so to speak, had left its imprint on the vista. Yet for all its beauty and incredible wealth, the Pasadena Julia found when she returned in 1937 was a city she barely recognized. While she was away, the floodgates had been opened—the hotel and tourist industry had spiraled to meet greedy demand, Caltech was spreading across the landscape faster than lungwort, a freeway to Los Angeles—the first of its kind on the West Coast—was nearly finished, the Palomar telescope newly perched atop Mount Wilson staked its claim on the stars, and smog—the first faint wisps of smog, like Morse code—backed up against the mountains, spelling out a portent of the changes to come.

Eager to resume her old friendships after a four-year absence, Julia

At the beach in San Malo, California, late 1920s

reached out to the few pals who still lived in town. But while Julia was struggling to carve out a career, they had begun to form couples, families, with their own tranquil lives and built-in interests. In the midst of deepening social imbalance, Julia's insecurities quickly resurfaced. She felt the widening gap that separated her from the others, and her relationship to them that summer, while pleasant, was never entirely comfortable.

The circumstances only sharpened the old conflicts inside her—the collapse of her love affair with Tom Johnston and her seeming inability to focus on the future. Both regrets continued to haunt her in Pasadena. "I really had no idea where I was headed," she recalled, "and it frustrated me, really frustrated me for awhile." Tom's rejection, combined with the mounting frustration, professional as well as sexual, cast Julia into an uncharacteristic state of unease. "It was one time I can remember feeling hopelessly lost."

Caro responded with an outpouring of encouragement to shore up Julia's sagging spirits. For years, she had exhorted her children to make the most of their lives. "Stand up straight. *Be* somebody!" she'd implore, catching them in moments of slack disregard. Now, however, she soothed Julia's setback with more sympathetic tones and turned her considerable skills as a mother toward rekindling her daughter's spark. But Caro's efforts, well-intentioned though they were, lacked her trademark vitality. That spring, especially during Julia's last weeks in New York, Caro's health had begun to fail. The ravages of stroke and high blood pressure had taken their toll, both visible and invisible. Only sixty years old and physically sturdier than her children, the strain on her vital organs crept treacherously toward cliff's edge. "Indigestion" was how she explained her persistent maladies to Julia. "A touch of the flu" was offered to mask the grimaces and sallow complexion that had marred her features. Frequent weak spells and bouts of nausea seemed to support these diagnoses, but even Julia could tell her mother's condition was more serious than flu.

Several times that spring the family's anxiety level had been raised. Caro fought through increasingly severe spells of anemia, dizziness, nausea, and shortness of breath. Alarmed by a sudden increase of jaundice in her face and eyes, John sent Caro to La Jolla for emergency kidney treatment. In early July, when her temperature spiked and her blood pressure plummeted, he rushed her by ambulance to San Diego. Both times, Caro returned home with a clean bill of health, but it was clear to those closest to her that her condition was deteriorating. Even so, Julia painted the situation with a rosy veneer. In a letter to Dort, on July 10, she downplayed the seriousness of their mother's illness, going so far as to declare Caro "100% better." In fact, her doctors—and presumably both Julia and her father—knew that Caro was suffering from uremia; her kidneys were shutting down, dangerous toxins poisoning her vital organs. There was little that could be done to prevent the contamination of her bloodstream. As far as Caro had traveled from the inbred limits of Dalton, as hard as she had worked to be a doting mother and a devoted wife, as much as she had prospered, spiritually and financially, in the California oasis she adored, she could not, in the end, escape the "Weston curse." It had claimed her parents, three sisters, and two brothers. And on July 21, 1937, around ten o'clock in the morning, Caro's heart finally gave out.

Julia was at her mother's bedside when she died. There were so many memories, so many things she still wanted to say to Caro. Her heart was flooded with undue guilt. "I could have been much nicer to her," Julia thought. "I could have been with her more." Her mother's death summoned an outpouring of grief. For Julia, it was especially devastating, coming on the heels of her recent heartbreak. She had never stopped mourning Tom Johnston; now she'd lost someone else she dearly loved.

Gratefully, her brother and sister returned home together a few days later, Dort from New Hampshire where she was working in summer stock theater, John from an apprenticeship at Byron Weston Paper in Dalton. For father and son, it would be an uneasy reunion. Pop had always counted on John's following in his footsteps—going to college at Princeton and, afterward, managing the family portfolio. The dyslexia, however, had kept him from meeting most challenges. In school, John kept flunking until he was in the same grade as Dort. Small wonder, then, that Princeton wouldn't accept him. "Father was furious with Princeton because he donated quite a bit of money," says a close relative, "plus he was the college's representative, interviewing future students on the West Coast." There had been talk of stashing John in Arkansas to run the family rice farms, but his girlfriend, Jo, whom he would soon marry, "put the kibosh on it." Dalton, as she saw it, was the lesser of the evils. John was a gentle soul, whose disability was totally misunderstood, but the paper business might provide him with a trade. In any case, he was a failure in his father's stony eyes; nothing he could do would satisfy the old man.

For the time being, however, they'd put their differences aside. The loss of Caro had given them both a serious jolt. "Father, more than anyone, was in terrible shape," says Jo McWilliams. "He'd adored his wife;

she kept him kindhearted, to a degree. What little warmth he had went out of him when Caro died." There was an emptiness inside him he could not reconcile. His spirit had cracked. The funeral, a simple, private service in the parlor of the house, was about all he could withstand. Even there he looked frail, his shoulders sunken, thronged by his children—"all eighteen feet of them," as Caro liked to remark—this once-strapping tower of a man, whose fearsome glare was blunted by sorrow.

His care, as it was, now fell entirely to Julia. Dort and John had lives back East; they would be leaving Pasadena soon after the funeral. Dort, however, had second thoughts. She was beginning her junior year at Bennington and offered to take a semester's leave from college to help out at home. Julia wouldn't hear of it. She knew her sister needed some distance from the family—to grow up independent of the family crucible, to put her own life together. There had always been some friction between Julia and Dort, the normal sisterly rivalry, but also petty jealousies. Distance had given them adequate breathing room. In fact, the farther apart they lived, the closer they managed to become. They'd gleaned a newfound enjoyment in each other's company. Living under the same roof again might go toward fracturing that accord. Besides, Julia had never stopped angling for her father's approval. The time alone with him would give her an opportunity to stake her claim anew.

Proximity or not, John McWilliams wouldn't be an easy nut for her to crack. His rigid shell had only gotten harder over the years. Pigheaded, contrary, intolerant, demanding, uncooperative—all these invectives could aptly be used to describe him. Ultraconservative: "He was to the right of Attila the Hun," Julia liked to say in later years. And it came at a time when she herself was leaning leftward. Politics—that is, Julia's politics—set him off in a rumble of explosive outbursts. "He *hated* East Coast liberals," says his granddaughter, Rachel, and now his daughter, of all people, had gone over to the enemy. One thing was certain: Julia's Pop was a cantankerous old man. They had very little in common, even less that they could find to agree on.

The only thing they enjoyed together was a round or two of golf, which Julia played with her father as a form of therapy. In the weeks after Caro's death they played well and often, trolling the fairways at the Midwick Country Club in the dry summer heat. Here John McWilliams felt at ease among his peers, the plutocrats, the retired millionaires, those "amiable old rogues." He'd drifted into their orbit and courted their stars. But, almost exclusively, he kept his own counsel. His business was personal, sub rosa. There were no corporate entities, no boards of directors, no shareholders he answered to. It was a point of pride, in fact, that he answered to no one. Men who played by his rules knew the score. In the meantime, he'd created a parallel universe that, in many cases, rivaled their triumphs and wealth.

John McWilliams had become a quiet force in Pasadena. His private portfolio returned more than substantial dividends, embellished by shrewd but oh-so-sound, *conservative,* investments. His contacts extended across a vast and varied community. He sat on the boards of the Polytechnic School, the library, and the hospital. In 1934, out of recognition for his prominence, he was appointed president of both the local Board of Trade and the Chamber of Commerce, positions that gave him even greater municipal influence. The combination of his business acumen and near-obsessive restraint—along with his extremist views of politics—was a magnet for the kind of visionaries and power brokers with unshakable views of their own moral superiority.

A beneficiary of this largesse was J. G. Boswell, a neighbor of the McWilliamses in Pasadena and, later, Santa Barbara. Through his enormous landholdings and political clout, Boswell planned to build an agribusiness in the San Joaquin Valley the likes and size of which had no precedent. To do that, however, he needed water, a scarce commodity, and the ability to bypass local ordinances to get it. As it happened, John McWilliams was one of the principal investors in Boswell Farms. He knew his way around the labyrinthine departments that oversaw these resources and lent his muscle to the legal hurdles necessary to protect his business interests.

"My grandfather made sure Boswell got what he needed by diverting water into the Central Valley," says Phila Cousins. They leveed and damned Tulare Lake, the largest body of fresh water west of the Mississippi, to the point of extinction. In its six-hundred-square-mile basin, Boswell grew cotton. "It was the whole *Chinatown* thing. He was part of the ultra-right-wing men's club the Grove, all these high-powered guys behind closed doors, pulling strings about the water supply."

Although largely ignorant of her father's involvement in Boswell's affairs, Julia continued to struggle with his notions of principles and politics. She couldn't fathom his seeming hostility toward progress. He opposed the building of the Pasadena Freeway, opposed Social Security, women's rights, racial equality, minimum wage, anything that smacked of social reform. Meanwhile, Julia had developed her own strong opinions, opinions that hardly resembled Pop's dogma. Yet, it was impossible to discuss them without risking an emotional tirade. There were nights, during dinner, when her father stormed from the table rather than tolerate Julia's point of view on a subject. There was no agreeing to disagree, no concept of mutual respect. It was Pop's way or the highway—except that he opposed the highway.

Living alone with him, in their new arrangement, brought a fresh perspective on her father. "He is a strange but wonderful man," Julia wrote, "and doesn't have much of the light touch or the abandon that would make this easier." It baffled her that anyone with such "wit and humor" could also be so downright disagreeable. Yet she was able to rationalize his curmudgeonly nature. "He does not have an abandon for life. He sees it well-planned and sober, and, I think, pretty unexciting."

In any case, they would coexist peacefully. Julia would see to it that they did. It didn't behoove her to disturb the gentle groove they'd established. Without the remotest possibility of a job, Julia spent much of the year at her father's house on Hillside Road. Aside from golf and tennis, there wasn't much for her in the way of responsibility. They had a live-in butler and a live-in cook, as well as a gardener, a laundress, and a seamstress who came in a couple of days a week. It was the perfect situation for an otherwise pampered young woman who had just lost her mother and was struggling with her identity. Work was not a priority, at least not for the time being. The Smith alumni office sent Julia two attractive job opportunities—at Harcourt, Brace in New York and at Reid Hall in Paris—but neither struck her fancy, or if they did, she lacked the initiative to respond. By the end of summer, Julia and her father's life together had settled into a leisurely routine that neither had the energy or the desire to interrupt.

Soon Julia felt the drag that comes with lingering idleness. Her dynamic spirit, bottled up for months, was stymied. To occupy her time, she took a part-time job writing a column for a start-up magazine called *Coast*. She already had a breezy, if slapdash, writing style, acquired from her job turning out ad copy at Sloane's, and she plied it lavishly in articles about fashionable apparel. "On this matter of ski wear," she wrote in the January 1938 issue, "I should like to say with sepulchral firmness: Don't dress yourself up like a bloody Alpine Christmas tree." It wasn't literary by any stretch of the imagination. But at least the column alleviated the boredom she felt without infringing on her leisure. "All I want to do is play golf, piano, and simmer, and see people, and summer and live right here," she wrote in her diary. When push came to shove, Julia realized she was "really only a butterfly"—a social butterfly, no less.

Over the next year or so, she developed a solid social circle, assembled from among the other butterflies her age and status who flitted from country club to country club, living the good life at high speed. "Julia ran with a fun upper-crust crowd," recalls Jo Duff, a lifelong friend. "There were three or four groups, at least, whose members were interchangeable. They were all wealthy, very attractive, and they threw a lot of parties." The women were native Pasadenans—Gay Bradley, Mamie Valentine, Betty Washburn, and Katy Gates—childhood friends who had known Julia forever. They gave the local men the cold shoulder, for the most part, in favor of a "group of boys who came out from St. Paul's in New York, happy-go-lucky guys, who played fantastic jokes on each other." And every one of them belonged to the Valley Hunt Club, that bastion of *prah-puh* Pasadena society, which prided itself on having rejected John Roosevelt because he was FDR's son. Of course, he wouldn't have fared better at the Annandale Country Club, where Julia played golf on a regular basis. There, a Good Samaritan had stuck signs in the lockers of suspected Democrats that said: COMMUNIST: RESIGN! Then, again, "anybody who was anybody belonged to the Midwick," says another friend, which drew its clique equally from the Pasadena and the L.A. blue books. Darryl Zanuck was a member, as were Will Rogers and Walt Disney and the Chandlers, who published the *Los Angeles Times*. With several pals trailing her long strides, Julia would blow into Midwick's colonial-style clubhouse, a citadel of privilege, most afternoons, where they drank martinis, one after another, in a banquette overlooking the manicured polo fields.

Julia liked the high-toned surroundings. And she seemed comfortable around the captains of industry, who enjoyed riding to hounds, and the steam they generated. "I want lots of people around, who are stimulating and with whom I feel intoxicated and clever and charming and a part," she spelled out in demonstrative, wiggy fashion. It was a typical Julia manifesto: clear, practical, demanding, and for the most part unobtainable. Like the job at Sloane's, country-club life offered Julia a chance to bide her time in a nonthreatening milieu, somewhere she could avoid the anxieties of her stagnant situation, away from more ambitious friends who were making something of themselves. But it wouldn't provide the lifestyle she craved—a fascinating job, intellectual excitement, an alluring, articulate lover, the whole package. For all Julia's vows to have it all, she had insulated herself from the outside world.

At least money wasn't an issue. Julia wasn't a material girl. Her father saw to it that she had "an allowance," whatever she needed, and by the end of 1938, there was an inheritance from her mother, as well, and quite a large one, at that. "Somewhere between $100,000 and $200,000," says Phila Cousins, "and a lot of stock, all in IBM." Suddenly, Julia had money to burn, the kind of money that Pasadenans understood. Not that she flashed it around or even spent it in an ostentatious way. She didn't do anything of the sort, but it gave her the wherewithal to play with that rich go-go crowd.

At her father's house in San Malo, one of the few places where Julia felt relaxed, she entertained a steady stream of guests—a handful of regulars as well as a changing cast of young bons vivants who horsed around on the beach during the day and did some serious carousing once the sun went down. One frequent visitor was Harrison Chandler, a Stanford grad she knew from the Midwick Country Club, whose father ran the most influential newspaper in California. Chandler lacked everything Julia was looking for in a man: wit, intensity, eloquence, and vivacity, although he could hold his own among the gilded country-club set. She thought he was "nice," but "somewhat stiff," not a glowing review. His pedigree, however, was impeccable—within limits. "He was not considered by the other members of the Chandler clan to be particularly bright," says Chandler family chronicler Dennis McDougal. "In any case, he was never in serious contention to take the reins of the company." Still, he had gravitas—and, above all, "he was crazy about Julia."

The suggestion that Chandler and Julia had anything that resembled a serious relationship would be stretching the truth. He was always around, part of the gang, and openly attentive to her. Very attentive. Friends could tell that Julia had caught his eye. A notable interest soon turned to outright infatuation. At social events, Chandler made sure they were paired up. "It was easy to think of them as a couple," recalls Katie Nevins. "He followed her around like a puppy, so solicitous it was almost comical." And so persistent that Julia often felt the need to put some distance between them. She avoided certain functions where he was sure to turn up, and she refused his offer of a job at the *Los Angeles Times*. In her no-nonsense way, Julia sought to avoid anything that might seem like commitment on her part.

But that didn't rule out a passable interest in Harrison Chandler. He was *nice,* as she'd already noted, and presentable and polite. God knows, he was assured of success and as good a catch as they came. Her father strongly approved of him; he made no secret of that. John was personally friendly with several of the Chandlers and embraced their widely known political bias. Unfalteringly, he encouraged Julia to give Harrison a chance. The more she did, however, the more indifferent she felt. He lacked spirit, that essential *je ne sais quoi.* It wouldn't hurt her to enjoy Harrison's company once in a while. But she doubted that he would ever have her heart.

FOR THE LONGEST time, Julia feared that no one special would claim her heart. Her height, it seemed, scared off eligible men. Why else were most of her friends either engaged or married, when she had it all over them in so many ways? Men were intimidated by big women, she concluded, and at six-three she gave them a handful to deal with. Dort, at six-five, grappled with the same issue, even worse. "She felt like she was a freak," according to her daughter, Phila. "It dealt a huge blow to her confidence. People often mistook her for a man because she was so tall and wore pants a lot." That had happened to Julia, as well, and it hurt her more than she was willing to admit. It confused her, damaged her self-esteem. But Caro's death, along with some serious introspection, had helped guide her toward a fresh new outlook. Months spent alone had taught her the value of acceptance and contentment. She was no longer tormented by her appearance, no longer blamed it for her funk. Julia had learned to grow more comfortable with herself, especially where her height was concerned. "Thank heaven I am getting over that fear and contempt of single maidenhood," she wrote in a diary entry. "I am quite content to be the way I am—and feel quite superior to many a wedded mouse. By god—I can do what I want!" There were many things associated with marriage she could easily live without, although, she admitted, "sex is nice."

So, she decided, was a more challenging job. And after months and months of coasting at *Coast,* she was finally ready to tackle one.

On the recommendation of A. W. Forester, her old boss at W. & J. Sloane, Julia applied for a position in their West Coast offices, where most of the company's administrative services had been relocated. The job was a good opportunity in a business she was already familiar with, even if it meant a rush-hour drive over the hills to L.A. It would be a good change of pace for her. The routine at home had grown deadly dull; she'd become antsy, eager. And by September 1939, Julia was working at Sloane's again, this time at their Beverly Hills store, with a clientele whose tastes she knew and understood. It was a large step up from her New York responsibilities—managing the company's PR and advertising departments—accompanied by a huge increase in salary to $200 a month, twice what she'd made before.

But almost from the start, Julia was in over her head.

Her duties were considerable—and complicated. Not only was she required to plan a local advertising campaign, but also to execute it, which meant hiring the layout artists, the typographers, writing the copy, and coordinating the whole shebang with the media. What's more, she was expected to oversee the window and floor displays throughout the store. There was no orientation process, no gradual transition into the job. It was assumed that Julia already knew the ropes. She may have given Sloane's top brass that impression during her interview or perhaps she assumed her New York experience would cover most bases. Alas, she was flying by the seat of her pants.

And she knew it, too. "One needs a much more detailed knowledge of business, buying, markets, and more experience in advertising than I had had for so much responsibility," Julia conceded in a future evaluation. Still, it excited her to take on the challenge. It spoke to the determined part of her that believed she could do anything. And for a while she managed to bluff her way through the maze of advertising details. She came to grips with "the mechanics of the office and the business personnel." It was all sailing along smoothly, if somewhat serendipitously. But regardless of Julia's guile and luck, sooner or later her lack of experience was bound to catch up with her.

That moment came in the spring of 1940, in the middle of an annual promotion that Sloane's was running. Julia had prepared ad copy for a furniture sale that would run in a series of newspapers. At the bottom was a paragraph of fine print defining the terms of the sale. It was pretty standard stuff, a routine she'd handled at least a half-dozen times. Julia approved the layout and had it sent out to be typeset. In the meantime, headquarters made a change or two in the wording, which eventually crossed her desk. It was a fairly straightforward matter. The typographer could reset the ad without much delay. But Julia, in her infinite wisdom, decided the changes were too insignificant to bother with—no one would notice them anyway—and placed the ads without the changes.

Unfortunately, the suits in the New York office noticed in a big way. And once the flames subsided in their eyes, the first thing they did was to deal with Julia McWilliams.

"Fired," she wrote in an explanation, "and I don't wonder." There was no gentle rebuke or second chance. Julia hadn't slipped up, this wasn't oversight. She defied her superiors, plain and simple. That was enough to warrant her immediate dismissal.

Having recently found belief in herself, Julia hit rock bottom again. She was back where she started, back at her father's house, without much in the way of prospects. All the wasted time, the false starts, began to pile up on her. These years had been counterproductive, she decided; they tended to "dissolve nobility of spirit." A few weeks before her twenty-eighth birthday, Julia's frustration and disillusionment grew more pronounced. A wall of self-doubt began to brick up around her. "When I was in school and later, I felt I had particular and unique spiritual gifts," she wrote in a burst of self-reproach. "That I was meant for something, and was like no one else. It hadn't come out yet, but it was there warm and latent. Today, it has gone out and I am sadly an ordinary person."

Less than two years after returning to Pasadena, Julia began to repeat the pattern of uncertainty and discontent that she had left New York to break. Her waking hours passed as an uneventful blur. She found a bit of daylight volunteering with the Junior League, whose do-good projects included a cookbook, of all things, filled with the kind of gloppy condensed mushroom-soup recipes that, as Julia Child, she would strive to annihilate. (Thankfully, none of her personal dishes appeared in their pages.) Instead, she reserved her energy for the plays the League put on, dramatic interpretations of children's classics, in which Julia often starred. Friends remember her "flying across the stage" at the Civic Auditorium—literally *flying*, harnessed by a series of pulleys and ropes—and "cracking up the audience with that waffley voice of hers." To fill the long, solitary nights, she hopped back on the boisterous Pasadena party circuit, which seemed to have grown and thrived in her absence. There was more of an L.A. presence in the scene than before, thanks to the new freeway, which made the towns chummy back-door neighbors. Now, everywhere Julia turned she kept bumping into Harrison

Chandler—at the country clubs, in San Malo, and at a weekend retreat they frequented in Rancho Matilija, a development near Ojai, where "some serious drinking" fueled the fun and games. Nothing had changed in her attitude toward him. He was a handsome guy, no doubt about that, and well-off, probably set for life. But he had no charm and, thus, there were no sparks, nothing that indicated traces of spunk beneath that stodgy outer shell, no pentimento. Still, his companionship satisfied Julia's need for intimacy and, at the same time, attested to her desirability.

One dividing issue between Julia and Chandler was the inevitability of war. All signs pointed to America's entry in the crisis that had cleaved a path through Europe and was spreading with intractable force. FDR's speeches intimated as much, as did his maneuverings in the shadows of diplomacy. Following Germany's invasions of Scandinavia and the Benelux countries in the spring of 1940, FDR established the first peacetime draft while overseeing the rapid buildup of the American military complex. War—its advantages and drawbacks—dominated all conversations.

As of 1940, Julia was still struggling to find her political voice. For the longest time, she had echoed her father's boisterous rhetoric until she returned from Smith with a head full of her own views. Somewhere in Northampton, she'd made a sharp turn to the left. From her professors and their disciples, she learned about New Deal initiatives and the promotion of social justice. "She was quite outspoken, when it came to progressive reform," recalls her friend and neighbor, Katie Nevins. In her spare time, Julia pored over Walter Lippmann's columns and parroted their opinions. "Julia loved to talk politics. It gave her great satisfaction, a kind of wicked joy, especially in heavily Republican Pasadena, where her beliefs antagonized most people."

One person particularly offended was Harrison Chandler, whose family's hatred of FDR was almost religious in scope. The *Times* was famously ultraconservative when it came to politics and Harrison stood somewhere to the far right of the paper. "He was a total reactionary," says Dennis McDougal. In *Privileged Son,* his biography of the Chandler empire, McDougal writes of Chandler: "He was a leading light of L.A.'s [Abraham] Lincoln Club" and spent "an inordinate amount of time . . . talking politics at the California Club or the even more exclusive and secretive Sunset Club." In any case, he and Julia were at opposite ends of the political spectrum.

Not even politics, however, could intrude upon matters of the heart.

In late August 1940, after a delightful weekend at the beach among friends and family, a visibly discomfited Harrison Chandler proposed to Julia McWilliams. It must have seemed the perfect setting for such a momentous event: a gorgeous summer evening, the gentle lapping of surf against sand, the serenade of neighbors deliberating over outdoor barbecues. Seemingly perfect—though anything but. Julia fumbled the moment with uncharacteristic awkwardness. "I found I was just as embarrassed as he was and didn't know at all what to say," she recalled. Perhaps she hadn't seen it coming or, more likely, she considered it mistaken. But there was a lot of hemming and hawing, dancing around the great question. In the meantime, a few issues were raised. Was he willing to live in Pasadena? How did he feel about children? (Julia told him she wanted three or four.) Chandler may have answered to her satisfaction, but Julia did not share his feelings—or his heart.

Julia needed time—to think, to gauge her feelings, to consider all the factors and the ramifications. On the one hand, marriage would answer all her problems: about the future, stability, money, status. On the other hand, she wasn't in love. On the one hand, he was a Chandler, L.A. royalty; her father approved. On the other hand, she wasn't in love. On the one hand, Harrison adored her just the way she was—curious, fun-loving, outspoken, slightly wacky. On the other hand, she wasn't in love. What to do? What to do?

In her diary, Julia wrote, "I have an idea I may succumb," but when push came to shove, she exhibited great restraint. There wasn't any need in rushing such a momentous decision, despite being the only unmarried woman among her inner circle. She refused to act out of desperation or be influenced by family and friends (although she was curious to know what Dort thought). Even her father got nowhere in his entreaties. "He made himself very clear," recalls Jo McWilliams. "Father wanted Julia to marry Harrison Chandler. He encouraged it. I think he counted on it."

By all accounts, Chandler put no undue pressure on Julia. It seemed they were both willing to continue seeing each other casually without altering the trajectory of their relationship. For the time being, at least. Besides, Julia was setting out on another kind of life-changing path.

In September 1941, bored and pensive, she joined the Pasadena chapter of the American Red Cross, volunteering in the office pool. It was mostly grunt work: typing, copying, and filing, with little opportunity to utilize her talents. She was basically a clerk. Months passed without a break to this routine. But all that changed on December 7, 1941, following the Japanese attack on Pearl Harbor.

Like millions of Americans everywhere, U.S. entry into the war galvanized Julia. It drew her into the spirit of a unified civilian effort that was mobilizing across the country. Week after week, as newsreels carried images of "a clear demonstration of national power and purpose . . . that linked [all Americans] to both those on the battlefields that ranged across the globe and to one another in common cause," Julia deliberated how to best play her part in the endeavor. A few weeks after the New Year, she fixed upon her role.

In California, especially in communities along the coast, there was a heightened urgency about enemy attack. Shockingly, there was little or no safeguard to defend almost twelve hundred miles of exposed coastline, along which were located strategic refineries and important aircraft plants, including Douglas and Lockheed in L.A. and Consolidated in San Diego. If an attack were directed at the United States, army commanders theorized, there was little doubt it would come from the west. A kamikaze pilot, a combat sub—America's borders were defenseless against them. By 1942, there was an overriding public sense of dread. "Invasion fever" spread as fast as rumors of enemy sightings, prompting the formation of the Aircraft Warning Service (AWS), in which civilian volunteers acted as spotters. If and when an enemy combatant was observed, word would immediately be passed to a filter center so that the military could take appropriate action.

Sometime in early March of that year, Julia and a neighbor reported to a nondescript loft building on Flower Street, in downtown Los Angeles. There, at one of the secretive Information and Filter Centers that processed data sent from AWS observation posts, they joined a young volunteer group that kept track of all the shipping up and down the California coast. "We sat in a dark, windowless room in front of a plotting map spread across a huge, flat table," recalls Katie Nevins, who says she was "recruited" by Julia. "It would be radioed in where there was shipping, and we had little pips that we moved around to chart the course." From balconies overlooking the action, military personnel studied the nonstop movement, transmitting pertinent details to operatives in the field.

This wasn't some gratuitous war game to appease the natives. Just two weeks earlier, on February 23, during one of FDR's fireside chats, a Japanese sub had risen out of the water just north of Santa Barbara and fired three shells into tidewater refinery installments. The spotters who manned the Information and Filter Center post knew what the stakes were. They threw themselves into the work, and they took it seriously.

"Julia loved the work," Katie recalls. "She loved the top-secret aspect of it, how it related to the national defense, even to our own families. It was wartime and this was a pretty exciting job." Exciting and demanding, with its mixture of details and intrigue. "We worked long, eight-hour shifts, often in the middle of the night. We knew the position of every ship, boat, whale or log that was in the water off the coast. And when something unusual happened that place would jump into action."

For Julia, the job was her first taste of intelligence work. She loved being "in the thick of things." It combined her fascination with politics and world events and stirred up the sense of purpose she'd been burying all this time. At the age of thirty, she'd finally managed to do something meaningful, and now she longed to do it on a larger stage—in Washington, D.C., perhaps, where many of her friends had recently landed, or maybe in the service, where the real action transpired. There was nothing holding her in Pasadena anymore. The obligation to care for her father was strong and sincere, but Dort had decided to move back home for a while, freeing Julia to explore other options. And Harrison Chandler—that was an easier decision. On April 10, 1942, she made it official, issuing an emphatic no. She didn't intend to marry him, not now, not under present circumstances. "And I hope I shall maintain this position," she concluded in a diary entry. "It is a sin to marry without love. And marriage, while utterly desirable, from my point of view, must be [with] the right one. I know what I want, and it is 'sympatico' [sic]—companionship, interests, great respect and fun. Otherwise and always—no."

WHILE CHANDLER COULD not give Julia his heart, he gave her a hearty piece of advice. If she was determined to have a greater role in the war effort, he suggested, she should quit doing volunteer work and take the Civil Service exam. With the war creating a shortage of men across all government agencies, there was an urgent demand for able-bodied women. This made good sense to Julia, who took the test in June 1942. But civilian jobs sounded too much like candy-striping. Julia was raring to do something that demanded more of her, something that involved more ingenuity, more action. Being in the navy had a special appeal, so she applied to its women's auxiliary, Women Accepted for Voluntary

Emergency Service—the Waves—and while she was at it, she also applied to the Wac, the Women's Army Corps.

In the meantime, several friends urged her to head to Washington, D.C. "That was where the action was," according to Katy Gates, who was already stationed there with her husband, a navy strategist. Janie McBain, whose husband was off on military assignment in Italy, offered Julia a place to stay, with her. The war wasn't coming to Pasadena anytime soon. Why remain there, waiting for an answer from the navy, when she could wait in Washington just as well? Besides, Julia's father was putting pressure on her to reconsider Chandler's marriage proposal. And Harrison was still everywhere on the scene. Between him and her father, Julia felt there was too much complicity among self-interested parties. "A change of scenery," she concluded, "would do me a world of good."

It wasn't exactly clear what Julia expected to see. But the new world that greeted her was about to change her life.

The social butterfly, Pasadena, 1939

Five

Keeper of the Secrets

Washington, D.C., must have brought great relief to Julia McWilliams as she emerged from Union Station into its teeming maw. From the steps of the station, the outlines of marble monuments, rising high above the bulwark of Federalist cubes, hovered in relief, sage figures against the summer sky. The snarl of traffic below blared like noisy vendors announcing a new age for the nation's capital. With its streets bulging from the recent influx of civil servants wedded to the war effort, Washington looked to Julia "like a scaled-down version of New York." But just as vital—positively percolating with vitality. Everyone seemed "headed this-way-or-that-way" to an engagement of great importance. But if she felt overwhelmed or unsure, she gave no sign of it. There was an exuberant spirit in the air—of extraordinary people in extraordinary times—and she desperately wanted to be a part of it.

After a weekend as a guest of her friend Janie McBain, Julia moved to a shabby residence hotel on California Street, just a bare cell of a room with mismatched furniture, whose cracked, paint-stained window looked out across a service alley onto the back of an adjacent brick building. Only temporary, she hoped, just long enough for her to hear from the Waves, after which she would most likely be deployed to a post on one of the navy bases. Friends who had enlisted had already shipped out to places as exotic as Banana River, Florida, and Olathe, Kansas, and Pearl Harbor, Hawaii. And while they would never set foot on an actual ship, other than perhaps to swab its deck in port, there were plenty of meaningful jobs—tending to carrier pigeons, rigging parachutes, manning control towers, washing planes.

None of them, it turned out, suitable for Julia McWilliams. Her application came back with an "automatic disqualification" on physical grounds. There were parameters that all candidates were expected to meet. Julia had examined them and presumed she met all criteria, certainly where it came to health and size. She had been under the impression that only very short women—those under five feet—were restricted from serving, but in the space where she had entered her height, six one, some anonymous hand had circled it. "I was too long," she told a previous biographer—too long at six one and even longer at six three.

Despite her rejection, Julia was in Washington to stay. She had gone there determined to do her part for the war effort, determined "to see action," and do it she would, even if it meant taking a less exciting job until something more action-packed came her way. Government offices all over the capital were frantically staffing up—the War Research Service, Office of Civilian Defense, Board of Economic Warfare, National Defense Research Committee, Alien Enemy Control Unit, Center for Regulatory Effectiveness, on and on it went, infinite titles of official mumbo jumbo that only a bureaucrat could decipher. Most she had never even heard of, nor did she know what they did or the people who ran them. Often those in supervisory positions were equally in the dark; they had only recently been funded and directed to hire, hire, hire. And still, competition was fierce. There were thousands of young, educated, ambitious, *shorter* job-seekers on the prowl, though few were more resourceful than thirty-year-old Julia McWilliams.

She hit the street running, scrabbling in and out of strange buildings, up and down strange corridors, in and out of strange doors, waiting in lines, dropping off résumés, filling out forms, pleading her case. Finally, on August 24, 1942, Julia got an offer: a position as senior typist for the Research Unit of the Office of War Information (OWI) at the Department of State. The OWI had only been in existence since June, but already it was churning out an avalanche of propaganda—flooding Europe with posters, warning citizens about foreign spies, producing radio broadcasts (including *This Is Our Enemy* and *Uncle Sam*), and promoting patriotism abroad through a new effort called the Voice of America. The Research Unit was its in-house database, a mash-up of the former Office of Facts and Figures and the Office of Government Reports.

Julia could not persuade its flaky director to see her, but his assistant was none other than Noble Cathcart, the editor who had assigned her the ill-fated book piece at *Saturday Review* and just happened to be married to her cousin Harriet. This assignment was more to her ability; in fact, it was considered idiot-proof: Julia's job was to page through reams of newspapers and official documents noting any mention of a government official, then typing his or her name and rank on a three-by-five card. Idiot-proof—and then some. But after two months and ten thousand cards—an amazing output, by all estimates—she'd had enough.

Depleted but not daunted, Julia looked for another job that would neither drain her physically nor regard her as a machine. Ideally, she wanted to work in intelligence, which required more insight and attracted a brainier crowd. Its objectives fascinated her: espionage, propaganda, subversion, forgery, sabotage, even murder were all facets of the novels she consumed. There were several agencies that addressed these ideals, all couched within the overstuffed Department of State. Julia had familiarized herself with most of them. She did her due diligence. There were a lot of possible matches, there was a lot of overlap. But one branch kept standing out: the Office of Strategic Services (OSS).

Julia knew a handful of people who worked for the OSS, elite grads like her, who had come to Washington determined to see action abroad and got co-opted by the insatiable intelligence machine. The job, which ranged from research and analysis to clandestine operations behind enemy lines, demanded smart, resourceful self-starters with a dash of maverick in their DNA. Professors were among the agency's earliest recruits, many of whom attracted their brightest students. An educated woman especially fit the director's ideal, which he described as "a cross between a Smith graduate, a Powers model, and a Katie Gibbs secretary." Julia must have figured she had two out of the three, with the potential to hit the trifecta. She also came from old money, which helped her cause, the thinking being that those who were financially self-sufficient were least likely to take a bribe.

The Office of Strategic Services wasn't established as a result of the war, but actually six months *before* Pearl Harbor, in June 1941, when FDR ordered William Donovan, a longtime legal adviser and a decorated veteran of World War I, to form America's first intelligence-gathering agency. The United States had always been satisfied with its national security. Now that it was almost certain the country would be drawn into World War II, "enforcing our will upon the enemy by means other than military action" was crucial to the president's objective for victory, to say nothing of America's well-being.

"Wild Bill" Donovan was the right man for the job. Described as "a rosy-cheeked smiling gentleman with a voice as soft as the leaf of a shamrock . . . and a punch in each hand like the kick of a mule," he was an unrelenting warrior who had hunted down Pancho Villa in 1917 and led the Fighting Sixty-ninth Regiment through some of the bloodiest battles of World War I, for which he was awarded the Medal of Honor. In the years between the wars, he prospered as a high-powered Wall Street lawyer, but he'd always kept a hand or three in global affairs.

Roosevelt gave Donovan what Capitol Hill called "carte blanche": permission to use his office—Room 122, in the basement of a central building on the Naval Medical Campus on E Street—for anything he saw fit. *No strings attached!* The spy business demanded a free hand to conduct its "sensitive" affairs. As such, Donovan was exempt from the usual red tape that ensnarled most federal programs, and he answered only to the president. He may, in fact, have been the only person to be given such authority. This meant staffing his office with fiercely loyal operatives, smart cookies of unquestioning obedience and above reproach, with allegiance to one god: Bill Donovan.

"He attracted the top lawyers and the nation's top public servants, and they brought their brightest and most congenial people into it," recalls Fisher Howe, a high-level career diplomat who gained his own rite of passage in Room 122. "There was no question that the OSS was packed with congenial, college-educated people who enjoyed working together, motivated by their glamorous leader." So congenial, in fact, that grudging outsiders claimed OSS stood for "Oh So Social." According to Howe, "It was the envy of everybody—but also the disparagement."

To those outsiders, the agency seemed elitist, unwieldy, a government boondoggle that, in time, would employ more than 21,000 dilettantes. It was impossible for antagonists to wrap their arms around such an entity, especially one that operated outside the system and "where standard operating procedure was almost taboo," and that had "an unvouchered budget that ran into the hundreds of millions [of dollars]." The military decried its lazy discipline. Bureaucrats were unable to penetrate its apolitical ranks. Rivals, like J. Edgar Hoover, despised the Almighty Donovan. The proletarian Hoover resented Donovan's disciples as a bunch of "amateur playboys." Moreover, its credo was nondenominational, its ministry open to all, including Communist sympathizers, Marxist enthusiasts, right-wing extremists, and leftist idealists. All one needed to join was to sign an oath of secrecy. "The O.S.S. was a fraternity—a fraternity of Ivy League upstarts," says Fisher Howe. "No question Julia would have found like-minded people there."

In fact, the OSS was a perfect fit for Julia McWilliams. She knew it, too, her first day on the job—December 14, 1942. Loping across the majestic E Street complex in a standout new leopard-fur coat, she had great expectations of what lay ahead. Friends who'd been working there since the bureau was formed painted a sanguine picture of their utopian circumstances. The office was more or less run by "very bright girls engaged in cloak-and-dagger activity, working not for the money, but for the thrill" of doing something clandestine. The whole scenario was in full swing, fairly "buzzing," upon Julia's arrival at OSS. "Walking in, there was a feeling of excitement in that office," she recalled. "It was a special place, filled with special people doing special work—*top secret* work."

On first blush, her job seemed less than glamorous. She was appointed a junior research assistant to the director himself, which involved organizing his prodigious files concerning the Secret Intelligence (SI) branch of operations, its personnel, encoded messages, and the documents detailing war plans. During most of the time, Donovan was away from the office, cultivating shadow agents and the cooperation of generals. Julia would work unencumbered by pressure, alongside a coven of Donovan's "glamour girls." It was donkeywork for the most part, organizing and filing, filing and organizing, but Julia was content just to be part of the team. "My typewriting helped a great deal, and I was used to office procedures," she recalled, "—and I was responsible," which added to her well-being. Perhaps a weightier perk was the impact of her co-workers—"so many interesting people"—whose intellects and imaginations fascinated her no end. "It was my first real encounter with the academic mind," Julia recalled. Especially the wonks in Research and Analysis, who evaluated the covert material used in planning subversive operations. She loved listening to them sift through and discuss the variables in vigorous, scholarly choctaw, most of which sailed right over her head. Despite her elite education, Julia still nursed an inferior view of herself. "I was sort of a plain old middle-class *bourgeoise*," she said. "I was not an intellectual type." She felt humble in their presence, unlicked and unformed. But she had the desire, a craving for something more. She was hungry for stimulation of this sort and sensed, perhaps for the first time, that she was around something that would change her, reshape her, in substantive ways.

And she was willing to work hard, six days a week, because there was so much at stake. By the end of 1942, OSS agents were buried deep in all key European cities, as well as across Southeast Asia, where "bodies" were stationed tactically to identify enemy arsenals, munitions dumps, industrial facilities, and supply routes. Information of all kinds was the currency on which the agency thrived. A flood of information—of even the smallest, most insignificant intelligence—flowed into the office each day. And not only was every word of it analyzed for content, it had to be sorted, filed, collated, and routed to the proper office where military experts would know how to utilize it.

Most all of the classified intelligence passed through Julia McWilliams's hands. As she opened dusty pouches and sifted through coffee-stained reports, there would be code names necessitating identification, phrases that required flagging, words that triggered critical responses, photographs that demanded studying, intercepts combed for names and contacts, charts, maps, diagrams—transcripts full of material involving some understanding of the entire American intelligence operation. The work was painstaking, elaborate, complicated, often convoluted, but it wasn't long before Julia mastered the office's bewildering maze.

All the more remarkable considering Julia had shown no previous evidence of accomplishment, not for work, not for discipline, not for exploring her potential. Up until then, Julia lamented, "I never had any brilliance whatsoever," chiefly because her left-brain generator, so to speak, "was only working on half cylinders." But something had changed in the process. Almost overnight, Julia morphed from a self-proclaimed dilettante into a dedicated civil servant, managing deadlines and supervising personnel with relative confidence. She labored long hours in that airless office, helping steer more than forty colleagues through the bureaucracy. Took care of managing her professional approach, to the point that OSS became a transforming experience, what Julia later called "my growing-up period."

In early 1943, her diligence paid off. Julia earned a promotion, first to the position of clerk in General Donovan's office, and eventually to senior clerk, overseeing his administrative support staff. She was clearly on an upward trajectory, taking a firm, if arm's-length, grip on her life. Washington "intrigued and amused" her. Living on her own "seemed civilized," better than she'd expected. A good crowd her age was doing important work there. She enjoyed an active social life, if not yet a meaningful relationship, merging a clique of educated peers with more proletarian émigrés. Even relatively recent friends from different State Department units played repeating roles in an endless engagement of parties. Yes, it was Oh So Social in those growing-up years.

AND THE GROWING wasn't finished yet.

A mid-year move to a new department placed Julia in one of the more hands-on experimental programs on the government's wartime drawing board. There was a furious urgency to the endeavors of the new Emergency Rescue Equipment Section (ERES). Its mission was to prepare fliers downed at sea for survival, and with each new campaign more pilots were at risk as the war spread across Asia and the Pacific theaters—ERES was working against the clock. They weren't concerned with the traditional gear used for rescue and recovery: flares, flotation rafts, wetsuits, transmitters. Those were already operational and sufficient for the short term. Instead, they anticipated the problems a pilot might face should he be stranded in a remote location, where assistance or food wasn't available.

The OSS encouraged "unconventional" approaches to seemingly straightforward problems, even those as critical as survival, and since Strategic Services was funding ERES its experiments were often conducted by "eccentric schemers" and leaned toward the "harebrained." Julia discovered these screwball methods almost as soon as she joined ERES. Along with a colleague, she was dispatched to the market and ordered to buy fish. Why? So researchers could test whether it was possible for a soldier lost at sea to sustain himself by squeezing the liquid from a fish into his mouth. Thereafter, Julia referred to her department as "the fish-squeezing unit," although its think tank was also engaged in more fundamental aspects of rescue work, like developing shark repellent, exposure suits, and rescue kits.

Among the characters she met during her tenure with ERES was Jack Moore, a talented illustrator who had left art school to join the army soon after war broke out. Moore developed maps and other graphics for the Presentation Division, a branch of Research and Analysis under the State Department's umbrella. Despite the comfort of his job, he was awaiting assignment overseas, most likely to India, where his boss, Paul Child, was setting up shop, in service to Britain's Lord Mountbatten, Supreme Allied Commander, South East Asia Command. The change of scenery would be welcome; he couldn't wait to get over there, closer to the action but still out of harm's way. Julia was drawn in by Moore's musings about working abroad. He made it sound more like an exotic adventure than a military posting. To a woman who had been searching her entire life for something meaningful—for spiritual growth, for contentment, for her identity as a woman—the prospect of foreign travel was not only alluring but constructive as well. A posting abroad offered an antidote for Julia's lack of initiative thus far.

Coincidentally, the OSS was establishing new bases in Southeast Asia, to facilitate vital field operations surrounding the fighting in Burma. "They began sending people overseas," Julia recalled—researchers, interpreters, provisioners, administrative personnel—to get the intelligence apparatus moving before installing key operatives. At Jack Moore's urging, Julia expressed her interest.

Overseas: a transfer that radical might work to expand and enliven her world. Her situation in Washington, at least professionally, seemed to have hit a wall. "I was just doing office work," Julia conceded of her three years at OSS. Further advancement, she realized, was going to be a slow, if impractical, process. "I didn't have any languages. I naturally wasn't trained as a spy. My history background didn't amount to anything." When you looked at her résumé, she had nothing distinctive to offer. Another promotion, as administrative assistant in the registry, amounted to nothing more than a fancier title and a raise—which was appreciated. But when she came right down to it, Julia was still *just doing office work.*

She needed to break the chain. Getting away—overseas—might be a good first step in that direction. Europe was the most sought-after posting. It was the logical choice for someone without much of a specialized background. But Julia saw no possibility of an opening there. Choice jobs like that were out of her reach. Besides, Europe wasn't that exotic, it wasn't that far off the beaten path. Plenty of her friends had spent holidays there. "I knew I'd sometime get to Europe," Julia reasoned, "so I signed up to go to the Far East."

JULIA ASSUMED FROM the start that she'd be posted to India. The OSS had established an outpost there in August 1943 with a mandate to gather intelligence that would ostensibly help liberate Burma, across the Bay of Bengal. Holding Burma was a buffer, critical to "keep[ing] the door open to China," so there was plenty to be done on that busy, chaotic front. At the same time, however, there was a proviso to monitor another vital interest: it would be a perfect opportunity for OSS observers to provide Washington with updates on the nationalist movement in India. British colonial power was in its last smoldering throes. With the country in turmoil, politically and socially, with the British Raj on the ropes—with warfare raging across the Pacific theater—the situation threatened to destabilize further the entire subcontinent.

On February 26, 1944, Julia left Washington on a troop train bound for California, the first leg of a journey that would take her halfway around the world. For Julia, whose only travel experience outside the United States was that Caesar salad in Tijuana, the idea of entering the land of spice and yogis—where it was known that Westerners often disappeared for good in the fetid, human sprawl—was pure excitement. She knew this would be "the adventure of a lifetime." It meant "taking each new experience as it came," which Julia was up for, "come hell or high water."

Hell came first. The trip west was a gauntlet of sorts, with three women riding solo among cars of swarming soldiers. A gallery of admirers soon sprung up, a gallery of men to whom these civilian gals were an anomaly—and an enticement. The women were constantly hit upon, not harassed, but pestered—incessantly. Be that as it may, Julia loved the attention. She loved men, felt comfortable around them, men of all shapes and sizes (but especially the virile and handsome ones). The exact nature of her interaction with this contingent isn't known, but Julia's reference to "more handsome men than you could shake a stick at" in a letter to her father suggests that it involved all the elements that, throughout her lifetime, demonstrated more than a keen fondness for the opposite sex. This, in direct contrast to the sympathies of her traveling companions: Ellie Thiry, who was overwhelmed somewhat by the unnatural imbalance of the sexes, and Cora DuBois, a lesbian who couldn't have cared less. All three, though, made the trip without undue complication or incident.

And then came the high water. On March 9, 1944, following an orientation that approximated boot camp, with orders, briefings, and survival training, Julia sailed from Wilmington, California, aboard the SS *Mariposa,* a former Hawaiian Islands luxury liner that had been pressed into military service in the aftermath of Pearl Harbor. It was to be a month-long voyage, zigzagging furtively across the Pacific, where Japanese subs had already sunk nine such troop transports. On board, the journey was an expansion of Julia's fanciful train ride west—with nine women this time and more than three thousand male admirers, mostly GIs, a state of affairs that gave rise to a rather rowdy departure. In the profusion of high-polished decks and hastily converted quarters, thousands of excitable enlisted men, single and married, surrounded the huddled distaff, serenading the women with "wolf calls and whistles," to say nothing of propositions that came with the fanfare. It was, according to Julia, "an utterly strange experience," though nothing that intimidated her or that she couldn't handle. Still, several of the other women weren't as adept. If they had hoped to avoid the lusty push-and-pull by melting invisibly into their surroundings, it soon became clear there was nowhere to hide. "Julia launched a rumor that we are missionaries, which has helped curb the outbursts," a passenger noted in her diary two days out to sea, but if the men were at all savvy, they weren't buying. That left only the cabin for refuge—*one* cabin shared by all nine women, another world entirely, with triple-decker bunk beds pushed against two walls, clothes and bags strewn everywhere, severely overcrowded, like Calcutta, which was where they were headed.

As Julia discovered, there was nowhere to think in that compact slip of space. The cabin was not a place for the restless or the curious—and she was both. Nor would it do for her to spend the voyage in seclusion, which is what some of the women chose to do to protect their privacy. Instead, Julia mingled with the civilians on board, many of whom were the brightest minds on the government's payroll—linguists, diplomatic attachés, scholars, correspondents, anthropologists, photographers, economists, cartographers, historians, and specialists in Asian and especially Indian culture. They had begun to form their own independent intellectual circle, comparing notes and waxing eloquent about subjects that bisected their individual areas of interest as they ignored the potential dangers of crossing the ocean during wartime.

This was a far cry from the Pasadena country-club set, even from the marriage-minded party crowd at Smith. These people were a world apart—they were informed on the issues of the day, on the arts, on culture, on a far deeper level than the parochial planes of Julia's usual acquaintances. Julia had never taken an interest in such business before, but everything they said, the way they looked at things, fascinated her. These people stimulated something in her brain that none of the private schools or elite colleges had been able to do. Julia had developed as someone who took an interest in the life of the mind, but in a social setting as opposed to an academic setting. Someone droning on about the indigenous sects of India in front of a blackboard set her to daydreaming; but around a table and over navy grub—that was an altogether different story! Perhaps there had been a capacity in her all along to appreciate a wider world. It was all in the presentation. There was no getting around the fact that Julia was a social animal.

In the midst of so much brainpower, Julia's insecurities quickly resurfaced. The way this crowd expressed itself had underscored her shortcomings. "What kind of mind do *I* have?" she wondered in a shipboard diary entry larded with misgiving. What was she meant for? Where was she destined? In page after page of reflection, everything she believed in had suddenly come under scrutiny: her politics, religious beliefs, sexuality, upbringing, especially her potential—all of it now thrown into uncertain disarray. It was as if she had had her footing kicked out from beneath her. Not on terra firma, but in the middle of the Pacific Ocean, surrounded by "world thinkers," and on her way to God-knows-where—a hell of a place to start questioning your existence!

Still, she always struggled with what she considered to be her intellectual inadequacies, which were now brought out by this crowd of super-smart people whom she admired, causing her to reevaluate and revise long-held beliefs. Fortunately, Julia McWilliams wasn't undone by candid appraisals; she wasn't someone who crumbled under doubt. Rather, she drew strength from challenge and ever-changing situations. Her clear-eyed contemplation was direct and earnest. She had enormous reserves of raw untapped intelligence that would reveal itself in many ways—but always from a position of a late bloomer. "All my life I've had to push myself," she allowed, "to keep up, to earn my place at the table." Interestingly, it was a place at the table she coveted, not a place behind a desk or at the head of a class.

Through the rest of March and into the ripeness of early April—every day for two weeks brought nothing but sunshine and star-filled nights—Julia gorged herself on the scholarship of her brainy shipmates, monitoring their charged conversations and dissecting their views. Mostly, she gravitated toward the anthropologists, whose abstracts about relationships and society she grew to adore. Julia was particularly attracted to an extravagantly tall, horsy man with a posh British accent who was engaged by the Morale Operations division of OSS to develop psychological warfare. Gregory Bateson had been to New Guinea and to Bali with his wife, Margaret Mead, where they studied the effects of outsiders on native cultures. Julia was entranced by his experiences and intensity, as well as his eloquently articulated ideas about developing societies. She remembered their conversations as "head-turners" that introduced her to concepts such as national character and genetics. Julia wrestled with the ideas, which she entered in her diary, trying to bring her own thoughts and opinions to them as best she could. Following one such conversation, thirty-one-year-old Julia came to the conclusion that she'd been seriously adrift, just "vegetating" all these years. "None of my college career or anything I had done in the way of work was of any use at all," she realized. And she made the choice, then and there, to cultivate her mind.

Any metamorphosis would have to wait, however, as the *Mariposa* approached the Indian coast. The troop transport had been at sea for thirty-one days and the anticipation and suspense of touching down on Indian soil was all-consuming. Word had begun circulating miles from shore that the ship's landing orders were in flux. In fact, there was a last-minute detour, from Calcutta to Bombay, and as the ship drew near, preparing to make berth in the harbor, everyone on board came topside to take in the scene. Bombay: primitive yet contemporary; opulent yet riddled with poverty. Julia got the whole samosa in a sensational sensory blast. She "could see and smell the haze," patches of dense, ashen smog that hung over the city like porridge from a spoon. It was a sight that cowed even the most worldly travelers. The stretch of landscape on the shore was an unholy congestion, its banks clogged by the bulk of a magnificent fleet, a treacherous labyrinth of ghats braced by countless matchstick planks, and a human eddy—thick swarms of dark- and light-skinned people milling, thronging, through the soupy setting. Clinging to the guardrail that encircled the deck, Julia gasped: "Oh, my God, what have I gotten myself into?"

Culture shock abounded as the ship's passengers stumbled down the gangplank into the maelstrom that was Bombay. Fisher Howe, who had arrived months earlier, recalled how "the swell of sensations just hit you like a sledgehammer." It was stimulus overload, he said, "filthy, sweltering, foul-smelling, blinding, everywhere you turned was another thrilling effect." On Easter Sunday, April 9, 1944, Julia surrendered herself to the mysteries of the city. For eighteen days, until new orders were drawn, she soaked in as many aspects of this new exhilarating experience as she could, sightseeing, eating, dancing, eating, golfing, eating some more, even swinging through Bombay's notorious red-light district. It was great theater, an education like she'd never experienced before. Not that the others in Julia's traveling party shared her fascination. "Have met practically no one who likes India," she wrote in her Bombay diary pages, though typically, gamely, she insisted: "*I do!*"

When her orders finally came through, however, she was downcast. India, it seemed, was now off the table. The situation there had become too explosive, too unpredictable. As a result, Lord Mountbatten, who oversaw the South East Asia Command (SEAC) as well as consulted with the OSS, decided to relocate his headquarters from New Delhi to Ceylon (now Sri Lanka). Julia's papers had a new destination inscribed on them: she was due in Colombo on April 25.

CEYLON WAS EVERYTHING India wasn't—peaceful, temperate, fragrant, *civilized,* a tropical paradise far removed from the wages of war. Long coveted as "a beautiful place to work and play," Ceylon provided a safe haven for the Americans who were starting an intelligence office there under the vast umbrella of Mountbatten's central command. Its focus was in support of SEAC's ongoing operations in Siam, the crossroads for Japanese troops traveling between Indonesia and China and the seat of the Allies' organized resistance. In the chess-like gambits of its high-stakes spy scheme, OSS dropped agents and equipment into jungle hideouts, from where they filed reports detailing, among other things, troop locations and bombing targets. Where specifically were the Japanese stationed? Which local people were assisting them? Julia McWilliams would be responsible for the dissemination of these reports. As head of the Registry, she was privy to the most sensitive intelligence—and in charge of who else got to see it.

Fortunately, the headquarters wasn't in Colombo, a bustling port town not unlike Marseille or Newark, but in Kandy, seventy-five miles inland, nestled atop a heavenly mountainous range. From the moment she and her colleagues climbed on the old-fashioned train out of Colombo, Julia entered another world. The scenery was breathtaking as they wound through palm groves, tea plantations, wild bush, and lush jungle, across mountain streams and under the crags of ragged limestone boulders. Adam's Peak, around which Buddha is said to have walked, loomed conspicuously on the horizon. Their arrival in Kandy, two hours later, was even more of an eyeful. The town was "like Shangri-La," Julia thought, right out of a fairytale. No wonder it was the stronghold of the ancient Sinhalese kings. As her eyes adjusted to the sun-flecked spectacle, she could see dense groves of coconut palms and papaya trees that bordered the town, a few Buddhist temples in the foothills above a terraced rice paddy, and thick folds of exotic vegetation all around. Monkeys played in the branches above the roofs, while "monks in bright saffron robes and shaved heads" threaded through the narrow weave of streets. The almost intoxicating spicy-sweet nectar of cinnamon blossoms filled the air. At more than 1,700 feet above sea level, the air was thinner and drier than on the coast, a condition Julia luxuriated in as being "skin-warm," perfect to the touch. Mountbatten considered Kandy "probably the most beautiful spot in the world," and from where Julia stood she would have had to agree with him.

Since money was no object when it came to the war effort, OSS rushed to create the kind of cushy lifestyle that, back home, had been reserved for the country-club set. "Mountbatten's headquarters became a byword for elegance and luxury," an eyewitness observed in a chronicle of the campaign, "a place where well-groomed staff, many of them titled, were chauffeured in shiny limousines to offices scattered throughout the lush tropical gardens." Dress was casual, formalities were few. The OSS sector, unlike most posts that served the military, was housed in a colonial estate on a tea plantation called Nandana, on the shore of a gorgeous artificial lake. The way one officer described it, that facility "was nothing so much as like a western university in summer session." The campus itself resembled a tidy village green, crisscrossed by a grid of inlaid walks. The civilian staff worked in palm-thatched huts, or *bashas,* which had just enough conveniences to create the illusion of comfort. An open-air officers' club overlooked the water, a communal mess hall stood a short walk away. Aside from the scorpions and cobras, the place felt just like home. "It is somewhat primitive, but airy and far from dressy," Julia recalled. All in all, however, she found the life there "pastoral."

If only her work had given her as much pleasure. The Registry, Julia discovered, was no more than a euphemism for "running the files," a job she'd loathed back in Washington for its "menial" routine. The grind in Kandy was no different—it bored her silly. Two days into the operation was all she needed to realize it.

Exactly how she managed to deal with this isn't known, but Julia determined to make the most of a tedious situation. One thing is clear: her sense of humor came in handy. Nothing crossed her desk that wasn't worthy of a poke in the ribs. Fake missives, especially, became her stock-in-trade. She bombarded department heads with official-sounding memos detailing rule changes that were obviously a goof. A new file system, for instance, in which all documents were classified under the first letter of their last word. Or a directive warning recipients that when the files were full they would be sealed forever, in a vault. All of these had to be read and initialed, and it amused Julia no end that they came back approved. Other barbs served as her way of dealing with all the infuriating red tape. "If you don't send Registry that report we need," she warned a colleague in the States, "I shall fill the next Washington pouch with itching powder and virulent bacteriological diseases, and change all the numbers, as well as translating the material into Singhalese [*sic*], and destroying the English version."

In any case, by October Julia had the Registry up and humming. "Our in-and-out material has been snowballing," she reported to headquarters, in D.C. "Of 365 Washington pouches received in September, there are about 600 pieces that had to be accessioned, cross indexed, circulated, filed. This figure does not include our operational and intelligence input from the field." A further description reveals her high level of clearance: "We keep master cards on each current subject, which means my staff must be completely familiar with what's going on. For example, cards for S.I. [Secret Intelligence] include names of all agents, student recruits and their various code names."

As one operative put it: "Julia McWilliams was keeper of the secrets." She knew who all the undercover agents were, where they were located, and what they were engaged in for the OSS. All the more tactical, as their instructions were also channeled through the Registry's confidential filter system. Throughout her life, Julia insisted she was nothing more than a file clerk, but "that was so much poppycock," according to Fisher Howe. "Those files practically ran the Secretariat, with all its operational and sensitive intelligence. It had to be handled very carefully, which was entrusted entirely to Julia." She wasn't a spy, if that was her criterion for professional stature, nevertheless OSS classified her as a senior civilian intelligence officer: keeper of the secrets.

While the job required resourcefulness and precision, life in Ceylon was anything but taxing. "Everybody in OSS had a very social time of it," Howe says. "We were a congenial group of people and kept pretty close together." A lot of festive meals were shared on that faraway outpost, even though most of the restaurants in Kandy were off-limits to Americans due to the fact that they served cat on the menu. Still the nightlife provided suitable diversion. "There are movies and dances twice a week at the American officers' club," Julia recalled, "walks in the moonlight. On Sundays there are picnics, golf, tennis, swimming, or a weekend down in Colombo, depending entirely upon the enterprise of yourself in enticing the enterprise of the other gender."

How clever Julia was at that enterprise, as she put it, isn't known, the accounts having been excised from her diary. There were a few superficial crushes that weren't acted upon, several platonic relationships that sufficed—for the time being. Two, in particular, that she rekindled in Kandy were with her recently acquired friends, Jack Moore and Gregory Bateson. Moore worked across the quad from Julia's *basha* in the Visual Presentation unit of Research and Analysis, where he ministered to the War Room with maps and diagrams. Bateson was a regular drinking companion, who beguiled her with his enormous brain. Together, they often picnicked in a clearing of jungle palms, with "a breathtaking view practically all the way to the sea." They may have accompanied others to Colombo or Trincomalee during the spring of 1944. By the beginning of May, however, their friendly outings took an intriguing detour when both men began inviting a mutual acquaintance to join them. In a matter of only a few weeks, Paul Child would turn their foursome into a twosome.

Six

Paul

A twosome. No configuration meant more to Paul Child. From the moment he was born, the power of two was implanted in him like a unique component of DNA.

According to family records, he was born in '02, just a few minutes after two on an icy winter's morning in Montclair, New Jersey. It would always be noted that Paul arrived first—"the first out of the womb"—followed by his twin brother, Robert, two minutes later. There, in the hospital, surrounded by family and curious staff, small crowds pressed against the glass to the ward where the newborns lay swaddled, looking from Child boy to Child boy with utter delight. One word echoed repeatedly through the well-scrubbed corridor: *identical.* It was impossible to tell them apart. But while Paul and his brother may have looked the same, sounded the same, deep down they were anything but identical—an issue that would complicate the rest of their lives.

And life for the Childs was already complicated enough. Paul's parents struggled to keep the family intact while they managed a schedule of nightmarish logistics. Each week, Paul's father, Charles Tripler Child, left their split-level home on Clairemont Avenue and made what was then a grueling six-hour trip to Washington, D.C., where he was director of the U.S. Astrophysical Observatory at the Smithsonian Institution. His wife, mustering her resilient New England spirit, played her part as

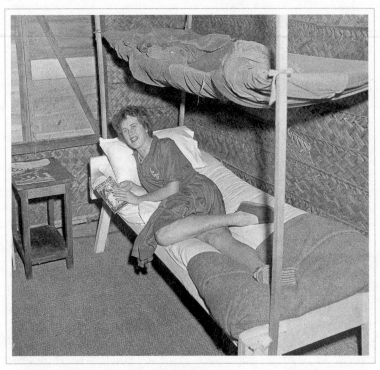

Julia in Kandy, Ceylon, with the legs that transfixed Paul, July 19, 1944

the dependable housewife during her husband's frequent absences, but it wasn't without great effort—and she wasn't happy about it.

Bertha Cushing Child had "given up her soul" for that family, at least that was the way it often felt to her. In her youth, she had been teeming with promise, a potent mix of beauty and talent that ran counter to the profile for an itinerant minister's daughter. There was a time, early on, when Bertha shared her father's Christly piety, but gradually her ambitions fastened on more worldly pursuits. Like the Boston Brahmins whom she envied and in whose shadow she had grown up, she longed for a life of refinement, a life of music and culture, salons and soirées. The men closest to her, however, seemed more inclined to bollix up those plans. Her father spent much of each year traveling the back roads of New England, preaching to wayward communities in need of salvation, while Bertha and her siblings handled the mundane household chores. Now her husband was gone for long stretches, as well, stranding her in a suburb with a family to raise, but she never stopped longing to be a part of another, very different world.

Bertha's circumstances hadn't always felt that bleak. For the longest time, Charles's career had been on a steady upward trajectory, its influences reaching into all levels of society. As a result, Bertha set her sights on a more cultured lifestyle—and for good reason. Electricity was the rising technological sensation and Charles Child, riding the current, was poised to release it into the new century. When it came to the cutting edge of science, no one, other than perhaps Edison, was more learned, more inventive, more visionary. Before the age of twenty, Charles had already earned graduate degrees in physics, chemistry, and mathematics from Johns Hopkins University, with language proficiency in French, German, Italian, and Greek. In 1888, he designed and supervised construction for twelve electric railway systems and set up the first storage-battery traction lines at Toledo, Newark, and New York. He then formed his own company for manufacturing power supply stations, inventing much of its equipment, before joining the Smithsonian, where he directed experiments on the infrared solar spectrum, whose space-age instruments he constructed from scratch. In his spare time—*spare time!*—he edited the *Electrical Review* and published *The How and Why of Electricity,* the preeminent work on the subject.

The diligence needed to maintain his thriving career left Charles Child little time for his wife, who was starved for cultural and social stimulation. "He was a driven man," said his grandniece, Rachel, given to bouts where he shut out everything—and *everyone*—to focus exclusively on his research. He missed much of his daughter, Mary's, early childhood while off streamlining the complex circuitry for an ultramodern telephone company in Richmond, Virginia. But as Bertha must have sensed, her husband's professional curiosity was piqued when his boys were born. Charles took a vigorous interest in the infants' development, drawn to them more perhaps by their sameness than any paternal connection. The idiosyncrasies of twins were irresistible, catnip for a scientist. Innocently, Paul and Robert fed their father's inquisitive mind.

Nevertheless, Charles became more available, much to everyone's delight, and then, suddenly, without forewarning, he was gone: dead at age thirty-five. The official cause was "a combination of malaria and typhoid," but apparently that was so much officialese. In various interviews for this book several subjects contributed, on condition of anonymity, their own addition to the lore. According to a "family witness," Charles died of thyroidism, a disease associated with the thyroid gland. Another family member insisted it was "the surfeit rum." And still another confided: "It was syphilis." Erica Prud'homme, Charles's grandniece, believes it may have been a combination of symptoms. "All told," she says, "his death was a shock. It was very mysterious."

Mysterious—and with devastating repercussions. Bertha was left with three young children—two of whom, the twins, were only six months old—and no means of financial support. Charles, in his electrically induced myopia, had left her near-destitute. In New Jersey.

By the summer of 1902, Bertha Child moved what was left of her family to a more culturally promising address. She found a rooming house in Newton, Massachusetts, that was close enough to Boston, where, with reasonable access to the arts, she could pursue her dreams. The family moved around quite a bit in the years between 1902 and 1916—to Brookline, Wellesley, Worcester, Cambridge, even Boston proper—wherever Bertha suspected she could gain entry to the right circles. Effortlessly, she threw herself into the swirl of artistic and cultural salons and, with her extreme New England beauty and natural charm, quickly became a fixture of the Boston social scene.

"Their life became very insular," says a niece with a direct pipeline to the Child ancestry. Bertha was "esoteric, in the style of Isadora Duncan, very bohemian, which people found difficult to identify with." She also became a disciple of Theosophy (meaning "divine wisdom"), a kooky movement with roots in Eastern mysticism that preached evolution through various levels of spirituality and the divinity of Nature. This left her alienated from all but the pithiest of social circles. No doubt her family bore the brunt of this unconventional lifestyle. Mary, nicknamed Meeda, grew up petulant and withdrawn. The boys, with their uniqueness, became especially codependent. In place of fatherly influence, they depended on their own resources, their own inventive devices to navigate their world. They supported and compensated for each other's particularities—Paul reserved and introverted, some who knew him going as far as saying "dark"; Robert (who was now called Charles after his father) easygoing, gregarious to extremes. Both, however, developed strong streaks of independence. Even as tots, the boys were left by themselves quite a bit while their mother carved out her niche in the arts.

As a result, Paul and Charlie became inseparable, almost indistinguishable. They shadowed each other "like two halves of one person," according to a relative. "The twins," as everyone called them, existed as a single entity. Paul's shadow, however, was fractionally longer, owing to his status as the "older" twin. "If he went anywhere," says Rachel Child, "even around the block, two steps ahead of his brother, Charlie would come around screaming, '*Don't go away!*'" Charlie looked to Paul for everything growing up, and, in turn, Paul gave him the attention he craved.

They loved each other, that much was clear, but they also fought like gladiators. It seems almost unnecessary to note that they both studied ju-jitsu. "They beat the crap out of each other," says Charlie's son, Jon. "My father had a cauliflower ear he got from Paul, and, in turn, he did a number on Paul's eye." *A number* makes the mishap sound more willful than it actually was; as far as anyone can tell, the number in question was an accident, nothing more. According to family lore, during an afternoon of play when they were horsing around, Charlie stumbled and banged into Paul, who happened to be holding a needle in the vicinity of his face. It isn't entirely clear what happened next, but the needle punctured Paul's left eyeball, thus limiting his sight forever. Later, on a different occasion in a reenactment of a tale from Arthurian legend, Charlie wound up with a hatchet wound to the forehead. Still, even in play, or swordplay, or whatever it was rightfully called, they remained, always, two halves of one person.

Although they were happy in their own rough-and-tumble world, Bertha steered the twins toward her ideas of refinement. From an early age, she took to molding them in her high-toned image—intellectually as well as physically. She read to them every chance she got, and not just children's books but avant-garde poetry, essays, commentary, and philosophy. She let their hair grow long and dressed them in matching Little Lord Fauntleroy outfits. "They were brought up as sort of a couple and shown off as a couple because they were so good-looking," says a niece. Noticing that her boys enjoyed drawing and singing, Bertha fanned every faint spark of artistic talent with private instruction—singing lessons, music lessons, drawing lessons, languages. Never mind that Bertha had no money for these extravagances. Because of her beauty and charisma, because she was "one of those women who attracted interesting people" wherever she went, she had cultivated a group of "sponsors" who supported her conceits and were willing, at her behest, to underwrite the training of her sons.

These lessons, while mostly modest, often came at a dear physical cost. Invariably, the twins were sent off through Boston Common, clutching their musical instruments dutifully to their chests. Their teacher's studio was only a short distance from home, but that grassy span of the park was as treacherous as crossing a minefield. Dressed preciously, Paul and Charlie were sitting ducks for the roving band of Irish toughs who patrolled that turf like sentries. Paul would keep his eyes peeled as he led the way along the paths until, at a certain strategic spot, he'd yell, "Run, Cha, Run!" The twins were fast and clever and often eluded their assailants, but sometimes they didn't and were punished on account.

"It didn't matter," Paul later wrote of the experience, "we were talented, undeniably so," a development that did not escape their mother's notice. Eager to show off their artistry and help make ends meet, she formed a musical group—Mrs. Child and the Children. It was a classic piano trio, with Meeda at the keyboard, Paul on violin, and Charlie the cello. Bertha, "who had a lovely voice [and] could work the charm," sang bel canto—hymns and arias—that showcased the novel ensemble with the help of Master Bach. "They went around New England," says Rachel Child, "playing in nice locations wherever they could get a gig—at ladies' groups, for weddings, in tea houses, and certainly in other people's homes. Boston society gave them ample opportunity to perform."

Bertha was a natural when it came to the spotlight and apparently she had the vocal chops to back it up. No less an authority than *The New York Times* referred to her as "the well-known Boston contralto." In addition to a rather well-trained voice, she had presence, a real allure, none of which was lost on her coterie of sponsors, all gentlemen of a certain age and means. One, in particular, developed a special enchantment with Bertha that guaranteed her a place in the society she dearly courted. Edward Filene was the general manager and president of the women's fashion store that bore his family's name and quite a fixture on the Boston social scene. He was well into his fifties when he met Bertha Child and was, outwardly at least, everything she longed for in a man: fabulously rich, debonair, well-connected, and unmarried. They became lovers, and in the parlance of the day Bertha gained notoriety as a kept woman. Not known for his generosity, Filene made sure she was provided for, and he took an earnest interest in the twins, as well. He may have been "penny-pinching... troubled... obnoxious... heedless... insecure" or any of the other traits attributed to him by a biographer; still, he had a soft spot for children and enjoyed their company "in a way that he could never do with adults."

For Uncle Ed's favor, the twins competed on a level playing field. From the outset, Paul and Charlie felt a mutual, albeit unspoken, acknowledgment that they were on the same indeterminate path, each gambling on the outside chance that Uncle Ed might endow their uncertain futures. Their talent as serious artists was emerging as an undeniable strength. Paul had an eye for the atmospheric and the romantic; his paintings, exquisitely rendered, captured the expressive power of landscape. Charlie, less affected and more practical—his son, Jon, calls it "slapdash"—was developing a real flair for illustration. Together, they mined a vein of gifted ambition that struck pay dirt in all aspects of the arts. Each boy could draw, paint, take gorgeous photographs, write poetry, play classical music, and express himself beautifully on the printed page and in conversation. It didn't take a genius to see they had talent in spades. An investment in their future was sure to yield favorable returns.

Beneath their similarities, however, lay a contrast of personalities that weighed disproportionately on Edward Filene's largesse. Paul was shy, cool, pessimistic, precise, qualities that, at times, made him seem condescending and smug. Especially when juxtaposed against Charlie's animated nature. In those cases, Charlie was a breath of fresh air—"eternally optimistic," exuberant, undisciplined, outspoken. You could always count on him to brighten up a room.

This must have been how Edward Filene sized them up, too. Still, it seemed cruel when he agreed to send Charlie to Harvard to study painting, without so much as a nod in Paul's direction. Whatever the reasons for Filene's rejection of him, Paul was crushed. He became demoralized, insecure. He considered himself "the real artist" in the family, the real intellect, the brother whose promise was infinitely greater. He was smarter than Charlie, cleverer than Charlie, more levelheaded, more focused. But Charlie managed to shine in school, Paul noted, "where his marks were better than mine; in amateur theatricals where he memorized with more facility." And he was likable—Goodtime Charlie, eager to please—whereas Paul's finchy nature kept people off-stride.

Whether out of resentment or envy or defensive backlash, over the next few years Paul's efforts to cultivate his own identity—and, in the process, to displace Charlie—proved useful, if only to break from their codependence. But it came at a price. Paul developed "a sense of inferiority and injustice" that compelled him to prove himself in ways, overcompensating and defiant. And it altered things forever with Charlie—"loving him on the one hand," as he explained to a therapist, "and hating him on the other."

In any case, while they were still young teenagers, Charlie went to college, to Harvard no less, and Paul went to work. He bragged to a biographer that he "joined the Canadian Army at 16," but that was just an effort to create a mystique. Instead, he "floundered from one piddling job to another," initially trying his hand in retail work before bouncing around New York, New England, and Europe for the next twenty years. His résumé reads like a fractured mosaic. He dug ditches in California; made reproductions of furniture in Cambridge; ran training courses on a three-masted schooner from Nova Scotia to Bermuda; served as in-house photographer for an advertising agency in New York; handled stained-glass production for the American Church in Paris; tutored a family's privileged children in Asolo, Italy; taught public school in the Dordogne; all before serving two long terms teaching at private schools in New England. If anyone had embraced all that life had to offer—and had little to show for it—it was Paul Child.

During one of his assignments, teaching art and French at the Shady Hill School, an ultraprogressive, back-to-nature academy in Avon, Connecticut, Paul's life was pulled off the track he was laying for himself. One of his students was a boy named Robert Woods Kennedy. The Childs and the Kennedys had been friends in Boston and had seen each other on and off over the years. Paul was especially enamored of Robert's mother, Edith, an accomplished writer, painter, and musician who was ten years his senior. He'd recently bumped into her in Paris, where she'd gone to recover from a divorce and a subsequent heartbreak with the Irish writer Seán Ó Faoláin. She and Paul were reunited during her son's tenure at Shady Hill, and in no time she and Paul became lovers.

Although Edith Kennedy had the bearing and personality of a Boston Brahmin—an extremely sophisticated and socially superior Brahmin—those closest to her knew she was anything but that.

"She was cool, ironic, self-sufficient, and insanely independent," said her grandson, Duncan. "She had impeccable taste—art and taste to her were the supreme criteria of all accomplishment—but more than anything, she was riveting in some complex way," an attraction not lost on Paul Child. In an era when women weren't quick to call attention to their brainier qualities, Edith did not try to hide the fact that she was whip-smart and talented—easily as intelligent as the company she kept. And the company she kept was world-class. She was a Mozart fanatic, but developed an appreciation for modern music, first from Nadia Boulanger in Paris and later from her friend composer Elliot Carter in the States. May Sarton was in love with Edith and wrote extensively about her in poetry and stories. And she loved brilliant talk, promoted it, participated with gusto. Regularly, Edith hosted salons with some of Harvard's leading lights: F. O. Matthiessen, the renowned historian and literary critic; the modernist academic scholar Harry Levin; and Perry Miller, whom Alfred Kazin called "the master of American intellectual history." These were the kinds of brilliant people with whom Edith routinely filled her house—and Paul's greedy hunger for enlightenment.

At first, Paul had seemed out of his depth. Edith had more experience with the creative arts, was so sophisticated in ideas and expressiveness, knew more highbrow people from the academic fold, and held her own when it came to conversing on their level. Paul was mostly self-educated and a gadabout—but he had potential, loads of potential, and he was a quick study. He may not have gone to Harvard, but he was a top-notch student, able to absorb and interpret big, elaborate ideas. It was all there in front of him, too, laid out like a smorgasbord—the recitals, readings, lectures, exhibits, debates. A king's banquet of information and knowledge! He gorged himself on everything this university-without-walls had to offer. Gorged himself! He couldn't get enough. It enriched him in ways that he'd never before experienced. And with a woman whom he would describe to others as "life-affirming." *Life-affirming!* Edith's world, he discovered, was the utopia he'd been searching for all his life, a world of intellect, sophistication, attitude, and exploration.

And love. Paul adored Edith. There was little doubt that he was in love with her world, but he loved Edith more. Their passion was grand, intense. And Paul wasn't discreet about expressing his feelings. He was magnanimous in every display of his heart. And what he couldn't express with physical affection he put into words, writing sonnets to Edith, like the one he composed in 1938:

> *If swamp mire nurtures golden flowers,*
> *And butterflies can grow*
> *Like folded blossoms in a web,*
> *And diamonds made of snow*
> *glint lovely through the bitter wind,*
> *I think perhaps I know*
> *the miracle that lets you walk*
> *Where other women go.*

A lesser man might have kept such feelings to himself, but Paul was comfortable with his softer romantic side. And Edith enabled him to bring it out with no inhibition. They rented a cozy little house together, on Shepard Street, in Cambridge, for about twenty dollars a month and built a life together filled with music, art, and love. Paul had real affection for Edith's three sons, Edmond, Fitzroy, and Robert, with whom he formed strong relationships that lasted his entire life. The only thing missing was marriage, which Edith refused to discuss. It was one thing for her to have a much younger lover—but another thing altogether to marry him. She wouldn't hear of it. Was it an unnecessary formality? Edith's answer was to point to her ex-husband, Arthur, a man, it was said, whom marriage had transformed from "an extremely sophisticated soul" into "an abusive taskmaster, a brute." She wasn't about to put herself in a situation like that again. And it made sense to Paul. He didn't need marriage to have Edith to himself. She'd given him her word—and her heart—and that was good enough for him.

They were a *twosome*.

And for a while, Paul and Edith had everything they needed. They had the house on Shepard Street filled with people and love. Edith wrote short stories for magazines and painted. Paul got a better teaching job, at the Avon Old Farms School, just west of Hartford in Connecticut. They traveled cross-country with Charlie. Edith taught Paul about food, serious food, the kind he'd eaten rapturously in France. And they spent summers at New Boston in New Hampshire, "a kind of hyper-arty universe" inhabited by musicians, painters, and writers who shared their creative interests.

In fact, Paul's own art had progressed to the point where it gave him a new sense of untapped potential. What he lacked in training, he made up for in confidence, and the quality of his work showed great improvement across the board. His paintings were "damn good," as one observer summed them up, darkly sensual landscapes, demonstrating enormous reserves of raw artistic promise. His photographs, "gorgeously composed, beautifully made," drew even higher praise. Photography intrigued Paul the way the universe intrigued a scientist. He studied it exhaustively, combining the collaborative aspects of technology and art, subject matter and technique, arrangement and spontaneity. He'd begun working seriously with a reflex camera in Paris, where he'd befriended Edward Steichen and Henri Cartier-Bresson. From them, he learned the secrets of perspective; he learned how to capture energy and expression through composition. He became absorbed in it, almost to the point of obsession.

But for all the steam it created, for all his dazzling facility, Paul's art remained a hobby, nothing more. No matter how Edith encouraged him, no matter the embarrassment of praise friends heaped on his striking work, Paul refused to put it on the line. He couldn't bring himself to show it in public. He didn't have either the confidence—or the courage—necessary to withstand critical response. Which was sad, because it kept him from making a career leap, the way Edith had—or Charlie.

Charlie was painting, painting, painting, pulling down hefty commissions for illustrations and portraits. "My father was very skilled at portraiture," says Rachel Child, Charlie's daughter. He'd studied it in Paris in the twenties, on a Guggenheim fellowship, and parlayed it into a flourishing career. One of his more promising commissions, in fact, was the college roommate of their sister, Meeda, a bookish, crimson-haired beauty who'd studied business at the London School of Economics. Fredericka Boyles was possessed of great poise and pragmatism, "an emotional anchor"—and an oil heiress—both of which suited Charlie Child to a tee. Her pragmatism gave him grounding and her money gave him freedom—freedom, at least, from money issues, because not long after their meeting, Charlie and Freddie were married.

Paul, on the other hand, was very single and very frustrated. Edith persisted in her refusal to marry him, and his job at Avon continued to perplex. He loved teaching there, more so than ever. But teaching subverted his art, pushed it into the margins—or perhaps it served as a convenient excuse. In any case, Paul waived what he had once dreamed of: supporting himself through artistic self-expression. He failed to pursue a career in the arts in any substantive way. Instead, the center of his life became his students, to whom he was "beloved" and "heroic"—and, of course, Edith, "who spoiled" him and "made [their] relationship so valid and rich."

But in the spring of 1942, that relationship would start to unravel—not suddenly or carelessly, but steadily and involuntarily—while Paul stood by helplessly. Edith's insatiable hunger for culture and knowledge had begun to take a visible toll as she endeavored to have it all at once. Weeks went by when every waking hour was occupied by a full load of the arts, with just enough left over to tend her family. She whirled from one salon to the next, from concert to exhibition to lecture to performance, as if some personal demon was hot on her trail. No matter how hard she pressed, how much she savored, a creeping strain chipped away at her irrepressible spirit.

Whether or not Paul knew Edith had a history of heart disease, he could see the residual effects. She tired quickly, looked haggard and ghostly. Her breathing became labored, so much so that it was described as "a horrid fish-out-of-water gasping" that was painful to nearby ears. By June 1942, Edith's condition turned even more serious. "She can't read," Paul wrote his new sister-in-law. "She can't listen to music. She can't write. She just lies in bed and suffers." The diagnosis was edema— a swelling of the tissues with water, which pressed on the lungs and had to be drawn off every few days. Worse perhaps, her heart didn't pump enough blood to the organs—and she hallucinated, which Paul described as "waking nightmares." Best-case scenario: she had to remain in bed for six months, get plenty of rest, recuperate.

Paul did his best to make Edith comfortable. He waited on her hand and foot, day and night, during "that dreadful summer in Cambridge." He never left her room. To distract her, he even took up mechanical drawing, drafting his textbook studies on a shaky card table in the corner of the bedroom, and then offering them to Edith for a pithy critique. But her breathing and hallucinations only grew worse. At Edith's urging, Paul spent a week in Lumberville, Pennsylvania, where his brother, Charlie, and his wife, Freddie, had just bought a house. It would be good to get away, good to see Charlie again, if only to recharge so that he could return with renewed strength to devote to Edith's care. Admittedly, Paul needed some breathing room, but he worried about Edith, who assured him, all too convincingly, she'd be fine while he was away.

Sometime in early August, Rachel Child remembers looking out the window and noticing her father and Paul sitting in the family station wagon out by the garage. "It was strange," Rachel recalls. "It looked to me like Paul was crying, and I wanted to go out there and see what was going on." Her mother restrained her, explaining that Paul had a "very good friend named Edith, and that she had died." Charlie was in the process of breaking the news.

As one might expect, Paul was distraught, shattered. Edith had been only fifty years old. Gone. Emptiness took hold, the kind of emptiness and heartache he'd never experienced before. Edith had been his beloved in every respect of the word. "I suppose I shall never again have the kind of companion," he wrote, "who . . . knew and appreciated both the latest jazz and the opus numbers of Beethoven quartets, who could talk lovingly about the art of writing, who was a master cook and gourmet, who could manage a household of complicated people with a sincere artistry, who enjoyed a wrestling match or the shape of a flower, who knew the vagaries and depths of the human heart, who could be completely objective, who had infinite courage, energy to expend, complete self-mastery, magnificent wit, an ironic yet understanding outlook . . . an Ali Baba's cave of the best human qualities."

Mourning Edith, Paul concluded that a love like hers only came around once in a lifetime. That was it for him as far as romance went. No woman alive could measure up to her standards. Just as his art could no longer ignite any sparks, all comparisons to Edith, after ten years of bliss, fell agonizingly short.

Two years later, not that much had changed. When he met Julia McWilliams, she might have been a fly on a drape for all he cared.

WHILE EDITH CONTINUED to haunt Paul's memory, the war provided a modest distraction. Every able-bodied man was signing up to do his part, and the Child brothers were no exception. They made a beeline for Washington, D.C., "out of a sense of patriotism," sharing a fetid basement apartment where they scratched out a plan. Neither Paul nor Charlie was eager to see action. Nevertheless, they attempted to enlist in the armed services, knowing full well they'd be rejected because of their age. Still, they conspired to find suitable civilian roles. Charlie struck first. He turned to an old Harvard buddy, Paul Nitze, who set Charlie up at the National Planning Association, a forum for business, labor, agricultural, and academic leaders to solve issues of national significance. Paul, whose bad eye precluded his working in a rigorous physical role, fell willingly into the hands of the OSS.

By December 1942, Paul was engaged in its Visual Presentation (VP) branch, in a job that seemed tailor-made for his talents. VP consisted of a small band of "creative misfits"—among them film director John Ford, screenwriters Budd Shulberg and Garson Kanin, architect Eero Saarinen, and journalist Theodore White, all of whom brought imagination and artistry to an otherwise brutal war. Instead of weapons and battles, they made maps, charts, diagrams, illustrations for manuals, and designs for "super-secret war devices" in early stages of production. Unlike Charlie, whose expertise came gift-wrapped in a college degree, Paul relied on uneducated instinct. He had a natural gift for the technical and the concise, along with a good eye—well, one good eye—for aesthetic appeal that often eluded trained draftsmen. Predictably, Paul flourished in VP, and spent a productive year there, producing graphics for various government agencies, as well as animation for wartime instructional films.

He and Charlie thrived in D.C., where a community of intellectuals and artists drew strength from their common refugee status. It seemed the whole of academia was involved in some aspect of the war, along with the leading cultural luminaries: writers, journalists, filmmakers, painters, broadcasters, publishers, a melting pot of the clever and the articulate. These were people eager to talk, eager to rub shoulders and exchange ideas outside the confines of their war work. There wasn't a night when the Child brothers weren't engaged in some intense social interaction—a dinner party or embassy soirée, a mixer, a full-on intellectual conversation. And the conversation was meaty and well-cooked. One entry in Paul's Washington journal provides an example of the nightly dialogue: "This highlights the ideas we were discussing the other night . . . [how] context and relationship are what create moral structure." A bit highfalutin perhaps, but Paul feasted on this kind of chin fare.

Weekends were free. Each Friday afternoon, Paul and Charlie would hop on a northbound train headed for Bucks County, Pennsylvania, where they aired out their tired brains at Charlie's house in Lumberville. Freddie would cook, while the brothers painted and read and generally argued, butting heads over some trivial philosophical point. There was still a lot of tension in their relationship, still plenty of twin-related differences they needed to work out.

In Washington, they'd already taken a semi-serious first step in that direction. Together, they'd been consulting a noted astrologer, Jane

Bartleman, who made a series of "startlingly accurate predictions" that appealed to their inner unrest. One, in particular, caught Paul off guard. Months earlier, in the summer of 1943, Bartleman had told him that a new opportunity would soon reveal itself, "something unexpected and terrific, that it would involve a secret mission, [and] that it would require a very lengthy journey to the Far East." In any event, she assured Paul, "it would switch the whole course of [his] life."

At the time, he dismissed her prophecy as pure guesswork, the crystal-ball musings of a fortune-teller, nothing more. But on November 5, 1943, he had an epiphany. Earlier in the day, Paul had taken a call from General Donovan's office, asking if he'd consider a position as the OSS representative to the staff of Lord Louis Mountbatten, in New Delhi. Mountbatten—the Supremo! Paul could hardly believe his ears. No one was more crucial to this entire world war. He immediately reflected on Jane Bartleman's prediction. "This could be it," he concluded. "I am gasping and unbelieving. I feel shaken at this turn of affairs."

Bartleman had been languishing in his crackpot file. But the next morning, bright and early, he was seated in her office, wondering "if she could add anything to [his] general state of nervous anticipation." In character, she consoled him with all kinds of assurances. Yes, of course, he'd get the job. His work would be of a highly secret nature. He would make many invaluable friends. All sorts of obstacles would be thrown in his path, but not to worry. There would be adventure, excitement, and profit on a tremendous scale. She knew this because he was coming, she said, into wonderful planetary positions. "And, by the way, *you'll fall heavily in love in about a year.*"

He was smart enough to realize that "none of it may happen," that he had been right from the get-go, that she was a soothsayer, a quack. But . . . *You'll fall heavily in love in about a year.* "That was worth paying for," Paul concluded.

In fact, Paul couldn't pack his bags fast enough. He was desperate to leave D.C., desperate to be overseas, desperate to put some distance between him and Charlie, desperate for adventure, desperate to forget, desperate to turn a page. As far as falling in love went: *not* so desperate. It was a long shot, considering the memories that lingered of Edith. They weren't to be forgotten anytime soon. But he was intrigued, all the same. Love was a powerful drug. If it came his way, if it materialized as Bartleman had said, he'd stand up to it, he'd "look it in the eye."

To do that, however, he'd need a step stool.

Julia and Paul reading proofs of her recipes

Seven

A Diamond in the Rough

Despite the intensifying warfare in Southeast Asia, still the focus of Allied commanders, and critical to the resistance against Japan, Ceylon remained an oasis of calm. It existed almost by oversight, "far removed from reality," as one of the "Kandy Kids" wrote, "where everyone had an academic interest in the war but found life far too pleasant to do anything too drastic about it." Distractions were plentiful at the OSS outpost. Between the sightseeing excursions, the steamy social scene, and fertile romantic plunder, there was hardly enough time to attend to the war. For Julia McWilliams, however, the spring and summer of 1944 had been a total grind. Her responsibilities at the Registry overwhelmed. So much classified information was processed by her office that, at times, she seemed to be the sole conduit for the entire South East Asia Command. Her schedule was tedious, brutal; in addition to the daily chores, which were mind-numbing, she worked most nights and half days on Sunday, filing, filing, filing. The paperwork was endless. "Why did I come over as Registry?" she complained in her diary. "I hate this work."

Despite that, the reason Julia came over, and not only came over but adored the overall experience, was her colleagues. She was in a swoon over them. They were everything she wanted to be in life—they were smart, sophisticated, opinionated, imaginative, adventurous, and witty; they were free spirits, highly competitive but in a challenging way, so that one's probing question stimulated another's thoughtful response.

And what minds she encountered in Kandy! Professors, engineers, artists, anthropologists, ornithologists, biologists, cryptologists—why, every kind of ologist one could think of was there. Julia loved the way they approached life, loved the way they expressed themselves, their insights and outlooks. Eager to quench her thirst for knowledge, she drank in everything they said, guzzled it like a rummy with a wooden leg. "I was a playgirl looking for the light," she proclaimed—in jest, yet with a telling note of candor.

In fact, the light hardly registered as a glow when it came to Paul Child. "It wasn't like lightning striking the barn on fire," he recalled of their meeting in May 1944. Neither he nor Julia felt the proverbial thunderbolt. When she first encountered him at headquarters in Kandy, she wrote, "I thought not at all nice looking." He was too old for her, already past forty-two, rather balding—and *short*—with "an unbecoming blond moustache and a long, unbecoming nose." His first impressions of her were even less positive. But later that month, on a steamy Sunday afternoon, Julia and Paul, along with a small group of friends, crammed into a mud-caked jeep and drove north, through jungle roads, to Dambulla, to explore the ancient cave temples. The exhibit, a circuitous stroll through five well-preserved shrines, made a huge impression on Julia and the others. She could not have been prepared for such a lavish display of artistry, a riot of murals and statues—more than 150 of Buddha alone. Her response was a breathy chorus of astonishment and bluntness, and that enthusiasm, however unpolished, attracted Paul. Afterward, he weighed in with an opinion that showed intrigue. "She has a somewhat ragged, but pleasantly crazy sense of humor," he observed in a letter to Charlie in early July. Still, he wasn't knocked out by Julia McWilliams, and it would be safe to say the feeling was mutual.

While Julia was unrepentantly "fun . . . always the most personable" member of any group at Kandy, Paul was what some people refer to as a *difficult* man. He was precise and uncompromising, "a bit of a know-it-all," whose body language expressed a weatherproof rightness that often passed for arrogance or imperiousness. A man of distinct physical appearance, he carried himself with the upright authority and thin-lipped skepticism of the teacher he had once been. He scorned indecisiveness, demanded perfection, and made no effort to disguise his displeasure with those who didn't measure up. Already he believed that "I am one of the few really mature people around here" when contrasted with "the adolescent confusions" of his colleagues on the base, "men of forty who avoid responsibility, are emotionally unhinged by non-essentials," and, in general, lack common sense.

He considered himself cultured and a sophisticate and he behaved like one, with all the pretensions that accompanied such an image. He had a temperament, an edge; it was one of the first things people sensed when they met him. And so there was always a little tension in the way he comported himself with others. But, *my*—that man had charm. He was debonair, unashamedly romantic, with the luxurious appetites of a bon vivant. Women captivated him, and so did food, both of which he held in the same sensual esteem. His use of language, the way the words flowed out of his mouth, the range of topics he spoke about with undisguised passion, all were like music to Julia's untrained ears. He expressed himself clearly and with great perception, both on subjects that related to his expertise and those that caught his fancy. Every observation came studded with gems. Though he never went to college, Paul was dazzlingly well read and he spun what he learned into fascinating threads of conversations. Listening to him enthralled Julia, not just because what he said was new and thought provoking, but because he brought so much of himself to it.

Their encounters, at first, were casual, innocent—a picnic, a concert, or a meal in the company of several OSS friends. They traveled as a group, not as a couple, nor were there any outward signs of attraction between them. In fact, Paul had designs on several other women—*many* other women, including the wife of a British officer—although none that he'd acted on, either out of inhibition or reluctance. He was still grieving over the death of Edith Kennedy, but slowly, unwaveringly, emerging from a self-imposed hibernation. "What I want, I miss, I need more than anything," he acknowledged in a letter to Charlie, "—an intimate, intelligent, and understanding companion (female gender)."

Julia's name didn't appear on his wish list, although she'd obviously registered somewhere in the back of his mind. In July, Paul sent Charlie a grainy snapshot of her—pin-ups routinely illustrated his letters—in which he drew extra attention to her fine long legs. Stretched across a rickety *basha* cot, her king-size frame an obvious spectacle, Julia looked resplendent, decked out in a cotton print dress, a strand of pearls suspended loosely at her neck, with fresh coats of lipstick and nail polish for good measure. She was propped on an elbow, wearing a dreamy, flirtatious expression—her "look of anticipatory lechery," she called it—that signified, somewhat bashfully, her willingness to play the part. But—those *legs*!

They seemed to go on forever and must have made quite an impression, because six months later they were still on Paul's mind. In another letter written from Kandy, he described her thusly: "lovely legs, very tall, 31 years old, a darling warm girl, but with a slightly girl-like overtone in relation to age."

Julia's interest also began to bloom. Following a "lovely Sunday" outing, in which Paul had invited friends to join him as he photographed elephants parading along a palm-lined ridge, she had what amounted to a romantic epiphany. "I decided I thought Paul was really very attractive," she said, while bemoaning the fact that his interests seemed to lie elsewhere. From what she could tell, he desired women who were "more worldly Bohemian types." She, alas, was the polar opposite, a veteran of the big leagues—Junior and, socially, Ivy—which had begun to seem as frivolous to her as surely they must to someone like Paul Child. Intellectually insecure, she seldom gave herself much credit for having the right kind of allure. By her own account, she lacked charisma, gravitas. How could she expect him to take notice of her? That night in her diary, she wrote: "Wish I were in love, and that what I considered *really attractive* was in love with me."

Maybe someone like Paul's astrologer might have noticed their stars were aligning, but Paul and Julia didn't. Not yet, at least, not with the winds of war starting to swirl around them.

By late 1944, the campaign in China was heating up anew; fresh strategies were essential, "desperate remedies" necessary to keep China in the war and to offset threats against America's efforts on the mainland. To that end, Paul was working under the gun, "fourteen to sixteen hours a day," building a war room—including specialized graphic presentations used in counterespionage, destructive devices, air-supply drops, and paratroop operations—for Mountbatten's American chief of staff, General Albert Wedemeyer. Julia saw Paul almost every day, but they were both too involved in their work to respond.

Yet the relationship began to change. Paul's brother, Charlie, was the first to sense his interest, even though it was insulated with ambivalence and disclaimers. In a long, rambling letter from Kandy, Paul told him plenty about Julia McWilliams, that "warm and witty girl" with the legs from Pasadena, with whom he spent quality time whenever they got the chance. "I believe she would marry me," he said archly, "but isn't the 'right' woman from my standpoint." Nevertheless, he found her "*extremely* likeable and pleasant to be around." He appreciated her passions, especially for music and food, but questioned her maturity, "the lack of worldly knowledge, the sloppy thinking, the wild emotionalism, the conventional framework," the fact that she "had almost no challenge in her life" up to this point. That was a deal-breaker for someone as sophisticated and urbane as Paul. The teacher in him thought that she had limitless potential, but it would take work, too much, perhaps, for him to take on; all the "training and molding and informing" would be daunting. And sex—sex was an altogether different concern. Julia's status as a virgin was particularly unappealing. He sensed real conflict, her "fear" and "fascination" with sex. "I know what the cure is," he boasted to Charlie, "but it would be too much for Dr. Paulski to risk attempting."

For the time being, Dr. Paulski was content to play the field. There were several women whose company he kept on a regular basis, all OSS colleagues, all friends (Julia among them), who continued to meet regularly for a movie or a meal. There was hardly an opportunity for anything serious to develop. But Julia kept a close eye on Paul throughout the fall of 1944, as developments on the base at Kandy tightened around them.

On October 19, after a flurry of high-level meetings in Mountbatten's pavilion, word passed through the ranks that General Joseph Stilwell was being recalled from China, a victim of his personal war with Chiang Kai-shek. Paul's boss, General Wedemeyer, would succeed him as chief of staff. The implications sent shock waves from *basha* to *basha*. Many of the "Kandy Kids" would be packing as a result, moving from their tropical paradise to a posting in Chongqing, China's wartime capital, a remote, provincial city that Stilwell considered a "sloppy mess." The first prominent transfer was Julia's boss, Richard Heppner, who immediately recruited Paul for a critical job. In January 1945, after a nostalgic New Year's bash, Paul left Ceylon "on two hours' notice," and flew to Chongqing to set up a war room for Wedemeyer largely modeled on his successful design in Kandy. It happened so fast, Julia hardly had time to say goodbye.

For Julia, Paul's sudden departure was almost as crushing as Tom Johnston's rejection nine years earlier. For nearly ten months in Ceylon, through a succession of increasingly warm encounters and shared intimacies, Julia had never stopped angling for a way into Paul's heart. Lately, she felt as though she'd been making some headway. They'd grown closer, confided in each other, talked and talked and talked some more. On more than one occasion a friendly kiss had turned serious. His standards for women were often severe. But there were qualities about him she grew to treasure—assuredness, expertise, gentility, character. Paul Child was the kind of man who could captivate her forever. But—China? Chongqing? They were separated by the Himalayas, a world apart. Her prospects, it seemed, were doomed to failure.

After almost a year abroad, Julia was suddenly adrift again. She relished her experience in the OSS, but the team she'd come to love and respect was splitting up, moving on. Few familiar faces were left on the post. The replacements were younger, more independent. The camaraderie she thrived on was gone.

Long frustrated by her repetitive workload, Julia put in for a change of scenery. For a while, it appeared likely that she'd be relocated to Calcutta. There were also some rumblings—Julia called them "propositions"—about a job with the Secret Intelligence branch. A spy! At last, the dream job she'd always fantasized about. Unfortunately it was offered too late in the game. "By the time I learned anything about China," Julia decided, "the war would be over." Still, it was determined that she could do a lot of good there, if not as a spy then in an administrative role, and in the spring of 1945, Julia was transferred to the OSS advance base in Kunming, four hundred miles south of Chongqing.

China would be a new adventure. Yes, she'd still be mired in the Registry, still be snowed under huge drifts of paperwork, but the exotic locale, the unfamiliarity of it, would go a long way toward relieving much of the tedium. Getting there, however, was an entirely different matter. On March 15, 1945, with a contingent of transfers from Kandy, Julia flew from Calcutta to Kunming, a route known affectionately as going "Over the Hump." The name may have sounded like an amusement park ride, but in point of fact it was anything but that. It was death-defying in the most literal sense, a 550-mile adventure over jagged 15,000-foot spurs of the Himalayas, "through air currents so turbulent they could break up an airplane"—and often did just that. "You could look down and see the twisted wreckage of planes that didn't make it," recalls Fisher Howe. More than four hundred were lost there during the first four years of the war, which is why pilots considered it "the most hazardous flight route in the world."

If the Hump was that much of a calculated risk, no one seems to have told Julia McWilliams. She seemed oblivious to the danger during the treacherous three-hour flight. "We were caught in a storm the whole way," recalls Betty McIntosh, who sat opposite Julia in a cramped jumpseat. The plane was a rattletrap, an unpressurized Douglas C-54 troop transport, forcing the passengers to wear parkas and carry oxygen masks. McIntosh says, "People prayed during the flight. You could see fear on their faces, especially during the descent. No one was sure whether we were landing—or crashing."

The plane hit an air pocket and went into a steep dive over the West Mountains, bucking hideously as it plummeted toward the ground. The lights went out inside the cabin. Gasps echoed through the darkness and worse—a few muffled shrieks, some crying. In the mayhem, Betty McIntosh remembers looking across at Julia, "who calmly read a book, while all the rest of us were preparing to die." Jacques Pépin would later joke that Julia had sweet cream running through her veins, but at the time McIntosh was convinced it was ice water. "She was one cool customer," McIntosh says. "It surprised me that anyone could contain themselves to the extent she did."

China was odd, oddly familiar, more formal, Julia thought. From what she could see, a wounded beauty blanketed the crenellated landscape where the conceit of ancient civilizations had left its indelible mark. There were crevices of dry red clay etched in the rain-washed earth and a supernatural stillness in the air. The climate and vegetation might have initially suggested Pasadena, but Julia, who had an eye for nature's subtle distinctions, could see clouds clinging to the temples carved in the rocks surrounding the city and, beyond that, the fertile lake basins at the foot of the Mazong Ridge streaked with the muted indigo of a Chinese calligrapher.

Kunming was a medieval walled city, whose importance to the war had left it a vestige of its former status as a go-to destination: the City of Eternal Spring. Before the Japanese incursion it had functioned as a resort for French colonials thanks to its location at the terminus of the Yunnan–Vietnam Railway and a gateway to the Burma Road. Now there was something "ominous and austere" about it, a burden that had sucked the life out of Kunming. The war: it had stripped the city of its dignity. The Chinese lived in coolie conditions, mudcaked villages with barely enough to sustain. A governing infrastructure was blatantly corrupt.

The OSS was headquartered outside the city, in a compound surrounded by towering walls. In a matter of days, Julia had the Registry up and running, a super-sized version of it, with a staff of ten. It was a sleeker, systematized operation thanks to Julia's know-how and a proximity to the war that made precision more urgent. This wasn't Kandy, that much was clear. Nothing was laid-back or remote, the way it had

been in Ceylon. In China, the war was on the Allies' front doorstep. The
Japanese were all around; their presence was felt, if not their actual hostilities. The Allied field operations, once deployed in far-off positions,
were launched directly from headquarters in delicate detail.

Julia's responsibilities became more elaborate. In addition to han-
dling all the encrypted intelligence reports—dispatches from Washington, information about the position of all OSS agents, and bulletins
pinpointing the enemy's positions, to name but a few—she also dispensed
the reserves of "secret currency," chunks of "operational opium," paid
directly to the spies. Every measure and stratagem was channeled through
the Registry in Kunming. As such, her judgment of who saw what information was a highly sensitive, if not tricky, task—not too shabby for a
woman who, only a few years earlier, was fired for incompetence by a
furniture showroom.

Intrigue aside, Julia still hated the work. She hated the tedium, hated
what she considered an unimaginative clerical desk job. Her colleagues
at the Registry were "dull, slow, dense." Her social life could also be
described in the same terms. Since arriving in Kunming, entertainment
was reduced to a succession of endless cocktail parties or dances with
unstimulating men to the same scratchy recordings of "I'll Be Seeing
You," "Lili Marlene," and "Don't Sit Under the Apple Tree."

Julia's OSS adventure had lost its pizzazz.

In April, however, an unexpected turn of events reversed her creeping
malaise. The war room was moved from Chongqing to Kunming, accompanied by its chief architect, Paul Child.

ENCOUNTERING PAUL AGAIN lifted Julia's spirits. He brought excitement back into her life, with his easy mix of wit and wisdom. And always
in the background: the possibility of romance. It was a breeze picking up
where they'd left off in Ceylon, getting back into the groove with him,
socializing and talking. Paul was an amiable conversationalist, Julia a
devoted listener. Both seemed eager to enjoy the other's company. But
nothing more than that at the present time. Paul was "extremely fond of
her," as he wrote to his brother, but in no more capacity than that of "a
very good friend." Warmth, humor, and intelligence aside, she was "limited in relation to [his] concept of *la femme intégrale.*"

He had missed Julia while he was in Chongqing, but in the interim,
apparently, Paul had had a fling or two. Julia knew the score. "There were

a lot of attractive women around," she acknowledged. No getting around it: "he loved women." He'd spent January romancing Julia's friend Rosie Frame, a young, pixie-like OSS agent who spoke eleven Chinese dialects. But while he found her "wonderfully interesting and *alive . . .* very attractive physically," theirs was nothing more than a "passionate friendship." The same could be said about his involvement with Jane Foster, "*une Bohémienne* of a fine sort," with whom he entertained only a mild flirtation. Despite these dalliances, for that is all they really were, Paul was increasingly frustrated in his pursuit of the perfect mate. "When am I going to meet a grown-up dame with beauty, brains, character, sophistication, and sensibility?" he wondered.

He never dreamed, at the time, that she was right there in front of him. Julia and Paul each knew they had met someone remarkable, but couldn't quite get to the heart of their interest. Julia suffered from being compared to Edith Kennedy. "Christ, there are only a few people like that," Paul bemoaned to Charlie in early 1945, acknowledging, as a result, that he was "really spoiled for other women." The more Julia tried to measure up, the more she stumbled, either expressing herself too vehemently in that high-strung comic warble, or else blurting out a whopper that betrayed her uninformed worldview. On more than one occasion, Paul scorned her incautious tongue. "I don't see why the Indians just don't throw out the British!" he reported her saying, topping it (if that were at all possible) with: "I can't understand what the Indians see in that horrid little old Gandhi!"

True, Julia often said whatever was on her mind—but so did Paul, who was quick and opinionated, especially when it came to his criticism of others. Clearly, he did not give Julia enough credit. She was *not* Edith Kennedy, that much was certain, not as deep or as polished to that degree, not by any means. But Julia McWilliams was a diamond in the rough: curious, open-minded, high-spirited, witty if not yet clever, with personality enough to light up any room. She didn't have a mean bone in her body. She wasn't at all pretentious, like some of Paul's friends. She may not have been discriminating—yet; or an intellect—yet; or an authority on some aspect of the arts—not yet. Still, she had a lot to offer, though his assessment of her was instinctively narrow. After months of heart-to-hearts, their hearts seemed far apart.

It is only fitting that what brought them closer was food.

First, "the terrible army food," as Julia adjudged it: "rice, potatoes, canned tomatoes and water buffalo." She and Paul could barely put it in their mouths. Even the local Chinese cooks hired to work the mess lines were unable to give the food a discernible makeover. It was nasty, beyond inedible. Fortunately, there was a Plan B they put into motion. "The Chinese food was wonderful," Julia said, "and we ate out as often as we could."

Kunming was the capital of Yunnanese cuisine, traditional savory dishes that lean heavily on bold flavors. In the warren of restaurants tucked back along the narrow dirt streets, Julia and Paul encountered dishes like *guo qiao mi xian*—rice noodles in a dense stock beneath a layer of oil served with a platter of thinly sliced raw chicken and vegetables that, when tipped into the broth, cooked instantly at the table. They also could find *qi guo ji,* a well-spiced chicken stew cooked in a clay pot with a steam-chimney venting up through its center, as well as the ubiquitous leaf-wrapped dishes, such as *ba jiao ye zheng yu* (fish steamed in plantain leaves) and duck with bamboo pith fungus. The more adventurous palates ordered Yunnan delicacies such as snake, civet cat, and even black bear.

The Chinese food was a revelation to Julia, with its extraordinary infusion of ingredients and aromatic spices. She adored the exotic preparations, the barrage of new textures, new tastes, new combinations. They defied all expectations. Each plate held another wonderful surprise. It's hard to imagine how appealing this experience was to a young woman who enjoyed eating as much as Julia did, how different Chinese cooking was from anything she'd eaten before. The dining experience itself was a source of endless discovery. The restaurants were noisy and chaotic: cleavers chopped, woks sizzled, pots bubbled, and the clatter of rickshaws rumbled in through the open windows. Waiters would yell orders to the cooks across the din. Even the local Chinese contributed a persistent throaty accompaniment, "making these great swooping, slurping noises as they ate," Julia recalled.

Paul was a good guide for her in this mysterious new milieu. He knew his way around the restaurant scene, thanks to some guidance from his friends, journalist Theodore White and the United Press International correspondent Al Ravenholt, both of whom had been in China since before the war began. And he was a virtuoso when it came to using chopsticks, teaching Julia how to wield them with workmanlike finesse.

Throughout April and May 1945, as the strains of war reached a final crescendo, Paul and Julia shared myriad meals together, taking great pleasure in the Chinese cooking—and in each other. They spent hours,

nights, weeks hunched over food-laden tables, exchanging the most intimate details of their personal sagas. Everything came pouring out: the
intransigencies of Julia's father, the twins' difficult rivalry, Tom Johnston's breach, Edith's death, their similar dilemmas at midlife—without
a peacetime vocation, without a partner, in personal purgatories of sorts.
"I feel lost," Paul admitted; no doubt Julia echoed that sentiment. They
debated what Paul considered "one of the clichés of human life: how to
have one's cake and eat it too?" Was there a plausible way "to spend half
one's time making money, and half in cultivating the intellect and the
arts?" Julia turned this same question over in her mind, as well. Now
that she'd acquired a taste for something more stimulating from life, was
there a way for her to improve herself when she returned home, after
the war? In time, they discovered themselves to be soulmates, not only
understanding each other's respective circumstances, but also appreciat-
ing the way the other felt.

This rapport continued to develop as both Paul and Julia were transferred to Chongqing: another war room, another Registry, another stop
along the war itinerary. Chongqing was "a wildly stimulating spot," the
provisional capital of free China, built on what seemed like hundreds of
extruding hills, with the Yangtze flowing through the center of town.
From 1939 onward, the city had been beaten to a pulp by the Japanese,
leaving the skeletons of bomb-shattered houses amid creeping filth and
pollution. Still, the remains of natural beauty shone through the misery.
By the time Paul and Julia arrived the plum trees were in blossom, the
warm, thick air made eminently thicker by the gusts of spicy mimosa.
"This busted and ragged city . . . is tenfold over-populated," Paul wrote to
friends. There was "an almost frenetic overtone of energy" in the air, with
a marked duality that mystified him. One could walk down any street and
sense a cosmopolitan spirit, yet see a "moss-covered thousand-year-old
pagoda standing alone in the mist." Somewhere between those extremes
lay the character of China.

Without ceremony, Julia reestablished the Registry. If anything, the
eleven months of managing those blasted files gave her even more perspective on the trajectory her life was taking. There was real know-how
in the way that she handled her job, know-how mixed with instinct
and practice. In the past, she had always wrestled with initiative: Was
she willing to take on responsibility, and if so, would she take it—or
herself—seriously? But the OSS had changed that for good. No longer a "social butterfly," she had a whole new sense of her potential. The

fact that she'd formed a friendship with such a smart man was evidence enough that she was headed someplace important.

Certainly, Paul had begun to take her seriously. In Chongqing their friendship continued apace. The social life hummed at a fairly high level, so they saw each other with clockwork regularity. There was the usual surfeit of dances and cocktail parties on the base, plus weekend getaways to the countryside at a favorite hot springs resort, visits to temples, walks through the rice paddies and along the mist-shrouded hills. But—always with a group, always perfectly platonic. Yes, Paul took Julia seriously, but it was all on the surface; there was no evidence of a deeper emotional response.

Food seemed to be their common aphrodisiac. If only they could launch another Chinese restaurant junket, perhaps spring rolls and spareribs might rekindle the spark, especially in Chongqing, where fiery Sichuan dishes ignited a provocative culinary heat. During the war, when Chongqing became the headquarters of the Kuomintang, the elite from all over China flocked there, toting their private chefs and secret family recipes. In the interim, Chongqing had become a melting pot of flavors. But to Paul and Julia's great dismay, restaurants were strictly off limits, thanks to an outbreak of cholera in the city. Any heat would have to be self-generated.

But heat needed combustion, some kind of chemical reaction. If there was anything simmering between them, it was hard for Julia to gauge. She sensed Paul's resistance to anything deeper or more heartfelt. Apparently they were buddies, nothing more, despite such obvious compatibility. She summed it up perfectly in her diary, calling it an "affair of friendly passion and companionship," which was acceptable for the here-and-now, if that were all he had to give. Whatever the extent of Paul's affection, Julia reveled in it. Deprived of a significant male relationship for so long, she found in Paul's sympathies the kind of attention that had always eluded her.

Something more meaningful might develop over time. But on August 6, after the OSS unit had returned to Kunming, news arrived that would affect every timetable. An atomic bomb had been dropped on Hiroshima; on August 9, a second bomb was dropped on Nagasaki. Japan surrendered on August 14. The reaction in Kunming was restrained, even detached. A different kind of shell shock silenced the Americans. The end of the war meant the end of the unit. What would happen to everyone now? Many would be going home to resume their routine lives, but for some, like Julia, it was almost an unthinkable step backward. The war had utterly changed her; she'd become a different person while serving her country, part of a mission, part of a community. What would she do with herself once she got home?

Two days earlier, Julia had turned thirty-three, an age when most of her friends were already married, with children. There was no family waiting for her back in the States, no husband, no job, no place to call her own. It seemed almost cruel to celebrate this birthday. In fact, it passed without fanfare. But on August 15, Paul came forward with a sonnet he'd composed to mark the occasion. One can only imagine Julia's reaction as she read through the ornately handwritten verse:

> How like the Autumn's warmth is Julia's face
> So filled with Nature's bounty, Nature's worth.
> And how like summer's heat is her embrace
> Wherein at last she melts my frozen earth.
> Endowed, the awakened fields abound
> With newly green effulgence, smiling flowers.
> Then all the lovely riches of the ground
> Spring up responsive to her magic powers.
> Sweet friendship, like the harvest-cycle, moves
> From scattered seed to final ripened grain,
> Which, glowing in the warmth of Autumn, proves
> The richness of the soil, and mankind's gain.
> I cast this heaped abundance at your feet
> An offering to Summer, and her heat.

Paul had thrown her an unexpected curve. For someone whose ambivalence was an established facet of his persona, the poetry was filled with romantic imagery. No matter how Julia construed the beautifully crafted phrases—"warmth is Julia's face . . . heat is her embrace . . . her magic powers . . . her heat"—the underlying message was unambiguous. The "sweet friendship" had somehow blossomed into "final ripened grain." Inevitably, Paul was falling in love.

Whether or not Julia sensed this right away, Paul was coming to terms with it. The next day, in a letter to Charlie, he devoted a paragraph to Julia's virtues, admitting that, over time, he had "become extremely fond of her." She might not be his ideal, his dreamgirl, he said, but she was "understanding, warm, funny, and darling."

In his newfound enthusiasm, Paul made the most of whatever time they had left together. He took Julia on "a terrific binge" of Yunnanese food—to "eight or ten different regional restaurants"—and spent hours reading Hemingway's short stories aloud to her on the veranda of the old tea plantation. "One was about sex," a friend remembered—a lesson courtesy of the old schoolteacher.

Yet, despite all the spirited attention she received, Julia still anguished over the feasibility of their relationship. She remained unconvinced of her appeal to such a fascinating man or the alien world from which he came. "I am not the woman for him as I am not an intellectual," she confessed during a full-scale meltdown in the pages of her diary. How could she expect anything more? There were too many obstacles in each of their paths. And he wasn't the only one who had reservations. Yes, Paul enjoyed her company and they could "talk about anything"—politics, philosophy, literature, sex, emotions, nothing was off-limits—but when push came to shove he was "not essentially vigorous enough" for Julia, he "seem[ed] to lack the male drive"—in other words, he'd never made a move. That didn't bode well for her future prospects.

Their other colleagues seemed to be pairing up before heading back to the United States. Almost all the women Julia had deployed with had found lovers or husbands during their Asian stay. There was any number of weddings scheduled for the months following their return. Everyone's status was in a state of flux.

Julia and Paul may not have resolved on anything more definite than friendship, but there is every indication they discussed the future. Paul's situation was changing—fast. "Everything is shifting and rearranging itself a dozen times a day," he wrote his brother. On October 12, his Presentation outfit was moving to Peking in the army's effort to reoccupy the major cities before the Communists had time to move in. With little time to spare, he was drawing maps for the "humanitarian teams" being dropped into the POW camps. Julia's tour of Asia was over. She was headed to Calcutta on October 16, and then back to the States—exactly where, she did not know, but it seemed probable that she and Paul would both eventually wind up in Washington. They made tentative plans to have Thanksgiving together, with his brother and sister-in-law, in Pennsylvania. But after that—it was difficult to say.

Everything is shifting and rearranging itself a dozen times a day. It was impossible, crazy, to make serious life-changing decisions in such an uncertain, unstable world. Anything could happen between one moment and the next.

On October 7, with very little time left, Paul and Julia enjoyed a farewell dinner at their favorite Kunming restaurant, Ho-Teh-Foo. In order to satisfy their powerful Chinese food fix, they pulled out all the stops, ordering enough from the menu to feed their entire OSS unit. The tiny tabletop was covered with heaping, steaming dishes: crispy fried spring rolls, long-leaf cabbage studded with bits of salty Yunnan ham, winter mushrooms flecked with the piquant tops of beets, sizzling-hot Peking duck on a bed of glass noodles, and meaty, scented egg-drop soup—a veritable banquet, not soon to be forgotten. The atmosphere was festive, if somewhat forced; in the backs of their minds, each was aware of the possibility that this might be the last time they would ever see each other. Their tentative plans, while upbeat, were no hedge against fate. So often people in such extraordinary circumstances, in such intense situations, formed passionate connections that didn't sustain in the everyday world. A war relationship was beyond extraordinary. "It was a strange life, dislocated," Julia recalled. Who knew how they would feel about each other once they got home? Besides, there was no need to rush into anything. "We were, by that time, fairly grown up and mature," Paul recalled. "So we pursued the plan we had in mind, which was to get through with the war and see what we looked like in civilian clothes." It would be better, they decided, to meet each other's friends and families and, after that, see if the magic remained.

It wasn't nearly that long before the spell took hold. Two days after landing in Peking, Paul had an epiphany that would redefine his life. He had been sitting in his new quarters, "a splendid old palace" surrounded by three large gardens and an orchard of ancient persimmons, staring out over the treetops at the rose-colored walls of the Forbidden City. Its complex of courtyards were eerily deserted. The architecture filled him with "a nostalgic sense of forlorn majesty" that conjured a similar feeling for the love he'd left behind. All those doubts that had been churning around inside him, from Kandy to Chongqing to Kunming, began to dissipate like the "blue smoke that sifted" across the "timeless" horizon. His mind came to a clearing: visibility washed over him. Picking up pen and paper, he began a letter: "Beloved Julie," he wrote in a hurried script, "at the risk of sounding trite, *I wish you were here.* I need you to enjoy these marvels with, and I miss your companionship something awful. Dearest

Julie, why aren't you here, holding my hand and making plans for food and fun!" He signed it: "Love, Paulski." He posted it at once.

It took more than a month for the letter to reach Julia's hands, in Washington, where she'd come to complete the formalities of her discharge. After years of searching for a vocation and a man, she was now once again out of a job—but she knew she had finally found the man.

Eight

Lucky to Be Alive

The sun burned high in the sky above Mount Desert Island. Julia and Paul had been driving all day, urging her beat-up old Buick along the homestretch of Route 102 in Maine. It was the final leg of a nearly four-thousand-mile journey that had begun a month before in Pasadena, in early July 1946. They'd set out on an expedition that might have been called the Julia and Paul Getting-to-Know-You Tour, a cross-country lollapalooza, of sorts, designed to show themselves off to their respective friends—and, more importantly, to each other.

In the space of half a year, since their return from China, Julia and Paul's relationship had gone from tepid to sizzling hot. Undaunted by the distance between them—Julia was at her father's house in California, Paul in Washington, D.C.—they summoned the courage to express their hearts honestly and with abandon in a rash of long, uncensored letters that might, in some circumstances, set the postman's hands on fire. They had begun tentatively enough, exchanging bits of personal news: gossipy observations, reviews of books, personal insights, this and that. Julia toyed with seeking work in Hollywood; Paul seemed headed for something more banal, with the State Department. They filled each other in on friends lost and found. But between the mild lines of chit-chat, things started to heat up. "What have you done to me," Julia teased, "that I continue to long and languish for you?" Paul picked up the forward pass

Julia and Paul's wedding reception, September 1, 1946

and ran with it: "You play a leading role in my fantasy life," he admitted, imploring her to read *Tropic of Cancer* and de Sade.

Finally, in a letter dated February 10, 1946, Julia McWilliams took off the gloves. Beginning it "Dearest one," she launched headlong into a description of a photograph Paul had sent her, of one of his tempera paintings depicting a familiar Chinese landscape. "I love your style . . . I love the sturdy warmth of the tree . . . " and then—*whammo!*—she dropped the big one: "I love you." She just snuck it in there. In fact, she might have slipped it by him, drawing little attention to it, had she not underlined the phrase a few times. I love you. There was nothing ambiguous about it.

Was it too much? Would it scare Paul off? One can only imagine that Julia held her breath until his next letter fell into her hands. Paul's response, as it turned out, was as equally free-spoken as hers. "I want to see you, touch you, kiss you, talk with you, eat with you . . . eat you, maybe. I have a Julie-need." Aside from the irresolute "maybe," there was nothing ambiguous about his position, either. Things had taken a turn for the steamy.

And—steamier. "I feel that I am only existing until I see you, and hug you, and eat you," Julia responded. Paul suggested that she move to Washington and become his cook. "We can eat each other," he said.

Clearly, they were preoccupied with their hunger.

Urgent measures were needed to satisfy their appetites. It was decided that, sometime after the July Fourth holiday, Paul would travel by train back to Pasadena. Aside from some basic touching, kissing, talking, and eating, Julia wanted him to meet her father and Dort. Afterward—that is, if there *was* an afterward—they'd set out across the country together, stopping to visit each other's friends, before winding up in Maine, at Charlie and Freddie's lake house. It would be the ultimate test to move their friendship along, hopefully into more serious territory. No doubt by the time they reached Maine, every lingering question would be answered.

The time was right for such a pivotal experiment. Both Julia and Paul's lives were in limbo at the moment, each unsatisfied with his or her respective role. Neither had come home from the war with specific plans for the future. For Julia, Pasadena was a rest stop, nothing more. She found her hometown much as she'd always remembered it—"comfortable and lovely, but not for me." Yet by the summer of 1946, she still had no idea of where to plant her flag. "There is always Washington and the government, both of which I like," she confided in a letter to Paul. But she was tired of secretarial work, and a dead-end job like the Registry was out of the question.

Unfortunately, Paul was in no better shape. He'd had an offer to teach in Peking, at Yenching University, but the situation in China had grown progressively too dangerous for him to remain. Instead, he headed home, to Washington, D.C., but even "home" was a concept that had no real meaning. Where was home? In a rented basement apartment—in a city that meant little to him? He had no roots there, no friends, no support system of any kind. And what was he to do? Teach school or work in a photo lab? He was forty-four years old, the world was passing him by. "I should have been making contacts for such a possibility," he related while still in China, "but I've kept too much in the groove"—by which he meant "in a rut," out of the mainstream. He had no job to speak of—and he had no family, aside from his brother. Now he faced the even more unnerving prospect of reinventing himself. Again. It exasperated Paul that, for all his sophistication and "unusual number of talents," he'd failed to translate them into a useful and rewarding career. So far, at least, but—*he was forty-four*!

These frustrations of Paul's were glaringly apparent to Julia. "If you could find your niche, I should think you could find your life," she said, comforting him as best she knew how. But the pep talk was a tough sell. In reality, they were at different crossroads in their lives. At thirty-four, Julia was finally "coming out of [her] cocoon," blossoming in a huge, exciting way. The new experiences she'd undergone had turned her inside-out; she couldn't process them fast enough. Since coming home from the war, she'd become her own personal reclamation project, devouring anything she could find that enlarged her already expanding universe. "I am starting on *The Cosmological Eye,* and also reading some elementary psychology, of which I know very little," she reported soon after she got back. She'd already clawed her way through a stack of books on semantics, including S. I. Hayakawa's *Language in Thought and Action,* which Paul had recommended when they were in China. In between tomes, she combed through three dailies—*The Washington Post, The New York Times,* and the *Los Angeles Times*—surveying the political landscape, which, for her, was rapidly moving from the right to the left. There was so much information for her to absorb. "Ah, life," she sighed, "will one ever learn to live it?"

With Paul, she'd be linking her future to someone who could teach her how, but also to a man who was relatively lost—at the very time she was finding herself.

By the time they hit Maine, however, Julia knew her fate was cast. The trip east had been everything she'd hoped it would be—and more, much more. After nine months apart, she and Paul fell into each other's arms, and that's where they remained throughout most of the month-long journey. They were together all day, every day, under insufferable conditions: long, hot days in the cramped car, lackluster meals at roadside diners, stuffy nights spent in cheap, dingy motels—all perfect, just perfect. They talked about everything under the sun, they took in a glorious assortment of sights, and they made love, often and splendidly, with none of the "measly Mrs. Grundyisms concerning sex" that Paul had expected of Julia. "She loves life and all its phenomena," he informed Charlie. Plus, he was in love again. With Julia. Everything was perfect, just perfect.

Their friends along the way had given them enthusiastic thumbs-ups, everyone, that is, except for Julia's father, who saw in Paul everything he despised—but that was an endorsement in its own, twisted way. In earnest, Julia had been moving away from her father, physically as well as philosophically, but now she faced an additional dilemma. Dort had been staying with Pop since 1941, running the household and looking after his general welfare. As a consequence, Julia felt her sister had become "quite stale and stultified." Everyone agreed with Julia's opinion that "she needs to cut loose," and the logic finally resonated. Dort announced that she was leaving for New York to pursue a career in the theater. In her absence, she felt "someone should live with father"—that someone, of course, being Julia.

John McWilliams, now sixty-five, hadn't softened with age. He was still, according to Julia, "a vigorous and attractive fellow," but if anything, he'd grown more opinionated, intolerant, stridently cantankerous, and autocratic. His right-wing politics especially disturbed Julia, particularly his latest protégé, an ambitious young lawyer named Richard Nixon, who'd just won a seat in Congress by smearing his opponent, Helen Gahagan Douglas, as a Communist sympathizer. And John had become a member of the so-called Bohemian Club, in Monte Rio, California, a secret, cult-like retreat for the conservative Old Guard power elite, whose members wore hooded robes and participated in pagan rituals. Pop was hard-core when it came to his "Republican attitudes," a posture that leaned heavily on his daughter. "Julia and her father just disagreed about everything," says Jo McWilliams, who had married Julia's brother, John, and saw them often during this time. "They fought like cats and dogs. No matter what subject came up, a war of words broke out." They weren't strong-minded so much as uncompromising, obstinate. Neither one of them gave an inch, Julia recalled, to the point that "we ended up not being able to agree on the weather."

One can only imagine the fallout if she were stuck in Pasadena, taking care of Pop. There would be bloodshed in that house, that much was certain. Paul warned her against such an unwise move, for her own well-being—and for his. He had heard the chilling stories of John McWilliams's behavior, the diatribes and rages, his refusal to respect any opinion of Julia's or anyone else's, for that matter. Their relationship wouldn't stand a chance with the old man breathing down their necks. Paul wouldn't stand for it. Besides, living at home, with a parent, was counterproductive, he argued—it was an extension of one's adolescence and offensive to him.

Suddenly, Julia found herself in an uncompromising position. If she abandoned her father, she might possibly lose his love—and if she didn't, she might lose Paul.

Kismet intervened in the person of Philadelphia O'Melveny. "She was a lovely woman who lived across town, whose children had gone to school with all of us," says Jo McWilliams. Phila (pronounced *fi*-luh) was elegant, outgoing, and, at fifty, a young, attractive, well-to-do widow who had caught Julia's father's eye. In fact, they had been "going steady" on the QT for two years and decided, quite impulsively, to get married. The match couldn't be more perfect, Julia reported. "I think they get along with each other wonderfully, have the same friends, like the same things. It's a great load off my mind, because I hated to think of leaving him all alone."

Even better, they were married by the time Paul arrived in Pasadena. He and Julia left town with no strings attached. She felt more at peace in her relationship with Pop—now that there were three thousand miles between them.

THE HIKE FROM the town road to Freddie and Charlie's cabin was exceedingly strenuous. If Julia and Paul hadn't been in such tip-top shape, the rocky path might have presented a greater challenge, but they swung along the trail, dragging shopping bags and luggage, with the flush of rapturous children on their way to summer camp. The sylvan Maine setting that surrounded them was almost as bucolic. The air had a crisp, briny freshness. Lacy shadows shifted playfully with the breeze. Through the tunnel of tall pines that framed the trail, Julia could glimpse snatches of steely-blue water that stretched out below like a living map. It was impossible to gauge the heroic sweep of the Atlantic, but one could hear its emphatic pitch, the force of its tides.

It was the perfect soundtrack to accompany Julia's visit. For almost two years, she'd heard nothing but Charlie, Charlie, Charlie. Paul talked about him incessantly, wrote him daily epic letters, insisted everyone in the OSS unit visit his brother when they were Stateside (and many of them did, with Paul synchronizing stopovers from eight thousand miles away). Charlie's name came up in almost every conversation Paul had; there was something almost disturbing and obsessive about the frequency he was mentioned. But, in any case, Julia was intrigued. No, intrigued was too feeble to describe how she felt. She was flat-out burning with curiosity about this Doppelgänger of Paul's.

The spirit in the cabin was almost as feverish. The whole Child family—Charlie, Freddie, their daughters Erica and Rachel, and son Jon—had been waiting all morning for the couple's grand arrival. Everyone had seen Paul's letters about this "quite a dame!" he was bringing to meet them. His last missive was unpredictably up-front. It was a glowing roundup of Julia's best qualities, the kind of testimonial one's mother might write, or a eulogy delivered at a wake. "She's direct and simple . . . she is unusually strong physically and marvelously healthy . . . she has a firm and tried character . . . she has a cheerful gay humor with considerable gusto . . . she has a frank and warm liking for men . . ." The man was out of control, he was besotted. "She has a deep-seated charm and human warmth . . . she would be poised and at ease anywhere . . . she tells the truth . . . and I find her interesting and fun to talk to at any time. And I love her dearly."

I love her dearly.

That last phrase caught them squarely on the chin. "We had heard about Julia in the letters," recalled Erica, who was fourteen at the time, "but there were a lot of other women in the letters, as well. Paul was always apprising: 'this one has wonderful breasts, that one has wonderful legs, this one is a gossip, that one is beautiful.' He had been auditioning for a partner for years. But . . . *love!* We just assumed he'd always be a bachelor. The fact that he was actually bringing a woman home to meet our family was a very big deal."

Rachel, who was twelve, saw them coming through the woods. "They looked so happy," she recalls, "and I hadn't seen Paul looking happy for a long while. He seemed proud, with his chest puffed out, as if he were bringing home a prize trophy he'd won."

They'd been warned in advance that Julia was tall, but no one realized how tall that meant. Rachel, who was struggling with height issues, towered over her father at that point. "But Julia was—*tall!* She was extraordinary, the tallest woman I'd ever seen. And her feet were huge. She moved in an awkward, completely unself-conscious way. And I remember thinking to myself: 'It's going to be okay to be tall.' "

Charlie and his family stormed outside to meet them. They still weren't quite sure what to expect from this dame. "We had heard she'd been conventionally brought up, a lady in a large Republican family," says Rachel. "And we were bohemians, fiercely progressive, living in a cabin in the woods, with logs being cured out back and mud everywhere." Everyone was on his or her best behavior—for about a minute. That was all it took for Julia to win over this crowd. "I liked her from the moment I laid eyes on her," recalled Jon Child, then six. "She had this amazing personality, her *joie de vivre.* She was fun—and funny. She became part of our family the instant she arrived, just like that."

Julia spent the next ten days suspended between the Child family's unadulterated affection, which was heartfelt, and this misfit house of theirs growing up around them. From the start, she was determined to endear herself to the family. It was essential to love what Paul loved, and, in this case, he couldn't have given her an easier assignment. Julia and Freddie hit it off immediately. "Mother needed someone to relieve the blustery despotism of my father," says Rachel, "and Julie was exuberant, she was a positivist, with none of the New England doom-and-gloom." A lithe, strikingly attractive woman, with hazel eyes, dramatic scarlet hair, and freckles, Freddie's reserved manner belied the rigors of keeping her family on an even keel. The personalities in that house were combustible; the teenage girls were especially sensitive, but Charlie, as advertised, was a force to be reckoned with. "He was very gregarious," recalls Erica, "very smart and cultured, but very childlike. The whole world had to revolve around him." Friends pegged Charlie as "self-centered and cocky," but fascinating nonetheless, forgiven for his arrogance and vanity because of the way he allowed himself to be scoffed at, in good fun. In Charlie, Julia found a man who "was an exact copy of Paul, who looked and spoke with the same intonation, had the same body language—but was a completely different person." There was a steadiness in Paul that Charlie lacked. Charlie had never suffered; he was indulged. Paul painted with great restraint; Charlie painted expressively. Julia liked Charlie's red-hot spirit, but she was wary of his volatile emotions, which tended to surge and gather force.

Charlie strode through the cabin with unmistakable pride, pride in all the ingenuity and elbow grease that had gone into it. The house was a "terribly rudimentary" one-room log structure with a back porch that doubled as a sleeping loft. An unsurpassable view in the front came with the property: a horseshoe swath of virgin seashore and the Atlantic Ocean, in all its grandeur. Charlie, who "had a Thoreau complex," had stumbled upon the site in 1939, a ledgy rise ten feet above the water, on a gorgeous promontory called Lopaus Point. The next summer he moved the family there, ensconcing them in tents, while he and Paul cleared the land, dug the foundation, and put down the basic framework. "We all worked on it," recalls Erica. "We cut down the trees, peeled the bark off, and then sawed them into lengths. Meals were sandwiches on a big board that we took to the beach."

By August 1946, when Julia arrived, the house was slightly further along. The log walls remained unfinished except for oakum, which was used to caulk the holes. There was a big coal stove in a designated kitchen area at the front and a beast of a fireplace in the living area made from stones that Erica and Rachel had hauled. Otherwise, there was no electricity, no refrigerator, no bathroom facilities. Milk and eggs sat on a little shelf that had the benefit of a natural breeze. Water was brought in from a nearby spring. "There was a system," recalls Jon Child. "Everybody had two buckets, water was heated on the stove. If you needed the bathroom, you'd go to the beach with a roll of toilet paper."

Julia loved the house from the get-go, even without plumbing and electricity. The whole notion of living in the woods, practically on top of each other—roughing it—spoke to her romantic side. She loved how welcoming the house felt, how everyone slept in the same room and shared meals at a communal table that Charlie had made, and read by the light of a kerosene Aladdin's lamp that cast a beautiful soft glow. She loved the energy in that house and the way Paul was in it. "She loved the house because she loved adventure," Rachel says. "The way we lived in Lopaus was just more of the same."

Freddie recruited Julia to help prepare meals, but it was clear the new guest was a pitiful *sous* chef. Freddie had to walk her through the most basic tasks: chopping vegetables and cutting up a chicken. "Word around our house was Paul's girlfriend couldn't cook," says Jon. "The joke was: she could burn water if she boiled it."

In the Lopaus kitchen, Julia was all thumbs—she had no ability—but she knew more about cooking than she let on. During her stay in Pasadena, Julia had enrolled at the Hillcliff School of Cookery in Beverly Hills, run by two dithering British women, Mary Hill and Irene Radcliffe. It was a classic Intro to Cooking course, combining commonsense skills with hands-on preparations. To its credit, the school rejected the numbing unoriginality of home-ec cooking, which staked its claim on convenience foods and kitchen shortcuts. There were no canned-soup casseroles or gelatin salads on its syllabus. It was, in the words of a brochure from the mid-1940s, "in service to old-fashioned culinary techniques using the freshest ingredients."

Julia was determined to cook—and cook well. Paul loved good food, and her desire to please him was great, which meant that she needed to develop the skills to meet his exacting standards. It wasn't a chore. "I do love to cook," she acknowledged earlier that summer. But Julia wasn't a natural when it came to the kitchen. She didn't have the instincts that some women were born with, the ability to throw something together and make it jump off the plate. Cooking, for her, necessitated a logical set of instructions: measure the ingredients, boil the water, mix well, cook until done. But, as Julia soon discovered, it took more than simply following a recipe to create a delicious dish.

Her first few experiments were unmitigated disasters. A soufflé she made had the weight and density of a brisket. A dish of brains turned to mush when she stirred it to death. Another time, friends brought her several ducks, which blew up in the oven when she forgot to prick the skin. Nor did she fare better as a *saucier*. Béarnaise, according to Julia, was "awfully easy when the tricks are known," but if they weren't known—that is, if one happened to improvise, substituting lard for butter, as Julia did at a dinner party in March—chances are the sauce will become a solid block of grease. With all that energy and fumbling in the kitchen, there was always a soupçon of hysterical nonchalance.

And no beginning cook was more nonchalant than Julia McWilliams.

Almost two decades before she diced, chopped, and minced her way into America's living rooms, Julia's inimitable kitchen etiquette was already talking hold. She and Freddie Child developed an easy rapport over meal preparations that became a hallmark of Julia's ebullient style.

They laughed and drank wine while they cooked. They told each other marvelous stories. If one of the ingredients happened to hit the floor, Freddie instructed Julia to brush it off and toss it into the pot. They made recipes that Freddie had learned while living in France. "My mother taught Julia how to cook coq au vin," recalls Erica, "and she taught her how to relax and have fun."

Freddie took the hysteria out of the hysterical nonchalance and gave Julia the keys to the kitchen.

THROUGH THE REST of the Lopaus visit and into the late-summer chill that came early to Maine—every day for two weeks, the temperatures dropped by two or three degrees—Julia and Paul integrated themselves into this warm, inviting family. They pitched in with the daily building chores, organized picnics at the beach, told endless war stories about "the clack-clack pandemonium of China" that got an animated retelling among the kids at bedtime. Julia quickly became the girls' favorite aunt—Aunt JuJu—winning their affection with her irresistible enthusiasm. "She was fascinating to us," says Erica, "and game to do funny things." Whatever the caper, she was the perennial good sport. Rachel and Julia began making funny hats for each other out of seashore detritus, such as seaweed and lobster claws. In an oft-repeated Chaplinesque pantomime, Julia would pretend to lose her footing and slip off a mossy rock, plunging comically into the surf. Such lavish attention wasn't skimped on young Jon, who got a haircut courtesy of patient Aunt JuJu, while he blew a toy bugle into her ear. "She possessed more than a touch of the unexpected," Charlie wrote in a memoir, and it is fair to say that he understated her impact.

The ten days Julia spent at the cabin on Lopaus Point provided the Childs with a view of Paul unlike any they had experienced. He was a different man with a different outlook. Instead of brooding conversations and cloudy discontent, there were plans laced with promise and hope. The kids noticed there were fewer flare-ups between the brothers, none of the tension that marred earlier visits. Everything he did took on a lighter, brighter twist. "It was nice to see Paul happy again," says Erica. "We loved it when he and Julia kissed each other and hugged. They were very open about it. He had never been that way with Edith so, of course, we credited Julia."

They all had been holding their breath around Paul for such a long time. Now, they were holding out for something more, a sign, perhaps, that he and Julia would steer their relationship inevitably toward the altar. "We were all abuzz with anticipation," recalls Rachel. There would have been talk, lots of talk, behind closed doors, if only there had been doors to close in the open cabin. Instead, there were entire three-act plays plain-as-day written on everyone's hopeful faces.

Julia and Paul wasted no time in bringing down the curtain.

They had disappeared the last morning of their visit to Maine, leaving the cabin just after breakfast with instructions that they'd return in time for lunch. Paul never missed a chance to walk the rock-ribbed ledges that framed the beach below the point. "He loved to go out and look at the view," Rachel recalled. With Julia, he would sit on a craggy bluff sketching the spectacular Acadian landscape where glaciers had gouged freshwater troughs from breaches in the soft sea banks. In the distance, they could see the village of Blueville, sparsely settled like an undiscovered continent, where, before the war, Charlie had apprenticed for a professor from Harvard. Since then, little had changed. Nature had cast its sentimental spell on the cove, leaving it protected from the tourists who would invade in due time. An ever-present platoon of gulls stood sentry on the tide-lashed rocks, occasionally breaking rank to plunge for fish, while, above, almost motionless against the breeze, terns floated like delicate kites. It was tailor-made for inspiration, the perfect place to reflect and contemplate the future.

Julia completely shared Paul's attachment to this rugged sanctuary. Yet, it was enough that they had finally come to a lovely place in two lives that only a year before had seemed nothing but barren and desperate. "The war had opened them up amazingly," Erica says. "Now they were giving each other an inner worth."

That day it must have all made sense to them. The years of restlessness, frustration, longing, and discontent—"the pursuit of the perfect," as Matthew Arnold had alliterated it—became a blur they were leaving behind.

Over lunch, they waited for a lull in the conversation. Finally, Paul raised a glass and gazed meaningfully at Julia. "We're going to get married—and right away," he announced.

A joyous outcry resounded from the family.

Freddie Child waited until the congratulations died down. She clapped her hands in delight and leaned halfway across the table. "Well," she said, "we thought you'd never come out with it!"

PAUL WASN'T KIDDING when he promised a wedding *right away*. With little time left on their hiatus from real work and real life, he and Julia set the date—September 1, 1946—less than a month off, and plenty of arrangements still to be made. The only definite detail was the place: the garden of Charlie and Freddie's house, nicknamed Coppernose, in Lumberville, Pennsylvania, where Paul had his own room in an upstairs alcove. Aside from the cottage he'd shared with Edith, in Cambridge, it was the only place he'd ever called home. Julia was all for it, although the logistics created a sticky family problem. Her father believed it was his duty to make the wedding—in Pasadena, of course, on his turf, at the country club where he was chief. He had already taken the first steps in that direction, drawing up a guest list of prominent friends.

Paul was understandably opposed. Pasadena—and Julia's father—stood for everything he despised. What's more, the old man had made clear his distaste for Paul Child—the artist, the intellectual, the French food lover, the *liberal*. From the beginning, John McWilliams disapproved of the marriage. He believed that Julia could have done better by marrying that *Los Angeles Times* heir, whose politics were more in line with his own. As late as February 1946, Julia had again refused Harrison Chandler, making it clear that this was the last time he should ask. That certainly didn't endear her to Pop. The thought of sharing his daughter with Paul was bad enough; taking the wedding out of his hands, however, was the *coup de grâce*. It was an unprecedented act of disrespect—and of independence, another unsavory trait in his book. According to Dort, it "got Julia and Paul off on the wrong foot with Pop," but it wouldn't be the last time they stepped on each other's toes.

The wedding was going to be an intimate event: the immediate families and a small selection of friends. Julia's family promised to attend. Pop and Phila were flying in from California, Dort was driving from New York, and John Jr. and his wife, Jo, were coming from Massachusetts. Paul's relatives, aside from Charlie, were conspicuously absent. His mother, Bertha, had died during the war, and Meeda, who grappled with alcoholism, was off somewhere, "gallivanting around Europe, engaged in a string of liaisons with men." Aside from Charlie and Freddie, a group of Paul's extended family and friends from his Paris and Connecticut days rounded out his side.

At last, everything was set. The only remaining detail was securing the marriage license, which Julia and Paul had left until the last minute. On Friday, August 30, two days before the ceremony, they drove to the Doylestown town hall to fill out the requisite papers. Unbeknown to either of them, Pennsylvania law required that they take a blood test, which was fine, except that the results wouldn't be available for five to seven days. No matter how Paul argued, the registrar wouldn't budge: the law was the law. There was no way they could be married on Sunday, as planned.

What were they going to tell everyone? Guests had already started arriving from points far off, with schedules requiring they be back at work on Monday. Pop, of course, would think them both complete idiots. What a way to start their lives together.

In desperation, they enlisted Charlie and Freddie to help solve the problem. A few high-placed friends were called to no avail. An even better scheme was proposed: have the ceremony anyway, with a blank license, which would be signed a few days later when the test results were back; the plan seemed feasible, but the justice of the peace refused. Finally, Charlie realized they were only two miles from New Jersey, where blood, at least in terms of marriage, didn't seem to be an issue. Their friends the Seymours lived in Stockton, just across the Delaware River. If they were amenable, it would make sense to have the ceremony there, on the Jersey side, and the reception back in Lumberville.

Everyone was satisfied with the new arrangement. So on Saturday afternoon, with everything apparently settled, Julia and Paul left Lumberville, headed for New York City, where her father was throwing them a rehearsal dinner at the posh River Club. It was a beautiful day. The drive wouldn't take long—two hours tops, once they hit the main highway. A few miles out of town they came to an intersection where the road collapsed into a three-lane affair. As they slowed to accommodate the shift, Paul glanced in the rearview mirror and saw a huge truck coming up from behind, moving fast—*way too fast*. It was barreling straight toward them. There was no way to know its brakes had failed, nowhere to go on that cramped, unshouldered road. Paul jerked the steering wheel, trying to swerve out of its path, but—too late. The truck slammed into them on the driver's side, crushing the car into an accordion fold. This was long before the days of seat belts, so the car was a chamber of bodies in motion. Paul was flung forward into the steering wheel. The last thing Julia remembered was that she "hit the windshield and was thrown out the door." Fortunately, her outstretched arms broke the fall, protecting her from a more serious head injury. Still, "I was knocked out and covered in blood," she recalled afterward.

A couple passing by scooped up Julia and Paul and rushed them to the nearest hospital. An X-ray revealed Paul had no broken ribs, but Julia was in more serious shape. Shards of glass were painstakingly removed from her arms. Lacerations streaked one side of her face and her head required a Frankenstein track of stitches. They were a mess, but "lucky to be alive." Paul needed a cane to walk; the bride wore white—white bandages, white sling. It seemed a perfectly reasonable decision to postpone the wedding.

Julia, however, wouldn't hear of it. A few wounds weren't about to stop her from marrying Paul Child. Promptly at noon the next day, under a gorgeous sunny sky, about two dozen guests gathered at the home of Whitney North Seymour,* in a lushly planted garden at the back of the house. It was a conspicuously casual affair—no formal attire, no bridesmaids, no processional of any kind. Julia simply appeared on Paul's arm, looking "exuberant," according to a guest. She was dressed stylishly, in a brown-and-white polka dot pinch-waisted suit, with high heels that exaggerated her long, long legs. Aside from the bandage pasted to the left side of her forehead, no one would have known how close to a tragic end she'd come.

Jon Child, who held his mother's hand during the brief ceremony, recalled glancing around at the "insanely tall" crowd. The Seymours were tall people to begin with, but nothing compared to the McWilliamses. He gawked at Dort and John Jr., who were standing behind their sister. "Julia was tall," Jon says, "but these people were *tall,* really tall." John Jr., who was six foot four, stooped slightly as a result of a war wound he received in France. But Dort, at six foot five, seemed "gigantic" to a six-year-old. Paul, by comparison, appeared almost comically out of place. He was barely five foot nine and leaning on a cane, but this happened to be his lofty day. Julia McWilliams was becoming Julia Child, and from the look on his face he might have been seven feet tall.

---

* Seymour was solicitor general from 1931 to 1933 and later the U.S. attorney in the Nixon administration, a post that no doubt would have pleased Julia's father.

Menu from La Couronne: *that lunch* in Rouen

Nine

Devouring Paris Whole

S he smelled it before she saw it. For an instant, there was sweetness of a kind she had never experienced before—butter perhaps, but more full-bodied, like a butter bomb, with a smoky, scorched tang. An instant later, the sea—probably a briny fish *fumé* with a splash of white wine. Wait! A faint lemony whiff drifting by . . . now gone. The ensemble of smells was impossible to contain. Seconds later, a waiter set a large oval platter on the table, and all the aromas shot off like Chinese fireworks. But the scents refused to sync with the sight. The presentation was ridiculously simple: a fish on a plate, with a sprinkling of parsley. From the sides, tipped inward at an angle, a stream of molten gold pooled around the fish. Otherwise, there was nothing unusual about it, nothing to suggest the explosion of smells. She leaned over and inhaled with conviction. A delirious rush of pleasure filled her lungs. Wave upon wave: the aromas began to overlap and coalesce. The butter brought a richness to the fresh saltwater fish. By adding some wine to the sauce, the richness took on a honeyed brightness. Each ingredient influencing the aggregate.

Julia stared at it for a minute or two. Something undecipherable was churning inside of her. But what? With more than a trace of impatience, she picked up a fork.

A meal was about to change Julia Child's life.

IN THE YEARS before World War II, when travel to Europe was still at a premium for most Americans, French food existed as an idealization, courtesy of Hollywood. In many a bistro re-created on the MGM or Paramount lots, a stiff-backed man with a beret and phony French accent would serve snails or frogs legs or crêpes to snooty assembly-line Gauls, who ogled their plates with a couple of *ooh-la-la*s. Tourists, like Julia's father, who actually dined in an authentic Parisian restaurant, often fumbled over menus that offered nothing familiar. They told of nightmarish experiences, trying to order something French. "Duck *ah-rahnge*. Duck! Duh-uck! You know: quack-quack! Don't you understand French?"

Julia Child's lunch on November 3, 1948, was not the typical experience of a clueless American tourist. There was no need for her to stare squint-eyed at the litany of incomprehensible entrées on the menu: *Pigeonneau Cocotte Forestière, Rís de Veau Clamart, Ecrevisses Bordelaise, Canetons à la Rouennaise ou Lapérouse le demi.* Paul, who "spoke [French] beautifully," according to Julia, perused the offerings with an accomplished ease. There were so many wonderful selections to choose from, he assured her. It was his first visit to France in eighteen years, and the prospect of eating such well-prepared food again, after all that time in the culinary desert, filled him with anticipation and joy. He had been extolling the delights of French food to Julia since they'd met, in Ceylon. In lovingly minute detail, he'd described meals he'd shared with Edith or Charlie or his mother or friends, recalling each dish as if it were a work of art. Julia had never met anyone who held food in such esteem. It seemed almost "absurd" the way he went on and on, but Paul's exuberance, his impassioned reminiscence, was impossible to dismiss. There was something beguiling yet elusive about his attitude toward food that she wanted to grasp. "The French dining experience," as he called it, had intrigued her no end. Now, the long-awaited moment was finally upon them.

La belle France! Paul talked about it day and night—its abundant charms, the urge to return there—but earlier that year, in 1948, it seemed ever more a pipe dream. In the two years since their marriage, Julia and Paul had lived in Washington, D.C., where they were more or less wards of the government apparatus. The war had shielded them from the rising tide of anxiety that both of their lives were stalled in midstream. At thirty-five, Julia had nothing solid to fall back on, nothing to occupy her febrile mind. Her war experience, to say nothing of Paul, had opened her up to a world of new ideas that lit her from within. But—what to do about it? She had a burning ambition to do something useful, something important, but none of the training a meaningful job required. File clerks, however, were in great demand. The State Department was scooping up college-educated women for all kinds of administrative work. An intelligence agency gladly would have hired Julia to run its equivalent of the Registry. But she'd put her foot down: no more secretarial work. "There were days in the Registry when I thought I'd just scream," she recalled, describing the monotony of it as "the same damn thing, over and over, over and over." Nothing short of desperation could entice her back to that. And Julia wasn't desperate, not by any stretch of the imagination. Paul had a desk job with the State Department that paid a decent wage, and there was the inheritance from her mother that subsidized them very nicely.

In the meantime, she was content with being Mrs. Paul Child. There was plenty of busywork to occupy her time, setting up house and entertaining new friends. With the help of Charlie Child, who also worked at State in the Division of Cultural Affairs, they found a quaint nineteenth-century house of eight rooms in need of considerable repair on Wisconsin Avenue, in Georgetown. Paul and Charlie did a quick renovation, while Julia filled the rooms with their ragtag belongings, a combined eighty years of accumulated stuff: her clothes and books, Paul's cameras and paints, along with thousands of his photographs. "It was a lovely little place, just big enough for a couple," Julia recalled. "The rooms were small, but cozy. There was a fireplace in the parlor that we always used." The kitchen wasn't much, considering Julia's lack of cooking skills, but she made the most of it, putting up a pegboard to hold the pots and pans and "25 cookbooks on the shelf over the stove."

At Paul's prompting, Julia endeavored to prepare their dinners, but despite her considerable efforts, most nights were a struggle. "I was not much of a cook when we first married," she told a previous biographer. Her daily menus were culled from a miscellany of sources—women's magazines such as *Family Circle* and *Ladies' Home Journal,* as well as from *Gourmet* and *Joy of Cooking,* the most essential cookbook of its day. Even with these aids, however, Julia was in over her head. "I was doing fancy things," she recalled, trying to please Paul's refined palate. The elaborate recipes would take her all day to prepare and even then they never turned out anything like their scrumptious descriptions. The work involved was well beyond her means. "We would not eat dinner until around ten [o'clock] because it took me so long to cook."

Julia was better off when she kept her menu simple. Still, there was no guarantee things would turn out as planned. Her attempt to make broiled chicken was a complete disaster. At first glance, the recipe seemed idiot-proof: put the chicken in the oven, turn on the broiler, and—*presto*—broiled chicken. But, as it happened, the directions were inexact. "I put it in the oven for twenty minutes, went out, came back, and it was burned." Another convoluted recipe, this time for beef heart, prepared for a dinner party, took an early detour from the stove straight to the trash.

Paul reassured Julia that her cooking would improve, but all evidence weighed against a speedy turnaround. "I was hopeless," she recalled many years later. "Nothing I did seemed right. The kitchen was a place I truly enjoyed being, but I was convinced I had no talent for making food that tasted good."

For the rest of the year, Julia worked with her sister-in-law Freddie at her house a few blocks away on Thirty-fifth Street, where she was given daily tutorials, developing her cooking skills in exchange for her abundant good company. Starting with the basics, like chopping and marinating, then gravitating ever so gingerly into the province of uncomplicated sauces, they would prepare a dish using only several essential steps. Simplicity and taste proved remarkable bedfellows; there was no need to embellish a straightforward recipe. If the sauce was too thin or weakly underseasoned, Freddie taught Julia how to correct it without fuss. When bits of meat or fish stuck to a pan, the magic of deglazing was demonstrated, rescuing the dish with a little stock or wine. For the most part, they worked without recipes. Freddie cooked instinctively, from feel, just a sense of the finished product on the plate. After Julia's frightful encounters with challenging—bewildering—recipes, she must have thrilled at the relative ease of the cook's craft, at the satisfaction of throwing a few fresh ingredients into a pan and just *cooking*.

The highest good in cooking, the French food critic Curnonsky argued, was above all *simplicity*—"the simplicity of art, the purity and the spontaneity of the effect justifying any means." But while Freddie Child could prepare a meal relying on the "purity" and "spontaneity" of her imagination, projecting from the outset how it would eventually turn out, Julia's process was still wildly chaotic. Recipes demanded too much of her. The various steps came at her too quickly, the ingredients never seemed to do what she expected, the results were unlike those promised by pictures in the magazines. Often, a dish she was preparing would transform in the pot from whisk to whisk, altering its consistency as a result of nothing but heat and sometimes falling apart altogether, forcing Julia to start over, from scratch. A college friend, who visited at the Georgetown house, remembers Julia's frustration. "She made a chowder with cod that had dissolved into mush. The fish just disintegrated from overstirring and overcooking. It was obvious she didn't know what she was doing." Although Julia had incited any number of ugly kitchen upheavals that year, she wasn't about to admit defeat. Granted, her mechanics were clumsy, her creative instincts more suited to filing than filleting. Any "purity" and "spontaneity" were still lightyears away. But the challenge was ordained. Confidence, Freddie assured her, would develop in time. She wasn't yet comfortable with cooking, but she was excited by it.

Julia was much more at ease with the entertaining aspect of her marriage. Washington was brimful of friends that she and Paul had made and their house on Wisconsin Avenue became the hub for social gatherings. "Paul loved brilliant talk," Julia noted, and he filled their evenings with a revolving-door cast of distinguished conversationalists, mixing Washington intellectuals and artists in a fascinating nightly salon. Every type of character passed through their house, politicos—like Sherman Kent, the so-called father of intelligence analysis, and master international strategist Paul Nitze—and those in the arts, like Archibald MacLeish, John Ford, Stewart Alsop, Budd Schulberg, and Eero Saarinen. Plenty of Julia's Smith classmates also joined the get-togethers, as did Charlie and Freddie's academic acquaintances. "You'd hear the most amazing discussions in our house," Julia said. "Every night was an education for me."

For Paul, that education was a cornerstone of marriage. He craved the type of stimulation that Edith had provided, and his need for another "intellectual equal" became a dogged preoccupation. Julia, alas, was still a work-in-progress. "She was completely unmolded," according to Pat Pratt, a Smith alumna, who became close to the Childs in the ensuing years. "Paul was determined to create an adult Julia, to turn her into a more worldly and sophisticated person." Although he was ten years older than Julia and all-knowing in her eyes, when it came to his wife Paul did not condescend. "He always *suggested* ways she could improve herself, ideas she could embrace and adapt." By listening to Nitze, for instance, she could learn how Europe's post-war reconstruction affected America's financial stability; from Saarinen, an impression on reshaping our own mutable future. Julia's personal development became a fixation of Paul's. But as he well knew, there was plenty to build on. He loved her unbridled exuberance, her robust sense of humor, the no-bullshit way she said what was on her mind, but told her that he didn't like "the slight atmosphere of hysteria" that was an aspect of her persona. She confessed that she hadn't read much of the philosophers or great essayists; he gave her a reading list. The same with poetry; he read aloud to her, in a quiet, expressive voice, from well-worn collections of Millay and Sarton.

The remaining months of 1947 had passed in a blur of enchantment, as Julia and Paul strengthened the roots of their new marriage. Julia embraced her new role as a social hostess—and as a wife. She put finishing touches on the house, hanging curtains and laying rugs; white flowers were ever-present in a vase on the music console. In a moment of inspiration, Julia decorated the front staircase with a gallery of Paul's best photographs—whatever she could do to enhance their pleasure. Dinner was always an occasion, a ceremony, always served elegantly on a dining room table Paul had built, always with a bottle of wine she collected from his well-stocked cellar. In the evenings, after dinner, while Julia read, Paul would spend an hour or so painting in a special area she'd cleared next to the spice cabinet in the kitchen.

Finally, they had a place that felt like home, someplace comfortable and permanent and unmistakably their own. It gave them great satisfaction.

But the satisfaction was short-lived. In early February 1948, after a long night of merrymaking in the dining room, drinking Chilean wine and making valentines for their friends (a ritual they would celebrate annually), the house burned down. Julia and Paul had been asleep in the upstairs bedroom and were awakened around four o'clock by "the creaking of flames downstairs" that sounded like "someone smashing wood-work." They sat bolt upright in bed, thinking, *But this just can't be happening!* The lights were dead and so was the phone. In the increasingly smoke-filled dark, they spent a few minutes pitching whatever belongings they could lay their hands on into the street below. Should they jump? It was tempting, but too great of a plunge. There was nothing to break their fall. Instead, they decided to try to make it to the living room windows, which gave out onto a lower roof. "The belly-crawl in the dark, through hot smoke, knocking into furniture, and fighting with the window lock was the worst," Paul recalled. It was touch and go for a few hair-raising minutes. Flames shot up from between the old wood floorboards, thick smoke began to wreak havoc with their lungs. At last, they fought their way outside into a wintry, twelve-degree night, wearing nothing but thin cotton robes.

The house was uninhabitable, a complete disaster. The fire had burned entirely through the lower two floors, and firemen had "chopped through the walls" in an attempt to contain the spread of flames. The lovingly decorated rooms lay in charred, waterlogged ruins. Fortunately, Julia and Paul could stay at Charlie's while repairs were made, but it was hardly the cozy family affair one might expect. While Charlie and Freddie were obliging hosts, there were unresolved tensions between the twin brothers that had been accumulating over the years. The prospect of depending on Charlie's kindness really agitated Paul. He became more prickly and taciturn than usual. Compounding this vicissitude was news that on March 15, Paul and Charlie would be squeezed out of their respective State Department jobs. Homelessness and joblessness delivered a cruel one-two punch.

Julia did all she could to minister to his distress. Nothing surpassed her devotion to Paul. She was his greatest cheerleader—an indispensable cheerleader—especially while he grappled with moodiness and bouts of insecurity. She knew how much he had hated his job—*hated* it. He was stuck in the bureaucratic ooze as a desk monkey for a superficial government agency that refused to take advantage of his tremendous talents. It was a tedious, banal, soul-sucking job. Everyone felt he deserved more, better, something impressive, or at least to be free and clear of the "average men with average minds" who tormented him all day long. For a while, he'd toyed with starting his own firm, Paul Child Inc., to "do visual presentation graphics for big business." But that was a dream, just a big dream that he never pursued. "If you could find your niche, I think you could find your life," Julia had once assured him. Now seemed like the perfect time to break his dependency on Uncle Sam.

Julia secretly hoped that Paul could support himself by painting. She encouraged him to rely on his artistic talent, what he called his "not-yet-realized capacities," instead of looking for work in the public sector. His brother had already taken the plunge. The gregarious Charlie decided he was through with government desk jobs and was determined, from now on, to paint professionally full-time. Soon after their jobs at State had ended, Charlie announced that he and his family were headed back to Lumberville, *permanently,* where he would pursue portrait painting and illustration. But if this was meant to inspire Paul, it only served to fuel his "various anxieties and fears." All the old jealousies he felt bubbled up anew, and he began to resent Charlie for "marrying a girl with a good income, leading what seemed to be a protected life of ease and world

travel, while [he, Paul,] floundered from one piddling job to another."
It didn't seem fair that things didn't come to him as easily as they did to
Charlie. Yet without Charlie, Paul sank back into restless self-doubt, and
before the snows had thawed he was looking for government work again.

In the interim, Julia found a more presentable house in Georgetown, on Olive Street, in the shadow of the new parkway, less than a
mile from their old place. They moved in at the end of May, with plans
to paint and decorate, but within days they were on the road again—first
to Boston, for the wedding of Paul's nephew, then to Lopaus Point, in
Maine, where they dug in for a month of rest and relaxation. It was clear
they needed a change of scenery, while Paul contemplated his uncertain future. He had gotten a verbal commitment from the newly formed
United States Information Service (USIS), a propaganda arm of the
State Department authorized to develop programs to broaden the cultural dialogue between American institutions and their counterparts
abroad. It was a good position, with somewhat of an intellectual accent,
but for a forty-four-year-old man with a lifelong need to express himself,
it doomed Paul Child to a mundane desk job. He'd be "back sucking at
the govt. tit," he lamented—another functionary in a crowded field of
functionaries. Still, there was an upside: he managed to extract a promise
from those in charge of a posting somewhere overseas. Julia was game
for more foreign intrigue. Her own plans were hopelessly vague. To see
a new part of the world with a man like Paul—that was something she
could get behind.

From what they knew, foreign postings were discretionary; there was
no telling where they'd eventually wind up. While Paul waited for FBI
clearance, he and Julia studied the map, fantasizing about the places and
experiences they would share. Because of their war résumés, India was a
distinct possibility. So were Germany and Austria, where, courtesy of the
Marshall Plan, reconstruction was in full swing. There were also opportunities in the Benelux countries, where American embassies were operating at full tilt. When Paul's assignment finally came through it almost
knocked them off their feet. *Paris!* Was it really possible? Had they really
landed such a plum posting, the one place in the world where everyone
wanted to be? *Paris!* It was Paul's favorite place on earth, and now it would
be Julia's, as well. They were going to *Paris,* of all places! Julia was positively beside herself.

By early September 1948, just weeks before their departure, Paul's job
title was clarified. He was officially a Class 4 Foreign Reserve officer—a

mid-level diplomat, an attaché in embassy-speak—in charge of exhibits designed "to inform the French people by graphic means about the aspects of American life that the government deems important." As a matter of policy, it seemed expedient to spread American goodwill, but the agency's underlying objective was to counter the influence of communism. Since the end of the war, Russia had been on the move, consolidating its power, ideological and otherwise, in Eastern Europe and parts of Asia. Mainland China was on the verge of its own seismic shift to communism. Lines had been drawn: the bucks stopped fear. American embassies across the world were pouring considerable resources into battling the Red menace, and emissaries like Paul were being positioned to lead the charge.

In *Paris*! Julia and Paul were giddy with anticipation. They couldn't pack fast enough. They rented their house, gave away their cat, put their furniture into storage, and shipped their belongings overseas in a container marked as "household goods"—a bulky wardrobe consisting of fourteen suitcases and seven trunks. In addition, they were taking "the Blue Flash," a brand-new 1947 Buick that had been a wedding present from Julia's father, along with a gas refrigerator as a hedge against French iceboxes. After a year living like campers in Ceylon and China, they felt entitled to a few creature comforts.

Finally, on October 28, 1948, they sailed from New York City to Le Havre aboard the SS *America*. It was a brutal five-day crossing, through squalls that produced waves the size of skyscrapers and endless cloudbanks of fog, confining most of the battered passengers to their staterooms for the duration. As the *America* lumbered toward shore on the morning of November 3, the Childs, restless and bleary-eyed, dragged themselves to the porthole for a bird's-eye preview of Mother France. Water sluiced along the glass thanks to a deliberate drizzle. Dawn had not yet broken, and a backsplash of lights twinkled like fireflies in the windows of the wartorn city. They could just about make out the outline of the stubbled horizon. Beyond the harbor, where "giant cranes, piles of brick . . . and rusting half-sunk hulks" blighted the landscape, the last ripples of urban gloom evolved into the great Norman countryside. Julia stared out at the scenery with a feeling of presentiment. She had no idea what to expect, aside from what Paul had told her—and the garbled aspersions cast like mud pies by her father. From all that she'd heard, France was almost exclusively a man's domain. She had no work, she couldn't speak the language. But a break with the past, after all, was a chance to forge a new beginning. For Julia Child, who was now thirty-six and still adrift, the land outside that window might hold something better for her.

THE ROUTE TO Paris revealed evidence of the wartime scars left on France. Julia could see from the road the scorched remains of bombed-out châteaux, many of them several centuries old, where Rommel's panzer divisions had rolled over entire villages in an effort to stave off the Allied invasion forces. From her vantage in the Blue Flash, looking across the wobbly meadow lanes, she could survey the lush Seine-Maritime valley, from Balbec to Yvetot to Barentin, cratered from repeated assault and draped in skeins of barbed wire that bit into the trampled earth. Further still, the land suddenly leveled off and the vast countryside stretched into meticulously furrowed fields. Everywhere she looked, cabbages cropped up and flax plants flaunted their pale blue crowns. Rows of neatly flanked plane trees—called *allées* or avenues—stood like territorial sentries along the boundaries of neighboring farms. However much the view scrambled Julia's impressions of France, she had little time for them to register. There was "so much to see, so much to absorb" that each kilometer they traveled offered another revelation. Paul barely had time to explain one unusual feature, before the next was upon them—and the next and the next.

Before Julia knew it they had crossed into Rouen, the historic capital of Normandy, where Paul had decided to stop for lunch. Over the twisty cobbled approach into the *centre-ville,* Julia recognized from newsreels the remains of a neighborhood near the Seine where the city was burned in 1940, the damaged Notre Dame Cathedral from Monet's dusky studies, and the fabled Gros Horloge, the astronomical clock with its sun and moon phases in exquisite detail. Paul's destination was the place du Vieux-Marché, the medieval town square where Joan of Arc was burned at the stake in 1431. Nearly a century earlier, the Restaurant La Couronne had opened in a half-timbered house just opposite a stretch of tiny shops. According to the *Guide Michelin* it was the oldest restaurant in France, a detail that had no doubt attracted Paul's attention. The food earned a respectable "three forks-and-spoons" rating. What better place to introduce Julia to Old World charm?

In retrospect, La Couronne was the kind of conventional restaurant one found in every city in France—a rather drab, nondescript room in the street level of a rather drab, nondescript hotel, with an unfussy white-tablecloth décor, an older clientele, attentive, though humorless, waiters, and a straightforward traditional menu. While Paul schmoozed in French with the maître d', Julia perused the *carte*—a sepia-toned bill of fare adorned with an Elizabethan-style etching of the restaurant, showing servant girls in mirthful stages of hospitality, an animal roasting in the fireplace, and haunches of meat hanging from the rafters. She was tired and starving, and the blast of fragrances fulminating from the nearby kitchen made her stomach do somersaults. A selection of daily entrées had been typed to the right of the etching—not that they made a whole lot of sense to Julia. After years of practical French lessons, from grade school through college, she was no better equipped to read the menu than was, say, her father or her cat. No matter: Paul, to the rescue, did the honors.

In Rouen, he explained, duck was often the specialty of the house, just not at this house; oddly enough, there wasn't any duck on the menu that day. Chicken . . . perhaps . . . there was a roast chicken brochette . . . hmmm . . . no. The grilled steak and potato soufflé . . . too heavy for lunch. Fish—they'd have fish, he decided. The *Sole Normande-Maison* sounded good, but maybe too much of a production. The ship's food, barely edible, had done a number on their stomachs. All the window-dressing that came with *Sole Normande*—the garnish of oysters, mushrooms, and crayfish—might work as a depth-charge on their intestines. Endeavoring to keep it simple, Paul chose the *Sole Meunière*.

It was a stroke of genius. Sole as God meant it to be: practically naked, its flesh young and supple, cooked like an omelet in nothing but a bath of clarified butter. Then—*more butter,* brown butter as a finishing touch spooned decadently over the tender filets to bring out the toastiness, and a discreet splash of lemon and dusting of parsley. Perfect! Julia had never experienced anything like it. The sole was "so very fresh, with its delicate yet definite texture," she recalled, firm and yielding and succulent at the same time, not like the sheetrock her mother had made in Pasadena. This was—*fish*! It tasted like the sea. Juicy—*my God!*—it fairly oozed a geyser of juices. And the butter! It was sweet and creamy, loaded with butterfat, and caressed her tongue with a slick, silky richness. She'd eaten butter all her life, but this defied all her previous conceptions.

Much later, of course, she would learn that the butter was churned by hand from the finest, thickest Norman cream, unpasteurized and unprocessed, and produced with the kind of care you'd give to plutonium enrichment. And the sole was honest-to-God sole, Dover sole, as opposed to the flounder sold as sole in the States that dried out and flaked apart at the slightest contact with heat.

In the meantime, Julia tried to get a purchase on the sum total of their meal. They had started it with a half-dozen oysters on the half-shell—*portugaises* from the west coast of France that tasted fruity and yet "*very* strong of the sea." Their texture alone took Julia by surprise; they were smooth and swimming in a pool of delicious natural nectar that Paul encouraged her to drink as a chaser. Julia was already feeling the effects of a lightly chilled Chablis, whose inclusion at lunch she found wildly extravagant. "I had never drunk much wine other than some $1.19 California Burgundy," she recalled, "and certainly not in the middle of the day." But it amazed her how well the wine paired with the oysters—how well the wine paired with *everything*: a humble green salad after the fish, followed by a cheese course, dessert, and coffee.

What a revelation that meal was to Julia. It was like somebody had showed her what it really meant to eat, not simply to fill her stomach with food, but—to *eat*, to savor each glorious mouthful with gusto. She had enjoyed food all her life, but this was enjoyment of a different kind. This was food that had been prepared with real understanding of how combining the most flavorful, highest-quality ingredients with great care and respect produced a pleasure that was sensual as well as gratifying. "I was quite overwhelmed," Julia recalled of the experience, which was certainly no exaggeration. She was shocked and awed by the food at that table, to say nothing of the ceremony Paul attached to the meal. Each course was presented like a work of culinary art, each dish eaten at a leisurely, respectful pace. All of it made a life-changing impression on Julia. If there was one incident that led to her future distinction, "that lunch in Rouen," as she often referred to it, was the culprit. Plainly put: "It was the most exciting meal of my life."

The next days in Paris were no less impressionable. "That city took my breath away," Julia recalled almost fifty years later. They arrived at dusk, as the last whisper of daylight cast a glow behind the silhouette of mansard rooftops, framing the skyline in a dramatic crimson blush. In the distance, she spotted the Eiffel Tower, so familiar a symbol that it seemed almost preposterous just standing there in the middle of town. "I couldn't get over how gorgeous everything looked, the beauty of the buildings and the Seine and the bridges and the monuments—the majesty of it all. And the *people*—so chic, yet unusual, so . . . so indescribably *French*. I couldn't understand anything anyone said to me, but the way they said it was so musical and enchanting." The embassy had found them temporary accommodations, in the Hôtel Pont-Royal on rue Montalembert, just off the boulevard Saint-Germain. Paul stashed their car in a nearby garage, and came back with the news that, quite marvelously, Harry Truman had defeated Thomas Dewey in an upset election-night victory. Interpreting that as a good omen, they descended on Paris with open arms.

New to Europe, unable to communicate, a fish out of water, Julia spent that first week alternately agitated and exhilarated. Paul's new job at the embassy demanded all of his time, so Julia was left to chip away at the mountain of official paperwork required of foreign diplomats—presenting their business cards to every American functionary as a means of introduction, and filing forms in triplicate for their ration books, travel vouchers, leave sheets, *cartes d'identité,* and enough bureaucratic rigamarole to satisfy the French compulsion for efficiency. In her pidgin French, she arranged with a real estate agency to find them a flat on the Left Bank. She barnstormed boutiques for something *à la mode* to wear to Ambassador Jefferson Caffery's reception for Secretary of State Marshall, choosing an eye-catching green-feathered hat that Paul felt made her look "divinely tall and svelte." And she began making herself at home in a city in which, after two or three days, she "already considered [herself] a native."

Paris was catnip for Julia. It had everything she craved: gorgeous architecture, dynamic style, vivacious people, ubiquitous culture, an intellectual temperament, and a distinct recipe for living that seethed with passion. Nothing was ever done in a routine or halfhearted way; every gesture, no matter how trivial, seemed to necessitate great drama. A greeting—*"oui, monsieur, oui, madame"*—was delivered with exquisite panache. Discovery was as simple as waking, breathing, looking: around every corner, down each street, lay a new adventure. "History on your doorstep," Julia enthused like a lovestruck schoolgirl. A self-proclaimed "swallow-life-in-big-gulps kind of person," she embraced it all—and all at once—scouring Paris, end to end, in bold, giant steps.

Paul was her eager tour guide. As soon as each weekend arrived, he charted a two-day exploration through a designated section of the city, stopping at every memorable landmark from his last, lingering visit: his mother's flat on place Saint-Sulpice, the building on rue de Vaugirard where Charlie and Freddie had lived, the American Church on the quai d'Orsay, whose stained-glass windows he'd helped to install. They had breakfast, croissants and coffee, on the terrace at Deux Magots; perused the *bouquinistes,* the quayside booksellers, along the river; crossed the Seine, walked through the Tuileries, visited the Louvre, Palais Royal, and Sainte-Chapelle; ascended Montmartre to Sacré Coeur, then out to Versailles. And that was just *the first weekend.*

They became *flâneurs,* "aimless strollers in a town ideal for aimless strolling." Paul, eager as a schoolboy, his camera flapping around his neck, flew along the crowded sidewalks, narrating at Mach speed, with Julia two steps behind, goggle-eyed and openmouthed. It was a whirlwind immersion. And everywhere they strolled, evidence of "the convulsions of the war" confronted them. Four years of occupation had taken its grinding toll. By the fall of 1948, the recovery of Paris was only partially under way; it was still a city wounded and brought low. They could see it in the rubble-strewn lots blighting the streets in each arrondissement; in the long, endless queues of downcast French who stood for hours awaiting ration coupons for milk, bread, butter, cheese, eggs, sugar, and coffee; in the half-empty restaurants or cafés closed for lack of clients. The remnants of Gay Paree—where "good Americans go when they die," according to Oscar Wilde—had all but vanished. Instead, it was "restless, anxious, cantankerous, and convalescent."

Paris was the City of Light, Paul insisted, because the brightest people were drawn to it. They saw beyond the despair, the smell "of rotting food, burned wood, sewage, old plaster, and human sweat," even adapted to the "incomprehensible contradictions" of it all. They proclaimed themselves—like Nietzsche, Hemingway, Picasso, Cather, Gertrude Stein, and countless others in the insatiable pursuit of enlightenment—citizens of Paris and assumed the status of gratified émigrés. It was a city, wrote Ernest Hemingway, that would stay with you wherever you went, "for all of Paris is a moveable feast."

And no one craved a feast more than Julia Child.

BUT THE FOOD scene in Paris was still largely foreign to Julia. Intimidated by the devilishly perplexing menus, as well as the solemn table etiquette, she stuck with her go-to option: *sole meunière, sole meunière, sole meunière.* For a few days, that was all she ate. "I just couldn't get over how good it was," she recalled. The shock of that lunch in Rouen wouldn't wear off, and Julia gorged herself on sole as though she feared the world supply might dry up. Paul let her taste from his plate of *rognons,* sautéed kidneys, one evening and suddenly her food world expanded to two dishes. A day or so later a bowl of pale, plump mussels *marinière* in a luscious broth of lemon-infused white wine, with shallots, garlic, thyme, and parsley led her to believe that maybe the French were onto something, maybe something spiritual.

French food intoxicated Julia, who awaited the daily mealtimes with anticipation akin to addiction. "I found it hard to control myself," she recalled. "It was an awfully astonishing learning experience for me. We'd take ourselves into another lovely place, and I'd have something new and *absolutely delicious* to eat. I had to learn that this was the norm, not the exception, to slow down, to appreciate everything." Occasionally, however, she went overboard and paid dearly for her indulgence. Recounting an eating binge to her sister-in-law Freddie, Julia succumbed to "such a gorge of food. Lunch: *sole meunière, ris de veau à la crème.* Dinner: *escargots, rognons flambés.* Every day for four days, with a half bottle of wine at least with every meal, cognac after, aperitifs and cocktails."

The food was a gift from the gods for Julia, but the food *and* Paris—that was an unbeatable combination. Paul couldn't get over his wife's rapid conversion. "Julia wants to spend the rest of her life right here," he wrote to Charlie, "eating sole, *rognons,* drinking wine and looking at Paris."

It was true. She was digging in with a mole's determination. By December 1948, she had found a flat at the foot of rue de l'Université, in the Seventh Arrondissement, for the whopping sum of eighty dollars a month. It was a two-story five-room apartment in "the heart of Paris," about a hundred yards from the Assemblée Nationale and the Ministry of Defense, and within shouting distance of the Seine. Part of what had once been an elegant town house, the Childs' accommodations had been "carved out of another place." With its warren of odd, asymmetrically shaped rooms, fun-house hallways, and wobbly staircase into the alcove kitchen, it was a place that only an artist could love.

"You came up to it in one of those creaky cage elevators," recalls Rachel Child, "and then once inside there was a vast foyer that looked as if Charles Addams had drawn it." She called the motif "tawdry-elegant," which was no exaggeration, although Julia thought it had "Frenchy old charm." The walls were covered in faded etched leather that buckled with age and the curtains were of a heavy brocade, "old and dirty, peeling." Behind it, the *salon* was only a modest improvement, with its "faintly ridiculous" décor: garish gold moldings, water-stained inset wall panels (including a marble relief of a Knight of Malta over the fireplace), a tapestry out of the Dark Ages, and "shredded draperies—very dingy and ornate." The furniture was hideous, musty, on its last legs. There were enough hanging bibelots and *tchotchkes* to endow a small museum, most of which Julia banished to an attic room that she and Paul nicknamed the *oubliette,* or "forgettery." The upstairs kitchen—*la cuisine*—however, was a matter of some "remembery." Julia recalled it being "large and airy," but frequent visitors insist it was "absolutely tiny, less than a galley," difficult for two people to stand in at the same time. In either case, there was an entire wall of windows, which bathed the supremely drab kitchen in day-long sunlight, and a "monster" stove that "seemed ten feet long." (What in the world was she going to do with that?) From behind the soapstone counter, Julia could look out over the rooftops toward the place de la Concorde or down into the gardens of the Ministry of Defense. Regrettably, there was no hot water for the sink. There was electricity, at least, and occasional running water, but no central heating, which did not bode well for the winter months ahead.

And, yet, despite it all, the place was loaded with charm. There was something typically French, something *je ne sais quoi* that radiated from the flat. "Julia loved that old apartment," says her niece, Erica. To her, it was "our little old bit of Versailles." She would stand at the windows for hours, gazing at the stricken Parisian sprawl as neighborhoods slowly rebuilt the streets that had been torn away by war. In the distance, she could see children playing soccer in front of the green-steepled Basilique Sainte-Clotilde, whose plangent bells tolled every half hour. Or reflect on the comings and goings via the interior courtyard to their rue de l'Université building, which Julia called "Roo de Loo" for short.

Heartened by a nest to snuggle in with Paul and the joyous discovery of Paris, Julia began what was, probably, the happiest year of her life. She loved walking from neighborhood to neighborhood, poking into every interesting shop. She could sit for hours at a congenial outdoor café, nursing a coffee or *petit blanc,* enjoying the endless pedestrian parade that never failed to entertain. The baffling quirks that plagued disgruntled Parisians—the daily power failures, crazy traffic jams, the antiquated phone system, the infuriating bureaucracy—charmed her. The French themselves, not known for their warm and fuzzy nature, eased their way into Julia's heart. Not one to seclude herself in a social vacuum, she quickly made friends—a diverse group that included her landlady's daughter and husband, a Lithuanian art historian and his wife, columnist

Art Buchwald and his wife, Ann, and the Mowrers, Paul and Hadley, whose former husband, Ernest Hemingway, had befriended Paul in Paris twenty years earlier.

It was at the Mowrers' Thanksgiving party a few weeks after they'd arrived that Julia decided it was time to go native. A self-described "talker," she was forced to stand by silently, confounded, as pockets of French-speaking guests around her "strung words together with machine-gun rapidity." The same thing happened in her forays around Paris. She was unable to express herself in the most fundamental situations. Paul recalled how all that finishing-school French eluded her once they hit town. "She couldn't even hail a cab and give him an address or understand if he said anything" in response, he said. How preposterous: Julia was a participant, not an observer, *damn it.* It made her feel helpless and ultimately angry that she couldn't speak the language. That was the last straw. Later that evening, she threw down the gauntlet. "I've had it!" she announced. "I'm going to learn to speak this language come hell or high water."

At the outset, it seemed as if she'd need a pitchfork and a raft. Determined to master the tongue once and for all, Julia enrolled in an intensive course at Berlitz, but French, for Julia, was "a swamp of abstractions and ambiguities." Her tongue just refused to get around those unutterable phonemes and diphthongs. Her trademark warble, a curse to even the most gifted linguist, strangled any hope of developing a decent accent. And those tenses—*mon dieu!* There were scads of them: present, past, future, conditional, subjunctive, perfect, the more-than-perfect, the imperfect of the subjunctive . . . How could anyone expect to speak this unfathomable tongue twister of a language? Julia could more than sympathize with Mark Twain who had said: "In Paris they simply stared at me when I spoke to them in French. I never did succeed in making those idiots understand their own language."

Julia Child wasn't so easily deterred. Those idiots, as Twain called them, rallied to her stubborn endeavors to speak only French in her dealings with them. Along with her new friend, Hélène Baltrusaitis, Julia spent many afternoons engaging shop merchants in an ongoing dialogue to explain their daily lives. They weren't rude or disdainful when she insisted they speak *en français* while selling her oysters or wine or olive oil, or when she tripped over verb tenses or murdered the language in her thick, poky delivery. Even though, according to Hélène, "Julia spoke very poor French" at the outset, the effort she put in was heroic. Practice became second nature to her—speaking, reading, conjugating those damn verbs. She read Baudelaire and Balzac in their native tongue. Paul put her through the paces at home, with tricky linguistic exercises, correcting, correcting, always correcting her "gauche accent." Slang came easily to a gal like Julia, and Hélène gave her an arsenal of expressions to assist her on the street. "I worked on my French diligently, and was able to read better and say a little more every day," she recalled.

It wasn't long—not more than a few months, in fact—before Julia felt comfortable enough to use her French conversationally with everyone she met. There was no more corrupt, garbled dialect, no more *Où est les toilettes, mon-soor?* It was smooth, colloquial: *Ou se trouve les toilettes, m'sieur?* The locals, who would just as soon insult Americans as listen to their pidgin, gave her credit in spades; remarkably, they embraced her as one of them. It was an impressive turnaround by someone only months removed from ineptitude, and Julia felt the gratefulness of a woman made welcome. "I never dreamed I would find the French so *sympathique,* so warm, so polite, so utterly pleasurable to be with," she said with a conviction that would no doubt give her father apoplexy.

As a gesture of Julia's progress, Hélène loaned her a well-thumbed copy of her bible: *Gastronomie pratique: études culinaires* (Encyclopedia of Practical Gastronomy), published in 1906 under the pseudonym Ali-Bab. It was a treasure trove of kitchen lore, the author's "attempt to put the entire history of food culture, cooking and eating all over the world into a single volume." It was a doorstop of a book, as thick as the New York telephone directory, and it was legendary. Every French housewife had a copy on her bookshelf. Chefs kept one close to their stoves, knew each of the recipes by heart. And Julia devoured it as she might a morning croissant. She took to her bed, running through the chapters "with the passionate devotion of a fourteen-year-old boy to *True Detective* stories."

> Nowadays, hors-d'oeuvres are served at the beginning of a luncheon and after the soup at dinner. It is a preface, an introduction, a curtain-raiser, an operatic overture, a flirt, a bit of sentimentality, a passing love affair.

Priceless! In fact, the book was the work of Henri Babinski, a widely traveled mining engineer from the same French family credited with the Babinski reflex. On his business trips around the globe, Babinski collected recipes for his friends and conveyed them in a gruff, no-nonsense style meant to impress and amuse. Julia loved Babinski's snooty irreverence (those who arrive habitually late for dinner, he said, should "end up by staying home, and nobody would be sorry"), marveled at his exhaustive index—there were more than five thousand recipes, considering the variations of variations he included. *Truites au Bleu,* Truffled Beef Tenderloin, Braised Stuffed Shoulder of Lamb with Madeira, Wild Duck with Anchovy-Stuffed Olives, Seafood Torte, omelets and soufflés a dozen ways! It was Julia's earliest brush with food porn. But, most of all, she developed a curiosity about food that went beyond the confines of simply satisfying her hunger. Food *preparation*—now, there was a subject that intrigued Julia in new ways.

Food, of all things, was becoming her passion. It was everywhere around her, impossible to ignore. Bountiful markets were in the fabric of French life, and they fascinated her, with their myriad stalls of the freshest of everything. Vegetables! Julia was used to simply opening up cans, but in Paris she found fat, unblemished spears of green and white asparagus, turnips the size of softballs, dimpled heads of purple garlic, mushrooms in enough variety to stagger a cultivator, beans *still in their shells* (imagine that!), potatoes so creamy they could pass for flan, and produce she'd never laid eyes on before: shallots, chard, leeks, truffles, celery root, zucchini flowers (the French ate the *flowers*!). Over time, Julia became a fixture at her neighborhood market on rue de Bourgogne and, eventually, the protégée of a rumpled old character known as Marie des Quatre Saisons, who sold produce from a three-wheeled cart and dished out gossip and advice as freely as she dished out Brussels sprouts. She took an instant liking to this new, fresh-faced arrival from America. The two women often spent hours together talking—*in French,* no less—about getting around this peculiar broken city, its ins and outs, its ups and downs. Julia loved the sound of the woman's voice, the way her words ran together in a breathless fluency. A cook herself, with the ample figure to prove it, Marie was a natural teacher who picked up on Julia's unexplored enthusiasm. "She took great pleasure in instructing me which vegetables were best to eat, and when," Julia recalled, "and how to prepare them correctly."

She also pointed Julia toward a supporting cast of shops: the butcher opposite the market, where a menagerie of freshly slaughtered farm animals hung on hooks in the window; the *crémerie* and *fromagerie* a few doors down, whose fifty-megaton odor could take one's wind away, with a selection of cheeses that rivaled the surface of the moon; next door, the fishmonger, with box stands of fresh oysters and misbegotten sea creatures; the wine merchant, Nicolas, just around the corner, where Paul began building an unparalleled personal cellar; all became whistlestops on Julia's daily shopping circuit. Friends suggested she let their maid do the shopping, but Julia demurred. Shopping was her education; she picked up the inside scoop on the street. "Besides," Julia wrote to her father, "it is heart-rending not to go to the markets, those lovely, intimate, delicious, mouth-watering, friendly fascinating places. How can one know the guts of the city if one doesn't do one's marketing?"

The market on the rue de Bourgogne was her neighborhood haunt, but for a change of scenery Julia often walked up the boulevard Saint-Germain to the market in rue de Buci, or on Wednesdays and Saturdays crossed the Champs de Mars in front of the Eiffel Tower to the sprawling outdoor market off the Pont de l'Alma.

Food—"gorgeous food!" It was slowly taking over her life—where to get it, what to do with it, how to enjoy it. What a strange, tantalizing development this was turning into for Julia. She waxed rhapsodic about the extraordinary flavors she tasted: "tender escargots bobbing in garlicky butter," the air-cured sausages doused in strong red wine, ripe, runny Brie, chicken from Bresse, the capital of chickendom, "great big juicy pears," and grapes so sweet it was as though she'd never tasted grapes before. Julia devoted her long days alone to learning about new and nutritious produce, collecting bags full of goodies in her tour of the shops, then hitting the kitchen with her haul and beginning to experiment. With Paul tied up at the USIS office, she had plenty of time to test some of the recipes in Ali-Bab.

She attempted quenelles ("The smallest may be the size of a rooster kidney," Ali-Bab advised) and, of course, sole, sole, sole, struggled with calf's brains, made duck *à l'orange,* a saddle of rabbit with mustard, braised leg of lamb, *pommes* Anna, sautéed cauliflower, not to mention desserts galore—crème anglaise, crêpes, chocolate cake, and soufflés.

Cooking! A once-calamitous process started to grow on Julia. She loved making breakfast for Paul, fried eggs and fluffy omelets, but lunch gave her another excuse to spar with the redoubtable Ali-Bab. Some yeasty talent was brewing in the kitchen at Roo de Loo. Julia wasn't self-assured or spontaneous by any stretch of the imagination, but enough of her experiments turned out favorably to inspire those feelings. It inspired other feelings, too—her food served as an aphrodisiac. Before long, Paul started coming home for lunch—"followed by a brief nap," Julia always added with a saucy wink.

Food and love had become one rapturous province. Julia's marriage, to say nothing of her life, had blossomed and bloomed. In less than two years, all the stars in her galaxy had managed to align: first with Paul, then Paris, and now food sparkled with promise. It was an unprecedented turn-around to a once-shapeless, wayward life, and Julia was understandably ecstatic. She adored Paris for its "sweet naturalness and healthy pleasures of the flesh and spirit." And she adored her husband, whose affection for her abounded. "I love that woman," he gushed triumphantly in a December 1948 letter to his brother, enumerating Julia's many virtues, including her tendencies for "only pleasure and growing satisfaction, never once a harsh word, or a bitterness, or a sense of disappointment."

Their attachment to each other was enormous—and intense. They loved each other's company, cherished those occasions when they explored a new neighborhood, discovered a new café, tasted a new dish or made new friends. Neither had ever experienced a friendship so complete, or so fulfilling. Everything they undertook or encountered became a shared experience, even Paul's work, which was fraught with difficulties.

The USIS was a bureaucratic quagmire, and Paul a man up to his eye-balls in the morass. His office was understaffed, "a shambles . . . riven with petty jealousies," the assignments too demanding, his budget woefully insufficient. He was overworked, he complained, and seriously under-paid. And he bemoaned the tangle of official red tape that ensnarled every request, forcing him to go through "the channels, the *channels.*" The deplorable conditions irked Paul no end, and he decried them without letup for being "ridiculous, naïve, stupid, and incredible!" He regularly vented his frustration to Julia, but also to those whose jobs intersected with his office, a habit that didn't endear him to the team players. "Paul did not fare well with the career service boys," says an American col-league who knew him well in Ceylon and France. For one thing, "he was didactic," thorough, often perceived as condescending, and somewhat of a loner, steering clear of office interplay. "He was an unusual guy, a per-fectionist, too much of an individual to fit in," according to the colleague. Things had to be done the right way, *his way,* or else he'd take things into his own hands, always "covering for others," dissatisfied that nobody appreciated him. "He was too temperamental, definitely not a bureau-crat, and it used to affect him physically and really upset him."

Julia had her hands full keeping Paul's bitterness at a simmer. Despite his loving disposition, he was not an easy man. "He was so contrary, so anti-authoritarian," says his niece, Phila. And "methodical to a fault!" according to his nephew, Jon. Precision and rightness topped Paul's personal list of standards. His was a constant fight against undisciplined co-workers, the dullards and incompetents, and, as such, he had to be soothed, stroked, consoled, constantly reassured. But from the beginning, he responded to Julia's encouragement and love. She had the perfect touch for a man with Paul's prickly temperament, acknowledging his frustrations while exhorting him to persevere. "She was such a positivist, an energetic force of nature," according to Rachel Child. She had a wonderful sense of the mechanics of marriage that dovetailed perfectly with Paul's shortcomings. He'd written to friends that Julia "would bring out the best even in a polecat," an observation that suggests he was speaking from experience.

It couldn't have been easy for Julia, having to remain so positive morning, noon, and night while her husband battled the forces of gloom, real or imagined. Evenings and weekends were set aside so that Paul could decompress. He often spent long hours painting stylized cityscapes, mostly of Parisian rooflines, from an easel at the windows of Roo de Loo, while Julia read or fiddled at the stove. For the most part, they steered clear of embassy functions, choosing instead to dine alone or with their own group of friends. Their social circle was widening exponentially thanks to the efforts of ex-pats and introductions. Earlier in the year, they'd been co-opted into a salon known as *le groupe Focillon,* named in memory of Henri Focillon, a beloved professor and medieval art historian who happened to be the stepfather of Julia's friend Hélène Baltrusaitis. *Le groupe* was an oddball mix of Focillon's students, who drank themselves into a lather and argued over scholarly arcana—"a sociable, intellectually vigorous, and very French circle" that contributed to Julia's expanding enlightenment.

But her real education came at mealtimes. Of all the sights and sensations that abounded in Paris, the bistros and restaurants went straight to her core. They provided a sensory, social, and cultural experience that threw Julia a powerful curve. She had already gleaned some of its finer aspects from Paul, but nothing could have prepared her for the situation she encountered in Paris. The French way of life espoused what was, for Julia, a radical ideology: that a gastronomic experience was essential to eating, or as her future sidekick Simone Beck aptly put it, "a major

occupation and pleasure." Months after Julia arrived in Paris, this phenomenon continued to captivate her. "The important thing here," she
wrote, "is that food is a national sport, indulged in by all classes. One's
best evenings are composed of a good dinner, and nothing else is necessary, and it takes the whole evening." The act of dining out in Paris was
like good theater to her: the setting, the dialogue, the presentation, the
performance—pure entertainment. Divine.

The sheer number of restaurants boggled her mind. It seemed as if
there was a dining establishment on every corner, small family places
serving beautifully prepared, classic French dishes: *bœuf bourguignon, veal
blanquette, poule-au-pot, cassoulet, terrines, gratins, fricassées, rôtis, ragoûts* . . . "Good
food was everywhere," Richard Olney noted—and it was cheap, no more
than a couple dollars for a meal, and that *included* wine. Julia was beside
herself! She was determined to "devour Paris whole." She met friends for
lunch or dinner nearly every day, and dined out with Paul every chance
they got.

Such extravagance called for some fancy bookkeeping. Their lifestyle
was tricky on Paul's meager government paycheck. Most of his $95-a-week
salary was already spoken for, owing to rent, clothing, auto maintenance,
and staples. The rest got eaten up by their attachment to the good life.
Both Julia and Paul spent money lavishly. Julia loved clothes, well-made
French clothes, and had her hair done weekly at a Right Bank salon;
Paul's wine cellar rivaled that of any two-star restaurant. They continued to take side trips to Provence, Normandy, and Marseille, staying in
posh hotels and sampling all the best restaurants. Such tastes would have
driven most couples on a fixed budget to financial ruin.

Fortunately, there was a safety valve: Julia's inheritance, which they
dipped into whenever the situation arose, and it usually arose nightly, at
dinnertime, during their deliberation over where to eat. Having lost the
struggle over their budget, they opted to splurge when it came to food.
"The restaurants in Paris were irresistible," Julia recalled. "Each one
was better than the next." A few bucks for such pleasure wasn't going to
bankrupt them.

Their go-to place was Michaud, an old-fashioned neighborhood
restaurant a few blocks from Roo de Loo, which despite its unprepossessing appearance served imaginative French specialties sauced with
puddles of scarce butter and even scarcer cream. "It wasn't fancy," Julia
recalled, "but every dish was cooked well and delicious, absolutely *delicious*." Escargot d'Or became another favorite once Julia developed a taste

for its signature snails. Another was La Truite, where Julia gorged on the "voluptuous" *sole à la normande*; it was the "cozy place" behind the American embassy owned by the same family that ran La Couronne in Rouen. Her datebooks reveal the names of at least a dozen places they esteemed, along with meals that made Julia's eyes bulge and heart swoon: "truly elegant" shellfish *au gratin* at Lapérouse, oysters and desserts at Brasserie Lipp, *poulet gratiné* at Au Gourmet, sandwiches and beer at La Closerie des Lilas, dinners at Marius, Prunier, Pharamond, Pierre, Chez Georges, a riot of restaurants. Every place they ate tapped deeper into their savings and fanned their curiosity for the unique, the refined, the exceptional.

It was this sense of curiosity as much as their consuming passion for food that brought Julia and Paul to the doorstep of one of Paris's most vaunted temples of gastronomy: Le Grand Véfour, in the fluted arcades of the Palais Royal.

Le Grand Véfour launched their dining experience into a stratospheric level. The restaurant, a bulwark of culinary elegance, enjoyed a long legacy tied to its origins, in 1784, as the Café de Chartres, a boisterous watering hole. Its denizens then were a crowd of Jacobins, political radicals who advocated democracy. Later, following a gilt-edged makeover, Napoleon frequented it as a trysting place with Joséphine (supposedly, the kitchen created *la bombe* in the shape of her breast), and even later, after Jean Véfour took it over and rechristened it, writers began turning up—not your run-of-the-mill writers either, but nineteenth-century studs like Victor Hugo, Alexander Dumas, Honoré de Balzac, and Ivan Turgenev, followed by their twentieth-century heirs, Jean-Paul Sartre, André Malraux, and Louis Aragon. Paul and Julia encountered a grizzled Colette in a red-velvet banquette at the end of the dining room and, over the years, craned their necks as luminaries came and went.

But it wasn't celebrity-watching that drew them to Le Grand Véfour. This is where Julia and Paul learned about serious cooking. Until now, they'd dined in places whose menus featured what could best be called *honest* French food—classic dishes that belonged to every restaurant's repertoire, prepared in a refined, albeit straightforward way. Le Grand Véfour was considered a restaurant *gastronomique,* which was French for fine dining raised to the *n*th power. "The food is absolutely wonderful and ... costs a million dollars," Paul recalled, "but you are so hypnotized by everything that you feel grateful as you paid the bill." The presentations arrived tableside like works of art. Pigeon was deboned and stuffed with foie gras and forcemeat, lamb filets came entombed in a savory pastry crust with cranberry beans and dried tomato, turbot was poached in a truffle emulsion, monkfish roasted with zucchini in almond cream. If the *sole meunière* at La Couronne whet Julia's appetite for French food, what she ate at Le Grand Véfour pushed her to worship at its ovens.

But even a meal at Le Grand Véfour failed to slake Julia's greater hunger. As she approached her thirty-seventh birthday, she was feeling increasingly unfulfilled. Homemaking, after all, had never been her calling. She was a big woman with immense enthusiasms who needed an outlet for the energies that tugged and tugged at her. Motherhood might have sufficed. Julia was keen to have children, despite Paul's indifference. His aversion to kids was evident to almost everyone who encountered him. For one thing, he "didn't deal well with children." Gregarious, attentive, and naturally charming in mixed company, he turned "standoffish and gruff" toward kids who invaded his space. They got under his skin. All that neediness! Besides, he couldn't talk to them about issues that concerned him most, issues "of immense importance . . . people, ideas, gen'l semantics," and the like. And at his age, forty-seven, fatherhood seemed even less desirable than his crummy government job. Still, it was clear he and Julia were trying to conceive a child in Paris. Paul revealed as much in a letter to his brother, Charlie. And Julia's hopes were high. In the early spring, she began feeling "quite queer" and concluded: "ah, pregnant at last!" She "was delighted"; raising a child was something she could devote her life to. For "about a month" she allowed herself to contemplate the start of a family until a routine doctor's visit short-circuited the dream. The stomach cramps, it turned out, were nothing but indigestion, the result of overindulgent eating. "I was bilious," Julia recalled. "Too much cream and butter."

The diagnosis dealt her a crushing blow. It seemed to end her desire for having children, or, at least, the expectation that they were in the cards. There were no more queer feelings or false alarms during the following months in Paris—or ever again, for that matter—and evidence suggests that she and Paul began taking greater precautions when it came to contraception. Somewhere in the interim the decision had been made that their lives were just fine without putting children in the picture. Deliberate or not, Julia realized that Paul's so-called willingness to start a family was fraught with misgiving, and she abandoned her maternal yearning rather than jeopardize her relationship. "I would have been the complete mother," Julia lamented in a magazine article years later, but a vital marriage would have to sustain her for now.

Still, as spring lapsed into summer in 1949, Julia continued to search for her groove. Her conversations with Paul always boiled down to the same nagging issue: "How was she going to keep busy while he was working?" They weren't in any kind of conflict about it; both wanted something meaningful for Julia, something that gave purpose to her life. As before, she remained firmly opposed to taking an office job. That was for the politic and the tentative—and Julia was neither. The solution had to come from some deep-felt passion, they concluded. But—what? She was at an impasse again.

At the end of July, Julia's situation took an odd turn when she enrolled in a hat-making course at a boutique on the Right Bank. It was a strange pursuit for a woman with Julia's hearty interests. By her calculation, she only owned "the same two hats" since 1942 and "rarely" wore either of them. Why, then, devote her time to such a stodgy routine? Perhaps it had sprung from her summer at Lopaus Point, when she and Rachel Child made funny hats from detritus they'd salvaged on the beach. Or perhaps she'd grown desperate—desperate to get out of the house, desperate for something to fill the empty hours. In either case, the class, as a career path, was a complete waste of time. After a few lessons, Julia still felt indifferent toward hats in general and realized she "never was any good at all at making clothes." Three hats she designed were actually presentable enough to wear, but they "always looked as though I had made them," she recalled. The overall verdict, in a nutshell: "awful, awful."

What a misfire. There had to be something more gratifying in store for her. Again, she and Paul put their heads together, hoping to come up with a solution. "You *do* like to eat, Julia," he reminded her periodically— certainly an understatement considering the ten-month binge she'd embarked on in Paris. All joking aside, he had raised a new idea: that Julia should devote herself entirely to food.

But could an inexperienced cook—an American, no less—do something on a professional basis with French food? In Paris, of all places? Less controversial conceits had touched off international crises. "I wasn't sure that it would lead to a career," Julia recalled, "but I knew I wanted to learn how to cook. *French* food—a perfect place to start." Paul encouraged her to explore the possibilities, and Julia approved. She couldn't wait to get started. She'd already begun cooking in the French manner, respecting local ingredients and timeless recipes. Thanks to several friends, she had mastered a few mouthwatering dishes, like veal *blanquette* and *navarin printanier,* embracing the spirit of *la cuisine bourgeoise.* At the stove, she was learning to express herself in an entirely new way. "I had no qualifications," she admitted when asked about it later. "I wasn't really turned on by anything until I discovered cooking. And then I realized, 'This is what you've been waiting for all these years—you're obviously not going to be a great woman novelist.' It was just something that suited me, that I became absolutely interested in."

During a visit to England earlier that spring, Julia had cooked a dinner with her friend Mari Bicknell. "If you really want to learn how to cook," Julia remembers her saying, "you should consider taking classes at Le Cordon Bleu." Mari had graduated from their diploma course and dazzled Julia with her poise and technique. Paul had been given the same advice by the librarian at the USIS. Le Cordon Bleu, it seemed, was the only school where professional chefs taught traditional French cooking in a serious, hands-on atmosphere.

Julia hardly needed any further encouragement. She made a beeline for the school and signed up for its intensive six-week course, a soup-to-nuts affair, beginning in early October. Finally, Julia could focus her prodigious energy on cooking. Almost simultaneously, the aftermath of war began shifting patterns in the kitchen, whereby home-cooked meals depended more on modern convenience than on practical know-how. It would prove a fateful coincidence. As odd as it seems, Julia didn't try to bridge the two extremes. She didn't have to. They conformed to her.

Julia's 7:00 a.m. cooking class, with GIs at Le Cordon Bleu, Paris, 1950

Ten

Lady Sings the Bleus

The school itself was ridiculously hard to find. An oblivious student might walk right past the near-invisible sign identifying the "École de Cuisine," located in a mouse-gray Renaissance-style building on an unremarkable corner of rue du Faubourg Saint-Honoré. As Julia pushed through its weather-stripped doors for the first time, the atmosphere inside was no more reassuring. The four cramped street-level classrooms suffered from hard wear; the two kitchens, located belowground in the basement, lacked the modern appliances found in most cooking schools. There were no mixers or meat thermometers or mandolines or *chinois,* none of the new electric blenders that were all the rage, only a miscellany of "ancient, almost non-existent equipment." In the words of one student who attended, "the rooms swarmed with confusion."

This was the vaunted Cordon Bleu, if not the most respected cooking school in the world, certainly the most famous.

Julia began classes there on October 6, 1949. Turning up bleary-eyed and fighting a nasty head cold for a 9:00 a.m. tutorial, she assembled around a badly scarred wooden table in one of the tortured classrooms along with her fellow students—two young women, one English, the other French—neither of whom had the wherewithal to brew a pot of tea. As the class progressed, it dawned on Julia that the demonstrations were geared toward the clueless. *This is the way to peel a clove of garlic.* Or: *We will now hard-boil eggs.* Of all things, she realized, I've landed in a *housewife* course!

Her heart sank; it wasn't at all what she had in mind. After two days entertaining such drivel, she'd had enough. She decided to put in for a transfer to a more "rigorous" program, which required the consent of the school's autocratic director, Madame Élisabeth Brassart. Waiting outside the office in order to make her case, Julia got a preview of the muddle that lay ahead. She watched the willful chaos, the frantic back-and-forth, the to-and-fro, the "nonstop door opening and slamming" in the narrow one-lane hallway, reminding her of "a madcap bedroom farce."

Marthe Distel had never envisioned it that way when, in 1896, she and pastry chef Henri-Paul Pellaprat expanded the magazine they founded, *La Cuisinière Cordon Bleu,* into a cooking school for (mostly) high-society housewives. Rejecting the age-old tradition of *cuisine de grand-mère,* which held that women learned to cook from family elders, they set out to establish a structured, instructional environment based on the French *académie* system that stressed classic skills taught by professional chefs. Relying on a built-in clientele of nearly twenty thousand subscribers, the school prospered mightily and by the early twentieth century carved a preeminent niche in the world of culinary arts. Young boys who were serious about cooking careers still apprenticed themselves at age twelve to master chefs, who imparted their wisdom in exchange for extreme donkeywork; they wouldn't be caught dead inside Le Cordon Bleu. But women, who were barred from professional French kitchens, took refuge in the school's studio classrooms, where they mastered the skills denied to them by dint of sex. Utilizing the refined recipes inspired by Escoffier, they "bridged the divide between the *haute cuisine* of male chefs, generally restaurant-based, and the *cuisine ménagère* of the devoted female cooks who managed middle- and upper-class households." Unbeknownst to anyone but its graduates, Le Cordon Bleu had staged a quiet revolution in the halls of French cuisine.

But by 1942, forty-seven years after its founding, the school lay buried in financial shambles. The combination of Marthe Distel's death, in 1934, and her will, bequeathing everything to a charity for orphans, precipitated its downward slide to near-extinction. It took a mercenary like Élisabeth Brassart to nurse Le Cordon Bleu back to its feet. A finely wrought Belgian, impeccably turned out, with a rigid, thin-lipped smile and the disposition of a rattlesnake, she staged a scorched-earth assault on the school's runaway budget, hired three world-class teaching chefs, and instituted an in-depth course leading to the Grand Diplôme that guaranteed, she said, "a place of honor in the very best kitchens."

That's exactly what Julia was after—training that would bring her some acclaim at the stove, not a cream-puff class for dilettantes. Madame Brassart wasn't so sure. For one thing, she explained, Julia had little or no experience with elegant French food preparation, and for another, Madame disliked Americans, Julia included. So the *haute cuisine* course was out of the question. Besides, it was a six-week immersion for proficient cooks and Julia had signed up for a yearlong commitment. Madame gave her a look of sincere displeasure. *Americans—zut alors!* There was another option, she relented, one that Julia could likely pursue—a course for professional restaurateurs that had begun just that week. It was the best she could offer; it was either that or the housewife course. Madame Brassart was used to strong-arming her students, but it was hard to intimidate this six-foot-three American with the determination of a bulldog. Julia hesitated, considering her options. As a sweetener, Madame mentioned that the class instructor was none other than the school's star teaching chef, Max Bugnard. That sealed the deal. Julia jumped at the opportunity.

Madame failed to mention that the course began just after sun-up and was a repository for American GIs. The next morning, when Julia bounded into class, she was met by the stares of eleven hulking veterans in aprons and white caps. *Who was this intruder—this woman!—in their midst? And how did she expect them to make room for her?* It was obvious from the heavy vibe that she'd infiltrated a boys' club of sorts. They were a ragtag outfit, "very GI indeed," she thought, "quite like genre movie types." You had your army mess cooks, your butchers, your hot-dog vendors, your bakers. "Nice guys, and tough, and simple." There wasn't a gastronome in the bunch, that much was clear. They'd cooked the kind of food best called grub and only sought to build on that turf. Say all you want about *bœuf bourguignon*; to them beef stew was still going to be beef stew. Julia was not deterred. She'd spent a year and a half in Southeast Asia with just such a crew. She knew how to handle herself in mixed company—company mixed with a little grit. This wasn't exactly what she'd had in mind either, but she could live with it.

The chef, to his credit, made it work. Max Bugnard was "a darling," Julia thought, a sprightly little man in his mid-seventies with a dignified manner and a countenance to match. He had some meat on him, more roly-poly than plump, with bushy eyebrows, a wiry tobacco-stained mustache, and round horn-rimmed glasses that made him look rather scholarly. A gentleman and a gentle man, he was a natural teacher who had been around the butcher block. He had sixty-five years of cooking under his belt, working in small family restaurants, bistros, the galleys of steamships, even in London's Carlton Hotel, at the elbow of the great Escoffier himself. There wasn't a French recipe that Max Bugnard hadn't cooked with panache, and Julia came to think of him as her "guiding spirit."

In class, he would sweep through the kitchen in his chef's whites, pausing long enough to see that everyone had the ingredients before launching into several demonstrations all at once. He just fired away in his "rat-a-tat delivery," expecting everyone to keep up, "giving the proportions and ingredients, and explaining everything he [did], and making little remarks." So many of the basics to be learned, so many techniques mastered. Chef Bugnard didn't believe in gradual immersion. Right off the bat, he taught proper chopping skills before launching headfirst into master recipes. Students were expected to give all vegetables the classic seven-sided cut, making sure each was the same bullet size, perfectly peeled, perfectly shaped. *Sauces!* He ran through the entire *bourgeoise* repertoire, beginning with the fundamental elements of sauce bases—the brown sauces and *veloutés*—and right up the gamut: demi-glace, soubise, madère, Mornay, béchamel, rémoulade, bordelaise, hollandaise, béarnaise, all the -aises. *Custards!* Crème anglaise, crème caramel, buttercream, pots de crème. Julia's head swam. The course, it turned out, was rigorous and challenging. There were so many ingredients and ways to combine them! She found it "a bit confusing," especially that first week, with everyone clamoring for Chef Bugnard's attention, working, fumbling, firing questions *all at once.* "It's a free-for-all," she realized, fighting to be heard above the men while madly scribbling notes, trying to get it all down.

Being the only woman, she was careful not to come on too strong. She could tell that the others were not as committed. They worked hard, but clearly their goals were decidedly different from Julia's. "All have ideas of setting up golf driving ranges with restaurants attached, or road houses," Julia concluded. Their objective was to spruce up their cooking skills, to turn the grub into comfort food, whereas she aspired to master French *haute cuisine.* So a delicate balance had to be struck. She couldn't seem too ambitious, too possessive of Chef Bugnard's attention. "I am being careful to sit back a bit," she explained in a letter to her sister-in-law. She resolved to be "cold-blooded and realistic, but retain appearances of sweetness and gentility."

Julia loved Max Bugnard's classes. They held out the promise that one didn't have to be French to prepare classic French food. From what

she could tell, it was all about technique—understanding "the fundamental principles that underlie each and every recipe" and learning how to
execute them with proficiency and style. Everything depended on practice, practice, practice, executing recipes the "right way," over and over
again, and Julia was more than willing to put in the effort. The real work
was done outside the Cordon Bleu kitchen. The minute class was over,
at 9:30 a.m., she made a beeline for the market, scooping up the identical ingredients they'd worked on in class, before heading back to Roo de
Loo to duplicate a dish. She recalled how "after that demonstration of
Boeuf B. [as she called *bœuf bourguignon*], I came home and made the most
delicious one I ever ett." Every part of the recipe had to be broken down
into its basic ingredients and then reconstructed—from the fat content
in the beef to the type of red wine incorporated in the sauce. Tasting
as she went along was essential in order to "thoroughly analyze texture
and flavor." She worked all morning practicing what she learned until
her handiwork began to resemble the example from class. Almost immediately, she saw progress in the results. "I have noticed the most TRE-
MENDOUS differences already in my cooking," she noted. And Paul
agreed. "Julie's cookery is actually improving!" he informed his brother.
"I didn't believe it would, just between us girls, but it really *is*."

Julia's afternoons sent her flying back to the Cordon Bleu in time
for the demonstration classes that lasted until almost dark. In a small,
airless amphitheater on the first floor, the class had the air of "a teaching hospital," with an audience of thirty "interns" seated in rising
rows of chairs, taking furious notes while a rotating cast of local chefs
worked tirelessly under lights on the kitchen stage. Ten hours a week
were devoted to watching the demos, which were informal in the sense
that students were able to interrupt with questions, although they were
anything but relaxed. Cooking dishes in real time—that is to say, without anything being prepared in advance or precooked, as all television
chefs do today—the teachers fixed entire meals, emphasizing timing and
rhythm as well as ingredients and basic technique. Like a neat-fingered
juggler, the chef would have five or six dishes going all at once. One of
the first demos Julia monitored was a culinary three-ring circus, featuring a woodcock roasted with winter vegetables; rouget *en lorgnette* (which
entailed cutting out the backbones of tiny red mullet, rolling them up,
and deep-frying); glazed carrots; hand-churned chocolate ice cream; a
thick, spongy ganache to spread between layers of cake; and buttercream
icing as rich and dense as porridge. Julia's eyes darted everywhere at once,

trying to take it all in—and get it all down. She worked furiously, with almost desperate energy, so as not to miss a word. Her earliest notebooks are filled with barely legible scrawling, entire recipes and explanations jotted cryptically in a personalized shorthand.

As inscrutable as these demos must have seemed to Julia, she delighted in them. They were like great theater: dramatic, comprising several suspenseful acts, and a climax, always a surprise ending. She sat on the edge of her seat one afternoon early in October, as Pierre Mangelatte, a young almond-eyed chef from Restaurant des Artistes, raced through a menu that featured a lighter-than-air cheese soufflé, galantine of chicken breast, spinach *à la crème,* and charlotte *aux pommes. Whew!* It was so much to absorb in one sitting. Still, it was inspiring, watching it all come together with such finesse. "These are the best parts of the course, to my mind," Julia determined.

The master's touch was pure magic, but Julia just had to try these recipes herself, while everything was still fresh in her mind. As soon as the last course was presented, she bolted from class to test her powers of recall, fighting crosstown traffic before her favorite market closed. Demos became dinners at "La Maison Schildt," as Paul called their kitchen, using the French corruption of their name. Julia worked for hours from her notes, trying to re-create the dishes from that day's class in order that she could serve them, note perfect, later the same evening. Paul would waltz in from work just after eight to find his wife hunched over a grease-splattered cutting board, up to her elbows in exotic food scraps. It was a sight to behold, considering his wife's maiden plunge into *haute cuisine.* "All sorts of *délices* are spouting out of her finger-ends like sparks out of a pinwheel," Paul declared, unable to contain his delight. After just her first week at school, he shared his enthusiasm with the folks back home. "If you could see Julie stuffing pepper and lard up the asshole of a dead pigeon, you'd realize how profoundly affected she's been already by the Cordon Bleu," he quipped. Only a few weeks later, his admiration snowballed: "It's a wonderful sight to see her pulling all the guts out of a chicken through a tiny hole in its neck and then, from the same little orifice, loosening the skin from the flesh in order to put in an array of leopard-spots made of truffles. Or to watch her remove all the bones from a goose without tearing the skin. And, you ought to see that Old Girl skin a wild hare—you'd swear she's just been Comin' Round the Mountain With Her Bowie-Knife in Hand."

It wasn't just the prep work that impressed Paul. It was Julia's demeanor in the kitchen, her newly acquired body language, how she approached her cooking "with an air of authority and confidence." She was "pushing her cooking hard," he noted, as he scored her output from the first six weeks of school. In that time alone, he figured, she had turned out a fantastic array of dishes, including rabbit terrine, quiche Lorraine, spinach gnocchi, scallops in white wine sauce, *vol-au-vent,* Alsatian-style choucroute, seafood risotto, rouget in a saffron sauce, chicken Marengo, duck *à l'orange,* stuffed turbot braised in champagne, and a brochette of feathery-light pike quenelles laced with cream, a "delicate triumph of French cooking" that took Julia days, if not weeks, to perfect, but "which ends up on a plate as a sort of white, suspiciously suggestive thing disguised by a yellowish sauce for which, if you saw it on the rug, you'd promptly spank the cat." Not much to look at, even downright ugly, perhaps—but *so* delicious that Paul gobbled it up, followed by murmurs of ecstasy.

Julia was learning "how to feel her way through a recipe," which took skill developed over time, lots of time, and was ultimately the mark of a real cook. That goal seemed insurmountable at times, when everything overwhelmed her. There was so much to learn, so much to practice. Six weeks at Le Cordon Bleu, she lamented, was "nothing, nothing at all. I feel I am just beginning to be a cook." It exasperated her that it might take "two years of training and [another] three years of working" at a first-class restaurant until "you might have something. [Along with] cooking, cooking, cooking all the time at home." After seven weeks at Le Cordon Bleu, she realized "I may just have my foot in the door." But only a month later, an arm and a hip squeezed through. "It's beginning to take effect," she wrote her family. "I feel it in my hands, my stomach, my soul."

The mysteries of French cuisine were starting to make sense, bit by bit, but cooking was still a slippery slope for Julia. Occasionally, feeling overconfident, a misfire occurred. One afternoon her friend Winnie Riley came to lunch, and Julia "served her up the most VILE eggs Florentine I have ever imagined." It was as if she had forgotten everything that she'd learned at Le Cordon Bleu. Measuring? Who needed to measure ingredients, especially the flour when making a sauce Mornay? Julia just improvised, beating in the grated gruyère, until the *béchamel* congealed into a thick, gluey mess. And ingredients? Weren't most ingredients interchangeable, after all? That was her rationale when she couldn't find spinach at the market and substituted chicory, which was too tough and refused to wilt in time to complement the eggs. Julia stared at the plates she was about to serve and thought, "God, they were awful." The dish looked horrid—beyond a disaster.

Julia was mortified. She had to serve it as it was; there wasn't time to start anew. She was wretched with defeat, but why should her guest have to suffer for that? She'd be damned if she'd call attention to the disaster and ruin the social aspect of the lunch, as well. "So I carefully didn't say a word, while she painfully ate it," Julia recalled.

One can only imagine the women trying to make conversation while struggling to get that nasty glop down their throats. If it was inedible, neither let on. They cleaned their plates, without a word about the food. No excuses were made, no apologies offered, which, for Julia, became a lifelong doctrine. *Never apologize!* "I don't believe in these women who are always apologizing for their food," she explained. "If it is vile, the cook must just grin and bear it."

No apologies were made for her fixture fetish, as well. Julia loved cooking utensils almost as much as she loved the cooking, and she spared no expense when it came to stocking her cozy kitchen. "Why, the place is practically an alchemist's eyrie," Paul marveled. In her ramblings around Paris with Chef Bugnard, Julia had stumbled on two favorite haunts whose aisles were to French kitchens what Home Depot is to fixer-uppers. Le Bazar de l'Hôtel de Ville, or BHV (*bay-ahsh-vay*), across from city hall in the Marais, was an enormous department store where Julia literally bought carloads upon carloads of the bare essentials: frying pans, casseroles, pails, dishpans, a broom, and anything else she could stuff into the Blue Flash. BHV seemed to have all an aspiring cook needed—that is, until Bugnard took the class to Dehillerin, in Les Halles. Julia took one look at the wall-to-wall shelves bulging with shiny restaurant-quality merchandise and got the hot flush a gambler feels entering a Las Vegas casino. She'd hit the jackpot—"THE KITCHEN EQUIPMENT STORE of all time," she gasped, a cavernous place "stuffed with mouthwatering things" that were catnip to a gadget junkie like Julia Child. Chef Bugnard did her no favor by introducing her to the owner. In the weeks and months that followed Julia returned there again and again, relying on M. Dehillerin's savvy to explain the absolute need for each implement, until the shelves of Roo de Loo resembled a Dehillerin annex.

"Our poor little kitchen is bursting at the seams," Paul observed, citing the gridlock forming in their upstairs *cuisine. Where did all this cooking stuff come from?* Horrified, he inventoried the "pots, pans, vessels, sieves, measuring rods, scales, thermometers, mortars, timing-clocks, choppers, grinders, knives, openers, pestles, spoons, ladles, jars, skewers, forks, bottles, boxes, bags, weights, needles, graters, strings, rolling-pins, mullers, frying pans, double boilers, single boilers, marble slabs and fancy extrusion-dies" weighting down the plywood shelves. And it didn't end there. *My God!* "She's got special whips for sauces, long needles for larding roasts, a deep copper bowl for beating eggs, a *pèse-sirop,** a *chinois,* three little frying pans used only for crêpes, a copper sugar-boiler, stirring paddles made of Maplewood, tart-rings, and a whole gamut of flat long-handled copper pot lids."

The counters, which extended out from either side of the stove, looked like the lab of a mad scientist. "On one side there are seven Ali Baba oil-jars full of basic reductions, standing in a row like seven fat soldiers," Paul noted. "On the other, hanging from hooks, are pewter liter-measures, demi-liters, quart-de-liters, deciliters and demi-deciliters, [as well as] innumerable scrapers, choppers, cutter-uppers, rockers, crushers, and enough knives for a pirate boarding-gang." He couldn't even fathom the types of vessels on exhibit—copper vessels, iron vessels, stainless-steel vessels, aluminum vessels, glass vessels, terra-cotta vessels, tin vessels, enamel vessels, crockery vessels, and porcelain vessels "forced, jammed, and pushed" into niches that he never even knew existed.

A sterner husband might have enrolled her in Gadgeteers Anonymous, but Paul, if anything, was an enabler, not a regulator. He was tickled by Julia's cannonball into the deep end of cookery and eager to help her stay happily afloat. Watching her jackknife about at the stove was a meal in itself. Paul was mesmerized and aroused by the way his wife took the controls, turning out feast after feast with the touch of a virtuoso. It amazed him how she moved with assurance and grace, how "the oven door opens and shuts so fast you hardly notice the deft thrust of a spoon as she dips into a casserole and up to her mouth for a taste-check." His descriptions of Julia in a series of letters to his family are filled with admiration and wonder. And yet, as she dived deeper into the process, she never lost the wonderful wicked spirit that first enchanted him in Ceylon. It cropped up and charmed him at the damnedest moments. For instance, one night, while Julia prepared pasta for a dinner party of friends, she snatched a bit of cannelloni out of a pot of boiling water, and cried: "Wow! These damn things are as hot as a stiff cock!" Paul hooted at the outburst. He loved

---

* A hydrometer that measures the density of sugar, used in making sorbet and preserves.

her sense of ribaldry, loved the way she held nothing back, called it the way she saw it. The Old Girl was something else!

It appeared that the Old Girl was finally happy, *really* happy doing something she loved. If the definition of happiness is being fully engaged in something that one is good at, up until this point she'd been only sporadically engaged. Sure, Julia did things that she enjoyed, kept her busy, but she wasn't testing her abilities in any way. Cooking gave her structure, it was substantive, meaningful, it brought her accomplishment and independence, everything she'd long desired. The last thing she'd wanted was a conventional life. Julia dreaded turning into the obedient little woman. She had seen that happen to so many of her friends. Smart and sophisticated, they disappeared after college into the shadows of traditional home life, expected to cook, clean, and raise families, ceding the more challenging work to their well-paid husbands. For women, at that time, there weren't that many opportunities to fully engage. But cooking, for Julia, was engagement enough. Far from resenting the kitchen to which she was virtually chained, she learned to love the feel of food and to love working with it: "the variety of dishes and sauces and arrangements," she said, "are immensely stimulating for the imagination."

For those first few months, Julia was content. She went every day to Le Cordon Bleu's morning and afternoon sessions, returning to Roo de Loo to practice what she'd learned. "Am still spending most of my life in the kitchen," she admitted, in a letter to Freddie Child toward the end of 1949, "just can't stay away from it." It seemed the more she learned of practical technique, the more theory she wanted to know. Cooking, she determined, was more than simple mechanics; there was technology and science—chemistry—involved. It wasn't enough to just walk through a recipe without understanding how ingredients integrated and combined. That meant first understanding the characteristics of each ingredient—where they came from, what they were made of, how they responded to heat. In her spare time Julia studied the classic recipes from class, turning them inside out, in an attempt to understand how all the elements combined.

Mayonnaise eluded her for the longest time. Oh, she could make the stuff, great tubs of it, "in a flash, no trouble, perfect brew every time." The process was simple: all you had to do was beat salad oil into egg yolks until they creamed and thickened, forming an emulsion. A little salt, a dash of vinegar: *voîlà!*—instant mayonnaise. One day she even timed herself, whipping up half a creamy pint in seven minutes flat. But when the weather changed, her mojo changed with it, turning her mayo into a thin rheumy mess. *What gives?* she wondered, throwing out batch after batch. In her notebooks, Julia jotted down the details of her failed experiments, struggling furiously to forestall the accidents that ensued. But even as she seemed to solve part of a problem, others materialized, in which the ingredients produced a different consistency, another variable, or transformed mayonnaise into something else entirely. This confounded her; she refused to give in to the vagaries of chance—or, worse, to fall back on a bottle of Hellman's. So she began experimenting, "making vast inquiries and researches" in an attempt to understand the impact that the elements—things like temperature, moisture, solubility, texture, energy, and time—have on cooking.

"Must be the cold that had the bad effect," she presumed, "or the egg yolks. Perhaps the hard beating of the yolks 'cooks' them just a bit." Or maybe not—she wasn't at all sure.

Thus began Julia's involvement with the alchemy of cuisine, understanding everything that went into making a dish, the chemistry, the physics, the theory that allowed her to turn matter into food. She wanted to do more than simply follow a recipe as written, prep-by-prep, step-by-step—but to understand it inside out, to deconstruct the building blocks of cuisine, so that she could not only cook food, but *master* it. Mayonnaise didn't emerge from beating oil into egg yolks. There were physical properties involved: "Everything must be room temp," she concluded after much trial and error, "including the bowl," as well as the oil, the eggs, and the workspace. And tools: never any kind of beater—*heaven forbid!*—but a wire whip, a whisk, which enabled you to "moderate the pace and control the action." And proportions: the quantity of oil in relation to egg yolk. A formula of four parts oil to one part egg seemed ideal for the egg to act as a binding element. And catalysis (yes, *catalysis!*): the process by which a pinch of salt and a half teaspoon of vinegar are added to break down the yolk so it can absorb the oil and eventually emulsify.

Over and over, she continued to test, tweaking her master recipe to reflect each new discovery she made. "I made so much mayonnaise," she recalled, "that Paul and I could hardly bear to eat it anymore, and I took to dumping my test batches down the toilet."

Understanding mayonnaise, Julia discovered, took more than simple know-how, but once she grasped the process she felt she had "licked it" once and for all. Would all French cooking require a degree in molecular structure from MIT? she wondered. From her trials and errors, Julia worried that might well be the case. She "became a bit of a Mad Scientist," sitting for hours analyzing ingredients and their properties, playing with them as if somehow she could get inside them or spin them into gold. Recipes were complex, mysterious. They presented too many possibilities and raised the chance of accident that hovered over every meal she made.

And yet, sometimes, to paraphrase Freud, a veal roast was just a veal roast. Julia had made this revelation during a class with Chef Bugnard. Her approach to the dish had been fraught with complications, detail piled on detail, a veritable excess of veal. "I used to marinate it in 200 herbs," she acknowledged, stung by her naïveté. "Now, I put on salt and pepper, wrap it in a salt pork blanket, put sliced carrots and onions in the pan, a tablespoon of butter on top and let her go, basting." Such things were "awfully easy when the tricks are known."

When it came to French cooking, she needed to strike the right balance: to incorporate precise technique with instinct in order to simplify the process. Practice was essential, she knew that without question, but poise and assurance—*confidence*—was key. In just a few months, Julia had converted a semester's worth of lessons into a cascade of recipes. But as far as confidence went, she still had a long way to go.

Even outside of the kitchen, Julia's confidence remained frayed. She still felt cowed by the long intellectual shadow Paul cast, unsure of herself, socially inept. No matter how outgoing and personable she seemed, Julia was never entirely comfortable in the company of guests they entertained at home. And the Childs entertained like it was going out of style. A celebrated cast of visitors paraded through Roo de Loo in the months leading up to 1950. Paul's position at USIS brought him into contact with all sorts of visiting dignitaries, most of whom got an invitation to dinner *chez* Child. Julia prepared meals for America's greatest minds—politicians, sociologists, authors, journalists, philosophers, ambassadors, art historians, professors, cabinet members, friends, friends of friends, perfect strangers, *tout le monde*. Hardly a night passed that failed to require an elaborate dinner party. And the conversation, to Julia's ears, was always lively, always brilliant, though just out of her orbit. It never failed: strong opinions flew around her table, heated exchanges on the Marshall Plan, the global economy, the welfare state, and British socialism—subjects on which she felt inadequately informed.

"I am no good at verbalizing," she fretted, after one such get-together in late November. Her friends Winnie and Ed Riley had come over for drinks before heading to La Grille, the Childs' restaurant-of-the-moment, in Les Halles. For months, Julia eagerly sought out the Rileys, whose company she preferred among the community of ex-pats. Ed, especially, was a favorite companion. He had an unflagging, reflective brilliance, "the ideal U.S. biz type," according to Julia, "plus, so handsome and rugged," her essential criteria. The evening unspooled leisurely, with updates of gossip traded back and forth, but as soon as the conversation turned informed and serious, Julia foundered. She felt exposed, owing to what she mistook as a "confused mind." The issues of the day affected her strongly, but every time she waded into the discussion, it seemed she "managed to get [her] foot in [her] backside." She became flustered, "defensive about [her] positions," after which everything seemed to come undone—her grasp of facts, her coordination, and especially her emotions. Julia's fatal flaw was that she became too excitable. Paul had noticed it almost from the day they had met. No one could spot the warning signs more acutely. Her breath grew heavy, she batted her eyes like a Tiny Tears doll, sentences trailed off in a haze of mumbling, or became garbled and overlapped. It was the same sort of behavior that showed up in the first few episodes of *The French Chef,* fourteen years later.

Entertaining at home was still a performance. No matter how good Julia was becoming at cooking French food, there was another aspect she hadn't yet mastered.

IN THE MEANTIME, Julia received the confidence she needed from the steady progress she made at Le Cordon Bleu. Her second session began on January 4, 1950, putting her back in the basement studio bright and early each morning, with "my group of dopey GI's," as she took to calling them. Julia was impressionable and eager to please, not protesting, as others did, when the same recipes from the first session "began to repeat and repeat" like an interminable mantra. Quiche Lorraine sixteen times, veal *blanquette* twelve, *sole meunière* so often the students lost count. Unlike the others, she found the repetition instructive, disciplinary. "I'm gradually learning how to do things the professional way," she realized, bankrolling the experience for future dividends. It was all very fussy, even painstaking work, but it provided her with the know-how to master the basics of French cuisine: a decent piecrust, a crêpe suzette, a perfect omelet, in addition to sauces. "I am beginning to experience what Paul has always been saying about learning the techniques of the trade," she recognized—"practice, practice, practice." The results were too precious, too delectable to squander.

But by the spring of 1950, frustration had set in. Julia became "increasingly disappointed in that damn poorly managed school." Madame Brassart, a noted skinflint, kept her eye on every *sou* that went out the front door. "She was all-controlling and skimped on ingredients," says a former student, who echoed Julia's chagrin. "We never saw butter, only margarine. And the equipment—*ooh-la-la!*" The soot-stained pots and saucepans, some said, dated from the Pleistocene Era, and the stoves were a throwback to days when electricity was a key on a kite string. "Of the several electric ovens, only a few worked," according to another disgruntled student. "The long stove was dotted with electric burners which had an unnerving tendency to short-circuit and shock."

Julia could deal with the ancient equipment, but the tenor of the class was beginning to wear. The GIs' high jinks no longer seemed cute. They delighted in trying to confuse Max Bugnard with short-order pidgin, like "Voolez-voo two blindfolds on a buttered shingle, chef?" Or calling the white sauce *bécha*smell—for the forty-third time. Besides, they were more eager to bang away on the pinball machines in the bistro next door than to perfect a *financier* or *vol-au-vent.* "If the 'Boys' were more serious, it would be a different matter," Julia conceded, "but even now, after six months, they don't know the proportions for a *béchamel* or how to clean a chicken the French way." It seemed futile for her to keep her spirits up under such conditions. Julia could do it, she could put up a good front. "Being just as cold-blooded and realistic as possible, yet retaining sweetness and humanity" had served her through the intervening months. But the GIs had worn down her defenses, as had the grinding routine—"all this 6:30 a.m. rising and not enough sleep and not having enough resistance" to the germ-infested school.

She discussed quitting Le Cordon Bleu with Max Bugnard, who convinced her to take a leave of absence instead. For as little as a dollar, Julia could still attend the afternoon demonstrations and take brush-up pâtisserie lessons when the situation arose. Chef Bugnard even agreed to make occasional after-hours visits to Julia's kitchen for some private instruction, in exchange for a good meal. In the meantime, she promised to practice, practice, practice, boning up at home in order to prepare for the cooking school's final exam.

Julia had also grown disenchanted with her role as an embassy wife. Having gleaned satisfaction, if not pride, from the effects of her cooking, she resisted any return to her butterfly status. There was nothing wrong with the part of her that enjoyed playing housewife, hurrying home to fix her husband dinner. A strong woman could pull that off without suffering any loss of respect. But helpless or superficial Julia was not, and she bristled at situations that required her—or any woman—to function as window dressing.

At first, the embassy receptions were fun. On most occasions, usually at the ambassador's residence, the wives of bureaucrats were enlisted as ushers in the receiving line. "Husbands met guests at the door and introduced them to Ambassador Bruce," Julia recalled. "Wives then took them off the other end and introduced them around, got them a drink, and then came out and stirred things up." The bigwigs who attended were entertaining, larger than life, and the novelty of it provided a charge. But after a year marked by weekly receptions the thrill, for the Childs, had run its course. The profusion of special events, galas, benefits, and parties began to blur and fatigue. After a while, Julia considered them a wretched nuisance and chafed at the spectacle once inside the door: "Government wives freshly manicured, waved and perfumed, twitching and shaking in their off-shoulder dresses, pulling up front to cover titties, flushed with excitement; men all like crows in black and white." Everyone was limited to one dance with their spouse, then a few mandatory turns with a guest. It was nothing you couldn't square with several bourbon-and-ginger ales, but who needed all that fuss?

They went because they had to; all agency personnel were obliged to attend. Paul's attendance was inescapable, if not compulsory, but would not go toward improving his situation at work. Despite his wonderful facility with all things artistic, Paul's career as a bureaucrat was an unfolding disaster. Strong-willed, opinionated, prickly, and aloof, he was a lone wolf in an agency that valued team players above all. He ate at his desk instead of lunching with co-workers, didn't gossip or socialize "with the right people," after work. He had a highbrow—some thought pretentious—way of expressing himself. And, worse, he struggled with authority, a lifelong headache.

As of early 1950, Paul began reporting to a man named George Picard, who was given effective oversight of the Public Affairs (PA) division. Most PA personnel considered Picard a benign functionary with no personal agenda, either toward art or office politics. Yet, it rankled Paul that such an uncultured man was given sway over a talented creative team, and he was unable to hide the contempt on his face. From the beginning,

their encounters were awkward, undermined by a "certain roughness" in
Paul's manner. "I've been having a series of minor run-ins with Picard
since he became my boss," Paul confided to his brother, worried how it
would reflect on his advancement up the ranks. Paul had good reason to
be concerned; no one had more influence on his position, especially when
it came to salary. For months, Paul had been waiting to hear about a raise
that was tied to his annual efficiency rating. The final decision awaited
Picard's evaluation. "He is not competent to judge anyone's skill in art,"
Paul complained. "If [he] had a personal grudge against someone under
him he could affect his whole career by a few nicely chosen phrases."

As far as can be determined, Picard held no grudge. His report, filed
in mid-December, was an exercise in fairness—although peppered with
a few nicely chosen phrases. In it, he praised Paul, giving him a desirable
Very Good rating, adding that he was extremely competent in the field of
art, but conditions were raised: "Of course, it would be unfair to expect
as much of this employee in the field of Administration," Picard wrote. "I
feel certain that in time he will become more competent, therefore I do
not feel that a salary increase would be indicated at this time."

Paul was stung and dispirited by the tone of his review. "He doesn't
know about my 17 years as a teacher," he fumed, "or my war years with
the OSS." Criticism would have been easier to accept. To stem the bitterness and reinforce his sense of duty, Paul buried himself in several
traveling exhibitions that the USIS was underwriting in the upcoming
spring months. He was particularly proud of a retrospective he curated of
Edward Weston's photographs, followed by a series of poster and photo
contests that received good press. One knockout show in particular,
"U.S. Artists Living in France," kept him exhaustively engaged, selecting juried work from over five hundred candidates. Hanging the show in
Paris was a delicate undertaking, with so many egos in the balance. Plus,
it was a logistical nightmare coordinating the arrangements to launch the
exhibit on a six-city circuit. For that reason, among others, he was forced
to bow out of a social function with Julia that promised to be almost as
forbidding as his work.

In April 1950, John and Phila McWilliams were coming for a month-
long visit.

Despite Julia's deep-rooted love for her father, they had not seen
each other since her wedding two years earlier. During that time, they'd
exchanged regular letters, but nothing substantive, nothing more than
warmed-over pleasantries. Anything stronger might have sparked a

nuclear incident. Pop's "emotions and prejudices" bred incendiary responses. It went without saying that Julia found his right-wing diatribes unconscionable. He'd been a bully ever since she could remember, intolerant and dismissive of anyone whose views ran east or west of his own. Julia knew better than to argue with him. For a while she'd become expert at dodging his recriminations, but since her marriage to Paul she'd had difficulty holding her tongue, especially in light of the recent McCarthy hearings in Washington. Several of the Childs' State Department pals had come under the scrutiny of the man they were calling "that bastard from Wisconsin." It was open season on artists and intellectuals. Already there was a suspicion in the air that the House Committee's wrath might corrode Paul's agency. In all likelihood Julia said as much in her letters to Pop because, for a while, he stopped answering her altogether. But tensions had thawed in the intervening months, and his visit portended a truce of sorts.

In Pasadena, John McWilliams, now seventy, hadn't mellowed so much as he'd ripened with age. Subversives were everywhere, as far as Pop was concerned, even smack in his own backyard. He had no doubt that his intellectual son-in-law, Paul, "was a communist-type." And who knew about his impressionable daughter? But years of bursitis had left John physically weak, "stiff in the joints . . . unable to do much walking," as age caught up to his once-imposing frame. He'd also softened somewhat as a result of his second marriage, with a winning wife for whom family came first. It had been Phila's idea to visit Paris. To John, Paris represented just about everything he detested, art and culture, to say nothing of those infernal French fops. He much preferred to remain in Pasadena. "I've got my nice house and my friends, and I can talk the language," he told Julia. But Phila put her foot down. It wouldn't do for John to be estranged from his daughter—either of his daughters, for that matter.

Dort's crime, in her father's eyes, had been to fall in with the theater crowd, "a high-strung and emotional lot" of "artistic ne'er-do-wells." She'd worked in New York and London with ragtag troupes, producing pitifully little income and even less fulfillment. There were no prospects on the horizon for any kind of fruitful career. Almost thirty-two, Dort had run out of options when Julia invited her to visit in Paris. Julia regretted the physical distance between the sisters. "To be honest, when she arrived I felt as if I knew Hélène Baltrusaitis better than my own flesh and blood."

Once she hit Paris, however, Dort's presence was greatly felt. Julia's little sister had grown in the interim, maxing out at nearly six-foot-six. In fact, she was outsize in every way—animated, garrulous, bohemian, and irrepressible, tending an untamed exuberance that rose and fell in waves. "She was very, *very* mercurial," says her only daughter, "full of life, but with a wicked temper that would go off like *that*!" With her animal energy, Dort threw herself into resolving things with Julia. In late 1949, with only a suitcase under her arm, she moved into the spare bedroom at Roo de Loo, ready to embrace her sister's new world.

Dort fell willingly under the transformative spell of Paris. Within months, she was a fixture on the young ex-pat scene, bounding from party to bistro to nightclub to café, curled behind the wheel of an armadillo-shaped Citroën. She had real magnetism, a great liveliness that made her the life of every party. Although Dort spoke hardly a word of French, the language barrier was no problem for her. She simply twisted the language into her own inscrutable dialect. French never had a chance in her mouth. Shampoo became *champignon* (mushroom), a fender-bender became *craché dans ma derrière* (spat in my butt). And somehow she got away with it—atrocities for which most Americans would be summarily disemboweled. Dort's abandon had a way of disarming the most thin-skinned of Gauls. Even Julia and Paul were amused by her.

By 1950, Dort was working for the American Club Theater, a Parisian outfit whose plays put the *avant* in *avant-garde*. Samuel Beckett might have found their productions impenetrable. It was a thankless job—long tension-filled hours and little pay—but Dort loved every minute of it. Even when the company manager directed skeins of abuse at her, Dort never protested. She loved the theater and forgave it its indiscretions. But, like Julia, Dort couldn't resist the vise grip of her father, and when news surfaced of his imminent visit to France, she traded the theater for the family crucible.

The prospect of entertaining Pop terrified the McWilliams sisters. John and Phila intended to spend a week with them in Paris, then travel through the south of France into Italy, spanning Portofino to Capri, for most of a month. As the momentous day approached, they were "prepared for the worst." Julia, especially, had gone to great lengths to accommodate her visitors, but nothing seemed to measure up to Pop's finicky standards. "I think it is all going to be somewhat of a trial," she fretted, "as we have grown so far apart in our ways of life." She sought to "show him something of the life and the people that [she] found so heart-warming and satisfying," but knew how dicey a prospect that could be. One false move—a stray eye-roll or errant opinion—could light the fuse on a war of words—or worse. Julia had no illusions about reforming her father. The best she could hope for was maintaining the peace. She was determined to do her "damndest to be very, very nice indeed, and dumb, and amenable, and having no thoughts or ideas about *anything.*"

At least Paul was off the hook. He agreed to entertain his in-laws while they were in Paris, but anything more would be asking for trouble. Paul was no one's fool; he knew the score. John McWilliams had nothing but disdain for him. Paul could live with their obvious differences—he could tune out Pop's rants about commies and progressives, lefties and liberals, intellectuals and elitists—but the subtext of his enmity was too much to ignore. "He felt his daughter was supporting Paul," said a granddaughter, and to some extent, that may have been true. Julia's inheritance gave the Childs freedom to enjoy a certain Parisian lifestyle, but Paul thought "it was none of John's damn business."

The old man was just too damn condescending. Behind his fatherly, mackerel smile, John McWilliams had other fish to fry. His daughter, Julia, was in need of long-term security, and that meant making a respectable man out of Paul. Pop made no secret of his disappointment that the marriage would effectively end Julia's chances of a place in society. But perhaps he could rescue her from the depths of failure. Paul needed to step up in some way. Fearing that he didn't have what it took to do it on his own, John offered to buy Paul's successfulness. In a letter to Julia, he wrote "that if Paul needed money to launch himself in the big time, he wanted very much to help out in any way financially possible." Julia turned him down without another thought, but Paul never forgave John for his royal arrogance. He was almost fifty, for god's sake, convincingly his own man. As far as Paul cared, going to Italy was out, Julia wrote, "because he don't want to waist [*sic*] no vacation time"—and she "didn't blame him."

Remarkably, the McWilliams-Child reunion in Paris came off without a hitch. Everyone was on their best behavior, including Pop, who'd kept his mouth shut, though, from where Paul sat "it was hard to tell whether he's just determinedly trying to be nice for this visit, or whether it's a deep-seated change." Julia also noticed restraint in her father's demeanor. As she and Dort set out on their group trip south, she observed: "I suddenly realize[d] he is an old man, which he never used to be—and he seems to realize it himself."

At age seventy, John McWilliams was no longer the bogeyman of

old. Had he lost the propensity to intimidate and terrorize, the need
to stage "wild and bitter scenes," to mete out constant put-downs and
beratings that made his tall daughters shrink in his presence? Julia obviously thought so as they meandered south, on a route that paralleled the
Rhône. She was struck by her father's "niceness and complete naturalness," his attempts to charm the French with a chirpy "Bahn Joor" wherever he went before launching into long exchanges in English "as though
it were inconceivable *they* wouldn't understand." Even *that* she found
charming, in a roundabout way. At least Julia no longer felt humiliated
around Pop. Or perhaps she no longer took his blather to heart. All in all,
she managed to endure his "standard prejudices about 'the harps,' 'the
chosen people,' 'foreigners,' etc. etc. etc." Some things about him would
never change, but Julia let them roll right off her back. Whatever she'd
felt about her father in the past, whatever scars his bullying had left on
her, it came to her, watching him putter aimlessly through France and
Italy, that the world he'd created for himself, his "rich, upper-class conservative Republican" world, was small and sad. It was evident in the
way he viewed the riches of Europe. Pop had little or no regard for the
ancient cities they visited, no interest in their architecture and art, "those
dank cold churches or museums," no enthusiasm at all for the food and
wine, all the forces of culture that made Julia swoon. "We have just about
nothing in common anymore," she wrote to her family, after the trip, "no
reactions, likes, life, anything."

JULIA GAINED A kind of freedom from her past as a result of the trip
with Pop. She freed herself from the lifeline that had always tethered
her, from the stultifying place where children were *always* children, obedient, passive, seen but not heard. She spent the rest of the summer mostly
in splendid isolation, "experimenting at home," combing through her
collection of classic recipes and cooking them repeatedly to perfection,
until she was satisfied they worked. Increasingly, all that mattered to her
were the wonders of French cuisine—the technique, the science, the care,
the magic—"the enjoyment of producing something wonderful to eat."
More than merely fine-tuning the recipes, Julia's goal was to make them
her own, to develop versions whose details and procedures were absolutely clear. She still wasn't sure where all of this was headed, whether
she would eventually cook alongside one of her mentor-chefs or open
that fantasy restaurant with her sister-in-law Freddie, under a sign that

read MRS. CHILD AND MRS. CHILD: FORMERLY OF THE CORDON BLEU, PARIS, FRANCE. For the time being, she was content just to practice her craft. "My immediate plan was to develop enough foolproof recipes so that I could begin to teach classes of my own," she recalled.

At the same time, Julia sank further into her exuberant Paris life, overseeing the new housekeeper she'd hired to manage Roo de Loo and "a great campaign of refurbishment of the tottery furniture" they'd inherited. Like the recipes that occupied her attention, she aspired to make the place her own. "She wanted to brighten up the apartment, to modernize it," recalls her niece Rachel. Down came the heavy brocade drapes and the rococo sconces. Cracks in the ceiling were replastered. The water-stained walls were repainted—beige in the salon, white and sage in the kitchen. She made butter-colored slipcovers for the lumpy old sofa, whose arms were as frayed as a homeless man's coat.

The ongoing life there with Paul filled a hole in Julia's development. Marrying him and moving to Paris had been an act of rebellion, but it helped her enormously to establish an identity all her own. Paul never tried to domineer, to possess her. He never acted like his career was more important than her cooking. With everything going on in their respective circles, they had learned not to crowd each other. Apart from their "two official lives—cooking and government"—Paul and Julia remained committed to a carefully balanced marriage; it was something they pursued with respect and great gusto. Their social calendar—a dizzying cycle of non-stop receptions and dinner parties—was as active as any jet-setter's, yet they always found the time to follow their own intimate routine. Alternate Thursdays were reserved for a Ciné Club they had joined. A long-awaited subscription to the Comédie-Française finally came through. Paul continued to paint street scenes; Julia sewed. They even maintained their Sunday-morning tradition, exploring a section of Paris they'd never visited before.

For all the family visits, entertaining, and other distractions, the kitchen at Roo de Loo remained a hotbed of experimentation throughout the summer and fall of 1950. "I've been making so many meals," Julia observed, "it feels like I've filled half the stomachs in Paris." For Julia, whose cooking closely followed her personal development, the output was a badge of increasing satisfaction: all the efforts of the previous year had begun to find their way onto plates. Finally, in the spring of 1951, feeling the thrust of Paul's encouragement, Max Bugnard's approval, and friends' praise, she decided to take her talents to the next level.

The McWilliams sisters in Paris, 1950

Eleven

What She'd Gotten
Herself Into

With the vast reserves of training and knowledge that Julia had been slowly accumulating in the year since she enrolled at Le Cordon Bleu, her progress was so ferocious that the test kitchen could no longer contain her. Julia wanted validation.

Paul had exhorted her to "go for broke," maintaining that the meals she was making "were equal to anything served in the best Parisian joints." Right after New Year's in 1951, a mammoth *galantine de volaille* that took her three days to complete stood on the kitchen counter, its flourish of forcemeat and truffles marinated in cognac and topped with a clarified bouillon jelly a testament to the breadth of her virtuosity. Meanwhile, Max Bugnard continued to extol her talents, declaring she was "qualified to be chef in a *maison de la Haute Bourgeoisie.*" Buoyed by the accolades—from both friends and professionals—Julia rattled her credentials at Madame Brassart, demanding that a date be set for her diploma exams.

Normally, this would be a given. A course of study at Le Cordon Bleu always culminated with practical and oral finals. In fact, there was rarely an instance when a student didn't graduate with solemn heraldry, clutching a certificate signed by the despotic headmistress. But Julia Child was no ordinary student. To Madame Brassart, she had been trouble from the get-go—an upstart American, of course, but something far worse: a woman who knew what she wanted and stood up for her rights and, even worse, stood up to Madame Brassart. Madame didn't appreciate gals with gall. Who was this . . . this *American* with the temerity to demand a diploma from her? Madame wasn't going to stand for such effrontery. On the other hand, Julia loathed anyone who played petty politics, and she threw up a façade that radiated disdain. Each woman was repelled by the other's magnetic force. Their mutual distrust was palpable; they "got on each other's nerves." So when Julia petitioned Madame for a date for her exams, the request was ignored with resounding silence, as was every follow-up request.

Every few weeks throughout the beginning of 1951, she whipped off another letter to Madame Brassart, the tone growing "stern"—and sterner—with each new appeal. In the meantime, Julia studied like mad, convinced that when the time came, when Madame Brassart eventually caved in and administered the exam, it would be a ballbuster, designed to show her who was boss. She reviewed recipes, honed techniques, memorized proportions; she even timed herself cleaning, flaming, and cutting up a chicken, nailing the procedure in twelve minutes flat. Julia was ready—oh, she was so ready for anything that witch Brassart might throw at her.

She just didn't know how to penetrate the veil of silence. What was driving this woman to torment Julia like this? Julia suspected it came down to money. Had she taken the school's "regular"—amateur—course, the one in mid-morning, upstairs, with the clueless housewives, it would have cost two or three times what Julia paid for the "professional" basement program, which was supplemented by the GI Bill. "They didn't make as much money out of me as they could have," she decided—that must still be bugging the vengeful headmistress. And, perhaps, to some extent, she was right. That may have had some influence on the situation, but more than likely it was a good old-fashioned power play.

Well, two could play this game, Julia decided. In late March, with Paul's help, she wrote her stoniest letter yet, this time containing the whiff of a threat. She indicated that all her "American friends and even the U.S. ambassador himself" knew that she had worked diligently "morning, noon and night" at the Cordon Bleu, surpassing almost everyone else who labored at the school, and that "it is surprising to me to see you take so little interest in your students." Moreover, she was slated to leave for a vacation to the States in April and demanded to take her exams now, before they sailed. "If there isn't enough space at the school," she insinuated, "I would be happy to take the exam in my own well-appointed kitchen."

The ambassador . . . my own well-appointed kitchen. That must have made Madame Brassart's Belgian blood boil. To her credit, however, she refused to take the bait. Julia awaited a swift answer, while none, in fact, came. *Zut!* A week later, the gloves came off. Julia took her case to Max Bugnard, who agreed to run interference for her. Somehow, the old chef's plea did the trick.

By Friday, April 2, 1951, Paris was beginning to thaw from a particularly long and brutal winter. It was a beautiful day, a sweater day, cafés spilled onto the sidewalks. Sun streamed in the windows that fronted the rue du Faubourg Saint-Honoré as Julia took a seat at the counter in one of Le Cordon Bleu's upstairs test kitchens. She was prepared for anything, knew her coursework inside and out. The moment had finally arrived and there were no second thoughts, no butterflies. *Bring it on!*

The first part of the test, the written section, was a no-brainer. Julia was asked to explain how to make *fond brun,* a simple brown stock rendered from butcher trimmings and vegetables; the proper method for cooking green vegetables so they retained their color and flavor; and the exact preparation for a *sauce béarnaise.* Any cook worth her toque knew these basics by heart, and Julia scrawled the answers with precision and speed.

The practical cooking section was another story. One of Madame Brassart's factotums handed Julia an index card with a set of instructions typed on one side. It said: "Write down what ingredients you want for the following, for 3 people," and beneath that: *oeufs mollets, sauce béarnaise; côtelettes de veau en surprise; crème renversée au caramel.* Julia stared at the words with mounting alarm. *Oeufs . . . what!* What the hell was *mollet* supposed to mean? And what kind of *surprise* surprised a veal cutlet? None of these were dishes that Julia had heard of before. As for the exact proportions for a caramel custard, they weren't anything she could recall off the top of her head. This wasn't at all what she had been expecting. "My mind was on *Filets de sole Walewska, Poularde Toulousaine, Sauce Vénitienne,* etc. etc. etc.," she recalled, the classic dishes they'd practiced again and again. These came at her from out of *nowhere.* Except it wasn't from nowhere, but rather a throwaway Cordon Bleu booklet that was handed to the housewives when they signed up for their six-week course. Julia's practical, as it turned out, wasn't groomed for a serious cook but for "a beginning pupil who had never cooked before her six-week course."

She'd been had!

The realization slowly hit Julia that she was doomed to fail. Not only wasn't she familiar with the recipes for the aforementioned dishes, she had no idea how to cook them, which was the next part on the exam. "I just should have memorized their little book," she concluded ruefully. Now, there was only one thing to do—"make everything up"—and bluff her way through.

Wordlessly, she tromped down to the basement kitchen "in a cold and clean fury . . . and whipped up the stuff," with no prayer of being accurate. The eggs weren't even close: she poached them instead of coddling and then peeling them. And the veal missed the mark altogether. The recipe called for a sautéed veal chop, surrounded by duxelles, which were hashed, cooked mushrooms and ham slices. "Julia sautéed the mushrooms instead of making duxelles, and left out the ham entirely." As for the *surprise:* the whole conglomeration was to be reheated in a paper bag! Some *surprise,* Julia thought. "The paper is just a lot of tomfoolery, the kind a little newlywed would serve up for her first dinner to '*épater*' "—impress—"the boss's wife."

The exam was designed as an insult, she concluded. Madame Brassart knew damn well that Julia was a serious, dedicated cook, she knew how much a diploma would mean to someone who had put in the overtime at Le Cordon Bleu. "Me," Julia fumed, "who can stuff a sole with a forcemeat of weakfish, and serve it with a sauce *au vin blanc* such as they could never hope to taste the perfection of. Me, supreme mistress of mayonnaise, hollandaise, *cassoulets, choucroutes, blanquettes de veau, pommes de terre Anna, soufflés Grand Marnier, fonds d'artichaut, oignons glacés, mousse de faisan en gelée, balantines,* galantines, terrines, *pâtés, laitues braisées* . . . me, alas!" After all that, the upshot was a veal chop in a paper bag. She had to hand it to Brassart: that woman had stuck it to her good.

Julia could kiss that diploma goodbye. For all she knew, Brassart never intended to give her one anyway. "She feels a diploma is like being initiated into some secret 'rite,' " Julia fumed. Well, to hell with her and her school. "The main thing, of course, is that I know how to cook."

AND COOK SHE did. Julia continued to build on what she learned at Le Cordon Bleu, perfecting the lessons until they'd become second nature, after which she began working her way through *Larousse gastronomique,* the encyclopedia-size "wonder book" of French cooking that had become her bible. She had begun to experiment seriously with other recipes, other styles, other sources, as if they might lead her to the next phase of her romance with food. "I was no longer satisfied with being 'just' an accomplished home cook," Julia decided. It was too limiting, too unimaginative for her awakening ambition. "I wanted to make a career of it," she said. But how, if not as a domestic? There were no glamorous positions for people who made food, no celebrity chefs. She was already pushing herself to explore other realms, taking a few pastry lessons, corresponding with purveyors. Teaching continued to fascinate—nothing large-scale on the order of Le Cordon Bleu, but something more informal, and more *reasonable,* perhaps small, private classes for Americans in Paris.

Though how long she would remain in Paris was anyone's guess. With the rise of communism rampant since the end of the war, Paul was growing worried about a destabilized Europe. It alarmed him how Russia was forcing itself onto countries that had been weakened by the aftershocks of World War II. France was already grappling with its own brand of subversion, coping with the arm-twisting tactics of Soviet-influenced unions. A series of carefully coordinated, insidious strikes crippled the country in early 1951; gas, electricity, telephone, transportation, and dock workers all staged walkouts at the same time. Most of Paris ground to a halt, causing skeptics to predict violent change of some sort. "This seems to me one of the 'good' moments for the Russians to start something," Paul chimed in. He'd been keeping an eye on similar hot-button situations in England and the United States, both of which were preparing for momentous elections, along with the hostilities raging in Korea, where the Communist threat was all too real. "The Big War, as of now, seems about fifty-percent possible," he speculated. However, if the variables conspired to upend the fragile balance, "it will decimate much of Europe."

Where would that leave him and Julia? As far as Paul was concerned, their options were "turning more and more toward the USA." Any permanent return Stateside was further down the road, but he was already considering "certain places [there] for the storage of valuables . . . places that wouldn't be such obvious bombing targets as Washington or New York." They had a "home leave" scheduled for the beginning of June, four weeks of vacation split between Pasadena and Lopaus Point, after which he felt it was "going to be difficult psychologically—if it wasn't impossible physically—to come back to France for another two-year stretch in July."

Julia's view was more sanguine. She "didn't believe in the possibility of war right now," nor did she anticipate a rash move back to Washington. She saw it more as an "unsettled period," the result of "shuddering birth pangs" across Europe. Paul, as she well knew, got overexcited when it came to circumstantial matters, such as preparing for a "Russian invasion," whereas she held out hope that common sense would prevail. "I prefer her attitude," Paul confessed, admitting to his negativist bent; nevertheless, he remained convinced that war would eventually uproot them from Europe. "There is no possibility whatsoever that in five years' time Julie and I will be right here doing just what we are doing now."

In any event, they were homeward bound for a while. It would be good to touch base with old friends and relatives, "to see how the ol' country was holding up," look in on Pop, spend time with Charlie and Freddie at their seaside cabin, take a break from the bureaucratic grind. Julia was looking forward to some time away from the stove. The trip abroad would put some distance between her and the debacle at Le Cordon Bleu, give her a little perspective on the long-range plans ahead. Maine would be insanely beautiful in the heart of summer, when everything was in bloom and beach plums filled the margins of the lichen-covered fields. She could hardly wait to see the ocean again.

Amid the preparations and excitement, another distraction arose. Suddenly, Dort announced her engagement to an actor in her troupe, along with plans to marry him in New York at the end of June. While stirring and impulsive, the event itself was not unexpected. Dort had been seeing Ivan Cousins on and off "for a good year," ever since he turned up in Paris "to cool off" at the urging of his navy buddy, Lawrence Ferlinghetti. Dort had been attracted to the cherubic, pug-legged, bright-eyed Cousins, whom friends described as "boyish" and "roly-poly." Clearly, the two were an odd couple in person. Although Ivan stood almost a head shorter than Dort, he had a big personality that played gamely off this "large, robust, loud American girl." It helped bridge the obvious differences that they had the theater in common. Ivan had studied at New York's Neighborhood Playhouse and had some success modeling, doing commercials for clothes. Appearances in a few off-Broadway productions gave him cachet in the American Club Theater, where he played Elmer Kirby in Thornton Wilder's *The Happy Journey to Trenton and Camden* and other leading roles.

Dort loved Ivan's *joie de vivre,* the way he captivated any crowd with his easy mix of banter and bluff. She loved the "overgrown child in him," the imitations and the mimicry he segued into seamlessly. She loved his vulnerability, too, even though it often masked something darker.

The darker side cast a doubly long shadow. "Ivan was a notorious drinker and he led something of a double life," says Alex Prud'homme, a distant nephew who came to know Ivan well. The drinking may have not raised too many eyebrows, but it helped distract from the fact that Ivan was gay. In any case, Dort was undeterred. "She knew all of it was there from the beginning," says Prud'homme, "and chose to ignore it." Like Julia before her, Dort, in her thirties, was rootless and adrift. Her job, such as it was, had no upside or future, her crowd changed from one week to the next. Ivan had come into her life when she needed him most, and immediately she achieved a sense of stability. With her usual abandon, Dort threw herself into the relationship, and in 1951, when Ivan landed a day job at the Economic Cooperation Administration, they moved into a flat together on the boulevard de la Tour-Maubourg.

Paul, especially, was happy that Dort vacated Roo de Loo. He'd grown tired of the stagy theater crowd and the "fairies" that gravitated around her room. Their easy, empty utterances and affected gestures made "his blood boil." And though he wasn't privy to Ivan's sexual tendencies, he had his doubts. Oh, he had his doubts! In any case, Paul made no secret of his disapproval of Ivan. "He's a dreary, emasculated youth," he concluded, and urged his sister-in-law to break her engagement at once.

His sense of displeasure went almost unacknowledged at first. Dort was accustomed to Paul's finchy moods and probably assumed, like others, he'd eventually come around. The same with Julia, whom she fought with regularly, but loved unquestioningly nonetheless. Dort sensed the "slight undercurrent" of tension when Ivan was around Paul and Julia, but refused to let it intrude on the couples' otherwise pleasant coexistence. As far as breaking her engagement, Dort wouldn't hear of it. Marriage arrangements were already in the pipeline. In fact, she had made up her mind to remain in the States with Ivan, whose job was relocating him to Washington, D.C.

Some time before everyone left for America, the two couples—Julia and Paul, Dort and Ivan—attended a cocktail party at the Saint-Germain-en-Laye home of Ivan's boss, George Artamonoff, an American executive who helped administer the Marshall Plan in the Far East. It was a boisterous affair: more than a hundred people in a salon the size of Versailles. During the evening, another guest named Simone Beck Fischbacher regaled Julia with stories about an exciting, though "somewhat disorganized," French cooking club called Le Cercle des Gourmettes. That same night, Julia decided that she would join the group, too.

THE GOURMETTES WAS a renegade group of culinary anarchists who predated the French Resistance. It originated in 1927, when an American woman, Ethel Ettlinger, lobbed an oratorical grenade into the all-male Club des Cent, a handpicked society of windbag gastronomes. There were no casualties, aside from a few bruised egos, but the imbalance of power was never the same.

The insurrection occurred at the end of Le Club's yearly feast—the only one at which members were permitted to bring their lowly wives. The august president, Louis Fourest, offered a few closing remarks, including this doozy: "I salute the men at this table, without whose skill and knowledge, and whose capacity for appreciation, this truly noble feast could never have been created." His smug smile insinuated that women weren't able to pull off such a feast. Such impertinence! Such temerity! After a burst of macho applause, Mrs. Ettlinger, the wife of a prominent member, pushed back her chair and tapped her champagne flute for silence. Bristling with indignation, she announced in broken French: "And I wish to propose a toast to the women at this table. After all, it is we who run your households, we who order your food, we who see that it is properly prepared, we who keep you men happy and content. And furthermore, I have no doubt whatsoever that we could arrange a meal in every way as splendid and as satisfying as the one we have just enjoyed."

For a moment, in the stunned silence, you could hear a croissant drop. Then wild applause broke out from the gallery of instantly radicalized wives. On the spot, they decided to "throw one of the greatest banquets imaginable, invite the men"—the lowly husbands—"and show them what could be done."

In all respects a Hollywood ending ensued. One of the Gourmettes, as they now called themselves, offered the use of her country château, and the gals launched a showstopper that put Le Club to shame. Not only was the food an unqualified sensation, but the show itself a lollapalooza of a hit. Somehow, they'd gotten the Republican Guard to officiate at the door, resplendent in helmets, crimson jackets, white trousers, and black boots, with a *corps de chasse*—a horn quartet—to sound a fanfare, announcing each course as it was brought to the tables. The men gobbled up the food, including a forkful of crow, when forced to admit "the women knew their way around a menu" with great élan.

Naturally, Julia loved the whole suffragette aspect. Any time that women stood up for themselves and stuck it to the men was a red-letter day in her book. She wanted into the club from the moment she heard about it. As it turned out, all these years later, Mme. Ettlinger was still *la présidente,* and she governed the organization with ironclad rules: "Each *gourmette* must be able to cook—under her own steam; each *gourmette* must be able to order a perfect dinner and the perfect wine to accompany each course; service and table settings must match in elegance the meal itself; and discussion of politics or religion is taboo at luncheons." Well, Julia would have no trouble with three out of the four, but hopefully she could learn to keep her opinions to herself.

In any case, she began attending the luncheons. But Madame Fischbacher (*feesh-bah-shay*), her sponsor, had an ulterior motive. She'd turned up solely to meet Julia Child, but not with the intention of luring her into Les Gourmettes. No, Mme. Fischbacher was trolling the party for an American who cooked to help her resurrect a failed pet project.

With her friend Louisette Bertholle she'd cobbled together a small spiral-bound booklet of about fifty recipes called *What's Cooking in France* that was published by Ives Washburn in 1949. At the time, however, Americans didn't care what was cooking in France, damning the few thousand copies printed to the rubbish bins. Even Mme. Fischbacher recognized its literary shortcomings. "[I] am ashamed to say it's a pretty paltry cooking book," she said in retrospect, "full of mistakes, owing to a faulty translation."

Undeterred, she plunged back into writing, gathering old family recipes from every source she could think of and sending them to a family friend in New York who happened to be on the editorial board of the Book-of-the-Month Club. Same result: "This is just a dry bunch of recipes," the woman wrote back. But the assessment, while severely critical, offered advice to salvage the project. The recipes could benefit from a personal touch, little anecdotes that explained the French way to American cooks. "Get an American who is crazy about French cooking to collaborate with you; somebody who both knows French food and can still see and explain things with an American viewpoint in mind."

Mme. Fischbacher sensed immediately that Julia was the right person for the job. She seemed "mad about French food" and fairly radiated enthusiasm. It would be fair to say the interest was mutual. The project was exactly the kind of lifesaver that Julia was looking for, and the added option of "giving lessons in Paris" with this woman excited her even more.

"Why don't we meet at our apartment tomorrow," she said, extending a hand to Mme. Fischbacher.

The woman gave it a quick, crisp shake. "Please," she said. "Call me Simca."

SIMONE SUZANNE RENÉE Madeleine Beck Fischbacher deserved the nickname Simca. The daughter of a rich conservative Norman industrialist, she was as high-powered as the famous Fiat coupe, but also as economical, *bourgeoise,* with a large, well-designed chassis that admirers found handsome. On top of it all, she was built for speed. "She was always on the go," says a nephew, "a no-nonsense woman, kind of haughty but not condescending, very liberal, which was odd for a devout Catholic, and regimented, as regimented as a gendarme."

When Simone was born, on July 7, 1904, she was baptized with a few drops of Bénédictine, the herbal liqueur whose secret formula was owned by her family and thus endowed with riches beyond most dreams. Simone grew up in Babylonian splendor, raised in a fully staffed late-nineteenth-century château with turrets, moats, and stables, an English nanny to teach her carefully chosen phrases, and trips abroad to stimulate her intellect. There were boarding schools and winters on La Croisette in Cannes, where she ate bouillabaisse out of the hollowed trunk of a cork tree. Meals were mostly lavish affairs in a formal dining room that often seated forty-five. In the kitchen, she gamely pushed the family's longtime cook aside to prepare her own elaborate dishes, drenched in incomparably thick sauces of sweet Norman butter and luscious-but-deadly crème fraîche.

A life of splendid leisure was duly laid out for her, but deep down a sheltered future did not appear all that promising. She was "bored and restless," convinced of the fact "there was a lot missing," and "naïve"—seriously naïve. When an older friend of her father's asked him for her hand, she balked, never having had so much as a suitor, but she eventually relented after he promised that they would live in Paris. The fact that she neither loved nor even liked the man was beside the point. Escape was all that mattered. In Paris, she no doubt could fend for herself, though that outlook was entirely presumptuous: she was not yet nineteen.

It was a mistake, of course. The marriage was "dreary and fruitless." In Paris, she led what she called *la vie oisive*—an inactive life—though filled with discovery. Like Julia, she was a rich, pampered girl desperate to prove herself worthy of a meaningful goal. She learned to drive, hewed to *haute couture,* and apprenticed herself to a master bookbinder, whose folios she finished with gorgeous hand-stitched calfskin. Like Julia, she described her late adolescence as nothing more than that of "a social butterfly," and also like Julia, she endeavored to dispatch that image by taking cover at Le Cordon Bleu.

The cooking school in 1933 predated the tyrannical reign of Mme. Brassart. Back then, the founding Distel sisters ran it as a finishing school for domestics, as just a demo stage, without any of the hands-on classes that popularized it later on. In no time, Simone grew bored and discouraged with the pedagogical lectures. She already knew the basics that were being taught. The chef's recipes were nothing new: *daube, quiche Lorraine,* omelets, *pommes* anna, crêpes. *Sole normande*—really! The dish originated practically in her backyard. Instead of stomping out in a huff, Simone cornered the chef one day after his demo and explained her frustration. She wanted to cook in a more refined way than the simple meals he offered, elegant dishes *in her own home.* Would he agree to teach her there, privately, she wondered, and regularly, too, after his classes were finished?

That he consented was only overshadowed by the fact that he was Henri-Paul Pellaprat, one of France's acknowledged *maîtres.* Like Max Bugnard, Pellaprat was among the sage troupe of missionaries who brought the gospel of the great Escoffier to young Parisian chefs. Drawn to Le Cordon Bleu after years of cooking in celebrated European kitchens, he remained there teaching for nearly four decades, during which he wrote *L'Art culinaire moderne,* to this day one of the classics of French cuisine.

Simone learned magic at Pellaprat's elbow—not just little *trucs,* the tricks, that defined a master's skill, but the kind of grand illusions, entire elaborate dinners served in four-star restaurants. Working together, they made duck with turnips and green olives, lamb roasted in red wine, fish pâté *en croûte,* ballottines, terrines, charlottes, soufflés, the works. Cooking by upper-class women was "practically unheard of," she recalled, but at last Simone Suzanne Renée Madeleine Beck had found her calling.

Her timing couldn't have been better. As she became more accomplished, more confident, more directed toward scaling new heights, her marriage was going in the opposite direction. She and her husband "had arrived at a totally platonic relationship," but his nature had darker repercussions. "Simone's husband had a drinking problem," says a relative, "and the alcoholism, at its peak, was impossible for her to deal with." When she could no longer withstand his emotional abuse, she did what was foreign to French Catholic women: she filed for divorce after twelve years of marriage.

To Simone, those years of emptiness and alienation must have seemed a kind of penance for her adolescence as a dilettante. The years of amusement and self-indulgence had been relatively happy; the years of marriage nothing more than a "bedroom farce," a façade. "My life was almost at a standstill," she said. But by 1936, she was finally free, and for the next year she immersed herself in the family's main business, selling a silicate powder used in industrial ceramics. Sometime that September, she paid a call on a company that made perfume and cleaning abrasives, both of which also used silicate. The assistant director was a Spanish-born Alsatian named Jean Fischbacher. As the meeting wore on, their attention turned from business to mutual friends—and mutual attraction. Still, it took him almost two months after that to ask her out for a date, at the end of which he accompanied her to her car.

As she struggled to fold her gangly five-foot-eight frame into a rather compact Fiat, Fischbacher flashed an appreciative grin. She was something to look at, all right, "a terribly imposing, beautiful woman with deep, seductive arches in her eyes and so very shapely." Even though it was the middle of winter, she slapped open the sunroof to accommodate the long, stylish feather attached to her beret. For Fischbacher, this was the punchline to the visual joke. "What a big chassis for such a little car!" he exclaimed, laughing at the scene. He glanced at the bumper of the car and saw the model's name in script: *Simca*. That was all that it took. On the spot, it became her official nickname. "From then on," she said, "I told everybody to call me Simca."

WHEN SIMCA TOOK the rattletrap elevator up to Julia's fourth-floor apartment in June 1951, she couldn't have known the extent of the tall American's cooking obsession. According to those who visited Roo de Loo, Julia's kitchen had been outfitted so that it now "rivaled that of a fully-operational restaurant." At the top of the small staircase on the fifth level, Simca came face-to-face with a veritable wall of cookery—a giant pegboard Paul had erected on which hung dozens of strategically placed gadgets, each outlined in bold felt-tip marker so that everything could be put back in its proper place. Some were from America, others from Dehillerin; a few were scavenged from the stalls of the Marché aux Puces. A library of cookbooks teetered on several shelves. All in all, it was an impressive display, and Simca was duly bowled over. Here was another woman just like herself, a kitchen zealot who lived and breathed cooking, and they "talked almost exclusively about food for hours."

Both women wanted to harness their passion. They could keep making dinner parties until they were blue in the face, but something necessitated more of a challenge. The two self-confessed former social butterflies could no longer be contained. They needed to express themselves in other ways—to fly. There was more to be made from their cooking, they agreed. Julia loved Simca's cookbook idea. Explaining French cooking to Americans was such an attractive affair. Why shouldn't women back home discover the same pleasure and gratification that she had? And they kept coming back to some kind of a homey cooking school. Teaching others, sharing the wealth—yes, *yes,* this was everything Julia had dreamed about.

A few days later, Simca introduced Julia to her sidekick, Louisette Bertholle, an attractive, earnest, engaging woman with a girlish heart, whose travels abroad had confirmed her instincts that French cooking was primed for an evangelical crusade. The United States especially intrigued Louisette. "She loved America and all things American," says her grandson, Bern Terry. Politics, sports, the Social Register, you name it, she could recite statistics at the drop of a hat. She'd begun making trips there immediately after the war, staying with an uncle in Savannah, Georgia, while traveling throughout the North and East, making friends. One of them, Gladys Birch, who owned a bookstore in Greenwich, Connecticut, encouraged Louisette to write a French cookbook for the American palate. According to Birch, soldiers had come home after missions on the French front lines spinning tales of the indescribable food they'd eaten. The time was perfect to strike, she advised. Birch had contacts throughout the New York publishing world and introduced Louisette to Sumner Putnam, an editor at the Ives Washburn Company.

In retrospect, it was a mixed blessing. Ives Washburn was one of the smallest New York publishing houses, with meager resources and parochial tastes. It cost them practically nothing to put out *What's Cooking in France,* but, as Simca noted, "it was given no promotion." Louisette and Simca held out hope that their follow-up effort, tentatively titled *French*

Cooking for All, would produce more favorable results. The publisher had even hired a freelance editor to help whip the bulky, incoherent manuscript into shape, but the authors remained convinced that only a true American cook—someone like Julia—could give the book what it needed most: a soul.

One of Julia's great joys that fall was her afternoon get-togethers with Simca and Louisette. The trio sat for hours in the salon overlooking rue de l'Université glowingly talking food and commerce while occasionally collaborating on a recipe or two. This was what Julia loved most, cooking in which she could *mettre la main à la pâte*—to get one's hands on the dough—which was the only way to "learn, while watching and doing." That would be intrinsic to anything they did, whether working together, just the three of them, or with a class of students, as Julia had hoped. Small and intimate, as opposed to the free-for-alls at Le Cordon Bleu. Julia "liked the energy between Simca and Louisette, the way they interacted," their mutual respect. In the kitchen, they seemed to have "a short-hand" that allowed them to work in complete harmony, without competing or getting in each other's way. Where Chef Bugnard had taught a formal, classic style of cooking, these women personalized it, offering a more down-to-earth approach to true French cuisine. Their recipes were inspired by old family standbys, *cuisine bourgeoise* with a subtle refinement, not quite *haute cuisine,* but something just as classy. Julia had admired the honesty of their cooking from the moment they showed it to her and understood what it would bring to what she'd already learned.

For the first time in years, Julia felt in the grip of a rewarding career, and the satisfaction made her enduringly lighthearted and ultramotivated. During stretches when Paul's work plowed him under a dispiriting tangle of red tape, she played Puck to Paul's stressed-out Oberon, administering charm and entertaining almost every night of the week. Four or five guests routinely turned up for dinner. And these weren't potluck dinner parties thrown together at the last minute, but fabulous pull-out-all-the-stops extravaganzas with plenty of bang. "I'd never eaten food made with such honest intensity," says a Smith classmate who visited with her husband in December 1951. While everyone was eating and *oooh*ing, Julia leaned forward, propped her elbows on the table, and maintained a running dialogue throughout the evening. "She kept everything humming, in perfect control." But it was the food that always stole the spotlight. Once, "just for laughs," she roasted a leg of venison that had been marinated for three days in red wine, cognac, and spices and served it with a purée of celery *rave* and prunes stewed in white wine and meat stock. It was impossible to hold this woman back from stage-managing memorable nights. No one appreciated it more than Paul. "Good conversation, good people, good food, good wine—good God," he exclaimed, "what more can you ask?"

IN THE MEANTIME, the women pushed ahead with the cooking-school venture they were informally calling L'École des Gourmettes. On December 17, 1951, they gathered in Louisette's "rather grand apartment" at the far end of avenue Victor Hugo, near the Étoile, to discuss the parameters for their classes. They should be small, everyone agreed, "limited to four students," and be practical, covering everything, from basic technique to recipe preparation to pastry to wine. Since the emphasis would be on teaching Americans to cook French food, Julia insisted the classes should be given in English, in contrast to Le Cordon Bleu where instructors spoke only indecipherable French. Louisette volunteered her kitchen, which, at the moment, was under renovation to make it even more spacious and well-appointed than it already appeared. To attract potential students, Julia offered to place an ad in the *Embassy News,* which was distributed to the families of all government employees. Hopefully, they could begin sometime in February 1952, when work on Louisette's kitchen was due to be finished.

But by mid-January, they were forced into early action. Three women had answered Julia's ad, "money in fist and wanting to start." Three Americans, bona fide students: it was now or never, even if the instructors were not quite ready. ("But is one ever completely ready?" Julia quipped.) Louisette's kitchen was still under construction, and Simca worried that her heavy accent was a liability. "We've got to plunge right in, Simca!" Julia declared. Temporarily, they could hold class in the Childs' kitchen, which was small but roomy enough for six. As for ingredients, Paul had access to the army's PX, through his government job, where they could buy staples for less than they would cost at the market. Every savings helped. The price of a lesson was only 600 francs, which came to about $2.50—and that included lunch.

The first class was given on January 23, 1952, amid a haze of improvisation and fluster. Almost immediately, all sorts of hurdles arose. Since there had been no time for rehearsal or an actual run-through, it was difficult for the teachers to coordinate who spoke when. Recipes hadn't been adapted for American-style measurements, when exact measurements were made at all; whereas Julia and Simca were specific when it came to quantities, Louisette was an instinctive cook, using pinches and splashes instead of exact amounts. And the French instructors found it incomprehensible that American housewives didn't cook with a staff of servants. Shopping? Cleaning up? Why, just leave it for the housekeeper, *bien sûr*.

These flaws were only hiccups, however. Within a few classes, they had ironed out the kinks and the women performed as an effortless ensemble. Sessions ran for two hours, twice a week, capped by a formal sit-down lunch at 1:00 p.m. Paul showed up in time to join the meal, pouring generously from a sampling of Bordeaux aging in his cellar and "giving a little discussion on wines" to students whose "taste in reds," he presumed, "seems to have been founded in large part on Italian Swiss Colony gallon-jug juices." Paul turned out to be a star attraction. "He poured with a flourish and talked with eloquence, as if the wine were nectar," Simca recalled. The lunches were so successful, in fact, that the cooking school began taking on extra guests just for the meals as a way of showcasing and promoting their classes.

For the rest of the spring, Julia worked in her kitchen with Simca and Louisette, testing recipes in between teaching and shopping. Those cooking sessions were especially rewarding. Simca's baking was inspired, nothing short of divine, Julia discovered, and she was "full of ideas on cakes and pastries." Chef Pellaprat had unlocked for her the mysteries of puff pastry, which she shared while making piecrust with Julia. But the women stumbled on an obstacle of sorts that would alter the course of their cooking exploits.

For some stubborn reason, Simca's recipe refused to proof—"all her proportions were off" and her piecrusts crumbled like gypsum. Why? The recipe had been in her family for years and she'd made hundreds of pies that had turned out perfectly. It must be Julia's oven, that hulking monster from the bogs of Hell. But regulating its temperature failed to solve the problem. What, then, or perhaps *who* was the culprit? At the time, no one suspected the flour, which they'd been buying at the PX—Gold Medal flour, to be precise, imported in bulk from the United States. After a few experiments, however, the proof was in the piecrust. French flour, they realized, was "much fatter and full of body and seems to need as much as one-third less fat to make a nice short crust." Apparently, American flour was chemically re-jiggered to extend its life on a supermarket shelf. That meant processing out the natural fats to keep it from getting maggoty, as it tended to be in France. So all the pastry recipes had to be recalculated, retested, and rewritten for the American kitchen, as would every recipe for their prospective audience. Not to mention the necessity of a rethinking of all ingredients. So many staples of French markets were not available in the States. *Crème fraîche,* for one, was unknown, as were shallots and leeks and chanterelles, to name a few. Butter, too, was a whole different animal. And try finding Gruyère on an A&P shelf. There was so much to explain.

It was a lot of work—but worth it. Julia focused her attention on the differences between cooking in France and America. "From that time on I never lost sight of the fact that my sole purpose was to teach cooking to *Americans,* not the French," she recalled. "I had to find a way to translate everything into a pleasurable experience that a typical housewife could execute without fuss." So things like margarine had to be taken into account. And Crisco. And ketchup.

Meat presented another dilemma. The French cuts of beef were entirely different from those found in an American supermarket. How were they supposed to explain recipes that featured tournedos, chateaubriand, and *entrecôtes,* to say nothing of sweetbreads, *tête de veau,* kidneys, and tripe? Buying *lardons,* for barding veal, was next to impossible, even in New York, with its large faction of French ex-pats. The last thing Julia wanted was for their students to return home to America only to discover they were unable to cook any of the recipes from her class. She expressed these concerns in a letter to her sister-in-law, Freddie, and in no time, a packet of photos arrived in France resembling an undercover surveillance of butcher-shop cases. Every cut of meat was shown in explicit detail so that the women could make a suitable comparison.

Meanwhile, the next session of the cooking school began on March 1, 1952, with a slightly higher price—7,000 francs (about $20) for three classes—and a new name: L'École des Trois Gourmandes, whose official logo, a red "3" in a circle, was worn on a badge by the instructors. The class filled up fast with five students, "plus a small waiting list." Julia, Simca, and Louisette had launched the operation so that it would be self-perpetuating, an ongoing concern—a business, as opposed to a hobby—and legitimate competition for Le Cordon Bleu. As somewhat of a coup, Julia brought in Max Bugnard as a guest instructor, and they plotted to lure away other chefly studs from Madame Brassart's stable.

Throughout the spring and summer of 1952, when not cooking or teaching a class, Julia explored the new culinary landscape that Simca and Louisette had mapped out for her. Her days were filled with functions that involved food and eating—many of them revolving around luncheons sponsored by Le Cercle des Gourmettes. The club remained one of her go-to haunts. She adored the "gossipy cooking sessions and the dazzling food," the delight of rubbing elbows with so many women obsessed as she was. It didn't faze her that the members were mostly ancient relics, well into their seventies and eighties. She, Simca, and Louisette were among the club's young Turks—rising stars, but hardly arrivistes. Food savvy was currency in Paris, where Louisette, more than others, seemed to know everyone on the scene.

It was Louisette who brought Julia into the capricious orbit of one of Paris's most eccentric gastronomes: Maurice Edmond Sailland, otherwise known as the great Prince Curnonsky. Part poseur, part virtuoso, part gustatory mooch, Curnonsky, as he called himself to juice up his otherwise plain-vanilla byline, had an all-consuming passion for fine French food and an intellect that showcased a seemingly encyclopedic knowledge of the subject. Curnonsky had been a reporter, an influential food critic, a prolific author, and a philosopher whose ideas and critical monologues are imbued with tradition as well as controversy. His thirteen-volume manifesto, *La France gastronomique,* advanced the interpretation of three hundred years of French cooking. He was instrumental in founding *Guide Michelin* and, in 1928, established the Académie des gastronomes, the preeminent body on matters pertaining to French cooking. He famously observed that "good cooking is when things taste of what they are," which was typically Curnonskian: simple, authoritative, pretentious, unassailable.

At seventy-nine, when Julia met him, Curnonsky was still the *enfant terrible* of the French food scene, a voluptuous epicurean known to receive visitors in his bathrobe and to swoop into a three-star restaurant unannounced and expect dinner waiting for him, free of charge. He was no longer strong and sinewy, but the victim of indulgence, a "short, fat, eagle-beaked, triple-chinned, pale-blue-eyed, witty, spoiled and knowledgeable" man, whose "stories about food, wine, and people" were the assets he traded on. Julia reminisced how she "immediately fell for him." He seemed larger than life, "a spirited and charming old man," who amused her with untold numbers of sketches of cooking lore that grew increasingly more convoluted and contradictory the more he rambled on, until she began to regard him as "a dogmatic meatball," and "a big bag of wind."

Later, in July, Louisette invited "the girls" to lunch with Irma Rombauer, the doyenne of American cookbookery, whose *Joy of Cooking* was the undisputed reigning heavyweight champion. Julia thought *Joy* was "a wonderful book." It was chatty and social and much more readable than its crowd-pleasing predecessor, *The Fannie Farmer Cookbook*. The recipes were clearly better, more in tune with what people were eating—much more modern, more twentieth century. Rombauer, herself, had surprised Julia. On the one hand, "old Mrs. Joy was terribly nice, just a good, simple Midwestern housewife." And, yet, there was a steely undercore to her, a no-nonsense astuteness that Julia found refreshing. Mrs. Joy, as she discovered, was also Mrs. Irate—irate for having been ripped off by her publisher. Heatedly, she explained how "she'd been in some way weazeled [*sic*] out of something like royalties for 50,000 copies of her book, and she was furious," Julia recalled. Publishing, it seemed, was a cutthroat business, a tidbit Julia stored away for the future, just in case.

In any case, Rombauer set the bar high for Simca and Louisette, who were in the midst of polishing their "big jumble of recipes" for their upcoming anthology, *French Home Cooking*. The publisher, Ives Washburn, had hired a freelance editor named Helmut Ripperger to assist in the process, which seemed to reinforce the good intentions all around. But Ripperger turned out to be a goldbrick. He dawdled when it came to revising the manuscript and preyed on Louisette's moony good nature, borrowing money from her and cadging "delicious little meals." It made Julia's blood boil when she thought of "poor Louisette" being "pushed around by this egocentric pansy." This only soured her on Ives Washburn and the publishing game. Still, her colleagues pressed on, engrossed in their work. The book was massive, ambitious, revealing practically every recipe from their families' vaults, in addition to a complete overhaul of classical methods and technique. Nothing like it had ever been attempted.

Finally, on August 28, 1952, a letter arrived from Ives Washburn, in New York, that starkly altered the course of the project. It contained the news that Helmut Ripperger had either quit or was sacked, leaving the book without its American voice. The consequence spelled disaster. As much as Julia loved her two colleagues, as much as her respect for their work was deep and profound, she knew they were lost, lost, if left to their own devices. Her opinion was no reflection on their know-how as cooks, but rather on their ability to express themselves to an American audience. They discussed all this decisively one afternoon in Louisette's upside-down kitchen, acknowledging that it now seemed hopeless to proceed as planned. Of course, if someone were to come to their rescue, someone they knew and trusted, someone much like them, fiercely dedicated to the cause, who understood and appreciated French cooking . . . All eyes turned to gauge Julia's reaction.

"I'd be delighted to," she said without hesitation.

The decision needed no great reflection, but it would be some time before she learned what she'd gotten herself into.

Twelve

A Memorable Feast

The manuscript was a mess. Julia knew it almost from the moment she started to read. The "big jumble of recipes" that Simca and Louisette put together was incomprehensible: too long, too complicated, too French, too *too*. As a cookbook, it seemed "infuriatingly vague," so clumsy in its execution; she doubted Americans would find it very useful. Above all, the writing was "not very professional." Julia felt a sinking disappointment throughout September 1952, as she attempted to parse the various chapters she'd been given: sauces, soups, eggs, entrées, poultry and game, meats, and vegetables. The book sure didn't grab her the way she had hoped. "In fact," she said, "I did not like it at all."

But . . . oh, there was something so enchanting about the idea: a French cookbook for American housewives, "fully explained for the novice." Others had tried—and failed—to pull it off, ignoring what Julia called "the 'whys,' the pitfalls, the remedies, the keeping, the serving," all the nuances that made French home cooking so special. And the cuisine! "I wasn't aware of any book that explained *la cuisine bourgeoise* the way this one did." It is almost impossible to overstate the effect its dishes had on Julia. Simca and Louisette were such damned good cooks. She loved their food, loved their whole approach. They—all three of them—had forged a close, interactive bond. It seemed a shame to let such a project implode.

Julia thought long and hard about whether to get involved with this book. It would need an overhaul, a major rewrite, from top to bottom,

Les Trois Gourmandes: Louisette, Simca, and Julia, Paris, April 8, 1953

and she doubted that any of the recipes would make sense to an amateur cook. They needed to be deconstructed, rethought, to make them clear and more informative. And accurate: Julia would have to test all the recipes herself, test them from scratch, to ensure that they worked, that the measurements were precise. How many times would she have to cook them to determine that? How long would it take to work her way through six hundred recipes? "It needs an immense amount of work," Paul warned. "It'll be a colossal job."

Could she make that kind of a commitment at this point in her life? Only a month earlier, Julia had turned forty. It seemed fairly late to launch yet another new career. She'd already laid the groundwork for a French-based cooking school that, still in its infancy, was loaded with potential. And there was Paul to consider. His four-year stint with the USIS terminated automatically on September 15 and therefore his "future was anyone's guess." It seemed unlikely that he'd be renewed for Paris. That seemed almost too good to be true. There was some talk about a transfer to Bordeaux or Marseille, but Paul knew the score: diplomatic service was "a matter of slots and bodies"; he could wind up anywhere they needed a French-speaking desk jockey with a background in espionage and art. Madrid and Rome weren't out of the running, or they could "slam us off to Zamboan," he mused. He had just turned fifty, an age when most diplomats were either at the top of their departments or taking early retirement. Since 1948, Paul had been stuck in a mid-level post with "an anomalous rank: Foreign Service Staff Officer." The best he could hope for was a lateral transfer. In any case, he said, "I don't particularly relish changing my life-pattern again."

Julia wasn't so sure. "Meself," she wrote to Freddie, "I'd rather like to stay here just one more year." There was still much she wanted to learn about French cooking, but she was also feeling some nostalgia for the States. "Two or three years in Washington" sounded nice. It had been ages since she'd slept in her own bed, or cooked in her own kitchen in the Olive Street house. She was also curious about a newfangled sensation she'd been reading about: television. The magazines were full of its attractions. A box in your home that broadcast entertainment shows and the news! "How much do you really use it?" she asked her sister-in-law. "How do you like the programs?" *Television.* "My heavens, I am beginning to feel very out-of-date indeed."

No, she wouldn't mind moving back for a while. Besides, there were rumblings of another sort that had begun to give her pause. The State

Department had become a target for right-wing witch-hunters who claimed there was widespread Communist infiltration inside its offices. Anyone connected with culture or the arts was a prime suspect. Paul's friend Budd Schulberg had already been fingered, as had buddies of his and Julia's from the OSS. Who was next? Julia understood how anyone engaged in an intellectual life in the thirties and forties might have flirted with the same ideals as communism: collective bargaining, ending classism and economic inequality. "I'll bet I would have been a communist at that period, too," she speculated, "if I had been an intellectual instead of a well-to-do butterfly."

Not even the USIS had been spared the Red-baiting pogrom. In December, Representative Fred Busbey, a Republican from Illinois, had seen one of Paul's art exhibits when he passed through Paris that he later determined was "communist art." Never mind that the work had been done by fifty-six contemporary American artists and was on loan to the embassy from the Museum of Modern Art. Or that half the prints were abstract, a form banned in Soviet Russia. Or that the exhibit was underwritten by Nelson Rockefeller. Busbey, art critic and patriot, demanded an investigation.

All of this made Julia uncomfortable. But the book—*that* book—took her mind off the distractions. She kept returning to Simca and Louisette's manuscript with real alacrity. "The more I thought about it," she said, "the more this project fired my imagination."

She would do it, she explained to her two colleagues; she would join forces with them in making this cookbook the most important work of its kind. But there were conditions. They'd have to be equal partners. To ensure that the tone was right for Americans, Julia would do most of the writing. And the manuscript—well, it was out, for now; they'd be writing an entirely new book.

The recipes, she quickly determined, were its tent pole. Everything depended on their accuracy to begin with, and afterward, on the way, they were explained simply and logically. Julia wasted no time getting down to business. By mid-September, she started cooking through the wad of recipes, beginning with soups, which seemed fundamental and were started with all-purpose bases that could be used as building blocks to create variations when enriched with other ingredients. This wasn't done willy-nilly, plunge-right-in. Julia had a plan: she'd make one soup per day, consulting Simca and Louisette's recipe for, say, watercress soup, along with similar recipes from five classic cookbooks on her shelf:

Carême, *Larousse gastronomique,* Flammarion, Curnonsky, and Ali-Bab. After reading through each, she would make the soup three different ways to determine the best possible recipe.

It was a long, tedious process. Julia's days were filled with experimentation: cooking and making notes, more cooking and more extensive notes. She went about everything scientifically, subjecting each recipe to what she called the "operational proof"—that is, not relying on the published recipes or family traditions so much as concrete results from her very own stove. Recipes found in the American cookbooks presented the greatest challenge. They were so loosely written, so casual in their approach; measurements were listed in terms of "a spoonful," "a cupful," or "a medium-sized onion." That wouldn't do—no, that wouldn't do at all. It became even more apparent when Julia made *béchamel,* one of the most basic French white sauces. Even *Joy of Cooking's* recipe for it was way off the mark. For authenticity's sake, she weighed American tablespoons of butter and flour on the metric scale until the perfect balance was achieved. This took time and several misfires before she was able to rewrite the recipe to reflect the results. To most observers, this process may have seemed trivial or "arcane"; nevertheless, to Julia each outcome was "an exciting discovery."

The work consumed her. The cooking itself was a source of endless discovery, each new recipe an unfolding mystery, each new combination of ingredients its set of unifying clues. She sifted through the data like Nero Wolfe: methodically, open-minded, inquisitive, analytical. Nothing escaped her critical eye. Everything needed proper balance. The first time Julia made onion soup, for instance, the broth seemed pallid, lackluster. It had none of the sweet, buttery richness that onions demand. Subsequent tests produced a burned, almost tarry aftertaste. None of the elements seemed to harmonize. After several more false starts, she discovered her problem: it wasn't the ingredients, but time. The onions needed to be fully caramelized, to take on that sugary, almost sticky quality, which could only be done by "a long, slow cooking in butter and oil." There was no cutting corners. The only way to deepen the flavor, to make it perfectly, was time, nearly forty-five minutes of constant cooking, constant stirring, constant attention as the onions melted in the nut-brown fat. Oh, the smells that competed in her little kitchen! Piles of strong, astringent sliced onions, sizzling butter laced with salt and sugar, the toothsome fellowship of bouillon and vermouth. In the end, she produced a rich mahogany soup that seethed with intensity and deep flavor.

The cooking was invigorating, joyous. For Julia, the cooking fulfilled the promises that Le Cordon Bleu had made but never kept. Where Le Cordon Bleu always remained rooted in the dogma of French cuisine, Julia strove to infuse its rigors with new possibilities and pleasures. It must have felt liberating for her to deconstruct Carême and Escoffier, respecting the traditions and technique while correcting the oversight. "To her," as a noted food writer indicated, "French culinary tradition was a frontier, not a religion." If a legendary recipe could be improved upon, then let the gods beware. Julia lost herself in the process, often working ten-, twelve-, fourteen-hour days. There were nights she "sat up till two a.m. working on that cookbook," unable to put it aside in mid-stride.

Simca Fischbacher joined her on many mornings. Almost immediately they established a professional, if distant, rapport, cooking side-by-side though continents apart: Simca upholding her French heritage, Julia giving it an American voice. There was a practical balance to their collaboration. Simca was "equally hardworking and professional in her attitude," Paul observed. It seemed to him "they make a good combination." He was right, of course; they were suitably well matched—but he was also wrong. Simca was "a perfectionist," a vigorous, charming woman who impressed Julia with her knowledge of regional cooking. It was in her blood, it came second nature to her. But Simca was also hidebound, obstinate, determined to preserve the family recipes she inherited, adhering to them like scripture. It didn't suit her to see them emended by an American upstart, not even Julia Child, whom she liked and respected. As a result, there was a constant undercurrent of tension as they tested each recipe: Julia questioning its soundness, Simca defending the faith.

They pushed and pulled at those recipes, challenged long-standing methods, challenged each other. Give and take. Simca, highly excitable, often put her foot down. *Ahm-pah-ceeb! Non!* She couldn't cook in a way that made a mockery of French tradition. It was wrong. *Wrong!* It wasn't right, wasn't . . . *French.* When she did this, Julia would draw back into the hard-shelled Pasadenan who was just as obstinate, albeit without the blood and thunder. Like her husband, Julia practiced diplomacy. She knew better than to tackle Simca head-on. Nothing was more likely to make this feisty *femme* dig into her position than an outright refusal to see things her way. Instead, Julia would suggest they test a certain recipe two or three different ways, knowing the results would vindicate her and eventually defuse Simca's indignation.

It wasn't easy, but it allowed them to stay on track, pushing through the chapter on soups and then deep into sauces. Throughout the day, skillets sizzled, kettles burbled, blenders whirred, mallets pounded, and the low rumble off rue de l'Université rolled in through the open window. Louisette occasionally stopped by to pitch in, but her kitchen appearances had grown more infrequent, less productive. Louisette was grappling with a regrettable marriage—another regrettable marriage, as things would have it. Her current husband, Paul Bertholle, was a big, boisterous character with "a rhinoceros's thickness of skin and a cockatoo's preening egocentricity," who was "into horses and gambling and business deals that bridged the two." His slippery behavior was propelling Louisette toward another rancorous breakup. Whatever the reasons, clearly Louisette was distracted by the domestic fireworks. She agonized over the prospect of ending her relationship with Bertholle. Her first divorce—the result of an arranged marriage to a Vietnamese painter, Harry Chan—had led to her excommunication from the church. It was a punishment from which Louisette, a devout Catholic, had never fully recovered. As such, she drifted deeper and deeper into despair and away from the cooking.

Julia and Simca had great empathy for Louisette's struggle to resolve her situation. They knew she was timid to begin with, "a lost little flower," not especially as confident or as gutsy as her cooking colleagues. While Paul pegged her as being "shy," "sweet," and dizzily "romantic," he also considered her "a charming little nincompoop." But, oh, that woman could cook—she knocked 'em dead in the kitchen, with her dazzling takes on Burgundian and southwestern cuisine. She knew her way around most of the provinces, yet she wasn't always available to work as a productive teammate. Instead, from the beginning of August through the fall of 1952, Louisette withdrew into a shell of inertia and seclusion.

In the meantime, Julia and Simca picked up the slack. By the end of September 1952 they had demonstrated their prowess for reworking creaky recipes and making them hum with precision. Their work had already transcended the esoteric world of cookbookery. Each evening, after cleaning up the dinnerware, Julia withdrew to the bedroom and typed up that day's recipe, along with handwritten tasting notes buried in the margins. Within no time, Julia recalled, "a pile of wrinkled and stained pages grew steadily on the counter next to my stove."

By November, the pile began to feel like a cookbook. It had heft, as Julia had noted, but also real focus and direction. The sauces chapter especially seemed accomplished, exhaustive. There were brown sauces with untold variations: mustard, tarragon, capers, duxelles, and curry; tomato sauces; butter sauces; hollandaise; and vinaigrettes. And, of course, white sauces galore, including *béchamel* and *velouté*.

One white sauce, in particular, continued to elude her—*beurre blanc nantais,* "a wonder sauce used on fish" that originated in Nantes. It seemed like a simple preparation: an emulsion of warm butter flavored with shallots, wine, vinegar, salt, and pepper. But no matter how many times Julia made it, her sauce turned oily. It needed to be creamy and just warm enough to keep the butter from congealing, while ensuring the acids were well concentrated. But—*how?* It was an incredibly tricky process, and "the cookbooks were all vague on the subject." Julia remembered a bistro that prepared it to perfection, a small Right Bank *boîte* called Chez la Mère Michel that she'd eaten in once, three years earlier. On a crisp night in October, she and Paul returned there—to have dinner, certainly, but also for reconnaissance. During aperitifs, Julia came face-to-face with La Mère Michel herself, a stoop-shouldered crone with a penetrating stare, who ruled the place like a despot. The former OSS operative leaped into action. Paul watched in awe as his wife, "with her special system of hypnotizing people so they open up like flowers in the sun, talked her way into Mère Michel's kitchen, and inside of two minutes was watching them make *beurre blanc.*" Julia wrote the recipe on a napkin and stuffed it into her purse. Yes, the sauces chapter was coming together beautifully. Julia envisioned it as a model for the entire project.

As if on cue, a letter arrived from Ives Washburn, the New York publisher. Under separate cover, it said, they were returning Simca and Louisette's original manuscript, along with the revisions that Helmut Ripperger had made. No one was happy with the outcome, so far. "After a year of frustration for everyone concerned," the publisher wrote, "we are still a long way from a completed book." Louisette had obviously informed them that Julia agreed to come onboard, and a sigh of relief was reflected in that news. "The big job now rests on your shoulders, and you must be the absolute boss of what goes into the book and what stays out. Now that you, Mrs. Child, have taken over the helm, I am more confident than ever that a fine book can be made of this."

Julia was pleased—and puzzled. The tone and style of the manuscript had been deeded to her care: *the absolute boss.* That was excellent news. And Ives Washburn seemed intent on publishing the book, but—*ye gods!*—not a word about business. A lot of time and effort had gone into the research, to say nothing of the costs the three women had incurred. From what

Julia knew of these things, some sort of advance seemed appropriate. At the very least, she expected to hear about recouping their substantial expenses. Or be promised a contract. What to do? What to do? She was in uncharted territory.

To stall for time, she answered the publisher—a long, rambling letter detailing a revolutionary approach to the book. She promised a sample chapter "in about ten days," as well as an outline "explaining the conception and plan" for the entire book. But in any case, it would "build off the Bugnard/Cordon Bleu system of teaching theme and variation," she promised. All in all "a new type of cookbook." If everything went according to plan they could expect delivery on or about June 1953.

Meanwhile, she sought advice elsewhere, from anyone who could help her. Initially, Julia contacted Paul Sheeline. The son of Paul's sister, Meeda, he was an associate at the Wall Street law firm of Sullivan & Cromwell. Sheeline admitted he "had no experience with publishing contracts" but agreed to review the correspondence related to the book and give her an idea of their obligation to Ives Washburn.

She also outlined the situation in a letter to Avis DeVoto.

ON A CLEAR spring evening in April 1951, after the Cordon Bleu exam debacle, after the inaugural lunch with the Gourmettes, Julia curled up on the couch with the latest issue of *Fortune* and combed over a persnickety essay by Bernard DeVoto. It contained a litany of complaints about big business shortchanging consumers, particularly as it applied to the manufacture of general household goods, and specifically to cutlery. Julia had to keep herself from leaping up to cheer. Knives were a special pet peeve of hers. She'd been known to "let off a blast of cuss-words in the kitchen" during wrestling matches with extremely dull blades. Once, while sitting in a garden, Paul heard her scream through an open window: "God damn it!—I've *never yet* gone into a private French kitchen where the knives are sharp! How the hell do these people think they're going to cook when they can't even slice a tomato?" DeVoto's article had struck a chord.

That might have sufficed, the last word on such a narrow topic, but DeVoto was a notoriously cranky guy; no less than Wallace Stegner referred to him as an "angry watchdog." So a few months later, this time in a column in *Harper's*, he resumed his splenetic crusade. Knives: "They look wonderful, but they won't cut anything," he chuffed. "The chromium that makes them shiny . . . makes them incapable of holding an edge." On and on he went, burning through more words than anyone ever dreamed possible, certainly more than the subject warranted, including an aside that knife manufacturers should be referred to the House Un-American Activities Committee.

That did it! The article "smacked Julie right in her Achilles' (cooking) heel." She could no longer restrain herself. She dashed off a fan letter to Brother DeVoto praising his "diatribe," along with a "nice little French model as a token of my appreciation." Inside the envelope, against a piece of cardboard, she had taped a stainless-steel knife she'd picked up at Dehillerin for seventy cents.

A month later, Julia opened a letter from DeVoto, although not Bernard, as she'd anticipated, but his wife, Avis. And what a letter!—several single-spaced typewritten pages of beautifully wrought prose, not only thanking her for the knife but rhapsodizing about meals she'd eaten in Parisian bistros and asking for advice on several related issues. "She pours out words the way the waters come down at Ladore," Paul cracked. There was real warmth in her writing; it was personable and engaging, the type of letter that begged a response. Julia couldn't let it go unanswered.

Back-and-forth letters flew during the next few months, an exchange between the women of their dynamic lives. They shared family information, recipes, self-scrutiny, and political views, both consumed by the looming presidential election. Nothing was an unsuitable topic for consideration. "Before marriage I was wildly interested in sex," Julia disclosed, "but since joining up with my old goat, it has taken its proper position in my life." There was so much to say, so much to ponder and chew on. Avis DeVoto, it turns out, was the perfect pen pal for Julia, so confident, expressive, an outspoken free spirit who refused to stand by while events unfolded around her. "She had a very particular view of what was right and what was wrong," said her son, Mark, "and she put herself on the line for things that mattered, no matter how unpopular or against the tide." She was "a take-charge gal," a Renaissance woman—wife, mother, writer, editor, critic, volunteer for charities, political activist, and savvy cook, with more than a hand or two in the publishing business. She seemed to know her way around the various houses, dropping names of legendary editors and raising Julia's eyebrows.

By November 1952, Julia could no longer resist. She sent Avis a chapter of *French Home Cooking,* with correspondence covering her arrangement with—and misgivings about—Ives Washburn. Any critique, as well as advice, was welcomed. "And please," Julia implored, "be frank and brutal."

Avis wasn't one to mince words. She was "wildly excited" about what she eventually read. In fact, she was so keen about the book that she couldn't believe it was as good as it was. "There isn't any cookbook like it," she said, adding she was "absolutely convinced that you really have got something here that could be a classic and make your fortune and go on selling forever." As for Ives Washburn, it was as Julia suspected—they were "small, poor, and not well known." Avis thought the women should jump ship for Houghton Mifflin, the Boston house that published her husband. She asked Julia's permission to show the manuscript to Dorothy de Santillana, one of Houghton's leading editors and a former cooking student of Dione Lucas, the first female graduate of Le Cordon Bleu. "I'm quite sure she'd give her eye-teeth to get this particular book." Julia needn't worry about her fear that they "seem to be sewed up morally (not legally) with Ives Washburn." According to her husband, Avis said, "there is no such thing as a moral obligation to a publisher."

That was all Julia needed to hear. Houghton Mifflin was big-time, it was legit, a huge step up from the basement operation that was Ives Washburn. She had what she thought was "a major work" on her hands, and had "no intention of wasting it on a no-account firm." Houghton Mifflin would take her book seriously, they had a track record with cookbooks, would publish it with dignity, promote it, pay royalties—everything she wanted. But how would she convince Louisette to agree? Louisette had a relationship with Ives Washburn. Its publisher, Sumner Putnam, had "absolutely charmed" her during a visit to New York, and they'd become friends in the interim. She felt "they had an obligation to keep working with him," though Julia "was not convinced."

Besides, Putnam had never responded to Julia's letter. Two months had gone by and not a word from his office. Did it take more than a few days to read a chapter on sauces? Had he lost interest? Was he neglecting her on purpose? This was exactly the type of poor stewardship Julia had feared.

She continued to lobby Simca to take her side against Ives Washburn, decrying their mistreatment any chance she got. She brooded over the affair like a spurned lover. They had to protect themselves, she insisted, do what was right for the book. It wasn't enough to trust in the publisher's good faith. After all, Ives Washburn had hung them out to dry once before. Simca held out as long as she could, but she was no match for Julia's agitprop. In the end, she agreed they should test the waters. Louisette had no choice but to make the decision unanimous.

By January 1953, it was all but confirmed: Dorothy de Santillana was "tickled pink" about *French Home Cooking*, which she read and considered "an essential book." There was no doubt that Houghton Mifflin would acquire it. In fact, paperwork was already in the pipeline for a contract, as well as an advance of $750.

Avis, it seemed, had pulled off the impossible. "HOORAY," Julia scrawled as part of her reply. She was beside herself—thrilled to have a deal at last, delighted to be with a big-time publisher. It validated everything she'd been doing these last few years, everything she'd been working toward since graduating from Smith. At last, a career she could call her own, with a payoff, she figured, no more than two or three years off. *A writer.* It's what she had wanted for herself all along, ever since New York, when she had made the rounds of magazines and journals, begging for an editorial job. In New York, she had desired to become "a great woman novelist." This wasn't so far off the mark. It had taken her longer than she thought to achieve her goal, on a route that had taken her halfway around the globe, but none of that mattered anymore. She was a *writer,* with a contract. A cookbook writer, no less. Could life be any better than that? HOORAY, indeed.

ALMOST SIMULTANEOUSLY OTHER news arrived that elicited a weaker and halfhearted hooray. On January 15, his fifty-first birthday, Paul's new orders finally came through: he was being made a Public Affairs Officer, given charge of all southern France—from the Italian border to the Pyrenees—requiring an immediate move to Marseille. It was a huge step up as far as promotions go—and a huge step down in regard to locales. Nothing beat Paris as a foreign posting. Sure, as Paul noted, "it might have been Reykjavik or Addis Abbaba," but measured against Paris, Marseille was Dubuque.

Marseille. A move south threatened to undo all the blessings of the last few months. Still, Julia put the best face on the news. She "knew Paris could not last forever," knew, after four years in paradise, they'd "been living on borrowed time." But—*Marseille.* It was another France entirely, the other end of the country, where they spoke a dialect of French that sounded like Uzbek. An eight-hour drive from Simca and Louisette, from a restaurant scene that never failed to amaze, from *haute couture* on every street corner. At least they'd still be in France, Julia recognized, on the Mediterranean, no less. And it would "mean a wonderful acquaintance

with Provençal cooking," an invitation to road test recipes for bouillabaisse, ratatouille, tapenade, *moules frites, pissaladière, aïoli, pistou,* and myriad
dishes rife with tomato, garlic, onion, and pepper. As food went, it would
be a welcome break from the super-rich cream sauces that had begun to
do a number on her and Paul's stomachs.

"It means, of course, that we three G's can't work closely together, and
the school will suffer, and from the point of view of a cooking career, a
real blow," she lamented. Simca, especially, was "sad to see her go." The
two women had forged an extraordinary relationship both in and out
of the kitchen. After long days cooking, they still chose to spend most
evenings socializing, enjoying long dinners locked in noisy repartee,
their husbands developing a similar friendship. The couples vacationed
together in Normandy, exchanged friends and other intimacies. This was
going to be a difficult separation.

Even so, they'd press on with the cookbook. Most of the work, the
recipe testing, was done individually anyway. They'd have to post their
results for the time being. Besides, Julia planned frequent trips to Paris,
and the Fischbachers had a farmhouse they spent summers at, in the
countryside, near Nice. There would be plenty of opportunity for con-
sultation. "It's the personal getting together and quick exchange, and
experiments together that will not always be possible," she despaired.
Tant pis. C'est la vie.

Anybody else might have thought they'd been banished to the provinces, but Julia immediately embraced the move. Marseille was someplace different, someplace new, someplace else. It was a typical Julia
Child reaction: decisive, pragmatic, unemotional, and utterly selfless,
in particular when it came to her husband's welfare. Part of her behavior could be attributed to pride, with roots stretching back to the family
dynamic. Like her marriage to Paul, the move reinforced Julia's independent streak. Being open to change, exploring new cultures—it ran counter to everything her father stood for. At the moment, this reflex was
especially strong. In November, she had spoken by phone to her father,
who laced into her about her liberal views. "You wouldn't know how
the country feels," he sneered, alluding to the recent election in which
Eisenhower became president. According to Pop, Julia was an outsider,
un-American—"you people over there," as opposed to the patriots back
home. "This was hard to take," Julia admitted. She considered John
McWilliams "a darling man, a generous father, a real do-gooder in his
community," yet a person who refused to respect an opposing view. *Her*

view. Apparently, he considered her "persona traitoria," as she termed it, a reprobate better left to the French.

Still, Julia wrote to him "religiously every week," not so much a daughter's responsibility as a link to the family she missed and loved. He'd never understand her, that much she knew—or approve of her lifestyle or the choices she made. Be that as it may, blood was thicker than water. He was her father and the patriarch of the McWilliams clan and she loved him.

She would have gone on writing him, too, were it not for a letter from her stepmother that arrived the following week. In it, Phila warned her against upsetting her father, which meant saying nothing to him "about either politics or Charlie Chaplin." Another letter, from her brother John, a few days later, inveighed against the evils of foisting her ideas on other people. "Furthermore," he wrote, "the only real red-blooded Americans are the Republicans."

Okay, okay, she got the message. Nothing compelled her to win political points. Her family was what they were, she conceded: "Old Guard Republicans of the blackest and most violently Neanderthal stripe." Instead, she'd confine her updates back home to work on the cookbook. No, that wouldn't do either; her father would equate that with *French* cooking, another of his peeves. Paul's promotion was also off-limits since Pop disapproved of her husband—that "New Dealer"—almost as much as his job. Unfortunately, they were "on such different beams." All her remarks would have to be health- and weather-related from now on. And he'd hear about Marseille, like it or not.

There was so much to do to prepare for the move. Leaving Roo de Loo was a chore in itself, to say nothing of being a heartbreaking affair. Julia and Paul had loved the place. It was perfect, perfectly funky, a period piece with charm. Over the last four years they'd squeezed half a lifetime within those walls. They'd lived, loved, celebrated, dreamed, grown, discovered the beginnings of who they were meant to be. Now packing up had become a killer of a job. "Julie wants to keep everything," Paul noted. "I want to eliminate everything, and we meet in the middle somewhere, not without misgivings on both sides."

Paul had taken hundreds, maybe thousands, of photographs of Paris. They'd collected a similar amount of books and Venetian glassware. His wedge of easels lay stacked against a wall, his wine cellar stowed in crates beneath an eave. Julia's book research filled "two wretchedly heavy steamer trunks." And her cooking *tchotchkes*—she had enough to open her own Dehillerin annex. "*God*," Paul moaned, "what a pile of stuff!" Everything needed sorting—and culling. Space in their luggage was at an extra-precious premium. Paul's orders read "on temporary duty," which meant they would not be in Marseille on an "official" basis until his transfer papers arrived from the State Department. That could take a week—or an eternity, you never knew. Nothing, not even their income, was guaranteed. So they were in "one of those Kafka-like limbos"— neither able to give up the lease on Roo de Loo nor rent a place of their own in Marseille. For weeks, maybe months, they'd be living out of suit-cases in a hotel. It was crunch time: sacrifices had to be made.

One of the hardest things to leave behind was Minette, Julia's beloved cat, but there was no room in the car, nowhere to keep her in Marseille. Between the owner of Roo de Loo and a long list of friends, no one stepped forward to adopt. A shelter was out of the question; putting her out was unthinkable. Julia wouldn't leave Paris, she said, until a proper home was found. Unfortunately, she was running out of prospects—and time. She hustled up and down the rue de Bourgogne, looking for a suit-able candidate. At the last minute, she arranged to leave Minette with the concierge family that owned the charcuterie on the rue de Bourgogne. They had "a nice old dog," and Mini could patrol the shop for mice and scraps.

That left only the farewells to be made. Julia and Paul covered the city like "two steam engines," darting in and out of old haunts on both banks of the Seine in a concerted effort to tie up loose ends. Their last day in Paris was a whirlwind, as they called on Paul's teary staff at the American embassy; Madame Ettlinger, "the ancient Queen Bee of Les Gourmettes"; that old fox Curnonsky, who received them in long under-wear; Madame Focillon, the titular head of their art salon; Simca; Loui-sette; a half-dozen friends and acquaintances who made their stay in the city a memorable feast. Then a final memorable feast: supper—but *where*? There were so many choices, so many favorites. Which place deserved to host their gustatory send-off? Since that first life-changing meal at Rouen, dozens of restaurants had dazzled Julia Child, each one a price-less tutorial in the education of a cook.

Julia ran through all the obvious choices—Brasserie Lipp, Le Grand Véfour, Lapérouse, des Artistes. No one place could do the city justice. In the end, she hit on the perfect spot.

Sometime just after nine o'clock, after all the tears and goodbyes and farewell toasts, Julia and Paul, weary from their rounds, parked outside

Roo de Loo and took the rickety cage elevator up to the fourth floor. A soothing soup, a crisp salad, a baguette, a bottle of wine. There, in the candlelit glow of the three French windows that opened onto the garden, they enjoyed "supper à *deux* in [their] darling, soon-to-be-dismantled kitchen," oblivious to the stacks of boxes downstairs. The night was clear, the view toward Montparnasse a starry rooftop triptych. A montage of memories wafted through the room.

This, they decided, was the place to celebrate Paris, the city that made hungry where most it satisfied.

Thirteen

Frenchy French

As it turned out, Marseille wasn't Dubuque. There was no timber, no tech, no Mississippi, no John Deere. There was no Lapérouse or Max Bugnard, either, but some things don't signify once outside of Paris. Julia regarded her new home as "a great bouillabaisse" of a city, a place whose sensory mix was as different from Dubuque as it was from Paris—or Prague or Peoria, for that matter—yet every bit as vibrant. "Such a feeling of life and movement," she enthused, trying to describe it for the folks back home, "gurgling crowded streets, wonderful over-flowing markets ... great hearty, howling, laughing vendors." No doubt about it, Marseille was as raucous as it was colorful. Paul couldn't get over its symphonic din. "There seems to be ten times as much horn-blowing, gear-clashing, shouting, whistling, door-banging, dropping of lumber, breaking of glass, blaring of radios, boat-whistling, gong-clanging, brake-screeching, and angry shouting as anywhere else," he remarked.

The first time the Childs set foot in Marseille, they walked the entire city, from hilltop to hilltop, trying to gauge its mongrel sprawl, but ultimately they found there was no better place for people-watching than from a café table in the bustling Old Port. You could sit for hours on that horseshoe-shaped marina, gorging on freshly shucked oysters and a cool cassis, as its crazy-quilt community paraded by. And what a spectacular sight they were! "The Marseille-types are terrific in their variety and color," it was noted, "lots of *very* black Senegalese with tribal cicatrices on

In the Marseille kitchen overlooking quai de Rive Neuve, March 16, 1953

their faces looking like tiger-claw marks and Arabs in costume and wonderful Paxinou-like Spanishy women with breasts like headlights and bronze fishermen with tattoos and gamins galore and great mounds of fresh fish being unloaded and nets being dried and good solid waterfront stinks in multitudinous profusion."

To Julia's eye, Marseille stood as "a rough, rude, 'Southern' " town. Its people took "in pleasure through every pore, in every form, as much as they could," wrote Flaubert. Sailors crowded "into the cabarets, laughing with the girls, turning over jugs of wine, singing, dancing, love-making at their ease." The street life was vivid, there was a persisting tug of intrigue in the air, with its funneling mass of Italians, Russians, Greeks, Armenians, Corsicans, Algerians, Moroccans, and Tunisians. One heard "a hundred unknown languages spoken." Julia clearly felt the raw combustible energy in the city. "It struck me as a rich broth of vigorous, emotional, uninhibited Life," she said.

The robust character signaled a reawakening of Marseille. As France's largest commercial seaport, it had been bombed senseless during the war, first by German and Italian forces in 1940, then by the Allies in advance of the liberation. When Julia and Paul arrived, in March 1953, a noticeable rebuilding had begun, but it was a slog, hampered by graft and bureaucracy. The one notable development was Le Corbusier's "massive block of flats"—Unité d'Habitation—opened in 1952, but its severe, cell-like architecture eluded the sober Marseillais, who called it *la maison du fada,* slang for "the nuthouse."

At the outset, Julia and Paul were merely uneasy guests. They lived out of suitcases in a rather shabby, boxlike hotel room "covered with flowered wallpaper and twenty-five watt bulbs," with no kitchen, no view, nowhere to escape to collect one's thoughts. All their meals were eaten out, in one of the endless Provençal cafés whose regional dishes satisfied Julia no end. The varieties of fresh fish on offer aroused her relentless curiosity, especially the *loup,* a Mediterranean sea bass grilled simply over fennel. She knew enough to avoid some of the more exotic specialties. Years ago, on her first visit to Marseille, she had eaten the pleasant-sounding *tripou,* a variation on tripe wrapped around bits of pig and sheep feet, sewn into a pillow and boiled in bouillon. As far as its ingredients went, "there was something else," she suspected: "faint herbs, and, I am quite sure, a bit of pig shit rolled in also." She'd been looking forward to the dish until arriving at that conclusion. In any case, she determined it wasn't her style. "Possibly an acquired taste, pig shit." No doubt.

Marseille certainly had its share of character, but it wasn't Paris, that much was sure. From what Julia gathered on an initial look-see, "Marseille is a place where women are seen but not heard, and stick close to home"—in which case it had come up against the wrong gal. Muzzle Julia Child? Not in Marseille, not anywhere on the planet. On first impression, it seemed Marseille wouldn't offer her many opportunities. Only a week after they'd arrived, Julia was already bored stiff. Their first Sunday in the city brought it all crashing down. The cold, gray day, bleak and grimy, mirrored the lethargy she was feeling. Stomping around in a circle, she vented to Paul: "Well, dammit, we can't cook: no kitchen; can't paint: no paints; can't visit: no friends yet; can't drown sorrows either in bouillabaisse or wine because of our feeble guts; and I don't *want* to write any more. I'm wrote-out, and I'm slept-out, and I'm read-out—and still two hours to dinner time."

Julia's frustration was exacerbated by the scarcity of potential friends. The consulate was usually a touchstone for the fragmented circle of ex-pats, with plenty of Americans and their wives on staff. In Marseille, she found them to be "an awfully nice bunch, serious, hard-working and warm-hearted," but with no one destined to amuse or inspire her. "Very nice folk—" she reflected, "but no blood-brothers."

Everything Julia did in those first few weeks was framed by struggle. Her writing stumbled with self-doubt as she vied with her troubled mood. She grew peevish, distracted. "What with all this moving and settling," she wrote to Avis DeVoto, "I was becoming frantic, schizophrenic . . . combined with anguish, frustration and ill-temper."

All of that changed, however, when she found a suitable apartment. It was a charming little place on the quai de Rive Neuve, a sun-filled, fifth-floor railroad flat overlooking the Old Port, which Julia sublet from the Swedish consul, who was on leave for six months. From the tall parlor windows, there were views out to sea and an ongoing scene that filled her with delight. "There is a small, two-masted schooner filled with fish right under my nose," she reported, "little fishing boats parked across the way, seagulls flying." Dozens of sun-baked stevedores unloaded their catches onto the quay. Inside, the furniture was as Swedish as Ingrid Bergman: blond, pale, not a hair out of place. It was obvious from the layout that the consul was fastidious; odds were he'd never touched the gas stove. "Though the kitchen is presumably 'fully furnished,' " Julia grumbled, "it is more fully furnished like a eunuch." But—never mind. With a few clever changes she began cooking again, which banished the doldrums like a fast-moving cloud.

And more sun shone through: La Criée aux Poissons, the wholesale fish market, happened to be steps from her front door, which helped to jump-start Julia's work for the book. She had begun research on the fish chapter before leaving Paris, and, as March faded into April, she gunned it into high gear. "The French are magnificent with fish," she wrote as an introduction to the recipes. "[T]he art of its cooking and saucing is accomplished with great taste and skill." Such wasn't the case in America, she knew, where it was next to impossible to buy fresh fish in cities such as Minneapolis, Omaha, Phoenix, and, well, Dubuque. Even in Pasadena and Santa Barbara, within spitting distance of the ocean, McWilliams family fish dinners had been achingly grim. "We had broiled fish for Friday dinners, pan-fried trout when we camped in the High Sierras, and boiled salmon the Fourth of July. That was it." In early 1953, only the most adventurous Americans ate fresh local fish; otherwise, the choice was limited to frozen cod or flounder—or fish sticks, a brand-new phenomenon infiltrating supermarket freezers. It was unlikely that people knew the names of most fish, aside from the usual suspects, a local lake fish, perhaps, or shrimp—not much more. But ever since that *sole meunière* in Rouen—that *sole meunière* in Rouen!—Julia was sold. "I [never] imagined fish could be taken so seriously or sauced so voluptuously." And she was determined to spread the gospel to the flock back home.

But—how to convey all of this to the American cook?

There were more than two hundred recipes for fillet of sole alone in her food-stained copy of *Répertoire de la cuisine*. And all those masterpieces she ate in Paris—whole roasted fish, mousses, brochettes, bisques. *Bouillabaisse!* (Now that she was in Marseille, she intended to solve that shifty little fellow.) Trouble was, there was no way to identify the equivalent names for French versus American fish. "Many types of European fish did not exist in the States and vice versa," she discovered. For example, the sole found on American plates wasn't sole at all, but a version of flounder that was smaller and bland. *Lotte,* a staple of every French menu, was called monkfish in the States and rarely, if ever, served. What about langoustines? Neither shrimp (too small) nor lobster (too large); maybe a prawn, which was more British, but *prawns* wouldn't fly back home. And what the hell was she to do with *rascasse?* There was a West Coast fish called sculpin, or rockfish, that might do as a stand-in, but really just a second or third cousin, at best. Somehow, she had to find a reasonable American facsimile for each of the species so that the great French recipes could "be cooked in the USA with approximately the same end-result."

That goal wasn't as easy as it sounded. There were two books on her shelf that she drew on for basic facts—Milo Miloradovich's *The Art of Fish Cookery* and Louis Pullig De Gouy's *The Gold Cookbook,* which included a twenty-six-page index of French fish and American equivalents. For most people, that would serve as plenty to ponder, but Julia wouldn't rest until she had all the facts. "My, there is so much to know, and I keep bumping into things," she wrote to Avis DeVoto. There was no point, she said, in just taking "hearsay" out of a book or relying on advice from Simca and Louisette. Every time she intended to make a point in her writing, Julia stopped and asked herself: "Do I really and absolutely know that fact?" For Julia Child, the facts possessed almost a mystique. They were the key to her power as a cooking teacher, the key to having American home cooks trust in her authority. Too many cookbooks, she found, had recipes from so-called reliable chefs that were adapted, but never tested for accuracy. For a woman for whom facts were sacrament, cutting corners like that was an unpardonable sin. Getting it right meant all your facts were in order, and not only in order, but bulletproof, airtight. Damnit, she was going to squeeze every last bit of information out of sources before committing a recipe to the printed page.

To that end, Julia leaned on Paul's government access to agencies, offices, and bureaus that had collected and studied the facts. Fish . . . hmmm, let's see, she wondered . . . who would have data on everything to do with fish? Ahhh, of course: the Department of Fisheries, part of the new Interior Services. There was even a Deputy Fish Coordinator, imagine that. She fired off letters full of questions, great and small, about fish, as well as to the official's French equivalent. And answers came back with notable efficiency—reams and reams of information, everything you wanted to know about fish but were afraid to ask: which were firm-fleshed, which flimsy, which were saltwater, which fresh? She asked similar questions about meat, corresponding with personnel at the Department of Agriculture. "I loved this kind of research," she wrote in a memoir. Facts, facts as valuable as ingredients.

She also loved her guinea pigs—not of the whiskery rodent sort, but friends and relatives who tested her work and sent back detailed critiques. These guinea pigs were her personal pets: "very typical of most average Americans . . . not aware of the classical tradition of French Cooking."

Every time Julia finished writing a recipe, she opened the case of her Royal portable typewriter and banged out single-spaced letters explaining the technique in exquisite detail. "Woodpeckering," Paul called the sound she made tapping at those keys. It went on for hours, *peck, peck, peck, peck, peck, peck peck,* while Julia attacked her "flying wedge"—six or seven pages of onionskin separated by five or six sheets of flimsy carbon paper. The number depended on how many guinea pigs got a copy. On most occasions, one went to Dort in San Francisco, Avis in Cambridge, Freddie Child in Pennsylvania, Rachel Child at college, Katy Gates in Pasadena, as well as Simca and Louisette. *Peck, peck, peck, peck, peck, peck, peck . . .* It took some elbow grease to get an impression through all those pages, and also something entirely different—a fierce perversity—making correction after correction. "It was terrible, just awful," she complained of the job, in retrospect. But it was the only way she felt able to maintain perspective.

Perspective skewed by a bit of paranoia. Julia anguished over sharing several "real innovations"—recipes she and her colleagues had developed that, as far as anyone knew, hadn't appeared in any other cookbooks. From all she had heard about the publishing business, these recipes were essentially fair game, so better to keep them from the grabby hands of rivals lest they wind up in some rag and "become old stuff." It would just kill her to lose the *beurre blanc* recipe she'd cadged from La Mère Michel in Paris. And her "beloved mayonnaise" was as confidential as the nuclear launch codes, although an almost identical version appeared in Madame Saint-Ange. Nevertheless, she made her guinea pigs swear an oath of silence. And just in case they hadn't gotten the message, Julia buried these recipes between special colored sheets and scrawled *Top Secret* across the tops and bottoms of each page. "This may sound overly cautious," she apologized to her sister, Dort, "but I don't want to take no chances, after all the work we've put in."

For a few weeks, after she'd moved into the apartment on the quay, Julia had the place almost all to herself. Paul was working endlessly, brutal fourteen-hour days, including weekends, so she plunged into the proverbial soup to demystify bouillabaisse. One can only imagine the trapdoor that recipe opened. In Marseille, where the dish originated as a fisherman's stew, everyone and his brother claimed to make the only authentic stuff—*la vraie bouillabaisse*—but Julia, characteristically, pronounced that "a lot of bushwah." She knew "a 'real' fisherman would make a 'real' bouillabaisse with whatever he had on hand," the bony unsalable leftovers from the day's catch, along with a brothy Provençal soup base of garlic, onions, tomatoes, olive oil, saffron, thyme, and bay leaf. *La vraie bouillabaisse?* Julia's response to that was: "Balls!"

Bouillabaisse wasn't a stylish soup in the gastronomic sense: the stock was water-based, the vegetables coarsely chopped, fish flaked inelegantly apart, herbs as sharp and musky as pipe tobacco. It was nothing like the *potages* Julia had mastered at Le Cordon Bleu, with their fine, rich creams and clarified stocks, or Simca's vichyssoise so dense with minced chives it resembled a work of pointillism. But bouillabaisse possessed an undeniable intensity: it filled the mouth with an explosion of flavors, a splendid example of culinary anarchy. Provençal people were as passionate about it as American Southerners about their barbecue.

Julia wasn't intimidated. She went right at it, canvassing the boats that docked off the port, buying catch-of-the-day from a gang of burly fishwives, discussing her options with various local restaurateurs. If she was going to make bouillabaisse, it would be the real McCoy—or as close to that target as was humanly possible. A traditional specimen, she knew, had at least three kinds of Mediterranean fish, typically *rascasse* (scorpion fish), *grondin* (sea robin), and *congre* (eel). But Julia had seen it made with lotte, red mullet, hake, Saint-Pierre, and mussels, even langoustine, if one were feeling particularly flush. The rules were fast and loose when it came to this soup. Some recipes called for tomato, some for potato, some no saffron, others for *rouille,* a peppery *aïoli* floated on top, as a garnish. "Some people also say that if the fish are caught and eaten immediately, they have enough taste so you don't have to make a stock," Julia said. "Maybe that's true, but who lives by a fishnet all the time?"

"How in the hell are we ever going to make bouillabaisse in [the States]?" Avis prodded her.

Whatever the eventual recipe, Julia knew it had to remain authentic but accessible to the American cook. That meant experimenting—she called it *bouilla-ing*—like mad in her new kitchen. First up was bouillabaisse *borgno* with fennel, saffron pistils, bay leaf, and thyme. She made it for lunch one day and, at the last minute, decided against straining out the vegetables, which was a standard of Marseillais style. The next day, she processed everything through a food mill, to thicken the broth. To potato or not to potato?—that was the question, so she made it both ways, with and without. Later, she cut lobsters and crabs into pieces to gussy up the dish. Who knew there were so many variations?

The book was taking an enormous amount of research. Each recipe required endless preparation—shopping and cooking, testing and note-taking, scrutiny and analysis—much like the development of any master's thesis. Readers, Julia knew, would demand such thoroughness. An American cook had to be able to follow each recipe. It had to be logical and establish a sense of confidence that everything the cook made, while not necessarily easy, would at least be foolproof. Everything had to come together just as the authors promised, and it had to taste good, taste *French*. Even if a modern lifestyle tended toward the fast and the easy—casseroles had become all the rage back home—there was an appreciable interest in entertaining with flair. French flair. It seemed to prove everything Avis had been saying about American housewives and a new kind of cook. They wanted to educate and enchant their families, to impress their guests. "Don't compromise—," she warned Julia, "you know what you are doing, and you don't want to turn out a hybrid cookbook. This is a discipline, and it mustn't be watered down."

Julia recognized the difference between the so-called reliable cookbooks in American bookstores and the one she'd always intended to write. For the most part, the reliables were "not well-written"; they were slapdash and full of holes. "I want ours to be way ahead of everything in accuracy and depth and perception," she declared. "Otherwise you get just an ordinary recipe and that's not the point of our book." And if Julia happened to overlook the refinement of a recipe, the rigor of a technique, the quality of ingredients, or a venerable age-old rule, Simca and Louisette were on hand to point them out and offer explanations, even if they were often contradictory.

Letters flew back and forth between Marseille and Paris, where Julia's co-writers were at work on their own set of classic French recipes. Simca, it turned out, was "a real workhorse," an extraordinary cook, who, according to Julia, put in "five solid hours of bookery a day no matter what happened." But Simca's personal recipes, the ones in her repertoire that she cooked from memory, since childhood, were not precise. They needed testing, retesting, tweaking, and revision before they were deemed suitable for the book. It just wasn't in her nature to work from a recipe, much less to measure ingredients. Like most Norman women who had cooked all their lives, she "knew in her bones why and how certain things are done." It befuddled her how Americans needed everything spelled out. "She is inclined to think that written rules, accurate measurements, and detailed explanations are a lot of hooey," Avis DeVoto wrote of the collaboration.

Julia constantly had to stay on Simca's case, and not only about writing clear, orderly—perfect!—directions. Their *scientific* approach to recipes—that is, their method of testing and retesting until each dish was flawless—often contradicted old masters like Escoffier, Carême, and Brillat-Savarin, whose recipes were anything but scientific. Those "boys," as Julia referred to them, got away with murder in print, using vague, often elusive instructions. Just because they were renowned didn't mean they were right. Who said they knew more than Julia and Simca? "I consider ourselves just as much AUTHORITIES as anyone else," Julia insisted. It seemed like a perfectly good point, but Simca worried that they'd come off as fools. After all, who were she and Julia to be so cocksure, so insolent? They were only home cooks—and *women,* to boot.

"I keep forgetting that in the European tradition women are not used to taking on authority themselves," Julia reasoned. But Julia was American and didn't lack for confidence. She was ready to take on all comers, the bigger the better. It irked the hell out of her how so many liberties were taken by established cookbook writers. One book, in particular, *Bouquet de France* by Samuel Chamberlain, drove her nuts. It was a follow-up to his beloved best seller, *Clementine in the Kitchen,* and Julia saw it as "big competition." "It is a wonderful and beautiful book," she acknowledged. "I just regret that the recipes are not more professionally done." *Poulet à la niçoise,* for example, made absolutely no sense. "Cut a 5lb. fowl for fricassee," Julia narrated, "cook for an hour." *Hmmm.* "How old the chick . . . 5lb. pretty big, might be an old hen, an hour wouldn't be enough, probably . . . and it would be pretty tough eating anyway." Other recipes—for *langouste à l'américaine* and *escalope de veau,* both of which she and Simca were testing for their own book—were equally careless, full of "little slips" and "pitfalls."

That would never be the case for *French Home Cooking. Never,* even if it meant policing her colleagues. "We must be Descartesian [*sic*]," she insisted, "and never accept anything unless it comes from an extremely professional source, and even then, to see how we personally like how it is done." To that end, she sent Simca three rules to live by:

Stand up for your opinions as an equal partner in this enterprise.
Keep the book French.
Follow the scientific method respecting your *own* careful findings,
     after having studied the findings and recommendations of other
     authorities. Work with exact measurements, temperatures, etc.

And, once having established a method, stick to it religiously unless
    you find it not satisfactory.

Simca stubbornly clung to the old traditions, but steadily, surely, Julia
brought her around. Louisette, however, was an altogether different story.
    Louisette enjoyed the business of the book, its conceptualization, the
camaraderie of working on it. She got a kick out of the back-and-forth
with the publisher; the idea of being in print thrilled her. But unlike
Simca and Julia, who were engaged in a process of discovery, Louisette
was oh-so-casual about everything, especially when it came to the cooking. Her recipes were good ones and she turned them out with flair, but
they were incomplete, too incidental, haphazard. How she arrived at
results was often inexplicable; she seemed incapable of describing the
procedure. Where Julia and now Simca were driven to experiment and
understand, Louisette was unconcerned. Whether she wasn't willing to
put in the time or merely didn't have the curiosity is difficult to discern,
but the imbalance was surely felt. Julia, especially, was growing disenchanted. "I have a strong feeling that this book we are doing is not at all
the kind of book that is her meat," she wrote to Simca, which was another
way of saying Louisette was a lightweight. "I think she is temperamentally
suited to a gay little book, like *What's Cooking,* with chic little recipes and
tours de main [tricks], and a bit of poesy and romanticism. The kind of recipes in *Vogue, Harper's Bazaar,* and the smart little magazines." Otherwise,
Julia acknowledged that Louisette's "role in our bookwork was minimal."
    Louisette had her usefulness, however. Julia saw her as the public
face of their book, "everyone's dream of the perfect Frenchwoman." If it
ever came to pass that they were invited to be on television, an American
audience would love Louisette. And she was "a good natural promoter,"
plugged into the right kinds of people, with "all those women's club connections" that would help to sell the book. Later, Julia's party line would
be that Louisette was too wrapped up in her family to contribute equally
in the work, but truth be told, she lacked Julia's and Simca's commitment.
Not to mention their talent. When push came to shove, Julia couldn't
avoid the hard truth. "Louisette, sweet as she is, is just unable and incapable of doing any serious work, and never has," she wrote to Avis DeVoto.
"She is the complete amateur."
    Even though Julia insisted that the book was "most definitely a joint
effort," it dawned on her that she was carrying the brunt of it. She steered
the direction of the content, arranged its hefty format, gave it shape and

style. The voice throughout was mostly hers, but the spirit, she knew, "must be French," even "Frenchy French." Although she shared the cooking with Simca, "the writing has to be done by Julia because the book will be in her language," Paul explained. She typed all their respective research, then the recipes, and finally the finished chapters. When Simca and Louisette drifted, she pulled them back on course with rallying encouragement. "We are a team!" she reminded them again and again. She collated the input she received from her litter of guinea pigs. She was the go-between with Avis DeVoto and Dorothy de Santillana at Houghton Mifflin in Boston. The work involved was all-consuming.

By the end of 1953, the cat was out of the bag: the girls were constructing a monster of a manuscript—"maybe 700 pages," Paul surmised. Maybe more. His crack that "it ain't going to be no brochure" was an understatement of colossal proportions. The sauce chapter alone ran more than a couple hundred pages. Julia had "put herself on a relentless five-hours-a-day regime for the book," but that was only for starters. Five grew to eight, then to nine and occasionally twelve. As the days passed, as the work snowballed, the book—*the book*—gradually took over her life. Still, Julia refused to scale back. "She's determined to be author, foreign-service wife, cook, bottle washer, market buyer, and sophisticated hostess," Paul marveled.

Never before had Julia worked more diligently than in that tidy apartment overlooking the Old Port. There, and in another, more spacious apartment they moved to in early March 1954, she juggled the challenges, keeping them all in the air. In this hothouse of Paul's devotion and her own engrossment, Julia thrived. As the challenges shifted and overlapped, Julia kept everything spinning. There, in the midst of apocalyptic disarray, she displayed the full range of her multitasking powers. The crush of responsibilities somehow didn't overwhelm her. The move to Marseille, in fact, marked the high point of a period of unparalleled emotional tranquillity and productive output.

Everything seemed to be going right for Julia and Paul. After a long delay, the Houghton Mifflin contract finally arrived, along with a check for $250, the first of three installments toward the $750 advance. Paul's boss, the consul general, a man he despised and privately called Queeg, was replaced with a man he considered "a wonderful guy." For a change, he began to enjoy his job, "his contacts around the region just blossoming into real usefulness." Julia finished a chapter on eggs that took Avis DeVoto by storm. "Swept off my feet," she wrote in response to a sneak preview. "Knew before how good the book would be but never felt it quite this way before. Masterly. Calm, collected, completely basic, and as exciting as a novel to read."

To celebrate, Julia decided to take a few days off and accompany Paul to a government conference in Paris. It had been a few months since her last visit there, and she longed to spend some face time in a kitchen with Simca and Louisette. Despite her fondness for Marseille, Paris enchanted her. "Paris is heavenly," she wrote to Avis from her hotel on the Left Bank. "Such fun to wander around it again." She had never found any place more suitable to her tastes. "Every thing about it satisfies everything in me." Old friends came out of the crumbling woodwork to see her. Louisette entertained; a gala dinner included Julia's old Cordon Bleu chefs, Max Bugnard and Claude Thilmont. Not even the weather, a raw, rainy spring, could dampen such pleasure.

It took more than weather to douse Julia's spirit.

The look on Paul's face was the first sign that something was wrong. He'd gone to see Charlie Moffly, his old liaison officer at the USIS, about some summer home leave for him and Julia. It had been a while, almost three years, since they'd been back to the States for Dort's wedding. Julia wanted to see her father, who was struggling with the impediments of old age, and her sister, who had had two children. If possible, they planned to build in time to finally meet Avis in person at her home in Cambridge, then head up to Lopaus for a rest on the beach with Charlie and Freddie. Moffly approved the home leave without blinking, but intimated they wouldn't be coming back to Marseille. Most likely, Paul would be transferred, by the summer at the latest. Nothing was certain yet, but "the likelihood," he said, "is that you will be transferred to Germany."

Oh no, not Germany, Paul thought. It hasn't been ten years since that savage war, since Hitler.

"Or an opening may exist in the Middle East."

Could it get any worse than that? *Why?* Paul wanted to know. What had he done to deserve such a posting?

A letter arrived shortly that laid it all out. "It has been the fixed policy of the Agency," it read, "to rotate the assignment of personnel after they have served more than four years in a given country." Paul had been in France for almost six years. It was time to pack up and move somewhere else.

"God damn it," Paul groused, "we just aren't ready to move again." Especially to Germany, with "its conquered-country neuroses," where he couldn't begin to speak, let alone fathom, the language. One thing was certain: "This is hard—hellishly hard—on Julia's bookery. Every time she just gets settled-in, establishes a time schedule, gets her pots and knives and spoons hanging: *Wham!*" They were back on the road.

Julia found it difficult to conceal her dismay. She was "just sick" about the prospects of a move, leaving Marseille—leaving *France*. "To think of living in Germany," she wrote to the gang back home. "Will I ever get over the imagined smell of the gas chambers and the rotting bodies of the concentration camps?" It wasn't likely. But, she admitted, "this is Paul's career, and if he wants to stay in it, we've just got to resign ourselves to abrupt changes."

She was also anguishing over the specter of McCarthyism. For the past year, it had dominated the American headlines, with nauseating tales of respectable citizens hauled before the House Un-American Activities Committee and accused of being Communists. It was a witch-hunt designed to ruin anyone whose values were different than McCarthy's— which is to say, arch-conservatism of the blackest stripe. Writers, artists, teachers, intellectuals, *liberals* were all prime targets of his smear campaign. Lately, he'd been rooting through the State Department, which he was sure was in the grip of Communists incognito. He'd already sent two notorious hatchet men, Roy Cohn and David Schine, barnstorming through Europe, to purge libraries of the USIS of books written by authors they deemed Reds. The diplomatic corps was riddled with them, they maintained. They'd ransacked Paul's office in Paris just weeks after he'd moved to Marseille, and Avis had cautioned Julia that the situation was uglier and more toxic than she realized.

"I must warn you to be careful about what you say about McCarthy," she wrote. "Paul has a job. And he could lose it. You two are particularly vulnerable because you are connected with State, so for heaven's sake, watch your step."

Lately, there was more than good reason for concern. McCarthy had begun to televise the so-called hearings, making entertainment out of what were really public lynchings. Many of those who lost their jobs had served with Julia and Paul in China during the war. "I feel, actually, that at any moment we may be accused of being Communists and traitors," she wrote to Dort in March 1954. Even her father had turned against them. "My dear old Pop . . . feels we are supporting the Communist line," she lamented.

Visiting him was always a delicate affair. They stayed eight days in

Pasadena, but they were far from enjoyable, with the old man on the war-path, gunning for fascists and Reds. Having Julia and Paul in his home was an affront to decency. To him, they were "nasty *foreigners,* intellectual eggheads, who have always caused all the trouble." It was consorting with the enemy. What a relief it was when they finally left.

By contrast, meeting Avis felt like a breath of fresh air. The two women had forged a close, improbable bond. They had been corresponding for almost two years, building a friendship that seemed extraordinary for all its drawbacks. They had never met, lived continents apart, needed to make extra effort to write to stay in touch, depended on each other's good judgment not to misinterpret any number of strong opinions, endured long intervals between letters. And, yet, with each new letter, each new opus (some ran ten to twelve pages in length), the friendship became stronger, more intimate, more essential to their welfare. Food and cooking formed the heart of their interplay, but by 1954 their letters were like therapy, almost confessional and unburdening.

Avis lived with a difficult man. Bernard DeVoto was a dazzling intellectual, well read and read well by others, with an enormous scope of attitudes and opinions—and an ego to match. His blustery nature was notoriously tyrannical: DeVoto the Magnificent, DeVoto the Impaler. "He is a man of violent dislikes," Avis warned, "he does not suffer fools gladly." Those who were not well acquainted kept their distance. "If there is such a disease as infectious high blood pressure, he had it and communicated it," wrote his biographer, Wallace Stegner. "He had Avis lying awake at nights" as she absorbed his atomic intensity, even while at rest. She always referred to her husband impersonally, as DeVoto—a nod to his force, and perhaps as a shield from it.

It would be fair to say that Julia, too, lived with a difficult man. Paul wasn't a tyrant or high-strung, like Avis's husband, but he was every bit as opinionated and aware of his effect. "He was quite intimidating," says his niece, Phila, "and demanded your respect. If he didn't agree with you, he'd let you know about it, pronto." And he was compulsive: compulsively neat, compulsively fastidious, compulsively precise, especially about language. He was forever educating Julia, correcting her. Plus, he had phobias—about his bowels, about illnesses—and mood swings; he was "chronically depressed."

The women shared the innermost details about their lives, confiding in each other, as sisters might do. Pen pals. Perfect strangers, except on paper. And now that was about to change.

Julia and Paul were determined to stop in Cambridge on their way to or from Maine. Still, they didn't want to impose. "I got a letter from Julia asking if they could come and stay with us as cook-butler or as paying guests," Avis recalled.

Benny DeVoto was finishing a manuscript and dead set against an invasion by total strangers. "I don't want to meet those people," he grumbled to Avis.

"Well, all right," she said, "[but] this time we're going to."

Julia was so excited to finally meet her pen pal—and more than a little anxious. There was so much riding on their relationship. She'd invested so much of herself in it, something Julia rarely did. What if they met and it just didn't click? What if Avis was prickly in person, or absentminded—or unnaturally short? Until now, they'd only exchanged pictures. "I feel that we do not have the definitive Avis here," Julia said, gazing at the photo her pen pal had sent. "You are dark, anyway. That is a wonderful worldly expression you have on." To hedge against an adverse reaction, Julia felt it necessary to describe herself in advance of sending a return photo. "Julia: 6 ft. plus, weight 150 to 160. Bosom not as copious as she would wish, but has noticed that Botticelli bosoms are not big either. Legs OK, according to husband. Freckles." Even so, Avis was unprepared for the Amazon smiling back at her. "I am rather astonished that you are such a big girl. Six feet, whoops," she responded.

The combination of photos sharpened Avis's perceptions. Big women cast big shadows, she thought—the better to make an impression with the public. In any case, Avis was on tenterhooks to meet Julia. "Hurry, hurry," she pressed her friend.

Since arriving in the East, Paul and Julia had been "hopping about," visiting friends and family wherever possible. They were amazed at how much had changed since they'd left the States. "Everything seems bigger, shinier, faster, and I barely recognize anything I used to know," Julia said. American food, they discovered, was completely unmemorable, especially when compared to French cuisine. Nothing they'd eaten had whetted their appetites, aside from a Nathan's foot-long slathered with sauerkraut that Julia devoured with great gusto.

The day the Childs finally hit Cambridge, July 11, 1954, Avis and Benny DeVoto were otherwise engaged. "We were having a Sunday cocktail party," Avis recalled, "and a large station wagon drove up, loaded to the roof with pots and pans and equipment of all kinds." To the ever-so-genteel Cantabrigians, it looked like the Joad family had come a-callin'. "There were seven or eight people sitting around [our place] drinking martinis, and Benny wasn't very happy about strangers." He sulked like a discontented boy, while Avis and Julia fell into each other's arms.

At last! They were no longer "words on paper," but flesh and blood, "perfectly familiar." It was, as Avis put it, "love at first sight." The women hit it off like long-lost friends. For five or eight days, they were perfectly in sync, inseparable. Together they scoured the local supermarkets, whose overstocked aisles fascinated Julia. They pored over the manuscript. "And Julia took over the kitchen immediately," making garden-fresh soups and skinning fresh halibut—"all very dramatic," Avis recalled. Even Benny DeVoto was charmed. Avis was particularly struck by "his whole-hearted acceptance of the Childs." It was a blessing, she reflected. "What could be sweeter?"

In the many hours they had spent together, Avis became more than a pen pal. She was the first to understand the potential of Julia's cookbook, the first to express, distinctly and unconditionally, that it just might change the way Americans ate—and lived. It was hard for most people to appreciate the importance of Julia's work—it was so different from what anyone else was doing at the time. But Avis could appreciate it. "My mother was the *catalyst*," says Mark DeVoto. "She was the person who lit the fuse."

It was Avis who'd fired up the interest at Houghton Mifflin, Avis who promoted Julia, Avis who believed the book would be taken seriously. Avis had taken Julia under her wing to the point of introducing her to Benny's coveted magazine editors in New York—"for later, after you're famous," she said. "I have never known anyone so selfless and so generous," Julia exclaimed. She felt a surge of confidence from Avis's friendship, felt its impact "with an all-embracing bang." Until now, it had been the one thing sorely missing in her life. She had many close acquaintances, but no one great intimate friend. She had found Paul, the intimate love of her life. And now Avis, the intimate female friend—the kind of person you could rely on in any circumstance, who gives you unquestioning support through difficult times. A person to talk over thorny situations and to help you decide which path to take. An outlet for humor, to help let the steam out when there was pressure. Before working on the book, Julia had never in her life taken on an all-consuming task that stretched her abilities to the limit. Having a friend like Avis made the task so much more manageable.

IF ONLY AVIS could do something about Germany. Julia and Paul dreaded the move. Leaving France was "painful" to them both. "We accept the concept intellectually," Paul wrote to his brother, "but I expect the emotional aspects will hit us more . . . when we hear chimes at midnight or taste a Pouilly *fumé* or hear somewhere a snatch of that lowbrow tonk-a-tonk music that's so typically French."

No question about it, all those years in France had left their mark. It had become a part of them, a measure of who they were now. Julia had "grown up" there, discovered her passion, spoke the language fluently, dreamed in French. She was writing *French Home Cooking,* for god's sake. How would that function from an outpost in Germany?

They flirted with bagging the Foreign Service altogether, taking early retirement and staying in Paris. Julia could finish work on the book with Simca and Louisette, she could resurrect her cooking school, and Paul could embark on a new career. Even at fifty-three, there were other things he could do. Something more exciting, something with photography, perhaps, his lifelong passion. Magazines were always looking for someone with his eye. While in the States, he'd seen Benny DeVoto's literary agent, who had set him up with photo editors at *Esquire* and *Holiday.* All he had to do was pitch a story idea and the job would be his, easy as that. But that took the kind of initiative Paul didn't have. He needed structure, guidelines, a steady paycheck—a support system. The Foreign Service had those in spades. In the end, the answer was a foregone conclusion: "We'd stick with the government," Julia said, "and see where it took us."

Fourteen

This Elephant of Ours

G *awd,* how did we ever get ourselves into this pickle?"
On October 24, 1954, Julia and Paul arrived in the district of
Plittersdorf, on the fringes of Bonn, and immediately sized up the situation. It wasn't much to look at, that was for sure. The American Sector
was nothing more than "a great big housing project"—a cluster of boxy
white stucco low-rises, with garish red trim and brown tile roofs, from
which radio antennas protruded like antlers—built to order and surrounded by sterile German housing projects on a plain near the Rhine,
as if Oceania had been set down in Hansel-and-Gretel country.

"Our hearts sunk at the sight of it," Julia explained. She expected a
slice of Germany that would enlarge her view of Europe, where she could
wrap herself in the country's cultural fabric, as she had done so luxuriously in France. But Plittersdorf was more polyester than cashmere.
It had been rebuilt quickly after the war with Marshall Plan money,
so the architects naturally created it in their image. There were pizza
parlors, movie theaters, a five-and-dime, and colonial-style churches.
Because no frame houses were available, American personnel were
quartered in dormitory-style apartments—cubicles so dark and charmless that lights were left on day and night, giving it the timeless effect of
a Las Vegas casino. Perhaps worst of all, everyone stationed there was
American—make that: American military, a species somewhat alien to
the Childs. These weren't OSS operatives, with college degrees and intel-

In the kitchen at Roo de Loo, Paris, 1950

lects to match. There were over 250,000 U.S. soldiers in Germany, most of them meat-and-potatoes GIs, thick and plodding, who preferred cases of thin, pale Budweiser from the PX to the exquisite nectar-like Lederbräu on tap at every pub. Who would Paul talk with about art or semantics or fine wine or Boswell's years in Holland? Or even about Germany, which those stationed there knew nothing about. It infuriated Julia that the Americans in "sad old Plittersdorf" practiced a kind of post-war isolationism; they were obtuse, the quintessential Ugly Americans, confining themselves to the Sector and insisting on speaking English to the natives, while acting disdainful of the culture. Most people she encountered "just hate the Germans." It embarrassed her to be a part of such a scene.

"We feel as though we are on the moon, somehow," she wrote to Avis DeVoto. The atmosphere was unnatural, un-foreign; there was nothing *authentic* about it, nothing to embrace. "I feel too weird and uprooted."

Determined to improve the situation in any small way possible, Julia made an effort to study German, taking lessons at a university in Bad Godesberg. She felt that in order "to function at all properly as a *cuisinière,* I must absolutely learn the language." As in France, she practiced it by frequenting local markets, relying on her phrasebook and ingratiating personality to get by. There was nothing instinctive or beautiful about the way she spoke; she mangled those consonants as if they'd been put through a meat grinder. But she charmed the Germans, who were eager to help.

The Germans, as a tribe, actually exceeded her expectations. They seemed to be decent, upstanding, law-abiding people, much like the proud *bourgeois* she encountered in France; not the "half-savage" Krauts who had worshipped Hitler and brutalized the free world. The whole thing flummoxed her. "How can Germans, who are, as I know, monstrous people, be lovely people? Or are they not monsters?" She admired how they were struggling to emerge from the wreckage of war. Julia seemed especially susceptible to their upward surge. "They are building like mad, so things don't seem to have been devastated somehow," she wrote. "One's impression is of immense vitality, vigor, bustling activity, prosperity."

Too bad some of that "great surge of creativity" hadn't rubbed off on new construction. The only housing available to Julia and Paul was, well, jerry-built—bland pre-fab apartments, "very much like a Statler hotel," as Julia described them. You couldn't tell one from the next, aside from the wood finishes inside: either blond or mahogany. No charm or character whatsoever on the premises. Otherwise everything operated with German efficiency (Julia called it "rigidity"). They chose a flat, Apartment 5, on Steubenring, from which they could just about make out the Rhine, if they stood on their tiptoes and squinted. It was one of the blond models, brand-spanking new: new heating, new plumbing, new-apartment smell throughout. Only the kitchen drew Julia's disfavor. "Not much room to cook much here," she complained. And the stove was *electric*—a word Julia uttered in the same way she said *Republican.*

By mid-1954, she was sufficiently comfortable with her new surroundings to resume work on the book, which was now being called *French Cooking for the American Kitchen.* With chapters on fish and eggs just about wrapped up in France, it was time to launch the next sections: Julia would focus on poultry, Simca on meats. For Julia, that meant researching and testing "some of the most glorious dishes of French *cuisine.*" There were literally hundreds of chicken recipes that would appeal to her readers. The old classics rolled off her tongue with assembly-line precision: chicken with tarragon, *suprêmes de volaille* (sautéed breasts in butter), *milanaise* (breaded breasts with Parmesan), *coq au vin,* fricassée, *à la diabolique* (deviled chicken, lightly breaded with mustard and cayenne), *chasseur* (with shallots, tomato, and cognac), Marengo (oil, tomato, and garlic), *poule au pot* (in the pot), *portugaise,* Kiev . . . You could seemingly cook a new chicken dish every day for several years. *Where would it end?*

She knew where it would begin. Roast chicken, especially, was the litmus test for any French chef worth her weight in schmaltz. Julia adored roast chicken, *poulet rôti;* it would stand as her favorite dish for the rest of her life. As far as she cared, there was nothing like "a juicy, brown, buttery, crisp-skinned, heavenly bird" done to perfection in the oven. She had learned the technique at Le Cordon Bleu, where the chicken was massaged lavishly with butter, then turned and basted continuously until it was done. But those were French chickens, mostly from Bresse, the capital of chickendom, where birds were bought live, then killed and plucked on the spot. Their succulence and flavor were exquisite, incomparable. The German chickens were store-bought and stringy and "didn't taste as good as their French cousins." Still, they were fresh, neither packaged, iced, nor shipped long distances, as in the States. They would do as adequate stand-ins for her recipe tests.

Julia experimented with roasting whole chickens for several weeks in November 1954, using different-size birds to gauge the best flavor. Her favorites were the roasters, weighing in at around three to three and a half pounds, with pale yellow skin that was young and supple. Not technically experienced with all things poultry, she had no way of knowing what type of chicken roasted best, so she conducted a series of tests with the entire range of birds: squabs, broilers, fryers, capons, old hens, and roosters, first learning to evaluate the characteristics of each, then determining their effectiveness as a mouthwatering roast. This, of course, took an enormous amount of time. Hour upon hour was devoted to cooking, analyzing, tasting, recalibrating, cooking again and again and again and again. She followed closely the classic recipes from such diverse authorities as Madame Saint-Ange and *Larousse gastronomique,* as well as younger phenoms like Dione Lucas, Louis Diat, and James Beard, whose books she imported through friends in the States. "There is no doubt," says Jacques Pépin, "that Julia intended to be the final word on the subject. She was relentless, just unstoppable, when it came to writing this kind of master recipe. At the time, no one had really done it so thoroughly, taking modern methods into consideration."

How could American cooks best roast a chicken at home? She kept trying to answer that question during each phase of her research. What type of chicken would one encounter at a supermarket? How could a consumer detect freezer burn or insipidness? Would it take a longer or shorter time to cook in an *electric* oven? Her early notes were full of such concerns. In the margins, she scrawled issues that were still on her mind. "How to defreeze—ice-box best?" "What should a good chicken taste like?"

She was relentless, just unstoppable.

Her curiosity was unquenchable—and not subject to compromise. If the butcher at Krämer's, in Bad Godesberg, couldn't answer a basic question, Julia launched an inquiry that knew no bounds. Any number of books were consulted at the local university, letters were dashed off to government agencies and food experts at *Gourmet* or *Woman's Day.* She took nothing for granted. "We must always remember that we are writing for an audience that knows nothing about French cooking," she would say. "Nothing goes in [the book] that isn't verified, beyond a doubt." Inflexible though that rule was, she never wavered, never cut corners—says one of her assistants: "She was anal when it came to researching. You could put money on anything in one of her recipes"—and she insisted that Simca and Louisette uphold the same standard. "Thank heaven we both agree on the effort to reach perfection," she wrote Simca.

In a letter to Louisette, however, she avoided making the same compliment.

Julia had always been so diligent in writing similar types of letters to both of her colleagues so as not to demonstrate any favoritism or cause a rift. From the beginning, they'd functioned like the Three Musketeers: "All for one and one for all!" But such codes of honor came with obligations. Louisette, as far as Julia was concerned, wasn't living up to them. She and Simca worked like slaves, putting in forty-hour weeks *at a minimum* on the cookbook; Louisette contributed a mere six hours, at best. The project, according to Julia, had "gotten beyond her anyway." She had "produced just about nothing except a long chapter on game, mostly copied directly out of a book." Sure, sure, there were complications in Louisette's personal life—a brute of a husband, two kids, trouble up the wazoo. She'd sung the same old song since they'd begun work on the project and they had made every effort to accommodate her. But when push came to shove, she was "not a good enough cook to present herself as an equal author," a fact, Julia said, that "stuck in my craw." It hardly seemed fair, and Julia said as much to Simca during a visit to France in early November 1954. She laid out her whole argument for redefining their roles, everything from individual responsibilities to credit and compensation.

In fact, Julia had drafted a letter to Louisette that she pulled out of her purse. It was a brilliant piece of writing, each word carefully weighed and calculated for its effect, each sentiment crafted for its ultimate aim—and diplomatic to a fault. She laid it on thick, praising Louisette up and down, her unique talents and dedication, her generous contribution, her charming personality. Louisette, she said, had such "nice little peripheral ideas." *Nice little peripheral ideas!* But—and here Julia began loading both barrels—"the major responsibility for the book rests on Simca and me," who, for all intents and purposes were the "Co-Authors," while Louisette was, let's face it, a "Consultant," nothing more. The credit on the book should read "by Simone Beck and Julia Child *with* Louisette Bertholle." Then she took aim and fired: the royalties needed to be readjusted for a "fair split": 45 percent each for Julia and Simca, and 10 percent for Louisette. These percentages more accurately reflected their collaboration.

Simca agreed with Julia—but soon began backpedaling. Louisette was her friend, she argued, they'd hatched the book together, taught classes shoulder-to-shoulder, that husband was a nightmare . . . *Arrête! Terminé!* Julia didn't want to hear it; she put her foot down. Hard. "We must be cold-blooded," she insisted. "I shall love her more once we get this settled."

But love and business do not easily mix. After having discussed the situation with Louisette in person and having sent the follow-up letter, Julia heard nothing from her itinerant colleague. Several weeks passed and still not a word. "This little business with Louisette is turning out to be something of a problem," she wrote Avis DeVoto in December 1954. Now Julia was good and pissed off. It was one thing for Louisette to disagree with the terms as proposed, another thing to ignore them entirely. Without delay, she dashed off another letter demanding that Louisette "come across with her opinions." It seemed foolish, Julia wrote, not to have sorted this out earlier. But she "also waved the big stick," suggesting that if an amicable arrangement couldn't be achieved, perhaps they were better off canceling the contract with Houghton Mifflin.

Over her dead body, of course. But the threat might extract an appropriate response.

In the meantime, Julia waded deeper into chicken, selecting recipes whose ingredients were accessible to American cooks but still a traditional French preparation. Simca's *poulet rôti à la normande* was a no-brainer. A roast chicken stuffed with sautéed liver, shallots, and cream cheese, and basted with an emulsion of thick, rich cream—talk about decadence. It was a dish that staggered, *literally,* friends and company, and she made it often that winter in Plittersdorf, for an ever-rotating ensemble of dinner guests. Occasionally, she tweaked the sauce with port and mushrooms, which threw the dish a musky curve. Or roasted the chicken in a covered casserole on a bed of sliced onions and carrots so that "the buttery, aromatic steam" created a sauna-like effect, tenderizing the bird beyond the limits of decency.

To Julia, every chicken inspired another recipe. She ran through thirty or forty different dishes in three months, amassing notes, a sheaf of notes thick as a book, on each one. Sometimes they were "fabulous," as she wrote in the margin of *poulet farci au gros sel.* Occasionally, "a complete disaster" ensued—"don't attempt," she advised. Avis followed her recipe for *poulet rôti à la normande,* using a gizmo called a roto-broiler, and wound up with pudding. "I made that chicken liver and cream cheese stuffing," she reported. "But after about an hour-and-a-quarter noticed stuffing beginning to ooze out, and in another fifteen minutes it was all out, the rear walls of the vent had collapsed and the damn thing was falling apart."

You win some, you lose some. Back to the drawing board. But Julia was neither discouraged nor distressed. Her response to fiasco might be a growl: a growl followed by a choice imprecation. She'd fix that chicken! She'd ram an onion up a cavity where the sun don't shine. Then it was on to the next dish, maybe *poulet d'Honfleur,* with cider cream and apples, or *poulet bonne femme,* with bacon, onions, and potatoes. The winter of 1955 kicked off an all-out chicken extravaganza.

With so much to cook, Julia was happy, even in godforsaken Plittersdorf, where there was no one to lean on and keep her entertained. "So many US army are depressing," she grumbled. "But I got quite a bit of working and cooking in, so it was not wasted!"

Paul was hardly around; lately he wasn't the best of company, up to his eyeballs in work as the USIA's exhibits officer for all of Germany. The job consumed him. This wasn't the ragtag operation he'd encountered in France. His budget was more than a hundred times larger, almost $10 million, and eminently more complicated. "The Information Operation is colossal here," Julia gasped. There was so much ground to cover. In addition to the main office in Plittersdorf, there were twenty-two centers called Amerika Hauses spread across the country, each one churning out cultural propaganda, with libraries, movies, lectures, bookmobiles, press sections, and student exchanges. Bonn, Nuremberg, Dortmund, Hamburg, Munich, Frankfurt, Cologne . . . Paul set out to another city each weekend, determined to visit one a month until he had covered all the houses—an impressive goal, what with his duty to provide constant programming for each.

He was working at an intensity that was stunning for its output. So on April 7, 1955, when he was ordered back to Washington on the next plane, Julia was elated. "I was sure he was going to be made head of the department," she said. At long last! After all the layers of bureaucracy—and the bullshit—he'd endured, he was finally going to receive the recognition he deserved.

Julia could hardly contain herself. This would give Paul some sorely needed self-esteem, something to reassure him that a life in foreign service was not all in vain. "He is not the kind of man who ever pushes himself, and he is not 'ambitious,' " she acknowledged. How sweet it would be to tell her father about Paul's promotion. This would show that old blackguard what her husband was made of. Maybe he'd finally shut up about what a good-for-nothing Paul was.

This called for a treat of some sort while Paul was away. Julia didn't hesitate: she'd run up to Paris for a little one-on-one with Simca. What better way to celebrate than cooking with her friend? But on April 9, in the midst of her packing, a telegram arrived. SITUATION CONFUSED, it read, in Paul's cryptic fashion. Somehow, no one in Washington could tell him why he was there. Even the director of Berlin's Amerika Haus, whom he bumped into at the State Department, had no idea. "He thinks it must be something special and secretive," Paul wrote Julia, "otherwise 'they' would certainly have told him. Ah me—what a muck-up.'"

Indeed. Paul got ping-ponged from one office to the next, from administrator to administrator, without anyone "so much as saying boo." "For God's sake," he wondered, "can't *anybody* in this outfit clarify the mystery? *Who* sent for me? *Why* am I here?" Old friends at State were suddenly not available or in a meeting or had just ducked out and couldn't be reached. A high-placed official, to whom he turned to for advice, said "there was a definite instruction to him to mind his own business." Another official "assumed I was a CIA agent all the time and that my job as exhibits officer was merely a cover—and that I was being hauled back on a secret mission."

In the meantime, Paul checked into the Gralyn Hotel, a fusty turn-of-the-century Georgian Revival on N Street, and tried to acclimate himself to being back home. It felt so strange, so alien after so many years abroad. "The city looks dirty," he wrote to Julia that first night in Washington. "Billboards stick out, strangely foreign. Everybody looks so *American,* it's funny. Lots of Negroes."

And lots of paranoia. Everyone in public service seemed to be looking over his shoulder, afraid to go on the record, afraid of his own shadow. *McCarthy!* Julia seethed—what a scourge on the landscape. How she hated that man! Hated his tactics. She put him in the same category as *Madame Brassart.* Ptooey! (Little did she know the hotel where Paul was staying was just three doors away from the senator's house.) "I think it best for you not to plan to go to Paris until I know more about how long I'll be here," Paul advised her. "It may well be that you'd better come back."

Come back? That didn't bode well. And right in the middle of her chicken research. Well, Washington would be a huge step up from Plittersdorf, she thought. And with Paul's obvious promotion, it would be a lot more affordable. She started to fantasize about living in her own house again. With a gas range and an outdoor herb garden. And having a steak—"an honest-to-goodness American steak."

By April 13, however, all that had changed. Another telegram arrived that put a new spin on the daydreams. SITUATION HERE LIKE KAFKA STORY, Paul telegrammed. I BELIEVE I AM TO BE PUT IN SAME SITUATION AS LEONARD. *Oh no,* Julia thought, *not Rennie Leonard.* He was a friend who'd come under scrutiny of McCarthy's Un-American Activities pitbulls. This was a security investigation! "Paul wasn't being promoted," she realized, "he was being *investigated*." Good lord! This had to be "simply one of those government mix-ups."

Not a chance. Her worst fears were realized over the next few days. Letter after letter arrived, describing the nightmare scenario. "This is curiously fantastic, unreal, frightening, and preposterous," Paul wrote. He racked his brain, trying to trace the origin of such a charge. "I have nothing to hide or be ashamed of. If I am backed into a corner by some false charge, I intend to fight my way out."

It was big talk, considering that Paul was a physical and emotional wreck. Since leaving Germany, he'd been on a steady diet of sleeping pills "to combat my nervous tension." He couldn't sleep. His heart pounded like a kettledrum.

It didn't get any better the next day, when he was led into the Office of Security for the USIA and worked over by two Special Agents from the FBI. They grilled him for hours, reading from a dossier they'd compiled on him "about four inches thick." What did he know about Jane Foster, his old free-spirited OSS pal from Ceylon and China? they wanted to know. And how about Morris Llewellyn Cooke, whose name Paul had given as a reference ten or fifteen years earlier? Cooke had headed the War Labor Board under FDR and later was instrumental in bringing electricity to rural American provinces. He was a Good Guy, Paul assumed. So was Jane Foster. In fact, he and Julia had reconnected with her while living in Paris, where she was engaged in the art scene as a prominent painter. State had also investigated his brother Charlie, that notorious *liberal*. The whole thing was outrageous, "preposterous," he chided them. But not half as preposterous as their next line of questioning.

He sat there, stone-faced, as they hedged, fidgeted, fingering his file. They were embarrassed, they said, about what needed to be asked. In the dossier was a charge that he was a homosexual. "And how about it?" they wanted to know. Paul "burst out laughing." These guys were chuckle-heads, "amateurs." It was clear they knew nothing about him. Still, when the joke wore off he grew angry, confrontational.

"According to the Constitution, I have a right to be faced by my accuser," he told them, "so who *was* he or she?" Put up or shut up.

If they knew, they weren't saying. Nor were they convinced that he was straight, despite his marriage to Julia. "Homosexuals often have wives and children," they said, returning to the issue time and again. Legend has it they asked Paul to drop his pants, but there is nothing in his letters or diary that confirms this.

After six or seven hours the ordeal was over. They thanked him for his cooperation *and cleared him.* Just like that. INVESTIGATION CONCLUDED SUCCESSFULLY FOR ME, he cabled Julia late the next day. Paul was so relieved, he said, it was cause to celebrate. "I am trying a bottle of Budweiser 'beer,' " a solution that he determined was "compounded of cold dishwater, with a dash of arnica to make it bitter and somebody's pale urine to give it color." He was grateful for closure, elated. And so was Julia. She, in turn, sent him letters with what Paul described as "libidinous hearts at the end, deeply stabbed with what appears to be a stiff cock."

She'd be ready for him when he finally returned!

Still, the entire matter was ugly and suspicious. "I have just been wondering today if someone is out to 'get him,' " she mused. Two reasons sprung immediately to mind. A few months back they had made a contribution of twenty-five dollars to something called the I Believe Fund, as in: I believe Senator McCarthy is a despicable insect, and here is twenty-five dollars for the express purpose of investigating him. Perhaps that had put Paul's name on a list. But could the Republicans be *that* petty—for a measly twenty-five dollars? Julia already knew the answer to that. What she didn't know was whether *she* had caused the difficulty.

A letter—it might have stemmed from a letter Julia had written. In October 1954, a woman named Aloise B. Heath, who happened to be William F. Buckley's sister, accused five Smith College faculty members of being "traitors" and the college of "knowingly harboring Communists." There was no evidence to support the claim, just her say-so. But it was enough to draw a fierce reaction from Julia. She immediately dashed off a letter to Mrs. Heath, announcing that she was "doubling my annual contribution to Smith" and that this type of character assassination sent a chill up her spine. "In Russia today, as a method for getting rid of opposition," Julia wrote, "an unsubstantiated implication of treason, such as yours, is often used." There was every reason to suspect the letter found its way into Paul's Washington dossier.

Of course, other peccadilloes might have also drawn attention. For instance, Paul's endearing nickname, "P'ski," which Julia always called him. He signed his personal letters that way, sometimes "Paulski" or "Comrade Paulski." Hadn't it ever occurred to him that Comrade Paulski looked the slightest shade of pink? How about his frequent tirades blasting government indiscretion? Lapses in judgment like that were reported to the proper authorities.

You never knew who was looking at you cross-eyed, Avis admonished

Julia. "I even wondered if your father had talked in the wrong places." Would Pop try to discredit his own son-in-law? Was he that ideologically rabid? Maybe it was simpler than that: "being so pally with the DeVotos." Benny had been subpoenaed by the House Committee in 1953 and refused to answer their questions. Guilt by association was a popular accusation.

Rather than stew on it, Julia put "the great investigation," as she called it, behind her. There was still too much duck and turkey work to be done on her poultry chapter, and by October "Paul's stock [had] risen considerably" as a result of several bravura exhibits that were credited to his stewardship. To Julia's delight, he began feeling as though he deserved more from his work—certainly more recognition, and even more respect, which was not in his makeup. "I have a feeling he may well, and at last, get a promotion this year, as he is making noises about it."

By September 1956, their lives seemed to be back on track—as far as their itinerant lives were ever really on track. They had grown reasonably comfortable in Germany, despite Julia's quibble that "Plittersdorf is a strange half life." "We both seem to be continually and hopelessly busy," she offered. Around this time she wrote her family a letter filled with enthusiasm for the German language and the rigors of her work. She had begun reading newspapers in the native tongue and hoped to wade into Goethe before too long. "I have been madly fussing around in the duck and goose section, along with running continuous experiments on making stock in the pressure cooker; how much water per rice is the right amount for risotto; and have also started a light round of entertaining again."

That same month Julia accompanied Paul to Berlin, where he was supervising three exhibits in the American sector. The trip coincided with their tenth wedding anniversary, and they celebrated in style, hitting a number of fine-dining restaurants that had resurfaced since the war. It was a lovely few days away together. Ten years later, Paul still found his wife "as astonishingly beautiful as ever." He considered her "a veritable goddess" and exulted in her company. "You've made quite a sacrifice for my career," he told her over *coupes de champagne* before dinner at the Dreesen. He had a surprise, a special anniversary gift for her, too: "I'm being transferred back to the States," he announced.

Julia could hardly believe her ears. The States! And after eight years in Europe. "Must feel a bit like an earthquake," Avis commiserated. How could it be otherwise? America would probably seem as foreign as, well,

Germany, she suspected. Living in a house again. *Their* house, in Washington, D.C. "Shall get a dishwashing machine first thing," Julia fantasized, "and I shall certainly get a new stove, a black one, *gas*. And it will be so heavenly to have some friends again!"

And family! It seemed like ages since Julia had felt that kind of intimate connection. Now Charlie and Freddie would be within a short train ride—and her brother, John, who was in Massachusetts, working for the family paper business. And Avis, in Cambridge; she was practically family. Her husband, Benny, had had a heart attack and died suddenly in November 1955. After all she'd done for Julia, it would be wonderful to provide some comfort and support.

The States!

After the initial "tingle of excited apprehension," Julia was left with a numbing fact: the move would delay the book. Again. The wonderful momentum she'd enjoyed would suddenly grind to a halt, as would her proximity to Simca and all things French. She'd finished the duck section in August and had started in on geese, but now everything—the boxes upon boxes of research, the towering stacks of notes, the dog-eared manuscript—had to be crated and shipped overseas, along with all her utensils and cooking doo-dads. And a new kitchen—*another new kitchen*—would have to be installed.

Nevertheless, it would give her a chance to apply all she had done, the cooking and the writing, to an American standard. "In fact," she realized, "this is just about the right time, from the point of view of the book, to be coming home." Her research may have been exclusive to France, but her audience was entirely back in the States. As was her publisher. Perhaps it was all for the best to finish the book at home, "where everything such as ingredients can be accurately checked."

A few weeks later, the preparations were complete. On the week of November 12, 1956, just as the leaves had fallen from the trees along the Rhine, Julia and Paul walked out of their Plittersdorf flat, into the midday darkness, and set out for Le Havre. The air was unusually frigid; a harsh winter wind had swept off the North Sea and, at the last minute, Julia, whose clothes had already been shipped overseas, had to borrow an extra coat for the trip. Their car would carry them across Germany into France. Then, home at last.

They never looked back.

————

ACCORDING TO JULIA, it took more than several months before her life returned to normal. Their 150-year-old house on Olive Street desperately cried out for a face-lift; the place needed repainting from top to bottom, the ceilings a replastering, the walls an up-to-date rewiring; the kitchen was enlarged, two bathrooms renovated, an attic studio remodeled to serve as Julia's office.

Her approach to cooking, American-style, needed a similar makeover. Everything had changed since 1947, when she had left for Europe, and it was essential to understand the shifting winds in the atmosphere. The post-war food industry stood poised to revolutionize home cooking, converting kitchens everywhere to a kind of instant, ready-mix fare. If Big Business had its way, traditional cooking from scratch would become passé by 1960. Housewives, they determined, sought culinary shortcuts, anything to help reduce the time it took them to prepare a meal. *Convenience* became the operational catchword, and with it came convenience foods: frozen fish sticks, milk in cartons, packaged cake mixes, canned vegetables—*TV dinners!* Could it get any more wretched? Julia was no stranger to the vagaries of convenience. She had made Paul a dinner that featured instant mashed potatoes, another with a helping of Uncle Ben's converted rice. *As an experiment.* Just to see if he would notice. (He didn't.) The phenomenon didn't intrigue her one bit, and yet it seemed to be sweeping the country.

Supermarkets were full of the stuff. "When the American housewife shops her supermarket," claimed an article in *McCall's,* "she has a choice of 4,693 short-cut foods—the most dazzling array of prepared, pre-cooked, and ready-to-eat foods the world has ever seen." The sensation wasn't lost on Julia. She swooned at the enormous selection of food available in an enormous M Street supermarket, around the corner from her enormous house. There was so much to choose from. So utterly . . . *convenient.* It was nothing like in France, where a few essentials were showcased on shelves behind a counter and the grocer always selected and bagged one's purchases. The supermarket experience was liberating to Julia. "You pick up a wire pushcart as you come in and just trundle about looking and fingering everything there is," she wrote Simca. How wonderful to pick out each asparagus spear or mushroom yourself.

As Julia knew, the rise of the supermarket was in no way analogous with an advance in American cooking. As early as 1953, *Esquire* had voiced the modern housewife's plaint: "Cooking, to her, is no longer an adventure. It's a chore, and she's sick of it." Women kept cooking, nonetheless, but with far less enthusiasm, less pizzazz. A post-war go-go lifestyle demanded a go-go kitchen routine. It seemed ridiculous to spend precious time making a roast when the family wolfed down portions of frozen prepared Swiss steak and Tater Tots. "It's just 1-2-3, and dinner's on the table," advised a magazine article designed for the modern homemaker. Opening a couple of cans and mixing the contents together, then popping the whole thing in the oven sure beat all the fuss that went into prepping a classic recipe. Why bother? Julia saw this reflected in "the most disheartening article" in *Woman's Day,* contrasting the output of a traditional cook who made things from scratch with that of "a smart young thing who did everything the 'New Modern Way' . . . using cans and boxes, and frozen stuff." It baffled her that this new-age gal would serve frozen asparagus—yes, *frozen asparagus*—with a blob of Hellman's mayonnaise atop instead of "silly old-fashioned Hollandaise sauce." It seemed counterproductive, if not silly old-fashioned dumb. The New Modern Way appeared to have factored out *flavor.* What is the country coming to, I'd like to know? she wondered.

In the end, Julia couldn't abide the supermarket ethos. The chickens on offer looked plump and beautiful—but had no chicken taste whatsoever. The butter had no creaminess, no body. The bread was unnaturally white, fluffy, and came pre-sliced, in cellophane wrappers. The fruits and vegetables were industrialized versions of garden-grown specimens. The lettuce was iceberg, full of water, all texture, no tooth. There were no cèpes, morels, or chanterelles, no shallots or crème fraîche. It was next to impossible to buy a calf's foot for making stock, or even decent veal. How did she expect to instruct modern cooks who used margarine and thrived on canned-soup casseroles?

More troubling, perhaps, was the absence of good wine. It wasn't a part of the American dining tradition. There was some cheap California jug wine—"hearty burgundy" or "fruity Chablis"—but it was rarely, if ever, drunk with meals. That meant there'd be nothing delicious on hand to cook with—nothing to deglaze a pan with or to flavor a sauce. "People just do not have bottles of white wine all the time to use in cooking," she reported to Simca. "If they bought one for a bit of cooking, they wouldn't know what to do with the rest of it." That raised a whole slew of problems. How could one prepare *coq au vin* with Italian Swiss Colony "chianti" or a sauce *à la livournaise* with Almaden "grenache"? You might as well forget about making fricassées or *moules marinière.*

Julia wasn't home very long before coming to the conclusion "that most Americans don't know anything at all, NOTHING, about the techniques of good cooking." There was none of the care or craftsmanship she learned at Le Cordon Bleu; the quality of ingredients was practically a nonexistent factor. Or the taste: it never occurred to the modern American cook that processed foods had little or no flavor. Wherever she went, Julia kept bumping into shortcuts and convenience food: frozen piecrusts and packaged fillings, dehydrated onion soup, instant coffee, pancake mixes, instant meringue, canned fruit cocktail, Cheez Whiz, Reddi-wip—the monstrous magnitude of it depressed and discouraged her. And the drivel she read in women's magazines! In one case, an editor's suggestion for a "Harvest Luncheon" included a recipe for Twenty Minute Roast, which featured slabs of Spam slathered with orange marmalade and a layer of Vienna sausages broiled with canned peaches. At the time, Julia was experimenting with duck *à l'orange*. She had typed an instruction for intensifying the flavor:

> Remember the sauce must be thick enough to withstand the dilution of the orange juice to come. Boil down to thicken more if necessary.
> Taste very carefully for seasoning and strength. It will receive some more flavor from the wine and roasting juices later, but should, even so, be almost perfect at this stage.

Normally, she would have just said: "Reduce to thicken if necessary and correct flavor," but would that be enough for a cook who slathers marmalade on Spam? Everything—every function and procedure, every baby step—had to be thoroughly explained. "So I am deeply depressed, gnawed by doubts, and feel that all our work may just lay a big rotten egg," she wrote to Avis DeVoto.

Even more vexing, she feared her collaboration with Simca would also come to naught. Initially nervous that no American would undertake one of Simca's rigorous, labor-intensive recipes, Julia had pleaded with her partner to simplify the process without losing any of the authentic French spirit. During their time apart, Simca obliged with her work on the vegetable chapter, a collection of recipes that would stand all the existing writing on its head. Now, every few weeks, another package arrived from France with a new sheaf of recipes that were as well conceived, logical, and streamlined as they were utterly delicious. Simca had managed to take all her old family specialties and reimagine them for an enthusiastic cook. Braised endive and leeks, glazed carrots, ratatouille, cauliflower au gratin, stuffed tomatoes, potatoes a dozen different ways—the output was extraordinary for its variety and inspiration. Julia was awed by her partner's contribution. No one worked harder preparing splendid recipes than Simca.

Despite their prodigious effort, however, Julia continued to be troubled. On the one hand she considered all the work they'd done to be something of a watershed in the history of American cookbookery. Nothing in print resembled anything they had achieved for its all-out research and thorough detail, as well as its exhaustively instructive style. It was revolutionary in the way it presented French cuisine, not with reverence or pomposity, but *joie de vivre*. And, yet, the apathy of the American homemaker seemed especially disturbing. All those cooking conveniences and processed foods! The magazines and newspapers were full of such blather. "There are loads and loads and loads of books and articles on how to do things quickly," Julia brooded, "and very very very few on how to make things taste good." Why, the sorry plague had even spread its tentacles to France. A new cookbook by Henriette Chandet called *Cuisine d'urgence*—or "Hurry-Up Cooking"—startled Julia for its insidious premise that classic French recipes could be accomplished by using . . . *shortcuts*! She found its techniques and cooking methods "horrifying" and "disturbing." It reduced culinary competence to shake and bake. "It will be the death of La Cuisine F(rançaise)," she predicted. The more Julia read and observed, the more discouraged she became. It seemed pointless to push ahead if the contrivances of modern cuisine pointed the whole practice on a downhill course. "HELL AND DAMNATION, is all I can say," she vented in a letter to Simca. "WHY DID WE EVER DECIDE TO DO THIS ANYWAY?"

Because it was undeniable, of course. Because there was no other alternative. "I can't think of doing anything else, can you?" she asked Simca.

Besides, the book they were writing defied convention. It was unique, she felt, in every way. There were plenty of so-called French cookbooks available on American shelves, but nothing so exhaustive, nothing so authentic, nothing "for people . . . who want to be able to produce the most delicious things it is possible to do."

Julia had spent considerable time studying the competition. So far, there was nothing that seemed to resemble their book. Overall, she wasn't very impressed with the quality of American cookbooks. They

were mostly condensed, slapdash affairs, with little instructional substance for the novice cook, not like the technically proficient models by
Madame Saint-Ange or Ali-Bab. There was *The Cordon Bleu Cookbook* by
Dione Lucas, the first female graduate of Le Cordon Bleu, who had made
a name for herself as a New York instructor. Julia didn't know what to
make of it. "Her technique is certainly not classical French," she grumbled. For example, the recipe for duck *à l'orange* was a single paragraph
long. There was no direction to season the duck with salt and pepper, no
orange liqueur, no vinegar for acidity. It called for stock, without saying
what kind of stock. No reminder to cut and discard the trussing strings.
No orange segments as an accompaniment to the meat, no butter added
to enrich the sauce. The new Lucas cookbook, *Meat and Poultry,* fared no
better in Julia's wary eye; she found it "sloppy" and "very poor in many
respects." Elizabeth David's *French Country Cooking* wasn't bad, as far as
recipes went, but the author was reluctant to provide specific measurements. "Her books were charmingly written," says Judith Jones, an editor
who would eventually play a major role in Julia's career. "But she despised
American cooks and their need for exact proportions, so you were often
in the dark as far as ingredients were concerned."

James Beard was an emerging force—*The New York Times* had recently
crowned him the "Dean of American Cookery"—and Julia considered
him "one of the best of the current cook bookers." His *Fish Cookery* was
becoming one of her all-time favorites. But Beard seemed more interested
in domestic regional cuisine, recipes like pot roast, turkey hash, meat loaf,
and bread pudding, and, therefore, was not much of a competitive threat.

Nor was anything written by Poppy Cannon, but for an altogether
different reason. It was hard for Julia to even get a grasp on Cannon,
the wildly popular "food expert" on NBC's *Home* show, the forerunner
of *Today,* and author of the best-selling *The Can-Opener Cookbook.* What
could you say about someone who made "vichyssoise with frozen mashed
potatoes, one leek sautéed in butter, and a cream of chicken soup from
Campbell's?" Or made a "French" variation of floating island with lemon
Jell-O in the shape of miniature hearts, roosting on a "small golden sea
of soft Royal Custard sauce?"

Only Louis Diat gave Julia pause. For years, Diat had been the chef at
the Ritz-Carlton in New York before landing at *Gourmet,* where he wrote
a series of articles on French recipes for the American cook. "He really is
the only good thing in *Gourmet,*" Avis insisted, and Julia agreed. She and

Simca thought he was "extremely good" when it came to preparing seri-ous food, but still a long way off from approaching their level of accuracy. Diat's measurements, in particular, drove Julia up a wall. His recipe for chicken *chasseur* called for a "half glass of white wine." But how large a glass, Julia wondered—a shot glass, a tumbler? Risotto with sausages sounded divine, but what kind of rice, and what kind of sausages? How stupid, she thought, to spend one's life juice on something, and have it a failure, just because of a faulty technical conception. She and Simca wouldn't abide such oversights. It would be negligent on their part, a disservice to their reader. Their book—"this elephant of ours"—had to be meticulous, pre-cise. "It must communicate and must be the cook's best friend."

BUT FIRST IT had to find its way into print.

They'd been grooming the elephant for six long years when the time came, at long last, to assess what they had. By the end of 1957 the book was far from finished. "Meat and fish are going to take several years, I think!" Julia admitted. Yet it wasn't like they'd been sitting on their hands. The manuscript had swelled to a whopping 750 pages—frightful, considering there were only two chapters, sauces and chicken. They'd figured on ten chapters in all to cover the ground. The way they were going, it would be a monster in the end, an encyclopedia, which would intimidate most cooks.

But maybe, just maybe, that was just what the book needed to become: an encyclopedia—if not in girth, at least in form. If it were published as a series, Julia mused, then Houghton Mifflin could put out the initial volume fairly soon. Avis DeVoto was not so sure. "I would sort of hate to see two volumes," she responded, "but then having too fat a book would be as bad, and hard to handle and use." Avis suggested they run it by their editor, Dorothy de Santillana.

Julia proposed to do better than that. Simca was due to arrive for a three-month visit in January 1958 and they planned to present the fin-ished chapters to Houghton Mifflin themselves, in Boston, on Monday, February 24. She would broach the format in person at that time.

One can only imagine the lead-up to the meeting. The women were "hard at it night and day," whipping everything—the gamut of recipes, the loose ends—into shape. Upon proofreading, they discovered the manu-script was a mash-up: the product of two women with vastly different literary styles working on vastly different subjects an ocean apart. When finally put together, it was like yin and yang. The sauce chapter alone was a recipe for disaster. It was written in 1952, before Julia knew much about cooking—or writing, for that matter—and lay untouched since that time. There were sections in the poultry chapter that still needed polish. Haphazard as it was, their efforts were not in vain, and on February 23 they set out for Boston to bridle the elephant once and for all.

When they got to Union Station, however, their plans went awry. Every train north of Baltimore had been canceled, due to a monster snowstorm battering the northeast coast. Boston was buried under a foot of fresh snow. There was nothing going in or out, they were told.

Zut and double *zut!* All that sweat, all that toil—the sum of which, *French Cooking for the American Kitchen*, rested in a cardboard box at their feet. Would a couple of tough birds like Julia and Simca let a mere snowstorm ground them? Not a chance, not after six years of exacting work. Julia spotted a Greyhound terminal adjacent to the station. For some mystifying reason the buses were still running, so they boarded a coach bound for Boston.

The trip took eleven hours in all, as the bus "chugged and slithered through the driving snow." Simca and Julia took turns holding the manuscript on their laps to keep it from sliding across the narrow aisle. The trip was grueling, draining. It was well after midnight when the bus finally pulled into Boston and another hour before they arrived at Avis's house in Cambridge.

It was still snowing the next afternoon, when Julia and Simca made their way downtown, to the Houghton Mifflin editorial offices. The meeting, with Dorothy de Santillana, was more social than businesslike, all three women gratified to have finally met after years of billowing correspondence. De Santillana's enthusiasm for the book was already well established. Not only was she "profoundly impressed" by the manuscript, but also delighted with the recipes, many of which she had tested with great success. She was gracious and agreeable, despite the elephant that had been dropped off on her desk. According to Avis DeVoto, Julia overheard various male editors express reservations about the book, saying: "Americans don't want to cook like that. They want something quick, made with a mix." But anything of the sort is probably apocryphal, the product of a memoir more than forty years later. Julia and Simca were treated warmly at Houghton Mifflin, introduced to staff around the

office, and left without receiving any editorial critique. It was an altogether superficial kind of meeting. "Neither of us said much," Julia
remembered, on the way back to Cambridge.

When Julia finally got critical reaction from de Santillana, in a letter
dated March 21, 1958, the book's fate took an ominous turn. "With the
greatest respect for what you have done (for the labor involved is gargan-
tuan)," it began, "we must state forthwith that this is not the book we
contracted for . . . It has grown into something much more complex and
difficult to handle than the original book." Julia kept reading but the
verdict was emphatically clear. Houghton Mifflin was rejecting the book.
After all that work, all that devotion. She was crushed, just *crushed*. How
could she tell Simca?

They had no choice but to absorb the impact of the decision. They
agreed that Americans probably desired a more "compact, simplified"
cookbook, something that hastened the trend toward convenience. De
Santillana had suggested they consider revising the manuscript, drafting
a much smaller book or "perhaps a series of small books devoted to particular portions of the meal," but neither plan lit a fire under the women.
It would mean watering down each recipe to a leaky helping of shortcuts,
nothing different from the atrocities offered in *Woman's Day* or *McCall's*.
After brainstorming with Simca, Julia dashed off a letter to her editor,
declining the proposal.

"The cook who interests us," she wrote, "is the one [who] . . . has the
time to devote to the more serious and creative aspects of cooking. She
has to have a certain amount of sophistication, and the conception that
good cooking, especially good French cooking, is an art-form requiring
techniques and hard work." Anything else was better left to the masters of abbreviation—the canned-soup connoisseurs and frozen-food afi-
cionados. "We therefore propose that our mutual contract for 'French
Cooking for the American Kitchen' be cancelled, and the advance of
$250 be returned at once."

That was it. They'd pulled the plug, they were finished. It seemed
incredible that their dream project was over *just like that*. But after sleeping on it, Julia drew a slash across the letter and backed away from their
hard-nosed stance.

"We'll just have to do it over," she told Simca.

Overnight, the two women had a change of heart. They'd come to
the conclusion that it made more sense to do what their editor asked—"to

compress the 'encyclopedia' into a single volume, about 350 pages long"—than to try and place the book with a new publisher. The new book, they proposed, would be "short and snappy," the kind of work that appealed to the "somewhat sophisticated" housewife. They might even take on canned soups and frozen vegetables—at least, ways to improve them using French techniques. "Everything would be of the simpler sort," she wrote, "but nothing humdrum." In any case, they promised to deliver a new, complete manuscript within six months' time.

Beneath the compromise, they saw that cutting was inevitable. The whole trend in America was for easy solutions, to pull off functions like dinner without torment or effort. One hugely popular craze did away altogether with the stove. Outdoor cooking, on the grill, was a post-war phenomenon that was as low-down and prevalent as TV dinners. It had even won endorsement from the culinary establishment. By 1959, no less a *maître* than James Beard had written four anthologies on backyard bar-becuing, and Houghton Mifflin had a Texas version on its current list. If Julia and Simca wanted to break into what they called cookbookery, they realized that French classicism needed a modern twist. Their "emphasis would [have to] be on how to prepare ahead and how to reheat." There was no middle ground. Julia had learned this much since returning to the States: if you can't beat 'em, join 'em. Nothing complicated or French about that.

"HOW TO SAUTÉ" was out; "How to Brown" was out, too. So was "How to Caramelize a Mold." "How to Boil an Egg" and "How to Boil a Potato" were also scratched, along with half the recipes for elaborate sauces.

Julia and Simca had taken a cleaver to their manuscript in an effort to trim and cut the fat. Anything that smacked of excessive labor was dis-patched to the bin. Jerusalem artichoke soup—gone. Oxtail soup—ditto. They bade *adieu* to fennel soup and tarragon cream. The *grande cuisine* of Escoffier and Brillat-Savarin was edited to reflect a simpler, more acces-sible *cuisine bourgeoise. Estouffade aux trois viandes*—a Norman three-meat stew—was dropped in favor of *bœuf bourguignon*. Fish aspics and quenelles gave way to more fundamental mousses. As for pressed duck, the authors recognized that it was a tall order for an American housewife to locate a bird suffocated properly so that its blood remained in its body for the sauce. Julia initially explained that they could use a French restaurant trick—substituting fresh pig's blood mixed with red wine instead—but there wasn't a snowball's chance in a hot oven of that one flying.

The revisions grew increasingly more difficult. How do you cut corners for a true French roast chicken? The original recipe ran more than five pages long, covering each essential point, from trussing through carving. For Julia, it was the ultimate ordeal. "I can't get oven-roasted chicken down to less than 2 pages," she protested. "If you leave out the basting and turning, it ain't a French roast."

In their new form, the recipes required retesting and rewriting, both of which took time and patience, and as far as patience went, Julia was down half a quart. The cookbook experience had been so damn *trying*. She'd put everything she had into it—and more. Now she was back at square one-and-a-half, giving it whatever was left in the tank just to make it to two. As a distraction, she decided to resume teaching. Throughout the spring of 1958, she conducted a weekly cooking class in Philadelphia, driving four hours each way to and from Washington, while preparing demanding French dishes that showcased her recipes. She also taught a group of women in her Olive Street kitchen, as part of L'École des Trois Gourmandes.

At some point in 1958, Julia began wondering where all of this was leading. The book contract was fine *in theory,* but she no longer felt secure in its outcome. And Paul, although secure, wasn't in love with his job. He enjoyed curating the exhibits for the USIA, but deplored the thicket of bureaucracy that constrained his every move. In another four years, he'd turn sixty and at that point he was calling it quits to work on his own art. Retirement wasn't a word Julia had given much thought to, not at fifty anyway. It wouldn't satisfy her one bit to sit around doing nothing, especially in Washington, D.C., which was a one-company town. There wasn't much in the city to feed her, socially or intellectually. When push came to shove, neither she nor Paul were keen on settling there.

In effect, they were rootless. So many postings had left them living out of suitcases and boxes, their belongings hanging on temporary hooks. Like summer-stock actors, they had learned to pack up and move on the spur of the moment, itinerant and adaptable. Paul had been on the move since the early 1930s, Julia following not long after college. The gypsy life suited them—seeing the world, sharing new experiences. But the thought of dropping permanent anchor gave them real pause. Where would they go? What place could hold them?

Paris was always a possibility. They had been happiest there; the city was even more of a movable feast than Hemingway knew. But it was so distant from family and friends, and no matter how enthusiastically they immersed themselves in all things French they would always be outsiders. Pasadena, as far as Paul cared, was enemy territory, conservative to the core, with a father-in-law from hell. And Julia felt about New York the way she felt about pudding; it was fine once or twice a month, but not as an everyday staple.

During a visit to Avis's, over the July Fourth weekend, the idea of Cambridge gradually entered the picture. It was a lovely, intellectual community, closely entwined with Radcliffe and Harvard. Paul had lived there, with Edith Kennedy, in the twenties, and had reveled in its bounty. Julia loved its "special, charming New England character," its proximity to Boston and Maine. Her publisher was fifteen minutes away. And, of course, there was Avis. There was no one in America whom Julia felt closer to, a devoted friend and trusted adviser. It was Avis who had masterminded the book deal with Houghton Mifflin and Avis who plotted to keep the deal alive. More than anything, however, Avis remained an indefatigable cheerleader, urging Julia onward, upward, to "keep trying and slugging away." True to form, Avis portrayed Julia's publishing defeat as a triumph of culinary integrity. "You have come nearer to mastering a good many aspects of cooking than anyone except a handful of great chefs," she reassured her, "and some day it will pay off. I know it will."

What a treat it would be to live close to Avis. Paul agreed, and all three spent the weekend house hunting in Cambridge. With a real estate agent in tow, they strolled around the sleepy, unspoiled, intimate community, with its cluster of irregular crosscut streets and colonial-era homes. The Childs were convinced: they'd found the location they were looking for, where they could work and thrive in meaningful ways. It would give them the long-sought sense of resolution. They made inquiries about several nice places, but none of the houses were apparently for sale.

Avis agreed to stay on the case—to notify them as soon as something suitable came up—but by summer's end, their plans had changed. Again. On August 6, 1958, the USIA sent Paul a new set of orders. The Exhibits Division was being shut down. He was being transferred, posted as Cultural Affairs Officer to Oslo, Norway, effective as of March 1959.

Norway! Halfway around the world. It struck like a bombshell, but Julia managed to take it in stride. Within days, she was telling friends, "I think this is wonderful, and we are getting excited." It wasn't permanent, and it certainly wasn't French. At least Norway was someplace new, someplace different, someplace else, another new horizon to cross in their ongoing odyssey. They would start all over again in the Land of the Midnight Sun. But Julia had to wonder where it would eventually end.

Judith and Evan Jones on their penthouse terrace

Fifteen

Julia's Turn to Bloom

Debby Howe, the wife of the Childs' old Ceylon intelligence pal, Fisher Howe, who happened to be the chargé d'affaires in Norway, told many stories about the "food obsessed" Julia Child. But her favorite had to do with the embassy wives' luncheon she made to welcome Julia to Oslo. "This won't be food you love," Debby warned her as they filed into the ambassador's private dining room. Julia reassured her friend with an easy, dismissive wave. She was tempted to remind Debby of her motto— Never Apologize—but refrained at the last moment.

"Big mistake," Debby said, nearly fifty years later.

The plates put in front of them looked like a six-year-old had gotten into Mommy's pantry. The main course was a cluster of grapes and sliced mushrooms floating in a kind of pink-gelatin amniotic sac with a crown of frozen whipped cream crusted with rock-hard fruit. This was followed by "a very thick slice of banana cake mix with a thick pale frosting," a blob of molded lime Jell-O salad, and a Norwegian's idea of key lime pie. A sticky cinnamon bun was served with tea.

Debby glanced across the table and caught Julia's eye. The look in it said: Down on your knees, friend—and *apologize*!

If Julia had come to Norway in search of a new culinary frontier, she came to the wrong place. She might have fared much better across the adjoining border in Sweden where *husmanskost*—their version of *cuisine bourgeoise*—featured meatballs, gravlax, and potato dumplings filled with pork. But Norway was another world entirely. The local fare consisted of either sweet-and-salt-cured moose, lobscouse, or ptarmigan, and a funky delicacy called *rakorret*—uncooked salmon trout, brined and pressed until it became fermented "like sauerkraut," eaten on flatbread, with a bracer. "If you had enough schnapps to go with it," Howe recalled, "somehow it tasted good," but others thought "the damn stuff stunk like a dead otter." Otherwise, everything else was "boiled, boiled, boiled, boiled, boiled." There were potatoes galore and a variety of berries, but very few fresh vegetables. And salad greens were practically extinct. Paul filled out his culinary scorecard with one word: "Vegetables: *lousy;* salads: *lousy;* meat: *lousy.*"

Still, Oslo was "a fabulous place to be posted," according to a diplomat at the embassy. World War II had left Norway relatively untouched. The German occupation invited minimal retaliation by the Allies, and a post-war resilience was evident across the kingdom. People seemed to enjoy a simple, uncomplicated lifestyle, to judge by their "relaxed, sweet, direct, at-ease-with-the-world healthy faces." There seemed to be an almost religious attraction to biking, hiking, or just strolling about. Soon after their arrival, Paul and Julia were struck by the Norwegians' communion with nature. "We both have an extremely pleasant sensation that we are now living in a place much like America 200 years ago," Paul wrote, "where nature is close about, where it is loved and used . . . where the nervous pressures and complications and Madison Avenue–inspired wants are relatively unknown."

Julia found Oslo to be "a great big old city of no distinction," "undistinguished architecturally," but "cozy"—a "family-oriented place, and small enough," with a population hovering around two million or less. "There are virtually *no fat people at all,*" Paul observed, an aspect he found "astonishing" after Germany and America. No doubt the environment contributed to a vigorously wholesome lifestyle. On the days when the weather cooperated, which were frequent, there was no finer place to dwell. "The whole glorious spread of spring" cast its spell—a "blindingly bright" sun, "air smelling magically of fir forests and blossoms." The view from almost any lookout was breathtaking. The city was a basin surrounded by dense, interlocking spruce-covered hills through which appeared the fjord, with its veiny weave of tributaries, inlets, and islands. Ferns and blueberry bushes abounded. The landscape reminded Paul and Julia of Mount Desert in Maine.

They settled in with spectacular ease. The Howes found them a white clapboard house "two steps down a hill" from their own place in Ullern, a neighborhood some distance out of town with "a heavenly view of the fjord." There was a sunken living room overlooking flowering fruit trees and a berry garden with rose hedges, and "an attic as big as Great Hall." The kitchen was sunny and large, although the "tired old Norwegian electric stove" was "preposterously unworkable," even for Julia, who had cooked on some broken-down beasts in her time. Ever obsessive, Paul hung her vast collection of pots and pans on a wall-size pegboard, each utensil given its own fixed place and then inventoried—"74 separate objects," he recorded, "arranged in a distinguished and classy fashion."

They were both eager to master Norse, a guttural Germanic dialect that swooped between low, flat pitches and high, sharply falling flourishes—not a bad approximation of Julia's trademark hooting. In fact, Julia picked it up quickly with her keen ear for language. In no time, she was making the rounds of shops and errands relying on a brand of "kitchen Norwegian" to see her through the day. Paul, on the other hand, had trouble communicating from the get-go. His ineptitude was baffling, considering that a battery of tutors had begun coaching him in Washington. "He'd made a real art of studying Norwegian," recalls Debby Howe—except it wasn't Norwegian, but *Danish,* and by the time he realized it, frustration had taken hold. After that, he could "never quite get the phrasing right."

Julia liked "the Wegians," as she nicknamed them, "very much," but realized there would be "no real soulmates" from among their new acquaintances. This was a blessing in disguise, as she soon discovered. "I am purposely being a bit of a mole, so I can get this book done as fast as possible," she explained. Great progress had been made since landing in Oslo, and throughout the summer of 1959 nothing interfered with the intense daily grind. "She was full-time occupied with it," says Debby Howe, who wandered over each day to observe "this dynamo" whirling through her kitchen. She'd be boning a lamb or perfecting béarnaise or peeling asparagus that her brother, John, sent by airmail, none of which Debby knew how to do.

"None of the embassy wives cooked French food," Howe recalls, "or any kind of food, for that matter." Later, in the fall, Julia would give them cooking lessons, but that summer distractions of any kind were strictly off-limits. There was more at stake than making new friends, she recalled. "After nearly eight years of hard labor, Simca and I could see the end in sight."

WHEN THE END finally came it took her by surprise.

Throughout Norway's unexpected summer heat wave—"one of the few in the memory of man"—Julia labored persistently over a blistering hot stove. Recipes that had languished in various stages of scrutiny were resolved, once and for all. It was her last chance to make crucial decisions. Her push to the finish line demanded total concentration. Even her forty-seventh birthday passed without note. But on September 1, 1959, thirteen years to the day of her marriage to Paul Child, the gears of cookbookery ground to a halt. It was time to celebrate—her anniversary, of course, but another event demanded an equal share of the spotlight: "The revised *French Recipes for American Cooks* was finished at last."

She and Simca exchanged their last set of notes and decided it was high time to lay down their tongs. The book was finished, but by no means complete. They'd made countless concessions in their push to edit and revise, with gems that wound up on the cutting room floor. It was no longer an *encyclopedia*, but a *primer*—"a primer on *cuisine bourgeoise* for serious American cooks." Nevertheless, it retained a certain heft: 750 manuscript pages of classic French cuisine, the same length as Madame Saint-Ange but without the esoterica, like thrush salami ("Take out the intestines, the liver, the head, and the feet for use in the coulis, and add a couple of whole thrushes to it, which will then be chopped and put through a drum sieve . . . ") or pork head cheese ("cut the ears off at their base . . . cut the tongue and lean meat into large cubes . . . "). No, it was pretty concise for 750 pages, and thorough and modern in its approach.

And *finished*!

"I can hardly believe it," Julia told a close friend. To another, she said in a jokey brogue: "It has weighed so like a stone these many years, but now it is off me back."

From here on in it was Dorothy de Santillana's baby to nourish and wean until publication. Julia was no longer on deadline. For the first time in years, opportunities beckoned away from the stove. She joined a class in Norwegian at a local university and played tennis daily with Debby Howe. Gardening engrossed her. There were receptions at the embassy, lectures, visitors to entertain, "so many office things going on in the evening," all done without preoccupation or guilt.

But—oh, the postpartum depression! Two weeks after delivering the manuscript, the vacuum it created had left Julia bereft. "Meself, am feeling quite lost without my book," she wrote to family in America. It seemed like the floor had given way beneath her. "I feel rootless and empty." Aside from Debby Howe there was no one to hang out with—"no friends," Julia lamented, "nobody to hug"; she missed that most at times like these. As such, she said, "I have descended into a slough of discombobulation."

There were still plenty of arrangements to look after back home. Before Julia and Paul had left Washington for Norway, Avis alerted them to a house in Cambridge that had come up for sale. "Drop everything," she advised, "and get up here right away." The Childs didn't immediately respond. "By that time," Avis realized, "they had almost given up the idea of Cambridge and were less than enthusiastic." Besides, it was sleeting and pouring, "the worst possible weather," but—what the hell. They jumped on a train to Boston, and the next morning, in a squall of wind and icy rain, poked about the rooms of 103 Irving Street.

It was an unprepossessing gray-shingled house on a rather prepossessing street smack in the middle of Harvard's Estate Row. John Kenneth Galbraith lived across the street, Arthur Schlesinger a few doors away, with distinguished professors and statesmen rounding out the roster. The place had been built as a cottage in 1889, then jacked up on posts and additions built under it. The last owners had left it in pretty good condition. Paul showed Julia the sturdy plaster walls and hardwood floors, and they all admired the well-appointed kitchen with a restaurant stove and double pantry. Out back, a good-size yard and garden came with the property. By the time they made their way up to the attic, the die was cast. "Well, this will suit us," Julia said, turning to her husband. "It's exactly the kind of house we want." But another couple was downstairs and had come to the same conclusion; they told the real estate agent they were going home to talk it over. In the interim, Julia and Paul bought it on the spot.

They had rented it back to the previous owner while they were posted in Norway, but agreed to give it a good updating, which required constant paperwork. Julia saw to many of the details while awaiting word from her editor.

The first critical response came in a letter at the end of September, and it left her "mightily encouraged." Dorothy de Santillana wrote that she was delighted with the book, "truly bowled over at the intensity and detail." She went on to say, "I surely do not know any compendium so amazingly, startlingly accurate or so inclusive . . . This is a work of the greatest integrity." She'd compared the manuscript to another recently published cookbook, *Classic French Cuisine* by Joseph Donon, and declared theirs the winner, hands down. Though she still needed her publisher and his beancounters "to do their figuring" before putting the book into production, the project, she said, looked good to go.

But nothing remained good to go for long. On November 10, 1959, a letter from Paul Brooks, Houghton Mifflin's editor in chief, arrived in the diplomatic pouch. "Your manuscript is a work of culinary science as much as of culinary art," he wrote. "However . . ."

However?

"This will be a very expensive book to produce and the publisher's investment will be heavy . . . It is at this stage that my colleagues feel dubious."

It was at this stage that Julia's heart began to sink. Still, she read on through the haze of hollow platitudes and backpedaling.

"I suggest you try this book on some other publisher," Brooks continued. "Believe me, I know how much work has gone into this manuscript. I send you my best wishes for its success elsewhere."

A *rejection* letter. Julia couldn't believe her eyes. It was the last thing she had expected after Dorothy de Santillana's praise. No doubt the manuscript needed a good cut, maybe even some heavy-duty editorial polish. But . . . *rejection?* She hadn't seen that one coming.

Avis had gotten the news earlier from Dorothy and attempted to give Julia a heads-up, but she'd sent her letter by post instead of the diplomatic pouch. When at last it arrived five days later, the blow had already landed. Julia was "devastated," "shell-shocked." She'd come to realize that the manuscript was "too difficult for Americans," too elaborate, too this, too that. "Quite possibly," she realized, "it is an unpublishable book." But Avis wasn't ready to throw down her cards. By the time Houghton Mifflin said no, she had other prospects in sight. Only recently, she'd become a talent scout for Alfred Knopf and his eponymous New York publishing house. There was an executive there she knew who not only "swings great weight," but was himself quite an accomplished cook. As a matter of fact, Bill Koshland had already seen bits and pieces of the manuscript during a visit to Cambridge. Without even waiting for Julia's approval, she'd ordered Houghton Mifflin to send it to him. "Do not despair," Avis declared. "We have only begun to fight."

But Julia wasn't so sure she had it in her.

THERE WERE CERTAIN realities that Julia needed to come to grips with. Literary pursuits were fine for dilettantes, but she was a practical person, not a dreamer, and refused to romanticize her prospects. Was the book, as Brooks claimed, too expensive to publish—or was it basically too time-consuming for Americans to use? Julia had come across a copy of *Helen Corbitt's Cookbook,* a Houghton Mifflin number that had already sold nearly seventy thousand copies. "It is such a wonderful example of easy looking recipes," Julia said. Take its recipe for *coq au vin,* only twenty-four words long: "Cut up two broilers. Brown them in butter with bacon, sliced onions, and sliced mushrooms. Cover with red wine and bake for two hours." Maybe that's all it took to make *coq,* she thought. At four pages, maybe she and Simca had driven that recipe into the ground. "Did the American public want nothing but speed and magic in the kitchen?" she wondered. Or was it the writing—was Julia just the wrong collaborator? "NOBODY has ever wanted to publish ANY of our recipes in *any* publication whatsoever thus far," she wrote to Simca, which "indicates that we're not presenting things in a popular manner."

Knopf was a "very interesting" prospect, but Julia wasn't about to fall down that hole again. "I refuse to let more than a coal of hope glow quietly," she said, preferring to let the publishing chips fall where they may. It was possible, just possible, that they were spinning their wheels. "So now what?" Julia wondered.

One thing was certain: she wasn't going to sit around waiting for the Good Cookbook Fairy to descend. "Having now started to re-arrange my life in case there is to be no published book," she reported in a letter to Avis, she decided that cooking would keep "the gloomies" at bay. She loved to cook. It was the one surefire way to take her mind off the perils of publishing, to "just continue on with my self-training." There was still plenty to learn about French cuisine, particularly pastry, which she began to circle with typical intrigue. She was dying to try her hand at some of Simca's sugary jewels—her *bavarois à l'orange,* a velvety mold of crème anglaise flavored with Grand Marnier; a thick, creamy, impossibly rich chocolate mousse; and the masterful *charlotte Malakoff,* an almond cream with ladyfingers that dazzled guests. Toward the end of November, Julia began baking in earnest—making petits fours and tuiles as a warm-up before moving on to tarts, using the berries from her bushes in sweet short-paste shells. It didn't take Paul long to appreciate his wife's resilience, as she took refuge in the kitchen, "clacking dishes and whistling like a magpie."

But the momentum of the cookbook could not be denied.

SELLING A COOKBOOK to Knopf in the late fifties was no mean feat. Unlike the novels of Sartre and Camus, cookbooks didn't carry the literary prestige that distinguished Knopf's list. Nor did they have the historical impact of *The War Lover,* by John Hersey, which the house had just published to great acclaim. They weren't exquisitely modulated like John Updike's *The Poorhouse Fair* or Roald Dahl's *Kiss Kiss.* Although cookbooks were far from finely wrought narratives, they celebrated food and captured the imagination through an engagement with sensual pleasure, creativity, culture, and an account of the good life. "You read them like fantasies," says Barbara Kafka. "They offered something different and exotic." But they weren't much of a factor in the overall publishing scheme. Of all the major houses, only Doubleday had anyone who functioned as a bona fide cookbook editor, a "good housewifely, home-ec type" named Clara Clausson, but the books she published were agonizingly simplistic, with "truncated recipes, no sensuous words, just straight directions, the most basic fare."

Alfred Knopf fancied himself a gourmet. He belonged to a tony food-and-wine society and cultivated an excellent wine cellar—but he never went near the kitchen. Never! As far as cookbooks went, they were dumped willy-nilly on any editor willing to send them on their way. Herbert Weinstock, Knopf's erudite music editor, got saddled with one of the company's earliest French cookbooks, and when he questioned why the recipes served so many, the author replied, "But you have to feed the help." Such was the state of Knopf's cookbook publishing.

The closest Knopf had come to anything of a cookbook editor was Alfred Knopf's wife, Blanche, an extremely charming but feisty socialite who was inexorably drawn to the cultural flame of Europe. She was the first person over there after the war and signed up every avant-garde author she could get her hands on. Cookbooks were something she handled by default; they fell to her because no one else dealt with them.

On Avis DeVoto's recommendation, Blanche had signed up Elizabeth David, Britain's leading culinary star, and *Classic French Cuisine,* the Joe Donon book that Julia had admired. Under her aegis, Knopf also put out *Cook, My Darling Daughter* by Mildred Knopf, Alfred's sister-in-law, and an Italian compendium by his brother Edwin, each of which sold a respectable ten or fifteen thousand copies. Yet food and cooking weren't on Blanche Knopf's radar, perhaps owing to an encounter with Joseph

Conrad. During a dinner party at the Knopf brownstone on New York's West Side, she overheard Conrad refer to her as *"Quelle belle Juive!"* To Blanche, *belle Juive* meant a plump Jewish dowager—and she immediately put herself on a fanatical diet. "Blanche knew nothing about food," says a colleague, "because she refused to eat it. She became anorexic." She took martinis at meals, but no food whatsoever. She was "a wraith, all skin and bones." This was Knopf's cookbook editor.

Normally, Bill Koshland would have sent Julia's manuscript to her, but he must have figured she would reject it, sight unseen. The Donon French cookbook had more or less tanked and Elizabeth David turned out to be "an incredibly difficult author." Word around the office was that Alfred Knopf had had his fill of cookbooks. But Koshland seemed to recognize the worth of this new submission. He'd taken home the manuscript and began cooking from it. He told Avis he was "impressed to death with it." In fact, he thought it was "the best damn cookbook he ever ran into, and unique."

Getting Knopf to publish it, however, would take considerable effort. The house was a very fraught little family business. "Alfred and Blanche were scratchy with each other, quite quarrelsome, and incredibly competitive," says a publishing colleague. They "liked their editors to be subservient" and kept them off-balance. "You could be up one day, and down the next." The Knopfs' moods were that unpredictable. But Koshland was something of a *grand vizier,* someone who knew how to work the margins by being diplomatic and cagey. "He could make things happen by being very circuitous—and playing Alfred and Blanche off one another." So instead of giving the manuscript to either of the Knopfs, he began testing the waters—seeing if there was a young editor who would feel as enthusiastic as he was and would go to bat for it.

Two agreed quickly to join his team. Alfred had recently hired Angus Cameron, a legendary editor who had fallen on hard times. An outspoken political gadfly, he had been fingered by McCarthy in a sweep of the publishing business and had resigned his position,[*] taking his family to live in the Alaskan tundra. Not only did he love to cook, Cameron had been an editor at Bobbs-Merrill for the launch of *Joy of Cooking* and knew what it took to market a cookbook. Koshland's other compadre was a less conspicuous choice. Judith Jones was a junior editor attached to Blanche Knopf's apron strings. At thirty-five, she should have been pull-

[*] At the time, Cameron was editor in chief of Little, Brown.

ing her own weight, considering her accomplishments in the publishing business. She'd rescued the manuscript of Anne Frank's *Diary of a Young Girl* from the scrap heap, worked with the translators of Camus and Sartre, and was currently working with John Updike on a new novel, *Rabbit Run,* as well as editing several of Elizabeth Bowen's books. But her editorial contributions were "strictly anonymous," passed along to authors as Blanche Knopf's ideas. Koshland knew Jones had two things on Blanche: she loved to cook and she adored French food. "Blanche wouldn't know a flounder if it bit her in the bum," while Jones would have pan-fried it in butter and white wine. But would she have the wherewithal to take a stand on Julia's manuscript?

It seemed unlikely at first blush. For one thing, she had no say whatsoever when it came to acquisitions. At Knopf, Judith Jones was "far too junior" to attend the "austere" editorial meetings, where book submissions were dissected and defended by one of the editors. And for another, she was a woman working in an old boys' club. In fact, Jones was the *only* woman in editorial at Knopf aside from Blanche, and Blanche didn't count because she ran the show. Still, they never failed to remind her of her lowly status. When Knopf moved to a new floor on Madison Avenue, it was announced: "Every office has a window—oh, except for Judith's."

And, yet, Koshland believed she would help his cause. She was ambitious and young. Cooking was a passion with her. So he deposited the manuscript on her desk with little fanfare. "Take a look at this," he said. "It came from Avis."

It hadn't taken Judith Jones long to appreciate that *French Recipes for American Cooks* was no ordinary cookbook. "I was surprised by it," she said. "I just couldn't put it down." It read "like taking a basic course at the Cordon Bleu." After flipping through the pages several times, her culinary instincts were more than aroused. As a young woman, she had lived in Paris and was well acquainted with the vagaries of French cooking. She and her husband, writer Evan Jones, made a practice of cooking *à deux,* preparing careful, French-inspired dishes adapted from the meals they'd enjoyed in Paris. Budding amateurs, they thought nothing about spending all day at the stove if their efforts resulted in an elegant French dinner. It seemed only fitting that she should take Julia's manuscript home so that she and Evan could work through the recipes.

After a month of experimenting from the book, Jones was sold. "She goes home for lunch and blanches the vegetables the way she learned from you," Avis reported to Julia, "then finishes the cooking at night."

Everything she attempted turned out a masterpiece. "It was revolutionary," Jones says of the book's expert approach. "It not only changed the language of cooking, it made the difference between ordinary cooking and cooking with finesse." The book was jam-packed with so much useful information, information she'd never seen in an American entry. The author wasn't just churning out recipes; she had "such an analytical mind." In some way, Jones saw this manuscript as being as important a document as Anne Frank's *Diary of a Young Girl.* It would be revealing, life-changing—a potential classic. "This was the book I had been waiting for all my life," she said. "I knew we had to publish it."

But first she had to convince Alfred Knopf. Although a lover of fine foods with a good palate, he endeavored to publish books that demonstrated more than good taste—they had to be profitable. And recently his cookbooks had performed miserably. He was "intensely gloomy" about business in general. At the moment, Knopf only had one best seller, *Home from the Hill,* by William Humphrey, which probably wouldn't sell more than fifteen thousand copies. He was convinced the house was "publishing far too many books, and they are not selling." Part of the blame he laid at Avis DeVoto's feet. Unlike most women Knopf dealt with, Avis was unintimidated and forceful when it came to defending her opinions. She was persuasive about the books she recommended to him, but her record as a scout had thus far been dismal. "I got him quite a few books and they all lost money," she recalled. Disgruntled, Knopf suggested it was time they part company, which is why Avis sent the manuscript to Koshland instead of to Alfred, as she normally did.

It would be better for Judith Jones not to mention Avis's name. Nor could she rely on Bill Koshland to make a strong case with Knopf. "Bill wasn't one to go out on a limb," she says. But Angus Cameron was. "He was a very persuasive man, and he enjoyed putting up a good argument for what he believed in." As luck would have it, he believed in *French Recipes for American Cooks.* He considered it "a remarkable manuscript" and "foolproof. The *best working French cookbook* I have ever looked at."

The night before the editorial meeting, Bill Koshland phoned Avis with encouraging news. "Well, *four* of us have been cooking with this book," he said. "We've cooked our way straight through it, and it works—and we're going to tank right over the Knopfs."

It was a bold assertion, if not quite plausible. Alfred Knopf was no mean pushover, and his wife, Blanche, could level a statue with a stare. She "hated the idea" of a cookbook that would compete with the others on their list, let alone one that might slip Judith Jones from her clutches. The nerve of that young girl to aspire to such a project! Blanche had already given Bill Koshland her opinion: "I don't think we need this, do we?"

It would take more than a tank to level the Knopfs.

Fortunately, Angus Cameron had time on his side. The weekly editorial meeting on Thursday, May 5, 1960, was a particularly long and weary one; it wore on and on before he raised the subject of acquiring the cookbook. It was getting toward lunch, toward martini time, and everyone had his or her eye on the clock. No one was up for a long, drawn-out debate. When Cameron finally launched into his presentation, the air got sucked out of the room. "This manuscript is an astonishing achievement and there is simply nothing like it," he said. "What these authors have done has never been done before . . . " Waving off superfluous discussion, Alfred Knopf relented. "Well," he said, gathering up his notes, "let's let Mrs. Jones have her chance."

For Blanche Knopf, it was the last straw. She had overlooked the fact that someone had "sneaked in" to her house and bypassed her with a cookbook submission. And she had overlooked it when Judith Jones responded to the manuscript with such unrelenting passion. But this was Knopf, *her* house, and being tanked over by underlings was more than she could forgive. She shot bolt upright and stomped out "in a snit."

Of course, none of that drama ever reached Julia Child. On May 9, 1960, the telephone rang in her Oslo living room. It was Avis, and Julia could tell something was up. Avis wrote. She never called unless there was trouble to report, like her last call, when her husband Benny had died. *Please God, don't let anything have happened to her sons!* Despite the transatlantic connection, Avis was breathless, all aflutter. There was a letter that day from Judith Jones, she said, launching into it without further explanation. "I am writing hastily to tell you our publication proposal for the Child, Beck, and Bertholle has just been approved," it said. "I can't remember when I've been as excited about a project . . . "

Did this mean what Julia thought?

Most of what Avis read to her zoomed by in a blur, but bits and pieces were unforgettable. "The enthusiasts around here are absolutely convinced that this book is revolutionary and we intend to prove it and make it a classic. We are hatching up all kinds of schemes . . . My everlasting gratitude for having brought us this creation."

Avis had done it—she had sold their book to Knopf!

THE DEAL CAME together very quickly. Knopf offered the authors what they considered to be "a perfectly fair advance": $1,500 for the book—twice Houghton Mifflin's advance—and a standard royalty rate. The only snag appeared to be Alfred Knopf's insistence that the deal be made with only *one* author, despite the three names on the title page. "It was unusual for Alfred to suggest such an arrangement," Jones says. But his instinct, in this case, was to avoid a contractual dispute among collaborators should the friendship go sour.

For Judith Jones, it was a foregone conclusion which author to sign up. "I realized while reading the manuscript that Julia was the driving force behind the book," she says. "There was a strong voice translating everything, which French women couldn't have done. I knew it instinctively—one woman had the vision for this book, and that was Julia. It was Julia Child's book."

That was fine and dandy as far as Simca went, but there were still questions about what to do with Louisette Bertholle. The women had negotiated an agreement that gave her an 18 percent stake in the book, which, at the time, seemed fair based on her early enthusiasm. But, lately, Julia had second thoughts about the distribution of royalties. Louisette's share galled her; it was "too damn generous," Julia decided. In a letter to Avis DeVoto, she wrote: "I think it is crazy when she hasn't done one single sentence of work on either of the two huge manuscripts we have prepared."

Amassing her greatest skills of diplomacy, Julia wrote to Louisette in August 1960 suggesting that before the contract with Knopf was signed perhaps she could consult her family and friends to come up with a more "fair and just" figure, something more in line with her contribution. Rather undiplomatically, she admitted, "We are quite willing to offer her 10% to shut her up, then have no further collaborations, and retain exclusive rights to 'Les 3 Gourmandes' as a trademark."

Otherwise, the remaining work was left to Julia and Simca. Throughout the summer of 1960, they cooked their way through the manuscript twice, refining details and fine-tuning recipes. Judith Jones requested that the size of certain portions be altered, especially in reference to recipes with meat. She had served *bœuf bourguignon* to a party of guests who adored it, but remained hungry after they'd killed off the dish. "Two-and-a-half pounds of meat won't do for six to eight people," she reported, particularly in America where beef was such a staple of meals. In any case, the book needed additional recipes featuring meat. She also appealed for "more hearty peasant dishes," the kind she remembered eating in Paris, which were less time-consuming and expensive to prepare at home.

Julia solved the meat problem by arriving at a formula—a half-pound per person—that became a standard in the food industry for the next fifty years. But as for peasant dishes, thank you, but *non.* "Neither Simca nor I are enthusiastic about including any more of these," Julia insisted. That ground had already been well-covered in the book, with recipes for cassoulet, beef daube, veal sauté, and braised lamb with beans. "Perhaps Americans think French peasants are more peasanty than they are," she argued. "Absolute peasants boil everything. But farm people, concierges, and policemen"—in other words, the middle-class and blue-collar populace—"cook like everybody else, with fricassées, *à l'ancienne, blanquettes, Bourguignons,* and Orloffs." Her point was that all Frenchmen, regardless of class, cooked with tradition and refinement. Had Judith Jones asked for more bistro-type recipes, which is probably what she'd intended all along, Julia's answer might have been different. But "peasant" dishes "set off something" that drew a line in the sand.

In any case, there was still plenty of work to be done before the manuscript was due, on August 31—mostly nuts-and-bolts business, including proofreading and minor edits. The only critical outstanding issue was the title. "*French Recipes for American Cooks* is not nearly provocative or explicit enough," Jones cautioned. A book of this importance demanded something classy and snappy, something immediately identifiable in the tradition of *Joy of Cooking.* Julia agreed. "The present title," she said, "had no sale appeal whatsoever."

But Julia, for the life of her, couldn't come up with anything better. God knows, she had tried. She and Paul had racked their brains, to no avail, for more than a year. They'd come up with forty-five potential titles, without a single winner. In fact, most were downright awful: *How It Can Be Cooked French, French Magicians in the Kitchen, Love and French Cooking, A Map for the Territory of French Food* (really!), *You Too Can Be a French Chef, How, Why and What to Cook in the French Way*—they went from bad to worse. Finally, she distributed a circular throughout the American embassy in Oslo offering a big *bloc* of foie gras to anyone who could come to the rescue. "All you have to do is think up a nifty title for the greatest French cookbook in the world today," it said. There is no indication they actually gave up the foie, but by November the situation was critical. Julia was leaning toward *La Bonne Cuisine Française,* which Knopf rejected as being "too forbidding." It wasn't certain housewives would want to cook French, let alone be able to speak it.

The folks at Knopf had "been talking about the *art* of French cooking, but even that seemed daunting," Jones recalls. The title needed to convey something fun, not imposing. "I'm not sure when I came up with *mastering,* but the minute I wrote it down, things began to click. *Mastering* implied a continuing process, with an emphasis on skill." Let's see: *The Master French Cookbook*—no, there was no rhythm to it, nothing magical. *The French Cooking Master, How to Master French Cooking,* none of them really captured the spirit of the book. Jones continued to play with a pattern of words, rearranging them on her desk like a baffling shell game. Finally, in a letter to Julia, dated November 18, 1960, Jones wrote, "I think we have now found the solution by calling it: MASTERING THE ART OF FRENCH COOKING. What do you and the other gourmandes think?"

They thought it was "a fine title." Julia loved it the moment she laid eyes on it. "It has all the elements," she said, "scope, fundamentality, cooking, and France."

The only thing left was to convince Alfred Knopf. He had the final say when it came to all titles on his list and was famous for being a difficult sell. Jones recalls being summoned to his office for the ceremonial presentation. "It was very old-world," she says, "with floor-to-ceiling dark bookcases and glass fronts." Knopf, who resembled the banker on the Monopoly Community Chest card, was seated behind a mahogany desk, with Sidney Jacobs, his production manager and fearsome hatchet man, in a chair to his left. Jones wasn't offered a seat. "It was quite daunting and disturbing. The two men wanted to intimidate me, and it worked very well." Even so, she believed in the book and decided to "stick to [her] guns" no matter how they responded.

Summoning up every last ounce of courage, she delivered the title with an appreciable flourish: *Mastering the Art of French Cooking.* Even in that chilly, godforsaken office it had the right ring. *Mastering the Art of French Cooking.* Knopf and Jacobs cut glances at each other, then the boss turned to Jones with a fearsome scowl. "If a book with that title sells," he bellowed, "I'll eat my hat."

IN THE MEANTIME, Julia and Paul finalized plans of their own. They ultimately acknowledged the inevitable truth they'd surmised more than a decade ago—that Paul wasn't much of a career diplomat. "He was an artist and an individualist," says his boss, Fisher Howe, "which didn't fly in a government bureaucracy. He was arrogant, he was prone to exaggeration. He was so much of a non-organization man, you were never sure what inappropriate thing he might say publicly. In Oslo, he put quite a few noses out of joint, including mine, and we had been acquaintances since Ceylon."

Paul saw himself as a soldier at war—"the endless war between bureaucracy and the individual"—and it was a battle he had been losing since he put in for Paris. He disdained "the crazy, intense, and hateful life of a bureaucrat," disdained himself for putting up with it for so long. In twelve years of service, he'd only received one promotion, and that came grudgingly after a long, noisy, self-financed campaign. "This God-damn job of mine is theoretically fascinating," he admitted, "but it should be done by *three* people, at least two of whom should be young, unshrunken, unwizened, and full of moxie." That wasn't Paul Child, at least not Paul as 1960 drew to a close. He was old, exhausted, bored—and cranky. "It affected him physically," says Debby Howe. "His stomach gave him a lot of trouble and he was uncomfortable. We all thought the job was killing him."

Figuratively—and literally. Paul always fashioned himself as something of a hypochondriac, but in Norway his anxieties grew increasingly dark. "Scarcely a month goes by that I don't believe I am dying," he wrote, "and though so far it has proved to be wrong I still go through the cruel preliminaries, inevitable if one fears death as I do."

It eventually dawned on Julia that "Paul couldn't take it any more," and the only way to save him was to leave Norway. *To leave the diplomatic service altogether.* They'd saved up some money; Julia's inheritance returned a fairly tidy sum on her investments. They had a new house waiting for them in Cambridge, Massachusetts. Julia could teach if things got tight. And who knew? Maybe the cookbook—*Mastering the Art of French Cooking*—might sell a few copies.

After the two years in Oslo were up, another posting in Europe was out of the question. Either way, they weren't leaving anything to chance. On December 12, 1960, Paul officially tendered his resignation. He'd been on the road since 1932. "After Avon, Cambridge, Washington, New Delhi, Kandy, Chungking, Kunming, Washington twice, Paris, Marseille, Bonn, Washington" again, and Oslo, he was headed home to America.

It was Julia's turn to bloom.

Sixteen

Taking Everything in Stride

There was no formal ceremony or brass band on that unseasonably warm afternoon, September 28, 1961, when the postman rang at 103 Irving Street. Boxes of furniture bearing the solemn STATE DEPT. seal were stacked around the doorway, still unopened, still waiting to be unpacked. The entrance hall was like an obstacle course. An old cracked urn lay upturned, headed for the dumpster; a battered screen door leaned off its hinges. Shouldering a hamper out of the way, Julia wedged her big frame awkwardly in the doorjamb and signed for the package, commiserating with the broad-jawed postman over the abominable humidity.

Gratefully, the moment was hers alone. Paul was in the basement, transforming a closet into his personal wine *cave*. A battery of carpenters buzzed around a shed in the backyard. The house was otherwise a silent tomb. Julia carried the package to a chair in the low-ceilinged living room, turning it over in her hands a few times. She felt anxious, the anxiety a prisoner might feel as the judge prepared to deliver sentence—someone ready to confront the inevitable. Her lips bit inward concernedly. The package was heavier than she'd expected, unadorned, unmarked. She ran her hand over its rough well-traveled surface. Nice, it felt nice, she thought. Without further ado, she ripped the covering away and let its contents fall into her lap.

Voilà!

Simca and Julia on *Cavalcade of Books*, Los Angeles, November 16, 1961

Mastering the Art of French Cooking
by
Simone Beck, Louisette Bertholle, and Julia Child

It was almost as if a nurse had purred, "Congratulations, Mrs. Child, you have a daughter." Instinctively, Julia tended toward a holler, but her throat produced a half-strangled gasp instead. Her book. *Their* book. It seemed hard to believe.

It was beautiful, just a beautiful thing to behold. For the first-time author, the feeling is almost indescribable. First you stare at the book, drink it all in. Then you run your hand over the cover a few times as if it were worsted wool, check out the spine, feel the heft. Inevitably, you trace your name with a respectful finger. A smile unfurls.

The book was "perfectly beautiful in every respect," she declared.

And such a healthy little critter—732 pages, longer than the Boston phone book. It "weighed a ton," she thought, hoisting it like a trophy.

Julia sat admiring it for some time, unable to let go of the satisfaction she felt. The overall impact was more than she'd bargained for. *Just look at it!* The cover was eye-catching, engaging, so strong in its design that it guaranteed to pop out on the shelves of a bookstore. The title vibrant, in black and red, was as distinct and resonant as they'd intended, with a reading line on the book jacket that left nothing to chance: "The Only Cookbook That Explains How to Create Authentic French Dishes in American Kitchens with American Food." Below, there was a drawing of a mouthwatering roast surrounded by a halo of sliced vegetables. And plenty of decorative *fleurs de lis,* just in case the French angle failed to connect. It obviously galled Julia that Louisette's name appeared equal to hers and Simca's, but she could live with it. For now.

Julia thought the jacket looked "handsome and distinguished." The way the publisher constructed the binding was admirable. The book could be opened to any recipe so that it lay flat on the table, allowing a cook to work without having to weight down the pages. They also had the good sense to waterproof the cover so that splatters didn't turn it into a Jackson Pollock painting.

The interior of the book was just as innovative. A so-called revolutionary cookbook demanded a revolutionary layout, new ways of presenting recipes, as a teaching tool instead of brief sketches. A cook should work the way any technician worked, Julia believed—methodically and logically. So in developing the recipes, she had used a "two-column" style, with the procedure, the practical application, annotated on the right-hand side of the page, and directly opposite the ingredients, *as they were needed,* on the left. This eliminated a lot of tiresome page-turning. Simple, but completely unprecedented, the design set a standard that became an enduring influence on successive generations of cookbook writers. But influence only counted for posterity. *Mastering*'s visual appearance was more immediately alluring. Its elements of beauty and style reassured inexperienced cooks, with ridiculously wide margins, a crisp, easy-to-read Granjon typeface, and detailed line drawings depicting intricate steps that eluded mere description.

Perfectly beautiful in every respect.

Julia couldn't wait to share it with Simca. But she hesitated—*why?* At first she wasn't sure. Simca was her inspiration, her guiding star, her compadre, her *chère chérie.* No one taught her as much about cooking as the Norman nonpareil. Without Simca, there would be no *Mastering.* They complemented each other, like strawberries and cream. But leading up to publication, the cream had curdled.

Julia had spent most of March and April 1961 in Oslo, reading the galleys of *Mastering*—answering editorial queries and keeping an eye peeled for errors. It was a painstaking, exhausting, "perfectly horrible job." Julia was up to her eyeballs in page proofs. The copy, she discovered, was loaded with mistakes, necessitating rewriting and correction ad infinitum. Certain passages that had looked fine in typescript appeared flawed and confusing on the printed page. Occasionally measurements were way out of whack. In one case, the recipe called for ¼ cup instead of ¼ teaspoon of an ingredient; in another, a scrambled number instructed readers to bake a cake at 530 degrees. More often, Julia simply hated her prose. The proofreading filled entire days on end. Julia stopped cooking and discouraged visitors. When she found a spare hour, instead of packing for the trip home, she sequestered herself at the embassy library, fact-checking in the reference stacks. "She was obsessed," says Judith Jones, "with getting things right."

If cooking brought out Julia's longing for perfection, Simca eventually brought out her rage. "I am just going WOOOOBIS with our dear old friend, Simca," she wrote to Avis in late April. With plenty still to do before deadline, the letters from France grew fraught with tension. Simca became difficult, demanding, downright perverse. According to Julia, "she was inclined to rush at things without half reading them, to forget what she has pronounced previously, and to act, in general, enragingly French." For instance, Simca insisted that almonds be deleted from a recipe for tuiles; otherwise, it would no longer be tuiles *françaises*. Never mind that Julia worked from a typescript of Simca's called "Tuiles Classiques *with almonds*." The same occurred with a half dozen other recipes. "*Pas du tout français*" Simca slashed across the margins.

"That old goat!" Julia fumed, when she saw the response.

In another instance, Simca wrote: "Why add a slice of bread to the *pistou* soup?"

"This was HER SUGGESTION, god dammit."

Still, long letters of comments and corrections continued to arrive daily from Paris. "This is not right. That is not right." "*Ce gâteau—ce n'est pas français. On ne peut pas l'avoir dans notre livre.*" In effect, she wanted *everything* changed, including the title, which she'd already approved.

Julia deftly put down many such insurgencies, but the Battle of Cassoulet nearly rent them asunder. Judith Jones demanded they include a recipe for the hearty southwestern meat-and-bean casserole, which, like bouillabaisse and barbecue, boasts as many versions as there are cooks. Julia collected twenty-eight recipes, all claiming to be authentic, even though they were as different as fraternal twins. Three towns in the Languedoc were especially certain that their cassoulet was the genuine article. So it goes: in the "pure" version served in Castelnaudary, the beans are cooked with chunks of fresh pork, a ham hock, sausage, and fresh pork rind. In Toulouse, they add either *confit* of duck or goose, and the cooks of Carcassonne throw mutton into the mix. Could Julia and Simca agree on a master recipe that would represent a classic cassoulet?

Not a chance. Simca insisted that no dish could be called cassoulet that omitted preserved goose. Without it, all you had was beans and charcuterie. Stubbornly, Julia conducted massive research, reams of evidence, documenting how cassoulet throughout the southwest was made regularly without preserved goose. Meanwhile, where did she expect American cooks to find goose *confit*? Instead, she offered a recipe that represented a perfectly respectable cassoulet. Simca dug her heels in. "We French," she argued, "never make a cassoulet like this."

"*Ce n'est pas français.*"

"*This is not correct!*"

"*Non! Non! Non!*"

"Fundamentally," says Judith Jones, "she didn't believe that an American could possibly have the finesse, the taste, the discretion, or the sophistication to cook French food with competency. And she became impossible. She drove Julia nuts."

Following a particularly scrappy exchange, Julia crumpled up one of Simca's letters, threw it on the floor, and danced a gavotte on it.

She was beside herself. "The big boob has had all this stuff for years, she has OK'd everything, again and again and again and again and again." *The French,* Julia huffed—why did she ever get involved with the French? "Reason has no effect, they have no memory of what they have done or said before, everything just comes out of the stomach and the top of the head at the moment—and with tremendous dogmatism."

Convinced that Simca was trying to sabotage publication, Julia decided not to send her the final galleys of *Mastering.* Instead, she dashed off a "pull-up-your-pants-for-god's-sake letter," urging her colleague to enjoy the publishing experience and to cool her jets. In any case, she refused to allow the bickering to scuttle their relationship. Julia was "far too fond" of Simca to let that happen. "Without her," she acknowledged, "the book would be nothing at all." Not only was Simca a masterful cook, "she works like a Trojan." They were a team, almost sisters.

Besides, her almost-sister was arriving to celebrate the publication. It wouldn't do if they weren't on speaking terms as the big day approached.

Judith Jones wasn't leaving anything to chance. She'd been working overtime to ensure the occasion would be memorable, beating the jungle drums up and down the avenues to stir up interest in the book. Novels and biographies were hard enough to promote. It seemed an absurd endeavor to create buzz for a cookbook. "There wasn't much of a food community," Jones says, "and I certainly didn't know anybody."

The most influential voice on the scene belonged to Craig Claiborne, the honey-tongued food editor of *The New York Times.* Jones didn't know him, nor did anyone at Knopf. But, in those days, if you wanted to reach Claiborne you just called him up. It was that simple. Jones told him, somewhat brazenly, that she had "a really remarkable book" that she'd share with him if he agreed to have lunch with her. And in those days, he would—as long as she was buying.

They went to a little French joint on the West Side, near the *Times,* where Jones made her pitch. "Craig didn't buy things easily," she said. "He was gentlemanly but tough, not easily influenced." And, for a while, it seemed she was getting nowhere with him. "He drank heavily, and I could see it was taking its toll." But during the course of the meal, she mentioned that her husband, Evan, cooked rather elaborately on a grill on their penthouse terrace overlooking East Sixty-sixth Street. Nowadays, that's as common a sight as satellite dishes and cell towers, but in 1961 it was quite a phenomenon. Claiborne proposed a little quid pro quo. "Tell you what," he said. "If you let me come up and do a story about you and your husband cooking, I'll look at this French book of yours."

On a sweltering August afternoon, she came across with her part of the bargain. Jones and her husband roasted a lamb on their terrace, while traffic blared in the streets below. Shortly thereafter, an article about it appeared in the *Times,* and a month or so later Claiborne wrote to Judith about *Mastering.* "He said the book was going to be a classic," she recalls. "He was as sure as I was."

THE PUBLICATION, ON October 16, 1961, was only the first but perhaps least dramatic in a series of events that spun Julia's life in another new direction. Two days after the book's launch, a review appeared in *The New York Times* that made the skeptics at Knopf "sit up and take notice." Written by none other than Craig Claiborne, it conferred heavyweight status on *Mastering the Art of French Cooking,* calling it "the most comprehensive, laudable, and monumental work on [French cuisine] . . . the definitive work for non-professionals." Claiborne was effusive—and then some. Its contents, he said, beheld "an embarrassment of riches." Everything was set down in easy-to-follow detail, the directions meticulous, infallible, eminently satisfying. "The recipes are glorious . . . written as if each were a masterpiece, and most of them are." Later on, in the *Saturday Evening Post,* Claiborne's pen ran wild with praise. "This work is brilliant," he declared, "the most lucid volume on French cuisine since Gutenberg invented movable type."

Julia was elated. "Once the *Times* had its say, everyone else jumped on the band-wagon," she told an interviewer long afterward. "It was so exciting, to be received that way."

But excitement didn't sell books. The *Times* catered to a rather concise, cultured, upscale readership. For *Mastering* to succeed in a meaningful way, for it to land on every Formica kitchen counter across America, it needed to find a more diverse national audience. The breakthrough came with an offer to appear on the *Today* show. Even in 1961, with a daily following fixed at around four million viewers, *Today* was an influential outlet for anyone with something to sell. Julia and Simca recognized its value to their cookbook, even though neither of them owned a television set, and they decided to make their appearance something to remember.

Interviewing a couple of authors, two middle-aged women, was boring, Julia decided. TV demanded something more animated, more dramatic. It needed energy, *action,* to create a little tension. Two authors *making an omelet*—that was more like it. Julia and Simca would do a demonstration so that someone watching at home could cook exactly like they did.

The day before, they crammed into a galley kitchen at Julia's niece Rachel Child's apartment on the Upper West Side, to practice in front of a pretend audience. If all went according to plan, they'd have slightly less than two minutes to answer questions, make the omelet, and plug the book, which meant everything had to be orchestrated with split-second precision. To make matters more difficult, there'd be no stove in the studio—only an electric burner. So Paul and Rachel sat on garbage cans, eating the spoils, while the women whipped through three . . . four . . . five dozen eggs, trying to cook while playing to the camera.

It was unfamiliar territory for these culinary countesses. Simca was nervous and "basically incoherent." Her usual exemplary English sounded like French-accented Ukrainian. Julia was forced to cover, taking over the narrative. There were moments when Simca looked lost, diminished. She rubbed her friend's shoulder in a soothing way. "Just stay calm," Julia said reassuringly. "We're going to get this done in the time allotted." For some strange reason, the thought of a television camera didn't intimidate Julia. It was a prop, nothing more, just another tool, like a whisk or a cleaver. She understood the illusion it was trying to create. What's more, she showed herself to be an intuitive, accommodating actor. The object was to relax, just be yourself.

The next morning, before sunrise, they marched into the RCA Building on West Forty-ninth Street and took the elevator up to Studio 3K. *Today*'s longtime host, Dave Garroway, had just been replaced by John Chancellor, the political correspondent for *The Huntley-Brinkley Report,* and it was clear he was uncomfortable in the new, more casual role. Julia let him know instantly that they had things under control.

The mood was set and the spot dominated by Julia's cool aura. Once the cameras began turning, she fell into a natural rhythm, instructing millions of viewers with the same intimacy she taught six in her kitchen. Her voice was arresting, encouraging, her instructions careful and deliberate. She took the reins and engaged the audience, while Simca melted into the background. "She just dominated the spot," recalls her niece, Rachel. "Almost immediately, she was so comfortable on TV."

The camera may have served Julia well, but it wasn't comfort she was experiencing. She told several friends after that first brush with television that the episode had been "simply terrifying." Afterward, when she stood back and thought about it, the two-minute spot had whipped by in a blur; she must have been "on automatic pilot." That may have been so, in which case she was lucky. Nevertheless the new medium changed everything overnight. It took her out of the dark bookstore corners where cookbook authors languished and cast her in a new spotlight. Suddenly, you could preach the culinary gospel to the masses and gauge an immediate impact. The day after the appearance on *Today*, a cooking demonstration at Bloomingdale's, which normally drew a handful of curious shoppers, attracted several hundred women who clamored for the book.

By the end of that first week, Julia was encouraged. "The old book seems, for some happy reason, to have caught on here in New York, and our publishers are beginning to think they have a modest best seller on their hands," she wrote her sister. "They have ordered a second printing of 10,000 copies, and are planning a third of the same amount."

The book's performance had actually caught Knopf off guard. "I thought if we sold 10,000 books the first year we'd be ahead of the game," says Judith Jones. "Maybe, in a few years we'd hit 25,000." The publisher's credo was "slow and steady"—to sell just enough copies year after year to earn the book a place on its backlist. That was how you established a classic, Jones says. Keep the book in print, sell a continuous, respectable amount. *Slow and steady.* "With any luck, it might last forever."

Marketing wouldn't be a factor. Knopf had no master strategy to promote the book other than "to put it out and hope to get Julia into a few bookstores." Such was the extent of the publicity machine. Avis helped by bombarding the press and the heavy-hitters in Benny DeVoto's Rolodex with copies of the book. But Julia and Simca had ideas of their own. They had a network of friends and family across the States with whom they made arrangements to stay for a few days that fall. Then, while in each city, they could promote *Mastering* by contacting newspapers and giving demos wherever possible. *A book tour*—although no one was calling it that. Nor paying for it—Julia would pick up the tab. Even so, their excursion would take them to Detroit, Chicago, San Francisco, Los Angeles, and Washington, D.C., dragging bags filled with cooking equipment and groceries.

In the meantime, Julia and Simca were being drawn into the small culinary community that was beginning to emerge as a force in New York. There was an elite coven of influential food editors at *McCall's, House & Garden, Ladies' Home Journal,* and *Gourmet;* there were a few innovative restaurants emerging, important chefs, creative cooks, food professionals, entrepreneurs. Most prominent among them all was James Beard, the king-sized, flamboyant, pleasure-loving figure whose penchant for self-promotion made him the master link in the food chain.

Beard's persona was inescapable. Twenty-five years before Julia Child sliced, diced, and grinded her way into America's kitchens, Beard had already begun sowing the seeds of gastronomy across the landscape of American food. "He was a man with great appetites, great intensity, and great passions," says Clark Wolf, a Beard acolyte in the mid-seventies. A self-created personality of "voracious charm," Beard fostered the idea that food and cooking were culturally significant, and that, together, they inspired the good life. "Food is very much theater," Beard once told a reporter, and his life, like his cuisine, was propelled by high drama. An early foray into opera (he studied with Caruso's vocal coach) ended in bitter disappointment; he lusted after stardom as an actor, appearing in notable federal theater productions and, later, DeMille and von Stroheim epics. But his size—a Bunyanesque physique whose weight careened between 250 and 325 pounds—precluded the meaningful, longed-for roles that sustained a career. He stemmed these setbacks by cooking, plying recipes acquired from his hotelier mother that relied on indigenous, fresh, *American* ingredients.

Beard's reputation as a talented cook skyrocketed among the denizens of café society. His food was elemental, but full of imagination—and delicious. No one cooked on a grander or more ambitious scale. He coupled kitchen savvy with his most abundant ingredient—charisma—and cultivated an image of flamboyance and sophistication. As a raconteur, a bon vivant, no one was in greater demand. He could hold a table of dinner guests in thrall with cultural and political commentary, laced with generous helpings of show-business scuttlebutt. "Jim was a very mischievous guy," Michael Batterberry recalls. He loved gossip and imparted it shamelessly, with great panache. But he could also be eloquent and thoughtful in his musings about food.

It was in this pivotal role that he made his greatest contribution to American cookery. Expressing himself on the page, Beard found, was easier than emoting from the stage. In a series of casual but wholly practical and indispensable books—*Hors d'Oeuvre and Canapés* (1940) and *Cook It Outdoors* (1941)—he established himself as an advocate for basic American food. Great meals, he argued, most often derived from "native cuisine" via fresh, local ingredients. Such was his innate gift that, despite volumes of recipes in magazines and newspapers, an entire post-war generation of fledgling cooks was converted to Beard's culinary gospel.

In the spring of 1946, with television emerging as a major modern entertainment medium, Beard seemed like the natural choice to become its first culinary star. What better combo than an actor who cooked to engage a national audience with recipes and repartee? The show, a fifteen-minute spot on NBC called *Elsie Presents: James Beard in "I Love to Eat!,"* was sponsored by Borden and debuted on August 30, 1948, at 8:15 p.m., as a lead-in to boxing from Madison Square Garden. Beard, however, wasn't exactly a knockout. For all his theater training, he was nervous, grim in front of the camera. A viewer's opinion summed up the general reaction: "He always seemed a little cross and petulant." In any case, "he wasn't any good on TV." But the show served to burnish his name.

James Beard became synonymous with good food. He wrote monthly articles for *Gourmet,* taught glamorous cooking classes, churned out myriad cookbooks, promoted endless products, hosted a daily radio program, syndicated newspaper columns, and developed menus for New York's toniest new restaurants, including the Forum of the Twelve Caesars, Brasserie, and The Four Seasons.

No one appreciated the power of Beard's enormous personality more fully or was more attuned to it than Julia Child. She had been following his exploits since returning to the States—his theories about food, his cooking techniques, the way he utilized the media. Beard was no hack. His recipes were well conceived. He had artistry, taste. Clearly, she recognized a fellow traveler in the struggle to elevate the way people cooked and ate.

Exactly when they first met is difficult to pin down, but it was sometime during the week before Julia and Simca left on tour to promote their book. Judith Jones arranged an introduction at Beard's town house on Tenth Street in Greenwich Village where he greeted the new authors with effusive charm. He laid out drinks and a little spread—a "Smithfield ham sliced so thinly you could breathe through it, Italian mustard fruits that made your eyes cross," and a purée of spinach—just in case anyone felt like a nibble. "Jim made sure that he didn't neglect anyone who might later become important," says Clark Wolf. He had respect for Julia and Simca's status, if not entirely for their book. "I only wish that I had written it myself," he told them. But privately, soon after *Mastering* was published, Beard's enthusiasm was more reserved. "He wasn't particularly excited about the book," recalls Barbara Kafka. "He'd seen all those recipes before. They didn't impress him." To his friend Helen Evans Brown, a respected food writer based in California, he wrote: "I think the Knopf book is wonderful, until they get into the chicken and meat department. The idea of cooking a piece of American boiling beef for four hours is insane ... And I think all the chicken recipes are over-cooked. Otherwise, it is a great book. Nothing new or startling, but a good basic French cookery book."

In any case, Beard kept any gripes mostly to himself and treated the authors with the same respect he reserved for culinary insiders with whom he was personally and professionally involved. Besides, Beard saw something in Julia that intrigued him right off the bat, even if he couldn't immediately put his finger on it. "Jim and Julia were meant to be friends," says Barbara Kafka. "If you looked at them next to each other, they were built on the same scale. It wasn't just that they were tall—they were big, with big bone structure and big personalities." They shared a West Coast sensibility, neither aggressive nor slick, and a background in classified military surveillance (Beard trained as an army cryptographer, focusing on codes and secret ciphers). Using intuition rather than powers of detection, he got an inkling of Julia's vast potential and decided on the spot to form an alliance with her. "He rallied colleagues" to her cause, Beard's biographer noted, calling Helen McCully, the excitable editor who had revitalized *McCall's* food pages, and Cecily Brownstone of the Associated Press, on her behalf. Julia recalled gratefully how "he took us right in hand, introduced us everywhere," opening doors for them throughout the New York food world.

One door led to the Egg Basket, a kitschy French-provincial café on Fifty-ninth Street, where Dione Lucas presided.

If Lucas was "the *grande dame* of the American cooking scene" through the 1950s, she was also one of its most divisive figures. An immensely talented chef with what Jim Beard called "the most wonderful cooking hands I have ever seen," she almost single-handedly created the American bistro menu. Still, her traditional heart remained with Le Cordon Bleu, where she had studied with Henri-Paul Pellaprat before opening an annex in London. By the mid-1940s, Lucas was *haute cuisine's* liaison to the small but growing community that craved French technique, conducting

"Cordon Bleu" classes in midtown New York, much to the chagrin of Madame Brassart and others, who felt she had "fraudulently appropriated" its name. She also had a cooking show, *To the Queen's Taste,* that aired on CBS-TV, but like James Beard, she "wasn't a gifted performer."

What she had, however, was expertise—"hands of gold"—and phenomenal skill. Lucas cooked like a musician who composed on the piano, not on the page—by touch, without recipes or notes. "She was encyclopedic," according to Paula Wolfert, who studied with Lucas and fell in love with cooking as a result. She believed cooking was an art form, a way to express oneself by creating subtle, simple, but gorgeous meals using flawless ingredients. Each plate was presented like an artistic composition. Michael Batterberry remembers her standing behind the omelet bar at the Egg Basket, "turning out a dish of scallops with mushrooms and tomatoes the way Renoir turned out a masterpiece." She *performed,* he said, as opposed to cooked. And sometimes those performances rivaled *Lucia.*

"She was a serious head case," recalls a restaurant consultant familiar with her behavior. She approached life like a warrior attempting to do battle with demons. Her life, according to a profile in the *Chicago Tribune,* was chaotic, "a veritable soap opera of eccentricities, feuds, dramatics, migraines, temperamental outbursts, rumored addiction to alcohol and pills." Others describe her as "impossible," "bossy and not very nice," "very neurotic," "a bitch," "off her head," and "downright nuts." James Beard, perhaps, summed her up best. He called her "sad and great," the kind of purist who reminded you how good she was each time out before throwing herself over a cliff.

Julia owned several of Lucas's cookbooks and was eager to meet her. She had learned an enormous amount from the recipes. And Lucas was another pillar of the food community to whom Julia was inevitably drawn.

Their meeting was cordial if not particularly warm. Lucas, a wiry pinch-faced Englishwoman with innate hauteur, seated Julia and Simca at the bar in her restaurant while she bent over a gas grill tossing off flawless omelets the way Bob Turley tossed off fastballs. The women were forced to watch her in a mirror hung theatrically over the stove, inasmuch as Lucas never made eye contact through the entire lunch. Even so, she delivered several "pointers on doing cooking demonstrations for an audience," and promised, at Jim Beard's urging, to host a launch party for *Mastering* in mid-December.

In general, New York's culinary stars were starting to align behind the new cooks on the block, and the French-tinged sparkle they gave off reflected outward, from coast to coast. *Mastering* ignited a budding interest in gastronomy, to be sure, but other factors contributed to the allure. The election of John F. Kennedy in 1960 has often been cited as a great watershed moment for French cuisine. The Kennedys embodied cultural sophistication at its most glamorous. They were arbiters of taste at a time when Americans were searching for taste. They advanced a fashion sense that celebrated *haute couture,* and fine dining—"food that could claim to be not just cooking but cuisine."

Stories abounded about Jack Kennedy's prejudice for good food. A fervid patron of the New York restaurant scene, he turned up frequently at Chambord and Lutèce and occupied a regular booth at La Caravelle, which not only catered to his preferences but had also plied his campaign staff nightly with refreshments such as vichyssoise and chicken in a creamy champagne reduction. And on April 7, 1961, Craig Claiborne announced in an article on the front page of *The New York Times* that the White House had hired René Verdon, a classically trained French *chef de cuisine,* to supervise its kitchens. Today that might be blasted as elitist, unpatriotic, but in 1961 it was the height of chic.

"People were reading about what the Kennedys were eating," Julia pointed out. "And I happened to come along just at the right time."

That was putting it mildly. By the time she and Simca hit Grosse Pointe, Michigan, the first stop on their whirlwind promotional junket, public interest had already reached a lofty pitch. The leading bookstore sold out its entire stock of 125 copies, and the same again in Chicago, where even the jobber's cupboards were bare. Their appearances in the Midwest were SRO affairs. "We are giving demonstrations twice a day for audiences of two- and three hundred!" Julia marveled, grateful that she and Simca had resolved to put their differences aside. It exhilarated her, especially in San Francisco, where a spot at the City of Paris department store turned into nothing short of a melee.

All over the country, anywhere Julia and Simca went, women were turning up in droves. Who were they? What were they doing there? Nobody was expecting them in any kind of number. There hadn't been that much publicity. There wasn't any sign that indicated such an interest existed, nothing to indicate that anyone would be interested in these two oddly matched women—one with a thick French accent, the other with a hilarious swooping voice—presenting recipes with all the complexity of the genetic code in this era of packaged food.

It was tapping into something women weren't doing—but something that, deep down, they wanted to do, which was to express themselves, to do something special. They'd been told again and again: live your life the easy way, the quick way, the ordinary way. They were like workers on an assembly line who took no pride in their jobs, just cranking it out like everybody else down the block. They bought the same appliances, wore the same housedresses, performed the same routines—the cleaning, the shopping, and the cooking, such as it was. They were ignoring one of the most essential human urges—to be creative, to be special. And suddenly, here were two women who could tell them how to do that, how to take themselves out of their constricting little lives. So at dinner, when they slapped down a duck *à l'orange* instead of Mrs. Paul's fish sticks, people might look at them in a new, admiring way. "You're somebody special, somebody talented." And even if nobody else said exactly that, they could look down at that duck and know it themselves.

In the same way that the space race tapped into Americans' desire to achieve something glorious in the realm of science, Julia tapped into a housewife's desire to expand the boundaries of her own world. Nobody knew American women were out there hungering for this, but out there they were. And Julia offered them an outlet for that pent-up ambition.

Not even the blaze of public attention could impress her father, however. Around Thanksgiving time, the *Mastering* delegation rolled into Pasadena, where the media was churning for the hometown author. The schedule was thick with luncheons, interviews, and book signings. In Los Angeles, there'd even been a television spot, seven minutes on *The Cavalcade of Books*. Friends competed to invite them to dinner, to toast their unfolding success. Instead of taking pleasure in the praise, however, "Big John" McWilliams hardly acknowledged Julia's accomplishment. A *cookbook*. His daughter had written . . . a *cookbook*. It wasn't as if she had rid the government of Communists or intellectuals. At eighty-two, Pop had more important matters to contend with. He was already recuperating from a strange virus that had kept him bedridden for weeks. He didn't have the time or the energy for such artsy-fartsy nonsense. A *cookbook!* Besides, he was preoccupied with damning society's ills, "tossing verbal stink bombs" at those atop his soaring enemies list. Paul kept a running account of "the old idiot's" favorite targets: " 'the chosen people' (he hates and distrusts all Jews), 'those people over there' (he hates and distrusts all foreigners), the labor unions (he hates and distrusts all unions)." Most of all, Paul realized, "he hates and distrusts his son-in-law," although they'd managed to carry off the visit without spilling any blood.

Even so, there was plenty of tension in the air. (Julia, as usual, was caught in the crossfire.) Pop's disgust was always visible on his face. And no doubt Paul contributed his own share of contempt. He hated Pasadena, the place gave him "the willies." He had just finished reading Lewis Mumford's *The City in History*, which held that art, culture, and political purpose—not numbers—defined a city. And in those areas, Paul was convinced that Pasadena was bankrupt. The people he'd met there were self-involved and unenlightened, their conversation frivolous, their lives "wrapped up in nothing much." The gift of nature had been ruined by "unrestrained commercialism." He couldn't walk anywhere, always fearful either the cops or "the John Birchers" would scoop him up. The whole West, to him, was alien; he felt like a stranger in a strange land.

Paul's mood, his dislocation, wasn't confined to California. Ever since returning to America, his letters to his brother and others were dark, pessimistic chronicles of a nation gone soft, of "an atmosphere of aggression, anarchy, and slackness of moral tone, wedded to ignorance and hedonism." He had little patience for Americans or for their lifestyles. Perhaps he'd been living abroad too long, he theorized. Admittedly, he was "nostalgic" for places like Norway, "with its simple life, its good sturdy folk . . . its un-spoiled nature . . . its non-hectic rhythms." The Americans he'd encountered seemed oblivious to politics and culture, "most of what makes life significant and interesting for us."

"He was so judgmental," as Judith Jones observed, but if the judgments were harsh and indiscriminate, they were also outward expressions of other turmoil.

The return to civilian life was particularly hard on Paul; it involved many tough transitions. He was almost sixty, "no spring chicken," according to a lifelong diplomat, "yet [it was] an odd point for a man of Paul's age to retire from government." Inexplicably, at least to colleagues, he'd lost his chance at a full pension by leaving before he was sixty-two, and he had no real money of his own to speak of. It would be difficult, he realized, to start anew as a private citizen, especially in Cambridge, in the heart of academia. How would people react when they learned he didn't have a college education? How would he stack up against the scholars and the intellects? Having made art the focus of his golden years, would he be able to practice it at a professional level?

It was these uncertainties that particularly tormented Paul as he reacclimated himself to life at home. Since returning, he'd put everything into Julia's new endeavor. He'd surrendered his own creative aspirations and turned his considerable skills as a painter and photographer to fulfilling his wife's ambitions. In a way, he'd stepped in as the stage manager for the *Mastering* book tour. He organized the itinerary, kept everyone on schedule, handled incidentals for the gigs. Who would have guessed that all his "years of experience in setting up exhibits and demonstrations under stress would be a help to the gals in being certain about microphones, stage lights, tables, ovens, placement of various objects, testing apparatus," and general emergencies that cropped up. Talk about "unpredictable situations!" Only a few months before, as late as May, he was the American government's cultural attaché in Oslo. Now, in November, he wrote his brother, he was "squatting on the floor behind scenery-flats of a theater in San Marino, California, trying to wash a heap of egg and chocolate-covered bowls in a bucket of cold water," while out front, "before an audience of 350 clubwomen, Julie and Simca were demonstrating *soufflé de turbot, quiche au Roquefort,* and *Reine de Saba* cake."

Go figure!

Judith Jones recalls encountering Paul in the ladies' room at Bloomingdale's on Long Island. The auditorium had been packed with women waiting to see Julia and Simca. "It had been shocking, unheard of, to see such a response," she says. "Authors in those days didn't draw that kind of audience." And during a lull, when she ducked into the bathroom to reapply her makeup, there he was, "happy as a clam," washing dishes in the sink.

Julia, for her part, was taking everything in stride. Despite all the hubbub, the precipitous shove from the kitchen into the public eye, she kept her cool, impervious to the surge of attention. She wasn't nervous, didn't suffer from stage fright or doubts, refrained from following the book's sales figures day by day. For all the draining energy it required, the hustle of the road, she remained upbeat, can-do, unruffled by the demands. She was the only one who didn't seem surprised or affected by what was happening to her. She was uncomplaining about the breakneck schedule—in fact, if truth be told, she secretly enjoyed it.

In the midst of all this business she took a step back to reflect. "What a life we are leading," she chortled to her family.

Julia Child had always been a person with a lot of excess energy and no proper outlet for it. All her life she had been like a high-performance race car perpetually stuck in traffic. No place to let it out, to make that baby purr. She had variously tried the life of a social butterfly, a government drone, an embassy wife, even hat-making, for god's sake, the most unsuitable miscue of all. So many stabs at a vocation that never tapped into everything she had to give—and always she had more, much more with no place to direct it. She had almost got there, finding some satisfaction cooking alone in her kitchen. But this new public arena demanded all of her talents—her skill at cooking, her stamina, her force of personality, her unflappability, her abundant charm. All of her undertapped abilities were finally put to the test, finally bent to a task that she was good at, great at. She was increasingly proficient in front of an audience, a natural, comfortable, clever. Imagine that! This crazy place was where she'd belonged all along. It was the kind of stretch she'd been craving, needing all her life. And just when she felt she was easing into the groove, everything was about to get stretchier. And groovier.

Seventeen

A Monstrously Busy Life

Americans who tuned in to their local CBS-TV affiliate on the evening of September 26, 1960, got a bracing glimpse of the future, what Marshall McLuhan labeled the Electronic Age. On screen, two men sat facing each other, each vying to become the next president of the United States. They were eager to debate—the first televised debate between two candidates for the office. The issues were incontrovertible—the Cold War, civil rights, Quemoy and Matsu, the economy. But issues weren't the issue as the encounter unfolded.

Richard Nixon, the current vice president, was the known quantity. For eight years, he'd been a fixture across front pages and on the nightly news as a stand-in for the oft-indisposed President Eisenhower, who had suffered several strokes. His challenger, John F. Kennedy, though a senator since 1946, was new to the national scene. For most Americans, he was an unfamiliar face, a glaring disadvantage in a contest that equated intimacy with confidence. Yet polls had the men neck-and-neck as they prepared to face off in a Chicago studio.

The outcome of the evening is one of those great American allegories—how JFK, who had worked on his tan on a hotel rooftop and patted on stage makeup to soften his image, charmed the discerning TV audience, while Nixon wilted sorrily under the hot lights, sweat beading up through the Lazy Shave powder that had been slapped on haphazardly to cover his beard stubble. How, before the camera's eye, Nixon

Julia with Ruth Lockwood and Russ Morash, on the set of *The French Chef,* 1963

morphed from a cool head of state into "an Armenian rug peddler." How the polls reflected that perception by the overnights that boosted Kennedy's numbers. How the balance of power shifted in the camera's telltale lens, which portrayed Kennedy as "boyish" and Nixon as "shifty," Kennedy as "a star," Nixon as an "assassin." In an eventual wrap-up of the debate it was noted: "The winner that night was not just Kennedy but the television image itself, which had, in a single stroke, demonstrated its new kingmaking power."

None of this was lost on Julia Child, who had watched a replay of the debates at a friend's house in Oslo. A relentless Democrat, she had "solemnly sworn [she] would never vote for a Catholic, as a Catholic could not be a free man." That left Kennedy out. Still, she said, "I don't want Nixon," who she thought was "smart—but really ruthless" and a darling of her father's. Television, the great game changer, sorted everything out for Julia. Nothing conveyed the personalities of the candidates as sharply as being able to see and hear them for herself. It was the launch of a new era when the images that flowed through a screen into people's living rooms became one of the most, if not *the* most, important determinants of how people thought and saw the world. Far away, in Oslo, reduced to watching this seminal event after it had already occurred, Julia couldn't have been more removed from the seismic shift that was taking place via the media. She could never have grasped TV's kingmaking power. Certainly she could never have grasped that, less than three years later, this shaky new medium would make her a queen.

THE KENNEDY-NIXON DEBATES announced to an otherwise ambivalent Julia that television had arrived. At the time, the Childs didn't have a TV of their own, nor would a set be found among the crates they unpacked in Cambridge, in 1961. Even so, Julia experienced pangs of interest in its evolving potential. In a letter to her sister-in-law Freddie, as early as 1953, she wondered: "How about TV? Do you find you use it much, and if so, when, how much, what for, etc?" At the time, it never occurred to her that one might *cook* on TV, let alone *teach* cooking, much less *French* cooking, to the masses.

Julia may have been impervious to the wiles of television, but cooking was a staple of local TV almost from the moment it first went on the air, in the mid-1940s. Daytime programming played almost exclusively to women. And cooking was a lure, a way for broadcasters and their sponsors to draw women to TV during the day. Even before Dione Lucas spun out her first soufflé, there were dozens of regional TV cooks from Honolulu to Hartford. You could turn on almost any station, anywhere in the country, and bump up against a homemaking show with a cooking segment. Hams were coated with tinted mayonnaise, gelatin eggs were piped into empty eggshells, canapés of curried peanut butter were topped with shrimp, sandwiches were assembled with tuna fish and crushed pineapple mixed with whipped cream, cabbages were stuck with bits of hot dog. Almost three-quarters of the country's 108 operating television stations were churning out these types of programs: Milwaukee's *What's New in the Kitchen; The Bee Baxter Show* in Minneapolis–St. Paul; *Cooking with Roz* and *Cooking with Philameena,* head-to-head in New Haven; *Chicago Cooks with Barbara Barkley;* Philadelphia's *Television Kitchen;* the ever-popular Josie McCarthy in New York; and the L.A. favorite, *Cooking with Corris,* which ran for almost three decades.

In the ensuing scramble, no one broke out of the pack to catch on nationally. Among America's leading culinary lights, the spotlight should have fallen on the avuncular James Beard, but he wasn't suited to the warm and fuzzy medium. Dione Lucas came close. She was extremely skillful and respected by her peers. By 1954, she was known widely, if not well, and generally perceived, mostly on the basis of her stagy British accent, as "the Sarah Bernhardt of the kitchen stove." But that's as far as her showmanship went. Described by an insider as "actively unlikable," her deadpan delivery couldn't ignite the audience's enthusiasm. She was contemptuous and "intimidating," a total turn-off when it came to personality. "She had the technique but not the charm," said Barbara Kafka, "no sense of theater."

Yet Lucas at least refused to dumb down her demonstrations. She stuck to classic French recipes, combining gourmet cooking with simple, store-bought ingredients in an attempt to attract the new breed of working women. But her aesthetic sensibilities were ultimately too highbrow for her to appeal to the traditional middle-class homemaker, who dominated the audience.

One TV cooking personality who struck the right note was Lillian Gruskin Cannon Askland Philippe White, known to the masses as Poppy Cannon. A food consultant by nature, a columnist by default, Cannon had published lighthearted articles in *Mademoiselle* and *House Beautiful,* where she promoted a time-saving process called can-opener cookery. Despite her fondness for fine dining in French restaurants, Cannon "reassured readers that packaged foods were as good if not better than their homemade equivalents." She was godmother to kitchen speed demons like Rachael Ray and Sandra Lee, "flinging" ingredients together, "whipping up" dishes, using a "splotch of wine," "a generous flutter of chopped chives," or "a great swish of sour cream" to tweak the flavors. *Bam!*

By 1954, almost a decade before Julia made her debut, Cannon forsook magazines and was launched coast-to-coast as TV's preeminent cooking guru. She oversaw a recipe every weekday on *Home,* an afternoon women's program, where her reputation as the "can-opener queen" flourished like food poisoning. She used Franco-American beef gravy for sauces, canned asparagus, canned macaroni and cheese, canned mushrooms, even Spam. For salmon mousse, she instructed the home cook to whip canned salmon, cream, red food coloring, and crushed ice in a blender for forty seconds. *Presto!*—salmon mousse.

There was nothing remotely epicurean about the food she prepared, nothing artful, nothing with "the French touch," as Julia romanticized it. Her dishes were a vivid diner-menu mix, relying heavily on shortcut cooking and close-ups of the sponsor's appliances—all the modern conveniences "needed to raise families and create a happy home life."

Such a slapdash approach only underscored the differences between Julia and her predecessors. They had none of the qualifications necessary to make viewers really *want* to cook. In fact, by the end of the 1950s, almost the opposite had occurred. The powers that be concluded that cooking segments were more diverting than useful. "I think that perhaps women just want to be entertained—not instructed—on television," said Arlene Francis, the game-show personality who also hosted *Home.*

Fortunately, Julia was oblivious to this current thinking, in the same way that she'd been spared the influence of the early TV cooks. Darned if she didn't want to teach people how to properly prepare French food, "to cook with distinction from scratch."

As luck would have it, she didn't know any better.

RUSS MORASH KNEW even less. Aside from the fact that his employer, WGBH, had ordered up three pilots featuring a local French cook, there wasn't a biscuit's worth of foodcraft that Morash could bring to this show.

Food was fuel; he ate to live, long and short of it. And he wasn't very choosy about what he put in his mouth. A bag of chips could see him through most of the day, a cup of coffee, a Coke or two, about all a man needs. "I couldn't tell a bouillabaisse from a coq au vin," he admits. And he'd had it up to here with those froufrou French restaurants. "The one or two I'd gone to in Boston were run by cruel men in tall white aprons who hated their customers and almost dared you to eat their food." No thanks. He'd stick to the stuff his wife, Marian, made. She did a wonderful thing with tuna fish and potato chips that would make Chef Boyardee cry.

Morash raked over these and other variables as he bounded up the front steps of 103 Irving Street. He'd gotten an earful about this woman, Julia Child. Ever since her appearance on *I've Been Reading,* the office chatter was "Julia this, Julia that." You'd have thought she'd discovered a winning formula for the Red Sox. He found out later, much later, that her gift was nearly as remarkable, but that afternoon, in late April 1962, it was all he could do to give her a quick once-over.

First impressions were pretty arbitrary. "I could tell right away she wasn't your typical Cantabrigian housewife," Morash recalls of the woman who greeted him that day. Julia, who would turn fifty that August, was a fairly ordinary, plain-faced woman, except that she towered over everyone in the neighborhood, aside from John Kenneth Galbraith, who was six foot seven. "She didn't look like people I knew, that was for sure. I assumed that she was a bit eccentric. Her manner and her conversation and her speech were all unusual. But she was a friendly character, and that appealed to me."

Julia already knew what Morash had come to offer: *her own show,* teaching cooking on television. Okay, it was educational television, the minor leagues. But plenty of people in Cambridge—the "eggheads," as Paul called them—watched only WGBH. It would give her a chance to promote *Mastering* to a wider audience and, who knew, maybe serve as a platform for private classes or a cooking school that she'd dreamed of starting. "Paul was all in favor of it," says Charlie Gibson, who would later introduce Julia's segments on *Good Morning America.* "She told me that, at the outset, she was undecided about being on TV, but he was the one who really encouraged her to pursue it." Television, Paul argued, would give her a distinct aura, the special something—like Kennedy's image or Fred Flintstone's *Yabba dabba doo*—that would be, for many Americans, an identifiable hook.

By the time Morash entered the picture, "she was all charged up about it." Over coffee and toast points, he explained that they'd do three pilots, but if all went well, the station would probably commit to a series, a full season of twenty-six shows.

Twenty-six shows!

"What sort of things would you like to cook?" he wondered.

Julia had given this some thought before he arrived. She wanted to make classic French dishes that would be recognizable to Americans—nothing too fancy, esoteric, or intimidating. Right off the bat, she thought: *coq au vin.* Chicken was an easy sell, and it was essential to Julia that Americans get used to cooking with wine. Once they got a taste of that rich, tangy sauce, infused with bacon and onions, moving them to hollandaise and mousselines would be, literally, child's play. And why not go for a soufflé while she was at it? They were basic and dramatic and so impressive to serve. Housewives usually avoided soufflés as too time-consuming and temperamental. But Julia's recipe was fairly easy to absorb. All you had to do was to master the base and learn how fold in beaten egg whites without letting them collapse. You pull off a soufflé, it's like catnip, a real confidence builder. So coq au vin and soufflés were definitely in.

"Could you manage that omelet?" Morash asked, referring to the demo she'd done on *I've Been Reading.* "You'll have to expand it to fill up an entire half-hour."

Julia waved him off with a nothing-to-it backhand. "Oh, by the time we talk about the various fillings and how we prepare them and the machinery we need and the pan and the technique and what the right flame is and how we serve it, I think we'll have enough," she said.

So the menu was set for all three pilots: coq au vin, soufflé, omelet. For the rest of the afternoon, they kicked around the format and the particulars. "You will have to practice speaking while you are cooking," Morash warned her. "That's not easy to do; it's two dissimilar acts, sort of like patting your head and rubbing your stomach. And the video side has to prove what you are saying. You can't say you are putting in one tablespoon of something if you're putting in six. Through it all, you have to concentrate, which isn't easy, either."

For most women, this would have been a daunting prospect. It meant retraining oneself at mid-life, mastering an entirely unfamiliar set of skills—and in public, yet, in front of a sophisticated audience. It would be like a stay-at-home mom suddenly finding herself in a high-powered financial job or an office worker becoming an emergency medical technician, and doing it while under the unforgiving scrutiny of a TV camera. Most would be too embarrassed even to try. But Julia Child was utterly unself-conscious. The possibility of falling on her face in public was something that, strangely, didn't seem to faze her. In her life she'd made a series of choices in opposition to social convention. She joined a secret intelligence agency, married a man her family disapproved of, lived abroad when most Americans were tethered to home, went to an all-male, all-French cooking school for professionals as a hapless female American cook, to forge a career that barely existed before, when most women were homemakers.

Her hunger for new experiences overrode any fear that would stymie any otherwise sensible person. Somewhere between the gawky, awkward Smith grad who fumbled her way through New York and the person offered a leap into the unknown ether of television, Julia had become confident in her ability to excel. It might be too simplistic to conclude that cooking gave her all the tools. But she had defied the prejudices of a tyrant like Madame Brassart, and, through hard work and countless hours in front of the stove, had transformed herself into someone who could hack apart a duck with her bare hands and turn out a *poulet rôti à l'estragon* as routinely as if it were a grilled-cheese sandwich. She had delivered the American bible on French cooking.

Pat her head and rub her stomach under the hot lights of a primitive television studio? Piece of cake.

Of course, it was harder than it looked. Julia and Paul rehearsed for hours in their Irving Street kitchen. "We broke our recipes down into logical sequences," Julia recalled, "and I practiced making each dish as if I were on TV." Over and over, they worked on those three recipes. She made very detailed notes describing every step of the process—the ingredients, the sequence of events, the logistics, the state of her delivery—while Paul stage-managed the performance, timing it with a stopwatch. It all had to be choreographed, right down to Julia's expressions. And, yet, she realized that sometimes things were better left to chance. "All the material within each section has to be pretty ad-lib, as one never quite knows what's going to happen on the stove," she explained. "The least one can say is that the shows will have a definite informality and spontaneity!"

But there were rules to follow—and words to the wise. "You've got to understand the way television works," Russ Morash warned her. "That metal box and piece of glass is your best friend. And you really want to let that person know that you care about them."

Morash had his own ingredients and logistics to worry about. There was no time or money to have a kitchen set built, which meant finding a suitable space already rigged up with appliances. "I had heard of a temporary kitchen the Boston Gas Company used to show contractors how to operate a gas flame," he recalled. It was in an auditorium in the Salada Tea Building, downtown, right off Park Square. *What a find!* Morash thought, while taking a tour around the place. It had a terrazzo floor at one end, ample cabinets, and a handy center island with a cooktop cut into it. The gas worked, of course, but there was no running water. With a little window dressing, it could be a perfect set.

The show also needed a title, something "curt, clear-cut, and concise"—not more than three words, one of which had to be French—that would fit into a single line in the *TV Guide.* That limited the choices somewhat to *gourmet* and *cuisine.* Among the thirty that Paul suggested, *Kitchen Matisse* was downright awful and *Table d'Hôte* too hoity-toity. They also rejected *Cuisine Magic, Kitchen à la Française, The Chef at Home, Savoir Faire,* and *Gourmet Kitchen. Cuisinavision*—really!—seemed almost too goofy to consider. It was either Russ Morash or his assistant, Ruth Lockwood, who came up with *The French Chef.* The simple, straightforward phrase seemed to say it all. There was nothing pretentious or off-putting about it. *The French Chef.* It had a nice ring to it. "Getting Julia to agree wasn't very hard—*at the time,*" Morash says. Later, she objected that it wasn't appropriate, as she was neither a chef nor French. "But our relationship was budding, it made a lot of sense, and she accepted it."

So did the honchos at WGBH. In a memo to everyone involved, the station manager proclaimed: "Let us call it *The French Chef* now and forever!"

Preparations for *The French Chef* ran through the spring of 1962. In addition to Julia's ongoing rehearsals at home, a small group of WGBH volunteers—mostly wealthy young women with time on their hands—saw to incidentals on the set, like putting up curtains on the fake kitchen window and choosing napkins and candles that would appear on each show.

In the midst of all this excitement and upheaval, Julia learned that her father's health was failing. Pop had never really recovered from the virus that had sidelined him during Julia's last visit. He complained constantly about shortness of breath and exhaustion. In the interim, he developed pneumonia and "a form of leukemia" that the doctors believed could be controlled for "five or six years." Lately, however, "he had lost forty-eight pounds" and taken a turn for the worse, which didn't bode well.

In Cambridge, the news stirred more melancholy than grief. Julia shared her feelings with her sister-in-law Freddie. In a rambling letter she said Pop was "a terribly generous father financially. Spiritually, however, something happened." He never forgave her for rejecting his way of life; the path she ultimately took was, in his eyes, "villainous." And he regarded her accomplishments with stony indifference. Still, Julia had never stopped angling for her father's approval. She sent updates of her exploits and clippings from her tour, cards on all the holidays. In the end, however, the alienation had been too great and she had cut off communications with him. He had forced her hand, first by his undisguised contempt for Paul, and finally when it became clear that she could no longer express herself openly, to share her "innermost thoughts" without risking his wrath. In any case, "old eagle beak," as she called him, would probably outlive them all—if not for love, then out of spite.

But by May, Pop's condition took another downward turn, and by the time Julia arrived in Pasadena, only hours remained in his life. Now there was no opportunity for anything but vigilance, no chance to reclaim precious years. Julia's feelings were mixed, as she joined her brother and sister at his hospital bedside. When it came to her father, she would always be conflicted. He was someone she admired for his success and generosity, and someone she deplored for refusing to accept who she was. He was never there for her when it mattered—*never*. Never in her corner, never on her side. She had lived her adult life without a parent she could turn to for advice.

"Frankly, my father's death came as a relief more than a shock," Julia said. As she and her siblings strewed his ashes at sea, along with those belonging to her mother and grandfather, an odd calm took hold. She felt something akin to closure. It was almost liberating. What Pop's oldest daughter was thinking only Paul, shortly afterward, was willing to admit: "That chapter of her life had finally ended"—just as a new one was ready to begin.

ON JUNE 18, 1962, Julia Child entered the Television Age. Having edged into the spotlight and savored its warm glow, she shelved the solitary art of cookbook writing and stepped out into the public eye, where she would no doubt rattle the spirit of John McWilliams.

Despite her adolescent flirtation with performing on the stage, Julia was a complete novice when she stepped in front of the cameras in the auditorium of the Boston Gas Company. What she lacked in experience, however, she made up for in determination. "I came prepared," she said later, reflecting on that day. "All the equipment and food was laid out where I'd find everything, I knew my lines, and Paul had mapped out a master plan, like an Arthur Murray dance diagram."

Before filming began, Julia fanned out her notes on the island with the cooktop. The pages were meticulously detailed, much like the recipes in *Mastering*: all her stage directions and dialogue ran down the right-hand side of the page, directly opposite what the camera would be showing, on the left. "Simmering water in large alum. pan, upper R burner." "Wet sponge in L top drawer." Paul, who would be operating behind the scenes, had his own set of notes. "When J. starts buttering, remove stack molds." "When Julie switches to ready-made *pipérade*: take off the hot no-stickum frying pan and its copper cover." It was an intricate pas de deux they'd worked out which, when performed, couldn't miss a beat.

There was a short rehearsal so that Russ Morash could give his crew a preview of what to expect. None of his technicians knew their way around the kitchen, so he had to lead them by the hand and walk them through the maze. From his command post in the mobile unit, the ancient Trailways bus parked outside, he whispered crisply into his headset, "Camera two, she's going to move from left to right, and when she does, please get a shot of the garlic press."

Over earphones, the cameraman replied: "What the fuck is a garlic press?"

It was that primitive. And to make matters worse, they were going to shoot it "live," straight through on tape, without stopping for glitches or retakes. There was no other alternative. Time was as tight as the show's meager budget; they had the cameras only for a fixed number of hours before the equipment was needed to cover the symphony orchestra. "We were too stupid to know how dangerous an undertaking this was," Morash says now. But at the time, he remembered seeing a segment of *Playhouse 90*, where Hamlet was downstage, reciting "Alas, poor Yorick. I knew him, Horatio," while upstage a stagehand walked across the scene; when he finally caught sight of the camera, the stagehand grinned and backed out the way he came. "Things like that happened all the time," Morash says, "and when they occurred there wasn't much you could do." So here he was relying on Julia, a rank amateur, to steer steadily through heavy traffic.

For all the uncertainty, for all its flouting of Murphy's Law, *The French Chef* proceeded along its course without a whiff of congestion. In fact, the show's intro was about as fluent as the lesson it hoped to convey. It opened on a tight close-up of butter blistering in a small, dark pan. An emulsion of egg was lapped in and coddled with a fork, and twenty seconds later a gem of an omelet was turned onto a plate. "It takes less than thirty seconds to make," a warbly female voice declared. "It is lovely to look at—soft and creamy inside—delicious to eat."

When the camera pulled back, the woman looming over the counter couldn't have seemed more inviting or reassuring had one's favorite aunt been in her place. "Hello. I'm Julia Child." The voice was as arresting as it was neighborly. "I'm going to show you how to make French omelets. They go like *lightning,* as you just saw."

And for the next twenty-seven minutes Julia was as good as her word. In a flash, she turned out herb omelets, cheese omelets, chicken liver omelets, *pipérade* omelets—a riot of omelets, each a masterpiece of eggdom. But her trick—and this wasn't an illusion or special effect—was the feeling that she was talking just to you. Not master and student, not performer and audience, but two gals chatting over the back fence. She let you know, right up front, that she'd been where you were, shared your fears about the calculus of cooking, the prospect of an all-out omelet debacle.

"If you've ever tried to make omelets in a sticky pan, you know what an impossible mess it is."

Not an "old" or "uncooperative" pan, but a *sticky* pan. Well—*exactly.* And nothing "untidy" or "ill-managed," but an *impossible mess.* This woman apparently knew what went on in our own cranky kitchens and she was here to help. Plus she made it look so damn simple!

The show on soufflés came off just as swimmingly. "Ordinary soufflés scare many people," Julia admitted, and no doubt the audience was nodding in agreement. "The timing is tricky, they fall before you're ready to serve them." *Uh-huh.* But Julia assured her skittish viewers that soufflés were a snap—and not only a snap, but "we'll go into all the little details so you can't miss on this." *Can't miss on this.* She made it sound like she was throwing together a bowl of cornflakes.

As for the sauce—a *béchamel.* French, but simple. And wouldn't you know it—Julia's *béchamel* came out thick and pasty, just like everyone's always did. Don't worry. "We'll thin it down and enrich it with cream. It coats the spoon lightly, see." *See.*

Afterward, Julia sauntered over to a table set beautifully for two. Pulled out a chair, sat down. *Poured herself a glass of wine!* "It's hard to believe, but here it is," she said as the steamy soufflé appeared at her elbow, on a trivet. "I want to cut this soufflé so you'll see it's real!" Not some TV prop, but an honest-to-goodness soufflé that she just made. *We* just made. *Together.* And she took a bite, savored it, smiled. Not only took a bite, but followed it with a nice slug of white wine. It was a bold move for TV, educational or otherwise. No one drank on live television back then, unless it was part of a drama, in which case the wine was a colored-water prop. Drinking for pleasure, as part of a meal? It just wasn't done in polite public, especially so casually, as an everyday treat. Not that Julia gave it a second thought. To her, wine with food had deep roots and a wonderful payoff. She couldn't imagine eating something delicious without a lovely glass of wine—and she wanted Americans to discover that pleasure for themselves. Having a meal along with wine was the perfect way to end the show.

Before she signed off, she looked directly into the camera, and uttered a line that Paul had written for her: "This is Julia Child. Thank you. *Bon appétit!*"

Bon appétit! For most viewers, that phrase was a complete mystery. It wasn't customarily said at tables—or anywhere, for that matter. The audience could only guess at its meaning, an expression for which there was no correlation in English. And, yet, it had such an exotic sound to it. *Bon appétit!* There was something musical about it, festive, something merry and playful. And when it rolled so exuberantly off of Julia Child's tongue, it felt as comfortable as a warm hug.

"This is Julia Child. Thank you. Bon appétit!"

Russ Morash thought "Julia sailed through the pilots." Rather surprisingly, "she was a joy to work with because she was so organized and efficient." There was a general feeling among the crew that Julia had acquitted herself capably, although they refused, to a man, to taste her omelets. Even so, the omelet show was such an enormous success that, right afterward, Russ rushed home and practically tackled his wife, Marian. "The omelet was terrific," he said, "and . . . *here,* let me show you how to make one."

A day or two later, Morash showcased the pilots for Bob Larsen, the program manager at WGBH. A shy, unflashy, cautious man out of the university setting, Larsen viewed new programs with considerable trepidation. Optimism meant obligation, and he was ever wary to commit the station's resources to something as experimental and precarious as a series. As Larsen watched Julia's tape with an impassive mask, Morash went slack with hopelessness. But when it was over, Larsen reran it—and reran it again. "She's terrific," he said, with deadpan enthusiasm. "I think we should go for a series."

On Irving Street, however, the scene was very different. The pilots ran in August 1962, and Julia watched the first two at home on her brand-new TV with a sinking dread. "There I was in black and white," she said, "a large woman sloshing eggs too quickly here, too slowly there." She felt oafish, like "Mrs. Steam Engine" the way she careened across the screen, "panting heavily." Mannerisms that were endearing in person appeared exaggerated and grotesque on screen. "There was a sense of breathlessness," Paul noticed, "due to her habit of gasping when she's self-conscious." Julia's erratic way of breathing functioned as a kind of pause or punctuation between phrases. "Also her habit of closing her eyes from time to time" drew attention to her inexperience with the medium. There was so much room for improvement, she thought. She was a long way from anything resembling professionalism.

The public couldn't have agreed with her less. Letters to the station professed their delight in her offbeat style. "Loved watching her catch the frying pan as it almost went off the counter," a viewer wrote. "Loved her looking for the cover of the casserole. It was fascinating to watch her hand motions, which were so firm and sure with the food." Another viewer wrote: "I loved the way she projected over the camera directly to me."

Morash knew almost instantly they had a hit on their hands. "I heard it at parties, people called me about it," he said. "We occasionally got invited to people's houses where they were trying Julia Child dishes. And we heard she was funny and entertaining from our Cambridge neighbors, which is where the money was." When WGBH got contributions, people wrote a note mentioning the shows they had seen with Julia Child. "That's what got the station's attention."

Should everything come together as expected, they planned to begin production in February 1963. But because of the station's paltry budget and its inability to come up with a viable sponsor, it meant conforming to "a blitz-type operation," taping four shows every week. The preparation that went into that was almost unimaginable. Aside from writing the script and planning new recipes, sequencing each step of a dish required timing much like air-traffic control.

"We knew very early on that we would have to prepare multiple copies of each dish," Morash says, "so that each stage of the recipe would display its progress so far." For *bœuf bourguignon,* the debut show, they got a fairly good idea of the maneuvering it would take. Julia needed to begin by braising a skillet of stew meat, which, at five or six minutes, took too much precious airtime. Off-camera, someone had to ready a second batch in an identical pot, so that when Julia came back and said, "Let's see how our *bœuf* is doing," it would be browned perfectly, leading to the next step—and so on. So *bœuf bourguignon* number two was only partially cooked, *bœuf bourguignon* number three needed another six minutes to cook and would be finished in real time. At the end, she would say: "Now, here's one that I've already cooked," and *boeuf bourgignon* number four had to look positively mouthwatering.

For Russ Morash, this overload proved a blessing in disguise. Invariably, Julia needed help with timing each stage of the recipes and would accost him at a chaotic point during rehearsals. "Russ, take this beef home to Marion with the following instructions," she'd say, thrusting extremely explicit directions into his hand. The recipe would be handwritten, with little line drawings and arrows showing Marian where the dish was in its progress and what remained to be done at home. "And have her call me if there are any issues." *Any issues?* Little did Julia know this was the same Marian Morash whose kitchen talent was limited to the wonderful things she did with tuna fish and potato chips. Issues would consist of doozies like "How do I turn on the stove?" "What is a bay leaf?" "Marian didn't know a thing about cooking," Russ recalls. "But she did exactly as Julia instructed, and as a result she learned how to cook."

Meanwhile, the Boston Gas Company's largesse was running on empty. They needed their auditorium back for another purpose and gave *The French Chef* its two-week notice. In consideration, they referred the show to their colleagues at Cambridge Electric Light Company, which just so happened to have a demonstration kitchen on hand. It was in a two-story timbered warehouse on the Charles River, where coal-powered fire had once been produced. Now it was used to introduce new cooking appliances. There was a little set made out of plywood, with a fake window and frilly curtains. The stove and refrigerator were finished in the latest avocado color. As a permanent set, it had a lot going for it, and it was Julia's to use, almost uninterrupted, anytime she needed it.

Naturally, Cambridge Electric had never put in a gas line, so she had to settle for using a clunky electric stove. At the outset, that was the least of Julia's worries. It took somewhat more doing to wrestle with the cable mike. The sound technician brought it up through her shirt and pinned it to her collar, while the rest snaked down her left leg and out behind her, to the mobile unit outside. But every time she touched the stove, she'd get a mild shock, which strengthened or weakened depending on how much Julia perspired. No matter how hard they tried, the crew was unable to fix it and, over time, she learned to live with it. But in the early shows, when it took her by surprise, you can see Julia twitch in response to an errant jolt.

The *French Chef* schedule was every bit as fitful. During the weekend, Julia wrote the scripts for her upcoming shows, then on Mondays and Tuesdays, rehearsed them with her production assistant, Ruth Lockwood, who paced the progress with stopwatch in hand. They shot two shows on Wednesdays and two more on Fridays, which left Julia almost no time to rewrite and get props—dishes, candlesticks, wineglasses, napkins, silverware, and tablecloths, as well as ingredients and equipment needed for each recipe. Eventually, she would farm out those tasks to a contingent of loyal volunteers, but in the beginning Julia saw to every detail herself.

Such were "the rigid necessities of television," as Paul saw fit to call them, which foreordained "a monstrously busy life."

It may have seemed that way at the time, but he didn't know the half of it.

Eighteen

A Law unto Herself

Monday evening, February 11, 1963, was a good night for Bostonians to stay home and watch TV. It was frightfully cold outside, and snow flurries had been falling since the sun went down. Checking the listings in the *Globe* revealed a mixed bag of prospects. The whole city was keyed up for the annual Beanpot face-off between Harvard's and Boston College's hockey teams, but it didn't begin until nine o'clock. To pass the time until the game, there was *I've Got a Secret* on Channel 5 or *The Detectives* on Channel 7. But the newspaper's "Hot Spot," the show it spotlighted that day, was a new series, *The French Chef,* on Channel 2 at 8 p.m.

The curious souls who tuned in to the educational TV station got more than they bargained for. Julia cooked her signature *bœuf bourguignon,* and for anyone watching at home there had to have been a terrible moment when hunger, uncontrollable hunger, gripped them like a fever and forced them to stage a manic raid on the family fridge. You could almost smell that meltingly tender stew in a "wine-dark sauce," as Julia described it, wafting off the screen. A fleet of onions and mushrooms floated luxuriously in the stock. "A perfectly *delicious* dish," she assured her audience, albeit needlessly. The proof was right there in black-and-white.

But while the stew was intended as the featured attraction, viewers found it impossible to take their eyes off the host. By the time she tasted the sauce, licked her lips contentedly, popped the casserole back in the oven, and said, "Hello, I'm Julia Child," there was already a sense that

With the Chicken Sisters, April 16, 1970

something special was cooking. Julia filled the screen with her easygoing presence and, without any artifice or affectation, upstaged the star braise burbling in the pot. Even on TV, she was larger than life. At fifty, she was a vibrant, vivacious woman, not obviously pretty or delicate, but handsome, and never more so than when she encountered food and her eyes sparkled. Julia looked at food the way some people looked at their children, and when she cast her adoring gaze at three pounds of raw beef chuck, the folks at home knew something was up.

It was impossible not to be drawn into her intimate fold. From the get-go, Julia radiated an enthusiasm that felt natural and approachable. When she pointed to a slab of steak and said, "This is called the chuck tender, and it comes from the shoulder blade, up here," indicating her own shoulder, one could understand in a way that was unmistakably clear. "And this is called the undercut of the chuck, and it's like the continuation of the ribs along here, where it gets up to your neck."

The rest of the show was just as straightforward and informative. Julia taught viewers how to correctly brown the meat so it wouldn't steam instead of sear or stick to the skillet, and how to deglaze the pan with wine, which infused the dish with rich, lush flavor. "It's called *a fleur* in France, when the meat looks like little flowers," she said offhandedly. Julia took great pains not to sound *too* French. Her goal was to demystify French cooking, not venerate it, and she knew there was a fine line between explaining a French tradition so that she informed and entertained without sounding pretentious. But her engaging way eliminated any chance of that.

The entire lesson was relaxed and entertaining. Her ongoing patter sounded casual, unforced; there were no awkward silences, no instances where she hesitated or lost her train of thought. The process seemed to come naturally to Julia. Occasionally, she looked into the wrong camera, but immediately caught the mistake without becoming flustered. She seemed completely comfortable in front of a demanding, invisible audience. *That metal box and piece of glass is your best friend. And you really want to let that person know you care about them.*

From day one, Julia's persona was already intact. She was, as one historian observed, "already recognizably Julia," charming, nonpatronizing, unaffected, inspiring. There was something intrinsically genuine about this anti-personality, this plain-looking, enormously appealing character in a boxy cotton blouse with a homemade badge—"École des 3 Gourmandes"—pinned to it. And that *voice*—that rickety gearbox of a voice! It may have caused some disgruntled viewers to jump up and adjust the sound on their sets. But long after the savage warble lost its power to distract, it was the image of Julia standing with her hands braced on the counter, rocking back and forth as she talked, eyes twinkling, game and encouraging, *all-knowing,* that lingered in the public imagination.

"You are the only person I have ever seen who takes a realistic approach to cooking," wrote a viewer after the first show was aired.

It was the *genuineness,* the Everywoman persona that came across on the screen. If the woman next door, that Julia Child, could cook up *bœuf bourguignon* one-two-three, then surely it could be done by anyone who watched her.

"We love her naturalness and lack of that TV manner, her quick but unhurried action, her own appreciation of what she is producing," another viewer wrote. "By the time she gets to the table with her dish and takes off her apron, we are so much 'with' her that we feel as if someone had snatched our plates from in front of us when the program ends."

The biggest fan of all was Paul Child, who kept up an endless stream of correspondence with his brother, Charlie, proudly relating every detail of Julia's "success-wave," with the cookbook and now her own TV show, but especially her "real pro's imperturbability" with so much busyness swirling around her.

Despite his obvious pleasure, it was by no means easy for Paul to figure where he fit in. After the pilots were finished, he wrote, "I have decided to keep out of this punishing new series and pursue my own life, though the temptation is great to lend a hand." But there was no escape. By the time *The French Chef* went on the air, he was an irreplaceable part of Julia's team. "Man can hardly catch his breath," he noted, describing his new role. Ostensibly, he was chauffeur and chief bottle washer, staying "after the shooting sessions to wash the mountainous heap of vessels and dishes, pick up and pack utensils," and anything else to "relieve Julie of the task following her all-day tension in front of the cameras." But Paul became obsessed with the necessity to prepare, prepare, prepare, relying on his display-making experience for choreographing Julia's scripts. For each show, he made a "diagram of the stove, the shelves, the sink, etc., listing on them every single piece of equipment, and every bit of food, spice, flavors, liquids, spoons, dishes, oven-temperature," the works, in order that everything should flow smoothly once the director called "*Action.*" So that if during the taping Julia reached for, say, the olive oil, she'd see a note that says: "shelf #1, left-hand side, glass bottle." Preparation aside—and the preparation was epic—Paul loved to observe how skillful she was "at covering-up when something goes wrong, as it inevitably did from time to time."

He didn't have long to wait. The second *French Chef* episode was onion soup *gratinée,* and Julia began to hit her stride. In addition to the basic recipe, the show was chock-full of valuable hints and tips—how to keep an edge on a knife (swipe it across a steel—a sharpening blade), how to get the smell of onion off your hands (wash them with salt), how to intensify flavor when browning onions (toss in a teaspoon of sugar), how to make a great beef stock, how to make croutons—delivered with chummy nonchalance. Julia's interaction with the camera was particularly smooth. In just two shows, her eye contact seemed instinctive, unstudied. She had really taken Russ Morash's advice to heart—and it showed. "She was locked in, not conscious of the camera," he noticed. Even a minor on-air slipup failed to rattle her. "You need some salt," Julia said when it came time to season the soup, but the box wasn't in the place where Paul had diagrammed it. Without missing a beat, she did a one-eighty and spotted it by the sink, on the other side of the set. "Now, I've left the salt way over here while I was washing my hands," she said, retrieving it as naturally as if it had happened in her own kitchen. Everyone watching at home understood; they got distracted like that every day of the year. Cooking wasn't foolproof, not even for Julia Child, a woman, apparently, just like them.

Later, however, she found herself really in the soup. To finish the recipe, she had topped the bowls with a slice of bread and a fistful of cheese and put them under the broiler to give the crust some color. In most cases, a cook would keep a vigilant eye on the oven, but Julia was busy chatting with the folks at home. Too much time had elapsed when she finally rescued the pot, which was all too apparent from the smoke rising off the rack. "That's really *browning,* I think possibly too much," she said, staring at the thick black cinders atop the soup, "—but it gives good effect."

It gives good effect! There was no way she was going to acknowledge the mistake. Instead, Julia carried the smoking pot to her dining room set, plunked it on the table, and caressed the aroma with her nose. "Ahh—there you are," she purred, digging through the char to the liquid center. "That's a wonderful smell, a very appetizing one."

IN JUST A few short weeks the verdict was in. "Julia was a sensation very quickly," Russ Morash says. "People were tuning in to WGBH in a way they had never done before." Word of mouth began to build steadily. Instead of a fragmented handful watching *Science Reporter,* *The French Chef* drew a loyal audience that rivaled the offerings of network TV. And when viewers dug in, when they decided to come back to the program week after week, sponsors emerged from the Boston fringe: both Polaroid and Hills Bros. Coffee ponied up grants to subsidize the show.

WGBH realized soon enough that *The French Chef* wasn't just a show—it was a phenomenon. The local audience, it seemed, was "just ripe" for good cooking, and not just cooking, but Julia Child cooking. After the fourth show had aired, the station was inundated with fan mail and letters pleading for the recipes. Six hundred envelopes sat piled on a desk, with more arriving by the day. The mail brought good news and bad. The good news, of course, was that people were watching. On the other hand, as Julia reported: "The station is getting a bit worried as it costs them about ten cents an answer, but luckily quite a few of the letters enclose contributions to the station."

There were also tremors along the syndication front. In 1963, WGBH was one of the few "producing stations" in the embryonic National Educational Television (NET) network, the predecessor to what is now PBS. Few of the fledgling sister stations had either the capability or the resources to produce the kind of programming geared for national distribution, but WGBH was already a prominent light in an otherwise dim canopy of stars. They'd fed a few of their series into the NET pipeline—a variety of dance, classical music, and fine arts shows. *The French Chef,* however, was something altogether different, something unusual, something distinctive, something extraordinary for its broad appeal. So they put out feelers to other markets. "We've got a tiger here," they reported to the stations. "We've got a show that people are watching. We're getting phone calls, our contributions are up."

Almost immediately, a half-dozen or so affiliates jumped on the bandwagon: KQED in San Francisco, WQED in Pittsburgh, WPBT in South Florida, WHYY in Philadelphia, WENH in Durham, New Hampshire, WCBB in Lewiston, Maine, and two small stations in upstate New York. That, as it turned out, was only for starters. This initial interest produced a snowball effect, picking up eleven more stations as *The French Chef* barreled east and west, north and south.

This was an extraordinary moment in the brief life of educational

TV. Never had a presenter caught fire like Julia Child. Oh, there was a children's show from Madison, Wisconsin—"a guy in an elf's suit, playing a Jack-in-the-beanstalk character"—that got some syndication here and there. But Julia was the first personality to emerge nationally—"she was the first educational TV star." And because public television never had quite enough programming to fill its broadcasting schedule, *The French Chef* was repeated three other times during the same week, which gave her even greater visibility. Many viewers reported watching her initial segment Mondays at eight o'clock, trying the recipe on their own, then catching a rerun to fine-tune their technique.

Julia wasn't immune to the wave of attention. Everywhere she went—"in the subway, or in stores, or on the street, or in elevators, or in business offices"—people stopped to congratulate her and tell her how much they enjoyed the show. To *thank* her for *The French Chef.* To *thank* her—imagine that! Even Paul got a taste of the billowing acclaim. During one of his routine medical checkups, a nurse pulled him aside and said, "Please tell your wife how *wonderful* I think she is! Even my *husband,* who *never* looks at television, says he wouldn't be *anywhere* Monday night at eight but right at home *glued to that machine!*"

The public reaction made Julia so appreciative, so gratified, that she refused to rest on her laurels. If people depended on her to teach them how to cook, she decided she owed them her best all-around effort. The show could be smoother, better. *Tighter.* Paul recounted their struggle to polish Julia's performance: "These evenings, when other folk are at the movies or the symphony or lectures, find Julie and me in our kitchen—me with stopwatch in hand, and Julie at the stove—timing the various sections of the next two shows. Over and over and over, with critical comments, and with suggestions for new language, or new demonstration methods." She was relentless in her persistence of perfection. Everything had to flow naturally. This was television, after all—it needed to look effortless, and to entertain. She even took to dispatching sixty strokes on a rowing machine every morning, so that when she beat egg whites during the show, she wouldn't get out of breath.

Smoother. Better. Tighter. *Looser.* Julia began to relax into the role, and as she did, another side of her emerged. It showed itself gradually, first as a kind of chummy informality in which she deviated from the script to deliver wry observations. Then, again, as Russ Morash said, "On live TV shit happens, and when it does the camera is on it and she learned to roll with it." For instance, during the making of *pommes de terre Byron,* a sautéed potato pancake, Julia flipped the concoction—*onto the stove.* "Oh—that didn't go very well," she murmured ruefully, fingering the mess back into the pan. "But you can always pick it up. If you are alone in the kitchen, *whoooo* is going to see?"

During a roasting episode, as the camera homed in on a chorus line of uncooked chickens, her voice sang out: "Julia Child presents—*the chicken sisters!* Miss Broiler, Miss Fryer, Miss Roaster, Miss Capon, Miss Stewer, and old Madame Hen!," giving each a playful slap, as though sending them out onto the stage. "The caponette," she pointed to a plumper bird, "is the same as the capon, but she's been 'on the pill,' instead of having the operation." Another time, she indicated the difference in sex between lobsters, flicking her knife across "the hard feathery parts" particular to the male, which, she admitted, "is rather fun." From time to time, she might "throw a pretend little fit," like with a rolling pin that didn't suit her. "Just throw it away," she'd say, flinging it over her shoulder to a thunderous *clank* off-camera.

Her humor was extemporaneous, droll and playful, occasionally blue. "But she had a black side, too," Russ Morash explained. "She was quite wicked, and she knew she was being wicked." He recalled a gala segment they planned for roast suckling pig. During a dry run, they went over the recipe to sequence the necessary camera shots. "When I show the suckling pig," Julia told him, "I will say something like, 'It's a bit like burning babies.'" Morash advised her against making such a remark, but he held his breath during the show, unsure whether or not she'd actually cross the line.

Morash knew he had a humorous personality on his hands, "but not nearly as funny as the audience thought she was." They caught on very quickly that Julia was a real character. She wasn't packaged or following anybody's script—not even her own—and that made for an anything-goes kind of show. You'd learn how to cook, but you'd also bask in her company. And, so, word spread that *The French Chef* was a different kind of educational TV—it was entertainment. But it was also different from entertainment as it was known on TV. It was real, it was unorthodox, it seemed spontaneous. It was a hoot.

Not only had Julia forged a vivid identity; she had broken through into a new dimension of success. Within a relatively short time, *The French Chef* had moved from a local novelty to form the tent pole of educational TV's amorphous network. In the first half of 1963, she taped an astounding thirty-four shows, two a day, with twelve-hour rehearsals—"the hardest work I've ever done," she wrote to a Pasadena acquaintance—that "went off like successful rocket launchings." She had become Boston's "fairy godmother," a high-profile presence who couldn't be ignored in a city where the prominent strove to keep their profiles low. *The Boston Globe* offered her a weekly column, featuring recipes and advice. And only a year after the rejection at Houghton Mifflin, her visibility had pushed the *Mastering* book sales over the 100,000 mark. Charlie Child, Paul's twin, who had watched the steam build from afar, wasn't off the mark when he quipped, "Julie could get to be a legend."

Even the nascent culinary community began to take notice. Fellow cooks like James Beard, who had considered Julia as, at best, an eccentric, Ivy League upstart in the trenches of *haute cuisine*—a former Cordon Bleu grad with a TV show—were suddenly obliged not only to acknowledge Julia, but to court her as an advocate who could give their projects credibility. That spring, Beard invited Julia to join the visiting faculty at his cooking school in New York, where she taught classes every few months, whenever her schedule allowed. And in no less than *The New York Times,* Craig Claiborne crowned her "the doyenne" of NET and allowed that *Mastering* "may be the finest volume on French cooking ever printed in English."

Everywhere the wheels of celebrity were turning. But in late July, Julia's chassis began to creak and sputter. The prodigious obligations piled one atop the other were "too much slogging work" for even the doyenne to cope with. She needed a break; so did Paul, who experienced a series of severe chest pains that he attributed to "a sort of pleurisy or inflammation of the something-or-other." In any case, it was enough to scare them into an urgently needed holiday, and without much advance planning they took off for Europe.

It had been almost two years since they'd been on the continent. Eager to revisit all their old haunts, the Childs mapped out a trip of grand scope—reunions in Oslo and Plittersdorf; a pilgrimage to London to meet Elizabeth David, "the foremost British food writer of her day," whom Julia considered "a kindred spirit"; a shopping spree at Dehillerin in Paris, where, according to half-joking Paul, Julia intended to "buy 10,000 more cooking vessels"; and restaurant-hopping at every locale and everywhere in between. But their primary destination was the village of Plascassier, a patchwork of rural farms in the southeast corner of Provence, the *arrière-pays* near Grasse, where Simca was quartered at a family retreat.

For Julia, the reunion with her old friend and collaborator capped off a year of startling success, both for their book and its glitzy half-cousin, *The French Chef.* The long separation from Simca had been hard on Julia. She missed the camaraderie of the old days, the creativity they shared in the kitchen, fine-tuning recipes and plotting book deals. But those had been simpler times, and much had happened in the interim. Julia had become the spokesperson for, if not the face of, *Mastering the Art of French Cooking* and an emerging force on the American culinary scene. Her celebrity at home had sprung in no small part from the success of the book. But Julia knew how much it all owed to Simca Fischbacher. Most of the recipes, after all, were heirlooms of Simca's family. And she had taught Julia everything she knew. The conceit of *cuisine bourgeoise,* the technique and the little *trucs*—a lifetime of Norman experience was absorbed into Julia's repertoire.

How her fame would affect their relationship Julia didn't know. Simca was a proud woman who knew her worth. Hands down, she was the better cook. But Julia was the better communicator—and the bigger dreamer. The concept of the cookbook may have been Simca's, but unless you knew how to package and sell it, all you had were some nice family recipes. Julia was clever. Her persistence and sacrifice had turned a pipe dream into a legacy, inspiring the show and the myriad perks it generated. She had courted the spotlight, and she had earned it. And it may well have thrown her relationship with Simca out of balance.

Stabilizing it was a focus of Julia's concern. For one thing, Julia loved Simca, whom she referred to variously as "my darling *cuisinière,*" "mon adorable amie," "ma tout à fait très chère and dearest Simca," and "my dearest *grande chérie et sœur.*" Simca was a tough old bird, but she was Julia's bird all the same; they'd come through the cookbook wars together and, despite all the bullets they'd dodged, all the mines they'd stepped on, their bond was solid, invincible. Julia wanted nothing to interfere with that.

She also had business to discuss with Simca. At several points during the editing of *Mastering,* they'd eliminated reams of material in order to trim the book's monstrous girth. "We always said, 'We'll do that recipe in another book,'" recalls Judith Jones, "as a way of letting go of some things." At the time, it was more of a device than a realistic expectation. But that was before *Mastering* became a runaway best seller. Now, those discarded recipes were like gold chips, ready to be melted into *Mastering, Volume Two.* "Financially, it made great sense," Jones argued in favor of a follow-up. Besides, there were plenty of other recipes that no American had ever tackled in a book, like making French bread, stuffing sausage casings, and roasting a suckling pig. Simca's family vault still contained dozens of worthy candidates. And it seemed prudent, reputation-wise, to finish what they'd started. At some point during the visit, Julia intended to gauge Simca's appetite for a sequel, but only after they'd had time to sink back into the comfort of their friendship.

Thankfully the sinking didn't take so much as a second. The moment the women laid eyes on each other, they fell into outstretched arms: two hearts in true-waltz time. No mention was made of *The French Chef.* Since the show was virtually unknown in France, Julia thought better of discussing it with Simca, lest her *chérie et sœur* feel *jalouse* and resentful. Besides, it was impossible to raise a flap in such a gorgeous setting. The family property—called Bramafam, which meant "the cry of hunger"—was the jeweled eye of a landscape dominated by nature. After a wondrous drive along a hilly weave of switchbacks, the effect of the homestead, a pastoral five-hectare enclave ringed by nodding olive trees and soldierly cypress, could not be more picturesque than if one were to blunder around a turn into the Deep Old South. The place was serene, enchanted. There was an eighteenth-century farmhouse—Le Mas Vieux—with its drapery of wisteria, a slim thread of woodsmoke unwinding from the stone chimney, and an immense garden. Everywhere the lavender was in bloom. A blush of roses twined along a fence, and a bouquet of pink mossy mimosa perfumed the air with a coarse sweet odor.

"Bramafam was very beautiful, but very simple," recalls Jean-François Thibault, Simca's nephew. "The house was rustic, with very few amenities, and everything was still done by hand." A local man cut the grass with a scythe; the Niçois olives were gathered with nets by family members and taken to a *moulin* in nearby Châteauneuf-Grasse. "Spending time there was like stepping back into an earlier century."

Julia and Paul were enthralled by it. They had visited several times before and considered it "paradise." There was their own little apartment in the back of the *mas,* from which they could see the distant snow-capped peaks of the Alpes-Maritimes, majestic yet foreboding like "a row of icebergs against the blue sky." Sun streamed in through an old timber-framed window, and at night they slept to the nonstop croaking of the frog-filled woods.

Everyone indulged their passion at Bramafam. In the mornings,

Paul roamed the scrubby hills with his treasured Rolleiflex and, when the sun cooperated, painted landscapes on the shaded terrace. Simca's husband, Jean Fischbacher, gardened. Naturally, Julia and Simca cooked. Later, after a long, extravagant lunch on the porch, they would climb crazily into one of Jean and Simca's cars and zigzag along the country roads, antiquing and collecting things for dinner. Those trips were hair-raising, pure "torture," according to Paul's letters written from France. Simca, who had been brought up in the thirties when there was no one on the road and had the attitude that *the road belongs to me,* drove like a "madwoman." She was "wild and aggressive" behind the wheel: "head-turning, brake-slamming, up-curve-on-hill roaring, through-marketplace-slaloming, talky-talky-talky (with high stridency), balling-out other drivers." If someone got in her way, she careened blindly around them, passed cars by fishtailing onto the shoulder. It was no surprise that "several of her friends had died on the road." It was an ordeal to be in the car with her and provoked silent prayer, as close to actual praying as Paul and Julia ever did.

But there were many pleasures on terra firma. Back down the Grasse–Cannes road, only ten minutes by car with Simca whipping through the gears, the leafy simplicity of Plascassier gave way to the gilt-edged Mediterranean, where yachts and sailboats crisscrossed lazily in the bay. Julia loved the Cannes markets with their surfeit of fresh fish, the sidewalk cafés, and her standing hair-do appointment at Elizabeth Arden. Or a few miles further east, above Mougins, the tiny commune of Mouans-Sartoux, where she found the kind of French butcher who would prepare a haunch for roasting in the classical way. Or the circuit of narrow trails leading from Bramafam up into the rock-ribbed hills that the Childs hiked with regularity. From a perch looking out over the verdant valley, cities seemed as far away as the business back home. A few days later, when a letter from "the TV people" arrived with the breathy news that *The French Chef* syndication was "catching, like measles," Julia and Simca were "up to their triceps in pastry" and didn't even respond.

No one was the least bit surprised when, a week or two after their arrival in Provence, Julia and Paul were already looking for land of their own. They'd always dreamed of owning a *pied-à-terre* in Paris for those leisure years ahead, but the idylls of Provence had an especially soothing appeal. In no time, they stumbled across "ten acres of long slope" with a copse of mature olive trees a mile or so from Simca's that "was especially attractive" for its serene exposures. "I could already imagine spending my winter months here, curing the olives from our trees, and cooking *à la provençale*, with garlic, tomatoes, and wild herbs," Julia recalled.

Could they afford it, considering their finances? They already owned houses in Cambridge and Washington, D.C. Paul's government pension was a pittance, it hardly made a dent in their expenses, and Julia's *French Chef* stipend was a pitiful fifty dollars per episode, which *also covered the food!* In fact, before they left the States Paul had laid down the law that her demo and lecture freebies had to cease. All such inquiries were now rerouted to Ruth Lockwood, who'd been instructed to quote a nonnegotiable $250 fee for Julia's services, "even for charitable considerations." Still, another property in Provence was not out of their reach. Julia had a bit of money left from her mother's bequest; she'd come into $100,000 from her father's estate; and her *Mastering* royalties had increased tenfold since the TV show aired. They could afford it.

But even before they crunched numbers, cold reality took hold. Julia was in the throes of scripting eight new shows as well as a month's worth of future *Globe* columns. Add to that an informal agreement with Simca to tackle *Mastering Deux*—they were already working on a recipe for it: *pâte feuilletée*, puff pastry—and the headaches involved with building a house felt positively suffocating. A day after their house-hunting, Julia and Paul came rudely to their senses. "We have decided not to invest in *any* land or property!" Paul reported to family back in the States. "It's terribly expensive (more than in the USA!), but mainly because of the horrendous complications involved." Besides, Simca and Jean had put a fanciful bee in their bonnets. Perhaps—just *perhaps*—if family entanglements could be unsnarled, there was an outside chance that some land on Bramafam might accommodate the Childs. There was an abandoned outbuilding about 150 yards from the house that Simca had long flirted with turning into a guest cottage. If they all agreed to combine resources, perhaps—just *perhaps*—the place could be shared.

"To be in Provence next to Simca would be a dream come true," Julia thought, ignoring the age-old warning to be careful what you wish for.

AFTER ELEVEN WEEKS in Europe, Julia was eager to resume her TV career: taping four shows a week, along with "extras," such as a Thanksgiving feast and *bûche de Noël* specials. Enthusiasm was growing for another new season of *The French Chef,* whose audience was expanding as fast as WGBH signed licensing agreements. By 1964, the show was seen in more than fifty U.S. cities, with the largest expansion west of the Mississippi—places like Ogden, Utah, and Norman, Oklahoma, where classic French cooking was about as common as bagels.

To everyone's delight, Julia sailed through a second series of twenty-six shows at her usual—puny—fifty-dollar fee. The process was becoming second nature to her, and she appeared "infinitely smoother, more integrated and more relaxed"—more *professional*—with a hoofer's flair for sidestepping potential disasters. "Her pacing is steady, rather than rush-here and hold-there," Paul reported. There was no more of the breathless vertigo that had paced her debut. As a crutch, she'd learned how to read Ruth Lockwood's "idiot cards," reminding Julia during demos what to say and do—*start heat under #2 burner with large frying pan* or *asparagus. set timer. front burner hot*—without tipping the audience, aside from the times she inexplicably grinned into the camera, when Ruth held up a card that read: *smile.*

Word filtered into the mainstream that *The French Chef* had caught fire, thanks in no small part to Julia's infinite charisma. Audiences loved her; they couldn't get enough. That loopy voice, those mannerisms, the outrageous *bons mots*—there was a campiness about her that partly explained her appeal, but people recognized there was substance behind it too, and that kept them coming back. It became clear that a new star had emerged, and soon enough "the Madison Avenue hounds" started baying at her kitchen door. The big agencies scrambled "to line her up for some sort of commercial deal." They dangled all sorts of "baited hooks"—offers to act as national spokesperson for a supermarket chain, to do a TV commercial for a detergent, even to jump ship to the ABC network. Posthaste, all suitors were turned away.

From the get-go, Julia had made up her mind to preserve her independence, "the freedom to plan her programs any way she wants, using any products that she feels are worthy or interesting," not just those that she was beholden to for an endorsement. "I just don't want to be in any way associated with commercialism," she informed a colleague. This was a noble gesture, virtuous, one that certainly defied accepted practice. The temptations, after all, were too delicious, too great. Every manufacturer and purveyor salivated over product placement on *The French Chef.* Was there a better arena in all of America to display new culinary wares, a more identifiable voice than Julia Child's to promote a new line? Really, how hard would it be for Julia to praise a Robot Coupe food processor or Waring blender, considering she used them in her demos week after week? Who would it hurt if she slipped in a word that her olive oil was Berio or her skillet Revere Ware? The fees for such plugs wouldn't hurt the Childs' pocketbook. Paul had let it be known: "We do not eschew cash!" But Julia, defiant, stood her ground. "We run the show to suit ourselves," she chastened a journalist who questioned her motives. "Nobody tells us what to do. There's no interference. What's the point?" This was educational TV after all, a cut above the commercial feed trough; to raffle off endorsements, she resolved, would degrade its purity. Besides, Julia had watched with distaste while a first-class cook like James Beard sold himself to any corporate overlord that dangled a buck before his eyes. Over the years, Beard shilled for Kraft, Corning, Borden, Spice Islands, Skotch Bonnets, Omaha Steaks, you-name-it, justifying it by saying he needed the money. It was crass, Julia felt, and demeaned him in the public's eyes. That wasn't going to happen to her.

Without much ado, products were banished from *The French Chef*'s homespun *mise en place*. Olive oil was poured from a simple glass cruet, dried herbs shaken out of bottles whose labels lay obscured in Julia's palm. The wine accompanying each dish was described in generic terms—a mountain burgundy, a nice crisp white. Even Hills Bros. Coffee, one of the show's early sponsors, never had its packaging displayed on air.

No, endorsements were out of the question, but Julia wasn't averse to the payoff of good publicity. By 1964, the media came a-calling, writing endless magazine and newspaper profiles that would ultimately frame her mystique. While not everyone appreciated Julia's elaborate menus, they were undivided over her gifted "sense of theater." In *TV Guide,* Judith Crist observed how Julia was "a law unto herself." She especially appreciated her endearing inartificiality, the way Julia "rattles saucepans, grunts when she lifts a heavy pot, mutters anachronistically about the 'icebox,' " and generally behaved in front of an audience the way Crist herself might act in her own house. Louis Lapham, then a mouthpiece for the Norman Rockwell bourgeoisie of the *Saturday Evening Post* who held out against the allures of fussy French food, suggested that viewers came to Julia as much for "her ingenious wit" as for the cooking. "Each of her cooking lessons," he wrote, "has about it the uncertainty of a reckless adventure."

Reckless, of course, couldn't be further from the truth. Julia's cooking owed its success to details, fundamentals, precision, practice—*mastering* technique. There was nothing reckless about it. She devised her recipes so that the enthusiastic cook would "know exactly what is involved and how to go about it." Nevertheless, even the best cooks suffered their share of mistakes; it was part of the process. Mistakes—and failures; they went hand in hand. "Cooking is one failure after another, and that's how you finally learn," Julia explained during a dessert show called "Gâteau in a Cage."

Yet the press continued to focus on her nimble wit. Here was a character that journalists could sink their teeth into: Julia Child, "natural clown."

In fact, her humor, such as it was on TV, was anything but buffoonish. True, she bumped around the *French Chef* set much as she did in her own kitchen. But Julia's mishaps were commonplace to the point of being mundane: putting away a colander and then forgetting where it was, hunting high and low for a utensil, reaching for the butter and finding a note that said "quarter pound of butter to be placed here." *Commonplace.* On her apple charlotte show, she instructed viewers to remove the mold carefully so the dessert wouldn't fall; then when it sank under the hot lights, exclaimed: "Well, for goodness' sake, it *did* fall!" *Commonplace.* On the endive show, she offered a Yogi Berra–style malaprop: "Now don't wash endive—that is, unless it's dirty." And during an episode of forgetfulness: "I did not have my glasses on when I was thinking." Once, she sorted through a jungle of seaweed in search of a twenty-pound lobster lurking in its folds; another time, she lifted the veil over a platter hunting for the "big, bad artichoke" lying furtively underneath. They were hardly the slapstick antics of Steve Allen and Ernie Kovacs, to whom one overheated writer compared her. Nor was she a descendant of Lucille Ball, as another claimed.

These high jinks, however, were irresistible to viewers, who retold and enlarged on them so often and so outrageously that they eventually became legend. "Sometimes she drops a turkey in the sink," Lapham wrote in his *Saturday Evening Post* profile. That never happened, Julia never dropped a turkey, but others recalled it gleefully as two chickens, or a duck—or a *pig.* They also remembered seeing Julia deglaze a pan with vermouth, then finish off the bottle herself, saying, "One of the rewards of being a cook." Actually, during a demo on juicing tomatoes she treated herself to a lip-smacking sip. But wine, of course, sounded funnier.

And made things trickier. "We had to continually defend Julia against those who thought she was staggering around the set," says Russ Morash. "Right from the outset, that was a problem."

Using wine and alcohol as savory cooking ingredients was unheard of on TV in 1964. Not only wasn't it done, it was an unwritten taboo on the same order of never showing a husband and wife sharing the same bed. Audiences were particularly finchy when it came to drinking alcohol; a *woman* drinking alcohol bordered on heresy. But as early as the first episode of *The French Chef,* Julia extolled the use of wine in her recipes. *A wine-dark sauce,* she had purred, before sloshing a third of the bottle into the *bœuf bourguignon.* The next show, too, she struck again, adding a cup of vermouth to the onion soup *gratinée.* There was no wine at all in her chicken casserole, but when she brought it to the table, her advice was clear. "You want a red Bordeaux wine with this or, as some people call it, a claret. It must marry with the chicken, not overpower it." Wine with chicken! Some viewers were outraged. And did that woman just say she would *marry a chicken?*

THE EXTREME REACTIONS, pro and con, only added to Julia's celebrity. "I can hardly go out of the house now without being accosted in the street," she wrote to a friend at Knopf. People recognized her wherever she went, and her lessons, from week to week, had a direct impact on business. After her show on broccoli aired, "the local supermarkets sold more of it in a week than they had all year long," an article reported. The same thing happened in the case of hardware stores when she mentioned a particular paring knife and rolling pin. "She told the audience they needed a good omelet pan," Russ Morash recalls. " 'Now, you need a fish poacher like the one I'm showing you here.' People felt like they had to rush out and buy one—for $112!" After her soufflé shows, when she beat egg whites with a wire whisk, "her followers," it was reported, "bought out every whisk in town." Pots and pans, rolling pins, good olive oil, vegetable steamers—*artichokes.* Items that stores never sold before were suddenly flying off the shelves.

Paul got a taste of Julia's influence when he was sent to pick up a meat order at their butcher in Cambridge. While Jack-the-Butcher, as Paul called him, was cubing a slab of veal shoulder, they watched a young woman approach, stoop down, and draw out a copy of *Mastering* from a little shelf below the counter. She flipped to the index, paged through a few recipes, made a shopping list, and waited her turn in line. "They *all* use it," the butcher assured Paul, who watched in amazement as the scene repeated itself over the course of a half hour.

He watched at the studio, too, as visitors and guests mobbed Julia after the taping of every show. He opened letters from viewers who wrote odes to her, sent her photos of their children and grandchildren, their crème caramels and their ratatouilles. He fielded phone calls from promoters at all hours of the day. And night. Sorted through offers for speaking engagements and personal appearances. Calculated her royalty statements every six months—the most recent one with a check for $14,000, more than three times what Paul had last earned in a year.

When he added it all up, the evidence was incontrovertible. No doubt about it, his wife had become a star.

Nineteen

The Mad Women of La Peetch

By 1966, the culinary world was ready for a star.

With America burrowing deeper into a war in Southeast Asia, the populace back home took refuge in a burst of new experiences. After an era of dreary button-down conformity, a longing for the Good Life had taken hold, with its roots stretching into almost every form of self-expression. People searched for something, *anything*, that would dazzle their senses, as "the everyday," according to a social critic, "was being converted into the extraordinary." The arts, sex, and drugs, especially, were in splendid flux; anybody with a whit of curiosity was seeking new direction and new inspiration.

The cultural upheaval that blazed new paths through the subconscious and the bedroom eventually reached the kitchen. It was no longer satisfying—or adventurous—enough to feast on casseroles or TV dinners. Americans began to crave food beyond mere subsistence. Suddenly beef Wellington was all the rage on the posh dinner-party circuit, as well as *ceviche,* with its nod to freshness, and custardy quiche. "The concern with good eating, which first became evident after World War II, has now swept across the nation," *Time* reported. Upscale ingredients were no longer solely for self-styled *gourmets,* as supermarkets realigned their shelves to meet the new popular demand. Where, only a year earlier, shallots had been as hard to find as a hairy-eared dwarf lemur, there were also fennel and endive and vanilla beans. Cheese departments offered

Sitting for the cover of *Time*, with Boris Chaliapin, 1966

Port Salut and wheels of runny Brie. Fresh herbs had pushed their way into the produce section, alongside the big, bad artichoke. Needless to say, there was a run on vermouth.

As the public caught on, restaurants responded in kind. The French restaurant business in New York—which had sprung from Le Pavillon, the sensation at the 1939 World's Fair—was still thriving. La Côte Basque, La Granouille, La Caravelle, Le Veau d'Or, Lutèce, and Chambord still drew the faithful older, fabulously wealthy crowds. But their menus were set in concrete; they all offered the same classic French fare. The chefs were invisible; people came because of the owners and maître d's who patrolled their front doors like martinets. That began to change in 1966, as the culture scanned younger and the young had money of their own to spend. Restaurants were no longer an indulgence only for the rich, but a *scene,* a place to eat, of course, but also to mix and be seen. The new crowd shunned places with flock wallpaper and snooty waiters, where they were looked up and down like common curs. Instead, they sought out places with personality, design, and flair—restaurants that were distinctive, with chefs who exerted a level of creativity making food that lit up people's appetites.

The shift away from French cooking began in the late 1950s with a man named Joseph Baum, who played a decisive role in the reshaping of the American dining experience. He had worked for Norman Bel Geddes, the great theatrical designer, and shared office space with architect I. M. Pei, so Baum came to food with a showman's sense of style. For Baum, food was spectacle. He "operated in the conceptual territory where food and theater overlapped." He understood that it wasn't enough to provide a menu of exquisitely made standards; you had to entertain the clientele, to offer exciting food in a unique setting. "Dining out, in Joe's view, had to be an unforgettable experience," says Barbara Kafka. "He was innovative, inventive. He brought the world of international upscale food to New York and beyond."

Baum's prescription was simple: restaurants with imaginative menus and gorgeous décor. In quick succession he opened the Forum of the Twelve Caesars, an Italian restaurant modeled on ancient Rome whose waiters dressed in togas and served exotic drinks in centurion's helmets; La Fonda del Sol, a splashy Latin American–themed *cantina* that resembled a Peruvian bazaar; the Hawaiian Room, all Polynesian razzle-dazzle, in the basement of the Lexington Hotel, with a slide for its entrance; and his masterpiece, The Four Seasons.

America had never seen anything like The Four Seasons before. Craig Claiborne, writing in *The New York Times,* called it "perhaps the most exciting restaurant to open in New York within the last two decades." Designed by Mies van der Rohe and Philip Johnson in the ground floor of the modernist Seagram Building, it featured a duet of dramatic dining spaces—the Pool Room, with its twenty-foot marble fountain and ornamental fig trees, and the Grill Room, with a Richard Lippold abstract metal sculpture suspended over the bar. There was a huge backdrop designed by Picasso and Joan Miró tapestries, chairs by Charles Eames and Eero Saarinen, and yet none of these visionaries managed to upstage the food. The Four Seasons redefined what restaurants served from that moment on. Its dishes emphasized fresh seasonal produce as opposed to a specific cuisine and introduced provisions people had never encountered before: snow peas, cherry tomatoes, baby vegetables, edible wildflowers, and a variety of rare mushrooms foraged by no less than John Cage.

The Four Seasons was a game changer for the American dining establishment, but sophisticated and expensive, like the other restaurants under Joe Baum's sway. It wasn't until April 1966, when Warner LeRoy, another incorrigible showman, opened Maxwell's Plum that the scene opened up to a younger, hipper crowd. Maxwell's, planted along a sterile outpost on First Avenue at Sixty-fourth Street, wasn't a typical high-toned expense-account restaurant. It was as much a scene as a place to eat—tables jammed shoulder-to-shoulder on multiple levels that revolved around a central bar, where singles and couples clustered five or six deep. The place was as loud and boisterous as its uninhibited décor: miles of brass railing, a jungle of enormous ferns, and ceramic animals underneath a Tiffany stained-glass ceiling that measured eighteen by thirty feet. There was no dress code, unless wide-lapeled flowered shirts and bell-bottoms counted as protocol. Its menu was *continental,* a term that, at the time, meant "potpourri" as opposed to "European": you could order a delicately stuffed squab, a grilled veal chop, or seafood crêpes, but also spareribs and hamburgers, and chili con carne—"not the *hautest* of *haute cuisine,*" as Craig Claiborne declared, but "amusing" nonetheless, and very much of it good.

Maxwell's Plum was an immediate hit, and it catapulted restaurants from stodgy special-occasion places into hot, trendy scenes. "It became chic to go out and discover these hangouts," says chef and cookbook author Rozanne Gold, who grew up in the revolution that realigned New York's kitchens and went on to become one of its illustrious figures.

"First it was Maxwell's, then Friday's, then soon afterward, Trattoria da Alfredo, which introduced regional Italian food—beautiful homemade pasta and pesto—to eager young crowds that only knew veal parmesan and spaghetti and meatballs."

New Yorkers in the know had easy access, but most of America, the people who were starting to take a real interest in food, didn't yet have the kind of places to indulge their awakening appetites. They would have a long wait until local restaurants would notice the trend. For the most part, menus across the country still offered a ghastly bill of fare: a wedge of iceberg lettuce slathered in Russian dressing, fruit cup, well-done prime rib *au jus,* sweet-and-sour chicken, baked stuffed flounder, goulash, fried shrimp, ham steak accompanied by a slice of canned pineapple, baked potatoes with sour cream, lima beans, coconut custard pie. In the early sixties, home cooking seemed like the only hope for anyone with budding culinary ambitions. The only strategy was to pick up knowledge and technique wherever possible, from a cookbook or, of all things, television. "Otherwise, it was still the Dark Ages," says Corby Kummer, a writer who would begin covering the food scene in the 1970s. "Everyone was waiting for the culinary messiah." A vision appeared on their TV screens: Julia Child was it.

TIME MAGAZINE DELIVERED the Word: they put Julia on the November 25 cover, where cultural, social, and political icons were celebrated. They anointed her "our lady of the ladle," concluded that the shows "have made her a cult from coast to coast," and declared 1966 "the year that everyone seems to be cooking in the kitchen with Julia." While they quoted Julia's standard line—"French cooking is easy if you get good working habits and stick to them"—the article was less about the cooking than it was about her persona, her "success as a showman," and the "flubs," "contretemps," "gaffes," and "goofs" that captured the public's imagination. There was something delightfully endearing about this anti-personality, this uninhibited, plainspoken, gentle giant with the warbly accent who "thinks nothing of belting down a couple of stiff bourbons at home" and admits that she "hates people who put on the dog."

Everything about Julia Child struck a common chord. Even though she was an unabashed Francophile—"I will never do anything but French cooking," she told *Time*—there was something as American as apple pie about her. Even though she lived in Cambridge, she was down-to-earth, not someone with Harvard pretensions. Even though she preached strict adherence to technique, technique, technique, it was clear that she relished breaking the rules. How could America *not* fall in love with her?

"That *Time* article catapulted Julia into a whole other stratosphere," recalls Russ Morash. "It made her the voice of American cooking," says Jacques Pépin, who had graduated from Columbia University and was emerging as a talent in his own right. "At last, there was someone who the public could turn to for advice, someone they trusted to teach them all about food, *not* a Frenchman or a tyrant, not a made-up figure like Betty Crocker—but someone very much like them."

It was the persona, the up-from-nothing spirit of America that the *Time* article celebrated—the idea "that the mistress of all this expertise could barely boil water when, at the age of 34, she married," that a "C average" student could become "the most influential cooking teacher in the U.S." and make herself a household name. *A household name.* Even if it hadn't been so before, it was so now. There she was—on the cover of *Time.*

The verdict was unanimous. The letters that poured into *Time* confirmed what the editors already knew. "Hurrah for Julia Child," wrote Robert F. Hever from Mettitt Island, Florida, after he arrived home from work one night and found *filets de poisson gratinés à la parisienne* on his plate. "Around our house she is spoken of as a member of the family," Frances R. Looney wrote from New Haven, Connecticut. "We just plain love her."

But the *Time* cover merely capped the year's media splash. In April, *The French Chef* was awarded an Emmy, the first ever given to an educational TV station. *Life* had also done a feature spread on Julia that appeared the last week in October, as had *The New York Times Magazine,* in which Craig Claiborne, now the most influential food critic in the country, referred to her glowingly as "one of the most extraordinary talents in the food field in America." Still, one jealous rival managed to get in her licks. The *Times Magazine* article quoted "another well-known professional cook trading candor for anonymity," whose resentment of Julia was all encompassing. "She's neither French nor a chef," the nameless source lashed out. "She hasn't worked as an apprentice, taken the examinations, and gotten her chef's certificate. It's a shame that the term 'chef' is used so loosely these days."

It didn't take long for Julia to unmask the scold's identity. Within days, word drifted back that the source was Madeleine Kamman, a "feisty," "fierce"—James Beard called her "peppery"—Cordon Bleu grad with a "psyche," she claimed, that "Americans do not understand," whose brilliance as a cook and teacher would forever be overshadowed by "the central question" in her life: "Why Julia? Why not me?" Kamman was French, she'd toiled in a one-star kitchen in Touraine, gotten her diploma, paid her dues. All admirable accomplishments, yet there was one affliction that stuck in her craw: "Why would they want an American 'French Chef'?" The question galled her. It didn't parse. For years afterward, she would openly deride Julia's tidal wave of fame; at the moment, however, it hardly caused a ripple.

Outwardly, Julia basked shamelessly in the spotlight. Wherever she went in the days after the article appeared, people stopped her to express how much they enjoyed what she did and who she was. Complete strangers called her by name—always "Julia," an instant familiarity. After all, she came right into their homes, looked them squarely in the eye, steered them through their family dinners, held their hand. She'd established something personal with them, a bond, a *relationship,* something more. Encountering her, people felt they could ask her anything—and did. "How do I roast my chicken to a deep golden glow?" But also: "How can I encourage my husband to participate in the family meal?" "How can I please my husband in other ways?"

Occasionally there would be a hiccup. The roast suckling pig show touched off a landslide of indignant outbursts reflected in the weekly mail. From the opening scene, viewers were startled by the lifelike little creature stretched out, peaceful and cozy, on an oval cutting board. It looked like the household pet was taking a little snooze, and Julia kept patting it affectionately as she described how she cleaned out *his* ears and nostrils and brushed *his* teeth. Stuffing it with vegetables seemed like a ruthless crime. Things got more gruesome later, when she hacked it apart with an electric knife. "I'm sure we shall get some angry letters from squeamish people," Julia wrote Simca, "as the little pig looks very much like a naked baby while he is being prepared."

Even that, however, couldn't dim Julia's halo. The fan mail at WGBH increased tenfold through the year. A mountain of letters poured in after every show, thousands of requests for the recipes. The station "has to turn away hundreds of people weekly, each willing to pay $5," *Boston* magazine noted, "for the privilege of watching the show backstage on tiny monitor screens." No matter. Everyone wanted to cook what Julia Child was cooking. A "horridly bulky envelope" reached Irving Street soon after

Thanksgiving, stuffed with *Time* covers that collectors requested Julia sign. *Collectors!* Whatever that meant for posterity, it touched off a fresh run on *Mastering*; the book's sales tripled in December 1966 and quadrupled the next month. Wisely, Knopf boosted its next print run from the usual ten thousand copies to thirty thousand, but it was anyone's guess where the demand would stop. Certainly not at the country's borders. There was new interest in licensing *The French Chef* throughout Latin America and as far off as Australia and New Zealand. These offers could have meant a small fortune for Julia. Since there was no educational TV in countries other than the United States, she was free to negotiate a *commercial* deal. There was no telling what a private broadcaster might pay! Reruns, she heard, were where the real money was. But, true to form, she decided to leave it up to WGBH and donate her percentage to the station's development fund, much as she'd been doing with the $500 she now received for public demonstrations.

The program's last season had been another runaway triumph. There were already 134 shows in the can that were being rerun in 106 cities across America, with plans under way for a fresh new stash. In appreciation, Julia had gotten a raise: she was now making a princely two hundred dollars a show instead of the fifty-dollar pittance allotted since her debut. And the production itself had gone big-time; the size of the crew shot up from five to a twenty-five-man regiment, with a dedicated auxiliary staff of volunteers. None of which really mattered to Julia. It was all just numbers anyway, not too earthshaking in the overall scheme of things. What she really cared about was how it looked, how she came across to the folks at home.

"I'm not going back until we get color," she protested, "so that we can at least get better looking food."

Julia firmly believed, as did most perceptive broadcasters, that by the end of the 1960s, just a few years off, most TV transmissions would be done in color. Black and white was still the norm, but homes were crawling with newfangled sets that turned drab two-toned images into brightly hued, if not garish, tableaux. The technology was changing and Julia wanted to change with it; otherwise, she feared competitors would leave her in the dust. A few months earlier, in fact, WGBH had tested the waters by taping a ten-minute segment of *The French Chef* in color. A thousand tons of highly specialized equipment were imported from New York, so-called experts converged on the set; several hundred NET "big-wigs" from across the country were invited to attend. Julia prepared a veal stew just for the occasion, along with a strawberry tart because, she said, "real strawberries look so much better than gray lumps." Two cameras—one color, the other black and white—shot the performance side by side, as the crowd watched the monitor, utterly fascinated. "They kept switching from one to the other, and it was like night and day." Julia was sold—and ultimately threw down the gauntlet: no color, no Julia.

"She was a tiger," says Russ Morash. "When any big change came along like that, Julia was out in front of it." She put pressure on cash-strapped WGBH to update its equipment sooner rather than later. With uncharacteristic aggressiveness, she went public with her point of view, offering interviews to "the right places" where opinion could be made. With few exceptions, columnists echoed her outlook that black and white was passé. The *Los Angeles Times* noted that *The French Chef* was "handicapped" by its outdated format. Cleveland Amory, in *TV Guide,* struck the same judgmental tone. "Lately they've been rerunning old tapes," he said, espousing an urgent upgrade to color. In the meantime, Julia Child was "a holdout."

The uproar was more a ruse than a demand. Julia needed time—to breathe and to lighten the insane schedule that was pressing around her. She had just wrapped up a taping blitz of twenty-two new shows, while consulting on the "difficult" pilot for a WGBH Chinese-cooking series with Boston restaurateur Joyce Chen. Now Knopf was after her to publish a paperback of some sort to tie in with *The French Chef.* Her *Globe* column was always on deadline; there were interviews galore, pleas for more demos. It was all too much to digest at once. Julia was swamped, exhausted. Paul worried constantly that she was "falling apart at the seams." She pulled any number of muscles, spent long, excruciating nights on a hot pad, nursed saucer-sized blisters, fended off cystitis, "the trots." Only recently, she had "busted her toe for the second time," this latest instance due to kicking their venal dishwashing machine. Besides, Julia had to get serious about *Mastering II,* which she and Simca had begun outlining in earnest. If it was to be anything like their initial blockbuster, it would have to be thorough, momentous—another *monster.*

By the time the clamor for Julia's attention reached its crescendo, however, she and Paul were tucked snugly away at Bramafam, in Provence, where they were consumed by a far more demanding concern: the building of their dream house.

IT HAD BEEN an ongoing process. Back in 1964, Simca's husband, Jean, had managed to unsnarl the entails that obstructed their claim on the family property. It had been left to him and his sister by a quirky cousin, along with a pile of debts that had accrued over the years. By paying off the creditors, Jean not only shrank the debt but increased his share in the estate until his sister, much to her chagrin, was entitled to spend only one month a year, in the summer, at Bramafam.

"So Jean and Simca became lords of the manor," says Jean-François Thibault, who, with his mother, felt like an interloper during their annual monthly stay. "Simca and Jean moved into the main house and basically did what they wanted with it. Simca redecorated without consulting my mother and made plans to develop the property as she saw fit."

Part of her objective was to offer a patch of land on the olive-tree terraces to Paul and Julia, where they could build a small house to use "when they need to get away from it all." The offer was generous—and complicated. Legally, the Childs would not own the property, but they would pay for all building costs and maintenance of the grounds. "The house will be ours, but revert to them," Paul explained. If Julia and Paul decided to move on—or if, for whatever reason, the Fischbachers wanted them gone—they'd leave their investment behind.

Initially, Jean's sister disapproved of the arrangements, which he conducted behind her back, but once she was brought into the discussions, she relented. "My mother decided to let Julia build," recalls Jean-François Thibault. "It was going to be a small house, just for them. We knew the builders, a local family, and we were assured the house would be constructed with old stones and covered with old tiles and would not protrude on the landscape."

After much back-and-forth, a blueprint emerged. The structure would be a one-story cottage with French doors that opened onto front and back terraces situated a stone's throw from the old *mas*. Shutters on the windows, two fireplaces for warmth. A few olive trees would remain along the gently sloped yard, fortified by new plantings—roses and bougainvillea—"which would be gorgeous in a year or two." Everyone—the Fischbachers, the Thibaults, and the Childs—signed off happily on the plans.

"The agreement was made with a handshake," Julia recalled. "It would be a house built on friendship."

Ground was broken in the winter of 1965 and continued, French-style, at an infuriating snail's pace, throughout the rest of that year. When they saw it in the spring, the foundation was only roughed in—"a shell of cinderblock, concrete, plaster and stones." Still a work-in-progress, it looked bigger than what they had anticipated, and gave off "a feel of comfort and good proportion." Even unfinished, Julia thought, the house was "a little jewel." The setting was pastoral, spiritual, a "psychological island of safety," and the weather a welcome relief from New England's glacial constraints. Spring had come early that year thanks to the warm escorting winds off the Mediterranean. "Mimosa trees are in full flower everywhere," Paul observed, "as are violets, narcissus, quince and almond trees, broom bushes, and blue iris," which carpeted the berms like a Bonnard landscape.

Lovely but modest, rustic but enchanting, they decided to call it La Pitchoune—"La Peetch," for short—which translated loosely as "the little thing."

Now, in 1966, it was finished, at last. Julia and Paul had rented a car at the train station in Cannes, and as they came up the winding drive that led from the N-85 into Plascassier, they could see the house in the distance, its lights ablaze to greet them. In their absence, Simca had taken care of everything—*everything*. There were curtains on the windows made from an old design from Les Baux, lovely bedspreads turned down just so for the night, old French table linens laid out, antique faience plates on the mantel, a wardrobe made from weathered oak door panels. It was everything they had dreamed of, and more, so much more.

Two days later, just as the mimosas were beginning to bloom, Charlie and Freddie Child arrived to celebrate the Provençal housewarming, and the brothers got Julia's kitchen up and running. Their first order of business: installing her trademark floor-to-ceiling pegboard with outlines of each object in bold detail "for permanent placement." The appliances were already primed for cooking. A great old iron Cornue stove with removable rings churned like a locomotive. It gave off a loud, indignant *pooooof* when first turned on, so forever after Julia referred to it as the Poof. "I cooked a *poulet* on the Poof," she would say with affection.

In the garage stood a Citröen Dix Neuf with automatic transmission that Simca had bought them as a special house gift. A thoughtful and gracious gesture, except that the Childs "absolutely hated it." It was an ugly metallic-beige color and shaped like a mollusk, which prompted another nickname. "There goes old Clam Face," Julia would say on the rare days when it was taken out for a drive. But Simca insisted it was "a

great car for them," much as she insisted on all their major decisions at
Bramafam.

"She was a very authoritative woman," says her nephew, Jean-François,
"bossy and inflexible and persistent, like a *gendarme*." There was a thoughtful and caring side of her—and a domineering side that ruled like a despot.
Julia and Paul were just beginning to appreciate her particular nature.
Gradually they came to realize that Simca the pen pal was an entirely
different creature than Simca the neighbor. "She knows everything about
everything," Paul complained, soon after taking possession of the new
house. He took every human effort to sidestep her blustery conceits. But
day in, day out, she busted his chops, issuing instruction after instruction
indicating he "knows nothin' about nothin'." Julia had encountered some
of this behavior before, in the days when the *Mastering* manuscript was
coming down the home stretch. But no matter how overbearing Simca
seemed, no matter how infuriatingly arrogant and *French* her asides, Julia
could tolerate her. Paul, on the other hand, was thin-skinned and easily
provoked. Steadily, ceaselessly, she began to grate on his nerves. "She's
rather like a French female version of General Patton," he said. "I can
take her for about ten minutes, then my dander begins to rise and I want
to shout (you *have* to shout to be heard above the riveting machine of her
voice), 'In the first place you don't know what you're talking about, and
in the second place *shut up!*' "

It would be a house built on friendship.

Julia both resented Simca's tenacity and fed off it. She considered
Simca an "opinionated French tyrant," according to a letter written to
Avis DeVoto, and became exasperated with her pushy behavior. But their
cooking partnership took precedence, and as 1966 lapsed into 1967, they
needed to pave the way for Volume II of *Mastering the Art of French Cooking.*
Julia had managed to divide the three months at La Pitchoune between
settling the house and cooking. Simca was spending more and more
time at the little cottage, and from the kitchen surged "a jolly, pleasant
symphony—sounds of frying, boiling, chopping, laughter, commingled
with the staccato sound of French sputtering out in the air." It was so
essential to keep everything copasetic; no need to scuttle the *Mastering*
juggernaut.

As weeks passed, as recipes evolved, Paul observed how Julia and
Simca "carry on a running battle about food and cooking, but are mutually admiring, appreciative, and non-jealous." He was astonished by their
ability to butt heads over procedure in a way that allowed creativity to

prevail. Julia remained the team's incorrigible scientist, insisting they test and test and *retest* the variables, but she allowed for Simca's instinct and spontaneity to make their marks. "Simca knew what to do, last minute, to pump up a dish," says Judith Jones. "She was always putting one more clove of garlic into a recipe; her food was pungent, lustier. Julia reined her in." Remarkably, their approaches complemented each other, even as far as temperaments went. "Somehow they manage not to tear out each other's hair," Paul concluded, "probably because—in the end—both have their eyes on the target rather than on themselves."

The target couldn't have been any clearer. During the weeks after the New Year, the cooking began in earnest. "The Mad Women of La Peetch," as they were called, started experimenting with a new vegetable soup recipe and talking, always talking, about the shape of the book. Based on detailed notes that Simca had submitted, Julia had already done "a tentative chapter list" for the book, as well as rough outlines so they had "something concrete to work on." Rather than meandering all over the culinary spectrum as they'd done in the days before Volume I, this new version would be broken up into seven clearly defined sections: soups, breadmaking, meats, poultry, charcuterie, vegetables, and desserts. "Julia was determined that it contain entirely different dishes from the original book," recalls Judith Jones, "but with the same basic premise: a realistic approach to French classics for the American cook, with an emphasis on theme and variations." While Volume I, however, reflected the traditions of French cuisine, Volume II was intended to drag it into the modern era—if necessary, kicking and screaming.

This time around, the work felt more focused, especially with Louisette comfortably out of the picture. They'd come to appreciate the old axiom: two's company, three's a crowd—especially in this case, where each cook's contribution was critical to the success of the book. For many reasons, Louisette just hadn't been up to the challenge, and her cooking, alone, was enough to exclude her. Julia always put a more gracious spin on it, saying that Louisette's tumultuous personal life required that she devote her time to family. In fact, as Julia and Paul moved into La Pitchoune, Louisette's personal life roared anew.

As Paul recounted it, "her monster of an [ex-]husband piled up debts of some 90,000 francs and then skipped the country to avoid payment. He's now living in Spain where he's already fathered several bastard children." The *scandale* might have ended at Paul Bertholle's doorstep were it not for French law, which mandated that a husband and wife who own joint property are jointly or singly responsible for accrued debts and taxes from the marriage. The very day Julia's *Time* cover story hit the Paris kiosks, fiscal agents descended on Louisette to grill her, her concierge, and her friends about L'École des Trois Gourmandes—the purpose of the school, the number of students, and the fees earned by the teachers.

Under no circumstances could she declare her *Mastering* royalties, all of which would have been seized by revenue agents as collateral against the debts. So Julia paid Louisette's share into Simca's account and cash was passed secretly to their erstwhile colleague.

Unfortunately, that wasn't the extent of Louisette's troubles. "Her hands are so twisted by arthritis," Paul recalled, "that she can hardly lift a glass of water, much less a casserole." She was due to get married for a third time, in March 1967, to Count Henri de Nalèche, making Louisette *une comtesse,* but the titles were deceiving. Count Henri had property near Bourges where woodsmen would assemble to hunt pheasant or take part in the sport of *la vénerie,* or stag hunting, but according to Paul, he had practically no money to his name. "They are both lonely, not too well, and reaching out for the dying embers of love before it is too late."

In any case, Louisette would continue to glean income from *Mastering*'s strong legs, and now from another source, as well: *The French Chef Cookbook.* Knopf had decided that launching a tie-in with the TV series was too good a publishing opportunity to pass up and rushed a compendium of its recipes from the 119 shows into print. Most everything in the book had a familiar provenance: they were simplified versions of the lessons in *Mastering,* and Julia felt an obligation to Simca and Louisette, cutting them in for a piece of the royalties. It would be a cushy payday for everyone concerned. Julia got an advance of $25,000—ten times what she received for *Mastering*—more than enough to spread around. Even Ruth Lockwood and WGBH were given a modest cut.

Knopf had an idea of the book's potential. For one thing, it had a built-in audience; there were now more than a million viewers who tuned in regularly to the show. And for another, a brilliant spokesperson to sell it: Julia Child. It was the perfect combination to assure its success. Judith Jones had extremely high hopes as she made her presentation to Robert Gottlieb, Knopf's new editor-in-chief. They were on their way to lunch to discuss the book's marketing plan when Gottlieb hesitated at the corner of Madison Avenue and Fifty-first Street. "How many copies are you printing?" he inquired offhand. Jones, a product of Knopf's conservative approach, was reluctant to admit that she'd gone for broke. "Forty thousand," she mumbled, hoping he'd somehow approve. Gottlieb wheeled on her. "Are you *insane?*" he bellowed. Jones hung back. Unyielding, Gottlieb bore down on her. "That's not *nearly* enough. Look at what we've got."

They were in a new era, influenced by television and publicity, he explained. It was essential, critical, they take advantage of all the elements. Gottlieb, who'd come to Knopf from high-rolling Simon and Schuster, had his sights set on a bolder publishing model than the cautious one his new boss had employed. "Bob was a publisher of this world," Jones deduced, "while Alfred was a publisher of the old world." Over lunch he boosted the initial print run for *The French Chef Cookbook* to 100,000 copies, with the presses poised to reprint without delay.

Julia had emerged as a powerhouse on Knopf's list, joining John Updike and V. S. Naipaul among their surefire bestsellers. This wasn't small-time publishing anymore. A six-figure print run put her in the same league as Arthur Hailey, Ira Levin, and Helen Gurley Brown. She could sell books merely by staying on TV and cooperating with all the requests for interviews. The *Time* article had, in Paul's words, "blasted *Mastering* off the pad," and now *The French Chef Cookbook* was set to launch into the stratosphere.

Julia had also taken on another culinary book project. With great fanfare, Time-Life announced it would publish Foods of the World, a series of eight lavishly illustrated volumes, each tied to an international cuisine. If Knopf's take on the business was either old or new world, this model was *out of this world,* with a projected print run of half a million, and a budget that knew no bounds. Money was no object. They'd hired the best food writers, cooking teachers, and experts in the field to give the work a prestigious as well as an authoritative glow, polished by Time-Life's resources for presenting stylized spectacle.

The publisher's resources also made it difficult for the culinary world's brightest stars to refuse its extravagant fees. Everyone signed on for a piece of the literary pie: James Beard "staged cooking classes for the Time-Life production team and acted as a general adviser"; M. F. K. Fisher, whose gorgeous prose, witty and sensual gastronomical books, and nuanced columns in *The New Yorker* earned her John Updike's designation as "a poet of the appetites," promised to write copy; the British kitchen diva Elizabeth David provided recipes and technical guidance; and the prize catch in the team: none other than Julia Child. Julia, who was basically lured by the $1,500-a-month premium and her gratitude to *Time,* agreed to act as consultant for the first volume, *The Cooking of Provincial France,* with the understanding that she "only had to read over everything," "to make sure what the writers have written is correct"—nothing more. The heavy lifting would be done by the book's editor, Michael Field.

Field, after all, had made quite a name for himself as the self-styled gastronome-of-the-moment on the New York food scene. He'd toiled as a concert pianist of some renown; had proved himself socially and politically clever; was an exceptional cook; had a fat Rolodex of top-shelf connections; and, best of all, knew James Beard, who had recommended he be appointed to the post at Time-Life. Even though he wasn't rooted in cooking, there was plenty on Field's résumé to vouch for his standing. Advocates like Beard considered him "serious" and "passionate," "an uncompromising traditionalist," with "a knowledge of cooking that was encyclopedic." He had a Manhattan-based cooking school whose pupils became devoted acolytes. And his gravitas landed him a column at *The New York Review of Books,* where he lionized cookbooks and their authors in arch academic tones.

But his prominence, however, had nothing to do with natural gifts. It had to do with ambition: Michael Field was as slick as they came.

"He had a flair, he was dramatic," recalls Judith Jones, "and ruthless." There was nothing he wouldn't do, no string he wouldn't pull, to throw a spotlight on his ascending star. No one wanted a position of power and influence more than Field. "He had to be Mr. Food, *the* authority, the ultimate word," says Michael Batterberry, who, with his wife, would eventually launch *Food & Wine.* Very intense, the way a panther was intense, Field made sweeping statements that were often meant more to provoke than to inform. "Cooks are not creative," he told a journalist from *Time,* "they're simply brilliant technicians." Needless to say, that didn't endear him to his peers, who bridled at his swollen theories. "He was an arriviste, another difficult spider," says Batterberry, "brilliant but ultimately so damn destructive."

Julia, to her credit, saw right through his act. She had heard from Judith Jones that "Field was kind of crazy" and tracked the rumblings from his cooking-school classes from one ado to the next. "They were *wild,*" according to a reliable observer. He was hyperkinetic in the kitchen, doing demo after demo at warp speed, prompting students to plead, "Please, *please,* just do one thing at a time." Another commentator said "he was almost fascistic" in his approach to hands-on culinary technique. Field "did not sentimentalize or romanticize food." Unlike Julia, he urged his students not to wash mushrooms, devein shrimp, or press garlic. She sensed he was "a romantic who got himself into the big-time before he was quite ready." Still, despite these misgivings, she signed on as his consultant for Volume One and let him move into La Peetch while he edited the book.

The Time-Life project got the culinary community excited. On the one hand, it was confirmation that their discipline had finally catapulted into the big time. Such attention elevated serious cooking from a quaint niche to a runaway trend, with a corporate imprimatur and corporate resources to fuel it. First the Time-Life media monolith put Julia on the cover of *Time* and now it was primed to launch her colleagues, as well. "They pumped so much money into this thing," says Michael Batterberry, "and everyone was feeding off it, financially as well as professionally."

But it also created rivalries and, with them, internal politics. "Alliances were being formed," says Barbara Kafka, who was writing culinary articles for *Vogue* and *Ladies' Home Journal*. Movements such as cooking required articulate spokesmen and characters to fire up the public enthusiasm. "Big personalities with big ideas began to surface—cooks and cooking experts, but also visionaries and self-promoters—and how one advanced often depended on who one's friends and mentors were."

There were two primary camps that vied for power: "the Jim camp and the Craig camp—and they were far apart," says an informed observer. There was no love lost between James Beard and Craig Claiborne. One-time friends, there had been a gradual falling-out over real and imagined slights. Beard had helped Claiborne get his first job at *Gourmet* and introduced him around the scene to the heavyweights who could help his career. But after Claiborne rose to power as the *Times*'s indomitable food critic, some say he "minimized Jim as an unsophisticated cook" and often claimed Beard took credit for recipes that weren't his. Personally, they had vastly different styles. They were both gay, both gentlemen who craved a loyal coterie. "But there was something cold and southern WASPish about Craig," says an acquaintance. "At parties, he restrained himself until he had enough to drink, and then he could get quite nasty." James was "a larger than life personality," says a colleague, more outgoing than Claiborne—but also more volcanic. "He could be a monster, just beyond the pale, but he loved people who were complex, difficult, and did something differently."

In the end, their incompatibility came down to cooking styles. Claiborne, who had been trained at L'École Hôtelière de la Sociéte Suisse des

Hôteliers in Lausanne, thought "French cuisine was not simply a taste preference but the gold standard of food against which everything might be judged." Beard was the acknowledged "dean of American cookery." They were as different as quenelles were to chicken potpie.

Even so, one had to choose sides. Jim's inner circle was Helen McCully, the influential food editor at *McCall's;* José Wilson from *House & Garden;* Sam and Florence Aaron, the owners of Sherry-Lehmann wines; Jacques Pépin; Barbara Kafka; and Madhur Jaffrey, whose upscale Indian cuisine was attracting huge attention. Craig's camp was Pierre Franey; writer Bryan Miller; Mexican chef Zarela Martínez; and Dorothea Elman, a Brazilian designer who cooked wonderful Latin-inspired recipes.

Julia was careful to straddle both scenes. She was fond of Jim Beard, whom she described as "always just darling," and continued to teach, every chance, at his cooking school in New York. "Their affinities for honest food transcended differences in their styles," wrote one Beard biographer, and to some extent their styles coalesced. In addition to trading the latest culinary information, Jim and Julia shared a love of gossip, which they practiced almost as much as essential knife-work. Craig Claiborne, on the other hand, eluded her. "He is sort of hard to get at," Julia explained in an interview. "He's kind of a loner. He's not helpful, but he's not inimical at all." In fact, it was a reckless statement, considering "he was the most influential voice" in the media and his review of *Mastering* practically launched her career.

Coincidentally, it was Claiborne and Julia, the two francophiles, who first became disenchanted with the Foods of the World series. From almost the get-go, Julia regretted committing to the project, which seemed "totally commercial," more flash than substance. "I wish I hadn't said I would act as consultant for the Time-Life books with Michael Field!" she wrote to Simca, as early as June 1966. To Avis, she wrote, "He is a dabbler, I think, a charmer, a wordmonger, a butterfly, and ambitious." Her "misgiving tremors" were confirmed by others watching from the sidelines. According to M. F. K. Fisher, who had ensconced herself at Bramafam during the research for the book, Field, now at La Pitchoune, was in over his head. The number of volumes under his stewardship had ballooned from eight to eighteen, making him "terribly high-strung and somewhat unstable," she feared. Meanwhile, there was every indication "he seemed to have a cooking block." Fisher, "because she was nosy," had stolen across the lawn to gauge his progress and found the refrigerator at La Peetch practically empty. "How can you allow someone to edit cookbooks who doesn't cook?" she wondered. Especially when it was Field's job to test all the recipes.

By November 1966 Julia had her own sad proof. "The recipes for the Time-Life French cookbook arrived," she wrote to Simca, and the verdict was in: "They are *awful.*" The recipes were riddled with "an inordinate number of errors." Most, she felt, were a "hodgepodge," demonstrating "tremendous incompetence and incomprehension," while many were lifted outright from *Mastering* and others. Perhaps an even greater offense, the book "had no zing."

Aside from the evident disappointment conveyed by letter to her usual pen pals, Julia was tightlipped on the subject. She followed the same rule of conduct that guided her through cooking disappointments: to never acknowledge or apologize for them. Claiborne, however, exercised no such restraint. In his *New York Times* review of *The Cooking of Provincial France,* timed to appear on the very day of its book-launch party, he excoriated Field for his slipshod work and called the book "the most dubious sample of the regional cooking of France." Field, who'd ceded much of the project to consulting editors, responded in kind in an article for *McCall's,* trashing Claiborne's beloved French restaurants. Back and forth it went like that, each response turning up the pitch, while the food community looked on with glee.

Months later, it was announced with great fanfare that Pierre Franey, the former chef at Le Pavillon, had signed a deal with Time-Life to provide a volume on classic French cuisine for the Foods of the World series. Claiborne let it be known that he wished to be Franey's collaborator, an unusual request considering the long paper trail of criticism he'd left. Pundits saw it as strong-arming the publisher; in effect, they "had no choice but to agree." A generous contract was signed, and outlines were approved, before they introduced Claiborne to his editor: for this volume they were bringing back Michael Field.

In the ensuing food fight, Julia Child remained above the fray. There was plenty for her to enjoy in the political intrigue, but there was plenty to distract also. She let the food community's shenanigans amuse her, but with all the recognition she had received—from her loyal fan base, the magazine profiles, the Emmy, the *Time* cover—she saw a different role for herself, not scrapping with colleagues for notice and stature, but as an authority, *the* cooking authority, someone who was doing this for the greater good rather than for fame or wealth. She kept her eye on her public, letting them see that she was serious about the food, but also about herself. Trust became an issue: for her audience to maintain their trust in her, as a teacher and entertainer but also a public figure, she couldn't push an agenda, she couldn't profit from endorsements, she couldn't pick fights. Her authenticity depended on it. Not only would she win the respect of the public, but the respect of the food community as well.

The culinary world had found its star.

Twenty

A Household Name

By the end of 1967, the *Mastering II* sweepstakes was off and running, with Julia and Simca sprinting through recipes at a breakneck pace. Their respective Bramafam kitchens, organized like laboratories in a research compound, were always cauldrons of enterprise, with big, heaping platters of meats and vegetables covering the counters and six stovetop burners perpetually chugging away. Dishes in various stages of deconstruction teetered on windowsills and chairs and atop one another, leading one visitor to describe the scene as "the spoils of a gastronomic orgy." Through clouds of steam at La Pitchoune, a leggy, hulking figure in a grimy apron, a pencil stub poking out from behind an ear, conducted a raucous symphony of pots and pans that sputtered and hissed like a Bruckner motet. Usually, Julia had three or four preparations going *fortissimo* at all times. She would concentrate on one recipe, while the others simmered, unattended, on their way to pulsing finales. For instance, in one pot she might begin boiling the tails and claws from a half-dozen lobsters for a main dish, *homard à l'américaine,* while in a stockpot, the chests, legs, and assorted "trash" parts were infusing a lobster bisque. In a frying pan, a mound of chopped shells in fat might sizzle for—what?—she hadn't decided yet. Even the Waring blender provided percussion, grinding a solution of tiny legs in a reddish-yellow froth that would develop into lobster butter. All represented only the first movement of testing. During an initial run, she might ignore the trace amount of meat from

With (from left) Jean Fischbacher, Simca's cook, Charlie Child,
and Simca outside La Pitchoune

the legs, while the next day reconsider, cutting through them and squeezing out every last fleck with a rolling pin. Every recipe, fanned out like a conductor's sheet music, would be cooked and recooked umpteen times. Julia worked through each set of instructions quickly but methodically, sampling and seasoning and making notes as she went.

Julia had always worked that way. Her earliest marginalia for *Mastering II* illustrate the struggle between recipes and technique, between instinct and precision. She wasn't about to subordinate her reliance on fundamentals to the unpredictable whims of the stove. The perfect recipe depended on what she called the *operational proof.* Trial and error, error and trial: there were no shortcuts.

However, in the burst of cooking that kick-started the book, Julia confronted an old problem. "I cannot trust Simca's recipes at all," she lamented. Once again, her co-writer's approach to the kitchen work was formless, erratic. Simca used the very methods—"unscientific, instinctive, verbal, and almost totally unbelieving in research, notes, order, [and] classical sources"—that Julia fought hardest to suppress. "Simca pays no attention to anything Julia tells her about all the researches she's done, the findings of the U.S. Department of Agriculture, or the careful scientific comparisons she's made," Paul grumbled in a letter to his brother. Indiscriminately he added: "*She drives me nuts!*"

Julia, who never edited his missives, resented his stinging characterization of her partner and asked Paul to modify his remarks. It was true that Simca's cooking technique frustrated her no end. They even set the new book's schedule back weeks, if not months. But she reminded him that Simca, while infuriating, wasn't incompetent; she was a "real half" of the *Mastering* team, with her own indispensable contribution. No partnership was perfect. Simca might have "zero interest" in the research, but deep down Julia knew that Simca was a pure cook—which she was not.

Julia admitted, however, that sloppy, even indifferent, work had led to errors in Volume I. There were three recipes specifically that continued to gall her. "I'm not going to have anything in this book that doesn't work," she insisted. "*Volume II* has to be better than *Volume I,* and I ain't going to be rushed over it."

The real snag came not from Simca but an unexpected source. In a letter to her co-author, Julia wrote: "Judith Jones says she wonders if we shouldn't have one good recipe for French bread." It was the magic phrase that Julia had been dreading.

Since *The French Chef* began in 1964, she'd received dozens of letters a week from viewers requesting a recipe for good French bread. It seemed like a natural part of Julia's repertoire and an essential element to any meal. But Julia knew better. Making French bread was an art not easily duplicated at home, much less with American ingredients and American ovens. God knew she'd never produced a decent baguette, nor, as far as she knew, had Simca. They'd given it a try together, during the posting in Marseille, going through fifty pounds of American flour with no good result. According to Simca, it was "a real disaster!" Since then, Julia skillfully avoided the issue, responding to requests for a recipe by saying "no French person bakes French bread in the home." In France it was customary to make a daily trip to the neighborhood *boulangerie* to buy delicious, freshly baked bread crafted by an artisan in specially designed ovens. Granted, that wasn't the case in the States. The so-called French bread found in American supermarkets was truly awful, a faux-crust with a spongy Wonder Bread core. It was nothing Julia could recommend. But baking it oneself was downright folly.

Viewers understood her reasoning—but Judith Jones was not to be dissuaded. No meal was complete without a baguette, she told Julia. "I thought it was absolutely necessary," Jones recalls many years later. "Imagine the bible on French cuisine without a recipe for French bread! I wrote Julia back and urged her to research it."

At the time, Julia was up to her eyeballs in puff pastry. She'd been busy baking fruit tarts, *mille-feuilles, Pithiviers,* petits fours, even beef Wellington and stuffed lamb baked *en croûte*—anything that mated with a fine flaky crust. She'd also been burning through a pack of chocolate cake recipes in an attempt to outdo the famous Reine de Saba that stole the spotlight in Volume I; it was a challenge, she discovered, "that was like trying to draw better than Leonardo." Instead of breaking stride, she fobbed the bread gruntwork off on Paul, who laid claim to a few loaves in his pre-Julia days and was itching to participate.

It was impossible to bake bread at La Pitchoune, where Julia commandeered every inch of available kitchen space. Besides, between epic cooking marathons the Childs were constantly entertaining a clique of ex-pat writers and artists who fed their intellects: author Robert Penn Warren, who lived in the nearby village of Magagnosc; Surrealist painter Max Ernst; and novelist Sybille Bedford, who with her lover, Eda Lord, lived in a hill town just behind Bramafam. Between the dinners and the late-night sessions banging out recipe notes at the typewriter, there was no time left to devote to bread. It was all Julia and Paul could do to catch their collective breath. Once back in Cambridge, however, Paul kicked off what Julia called the Great Bread Experiment with typical obsessive intensity.

Perfecting French bread, he found at the outset, was ostensibly a pipedream. Paul wrestled again and again with the overly fussy active ingredients: flour, yeast, water, and salt. Who ever thought that four basic staples could spark such conflict? There were so many factors involved, too many variables in the magic. For the bread to be ideal, it had to hit all the notes of its chief characteristics: "crust, crumb, flavor, and color," and, brother, that was easier said than done. Every baguette Paul made in those early attempts could have been stamped "Louisville Slugger" and shipped to the Red Sox for batting practice. "They were hard and heavy," recalls Judith Jones, who received meticulously packed boxes of his samples in the overnight mail. "I remember opening them up, thinking: 'Oh, dear—*no!*'"

He worked for months trying to perfect a decent specimen without much luck. By May 1967, Julia joined the fray, and independently, each employing their own systems and methods, they conducted "eighteen separate experiments leading toward the development of real French bread." Solving the chemistry of the flour gave them a light, moist crumb, but the outside of their baguettes remained pale and paper-thin. They tried to achieve a golden-brown crust by creating a steamy atmosphere in the oven, which was essential to texture, using every trick in the book. "How to get it and how to regulate it and how much for how long are the bugs in the steam business," Paul reported. A variety of contraptions were devised for just that purpose. First the obvious: a plastic spray bottle used to squirt the loaves proved grossly inadequate. A handful of ice cubes tossed into the oven fared no better. Their "wick system," which consisted of a wet bath towel protruding out of a pan of water, gave off substantially more steam but the crust was obstinate and refused to color. Finally, a wet whisk broom was dragged across the oven grate, to no better result. "We even researched the medieval method of dampening a bundle of straw and throwing it into the oven to keep the air moist," Paul recalled.

Julia got close when she heated an iron weight until it glowed red-hot and then dropped it into a pan of water. But "close" was a pedant's curse. She'd come this far in her work demanding no less than perfection; that baguette recipe had to hit the same peak.

"We'll lick it yet," Paul assured her, but by August he wasn't so sure.

He had done "thirty-one careful experiments, and Julie about the same, and we *still* have not been able to say objectively, '*this is it!*' "

What about Simca? Usually, she would weigh in where there were problems to solve. In her memoir, *My Life in France,* Julia wrote: "Simca had no interest in our breadworks and did not participate at all." But, in fact, it was Simca's resourcefulness that eventually put them over the top. Since 1958, she had been taking breadmaking lessons with a *boulanger* in Bourbonne-les-Bains, turning out dozens, if not hundreds of dozens, of croissants, *flûtes, bâtards,* and baguettes. Whether Julia asked her to help develop a recipe remains unclear. In their correspondence that summer there was a furious exchange of notes on the subject, dealing with flour, leavening, gluten content, and kneading. But there was no real break-through until Simca consulted the oracle.

In her time travels, she had come across the name of Professor Raymond Calvel, the head of the state-run École Professionnelle de Meunerie in Paris and perhaps the world's leading authority on French bread. Calvel had an encyclopedic knowledge of flours and grains and a sculptor's flair for giving them form. Simca suspected he could solve their outstanding problems and arranged a one-day tutorial in December 1967. The moment she learned of this, Julia decided that she would attend.

Calvel's advice was a revelation. It was as if he flipped a switch and suddenly the murky world of French bread zoomed into focus. "Every step in his process was different from anything we had heard of, read about, or seen," Julia recalled. For one thing, she'd been making "too stiff a dough." The mixing, rise, and shaping of loaves had been documented in the definitive *Boulangerie d'aujourd'hui* that had guided her through early experiments, but what inspired Julia most now was how Calvel applied the traditional protocols to the volatile dough.

Usually, Paul added a sprinkling of flour to the dough to make it more pliable and easy to handle. But for a perfect consistency, Calvel explained, the dough had to be sticky enough to create a sponge that would encour-age rapid rising. This usually occurred in a warm, dark place, but Calvel preferred a slow, cool fermentation to develop a riper flavor and maintain humidity. "This seems to be the trick that gives the bread its interesting taste and texture," Julia marveled. He also explained how a gluten cloak enclosed the loaf to protect its shape.

Julia hung on his every word. Calvel's version of the "arcane craft" may have gone against conventional wisdom, but at least it was a version that could be duplicated and taught. During a hands-on session that lasted more than four hours, he guided Julia through the entire process, so that she could "learn through eye, ear, and by [her] own tactile sense." The ultimate goal, of course, was to control all the elements so the bread would achieve the level of taste that Julia felt defined French cooking. "Each of the several steps in the process, though simple to accomplish, plays a critical role," she wrote in a related overview, "and if any is eliminated or combined with another, the texture and taste . . . will suffer."

Raymond Calvel provided the foundation for Julia's fussy standards. With a mix of fondness and contentment, she later recalled how by the end of the day, after "taking copious notes on how the dough should look and feel, and the position of the baker's hands," she began turning out perfect loaves of French bread. They were finer specimens than anything she'd seen in the States and comparable to the Parisian gems. A postcard to Judith Jones, mailed directly from the École, revealed a flush of exuberance in the card's single sentence: "It's all in the shape," which, of course, wasn't the case.

"What was lacking for our perfect loaves," Simca wrote, "was the right heat-and-steam combination." They still had to simulate the baker's oven to accommodate American cooks. "Paul Child's ingenuity finally helped us come up with the gimmick—to drop a hot brick in a pan of water." It worked perfectly, too perfectly, until Julia's niece, Phila, came to visit a few days before the manuscript was due. "I noticed the bricks they put in the oven had asbestos in them," she recalled. The discovery threw the Childs into "a complete tizzy." They'd read the recent warnings about asbestos exposure, how scientists believed it led to mesothelioma, a form of cancer that attacked the outer lining of the lungs. As the clock ticked toward deadline Paul flew madly around Boston ransacking the local building-supply stores, but there was a degree of asbestos in *all* brick. Ultimately, Julia gave her readers a choice: "plopping a heated brick *or a stone* into a pan of water," in addition to lining the oven floor with quarry tiles.

It had taken almost a year "and two hundred-and-eighty-four pounds of flour" to develop the master bread recipe with American ingredients. In the early rush to deliver it, so many mistakes were made. Paul recalled how "things were dropped on the floor, three times too much salt was put in, crusts were burned black, or the bread was only half-baked and the loaves were often rushed into the oven so fast they curled up like crullers." But finally the end results were perfect each time out. Even when

Julia got carried away with tweaks and fillings, the loaves emerged without a flaw. According to Sara Moulton, who assisted Julia later in her career, "what came out of her oven was better than *boulangerie* bread."

The question, now, was whether amateur cooks would actually make their own. Julia needed *operational proof,* in this case from her retinue of volunteer analysts who would test the recipe and offer concise feedback. She needed to know if the directions were coherent, and if her ideal reader, a typical American home cook, could follow them with success.

The verdict was in even before the yeast began to rise.

"I got this package in the mail, about an inch-and-a-half thick," recalls Pat Pratt, Julia's friend and neighbor in Cambridge. It was the final typescript for French bread. "I took one look at it and knew everything had gone bust: the recipe was thirty-two pages long."

BREAD! BREAD! BREAD! The whole of 1967 seemed devoted to the stuff. Baking, in general, seemed so damned ungovernable (a reason, perhaps, that it was Simca's specialty), but once demon bread had been exorcised, everything felt possible. If anything, the twelve months of unpredictability had given Julia and Simca even more perspective on the subject. In early 1968, they kept their ovens on overdrive, cranking out croissants, brioche, pound cake, spice cake, and a showstopper—a meringue-nut layer cake they called *Le Succès.*

Through it all, Julia persevered in her routine. Everything was geared to maintaining a rhythm. In the winter, she holed up in the south of France, away from the public hubbub, where she could bore undisturbed into *Mastering II.* Friends, even those who supported her through the first book, were astonished by the obsessively long hours she put in. (Simca's nephew quipped, "That's probably why Paul's such a grouchy bastard.") Mornings and afternoons were devoted to cooking. Then, after a dinner with guests that stretched long into the night, she retreated to a bedroom, dragged out her Hermès portable typewriter, and transcribed the day's notes into the wee hours of the morning. She had a klatch of pen pals—Judith Jones, Avis DeVoto, James Beard, Ruth Lockwood, her sister Dort—with whom she kept up a running correspondence. Whenever Paul wrote to his brother, she added a few paragraphs. Every so often, she filched an hour or two to work in the garden or steal into Cannes for her weekly hair-do at Elizabeth Arden. No matter what, she was always ready around five o'clock when Paul emerged from his studio—his *cabanon,* as he called it—in time for a reverse martini (one part gin and three parts vermouth) or a tumbler of bourbon.

Julia also kept the reservations book for the revolving-door calendar of frequent houseguests. The most frequent, of course, being James Beard, who came often for long stretches during the winter and summer. From a table on the porch, he worked on recipes and notes for what would become *American Cookery*, to this day considered his *chef-d'œuvre*, and whenever possible he cooked with Julia and Simca, with whom he enjoyed a flirtatious repartee. They also ate like royalty; their table spreads resembled those of the court of Louis XIV at Versailles—whole lobes of foie gras, ortolan, black and white truffles, Iranian caviar—with wines that, by today's standards, would cost $500 or $700 a bottle. M. F. K. Fisher was another of Julia's periodic guests, though at first Julia found her "too self-absorbed" and "didn't warm to her." But Fisher, an eloquent, sensual, *magnificent* interpreter of the culinary landscape, persisted in pursuing a friendship by subordinating herself to Julia's and Jim's distinction, which touched Julia, although the admiration was mutual. "I saw you once on TV and thought you were *exactly* right," Fisher wrote to Julia, breaking the ice, thus insinuating herself in the charmed Bramafam circle.

But once back in the States, Julia wasted no time in attending to a bulging calendar of obligations. In addition to preparing a full slate of new *French Chef* episodes, she also hosted a one-hour documentary special, *The White House Red Carpet*, a behind-the-scenes peek at its kitchen operation during preparations for a state dinner honoring Prime Minister Saito Makoto of Japan. President Johnson, she was told, would not appear, but as Julia and the crew were coming out of the White House flower shop, "a great field of blue" swept along the corridor with a dog in tow. "Mother of God, it's the President," Russ Morash realized, just as he and the blue blur collided belly-to-belly. Today, that would have sparked a code-one Secret Service intervention, but in less spooky times an introduction ensued. Morash recalled: "Johnson merely looked at us as if we were something nasty on his shoe, then at the dog—the same dog that he'd infamously lifted by the ears—and said, 'Come on, Yuki,' before hurrying away." At least the food was more inviting. "The food could not have been any better," Julia declared, much unlike her experience years later, when President Reagan's chef served chipped beef, cream cheese, veal madeleine *en croûte* with mayonnaise, and purple sorbet with canned peaches.

There was hardly time for Julia to appreciate the White House affair as she spun right into a series of high-profile magazine interviews. *The French Chef Cookbook* had thrust her back into the spotlight with a media groundswell that took everyone by surprise. *Ladies' Home Journal, McCall's, Vogue,* all the big-ticket monthlies were clamoring for her time. Just when it seemed that *Mastering* sales were tapering off into a slow but steady flow, *The French Chef Cookbook* came on like a gusher. The first edition—that 100,000 splurge print run that Bob Gottlieb had requisitioned—sold out on release, triggering another huge printing. "We were staggered!" Paul exclaimed in a roundup to his brother. Just the other month, he and Julia had detoured through the Harvard Coop, and saw two enormous stacks of the book forsaken on the floor. "Our hearts sunk," he recalled, "and we thought, 'My God, the poor bastards have got themselves way out on the limb and probably most of those books will have to be remaindered.'"

So much for prophecy. Only four weeks after its release, the cookbook shot onto the *Herald Tribune*'s best-seller list, the first of its kind on the vaunted registry.

The new wave of success got Julia to thinking. This wasn't some over-night sensation that would soon fade. In fact, if the critics were right, if *Mastering* and *The French Chef* were not just groundbreaking but acknowl-edged classics, then their predominance might live on well after Julia and Simca were gone. But in what shape? And to whose benefit? She wanted to avoid the fates that befell *Fannie Farmer* and the *Joy of Cooking.* Both those books were modified by their respective literary executors and watered down to a pale shade of their original editions. "This must not happen to our books," she insisted to Simca. They needed to address the future while they could still control it—perhaps decide who had the same sensibility as they and was qualified to re-edit the manuscript so that it maintained their standards, as well as how subsequent royalties would be dispensed. Even in 1968, at the age of fifty-six, Julia had already planned to leave her share to Smith College. Perhaps because of her mother's strong ties, she felt a deep allegiance to the school that failed her academically and only recently had refused to honor her with the Smith Medal. In any case, she hired a lawyer, Brooks Beck, to protect her interests and urged Simca to do the same.

There was also a wild card they needed to consider: Louisette. She continued to profit from *Mastering the Art of French Cooking,* which was fine by Julia; Louisette was entitled to her 10 percent share. But she remained part owner of the title of the book. Legally, that also gave her and her heirs the right to exploit and determine the future direction of the copyright, and that was *not* fine by Julia, not fine at all. In no way would she sign a contract with Knopf for *Mastering II* until that little road bump had been resolved.

The easiest way to settle it was to buy out Louisette, including all future royalties to *Volume I*. Julia had done some investigating and came up with a reasonable figure: $25,000. Louisette had more like $45,000 in mind, which Julia dismissed out of hand as too high; $30,000 was as high as she would go. In the end, Louisette sought advice from her son-in-law, Arthur Terry, who examined her royalty statements and calculated what she could expect to recoup. "You are at or close to the peak of sales," he explained. "If you sell"—and he was convinced that she should—"this is a good time to do so." In any event, Louisette needed money. She was in tax trouble with the French authorities, but figured out how "she could accept a sum [like this] without being taxed." Finally, she agreed to take the $30,000, which would be paid from the advance of *Mastering II*.

Julia and Simca wasted no time getting their new book back on track. Fueled by a new resolve, they wore out the path between their houses. Recipes they'd been testing for months took on a sudden finished shine: bread, ice cream, custards, soups, even the meat chapters started to gel. If the work continued apace, they could deliver a draft of the manuscript by year's end: *on time*.

Invigorated by the progress, Julia flew back to Cambridge for some unfinished TV business. A spirited voice-over was all that was needed to wrap up the White House documentary, after which she'd return to La Pitchoune for the final thrust. Before she left, however, there was time to squeeze in her annual gynecological exam, specifically to examine a small lump in her breast.

She called her friend Pat Pratt with the results later that day. "I've got breast cancer," she told Pratt matter-of-factly. "I'm going to have an operation."

A biopsy had revealed a mass of malignant cells in Julia's left breast and the doctor was worried about it spreading to the lymph nodes. The tumor was small, but he wasn't about to take any chances. Out of caution, he intended to perform a mastectomy.

"What a nuisance!" Julia huffed, informing Simca of her upcoming operation.

A nuisance! She might have been talking about a dough that refused to rise. "Julia refused to let health matters faze her," Pat Pratt explains.

"She treated herself like a car; if you had a flat tire you went and fixed it." Paul, on the other hand, envisioned a head-on collision. "He convinced himself she wouldn't make it through the operation and worked himself into an awful froth."

Paul had been burdened by death his entire life. His letters are filled with doomsday prophecies about his health and safety, not that the anxiety was completely unwarranted. Considering the fates of his family and friends, he had little hope to go on: his father's sudden death during Paul's infancy, the loss of lover Edith Kennedy to cancer at an early age, Bernard DeVoto, his mother and sister—all gone too soon. A friend from his government days, seemingly healthy, had recently dropped dead, and his brother Charlie's routine prostate exam sparked a new wave of fear. Following his own colonoscopy, Paul wrote: "One always feels that the doctor has made some dread error, pierced the peritoneum, and that the agony will continue until death releases one, finally." He was obsessed with dying, naturally and otherwise. Flying anywhere was out of the question due to his certainty that an airborne trip would end in fiery carnage. Simple aches and pains evolved into gruesome afflictions. In early 1968, while in France, Paul consulted his doctor about a stiff shoulder and was relieved at the diagnosis. "That angina pectoris running across my chest and down both arms to my little fingers . . . is a form of neuralgia," he exulted, "*not* my heart, *not* muscular dystrophy, *not* polio, *not* tuberculosis, *not* a circulatory impediment, not *death* waiting just beyond the door to kill me in agony." Just in case, he added: "Not today, anyway."

One can imagine how he twisted Julia's operation into certain death. The slightest rise in her temperature brought on a nightmarish vigil. "Death and degeneration sat on my chest like twin ghouls," he wrote, "and I had a white night in spite of a double dose of sleeping pills: planning the funeral, the disposition of La Pitchoune and of our house in Cambridge, who to send the necessary telegrams to, the problems of whether the ashes would better be buried in the Plascassier cemetery, in Pasadena, in Cambridge, or simply scattered somewhere." He couldn't control what he knew were his "damn-fool emotions."

By comparison, Julia was bloodless. "Left breast off" was the solitary notation in her datebook for February 28, 1968. To others, she was similarly stoic. "I'm going to get a false titty and I'll have to wear a plastic sleeve on my arm," she told a friend, "*and I'm going to be fine,* dearie." Simple as that. It wasn't grandstanding; Julia believed it with absolute certainty.

She was an incurable optimist—strong enough for two. "Whenever Paul began to brood about her certain death," says Pat Pratt, "she immediately changed the subject." Death wasn't going to creep anywhere near her. She wouldn't hear of it, she wouldn't allow it.

To Paul's utter amazement, the operation was a success. Julia came through it with flying colors: the cancer "wasn't life-threatening," according to the post-op report. It was crucial, however, that her lymph nodes not swell, which required endless months of physical therapy to rehabilitate her arm. Cooking became a huge pain in the ass—and exhausting: it took the steam out of her pipes. The fatigue and the sleepless nights were beginning to take their toll. Four months later, Julia still wasn't her old self. Avis DeVoto visited La Pitchoune in May and "was a bit taken aback" by her friend's appearance. Others thought Julia looked "very tired and depleted." Convinced that only work would reverse her condition, she plowed whatever was left in her tank back into cooking.

For the next year and a half, Julia worked like a dog, plying recipe after recipe to fatten the body of Volume II. It was a full-time job. She and Simca cooked around the clock, seven days a week, no time off for good behavior. Judith Jones had made it absolutely clear that Knopf intended to publish the book in 1970, no excuses, and the pressure was intense that the women meet the deadline: March 15, 1970. "They'd been working on the book for three years," Jones recalls, "and it seemed like, unchecked, they could continue long into the next century." Julia admitted they could use five more years. There was no time in the schedule for such indulgence. Especially since only three of eleven chapters were complete. Five years became five months, just like that, and the clock began ticking.

The deadline crunch gave new license to Julia's old nemesis. Simca, who had been stewing privately ever since a *House & Garden* contingent visited Plascassier for an article on the forthcoming book and basically ignored her in favor of Julia, vented her resentment through familiar passive-aggressive behavior. "This is nothing new, of course," Paul observed during their sessions at Bramafam, "but the difficulties seem more aggravated this year than last."

It was a constant struggle.

"Simca simply would not listen to anything I had to say," Julia recalled. "La Super-Française," as the Childs dubiously nicknamed her, cooked straight through the recipes, refusing to acknowledge any contribution Julia made. The precise measurements, the detailed notes, the scientific research, the operational proof—all went out the window during their trials down the homestretch. "Deep down, Simca has never been convinced that all the accuracy and measurement is anything but a crazy American idea," Avis DeVoto observed. Lately, in fact, Simca seemed almost to take a perverse pleasure in flouting Julia's orderly process. When she tossed a fistful of salt into a bisque it was tantamount to lobbing a grenade—and she knew it. Adding ingredients that were not in a recipe—a way to assert her leverage. Discussions about method erupted into florid scenes, Simca's voice leaping tall octaves in a single bound, "going on and on, floods of French" swooshing around the kitchen, Julia bleating "*oui, oui, oui* at intervals," if for no reason other than to calm Simca down.

Paul would shut himself in his room or move out to the *cabanon* to avoid the uproar, but a blustery backlash usually sifted through the walls. "Do it *this* way! Do it *that* way!" He tried to ignore the arabesques of Simca's harsh voice. "No-no-no-no! Impossible!" *Am-pah-seeb-luh!* It was maddening. He fought to take into account her generosity and creativity, but confessed, "I would strangle her if I were in Julia's position."

Even the Atlantic Ocean wasn't vast enough to stanch the divide. Simca's letters to Julia, now back in Cambridge, grew more critical, demanding, strident—*am-pah-seeb-luh*. Recipes that had been fully tested and approved for publication were suddenly sabotaged by last-minute irrational scrutiny. "*Ce n'est pas français!*" became an incessant mantra. "*Ce n'est pas français!*" "*Ce n'est pas français!*" The phrase made Julia want to pull out her hair. "I can remember—more than once—visiting in Cambridge when she opened one of Simca's long-winded letters and got angrier and angrier as she read through the pages," recalls Judith Jones. "Simca was so difficult and condescending. The hauteur—it was unbearable. '*Non, non, non—ce n'est pas français!*' We were idiots in the kitchen." One such missive was so infuriating that, after reading it aloud, Julia exploded. "I will not be treated like a dog!" she declared, balling up the letter and banking it into the bin.

As the deadline approached, Simca could no longer hide the real reason for her behavior—either from Julia or from herself. She was sliding into an ominous depression. Since early 1969, a series of misfortunes had been piling up on her. First, a kitchen mishap with a broken bottle sliced through a major tendon between her thumb and index finger. Despite an operation, it had never healed properly, causing numbness and limiting the use of her hand. Soon afterward, she learned of a chronic heart condition, which her doctor said would require a pacemaker. On top of that, she was becoming progressively deaf and wasn't responding to physical therapy. Her hips were giving her trouble, necessitating painful injections. And just for good measure, her husband Jean's new business was faltering, which added undue stress to the health issues.

Julia had a rare intimate talk with her before *Mastering II*'s publication and found La Super-Française feeling vulnerable and scared. "She feels that Fate is closing in on her," Julia told Paul. Nothing was turning out the way Simca had expected. There was even an outside chance that she might have to cancel upcoming plans to promote the book's publication in the States in the fall. A heart specialist in Paris would deliver the final verdict, but either way Simca was already plying the gloom. She'd been looking forward to that trip for all the obvious reasons, but also to show Americans that *Mastering* wasn't just Julia Child's book.

For some time, Simca had felt shunted to the background in this affair, playing second fiddle to Julia's star turn. The *House & Garden* episode was only the tip of the iceberg. Every journalist who came through Bramafam was looking for Julia. Every article she read featured Julia as its focus. It was Julia who was closest to Judith Jones, Julia who hung out with James Beard, Craig Claiborne, and Avis DeVoto. *Julia, Julia, Julia*—the TV star, the French chef. You'd think the cookbook had been her idea alone. Really, who was Julia Child to demand she cook a certain way? Page after page of niggling notes and instructions. It was demeaning for someone with Simca's expertise. Hadn't she taught Julia all the secret Beck family recipes? Hadn't Simca allowed her to build a house on Fischbacher land? It seemed easy to see how the resentment had grown.

Julia did nothing to help reduce this bitterness when she broached the subject of changing their fifty-fifty royalty split. "One thing we have never taken into consideration at all is my role in publicizing the book," she wrote to Simca. Ever since Julia looked over the full sweep of Knopf sales figures, a disparity rankled. There were times when it appeared that *Mastering* had run its course, only to be revived by *The French Chef* television series in 1963 and the *Time* cover story in 1966. The way she viewed it, the extra exposure exclusively promoted the book, and in every case, sales shot from a couple of hundred copies each month to several thousand. Not that the book didn't deserve the attention on its own merits. But it had been "a tremendous amount of work" for her, "almost without stopping." It seemed only fair that her efforts be taken into account with regard to future royalties. "If you hired an agent to do this work of promotion," Julia argued, "you would have to pay a minimum of thirty or forty percent of your profits for this kind of publicity."

If Simca had been stewing privately since the *House & Garden* article, she was at a full boil now. The request to alter their agreement was like a slap in the face. A visitor to Bramafam remembers how Simca "pored over the details of Julia's letter" as if it were an eviction notice. Periodically she rattled off lines from it that, in stinging French, seemed to emphasize the underlying selfishness and lack of generosity. "There was no end to the indignities she had to endure," the guest said, recalling how agitated Simca became over every perceived slight. Even the mocked-up book jacket for *Mastering II* had Julia's name first, not in alphabetical order. "Why not eliminate me completely?" she grumbled. "It's as if I don't exist."

NO MATTER, *MASTERING II* was shaping up to be another blockbuster. Its publication on October 22, 1970, was "heralded like the second coming" and the ensuing hoopla did much to ease Simca's discontent. She arrived in New York in time to join Julia for "a very swish affair" for 250 given in their honor at the Ford Foundation's mansion on the East Side. "*Le tout New York*" toasted them with icy flutes of Moët, followed by a buffet that featured the highlights from their book. The party was the perfect kickoff to the main event, although Simca, radiantly sheathed in a black silk dress with red chiffon scarf, observed circumspectly that "Julia was a celebrity."

Knopf had pulled out all the stops for the book launch. There was a first printing of 100,000 copies, with so many advance orders that a second run of 50,000 had already gone to press. The reviews were uniformly ecstatic, drawing apt comparisons to *Mastering I.* Gael Greene, writing in *Life,* called it "utterly intoxicating" and said, "No serious scholar of the kitchen will want to function without it." *Newsweek,* aflutter with breathy rapture, actually elbowed Volume I aside, claiming: "[Volume II] is without rival, the finest gourmet cookbook for the non-chef in the history of American stomachs." A burst of accolades rose from within the ranks of the culinary world: James Beard, Dione Lucas, and Craig Claiborne joined the growing hallelujah chorus. *McCall's* debuted its three-part cover story of Julia and Simca to coincide with publication, and, as a hedge against disaster, PBS began airing a new long-awaited season of *The French Chef*—in color, for the first time, with a new kitchen set "and a plethora of unbridled *joie de vivre!*"

There was so much anticipation for the show, in fact, that WGBH pressured Julia to get back to work, pumping new episodes of her series into the pipeline. They made no secret of the fact that her viewers were major PBS contributors and, in case she needed extra incentive, major book buyers. But Julia was in no hurry to meet the station's demands. More enticing, Knopf had set up a modest book tour for her. Actually it was Knopf's first book tour of any kind, considering the majority of its authors "were neither living nor breathing." As such, author promotion wasn't anything they'd ever given thought to. But an aggregate of PBS stations from around the country had called, asking Julia to do promos for the show and an assistant figured out how best to tie that to the book.

Jane Becker had come to the publisher two years earlier in the management shake-up that brought Bob Gottlieb to Knopf. She was only twenty-two; Judith Jones, who was now in her forties, was the next youngest executive to her at the house. But, like Jones, Becker had decided to speak up at an editorial meeting and was being given a chance—or some rope; it all depended on how her idea turned out. She proposed to send Julia, this time on Knopf's tab, to several cities where there were PBS affiliates and thriving department stores. "The TV people could host a cocktail party for her in the evening," recalls Jane, who as Jane Friedman later headed HarperCollins. "The department store would take out a full-page ad announcing Julia was coming, then the next morning she'd do a demo in their auditorium. In between, we'd do some local television and newspaper interviews. With luck, maybe we'd sell some books."

They decided to road test her idea in Minneapolis, at Dayton's department store, in November 1970. The night before the first demonstration, Julia, Paul, and Jane huddled in the lobby of their hotel across the street from Dayton's to go over a few last-minute details. "You know, nobody may show up tomorrow," Jane warned them. "I'd be very disappointed, but that's the reality. And if it happens, that'll be okay. We'll go into bookstores and sign books." Julia wanted to know how many copies of *Mastering II* were in the city. "About five hundred," Jane responded. Julia, she recalled, intended to sign every one.

The next morning, Jane got up early, in plenty of time to wake her author. The demo was scheduled for 8 a.m. in Dayton's famous revolving Sky's Restaurant, before the store opened for business at nine. At seven she glanced outside and immediately dialed Julia's room. "My God! Look out your window," she said.

Julia threw open her blinds. There was a queue down the block, what could have been a thousand women waiting to get inside.

The same thing happened at one of their next stops, Columbus, Ohio, where the Lazarus department store couldn't accommodate all the people who had come. Instead, at the last minute, they rented a theater down the block where, from a hydraulic lift hidden below the stage, Julia rose up through the floor like Venus to the crowd's wild delight.

In Cleveland, at Halle's department store, Julia's sense of mischief emerged. During a presentation for making homemade mayonnaise—her go-to demo for most of the tour—Julia eyed a store display of pots and pans just behind her. "How wonderful of Halle's to put these up here," she said, "so I can tell you *never, never* buy a pot like this." Without further ado, she picked up a pot, inspected it skeptically, and flung it over a shoulder onto the floor behind her—one by one until the entire display was scattered in a heap.

Julia had a Harry Houdini–like power over her audiences—and was eager to use it. "She became a dynamo once the lights hit her and the applause kicked in," Jane Friedman recalls. "I'd never experienced anything like it before—or since. More than anyone I've ever met, Julia was a true star."

She loved being in front of a live audience, *loved* it. But the book signings, most of all, were her payoff on the road. She planted herself at a desk next to Paul, while long lines formed with fans clutching both volumes of *Mastering,* and made sure she had a word or two with everyone who greeted her. "It became personal," Jane recalls. Julia would hold on to a book that someone handed her to sign, while she asked them something about themselves that humanized the encounter. "And what are *you* making for dinner tonight, dearie?" was one of her favorite icebreakers. Or: "Tell me, dearie, what dish do you enjoy cooking most?"

No feigned interest, no brush-off. She looked them right in the eye.

Occasionally, someone she'd met before would greet her and say, "You once told me to tie a veal roast in caul fat" or "You said it was okay to use bittersweet chocolate instead of semi-sweet in the Queen of Sheba recipe." Instead of trying to recall the conversation, Julia would say, "And how did *that* turn out?"

She was fast on her feet.

"I wasn't surprised that she could handle the crowds," says Jane Friedman. "She was a natural. Here she was too tall, gawky, squeaky voiced, not what you would call a pretty woman, and who had just had a mastectomy. But put the camera on her, and, man, she was a superstar."

After a few weeks on the road, Julia staggered back to Cambridge in time for the holidays—more than a star: "a kind of Public Property," a household name.

Julia and Paul lunching alfresco in Plascassier, Provence, May 6, 1970

Twenty-one

We Are Not All Eternal

The distinguished couple that stared into their plates at Lucas Carton on rue de la Madeleine one evening in September 1974 was flabbergasted by what they saw. On one lay six tiny slices of blood-rare pigeon pinwheeled like drops on a Miró canvas atop a bed of tender turnip rounds, a tang of anise rising off the surface. The other featured a cluster of roe-dusted lobster meat artfully arranged on a mound of spinach and watercress and drizzled with—could it be?—*vanilla* sauce. Around them other diners were *tsk-tsk*ing over similar concoctions. *Rouget* with black olives, capers, and lemon slices sauced with nothing but warm olive oil infused with *herbes de Provence*. *Loup de mer*—sea bass—wrapped in green lettuce leaves, barely cooked salmon in a satiny sorrel sauce. Julia and Paul looked at each other through scimitar eyes. What in the name of Escoffier was going on here?

Quite obviously, the chef had gone mad. But then all of Paris seemed to have gone mad for a folly they were calling *la nouvelle cuisine*.

No one seemed to enjoy it less than Julia and Paul. But only a week before, since arriving from the States, they had made the rounds of their beloved standbys. Le Restaurant des Artistes, where old Mangelatte came out of the kitchen to personally serve them *sole meunière*, was "no more, alas." La Méditerranée, on place de l'Odéon, was "slowly going downhill." Chez la Mère Michel, where Julia first learned the secret for *beurre blanc*, was disappointing and they "sadly crossed her off the list."

Michaud was dated, Brasserie Lipp a tourist trap, the riotous Les Halles now, *egad,* a cavernous construction site. Even at Le Grand Véfour, where they "always got the royal treatment," they now got food poisoning and swore off going back. It seemed only fair to try one of the temples of *nouvelle cuisine.* But even though they'd heard plenty about the revolution going on, the skirmish on the plates took them by surprise.

Nouvelle's flourishes announced to an unprepared dining public that chefs had arrived. For years—*decades*—the masters of restaurant kitchens cooked classic French dishes exactly the way they'd been codified by Escoffier at the turn of the century. That was the unwritten law: "according to Escoffier." It was unthinkable to vary the formulas, and no one dared question them. So, in effect, a chef produced *poularde Albuféra* at a brasserie in the Latin Quarter or at an *autogrille* on the A-1 motorway using the same ingredients and technique as the chef at La Tour d'Argent, and, as such, each toiled in virtual obscurity.

No more. Chefs became the *auteurs.* Like many waves of innovation, *nouvelle cuisine* sprang from the restlessness and disillusionment that sparked the cultural uprisings of the 1960s. In Paris, especially, orthodoxy was deemed corrupt, conformity a malignance. The *enfants terribles* of French cinema—Godard, Truffaut, Resnais, and Chabrol—had already made that clear. They broke all the rules with *la nouvelle vague,* rejecting classical forms by putting their personal signatures on the films they made, to great approbation.

In essence, they were the role models for a gang of disgruntled chefs who were raring to cut loose. Paul Bocuse, Pierre and Jean Troisgros, Louis Outhier, Alain Senderens, Roger Vergé, and Raymond Oliver, among others, abandoned the strictures of classic *haute cuisine* in favor of a less rigid cooking style that showed off their extraordinary artistry. Heavy cream sauces and overworked recipes were replaced with imagination and ingenuity. Fresh flavors were emphasized, new combinations encouraged. The revolutionary concept, this *nouvelle cuisine,* called for far lighter and more delicate fare—a white wine reduction, say, instead of flour and butter and cream, an infused oil, maybe, instead of, well, flour and butter and cream. Sauces *underneath* instead of obscuring the main attraction. Perhaps Asian accents, more spices and herbs; vegetables cooked only long enough to release their flavor, crisp to the bite. Dishes still acknowledged the Escoffier canon—the basic sauces, the *fumets,* the mousses, the *glaces de viande*—but also the personality of the chef, the anonymous toiler, who finally stepped out from behind the stove to acclaim himself.

It was a liberating moment in the annals of French culinary history. Chefs swept centuries of tradition aside and elaborate new preparations burst from their kitchens. Suddenly there were no rules, just foundations on which to build, using one's own intuitive gifts. After a brief period of unchecked anarchy, lorded over by the dour but supremely gifted Bocuse, the new movement coalesced around the proposition that French food, when inventively cooked, was not at the mercy of unique rules and ingredients; it was the means by which to *explore* unique rules and ingredients.

A pair of food writers—Henri Gault and Christian Millau—were the engines of the new movement. They published a manifesto committed to challenging the system fortified by Michelin, "the bastion of culinary conservatism" and the "pompous stars" it awarded to temples of *haute cuisine*. Gault-Millau had little interest in the perceived excellence of Michelin's three-star *corps d'élite*. They didn't want to celebrate dishes of the old masters; they wanted chefs to reinvent them: not absurdly, not by painting a mustache and goatee on the *Mona Lisa,* as the Surrealists had done, but with craft and subtlety, by pairing sole, say, with a wild mushroom reduction or even fruit, ingredients that *complemented* each other in new and exciting ways. They seized on the idea that there was a vast, untapped reservoir of talent in French kitchens that needed to be unleashed and encouraged to experiment and improvise. A chef who could liberate a recipe from heaviness, rigidity, and excessive complication would produce dishes that reflected a modern lifestyle. To make their point, Gault-Millau began publishing *Le Nouveau Guide* in 1973, identifying forty-eight practitioners of *nouvelle cuisine* who they believed could lead France into a new age of gastronomy and spur countless others to follow their toques.

"Up with the new French cuisine," they wrote in their introductory issue. "It is bursting with health, good sense, and good taste! . . . No more of those terrible brown sauces and white sauces, those *espagnoles,* those Périgueux with truffles, those *béchamels* and Mornays that have assassinated as many livers as they have covered indifferent foods. Down with veal stock, and down with red wine, Madeira, pig's blood, *roux,* gelatin, and flour in all sauces, and with cheese and starches. They are forbidden!"

By the following year, *nouvelle cuisine* had left its defiant imprint on the French restaurant scene. Most important head chefs, however hesitant or reluctant, had made some foray into the new expressive approach. Even if it meant nothing more than adding a leaf or two of fresh basil to an Escoffier-enshrined recipe, the act itself felt as rebellious and exciting as an adulterous kiss. In the rush to experiment, chefs sometimes got carried away, combining ingredients that were downright nutty. Kiwi fruit turned up in too many dishes. "I have heard of truffles served with lime ice," Craig Claiborne reported, "of grapes and other fruit served with sauerkraut in a red-wine sauce; ravioli stuffed with snails and peaches." There was plenty of room for error and forgiveness, but exquisite creations happened more often than not. After being tied to Escoffier's apron strings for years and years, chefs flexed their muscles in such a way that, for the most part, showcased their great ambitions and sensuous power.

Not everyone was appreciative or amused. Defenders of *haute cuisine*—and they were legion—deplored what they saw as *nouvelle*'s lack of discipline and unchecked improvisation. Purists like Simca dismissed its recipes as *ce n'est pas français*. To James Beard, it was "an indulgent hodgepodge." Jacques Pépin blamed it for "destroying the repertoire and nomenclature of French cooking." Others denounced it as "the worst thing to have happened to the entire culture of good cooking since the invention of the can opener."

Julia, for the most part, kept her opinions to herself. Her formal culinary training was entirely *haute,* but she looked at it always from an American point of view. "When it came to food, her sole criterion was good cooking," says Jasper White, the Boston chef who later befriended Julia. Still, it was clear the *nouvelle* concept bewildered her. "Is it a hoax, a public-relations snow job?" she wondered. "Does a new cuisine really exist in France?" She wasn't prepared to say. As far as she could tell, it wasn't "a cuisine without the fundamentals, without training in the basics." There were aspects, however, that were worthy of her opinion. "I don't like crunchily underdone vegetables," she objected. The same with meat that was "blood-red and then blue-raw at the bone." Besides, she was tired of going to a ridiculously expensive restaurant only to be served "the ubiquitous seafood poached with a julienne of carrots, celery, leeks, and a sliver or two of truffle." That was pipsqueak food, nothing that would satisfy Julia Child. You want to invite her out to dinner, make sure it's a place where she can dig into *œufs en gelée* flanked by a chunk of *pâté,* followed by a well-sauced haunch of meat and a stinky cheese course before dessert. And, brother, don't forget "a big dollop of thick French cream" on top of that tart.

"All this beating of poor old Escoffier over the head," she clucked sadly. It was shameful to see him discredited by young culinary mavericks, especially when they owed everything they knew to the master. Still, Julia had enormous respect for some of *nouvelle cuisine*'s brightest practitioners. The dour Bocuse was, by her measure, "a marvelous *marvelous* cook," and no praise was too effusive for Roger Vergé's "great skill in the kitchen." Both men were insatiably curious. The worst fate that could befall a chef, in Julia's estimation, was to "grow stale and jaded"—to become a chef who sacrificed "his own pleasure" in exchange for the safety of a steady clientele.

To some extent, Julia was emulating the young Turks. She had recently brought two mainstays of her career to a decisive end: her writing partnership with Simca ("No More!" she declared. "End of collaboration!") and *The French Chef* TV series, which had run its course. After eight years, the demanding shooting schedule had finally grown tiresome—and stale. "It's just too confining," she explained to Judith Jones, "and we are really prisoners, unable to do anything else." It was time for Julia to explore new possibilities—to take what she had done with French cooking and apply it to new realms.

But *what*? She wasn't sure. There was another book on the horizon, one of her own, without Simca. Perhaps a few TV specials in tandem with Jim Beard. Promisingly, ABC had offered her a prime time slot for a weekday morning show at a beyond-prime salary, but Julia turned it down, convinced that "all is for housewives in the daytime and that's not our audience."

Almost immediately the vultures started circling. Julia's old nemesis Madeleine Kamman got in touch right away. "Rumor has it that you are retiring," she wrote, hiding behind the all-too-transparent premise that the life goal of one of her assistants was to replace Julia at WGBH. In fact, Paul had already learned from contacts at the station that Kamman was "spreading stories that 'poor Julia Child has had a bad operation and can't possibly continue her *French Chef* program.'" Apparently, she'd made other calls to WGBH, spread other rumors bad-mouthing Julia, in the hope that one day she'd fill Julia's sizable TV shoes. When a particularly vexing story got back to Julia, she wrote a cautionary letter to her new lawyer: "[Kamman's] former story about me was that I was mortally ill, and dying. When I didn't die, she evidently decided to change it to the story that I was an alcoholic." This needed to be documented, Julia thought, in case it got out of hand. She also warned Simca, who had her own troubles with Kamman. "She is a trouble maker, an immense egocentric, and I think one should keep as far away from her as possible, always remaining polite, but remote."

Taking a page from her own playbook, Julia responded to Kamman's query with acid charm. "Thanks for your letter, and your concern about my 'imminent retirement,'" she wrote. "Neither Paul nor I believe in retirement, so you shall be seeing us around in one guise or another at least until the year 2001."

Julia could handle this difficult woman; still, the dispute upset her. There was plenty to be said in Madeleine Kamman's defense. She had grown up cooking, working hard in the trenches, living the life of a serious cook. Both Julia and Paul thought Kamman was "an excellent cook" who deserved wide acclaim. And word had it that she was a damn good teacher. When she opened her cooking school close by, in Newton, Julia gladly sent her a proprietary list of cooks in the Boston area who might throw some business Madeleine's way and promised to visit as soon as her schedule allowed. (This, despite credible reports that Kamman advised her students "to throw [*Mastering*] away or not to buy it because it was not authentic.") But Julia would no longer pretend a personal friendship where one had once rooted. From now on, not even Kamman's name would be spoken; she was reduced to a figure of speech: "that woman from Newton."

In any event, after wrapping up the last seventy-two shows, the ones shot in color, Julia turned her attention to a new pet project. There was demand for a sequel to *The French Chef Cookbook,* both from viewers who appreciated the easier, more informal lessons and from Knopf, which had sold a ton—*a ton*—of books. Drawing recipes predominantly from the final color shows, the book allowed Julia to spread her wings, veering outside the confines of strictly regional French cooking, while adhering to the French *approach.* So there was breathing room in its pages for crowd-pleasers like New England chowders, Belgian cookie doughs, curries, and pasta; for ingredients such as soy sauce and provolone cheese; as well as allowances for the microwave, the food processor, and the pressure cooker—all of which would have touched off a firestorm of *ce n'est pas français* a year earlier.

At least that monkey was off her back. In fact, Simca had her own book deal at Knopf, for a collection of old family recipes—*la véritable cuisine française,* as she put it, or "the true French cuisine"—and it was no small coincidence that Judith Jones agreed to edit it. With Simca busy working on her own opus, Julia could concentrate on flying solo for a change.

She began by deconstructing the shows, taking a master recipe that she'd perfected and seeing how multiple variations would alter it; making a modest poached salmon in a white-wine stock, for instance, and afterward flaking the fish into a pastry shell, adding three eggs, enough cream, some dill and parsley, and a sprinkling of Swiss cheese to produce a luscious quiche. Retreating from the rigid scholarship of the *Mastering* format, she turned to the chatty informality of a cooking school. Yes, *a private cooking school.* Just Julia and the reader noodling around in the kitchen—Julia Child's kitchen, to be exact—making something wonderful to eat. No need to call it *The French Chef Cookbook, Volume II.* That sounded too indistinguishable, too stuffy. Better it should be *From Julia Child's Kitchen.*

Julia took the opportunity to stretch out a bit, throwing an anecdote or a personal travel story in with a lesson. There, among the recipes for cheese soufflé and roast leg of lamb was a descriptive reenactment of that first lunch in Rouen at Restaurant La Couronne, of the characters at the Criée aux Poissons in Marseille, where she learned to make bouillabaisse, and a sampling of the hate mail she received for her method of killing lobsters, which, as a result, she now did in a more humane way. It was a refreshing experience for Julia, who, since college, had always wanted to write compelling narrative. For years, she'd always claimed that writing a recipe was demanding, an all-day affair, similar to writing "a little short story that you have to convey to the reader," but the book gave her the opportunity to take it one step further, blending in personal experiences with what one reviewer called "feisty prose."

Occasionally, Julia just let it rip. In one anecdote, she recalled meeting "a quite nutty woman" in the fruitcake section of her supermarket who explained how she cooked green beans according to Julia's technique *only on weekends,* while the rest of the week she used another chef's recipe (Julia deleted the culprit's name), boiling them for fifteen minutes so she could "be sure of getting all my vitamins." Rather than dismissing the woman as a crackpot, Julia, ever the empiricist, went home and put the process through the paces, ending up with "gray, color-bleached, taste-leached, miserable beans." She was disgusted, and characteristically blunt. "Anyone . . . who cons the public into acceptance of such culinary balderdash deserves to be disposed of, bit by bit, in an electric super-blender-food-processor."

The manuscript quickly developed into a more accessible tool—to teach, of course, but also to entertain. It was another way for Julia to engage people who were still scared off by the complexity of French cuisine. And as a result, she said close to the end of her career, "it was my most personal book," as well as her favorite.

She was working almost single-mindedly on the manuscript in September 1974, after she and Paul returned from Europe. Paris and Provence had been lovely, but too distracting. Jim Beard showed up, overweight and broken down, a sad figure, necessitating more hand-holding than usual. And their daily routine was interrupted by a steady stream of visitors.

Among the increasingly frequent guests who came to dinner at both Le Mas Vieux and La Pitchoune was Richard Olney, the forty-seven-year-old ex-pat artist and food writer, who lived hermit-like in a nearby mountaintop aerie. Julia had first met Olney in 1972, shortly after the publication of *The French Menu Cookbook,* his inspired collection of seasonal recipes and the first, perhaps, to introduce wine pairings with each dish. Julia said later: "He writes brilliantly, not a misplaced word." And his cooking, she felt, was "entirely honest, entirely serious." They had sampled it at his place in the village of Solliès-Toucas, which was no easy feat for aging adults. Their visit necessitated a steep trip up a rock-laden sheep trail on the edge of an abandoned quarry. But the setting was magical: a picture-perfect garden, a gorgeous arbor with grapes hanging overhead among the wisteria, a picnic table set impeccably with hand-pressed linens. Olney always received visitors in the same eccentric attire, wearing nothing but an unbuttoned shirt over Speedo bathing trunks and frayed espadrilles, which defined him.

He was a man who wore his odd identity oddly. In the fifties in Paris, where he hung out with James Baldwin, John Ashbery, and Kenneth Anger, Olney had been a promising protégé, neither conspicuous nor acclaimed; alone, in Solliès, he was a "genius," a badge he wore with conceit. In any milieu, he was a complex, difficult man—"a purist, a perfectionist, a sensualist," says Paul Grimes, who assisted Olney in Solliès, "but also cynical, bitter about people with pretensions toward food." He referred incessantly to the art of cooking—the *art*—which only the true artist was capable of understanding, and very few practitioners fit his idea of that archetype. Not M. F. K. Fisher, whom he found "sweet but essentially empty-headed with no palate . . . and her writing silly, pretentious drivel." And not James Beard, whom he liked personally but considered "irrelevant" as a cook. With regard to Julia, Olney was treacherous. Socially, he was outgoing toward her when their paths crossed in

Provence, but there was little about her that he liked or tolerated. He described her in his diary as "very bitchy" and considered the Childs "bitter," "destructive," and "irrationally anti-French."

At the outset, Julia had been "dying to meet him," having heard from Simca and others about Olney's exquisite culinary skills. She'd also read the manuscript for his new book, *Simple French Food,* which she found, like most others who came to admire it, "a remarkable achievement." But he brushed off several of her invitations to dinner with curt, almost dismissive replies. Bowing at last to overtures from his friend Simca, Olney could no longer resist without offending Julia, but the encounter, at La Pitchoune, left much to be desired. While most Americans were deferential, even reverent, toward Julia, Olney remained standoffish, if not insolent. He smoked Gauloises ceaselessly, drank scotch compulsively, both of which advanced his "nervous, high-strung" state. Neither Julia nor Paul found they could warm to him. "He is so self-engrossed, self-protective, self-laudatory that he has almost no outgoingness," Paul observed. Paul grew tired of listening to Olney "run down almost everything"—people, music, places, weather, architecture, there seemed to be nothing this poor guy found rewarding or desirable. Nor was Paul impressed by Olney's scene-making exploits in Paris; he'd been there himself thirty years before, often in more stimulating company.

Even so, Paul and Julia kept any resentment to themselves. Olney's prowess as a cook—and Simca's high regard for him—counted more than first impressions. They were willing to maintain cordial relations out of recognition for his growing influence and his importance in the community. Casting personal misgivings aside, in a particularly gracious gesture they invited him to stay *chez* Child in Cambridge, when his upcoming book tour took him through Boston.

Little did they know at the time that he'd accept—or that his visit, in the fall of 1974, would coincide with a cataclysmic event.

IN GENERAL, PAUL CHILD was a pretty cranky guy. Having spent a good chunk of his life babysitting schoolboys and bureaucratic drones, he had always been impatient, short-tempered, and caustic with those he considered vulgarians. He didn't suffer fools gladly or otherwise, a trait that earned him a good deal of antipathy. There was also an element of frustration to his nature that could best be illustrated by an encounter with a journalist.

The writer, on assignment from *TV Guide,* had been wandering around the Irving Street house, when she paused to admire the array of wood-carvings, etchings, woodcuts, and oil paintings that covered most of the living room walls. She lingered in front of a brooding forest landscape of slender trees submerged in pools of water. "All are by a painter who is a master of his craft," she noted. "Whose are they?" Hesitantly, Paul admitted they were his. "Why has no one written about you?" she asked. He smiled ruefully. "They don't see me. They only see Julia."

"You could tell upon meeting him that he'd once been the center of attention," says Sheryl Julian, the longtime food editor of the *Boston Globe,* "and he didn't quite know how to grab it back." Not that Paul really tried to the extent that it became an issue. But Julian was convinced it made him "ornery, grumpy."

It also still rankled that he got short-changed after high school, when Charlie got sent to Harvard. "Paul was really the intellectual of the two, he had a wonderful mind, but was forced to educate himself," says Pat Pratt. "And Charlie became a professional artist, while Paul, who was really much better, had to work a desk job. And I think it really got to him."

His irascibility seemed to build that summer. Pratt noticed it during a trip to Venice, where she and her husband, Herb, shared a suite with the Childs. The couples often traveled together; they knew each other inside and out. The Pratts were neighbors in Cambridge: Pat was another tall Smith alumna close to Julia; Paul had known Herb's brother, Davis, in Paris, and enjoyed the fact that they were twins, like him and Charlie. "So I could tell right away that he was out-of-sorts," Pratt says.

The nosebleeds were another sign that something was wrong. Paul had a series of them in July, in Provence, which Julia knew was "not normal." His left arm hurt constantly, which he attributed to lifting suitcases so often. And his sleep cycle was a mess, a turbulent nighttime grind in which he would "struggle awake to fight for air, heart pounding from adrenaline." Because they had separate bedrooms, Paul could hide this phenomenon from Julia, but she knew he was "cross and touchy" in the morning and had her suspicions.

She was completely in the dark, however, about Paul's persistent chest pains. He'd been having them since 1967, infrequent tingles at first, then more bothersome and more painful spasms, until, that April, they graduated to an everyday occurrence. When they returned to the States in

October 1974, Paul finally fessed up and found himself, "at once, without delay," in the intensive care unit of Beth Israel Hospital.

It wasn't a classic heart attack, with sudden wrenching symptoms, but rather one that "crept up on tiny padded feet"—two blocked blood vessels that needed immediate repair. Years later, that would be a relatively routine procedure, but in 1974 a bypass was revolutionary, rare. In any case, Julia explained, the operation was essential—Paul couldn't live without it. Still, she couldn't help but wonder how it would affect him post-op. "What changes in life and other habits this will entail—who can know," she mused.

Over the next month or so, she had a better idea. When Paul was discharged from the hospital on November 24, he was "still weak and groggy," which didn't bode well; so much time had elapsed and he'd made no strides. Still, Julia remained optimistic. "I think we shall see more definite progress from now on," she wrote to M. F. K. Fisher. But other, more alarming, symptoms became apparent once he got home. "He looked diminished," said Paul's nephew Jon, who was staying with his aunt and uncle. "He was bent over, he couldn't speak properly; it got tricky to understand what he was trying to say. And his frustration was terrible. He was angry about it." Paul's ability to speak French, in which he was fluent, had disappeared, as well as his taste for red wine. And reading became a problem. He said later, "Words seem to get stuck in my memory-box," slowing his ability to process information.

Julia told Pat Pratt he had "scrambled brain trouble," but she feared something else, something more insidious going on in Paul's head. Brain damage, perhaps, which might account for Paul's memory loss, and also explain his diminishing motor skills. It seemed incomprehensible that he couldn't operate his beloved Rolleiflex camera, turning it over in his hands like a Chinese puzzle box. His drawings, once museum quality, looked like a preschooler's doodles.

Anne Willan, the highly regarded cooking teacher who had dined at L'Ami Louis in Paris with Julia and Paul just prior to his surgery, visited after Christmas and was taken aback by his behavior. "He had no short-term memory and was having trouble speaking," she recalls. "My husband Mark knew right away. 'He's had a stroke,' he said."

In fact, they learned later, he'd had several, most likely during the bypass operation. According to Julia's niece, Phila Cousins, "After the surgery, a blood clot went to his brain and gave him aphasia," the loss of ability to understand or express speech. Any improvement he might make would take months, maybe years.

The recovery process took its toll on Julia, who split her waking hours evenly between finishing *From Julia Child's Kitchen* and caring for her disabled husband. "She spent most of her time just trying to calm Paul down," recalls Jon Child. "And I think it got to her somewhat; she was a bit of a mess for a while." Paul was demanding during the day, needing her for every little function. She couldn't cook, couldn't concentrate on her work. But Julia wasn't one to let the walls come tumbling down. At a point right after New Year's, she shifted into damage control. "Okay, we've got to get speech therapy," she decided. "We've got to figure out a way to get Paul up and down the stairs." To start, she reorganized the house from top to bottom and had an elevator installed for easy upstairs–downstairs access. She accepted her friend Rosie Manell's offer to help test recipes and hired Judith Jones to edit early drafts. Avis DeVoto was enlisted to type the manuscript. "Julia just bulled through everything," her nephew remembered. "There was no way she'd let this personal situation defeat her."

Besides, suffering and self-pity didn't pay the bills.

For Julia, who hadn't published a book in four years or appeared on TV in three, *From Julia Child's Kitchen* brought financial as well as popular success. The book, released in October 1975, was a huge hit with an American audience that had started cooking seriously when *The French Chef* debuted in 1964 and was hungry, starving, for new recipes from its guru. *From Julia Child's Kitchen* gave readers everything they wanted—a delicious new repertoire of dishes with a light touch and enough personal stories to entertain away from the kitchen. There was plenty to chew on in it for the serious cook, but also a feast of information for the newcomer or novice, plus pizza and hamburgers and coleslaw and even ideas for leftovers. For anyone who believed Julia's lessons were too complicated and unwieldy, the new book was a breath of fresh air.

Knopf flooded the market with the book and worked the press without mercy. "We knew the audience was there," recalls Judith Jones, "but since *Mastering II*, there was plenty of competition." Judith alone now edited cookbooks by Roy de Groot, Michael Field, Claudia Roden, Marcella Hazan, Madhur Jaffrey, Irene Kuo, Edna Lewis, James Beard, and of course, Simca. A full-out book tour was essential to making *From Julia Child's Kitchen* a success. But what to do about Paul? He'd made some strides toward recovery with his speech and coordination, but "his mind was still scrambled." There was a long, long way to go. He certainly couldn't fend for himself. A marathon stretch on the road would be a strain for Paul, to say nothing of a distraction and burden for Julia.

"There was never any question about that tour," says Pat Pratt, "or that Paul was going along with Julia."

"The doctor says he is just fine physically," she told Simca before they left, "but that his mental confusion will not get any better—alas." In any case, she felt "lucky" that he was doing as well as could be expected.

"I was determined that nothing was going to be different from before," she said years later, while reflecting on that period. "Paul loved the audiences and the travel. It just meant a little more work, making sure he was looked after properly." In fact, she thought the trip would be therapeutic; it would do "him good to be doing things, as long as we don't do too much, since it keeps him active."

It wasn't as easy as she thought it would be. Traveling with him was hard, *different*. Before, Paul had been her backbone, her enabler. He was always by Julia's side, never too proud to wash the dishes or jump in the car and go get something she forgot. "He'd even get down and scrub the floor," recalls Judith Jones. "But the operation had soured him in a funny way and during that book tour everything changed." Where once he had been "fun and flirty," full of fascinating stories, he'd become grumpy and antisocial—also occasionally irrational. You'd never know when he might say or do something inappropriate. At cocktail receptions in Julia's honor, he was known to grumble: "What are we doing here?" Seated in the audience of her department-store demos, there were times Paul would bark out directions—"Go slower, Julia!" "We can't see the chicken! *Hold it up, dammit!*"—or mumble criticism in a stage whisper that would carry several rows. Somewhere along the way, he'd picked up a stopwatch, and throughout the West Coast segment of the tour, he'd call out the time from his seat. Jones recalls how he would throw a tantrum during seating arrangements in restaurants if he wasn't put in an important place. But Julia always handled it with such grace. "Oh, P'skie," she'd say, "*of course* we'll put you in the sun." Except that moving him dictated where Julia would sit because he had difficulty using silverware and needed assistance. So there were times she'd be consumed with Paul's care, unable to answer a journalist's questions or cozy up to an important bookstore buyer.

The tour took everything out of him—and of Julia. She knew how important it was to promote her new book, and she loved those audiences—*loved them*! But being on the road wasn't fun anymore. It was nerve-racking. Paul was a handful—her dear, darling Paul. No man had ever been more appreciated. No marriage had ever been closer, no husband had ever done more to give a wife confidence, to give her life meaning. Now Julia was basically out there on her own. Traveling with him had become a chore rather than a blessing. Besides, the book itself had drained her. She'd poured everything she had into it, everything she'd learned and all her abilities as a writer. "This is the summation of my 25 years in the kitchen," she wrote to M. F. K. Fisher. "I have little more to say about anything. I'm writ dry. NO MORE BOOKS!"

TELEVISION, HOWEVER, WAS a whole other enchilada. Julia hadn't had a show of her own since *The French Chef* ended in 1972, and by the beginning of 1976 she'd sworn off TV as well. "It's gotten much more expensive to do," she told the *National Observer,* "and it involves a twelve-hour day and a seven-day week, and we've had it." *We've had it:* over and done with. She mostly meant it, too—*mostly.* But there was one realization that kept tugging at her: "if you're not on TV, people forget who you are." The last thing she wanted was to lose her audience. Only a lucky few had such a faithful following and she was determined not to squander it.

That goal wasn't as easy as she thought. Public television had grown exponentially over the last fifteen years, with a widespread impact and brutal competition. There were now two or three hundred program managers across the PBS spectrum, and if they didn't want to run your show, they didn't have to, simple as that. Which meant the underwriter disappeared and the show along with it. WGBH, in particular, held a prominent place of influence within the network, with its attention turned to mega-international programming, like *Nova* and *Masterpiece Theater.* In no time, they'd become a powerhouse, the largest producing station in the country, eclipsing even WNET in New York. Foodwise, the station had other things on its plate, in particular Italian cooking with a couple called the Romagnolis, Chinese cooking with Joyce Chen, and a smash hit called *The Victory Garden.* "And anyway, the people at the highest level there thought the how-to programs were passé," says Donald Cutler, who handled the station's literary rights. There didn't seem to be a place for Julia Child on their roster.

Julia had worked too hard for too long to cede the spotlight to others. If WGBH was hesitant to pull the trigger with her alone, perhaps there was more bump-and-bang with a double-barreled lineup. She and James Beard together were a commanding two-for-one, and their concept, in 1976, sounded unbeatable: a program about American food from the Revolutionary War period, featuring cooks who worked in what had been the original thirteen colonies. The *old* PBS would have eaten it right up, especially after viewing the slickly produced pilot, which spotlighted the two biggest stars in the culinary firmament. Julia sparkled on camera, she was back where she belonged, but Beard suffered from his longtime curse: discomfort on TV and overacting to cover it. He put out absolutely no wattage on screen, even less than the lusterless subject, and the *new* PBS refused to bite. Aside from WGBH, no affiliate signed up, damning the show to oblivion.

Julia was frustrated that she wasn't back on TV. She was viewed as an old network personality, like Milton Berle or Lucille Ball, someone from its glorious past, but not its future. "Nobody ever said, 'We don't want Julia anymore,' " says Russ Morash, "but that was certainly the feeling we got."

The Morashes and Childs were regular dinner companions throughout the seventies, assembling often to cook and talk shop. Their blowout bash was always New Year's Eve, when a full guest list was invited to round out the evening. "People who didn't know Julia very well assumed we were going to have a king's banquet," recalls Marian Morash. "But we'd have a nice oyster chowder—oysters and milk. And Goldfish for hors d'oeuvres, which Julia gobbled by the handful, always her favorite."

One night, right after their festive celebration in 1977, Julia was musing on her inability to break back into the WGBH lineup. "Isn't it funny that they don't want to continue where we left off?" she asked Russ. She wasn't offended or unnerved by rejection, he recalled, just confused by the changing tastes that were seeming to pass her by. Understandably, Morash was plenty "pissed off" at the station's outrageous indifference to reestablishing its biggest star. The underlying problem, he felt, had nothing to do with Julia but rather with their formula, which was worn around the edges. Sitting around the Irving Street kitchen table, they discussed rewriting the winning blueprint they'd devised thirteen years earlier. "Instead of a single recipe," he said, "why don't we do some menus building up to a party?" Julia loved the idea: "a meal-centric program for occasions, like birthdays, Sunday-night supper, or dinner for the boss." She could break "out of the French straitjacket" and do "a lot of plain old American cooking—like Boston baked beans, and a chocolate-chip rum cake."

It didn't take them long to polish the concept. In February, they pitched *Julia Child and Company* to WGBH, which agreed without hesitation to underwrite a thirteen-episode run. Morash worked out the details. Julia would only have to tape one show a week. There would be no shopping for her and Paul, no endless trial-testing at home; prep work would be delegated to a battery of assistants, with plenty of time set aside for rehearsal. To keep costs in check, Russ proposed that he build a dedicated set that didn't come down from one show to the next. "Julia loved that," he says, "because it meant she and Ruth Lockwood could come in and rehearse their brains out day after day without having to worry that it would put us over budget."

And what about a book to showcase the new recipes? Julia had already put her foot down—no more books—but at the time she must have had her fingers crossed. Don Cutler insisted on a companion volume for the show, and before he hung up the phone with her, Julia was back in the book business. An arrangement was made so that she wouldn't have to write during production, as before; instead, they hired Peggy Yntema, an editor at *Atlantic Monthly,* to produce a first draft using dialogue from the rehearsals, to which Julia would add recipes and tweak as she received fresh copy. "This way," Cutler explains, "the book would appear as the show went on the air, instead of months afterward, when the excitement faded."

Naturally, Judith Jones expected Knopf would publish the book. "A new cookbook by Julia!" she exulted. "Half of America would be watching, and at least half the audience would want those recipes." But a week or two later, she got a call from Bob Johnson, a lawyer from the Boston white-shoe firm Hill & Barlow, whom Julia had just hired to represent her. "He said that Little, Brown was very interested in publishing the book and that it might be of value to Julia to work with a Boston-based publisher instead of us." Jones held the phone steady, without responding, trying her best not to cry. "In any case," Johnson said, "I don't think Knopf's royalty rates are acceptable."

I don't think Knopf's royalty rates are acceptable. It was French for "You are screwing my client."

Johnson came on like a steamroller, flattening the dainty Jones. Stunned and dispirited, she enlisted the help of Knopf's financial hatchet man, Tony Schulte, and they flew up to Boston the next day. "We went to Bob Johnson's apartment," Jones recalls. He was a handsome, eccentric, volatile character who trod a treacherous high-wire between

Brahmin Boston on one side and the gay demimonde on the other. Julia was oblivious to his sexuality and never failed to introduce him, without any irony, as "my he-man." Her friends, like Russ Morash, failed to see the humor in it. "Johnson was the most miserable son-of-a-bitch you ever could meet," Morash says, "an odious creep, who had Julia locked in his clutches." Judith Jones seconded that opinion. "He was really quite crude, and vicious, not nice at all," she recalls.

From the opening of negotiations, Johnson refused to back down. He didn't give a damn about Julia's long-standing relationship with Knopf or her friendship with Jones. They meant nothing as far as the deal was concerned. He wanted more money for his client, both up front and on the back end, and if Knopf wouldn't give it to him he was taking Julia elsewhere. Tony Schulte had come prepared. He brought a complete breakdown of the company's profit and loss on a typical Julia Child book to explain the slim margins of return. Johnson hardly glanced at the wobbly math, throwing the profit-and-loss report back at Schulte. He didn't give a damn what the figures showed. "I don't believe your bottom line," he said, holding fast to his terms.

Jones knew it was a deal they couldn't make. "It was prohibitive," she says. "We wouldn't have made any money." After sixteen years as Julia's editor, confidante, and friend, she sensed the wonderful partnership was over.

But not without a fight. Desperate, Jones decided to break two cardinal rules of publishing etiquette: discussing business directly with an author, and using tears as a weapon. She picked up the phone and dialed the Irving Street number. "Julia," she sobbed, unable to check her composure, "do you know what Bob Johnson is asking for? I think you should, because he's making it impossible for us."

All warmth drained from Julia's voice. "I don't want to hear it!" she snapped at Jones. "That's why I have a lawyer." The silence that followed was thunderous.

Jones recalls, "It was like a knife through my heart." With Julia, she knew, there was always some element of mistrust with regard to publishers, dating from the early debacles with Ives Washburn and Houghton Mifflin. But she assumed Knopf had done everything to heal old wounds, and anyway, this went beyond publishing; this was Judith and Julia. Jones thought their friendship transcended business. It went well beyond the customary author-editor relationship. They had often served as each other's therapist. Jones freely offered advice on how to deal with

Paul's illness. When Julia learned the details of Judith's pitiful salary, she implored her, "Ask for more money! *Push yourself,* Judith."

This antagonistic book deal put everything in jeopardy. Knopf would make the deal; they had to. They'd cave in to Johnson's usurious terms. It was more important to keep their celebrated author. But as far as the relationship, it was forever changed. It would always be warm and cordial on the surface, but Julia had drawn the bottom line.

FINALLY, JULIA WAS ready to roll. Production on *Julia Child and Company* was slated to begin October 20, 1977. After a five-year stretch, she'd be back in front of the cameras and the anticipation filled her with a school-girl's enthusiasm. This show was going to gleam with polish. If anything, the long absence had given her even more perspective on the lessons from *The French Chef.* In the interim, Julia developed informed opinions that helped her differentiate between a seat-of-the-pants local show and a seamless national broadcast. All the elements were already in place. She and Russ had mapped out a strategy that would recapture the old glory in a new, modern guise.

The summer had been rough, a combination of rehearsal and family obligations. Paul's condition had started to improve. He began to draw and paint again with some degree of finesse, although his French remained rusty and his speech therapy leveled off. "My field of comprehension is murky," he wrote Charlie in July. "Numbers are stuck, rooms full of many people talking confuse me." He recognized, with regret and resentment, his best days might be behind him, but his will remained strong and he vowed "never to give up."

Julia was relieved by her husband's progress, so much so that they made a short impromptu visit to La Pitchoune. She needed to get away for a while, not so much to plan menus, as she told her staff, but to refurbish her image out of the public eye by having a face-lift and dropping fifteen pounds.

The weather was especially inviting that summer in Provence. Julia and Paul had both missed the balmy serenity that surrounded them in Plascassier. It was the perfect escape for them under the streaky Van Gogh sky, a place to relax and to collect their lives, "a little bit of heaven." They spent hours, sometimes whole days, sitting on the terrace beneath the mulberry tree, gazing out at the scenery, "the almost tropical growth" as a result of an unusually wet spring. The surrounding hills were "abstract swatches of pale-gold ginesta," the air intoxicatingly "sweet with com-mingled honeys"—heaps of lemon verbena and summer mimosa, spicy fig leaves, an extravagance of plush lavender, ambrosial roses everywhere. Paul never missed a chance to walk the gently sloping periphery and take pictures of the Impressionistic landscape. Occasionally he would try to read one of the books they'd carted from Cambridge, but gave up when the words conspired against him, and asked Julia to read to him.

Julia was still nursing her various ailments at La Peetch, when she picked up an overseas call from Erica Child. Her mother, Freddie, had suffered a sudden heart attack and was in the intensive care unit of a hospital in Maine. *Freddie!* The news struck Julia with grave unrest. They must go—immediately. But was she in any condition to travel? Her face was still purple and swollen from the surgery. And how would Paul bear the news? He remained in a fragile state and any sudden shock could trigger a setback. Erica did everything to assure Julia that her mother was all right. Freddie's condition had stabilized; they hoped to bring her home in the next week. Julia and Paul could wait to see her when they returned, the last week in July.

By then, however, it was too late. While they were en route to the States, Freddie had a second attack, and the impact of it had killed her.

They were heartsick. Freddie and Charlie and Julia and Paul—they had been a tightly tangled foursome for more than thirty years, the clos-est family Julia had known aside from Dort and John III—maybe even closer. Freddie had been her first cooking inspiration and her ultimate partner-in-crime: Mrs. Child and Mrs. Child; they'd never managed to pull that one off. But Freddie had always been Julia's go-to gal, the oracle she consulted when crucial advice was called for. And she'd always been Charlie's rock. What would become of poor Charlie now? He was "shattered," Julia realized. He was seventy-five; he was losing his eyesight, with a cauliflower ear he'd gotten in boyhood courtesy of Paul. And, "he hated to be alone, it gave him anxiety," says his daughter Rachel.

Julia already had some idea of what his decline might be like. She had seen it in his twin, who was crushed by Freddie's death. Clearly, Paul and Charlie were now shadows of themselves, their eggshell frailty all too apparent over the last pivotal year. "I can only thank heaven that I am ten years younger than Paul," she resolved. "*Dommage* that we are not all eternal!"

Julia loved Dan Aykroyd's impersonation: "Save the liver!"

Twenty-two

Looking Forward

Work was Julia's fountain of youth. All around her, the spoils of age were taking their toll. Ever since Paul's stroke, she had been especially attuned to the decline of others in her immediate circle. Michael Field, overwhelmed by work and penniless, dropped dead of a heart attack at the age of fifty-six. Ruth Lockwood's husband, Arthur, died suddenly, after having a pacemaker installed. Julia's editor at *McCall's*, Helen McCully, lay in a coma in a New York City hospital. Charlie Child lapsed into a "deep depression" before settling in an assisted-living complex. Jean Fischbacher had prostate trouble. M. F. K. Fisher developed "a kind of palsy, with cataracts in both eyes." And Jim Beard was his usual self, a walking, talking, physical mess.

Aside from her knees, which had tormented her since college, Julia felt like "a teenager" when she was working. Work invigorated her, kept her current, forward-thinking. Whether out of ambition, or distraction, or emotional need, over the next few years she buried herself in an avalanche of projects that, physically and mentally, kept her humming like a DeLorean. *Julia Child and Company* had reignited her star power. Her TV persona resurfaced in tip-top form, a larger, more sophisticated audience tuned in to embrace her, and the reviews confirmed the obvious: *Nova* may have been the station's latest star, but Julia was its supernova. The show's companion cookbook flew off the shelves—more than 200,000 copies before the thirteen weeks elapsed—and her backlist got a power-ful lift. *Mastering,* especially, found new life, necessitating a tour of book signings in the major PBS markets. On paper, Julia resented the constant grind, touring to support the book. "I am even hoping I won't have to go out and promote it this time," she wrote Simca. But, in truth, she loved the face-to-face contact with her fans. "It's where I learn what really goes on in American kitchens," she said. In between appearances, she wrote a column for *McCall's* and did demonstrations at a number of charity events for Planned Parenthood.

More than any other medium, however, Julia drifted toward televi-sion, and in late 1978 there were two appearances that elevated her image as a cultural icon. The first, in November, was a Thanksgiving guest spot with Jacques Pépin on *Tomorrow,* hosted by Tom Snyder. During prep for the show, which was rushed and chaotic, Julia cut herself with a borrowed chef's knife. "To Julia it was nothing, but it was a very big cut," recalled a publishing rep, who had accompanied her to the set. She spilled a lot of blood. Still, Julia, ever the trouper, continued to work through the show, with a towel wrapped around the hemorrhaging wound.

Snyder's late-night show, a mix of hard-hitting interviews and often bizarre and wacky personal observations, attracted a hip and countercul-tural audience. Among the media personalities he influenced over the years were David Letterman, Howard Stern, and Dan Aykroyd, the lat-ter of whom parodied Snyder's hearty, expressive laugh as the basis of a regular impersonation he did on *Saturday Night Live.*

"We saw Julia cut herself on Tom Snyder," Aykroyd recalls. "Every-body was talking about it." A few days later, *SNL* writers Al Franken and Tom Davis brought Aykroyd a skit based on the *Tomorrow* segment that would eventually become a classic. In it, he'd play a campy Julia Child demonstrating a roast chicken recipe, during which she cuts herself and bleeds out on camera. "I was a little reluctant because it seemed like one long blood joke and thought that it might not work, but Franken talked me into it."

Unbeknownst to his *SNL* cohorts, Aykroyd had a personal connection to Julia. His aunt, Helen Gougeon, the author of several popular cook-books, was known as "the Julia Child of Canada," with a long-running radio show, *Bon Appétit,* on CJAD, in Montreal, and a shop called La Belle Cuisine. Her recipe for bouillabaisse inspired his famous "Bassomatic" skit, in which he dropped whole fish into a Ronco blender. "Both my Aunt Helen and my mom had *Mastering the Art of French Cooking* and made recipes from Julia's books all the time," he recalls, "so as a kid I ate the kind of *belle cuisine* she was famous for. And, of course, I was totally a big fan of her show."

Aykroyd and Franken tinkered with the sketch, then performed it at the show's read-through on Wednesday afternoon. "Now, first, remove the giblets—and you should really *save* the giblets," trilled Aykroyd, dressed in a fright wig and apron. "*Save* the liver! *Don't* throw it away! I hope I've made my point. *Don't throw the liver away!*" A few beats later, while cutting out the backbone of the chicken, Aykroyd nicks his hand, à la the *Tomorrow* snafu, and blood begins to spurt. "*Crap!* Oh, now I've done it—I cut the dickens out of my finger." Somehow, the cut was as powerful as Old Faithful, with blood squirting on the chicken and pooling along the kitchen counter.

"The read-through went well," Aykroyd remembers, "it hit all the right notes, but when we did it in dress [rehearsal] on Friday before the show, it didn't work, the blood didn't pump right."

To save it, Franken decided to get into the act. When the show went on the air, he knelt under the table, running the fire extinguisher full of fake blood himself, pumping it like crazy while "Julia" started to reel. "Oh, God, it's throbbing!" Aykroyd blabbers, tying a tourniquet made with an apron and a chicken bone. "If you're too woozy to tie the tourniquet, you might call Emergency Help." But after picking up the phone and dialing 911, he realizes that it's only a stage prop and starts to hallucinate. "Why are you all spinning?" he asks the audience. "Uh . . . I think I'm going to sleep now. *Bon appétit!*" He falls headfirst onto the counter into the pool of blood, but jumps up one last time to say "*Save the liver!*" before dying in a series of twitches.

The skit was an immediate hit and a tape copy eventually found its way to 103 Irving Street. As a rule, Julia wasn't inclined to like parodies. For one thing, she took her cooking seriously, and for another, she didn't think she sounded unusual. Because any mimic immediately went for the voice, her reaction was usually unenthusiastic. But something about Aykroyd's performance struck her funnybone, most likely the darkness of it, the blood and twitchy death.

"For years she played that tape for any guest who visited," says Stephanie Hersh, who later became Julia's personal assistant, "or pantomimed it herself while preparing a roast chicken." Time and again, Julia would hold up a giblet, yell "*Save the liver!*" and collapse across the counter, writhing in laughter.

WORK SEEMED TO energize Julia's spirits, and at sixty-seven there was no evidence of a slowdown. She was constantly on the go. If she was thwarted by the crush of obligations it didn't show. In fact, when WGBH offered to renew *Julia Child and Company,* she jumped at the chance, even though it required a staggering amount of work.

Before production on the new series, *More Company,* could start, Julia had to create enough menus to fill thirteen shows. She could no longer rely solely on Simca's family dishes or simplifying the contents of *Mastering I* and *II.* This necessitated developing her own mouthwatering recipes, which "meant much research and testing," too much work even for one tireless dynamo. It literally became a function of Julia Child and Company—a team of semiprofessionals she assembled to streamline the process. Two women were holdovers from the first series: Rosie Manell, a talented painter Julia knew from the early days in Paris who did what was now called styling, arranging food artistically on the plate; and Liz Bishop, the staff's resident "wild woman and party girl," whose outrageous tongue and infectious laugh kept things lighthearted but on track. Unfortunately, neither of the women cooked, so "two professional chefs joined the team," Julia noted, although *professional* was a bit of a stretch. Sara Moulton "had no formal training" other than a degree from the Culinary Institute of America and two years of prep work at "dusty, old, not-great restaurants" in Boston. And her co-worker was none other than Russ Morash's once-cooking-illiterate wife, Marian, who, through Julia, had become an inventive, resourceful cook.

"There were no pros back then," Moulton recalls. "You were either good or you weren't good. You learned on the job, and we were *competent,* we were professional *enough.*"

As a cook, Julia could be a taskmaster and perfectionist; as a team leader, she was an incorrigible mother hen. Each morning, as her crew assembled in the studio kitchen, she'd say, "Let's start with a little *apéritif,*" pouring out tumblers of white vermouth "to steady the hands." After the little *apéritif*—or two—they'd get down to work. Julia began by providing a template—say, a vegetarian menu—and sketched out scenarios for appropriate dishes. She had a notebook just chock-full of half-formed recipes that she gathered from years of travels, and from these sketches a dish began to emerge. For instance, she might say, "I've got this idea for a *gâteau of crêpes* with vegetables and cheese." There would be some discussion about it, and everyone would contribute to build the dish. Gradually a recipe would evolve.

"We'd all work on it separately," recalls Marian Morash, who was given the title of executive chef. "It would go through many incarnations. Then we'd go give it a shot, we'd make it together, and finally taste it with the rest of the volunteers."

"There was a chocolate bombe cake that we did thirteen times before we even liked it," recalls Sara Moulton, elevated in the hierarchy to executive associate. "But ultimately Julia would have the last word." She'd usually say, "You know, dearie, I like it, but it still needs . . ." and she'd name a few ingredients that brought everything into sharp focus. "She always had a vision," Moulton says. "There was just one way to do it, and it had to be the best way. She was an absolute perfectionist. She knew what she wanted, or she found out what she wanted in the process."

Julia Child and More Company was an all-out group effort. The team worked on a breakneck schedule—cooking four, sometimes five, days a week in time to make the rigorous shoot, which taped at WGBH on Wednesday afternoons. There was always added pressure weighing on the production, the result of a tyrannical imperative imposed by Russ Morash, whom Julia nicknamed "the Ayatollah." In the intervening years Morash had flourished at the station, bringing in *The Victory Garden* and *This Old House* among other hits, and the status made him a demanding stickler. But the kitchen atmosphere was never anything but relaxed. Julia reveled in the new group experience. "This past week we did cassoulet," she wrote Simca halfway through the run, "and we all had so much fun cooking together to get everything ready." Having help took the pressure off, allowed her to concentrate on the script for the show.

Besides, she practically had her hands full with Paul. He was doing well, she acknowledged, "he gets along, he functions," but, alas, "he was not," as she put it, "remarkable in the head." It was futile, in the long run, to expect much improvement. "Mentally, he is no better, and never will be," she realized. The stroke had destroyed key elements of Paul's personality, but he was also seventy-eight, old and fragile. The evidence was everywhere now: his buckled posture, the way he lost his train of thought, nodded off at the table, intimidated guests. Physically, he was thinner, his gait an unsteady shamble. He was less able than ever to care for himself. "Up to now, Paul had looked after everything for Julia," says Anne Willan, "the business, the travel, the what-restaurant-should-we-go-to, the finances. From one day to the next, she took over all of that."

She couldn't afford to take her eyes off him for a moment. Even with all the work piling up, Paul's welfare was a full-time job. "After that," says Willan, "Julia always had a minder, always a friend enlisted to stay by his side." Julia understood what the situation called for: she needed someone nearby who could turn a blind eye to his afflictions but also handle the frustration that ensued. "It was always a happy person who could jolly him along," says Sheryl Julian, "someone who, after a particularly rude outburst, could laugh and say, 'Oh Paul, you are *such* a character.' "

Whether Julia admitted it to herself or not, Paul was becoming a liability. During the shooting of a TV segment for "Summer Dinner," he flew into a rage, demanding to taste the salmon she was making and walking into the frame. Later that spring, at a dinner with important California winemakers, he stormed out of a restaurant in Santa Barbara, shouting, "This place is too dark! I can't see the menu!"

Nevertheless, Julia refused to let the difficulties with Paul slow down her professional life. Julia Child, as a phenomenon, was growing bigger and bigger, even as her personal life was growing more fraught. And yet, despite widening opportunities, she was determined more than ever to keep Paul at her side. "He had brought out something in Julia that she never dreamed was there," says Marian Morash, "and I had the feeling she was eternally grateful and would never abandon him, no matter what." A thirteen-city tour for *Julia Child and More Company* in the winter of 1979–80 was scheduled strategically to provide significant downtime for Paul. But as Julia's appearances ballooned from drawing hundreds to several thousand, more events were added, booked back-to-back, with local talk shows and newspaper interviews sandwiched in the gaps. The schedule was punishing, but irresistible. Paul was just going to have to cope. More publicity meant bigger book sales, which had become the Childs' sole means of income.

Recently, Julia had grown concerned about maintaining her clout, which drew sharply into focus in the aftermath of *More Company*. The trouble had begun before the show went on the air, when WGBH first announced it to the PBS affiliates. If it had been commercial TV—CBS, NBC, or ABC—they would have demanded the show be run by local stations on a specific day and time—*or else*. PBS, however, didn't work that way. Their affiliates in the educational network were independent to a fault, and they'd broadcast Julia's program whenever they damn well pleased. And that wasn't limited to which day of the week they showed it. "Often, a particular market might put it on a month or two later," says Russ Morash, "a detail that Julia never understood."

The way she saw it, she and her entire team were on the road, promoting the hell out of it, and the show wasn't on the air in key markets. "We just *killed* ourselves," she fumed to a reporter covering the tour. "But PBS—I don't know whether they forgot we taped it or what, but it never even got on in New York, and if you're not on in New York, you ain't nowhere." She was hopping mad that several stations made out their seasonal schedules without adding *Julia Child and More Company*. She'd put in long days and weeks getting the series on the air. "I'm not going to go into that kind of thing and have it just lay an egg. That's a damn good book, and they were damn good shows and very original recipes. So I'm through, frankly."

In fact, New York and every major market eventually ran *More Company,* but too late, *too late,* as far as Julia cared. That was it for PBS! She made nothing for doing those shows, "not so much as five bucks" she could bank; whatever budget they gave her went toward food and expenses. She earned a living selling books; it was quid pro quo. The show sold the book, simple as that. Knopf certainly wasn't happy about the turn of events. "I'm not even sure we would have done the book if we'd known there was no TV," Judith Jones says in retrospect. "In any event, its sales were a bit of a disappointment."

PBS, as far as Julia was concerned, had let her down, left her vulnerable. After all she had done for it! Loyalty issues aside, the economics alone galled her. While she earned virtually nothing from WGBH, she had given the station 20 percent of her companion cookbook royalties *out of the goodness of her heart.* Knopf, her publisher, underwrote the subsequent tour. The least WGBH could have done was made sure she was *on the air.* Something wasn't equitable, that much was for sure. In a year or so she'd be seventy. She needed to take better care of herself, to look to the future. The way she saw it, PBS no longer had her best interests at heart. "This is THE END, finito," she groused to Simca.

Julia Child, supernova, was headed elsewhere.

ON A SPRINGLIKE afternoon in April 1980, George Merlis was sitting in his cubicle overlooking Broadway when his boss, Woody Fraser, poked his head inside.

"What do you think of Julia Child joining the Family?" he asked.

Merlis bolted upright in his chair. "I think it's the greatest idea ever," he replied. "Can we get her?"

Merlis was in charge of expandng the Family, and, no, he wasn't reporting to Carlo Gambino or Vito Genovese. His family was a rag-tag group of noted personalities who made weekly appearances on *Good Morning America,* ABC's news-variety entry that ran head-to-head against the almighty *Today* show. Since 1978, when *GMA* first went on the air, they'd been recruiting Family associates like greedy dons. So far they had enlisted Rona Barrett, who contributed Hollywood gossip; author Erma Bombeck, who did a twice-weekly humor segment; Dr. Tim John-son, who was beamed in from Boston whenever there was medical news; F. Lee Bailey, "who would stagger onto the set drunk as a skunk" for a legal briefing; Alvin Ubell, who instructed viewers on home repair; and Arthur Miller from the New York University Law School.

Merlis, *GMA*'s executive producer, salivated over adding Julia to that mix. Whatever pizzazz the Family brought to the show, Julia Child, he thought, would bring more, and in spades. He mentioned the possibility to Joan Lunden, who had recently been elevated to full-time host.

Lunden felt it would be a real coup for the show. "We were looking for star power," she says. "As well known as David Hartman and I were, Julia was that times a thousand. She was someone who would help put us over the top."

In any case, *Good Morning America* needed to spruce up its food seg-ments. Over the last few years, the country had whetted its appetite for good, inventive cooking—or, at least, a reasonable facsimile of what they imagined it to be. Food—*cuisine*—was storming the mainstream culture, and television was, in large measure, carrying the flag. You could turn on any channel at any time in the morning and encounter a chef demonstrat-ing a picture-perfect dish. *GMA* had already featured a dozen or so visit-ing cooks, but no one who measured up to Family standards. They'd used a couple of promising unknowns—Wolfgang Puck and Emeril Lagasse, for example, who, at that point in their careers, lacked TV personalities without the payoff of a permanent spot. "And they were nervous," says Lunden. "We had to walk them through their segments. Whereas Julia was a wonderfully funny personality and radiated more confidence than anyone I'd ever met."

But could they get her? The question lingered. A weekly appearance was out of the question. Julia couldn't commute from Boston to New

York with that kind of frequency; it would exhaust her and there was Paul to think of. She refused to consider the job without him by her side, so convenience would have to be in the details. Merlis had the logistics all worked out. He suggested she come in once a month, do a live segment, and tape four or five others, which they'd spread over the intervening weeks; they'd have her back to Boston on an afternoon plane. Physically, Julia could handle that, but it wasn't humanly possible to prep six dishes in one day. Six dishes meant cooking each recipe at least three or four times so that viewers would be able to see every stage of the process: assembling the raw ingredients, cooking them, and the finished product. *GMA* rehearsed at 6:30 in the morning and went on the air at 7 sharp. To be ready, she'd have to start cooking just after midnight.

There was a solution for that, too: Sara Moulton. She was young, ambitious, and extremely capable. They'd put her on the payroll to take care of the prep. That way, Julia could walk into the studio at 6:15, ready to roll. As for payment, they offered a king's ransom—that is, compared to Julia's take at WGBH. She'd get $605 per appearance, plus expenses. And think of all the books it would sell! Julia was still haunted by the hardest fact of celebrity: "As soon as you're off television, in a few months nobody will know who you are." This was network, coast-to-coast, five times a month.

Julia Child had been gotten.

IF JULIA HAD been seen as slightly wacky on her PBS shows, she really let it rip on *Good Morning America.* She came to cook and teach, her parallel *raisons d'être,* but also to polish and promote the Julia Child persona. It was no secret, especially to Julia, that her audience loved the "unintentional" humor. They still talked about the time she held up withering baguettes, referring to them as "limp ones" as they began to droop and shrivel. "You really want a stiff one," she said, winking. Or tossed things over her shoulder that she deemed shoddy. And now she was prepared to play it for all it was worth. If there was anything she hated more than dour, pretentious cooks, it was taking herself too seriously.

"I don't think we were prepared for how funny she was," says David Hartman, who often served as Julia's on-screen foil. "She'd blurt things out that had the whole place in stitches, and we were never sure whether she knew what she'd said."

But she did. There was method to the madness. "Julia loved the double entendres," says Moulton. "She went out of her way to make them. Above all, she knew what would get a laugh and how to milk it. And she was always aware where the line was drawn so as not to cross it."

Joan Lunden sensed something was up almost immediately after Julia joined the Family. In the midst of a Thanksgiving demo, Julia's eyes developed a mutinous gleam. "She grabbed that turkey's legs and she just spread 'em for the camera," Lunden recalls. It was wonderfully obscene—and funny as hell. A subsequent eggnog segment devolved into a raucous wing-ding when Julia's heavy hand laid on the rum. All morning through rehearsal she kept lavishing the bottle so that by the time they went on the air everyone was "incredibly giggly."

"Whenever we did spots that used any kind of alcohol, she just grabbed that bottle and poured," says Hartman. "And then poured more—*more*. There was no stopping her."

You couldn't tame Julia Child. "Americans, as a race, are too timid," she told Lunden, "especially when it comes to what they put in their mouths." One of her pet peeves was the country's phobia regarding fat. Real butter and cream were essential to good cooking, irreplaceable, and critics be damned. Despite the health and exercise revolution currently in high swing, "Julia would come into the studio and pour a whole pitcher of cream into a recipe." Or bind a sauce with three or four tablespoons of butter. No matter how often one of the hosts admonished her, she would argue, "A little fat is not going to hurt you. In fact, we *need* it in our diet." And when they didn't outwardly endorse that message, she'd cock an eye and add: "You could use a little yourself, dearie."

The audience loved her "wicked ways," and so did the network. "No one here minded that her act bordered on the risqué," says George Merlis. Still, they assigned a special line producer "to keep a rein on her—just in case."

Sonya Selby-Wright was a "tough, hyper-efficient Brit" who was in charge of Family and ran her segments the way a drill sergeant might run a squad of new recruits. She was a short, reed-thin woman with a laser stare that gave her face the waspish cast of a Gothic gargoyle. One well-placed look could snap the entire crew to attention. Although intensely dedicated to the show's split-second timetable, Selby-Wright's measured, orderly hand brought composure to the everyday chaos. "When it came to Family," Merlis says, "she knew innately how to juggle those trained seals."

Selby-Wright had one rule she stood by: no one came on *GMA* unprepared. The segments were relatively short—three, four minutes at the most—and every second was precious gold. By contrast, Julia's on-air persona was fly-by-the-seat-of-her-pants, hoping things came together at the last moment. But Selby-Wright knew the best performers gave that impression while knowing their material cold. As a result, she and Julia hit it off from the get-go.

"They became fast friends," Lunden says, "on- and off-camera." Sonya dedicated herself to protecting Julia's brand. But one thing continued to rattle Julia: Sonya's *ved-dy pra-puh* English comportment. There were no cracks in that genteel façade. It was time to have a little fun with that. Julia being Julia couldn't resist.

One morning, Julia had set up in the studio to rehearse a recipe for *croque monsieur.* The cameramen were swanning around her, adjusting lenses and wires, while Julia cast an eye up to the control booth above the set, where Sonya sat. When the signal was given to start the run-through, Julia cleared her voice and began. "Today we're going to do cock monsieur . . ."

"Just a moment, Julia," came the detached British voice over the PA system. "Let's do that again, from the top."

Julia gathered herself, took a breath, and began anew. "Today, we are going to do cock monsieur . . ."

"Hold on, Julia."

Sensing mischief, the cameramen began snickering and cutting glances at one another before looking skyward, in Sonya's direction. They knew she was uptight about the word *cock* and had convinced herself she was the only person who had heard it.

Julia barreled right ahead with the demo. "The first thing you want to do with your cock . . ."

Sonya's voice broke in again. "Julia, listen to me. It's *c-r-r-r-r*-oque monsieur."

"Well, dearie, that's what I was saying."

"No, Julia, you were not saying that. Listen again. It's *c-r-r-r-r*-oque, *c-r-r-r-r*-oque!"

Julia looked up and insisted they were pronouncing it exactly alike.

"No, you were *not saying that.*"

A look of exaggerated innocence played on Julia's face. "Well, dearie, what *was* I saying?"

By this point, the cameramen were beside themselves. They knew what Julia was up to and were laying bets whether she could get Sonya to say the word aloud.

There was a long silence before the PA clicked back on. "Julia. You were saying *cock*."

"What was that, dearie?" Julia played with the ingredients in front of her, distracted.

"*Cock*, Julia. You were saying *cock*."

Julia put down a few slices of bread and looked up at the booth with a rascally grin. "Well," she said in her swoopy drawl, "I'll bet it sure tastes better that way."

WHEN JULIA COMMITTED to working in New York in 1980, she knew in advance that the commute would be hard. All that travel back and forth, the disruption and the strain. There was no telling how Paul would take to it, and friends cautioned it could hinder his recovery. "She thought the activity would be therapeutic for him," recalls Pat Pratt. "That it might get his mind going, take him back to the days when they were on the go, that they'd have this project together, he'd start using his camera again, click into the old routine." Instead, unable to keep up with her or communicate effectively, he withdrew even further into his inner world. At ABC, where the hustle and drive were constant, Paul clung to the shadows. "He was very quiet, very reserved," recalls George Merlis. "He always stood off by himself, always sharpening Julia's knives in a kind of guarded, hypnotic way."

All in all, doing the shows was "rough," Julia reported to Simca, "but we do enjoy going to New York to do them." There was plenty of time to take pleasure in the city, see friends, catch up on the swiftly moving food trends. Typically, they'd fly in a few days early, have dinner with Judith Jones or a culinary grandee. James Beard, busy revising a manuscript for *The New James Beard,* always made time to see them. He seemed to be doing much better than when they had last visited with him in Plascassier. His seventy-nine-year-old body was still "dangerously overweight"; he was "slowing down a little," Julia thought, "but functioning." Whenever possible, she stole down to the Village to cook with him. "James *loved* cooking with Julia," says Clark Wolf. "Even after all those years, they always behaved like it was the first time, and it was always something of a performance, just the two of them at the stove."

Jim fantasized openly about returning to La Pitchoune. A lengthy visit usually succeeded in reversing his tortured decline. It was a place where he could recuperate, away from the parasites and jackals, the constant deadlines that shot his blood pressure into the stratosphere. In Plascassier, there was little reason for him to be on his feet. He loved to while away endless days lazing about on the porch, sipping martinis, cook with Julia or go across to Simca's. Christmas and New Year's there were always over-the-top occasions. And the cast of visitors refreshed itself regularly and was gossipy enough to suit him.

It was an idyllic thought—they always enjoyed each other's company—but Julia doubted they'd reunite there anytime soon. And it would be too difficult for Beard, "with his big old purple legs," to get around Plascassier on his own, without them. Paul had already made it clear that he wanted a change of scenery. He fared even worse than usual in the seasonal damp chill, making another winter in the south of France out of the question. In fact, Julia had laid plans to take him west instead for their three-month hiatus in early 1981. The warm, dry weather in California was better suited to their needs than Plascassier, marginally; than Cambridge, not even close. "Why spend the remainder of one's life in that awful climate?" she wondered. And the constant highbrow tension was fairly exhausting.

California was another world entirely. Where Cambridge and Plascassier were animated and intellectual, Santa Barbara was laid-back and economically diverse: a genteel but unpretentious community of oil barons and high-stakes investors intermixed with personal chefs, organic gardeners who supported the farmers' market, and film buffs. There were plenty of other incentives to go west, as well. Dort and Ivan were just up the coast, as was Julia's stepmother, Phila, in Pasadena, and they could reconnect with long-lost intimates from Julia's past. "Lots of my old school mates and childhood friends are there," she mentioned. A handful of Pasadena families still dominated the social scene. And all those memories—the idyllic summers on the beach in Sandyland Cove, the family drives through Montecito Park, watching her mother play tennis on the city courts. Her mother: when Julia pictured Caro in Santa Barbara she saw a vibrant, robust beauty with unconventional spirit. Julia's spirit. The city—its easy lifestyle—was a powerful draw.

It didn't take long to settle into a routine. Julia found Montecito "spectacularly beautiful, with the sea and the big rough green mountains in the very near background." The sun's heartwarming dry heat gave Paul an immediate lift; he seemed less reluctant, even willing, to participate in social situations, more responsive to Julia, which was encouraging for the long term. "We have found ourselves so happy here," Julia wrote to Simca soon after their unpacking. Everything seemed to fall right into place. So many friends came to pay their respects. Julia joined the Birnamwood Country Club, *the* club for old established families. She discovered a batch of reliable restaurants—nothing gastronomic, like Bocuse or Moulin de Mougins, not even innovative like Four Seasons, but "jolly places," she called them, where you could get a nice rare steak and an excellent local pinot noir. In fact, she'd become close to two winemaking artisans—Dick Graff at Chalone and Richard and Thekla Sanford, the young couple who owned Sanford Winery—and through them educated herself about the domestic wine industry, which was just coming of age.

Within a few months, the Childs decided to make the move more permanent. They bought an apartment in the Montecito Shores complex, across from the Biltmore Hotel where they planned to retire—eventually, some time distant. They settled in the top floor of a low-rise co-op, a two-bedroom space with a modest dining nook that Julia claimed as her West Coast office. A glassed-in porch overlooked a vast green meadow and beyond that the sea. Most important: "all on one floor," Julia gloated, "with an elevator near (for my knees!)."

Julia's knees were developing into a chronic problem. Since the accident on her wedding day they'd never been the same, and her ungainly size did nothing to help the situation. She was an enormous, big-boned, weight-bearing woman *on her feet all day long.* On top of that, crippling arthritis had set in, which only exacerbated the problem. She'd been warned by her doctor: she could only stand all day for so long with those knees. Twice already she had to have them drained, along with some microsurgery to scrape out and repair scar tissue. But Julia didn't intend to slow down anytime soon.

There were too many new places to go, too many new situations to explore, too many new people to meet in the lush lap of California. In the tradition of her grandfather, she prospected up and down the coast, mining experiential nuggets that yielded fat returns. The local wine industry was a particularly rich strike. Dick Graff showed Julia around the up-and-coming vineyards, through the Simi Valley north to Monterey and further into Napa and Sonoma, hoping to convert her to the sophisticated American-made product. Some fairly respected critics already claimed "that California wines . . . were as good as the French," but Julia's prejudices were pretty well fixed. "She and Paul were so negative about California wine," recalls Richard Sanford, who befriended them on that early sightseeing trip. Even though the industry had been growing more polished and innovative through the seventies, they only basically knew the swill that came in jugs and screw-cap bottles. "I'd grown up on that stuff," Julia recalled later, "and I knew better than to put much stock in it." But Graff's dog-and-pony show proved an eye-opener. They hopscotched across the vineyards tasting the California rising stars—Stags' Leap, Heitz, Chateau Montelena, Mayacamas, wines with great depth and complexity—and "found true religion in those cabernets and pinot noirs."

Julia learned an enormous amount from the charming and suave Graff. A "great artisan" in the precincts of new-world winemaking, Graff was another of the "really handsome, literate, but sexually conflicted" men to whom Julia was inexorably drawn. He was a glamorous and alluring conversationalist, strikingly muscular, with a black pencil mustache and sparkly eyes, and a knack for being more connected than an IBM mainframe. Plus, he was "wildly talented," some called him "a genius," and there was nothing Julia loved more than handsome, wildly talented geniuses.

Graff was Julia's liaison to the small but hard-charging wine-producing community that seemed to be marching in lockstep with local restaurateurs. He introduced her to his winemaking friends, not the least of whom was the enterprising Robert Mondavi, and initiated her—very, *very* gradually—to a culinary style that was being called California cuisine.

Like many revolutionary movements, California cuisine sprang from the innate drive to create something different and the sudden availability of the tools to facilitate it. The American palate, so basic, so pedestrian, and so uninitiated, had been awakened in the 1960s by Julia Child, James Beard, and their merry band of acolytes, who mentored legions of young people wanting to learn how to cook. They studied Julia's books, they watched her shows, inhaled every word she said; the serious ones went to France to learn more. They mastered the hands-on skills, the vocabulary, the cook's way of thinking, and they came back to America wanting to take it to the next step. It grew out of the sixties ethos of valuing creativity and the seventies ethos of wanting to express oneself. These trained young cooks hungered to put their own stamp on cuisine: French-based with a decidedly modern, American twist.

California cooks had a leg up on the process, owing to the state's luxurious year-round growing season and the stunning variety and quality of its produce. They had immediate access to the freshest and very best ingredients, most of them harvested on farms within a short, accessible drive. Leslie Brenner, who studied the phenomenon in her book *American Appetite,* noticed that local California greenmarkets overflowed with "a generous cornucopia of produce: six or seven types of exotic broccoli; juicy flavorful strawberries; tiny succulent mandarins; Haas avocados; Chinese water spinach; an heirloom variety of watercress; fresh fenugreek; even ripe flavorful tomatoes grown outdoors." There was goat cheese, artichokes, nasturtiums, lettuces—*mesclun*—and patches of herbs in constant bloom. Cooks could prepare their menus with produce picked just that morning and have it on the table a few hours later, whereas the top New York restaurants depended on produce shipped from the West Coast, which inevitably lost flavor by the time it arrived.

It was undeniable: fresh ingredients inspired creativity in inventive young cooks, who began to put their personal interpretations on simple French cooking. In time, they developed a style entirely their own: classically influenced, sexy, ingredients-based, and creative. Simple grilled food with an attractive presentation was the foundation of California cuisine. Fresh field salad and baby vegetables added a quiet, dressy touch. Of course, The Four Seasons in New York and Harvest in Boston had been featuring such food since they'd opened their doors, years earlier. But suddenly a pack of new practitioners took it to another level: Alice Waters, Jonathan Waxman, Jeremiah Tower, Michael McCarty, Mark Miller, and Wolfgang Puck burst out of the gate in spectacular fashion. Finally, there was a synergy to the cooking. Their food was more experimental, more assured, and more refined in its execution, throwing a spotlight across the fashionable terrain. And the innovation didn't stop at the plate. The restaurants they worked in were laid-back and casual instead of cathedrals to propriety. Before, any type of sophistication in regard to food in America was put through a prism that included an intimidating French waiter. Now, the *server* was likely to appear in a white shirt and jeans: "Hi, my name is Zachary. I'll be assisting you tonight."

California cuisine was a runaway success and the food press was quick to anoint the trend. Everyone, from Craig Claiborne to Mimi Sheraton to Jack Shelton gave it their blessing. Patricia Wells, writing in the *International Herald Tribune,* declared, "The cuisine generates an excitement about food, a sense of experimentation, plus an uncompromising concern for good food and good dining that seems to have been lost in much of America."

Julia wasn't so sure. Jim Beard had been cooking and promoting American seasonal cookery since his appearance on the scene, in the early 1940s. His food was elemental, it wasn't from the grocery store, and he made no compromise to freshness or quality. The same with Richard Olney's artisanal approach. Julia thought California cuisine was nothing more than southern French regional coupled with local cooking, and she said so whenever asked to comment. In a 1981 panel discussion sponsored by the San Francisco Culinary Academy, she responded to an address by Alice Waters that presented California cuisine as a simple, pure form.

"There is not as much of a California cuisine as you chauvinists would have us believe," Julia said. "It is actually such a mixture that definitions cannot be made. Although you mention simplicity, I think menus are so simple they can become dull. Sometimes I'm glad when I can go back to France, where they really *do* things with food." As far as the incestuous pact with foragers and farmers that made just-picked produce an almost religious requirement, Julia thought it was patently elitist. "You have an unduly doleful point of view about the way that most people shop for food," she told Waters. "Visit any supermarket and you'll see plenty of fresh fruits and vegetables. And if you don't like the looks of what you see displayed, complain to the produce manager. That's what I do, and it always gets results."

In the search for a genuine American cuisine, California cooks were viewed skeptically by the establishment, whose allegiance was to classic French food. But their impact was not to be denied. The "grill it and garnish it" brand of cooking was a welcome change from the monotony of lugubriously sauced roasts and leaden casseroles that epitomized most fine-dining pretensions. And by the time the new cooking caught on, its top-flight practitioners raised the bar to a new level of pizzazz. Jeremiah Tower began serving roast duck with fresh basil along with composed salads that owed plenty to modern architecture; Alice Waters offered buckwheat pasta with arugula and goat cheese, as well as lobster in cabbage leaves with roasted peppers; and Wolfgang Puck reinvented pizza—smoked salmon pizza, duck pizza, pesto shrimp pizza, *gourmet* pizza. And collectively, they no longer allowed captains to cook, *flambé*, and carve tableside as was customary in most fancy joints, but rather the chefs themselves *plated* food in the kitchen to emphasize presentation, often finishing dishes by squirting sauces from a squeeze bottle in Jackson Pollock–like zigzags across the entire plate.

It was the Wild West all over again.

Julia, understandably, had trouble dismissing the importance of California cuisine. The food was too well made and well-thought-out, and it conformed to her basic principle: "If it tastes good, it's good. Period. End of story." Jasper White says, "She was careful not to rail against the movement, although she called bullshit on grilled vegetables," but she was also not quick to jump on the bandwagon. There were too many shortcomings that curbed her enthusiasm, one of which was apparent lack of training at the stove. Above all else, she believed, chefs must master technique. Julia was dedicated to the old French system, where would-be chefs toiled for years in the back of professional kitchens, topping-and-tailing beans, peeling potatoes, or making vats of *vol-au-vent,* before they were allowed anywhere near a stove. But Alice Waters, from what she'd heard, "never attended cooking school or served some kind of rigorous apprenticeship," nor had Jeremiah Tower, a notorious head case. Jonathan Waxman put in some time studying cooking at La Varenne; otherwise, he'd kicked around in a series of amateur rock bands. At twenty-five, Wolfgang Puck, had he remained in Europe, would still have been apprenticing, still learning, still lightyears away from cooking, and even then, only cooking Escoffier-type standards. How could she endorse these young and reckless chefs? How could she forsake everything she stood for?

Even Sara Moulton had to pay her dues. Despite the fact that Moulton had graduated from the Culinary Institute of America, worked two cooking jobs in Boston—as the manager of a catering operation and chef at a restaurant called Cybelle's—and had served as executive associate for *Julia Child and Company,* Julia was convinced she needed more formal training if she were to get anywhere in the professional culinary world. She never came out and told Moulton as much. Instead, she said, "Dearie, *everybody* should go to France." Next thing Moulton knew, Julia had consigned her to an apprenticeship with a French two-star chef. "Her idea was that I go over and do a *petit stage,*" Moulton recalls. "He would pay for my room and board, and I would work for free. At the time, I was a chef at a restaurant in Boston, and *he wouldn't even let me work the line.* And he chased me around on my day off." Didn't mean a thing to Julia Child. When Moulton complained later on that she'd been fed to the lions, Julia replied, "Dearie, what did you expect? They're all like that. Get over it."

In her eyes, it had been a wonderful opportunity for a young, ambitious woman to learn, learn, learn.

Years later, Julia would refer Sara to a job at Chez Panisse, but in 1982 that restaurant was well off her radar. Still, she loved the fact that young people were interested in cooking. "No one was more encouraged by the new young wave," says Anne Willan. "Julia was their greatest and loudest cheerleader, even if she was unconvinced that their experience was sufficient." Despite the few talented artists who caught her attention, Julia suggested wannabes take up classic French training—advice that left most aghast. While their brash creations brought public attention, they reinforced Julia's impression that California cuisine was a craze that would stay fresh only as long as a squash blossom in July.

In the ensuing upheaval, Julia retreated to the sidelines. Rather than grapple with the new young upstarts, she became the food editor of *Parade*, the Sunday magazine supplement in hundreds of newspapers, where she proposed to blend French technique with "free-style American cooking" for the new generation of eager home cooks. The position served two burning purposes: the creative urge and visibility. First and foremost, Julia considered herself a teacher, and at last she had the forum to deliver a detailed and methodical weekly lesson. Space was not an issue; she could write as long and as freely as she wished. And a team of first-rate photographers was on board to capture every step of the process. The layouts were beautiful, attention-getting. Best of all, *Parade* delivered the kind of weekly audience that most writers only dream about. "They have, at present, a circulation of twenty-one million!" she reported to Simca. It would do more than keep her name in the spotlight—it would sell books! Recently, both *Mastering*s had "fallen off in royalties." A weekly column would go a long way toward reviving the franchise and keep Julia Child a top-flight brand.

But it had never been entirely about the money for Julia. Visibility meant power, the power to make a difference by using her persona for broader concerns, beyond the world of books and television. The election of Ronald Reagan had rekindled her political activism. His well-marked agenda echoed her father's arch-conservatism, but it was more than that. "It was her deep-rooted liberal disposition," says Judith Jones, often privy to Julia's political tirades. "She hated where the Republicans were taking the country, driving a stake between the left and the right. And she blamed Reagan for widening the divide." It gnawed at her insides. Everything about him seemed like a slap in the face, not the least of which was his immediate reach. The Reagans had a getaway, Rancho del Cielo, in the hills behind Julia's apartment in Montecito and Nancy was, of all things, a Smith grad.

The final insult came when Reagan stepped up his opposition to abortion. For the past few years, Julia had been supporting her favorite charity, Planned Parenthood, through a series of appearances and demonstrations. Her reasons for aiding the organization are difficult to assess. "To me, it's always been about the *wanted* child," she said. And yet it wasn't as though she had been around a lot of impoverished people who couldn't handle their kids or around anybody whose life was ruined by having kids. For Julia, this conviction that she had was a purely intellectual one. She believed in a woman's autonomy, in a woman's having control of her own decisions. She had always made her own decisions, and from a young age she had always charted her own course, often in defiance of expectations and her father's wishes for her. She strongly believed that women, in general, knew what was best for themselves and had the right to control their own fates. "If we really supported Planned Parenthood," she said, "we wouldn't have need for abortions. People would be educated and think a little before they had a child."

In any case, the more the opposition to abortion mounted, the more engaged Julia became. In April 1982, she staged a three-day fund-raiser at the Holiday Inn in Memphis, holding cooking classes to benefit the local chapter. This was the first time she'd ever met opposition. Each day, as she arrived at the hotel, a small group of protesters, women holding babies in their arms, converged around her. They chanted and waved signs that read IF YOU HAD YOUR WAY I WOULDN'T HAVE BEEN BORN. Julia was too startled or too tactful to confront them. "It was not the place to make a scene," she said, although she later described the encounter as "pathetic and infuriating."

She wasn't naïve. She knew abortion was a controversial issue. But Julia didn't give a damn about what other people thought. Instead of letting the matter die quietly, as most prominent figures would, she went on the offensive, taking it public. On July 15, 1982, a letter appeared nationally in the syndicated "Dear Abby" column. In it, Julia explained the situation in Memphis and her contempt for the women who picketed the event. "I did want to ask them this," she wrote. " 'What are your plans for these children once they are born? Are you going to help provide, for instance, for the child of a retarded 13-year-old daughter of a syphilitic prostitute? Or what of a tubercular and abandoned welfare mother who already has six children?'

"These are extreme cases, of course, but there are plenty of them, and these are our future citizens who, for the most part, end up in our juvenile courts and in our jails. If you insist on their birth, you must also assume responsibility for their lives."

Dear Abby's response was spineless to a fault. "Dear Julia," she wrote. "For the world's most famous cook to have whipped up a world-famous controversy is a case of just deserts!" Julia Child deserved more than that—and so did Abby's readers, right-leaners or lefties. The firestorm it provoked was impossible to ignore. In the days that followed, a deluge of letters poured in to the columnist, with each side duly represented by its advocates. Some papers, like the *St. Petersburg Independent,* printed only the right-to-lifers' responses, which detailed instances about children who endured grave circumstances and went on to lead fulfilled lives. Others, like the *Eugene (OR) Register-Guard* and the *Indiana (PA) Gazette,* included letters that supported Julia's outspokenness. "Three cheers for Julia Child!" one wrote. Another responded, "I would like to commend her for her guts and integrity."

Either way, this type of publicity could have proved devastating. In the past, political controversies had wounded the careers of Benjamin Spock, Anita Bryant, and Jane Fonda. Supporting Planned Parenthood, which encompassed the abortion issue, was playing with fire. Still, Julia took her celebrity and used it for something she believed in. It was ballsy, but potentially lethal, a terrain studded with landmines, yet a measure of her popularity that people let it slide.

By 1982, Julia had moved on, devoting her time to an issue closer to her area of expertise. The food frenzy in California had reawakened another facet of her activism. She became convinced that any *serious* cook needed to be an *educated* cook as well. Compared to her decades of hands-on study and scientific approach to gastronomy, the new generation's grasp of culinary arts was rudimentary and piecemeal at best. They had no connection to history or theory. She was frustrated about the lack of source material in the United States, that no academic institution paid it much attention. She'd received an honorary degree from Boston University in 1981 and yet there was no culinary degree program in force at the school aside from a few dissociated cooking electives. Or anywhere else, for that matter. It underscored how far the profession still had to climb, not just to achieve a level of respectability, but for basic knowledge, which would go toward developing a more sophisticated American cuisine.

In 1981, during a dinner in Montecito, Julia grumbled anew about academia's lack of support. A man named Robert Huttenback, who was seated across from her said, "Well, why don't we do it out here, at the University of California?" Huttenback was more than a casual observer; he was the chancellor of UC Santa Barbara, with land, a building, and an endowment to offer. Dick Graff, who also attended the dinner, volunteered to enlist important winemakers and restaurateurs, which ultimately set the table for an exploratory group.

The American Institute of Wine and Food, as it would come to be called, was born of noble intention. It was high time the kingpins of American cookery establish a professional alliance that would not only unite chefs and winemakers but set standards for cooks and schools, while establishing qualifications in all fields. A preliminary meeting at Julia's in July brought together an impressive core group: Huttenback, Robert and Margrit Mondavi, Alice Waters, Jeremiah Tower, Marion Cunningham, who had revised *The Fannie Farmer Cookbook,* and Graff. Julia hoped to attract her influential buddies, but "people like Jim Beard," she found, "have been very much against the whole thing." M. F. K. Fisher, for the most part a social hermit, was also reluctant to join, but eventually relented after some gentle arm-twisting. The old guard was coasting on the vaunted legacies. Instead, Julia focused on a new wave of younger faces, the up-and-coming chefs, who were edging into the scene.

Within the next few years, Julia would forge a personal relationship with virtually every rising star of the American food movement: Alice Waters and Jeremiah Tower, of course, but also Michael McCarty, Wolfgang Puck, Paul Prudhomme, Larry Forgione, Jimmy Schmidt, Jonathan Waxman, Mark Miller, Bradley Ogden, as well as an impressive group that was infiltrating Boston—Lydia Shire, Bob Kinkead, Jasper White, Bruce Frankel, Monsef Meddeb, and Jody Adams—all emerging as inventive artisans at the forefront of a neoclassical, *sexy,* American cuisine.

Like Julia, thirty years earlier, they were about to change the way Americans ate. She recognized what their contribution would mean. It was everything she wanted: new blood, fresh ideas, real commitment, forceful personalities, ambition, *youth.*

She may have been seventy, but old age be damned. Julia was looking forward, not back.

Twenty-three

Enough

Basic recipe shows were old hat, boring. Since 1963, Julia had done hundreds of them—*hundreds*—all within the same basic format, lurching ahead. They were straightforward how-tos and tightly scripted, no surprises. "Hi, I'm Julia Child, and today we're going to be making *blah blah blah.*" She'd roll out the ingredients, mix, sauté, roast, whatever, then pull the completed dish out of the oven for the big finish. And frankly, that didn't intrigue her anymore. Besides, television had come a long way since she had first hit the airwaves. More than just cooking lessons, it needed a strong entertainment value, an arresting diversion; throwing ingredients into a pot was no longer going to cut it. If Julia were ever lured back to TV again—a big *if,* considering she'd sworn off the tube—she'd need something more exciting to match the excitement that was fomenting in American food.

Enter Russ Morash, who was like the pitchfork-bearing Goofy on Mickey's shoulder. He tempted her every few years with another new offer for a series. WGBH wanted her back. Oh, sure, sure, the station had its fill of Julia. But that was then, after fifteen years and umpteen reruns; absence made the heart grow fonder. She'd been off the network since 1980. They felt the void and so did she.

"You know what would be fun?" Morash posed one evening, as the Morashes and Childs finished a casual Cambridge dinner. "A series based on events rather than simply a recipe. Something that would be appropri-

With Jim Beard at the market in place aux Aires, June 24, 1972

ate for a birthday party or a dinner with the boss. What about doing a whole menu for a significant event?"

Menus were only the bait on a hook. Morash had more on his line. He suggested they shoot the series in Santa Barbara, ostensibly to facilitate Julia's schedule during the winter months, but his ultimate angle was pure showbiz gloss. California as a backdrop would give her a glamorous new look. They could shoot outdoors, heighten the production. "We can even take you on some adventures," he said.

Adventures was one of those words that never failed to tickle Julia's follicles. After all, this was a woman who had flown off to Ceylon during World War II, married a Renaissance man of the highest order, hopscotched through unending new and unusual experiences throughout Europe, and appeared on TV without a stitch of training. Adventures were religion to Julia Child. Adventures? She was listening. What did Morash have in mind?

Now he was really cooking himself, improvising really. "How about if we have you forage mushrooms in the oak groves and make cheese in Atascadero?" he said. "We can go to Seattle for salmon."

Julia *loved* it. "She was game for it all," Morash recalls. "Going on location was like heroin for her. She had terrible knees and other medical issues, but she was living life large and wouldn't be denied." As for cooking, Morash proposed they open up the format to include local chefs and winemakers she admired and wanted to introduce nationwide.

Julia was hooked, but Morash continued to reel her in. "And let's finish off each show with a grand glittering dinner party. You can invite all your pals, Judith Jones, M. F. K. Fisher, anyone who comes to visit the set. And we'll all sit down to a sumptuous feast that shows off whatever was made on that program."

Julia's only hesitation was over a lingering squabble with PBS. Her previous series, *More Company,* was the victim of such erratic scheduling—on the air in Boston and Chicago one month, New York three months later. Who could keep track? Even worse, stations broadcast it in the *daytime,* which appalled her. Daytime labeled it a housewife show. She insisted it appeal to everyone.

"I'll take care of that," Morash promised. He had a title already in mind that dared the network to show it anytime but in the evening. And that's how *Dinner at Julia's* was born, as a high-concept, magazine-style format designed to change the structure of cooking shows.

Dinner at Julia's, which premiered in the fall of 1983, predated the

Food Network by a good ten years, but it contained all the ingredients that established the future phenomenon: a strong, super-personable host, travel and exotic locales, instructional cooking, celebrity guests, a reality-type atmosphere, slick production values, and the practice of taking viewers behind the scenes in each jam-packed episode. It opened up the TV kitchen to the culinary world at large, expanding the basic recipe Julia had practically originated.

"It was a fairy-tale production," Morash recalls. Everything came together rather quickly for television. WGBH signed on the moment it heard Russ's pitch, and Polaroid followed with an underwriting grant of a million dollars. The perfect set was located: an enormous mansion in Hope Ranch, an exclusive twenty-five-acre Santa Barbara suburb wooded by tall oaks on a hill overlooking the Pacific coast. The kitchen was "a chef's dream," a professional set-up, with restaurant-quality equipment, dual counters the size of the runways at LAX, and a fireplace to warm those toasty seventy-degree winter days. There was plenty of room to board the crew so they could live and work on site. Russ's wife, Marian, stepped in as Julia's executive chef, with a crew of kitchen assistants that was familiar and trusted. And Julia had an idyllic commute: the set was a mile from her place in Montecito.

Not everything, however, progressed smoothly. The bubble of friction began vaguely during preproduction when, in the interchange over particulars, Julia's lawyer, Bob Johnson, cross-examined Morash about every detail. Already peeved by his previous experience with Johnson, Morash, the Ayatollah, was hostile and dismissive. He didn't want any land sharks circling his tightly run ship. When he said as much to Julia, she put her foot down. "I need somebody to represent *my* interests," she insisted, "and Bob has agreed to come out to be with us and help out."

Come out and be with us. Help out. It sounded like a recipe for disaster.

A few weeks later, Johnson showed up on the set of *Dinner at Julia's* determined to exert his influence on the look and feel of the show. Naturally, Morash didn't want Julia's lawyer around, undermining him, trying to call the shots. Johnson was a flamboyant figure, "aggressively assertive," Morash says. Russ was surprised Julia was so devoted to her lawyer, because he'd often heard her say homophobic things and he knew Johnson was gay. "He was promiscuous; it was legend around town. The stories that you heard about Bob Johnson and his proclivities—he was *notorious*! I wasn't going to have any part of it."

It was an epic contest of wills. Morash refused to give an inch, and so did Johnson, who attempted to move into the Hope Ranch mansion. Morash effectively blocked the door. It was High Noon: Morash drew first. He confronted Julia with an it's-either-him-or-me ultimatum. In twenty years of their mutual work-lovefest, they'd never exchanged so much as a single cross word. Russ was certain Julia would cave.

But he was wrong. "I love Russ, but I am loyal to my lawyer," Julia replied in a note to would-be peacemaker Marian Morash. She had no intention of sending him home. Nor did she want to hear any more bickering. They had a show to do and she expected Russ to deliver it. "Bob," she said, "will deal with my personal matters and the staff."

This time the Ayatollah would be taking no hostages. Reluctantly, the two adversaries carved up the duties: Russ would oversee the production, while Bob would handle Julia's personal matters, like making sure her hair got done by a person she approved of and choosing her wardrobe, giving her a new look for the show.

That was right up Johnson's alley, Morash fumed, but he continued to wonder about Julia's relationship to this "character." Morash and others were often confused about Julia's attitudes toward homosexuality. To Julia, gays were always "something different"—"fairies" or "pansies" or "homos" or "fags," "light on their feet," even *pédés,* French slang for homosexual. To an assistant, she would "very often wink and say, 'one of the *boys.'*" Michael James, Simca's new protégé, was "another of them." And so was Corby Kummer, a young journalist Julia had befriended. "To her, homosexuals were like *the other,*" Kummer recalls.

On the surface, she came off as a raging homophobe, but her feelings were more complicated and often contradictory. James Beard was certainly one of her closest friends, whom she loved dearly and without reservation. His sexual disposition was never a factor. *Never.* He was a "soul mate," as some saw it. The same with Sybille Bedford, her neighbor in Provence, and Craig Claiborne and Dick Graff, and Richard Olney, for whom she gave a press party when he published *Simple French Food* and always expressed the greatest respect, though it wasn't always mutual, as she might have hoped. "Richard never forgave her for being homophobic," says Paul Grimes. "He was tired of all her veiled innuendoes and told people to *watch it* around her."

Clark Wolf, at the time a young protégé of Jim Beard, says, "It would be easy to call Julia a homophobe, but it depends on how you define that term. She was politically incorrect on a regular basis about a lot of things, propriety be damned." A handicap parking space was "where the cripples park," and she liked the way "colored people" cooked. Friends would cringe when these labels popped out of her mouth but knew that she was a product of her times, unaware of giving offense.

She certainly wasn't thinking when it came to Bob Johnson. "She never thought Bob Johnson was gay," says Jane Friedman, "and she was really shocked when she finally found out. I mean, *really shocked*!" He would always be her "he-man lawyer," a man she trusted unconditionally, and in her eyes every bit "as normal" as Russ Morash. The two men conducted a fragile truce.

Together with a staff of twenty-five, they put the show into production that January of 1983 and quickly resumed the frantic pace of previous Julia Child series: rehearsing, staging, lighting, editing, socializing, and occasionally cooking. "The house was utter chaos," Rachel Child recounted. "It was like Grand Central Station at rush hour. Friends, neighbors, even passersby with their kids would stop in to have a look at the proceedings, perhaps hoping to touch Julia or maybe her food. It seemed like the set was a big happy party; everyone was in pretty good spirits."

Julia's niece, who was living in Pasadena at the time, was enlisted to visit the set and stay close to Paul, muzzle him, she says, "because he would yell instructions to Julia during filming." In San Francisco, while Julia performed with René Verdon, the former White House chef, he'd shouted "Read your cue cards correctly, Julia!" from the back of the auditorium. At regular intervals, he'd shout out the time. *"Nineteen minutes!"* "Thank you, Paul," she'd respond, without lifting an eye from the cutting board. "That's my husband, Paul, our official timekeeper." Paul had just turned eighty-one, and though he was "quite well physically" in Julia's eyes, she knew he was "mentally often confused." Regularly, he fell asleep during dinner, just nodded right off at the table while the meal was in full swing, and Julia would order the person sitting closest to him to "kick Paul, *hard*." After being jolted awake, Julia usually chortled, "Ah, welcome back, Paul." It was age—*"c'est l'âge,"* she said—age was catching up to him. She wanted to protect him for as long as she could.

For the most part, her instincts were good when it came to Paul. She made sure he had enough distractions to keep him busy on the set and named him the official photographer for *Dinner at Julia's,* even though a young, talented professional covered the action. But on February 8, as production began on a new episode, they got news that would throw Paul a wicked curve. Charlie Child had died "very suddenly"—his *twin,* his echo, his other soul. "We were truly parts of each other," Paul explained to a friend, certainly no overstatement. Their relationship was symbiotic, though not always mutually beneficial. Paul wrote Charlie long, beautifully composed, introspective letters nearly *every day,* for forty-five years, though through them he was never able to reconcile their very complicated sibling rivalry. But losing Charlie was tantamount to losing a part of himself. "I suffer because of Cha's death," he scribbled across a page in his datebook. Confined to some dark, private place in his mind for several months afterward, he languished in despondency, alternately grieving and lashing out for no particular reason. Julia recognized the severe blow it had dealt Paul's condition. "Charlie's death really set him back mentally," she admitted.

Julia paid a high physical price for keeping Paul by her side. Throughout the taping of *Dinner at Julia's* her knees grew stiffer and more swollen, despite a steady dose of Indocin to reduce inflammation. Strong and self-reliant in public, in private she suffered excruciating pain after long days "slogging through viscous mud . . . to gather a basketful of yellow precious chanterelles" or braving choppy waters on a salmon boat in Puget Sound. There was no end to her grueling balancing act.

DINNER AT JULIA'S took her mind off the infirmities. "She had a ball doing it," Russ Morash recalls. The whole experience was "fast-paced and lively," different from anything she'd done before—and *new,* which was Julia's greatest delight. "It was great fun having visiting chefs," she said, in particular the four French virtuosos—René Verdon, Jean-Claude Prévot, Jean-Pierre Goyenvalle, and Yves Labbe—who'd updated Escoffier in ways her mentors might consider sacrilegious. Their food was inventive, trendy. The French were gamers, not at all uptight once they hit these shores, she thought. Meanwhile, it was "good to have some red-blooded Americans doing things," as well.

Each show was a lavish production. Besides the adventure and the guest chef and winemaker segments, the dinner itself was a glitzy, luxe affair. Guests didn't just arrive at the mansion in their own shabby cars; they were delivered in a Rolls-Royce sedan polished to a high-gloss sheen. There was a head butler named Ken to greet them and enough fresh flowers to dress a royal wedding. And speaking of dress, who was that dolled-up figure circulating as hostess? Dearie, it was none other than Julia Child. Not the Julia Child audiences had come to recognize and love, in her boxy skirt and frumpy blouse with the Trois Gourmandes badge pinned to it. She looked grotesque, like Jessica Rabbit, in a splashy caftan, her hair done with "every possible twist and turn and curl," and "tarted up" with way too much makeup. Russ Morash took one look at her and thought she "looked like a figure from Madame Tussaud's."

He pulled Bob Johnson aside and said, "This won't do," but neither Johnson nor Julia wanted to hear it.

The critics zeroed right in on Julia's startling makeover. She got pounded for her image as much as for the show's content, a pastiche of disconnected scenes that catered to the frivolous well-to-do. *Time* said her "wardrobe was worthy of *Auntie Mame*," while *The New York Times* saw it as "silly and distracting." Even longtime loyal viewers weren't buying into it. "To see this darling, feisty, gifted lady dressed up in cowboy clothes, tottering around in boots, swishing among rather wooden-looking 'guests,' and above all to see her modest, perfect little show given the Beverly Hills treatment, the ostentation, the waiters, the gratuitous free plugs . . . well, it's awful!" one fan wrote. Another begged, "We want you to be human," before pleading: "How *could* you?"

If Julia and her handlers thought they'd reinvented Julia Child, they'd miscalculated. "We were ultimately criticized because we'd gotten away from what viewers thought they wanted, which was more of the same," Russ Morash concluded. "Apparently, people hate change, especially when it involved Julia."

Even so, Julia wasn't bothered in the least. She'd had a swell time doing the series and if people couldn't adapt, then so be it. "We had such a good time making those shows," she told a reporter. Drawing from her principles of cooking, she clung to an old favorite: *Never apologize*. Serve it up and move on.

BUT BEFORE MOVING on—that is, moving on back to Cambridge—Julia kept a promise to the newly formed American Institute of Wine and Food (AIWF). The little engine that could, powered by $50,000 anted up by Julia, the Mondavis, the Sanfords, and a half-dozen other founders, had been chugging along slowly, gathering momentum where it could. An early meeting in Santa Barbara laid out the AIWF's mission statement: to create a national educational organization, a crossroads of professionals and laypeople, academics and practitioners, that would promote food and wine to the American public. It sure sounded good *in theory*, and so did its motto: *inter folio fructus,* "between the leaves there is the fruit," the grapes, which could also be construed as meaning "between the leaves of books there is the fruit of education."

Julia was excited. In a roundabout way, it was another form of teaching, her true passion, and she threw herself into it headlong, without reservation. Meetings, dinners, phone calls, appearances, solicitations, money—whatever they wanted from her she gave unconditionally. Promoting wine and food was a fine and noble cause, but she also had two other goals up her sleeve: to establish a college degree in the culinary arts and to make sure women got more involved.

The CIA—the Culinary Institute of America—which stood more or less alone at the forefront of academia, was "just a good cooking school," in Julia's estimation, no different from Le Cordon Bleu. But gastronomy and culinary arts demanded a broader perspective. What about the science of food, or culinary history? There was plenty to learn about nutrition and diet, even food writing. Julia envisioned a curriculum that covered all the bases, maybe even separated cooking and baking. *And treated women respectfully.* Even as late as 1983, she continued to rail against the CIA's attitude toward women. Oh, sure, sure, they were admitting more to their program, but the ratios were still way out of whack. "When I was there, women were not supposed to be in the kitchen," recalls Sara Moulton. "All the chef-instructors were European men who ran the place like a military academy. They ignored the women in their classes, for the most part. And Julia knew it." This was one injustice the AIWF would correct. You could count on it; she'd see to it herself.

First, however, you had to feed the beast. AIWF needed funds, donations, and a *lot* of them to underwrite its intentions. The founders had ponied up seed money, but it was hardly enough. More, *more,* MORE they needed—for a library and a newsletter, and a skeleton staff. It took money to grease the wheels of their culinary conveyance. The fastest way to a donation was through one's stomach, they decided, and God knew they had the wherewithal to mine that lode.

Julia made a lunch to benefit AIWF, but that was chicken feed. Along with Jeremiah Tower, she prepared a lobster bacchanal that succeeded in raising a few more shekels and cast the nets a little further, attracting fat-cat sponsors like Fritz Maytag, the washing-machine magnate, and comedian Danny Kaye. But they needed to make a splash; they needed to reel in bigger tunas.

Determined to pull out all the stops, the AIWF staged its first public bash on May 4, 1983. They called it the "American Celebration," an eleven-course feast held at the Stanford Court in San Francisco, prepared by a brilliant constellation of new American chefs who exclusively used homegrown American food. It was a way of announcing "we've got the stuff" to a fan base that paid dearly: $250 a head for the meal and various workshops. On the surface, as Julia noted, "it was a tremendous success." The event was a complete sellout; more than 370 people showed up. "But AIWF spent a fortune—it must have cost them a trillion dollars," says Clark Wolf, "and it was an event from which they almost never recovered."

Three weeks later, they repeated the extravaganza in Santa Barbara as a big outdoor garden party, with all the food and wine donated by local merchants. This time, seven hundred people attended, with hundreds more, cash in hand, turned away at the door. With such a smash turnout it felt like the big launch AIWF was hoping for. So why were the founders feeling ill at ease? Fund-raising, it seemed, meant staging big dinners. "It began to dawn on us," says Richard Sanford, "that all we were doing was throwing parties for wealthy people who had the money to participate—Julia referred to them as 'the robber barons'—and it was becoming more elitist than we liked." Julia loved the idea of presenting food to the people. "But she was afraid it was becoming pretentious and separatist, instead of inclusive."

No one was giving up the ship, as of yet. There were too many good ideas and resources to build on. But if AIWF were to succeed as a populist enterprise, they were going to have to retool in order to cast a wider net.

Julia took this sapling back to Cambridge with her, intent on laying down some fertile East Coast roots. The national organization of AIWF was to be built upon local chapters, and New York was already answering the call. Julia was hoping that Boston might step up to the plate, depending on whether its food scene had evolved.

Up until 1980, Boston's palate hadn't changed much since the Pilgrims landed. It had very little going on in the way of fine dining. Chowders, fish fries, pot roast, and puddings pervaded the Yankee menus. Dinner vegetables went on the stove sometime after breakfast. The most visible upscale establishment was a place called Locke-Ober, a wonderful old chophouse saloon presided over by cruel men who wheeled out stainless-steel trolleys heaped with mutton and the like. The Union Oyster House, adjoining city hall, was a classic Irish pub and bona-fide Boston legend. The dining rooms in the Ritz and Parker House were stuffy hotel restaurants that served *continental,* a posh name for stuffy hotel restaurant food. There were a few popular red-sauce Italian joints in the North End, where a plate of spaghetti and meatballs could sustain you through the winter. And Maison Robert—*Ro-bear*—which was Frenchy French, Escoffier-style, and a dinosaur among the fossils. Only Harvest's menu offered anything that could be construed as creative—a muscular French-style cooking uprooted with American ingredients that heralded the so-called New American revolution.

But by the end of 1983, when Julia arrived home, the revolution had stormed the citadel. "Boston was ready to eat," says Jasper White, who was leading the charge at Seasons, in the Bostonian Hotel. "Everyone here was breaking the mold—doing the same old shit, because our bosses insisted on it, but putting a personal statement on every dish." He hired Lydia Shire, whose wildly original cooking was already raising eyebrows in the city, and they did menus with regional ingredients designed to rattle the Puritans' diet, dishes like trout with fried grits that would seem timid today but were absolutely revolutionary in 1983.

But it wasn't White's food that transformed the scene; it was his banker, Jack Sidell. "*He gave me a bank loan!*" says White, incredulous to this day, because he hadn't "a pot to piss in," much less credit enough to get a car loan. Sidell, however, had some experience with restaurants and could smell what was in the air. He knew there was no revolution without financing, and when he gave White the money to open his own place, chef-owned restaurants became viable entities. "Once the chefs got their hands on restaurants, everything changed," White says. The money was put in the hands of the artist, as opposed to the businessman, and now the cooks could do anything they wanted.

White opened Restaurant Jasper a few months later with a power-house menu that kicked out the jams: ricotta-filled tortellini in a rich rabbit sauce; homemade garlic pasta with crayfish and fresh tarragon; rare, meaty squab paired with breaded oysters; and pan-roasted lobster with whiskey—yes, whiskey!

The inmates had finally taken over the asylum.

Across America the revolution stepped up its charge. A new style of cooking finally burst on the scene that would be embraced by a vast tide of young chefs at the helm of their own places. Within months of White's coup, Jeremiah Tower opened Stars, Wolfgang Puck opened Spago,

Jonathan Waxman opened Jams, Larry Forgione opened An American Place, and in the six months that followed there was an explosion of New American Chefs. "It was like a cauldron boiling over," White recalls.

Jasper sent another friend to Jack Sidell—Todd English, who borrowed enough to open Olive's. Lydia Shire also opened her own place, as did Michaela Larson, who introduced Boston to the kind of Italian food that hewed to Italy as opposed to Italian America.

Julia was absolutely beside herself. There was so much attention being paid to food in the city, so much high-pitched excitement. From what she'd heard, "it was still a pretty sloppy scene," but *explosive*; she was intrigued by its brashness. "She wasn't really prepared for the upheaval going on in Boston," says Sheryl Julian, "but she was determined to be part of it."

As soon as she'd unpacked, she grabbed Paul and their friends the Pratts and headed out into the thick of it. They began eating their way across the new landscape, beginning at Jasper's, through the middle of the lineup, and on down to the lowliest newcomer. "At first, she didn't like all the experimentation," says Corby Kummer, who occasionally accompanied the Childs on their rounds. "She didn't like the excess, there were too many things on the plate. But every so often we'd hit a real winner, and Julia would say, 'He has *technique*.' That was her highest praise."

No matter what, after dinner in every new restaurant she would head into the kitchen to seek out the chef. There would be an initial jolt of panic. One can only imagine looking up from the stove to find Julia Child staring over your shoulder. But she'd find a few kind words to say about the food, offer encouragement, "keep up the good work." She'd call them dearie, always dearie. "Tell me, dearie, was there a little tarragon in your mayonnaise?" "Was that your idea, dearie, putting celeriac in the potato puree?" No matter who the chef, she invariably wanted to know how many women were working the line, suggesting ever-so-gently that more be involved, never forgetting to throw her arm around the dishwasher before she left.

"She was always super-sensitive about what she said to young chefs," says Sally Jackson, an early publicist on the Boston food scene. One night Julia and Jackson checked out a new Cambridge restaurant that had been making noise on the culinary grapevine. "The chef didn't have any training at all, and when he came out to say hello, Julia very carefully said, 'We had a wonderful time, dearie. This is such a lovely restaurant.' But not a word about the food." As they were about to leave, she pulled the chef aside and said, "I do hope you get to travel, dearie. It's so important to experience cuisines in their native countries."

Again and again, she encouraged local chefs to find their own voices, to want to succeed, to be bold, to try to make a name for themselves. "Her disagreements with their style of cooking were minor compared to the idea that she wanted there to be independent chefs working in Boston who cared about making good food," says Corby Kummer. "She promoted the scene, made connections, sparked competition. And she would call up people and recommend these chefs; she wanted others to know them and to publicize them."

Jasper White, especially, sought her blessing. His new restaurant was a big financial undertaking; its success was riding on word of mouth. "I really needed Julia to love it," he recalls. "I needed her to put the word out."

She came in a few months after the kitchen got settled. "I was a fucking nervous wreck," White recalls. "The rest of the dining room could have gone completely to hell. We just focused on her." He and Lydia Shire personally cooked everything that got sent out to Julia's table; every single ingredient had to pass their approval. "If I don't see the bread," he ordered his staff, "you don't take it out to her." Twenty-five years later, he still remembers the order: "She had oysters, Paul had rack of lamb, Julia my pan-fried lobster. I grilled leeks and roasted her potatoes in lamb fat." After dinner, she came back in the kitchen to say she loved it. A week later she came in again and that pretty much sealed the deal. The jungle drums went beating across Boston.

According to White, Julia transformed the Boston food scene. "She became the tent pole," he says, "the anchor. Everything that went on in the city went through her. She took us all under her wing and was *thoughtful* about how she supported us. We got invited to her house; she made sure we all knew each other." When a young cook named Gordon Hamersley moved back to Boston, Julia sent him to Jasper and Lydia. Later, when Hamersley finally opened his bistro, Julia quickly gave it her imprimatur.

"If we were good, she made sure people knew," says Jody Adams, who worked for Gordon Hamersley before opening her own place. "Thanks to her, Boston became a major restaurant town with a close-knit group of chefs who helped build it together."

The benefits worked both ways. "Restaurant food was shifting from classic French to New American," says Clark Wolf, "and when the young chefs changed their styles, they dragged Julia along with them." Resis-

tant, at first, more as cheerleader than stovemate. "I will never do anything but French cooking," she told *Time* in 1966, during her cover-story
interview. But by the mid-1980s her curiosity was aroused. She quizzed
the young upstarts relentlessly about their technique and favorite recipes.
Her own cooking became looser, less observant of French dogma, more
improvisational. "She began updating the French classics," says Marian
Morash. "It was so much fun to watch her unwind."

That feeling spread as 103 Irving took on an informal open-house
policy. The young chefs dropped by regularly to talk, relax, and eat. Julia
always put on her trademark lunch—a tuna fish sandwich with homemade olive-oil mayo—and a mix of shoptalk and gossip prevailed. Even
the local press came by to socialize and eat instead of just seeking comment for the record. Sheryl Julian recalls taking time out from her *Boston
Globe* food columns to join the festivities at Julia's dinner table for the
camaraderie, if not always satisfying fare.

"One of the first times I went there, I had roast chicken with rice,"
Julian remembers. "There were ten of us packed in like sardines, as the
chicken came to the table. Now, I'm Jewish, so I assumed it was the *first*
chicken; she'd cut it and another would be coming out in a minute. But I
was wrong. Everyone's portion was the size of an eyeglass lens. Yet it was
one of the best parties I'd ever been to."

Practically every night was party night at Julia's. Her kitchen door
was always open and whoever happened by was invited to join the meal.
There was always some celebrated person at the table—David Brinkley,
John Updike, Charlie Gibson, Roger Vergé, whoever was in town—and
a giddy atmosphere was strictly enforced. Like every hostess in America,
Julia was always slightly behind schedule, so she put everybody, no matter
how famous or distinguished, to work. Everyone pitched in the prep, no
exceptions. A bowl of Julia's beloved Goldfish served as hors d'oeuvres.
Paul kept the wine flowing before nodding off at his place.

Celebrations were only slightly more formal. The food would be copious to mark the occasion and considerably dressy—oysters and foie gras
and truffled this-or-that and endless champagne. Only Thanksgiving
became a chaotic affair. On Thanksgiving, Julia's phone started ringing
around noon and continued steadily until eight that night. The callers
were all strangers, people in the throes of making their dinners who had
either messed up or needed rescuing. Julia's number was in the phone
book—it was a famous fact that she was not only listed, but picked up the

phone herself—so people took that as an invitation to call at will. She answered every single question, as though she were some sort of hotline. "Yes, dearie, you just put that bird right on the table."

"It was so charming!" says Sheryl Julian. "She was concerned that people were going to all this effort and their timing was off or they ran out of milk for the potatoes." She was determined to do the troubleshooting, figuring a sentence or two would turn their meals around.

"Dearie, you put that old sweet-potato soufflé right on the counter. No one's going to care." "Have you *ever* had hot turkey? No one eats hot turkey."

Occasionally, she'd call one of the emerging young chefs and pump them for answers to food questions. Jasper White recalls often picking up a call at home to find Julia on the line. "Dearie, last night I made red snapper. It was beautiful but turned out really tough. What do you think happened?" He'd gaze at the clock on his night table and think, "It's six-thirty Saturday morning. Doesn't she know I cooked until midnight?" Didn't matter. Morning, noon, night—if Julia had a question, she'd say, "Oh, I know who to call!"

Her life back in Cambridge only got busier and busier. Throughout 1985 and 1986, Julia immersed herself in a bruising cycle of work that would have derailed a woman half her age. She signed a whopping $400,000 deal with Knopf for a book and videocassette series called *The Way to Cook,* an encyclopedic instruction bible of everything she knew—recipes, ruminations, technique, and *trucs*—illustrated lavishly with photographs from her *Parade* columns. The book would take nearly five years to produce, but she completed the videos in practically no time, and supported them with a ten-city promotional tour. Even while she was on the road, she churned out weekly columns for *Parade* and flew back for regular appearances on *Good Morning America.* There were also fund-raisers for AIWF, the Women's Culinary Guild, the International Association of Culinary Professionals, Les Dames d'Escoffier, the Association of Cooking Schools, Smith College, Harvard, independent bookstores, and any other needy case that caught her eye.

There was no chance of her slowing down. "I have no intention of ever retiring," she repeated like a mantra to journalists, hoping they'd eventually take her at her word, and vows to surge forward "till I drop" became ridiculously routine.

Dropping had never really vexed Julia. Death was Paul's department, intensified tenfold since Charlie had died. But Julia never really paid it much thought. She seemed content to trundle on, convinced that one day "you just slip off the raft." And when that day came, it was fine by her.

But there were snags in the journey as it flowed downstream. On January 23, 1985, while the Childs were resting at La Pitchoune, they got the news that James Beard had died. His death caught Julia by surprise. She knew Jim had been ill—he had been fighting one ailment or another practically as long as she'd known him—but last she'd heard, before leaving for France, he was hard at work editing his newspaper column. Little did she know that, in the month before his death, Beard suffered from congestive heart failure, intestinal bleeding, and kidney failure, to say nothing of monstrous weight issues and alcohol excess. Years of self-abuse had finally caught up with him. At the end, his dissipated body just plain gave out. Still, Julia grieved, grew melancholy and contemplative. To her, just like to the rest of the culinary world, James Beard had been larger than life itself. He'd transformed how Americans ate; they'd accomplished that feat together. *Together.* Reflecting on Jim and the legacy he left was a long, plaintive gaze into her own past, which must have seemed as gossamer as a meringue.

If anything, it made her more aware of frailty and the ravages of aging. She only had to look around her to be reminded of its consuming effects. Simca's husband, Jean, was seriously ill with kidney disease and Avis DeVoto was battling pancreatic cancer. On top of everything else, Julia learned that her lawyer, Bob Johnson, who'd been fighting a stupefying disease he'd contracted in the Caribbean, was sick with AIDS and had no hope of recovering. All these friends on the periphery of her world! "It was heartrending to see someone going downhill before one's eyes," Julia said, "and to know there is so little one can do."

No one knew better than Julia how age and health conspired to lay waste. Paul, she finally admitted, was "in a gradual decline." He'd weathered a prostate operation, with a second one on the horizon. He was taking Ritalin, a powerful stimulant, to help control his attention deficit and narcolepsy, but "his receiving and processing of information has gotten steadily worse." His stamina and personality were certainly impaired, but other telltale signs served to raise Julia's fears. For one thing, his painting, what little there was of it, was crude, incomprehensible. Julia continued to assure friends that he was painting away, when in fact he rarely touched his brushes, much less put them to canvas. And his short-term memory was deserting him. In the summer of 1985, right before Julia left for Europe to shoot a travel segment for *GMA* called "Julia Child in Italy," Paul had gone out for a walk to pick up his morning newspaper, but returned minutes later saying he couldn't remember where he was going. He'd become frustrated, disoriented. Instantly, Julia realized that his mind, not just his body, posed a serious threat and that she could no longer chance to leave Paul alone.

It also meant she had to reconsider some of the clutter that dominated her day-to-day schedule. There was too much chaos in their home, contributing to Paul's confusion. Often 103 Irving seemed busier than the intersection at Copley Square, and she could tell the constant traffic made him agitated, addled. On any given day, there was a preposterous ongoing parade: Julia's secretary, the housekeeper, their gardener, a full contingent of women testing recipes and prepping demos and styling dishes, grocery deliveries, friends stopping by, journalists, chefs, messengers, Russ, Ruth Lockwood, Avis, neighbors. *Enough!* In particular, the photo shoots for her *Parade* column turned the house upside down. Once a month, in Julia's kitchen, they shot enough pictures to illustrate four columns. "The living room and hall become staging areas for plates, tablecloths, etc.," she explained. "All the dining room furniture [gets moved to] the piano room . . . and the kitchen is busy indeed." Then *Parade*'s crew invaded: Julia's editor, the art director, the photographer's assistants, equipment men. *Enough!* To simplify matters, she insisted they move the shoot to an outside studio, and eventually, in late 1986, she ended the *Parade* columns altogether, ceding them to the popular *Silver Palate Cookbook* authors, Julee Rosso and Sheila Lukins, a succession that signaled a generational shift.

Enough was enough.

There were times when one had to be harshly unsentimental, and moving on often meant first closing doors. It was obvious when Julia took Paul to La Pitchoune in September 1986, just after their fortieth wedding anniversary, that it would most likely be their last time there together. She would be unable to bring him back there again. It was just too difficult traveling overseas with Paul. He was eighty-four, and age alone had become a factor, but his mental state was altogether too unstable.

She had been wary of going back to Provence at all that year. Earlier in February, after years of pain and interminable suffering, Julia finally had her bum knee replaced, and the convalescence, typically, was a struggle to keep her leashed. On those rare occasions when she begrudgingly stayed put, there was hope that a litany of summer social obligations might be met. But Julia was beyond hope, untamable, too eager to "burst forth again like a tigress into the world of La Kweezeen," as she playfully called it. Besides, she needed to stay a step ahead of Paul. After he had that second prostate operation in June, his physical condition was precarious at best. He was foggy and took "many cat-naps which he is not aware of."

Life was tough enough that spring. Bob Johnson's condition grew progressively worse, necessitating his permanent move into a Boston hospital. The impact of his battle with AIDS dealt a double blow to Julia. First, she had to get over the shock that Bob was indeed gay. "She hadn't a clue," says Marian Morash. "Whenever he came to Julia's house for dinner, he always brought a dark-haired woman along with him, and Julia used to ask me, 'When do you think they'll get married?'" An assistant recalls her saying, "It can't be AIDS, dearie. AIDS is a gay disease, and Bob isn't gay." But now, no such revelation could temper her sorrow. She'd grown incredibly fond of Johnson over their sixteen-year relationship. He'd fought tough battles for her, often ruffling feathers, and often going up against her closest professional friends, winning important concessions she never would have achieved. He was her "he-man lawyer." She was "scared to death for him," she confided to a friend.

She was also scared to death of AIDS, a disease she mistakenly believed was airborne. There had been plenty of talk about it in the months before Johnson's diagnosis, uninformed debate as to whether it could be transmitted through food by chefs. According to a member of her staff, "Julia was close to what I would call obsessed over what we didn't know about this threat to our health." Fear: Bob Johnson brought it right onto her doorstep.

Was she going to contract this dreadful illness? That really didn't concern her anymore. She wasn't about to let Bob bear it all alone. He was only forty-five years old, practically a son to her. Knowing he wasn't going to survive, she visited him in the hospital, giving him a long, deep-felt hug, expressing her deep grief in no uncertain terms.

Bob's death that September seemed like a cruel, unnecessary blow. In August, Jean Fischbacher also died, from hepatitis C. The cumulative effect of these tragedies weighed heavily on Julia. She'd take Paul back to France for a nice long visit, but it would serve to close yet another door.

La Pitchoune had long been their little slice of heaven. This one last visit would have to be—*enough*.

Twenty-four

The End of an Era

For once, Julia was adamant. The publication of her next book, *The Way to Cook,* scheduled to be released in October 1989, would be her last. Over and done with. The reason she gave Simca was that writing had become "too confining," but that argument only scratched the surface.

This book, more than others, had been a slog, a seemingly endless five-year endeavor that, at times, felt more like forced labor than an exploration of cooking and technique. The sheer volume of recipes—more than eight hundred, culled from the *Dinner at Julia's* series, *Good Morning America* segments, and *Parade* columns—was a lifetime's work condensed in such a way that the recipes required extensive reevaluation and reediting. Deadlines came and went like overdue bills; all those years chained to a typewriter and computer really got to her. "Bookery is so damned solitary," Julia complained to M. F. K. Fisher, not "lively and fun" like doing a TV program. But a new TV series didn't seem to be in the cards. Prime time was angling for youth and flash—"the event," as Julia envisioned it, instead of good solid "straight cooking." The competition to land a new cooking show was fierce—and generally depressing. There were so many poseurs and rank entertainers on the air, galloping cooks and frugal cooks and sixty-second cooks and I-hate-to cooks. Besides, classic French cuisine was out of vogue, in Julia's estimation, "because of health and cholesterol fads."

Julia felt about health and cholesterol fads the way President Bush

On the set of *The Way to Cook*, with Russ Morash

felt about broccoli. So much fuss had been raised in the past few years that the kitchen had become an ideological battleground. George Carlin was right—there were seven dirty words you can't say on television, but if Julia were to enumerate them, they would be *butter, cream, veal, sugar, marrow, potatoes,* and *fat.* Everywhere she turned "the food police," a phrase she coined, were lining up to monitor what people ate. The organic proselytizers, the anti-veal fanatics, PETA extremists, anti-irradiation activists—*vegetarians;* Julia pronounced the word the way President Bush said *liberals.* "Whatever happened to good old moderation?" she wondered. "What happened to common sense—eating whatever you want, small helpings, combined with variation, exercise, and weight-watching?"

The diet gurus were always on her back about using rich, sensuous ingredients. Nathan Pritikin had accused her of promoting wine and fat, and one of his acolytes sent letters to Julia's WGBH underwriters claiming that her cooking contributed to obesity and heart disease. Typically, Julia was unflappable. "I must say," she wrote in response, "after learning something about the severity of his diet and knowing not only of Pritikin's long illness but of his relatively early death, I have often wondered if a good meal once in a while might have kept him going a little longer."

She'd always fought off the enemies of French cuisine, the Nervous Nellies, as she called them, claiming they made the dinner table "a trap, rather than a pleasure." But in *The Way to Cook* she held out an olive branch. "In this book, I am very conscious of calories and fat," she wrote, "and the major proportions of the master recipes are low in fat or even fat-free." Then, again, she also crusaded for a shelf of *indulgences* that would contain "the best butter, jumbo-size eggs, heavy cream, marbled steaks, sausages and pâtés, hollandaise and butter sauces, French butter-cream fillings, gooey chocolate cakes, and all those lovely items that demand disciplined rationing."

Under ordinary circumstances, *The Way to Cook* should have been a pleasure to compile. It was an encyclopedic work, of sorts, an A to Z collection of everything Julia cooked, everything she practiced in the kitchen, all her culinary knowledge adapted for beginners, as well as "the new generation of cooks who have not grown up in the old traditions, yet who need a basic knowledge of good food." Vaguely modeled on Jacques Pépin's 1976 masterpiece, *La Technique,* the ultimate kitchen reference and practically every serious chef's go-to guide, Julia saw *The Way to Cook* as "more recipe-driven than Jacques's book," according to Judith Jones, "more of a primer, so that someone interested in cooking could develop enough confidence using a master recipe to attempt variations on it." A lazy writer might have stitched together the contents of her recipe files or simply anthologized her previous books. But lazy wasn't part of Julia's makeup. If anything, the familiarity of the material drove her to seek a deeper understanding of it. Her curiosity, insatiable as ever, tipped toward the obsessive.

"[I] never feel I know enough," she lamented to M. F. K. Fisher, while researching the meat chapter, "and have to go out looking at chops, cooking them, etc."

Looking at chops, *cooking* them—after thirty-five years! How much more was there to learn about meat?

Plenty, apparently. The variety of cuts continued to confuse her—and, thus, her readers. Blade roast, tri-tip, shoulder filet, hanger, porterhouse, wedgebone, skirt, flap, rib-eye, flat iron, ranch, rump, flank—the possibilities were mind-boggling. She asked her butcher, Jack Savenor, to identify every conceivable piece of meat in an effort to reach a consensus, but there were so many other factors that needed to be addressed. What about freezing chops—or flanks, or tips? Julia identified with American home cooks who, out of convenience or necessity, cooked from their freezers. What were the best methods for defrosting? she wondered. At what temperature should the freezer ideally be set? These weren't questions to which she could ad-lib answers. Her advice had to be accurate, scientific. So she conducted in-depth research, first by contacting the National Livestock and Meat Board and then the folks at Amana.

The work began to consume.

If only that were the main focus of her worries. But personal issues began to intrude. In 1988, in the throes of manuscript rewrites in Santa Barbara, Julia was "plunging around" her office when she tripped over her computer wire and fell, breaking her hip. "She was furious with herself," recalls Nancy Barr, a kitchen assistant who had Julia's ear. "Her work on the book suddenly skidded to a halt." But she wasn't as concerned with either her hip or her work as she was about how they distracted from Paul, who was relying on her more than ever.

"[Paul], I am sorry to say, is not doing at all well," she wrote to M. F. K. Fisher in March 1987, just weeks after his eighty-fifth birthday. The move to Santa Barbara served to facilitate his comfort but did nothing to reverse the effects of dementia. "He was still *there*," says Rebecca Alssid, who ran the culinary arts program at Boston University, "but barely. At dinner, his head would practically fall into the soup." Charlie Gibson, who replaced David Hartman on *Good Morning America* that February, described Paul as "clearly not well and fairly unresponsive. As far as I could tell he was practically lifeless."

Week by week, Julia noticed more signs of his regression. "He lurches about when he walks now," she reported in a letter, "and the other day, although I had his arm, he plunged down some wooden steps onto the cement below." A year before, he might have broken such a fall, avoiding serious injury. But with his coordination no longer intact, he subsequently cracked a bone in his wrist, as well as a tooth and a rib.

Now, with *The Way to Cook* on the brink of publication, the usual hubbub was jacked up to a higher degree of intensity. There were so many last-minute details to arrange before going on the road. During a particularly chaotic week in Cambridge, before another trip out to Santa Barbara, Julia was engaged in back-to-back interviews intended to lay a little groundwork for the forthcoming book. While she was upstairs in the office doing several radio station "phoners," a cleaning company working downstairs left the front door unlocked. It was only a matter of time before Paul, in his usual state of confusion, wandered outside by himself. Coincidentally, someone was getting out of a taxi at the curb. Paul hailed it and apparently gave the driver an address of some kind, but sometime later, when it became clear he had no money, he was booted out on a street corner far from home.

It wasn't until several hours later that Julia realized Paul was gone. Since his stroke, in 1974, she had been terrified of his wandering off alone. She knew he'd be helpless in a situation that was out of her immediate control, and, now, it had finally happened. As unimaginable as that must have seemed, Julia managed to keep calm, organizing a posse to scour the neighborhood. The police were of little help. Fortunately, a neighbor recalled seeing Paul get into a cab and a taxi dispatcher eventually helped to pinpoint his location. He was safe—for now. But Julia feared it was only a matter of time before something more perilous happened, something life-threatening . . . or worse. That evening, after she helped put Paul to sleep, she made up her mind: he needed to be somewhere he could be watched at all times.

Julia couldn't handle him by herself anymore, not with a book coming out, not in his diminished condition. They had been the closest of life partners for forty-five years; he was her mentor, her lover, her closest confidant, the person who inspired her to be herself, to do great work, *more than that.* He was the force behind Julia Child's public personality. But he wasn't that Paul anymore, and Julia, being an eminently practical person, knew she could not continue her career if she had to be a full-time nurse for her husband. She told herself that he didn't really understand what was going on anyway.

"If I tried to take care of him at home and people stopped coming to visit, then chances are I'd become resentful of him," she concluded. "We had a wonderful time together, and I was very lucky, but the survivors have to survive."

In June 1989, while Paul was in the hospital for a prostate procedure, Julia made arrangements with a senior care facility in Santa Barbara to take him in on a part-time basis. Her new lawyer, Bill Truslow, supported the idea. "It was obvious Julia needed professional help," he remembers, "and I *strongly* urged her to organize it. Doing it saddened her, naturally, but she didn't hesitate. She was taking care of Paul—but also taking care of herself."

Julia tried to keep the arrangement as loosely structured as possible. Rather than hinting at any permanence, she told him it was "a place for him to recuperate." To a man who had only sporadic understanding, it seemed harmless enough. Every day, like clockwork, she arrived during visiting hours, always with a pint of his favorite ice cream. She often took Paul out to dinner nearby and dressed him for special occasions, when the situation allowed her to keep him by her side. In August, when the Southern California Culinary Guild presented an exhibit of his paintings, the Childs previewed it together before the gallery opened to the public. But Julia returned Paul to the nursing home before doubling back to arrive with the rest of the guests. As far as Paul knew, in those flickering interludes when his mind was lucid, he was in the facility for observation purposes only. He wasn't aware that anything more permanent had been settled. But Julia needed to finalize the situation.

Was Santa Barbara the right place to square him away? Julia knew that someday she would probably retire there. She loved the city and its sumptuous weather; the California spirit was still bone-deep, still an intransigent part of her makeup. But there was too much going on back East right now to consider making such a drastic move. Her gig at *Good Morning America* was especially precious, the only vehicle keeping her in front of a television audience. She hadn't had a show of her own since *Dinner at Julia's* in 1983, and the temptation was always strong to return. To be on the air again, with a new series, a new challenge—she couldn't shake that powerful impulse. Her chances would be lower if she relocated out West. Better to stay in Cambridge, near WGBH and Russ Morash, to see if something developed. There was also a commitment she'd made to Boston University, where she and Jacques Pépin were helping launch the culinary arts degree program. If Paul remained behind at the Santa Barbara facility, she couldn't see him on a regular basis. That wouldn't do—no, that wouldn't do at all. He was still too much a part of her life to put long distances and stretches of time between them.

Not long afterward, Julia broached the subject with Dr. Tim Johnson, a longtime member of GMA's Family who lived and practiced privately in Boston. "I've got to put Paul in a nursing home," she told him during a brief, businesslike phone call. "Would you help me scout out some suitable places?" The request wasn't unexpected to Johnson. "I'd gone out to dinner with them some months back," he recalls. "I hadn't seen them in a while, and I remember thinking, 'This guy's going downhill fast.' " As a favor, he made a few calls and discovered there were plenty of nursing homes in the Boston area, "many, however, that were not up to par." Too many were more profit-oriented than patient-oriented, employing people at the lowest end of the wage scale. Johnson wanted to make sure he recommended a place where Paul would get capable care. One place, the Fairlawn Nursing Home in nearby Lexington, got high marks in that department. It was a private, family-owned facility in a reconverted Victorian farmhouse set amid acres of lush landscaping where residents could relax. Julia already knew of it from her friend Pat Pratt, whose aunt and uncle were residents. Johnson drove out to Lexington to look the place over and wound up recommending it to Julia, who acted on his advice.

In September 1989, she and Paul flew back to Boston with Bill Truslow, who had agreed to help her get Paul settled at Fairlawn. Julia called Marian Morash and asked her to meet them there. When they arrived, Morash recalls, Julia was visibly agitated. "She told me Paul had been in a kind of quasi state, where sometimes he was with you and other times he wasn't, but that this night he was totally with it." Throughout the cab ride in from Logan Airport he'd repeatedly asked: "Why are we going out to Lexington? Why aren't we going home?"

Fairlawn had a private room ready for him near the nurses' station. Thoughtful as always, Julia had arranged to have pictures that were familiar to him already on shelves and the nightstand next to the bed.

Paul gave the place a cursory once-over and raised an objection. "This isn't our house," he argued. "What am I doing here?" Marian Morash recalls, "It was the worst possible scenario."

Julia assured him that it was a nice place to rest, where the staff needed to do some medical procedures. "It will just be for a while," she insisted, though unable to say for how long. "She didn't lie to him," Morash says, "but she didn't make it sound like he was going to be there forever." It was a difficult balancing act, and she worked hard to sell it.

It took more than an hour until she could find a way to leave. Then Julia climbed into Marian Morash's car, put her head in her hands, and wept all the way home.

JULIA FELT THE void right away. Although released from the constant worry that something dreadful would happen to Paul, she could sense something extraordinary ending for good. From Asia to Europe to Washington to Cambridge, Paul had never been far from her side. For the first time in forty-five years, Julia Child was alone, and the emptiness disheartened her. It was almost like grieving after someone had died, but without the rituals of grieving that can provide comfort. Some version of Paul was still very much around and she felt love for him, whatever version remained. There were so many conflicting emotions: relief at not having the daily responsibility, missing him even as he was now, guilt at not caring for him herself. But at the very core, grief for the real Paul who had given her so much.

However, friends who saw her that week recall no outward show of sorrow. There was no grieving, no moping, no self-pity. She put on a face and got right back to work. "Julia didn't dwell in the past," says Russ Morash, who checked in with her later that day. "She had no interest in yesterday, only in today or tomorrow; moving ahead was how she dealt with life."

Almost mercifully, the book tour for *The Way to Cook* began three weeks later. It was a grueling, two-month grind for a seventy-seven-year-old woman, hopscotching across the country, from Boston to Pasadena and back again, with an entourage of four or five women. Her schedule, a marvelous mix of media, was relentless, brutal. Often, she lumbered through five events each day: press and radio interviews, local TV appearances, guest spots on *The David Letterman Show* and *The Tonight Show*, luncheons, and bookstore signings, the latter of which was easily the most demanding. Julia hadn't lost so much as a smidgen of her appeal. Everywhere she went, the crowds "were incredible." Long lines of fans snaked out of the bookstores. "Hundreds of people showed up wherever we went," recalls Susy Davidson, a young cook who prepped for Julia's GMA segments and often assisted her for demonstrations on the road: "It was more like a ritual, a divine observance, than an ordinary signing." People's faces glowed, they were dumbstruck when they finally laid eyes on her, like encountering Santa. There she was in the flesh, Julia Child—make that *Julia,* just Julia; everyone was on a first-name basis. Signing three or four hundred books at a clip was nothing to her. She'd inscribe each one, often dispensing bits of culinary advice and answering personal questions. People repeatedly asked her about Paul. "Well, dearie, he's fine, just *fine,*" she'd respond, "slowing down a little, but aren't we all."

Except that there was no slowing down for Julia Child, who was nicknamed "the nation's energy queen." Throughout the holiday season she continued to stump for the book, which was picking up steam in proportion to her super-size efforts. There was no lack of incentive for her to give it extra oomph. Knopf had gone out on a limb, producing a rather lavish number. It was a doorstop of a book, weighing in at almost five pounds, with a similarly hefty price tag of fifty bucks. That was twice as much as what people were accustomed to paying for a cookbook, and there was competition up the wazoo. That season, cookbooks were ridiculously plentiful. Julia's friend Anne Willan had released *La Varenne Pratique,* a similar encyclopedic volume that was attracting serious cooks, and those *Silver Palate* gals had cranked out another best seller.

Julia was determined to sell the hell out of *The Way to Cook,* if not to vindicate her publisher, then to make a final grand splash. She held firm to the notion that this would be her last book, and everything, bar none, had gone into it to secure her legacy. *The New York Times* agreed, calling it "a magnificent distillation of a lifetime of cooking." Forty years of know-how sandwiched between two covers—it was a fitting knockout to a championship career.

She could also use the money to see her through retirement. Julia had a nice little nest egg to fall back on. Book royalties had made her a prosperous woman and there was an ample cushion from her parents' estates. Julia had never had to worry about money. But she was in excellent health—"from good pioneer stock," as she liked to say—and she fully intended "to run with the tide." Travel, lots of travel, was on her agenda. And there was Paul to think about. His care would require a constant infusion of cash. She'd spend whatever it took to ensure his comfort and safety. She'd already hired a special-duty nurse to join him at dinner, so he wouldn't have to eat alone. The provisions involving Julia were also expensive. While on tour, she insisted on flying back to Boston once a week, so she wouldn't miss an opportunity to visit Paul. And her long-distance bills were monstrous as a result of long, rambling phone calls to him several times a day.

The complexities of Julia's schedule were labyrinthine. Demand for her presence at events was absurd. Every women's group, from the Junior League to Hadassah to the Pillsbury Bake-off, invited her to their functions—and expected that she would attend. The same with nonprofit organizations. Her name was a beacon for any cause. Everyone felt as thought they had a *right* to Julia Child, and she did little to discourage that perception. If someone called her—which was easy; all anyone had to do was look her up in the phone book—and made a reasonable plea, Julia would try to accommodate. The Food & Wine Classic in Aspen—she'd shoehorn that in. A benefit for the Long Wharf Theater in New Haven—no problem; she'd hop in the car and drive right over.

Sometimes she worried that she spread herself too thin, but when push came to shove she was unable to say no. That was exactly what happened with the whole James Beard business. Julia had been at a luncheon tribute to her fallen friend in Seattle. It had been a weird afternoon. Madeleine Kamman had shown up to say a few words, and when Julia reached across the dais to grab her hand a collective gasp shot through the crowd. Everyone knew their thorny story, but Julia was determined to keep the mood congenial. It wasn't until word sifted down that Oregon's Reed College, which had inherited Beard's New York house, was planning to sell it along with his belongings, that things got overheated.

"You don't want to be anywhere near Julia when she gets her back up," says Nancy Barr, who had accompanied her to the event. "It didn't happen often, but this was one of those times and I could see flames shooting out of her eyes."

"We've got to stop this!" she huffed in a biblical rage, her face reddening with indignation. "We've got to stop it now! This is James Beard, a national treasure." Something had to be done and *right away*. The house, for one thing—it had to be preserved. It was a landmark, if not for New York City then for the culinary world, which had to step in and make things right. Julia pledged all her efforts to help, and Peter Kump, a Manhattan cooking teacher who was in the audience, took her at her word. Soon, the two were engaged in raising money toward purchasing the house and its artifacts—which is how the James Beard Foundation was born.

In addition to all Julia's charitable work, the American Institute of Wine and Food still had a powerful grip on her to help expand and shore up its growth. "The organization had lost its focus," says Thekla Sanford. "There were too many egos involved, and Julia was frustrated with it." Rich society ladies seemed to dominate its ranks. Endowments had been necessary to underwrite its goals, so fund-raising efforts were focused on getting the AIWF into wills and trusts. Even so, they'd sunk deep into financial difficulty. The organization had been undercapitalized from the start and, by 1989, its walls had begun to buckle. In one year alone, the AIWF's debt ballooned from $285,000 to $635,000. A bank loan became necessary to fend off creditors. Julia, Robert Mondavi, Dick Graff, Michael McCarty, and Dorothy Cann Hamilton, who ran the French Culinary Institute in New York, each put up $100,000 to guarantee the loan, and the bank demanded Graff's Chalone Vineyard stock, as well. "Now we all had real money on the line," recalls Hamilton, the group's newly installed chair, "so it was time to put-up-or-shut-up."

What they put up was Julia Child. Her name was worth even more than her equity stake and they traded on it incessantly to enlarge the membership. If she were signing books in a particular city, an AIWF event was cobbled together so that Julia could appear and raise some cash. "I sent her all over the country, to the individual chapters for dinners," says Hamilton—eight cities from March to July 1990; ten cities the following year. "She became our major fund raiser, and in no time we started swimming in money." Thanks to Julia, the number of chapters swelled from thirteen to twenty-seven, with each giving generously to the national organization.

One of Julia's appearances for AIWF dropped her squarely into an issue that weighed on her mind. Since Bob Johnson's death in 1986, she'd been haunted by the way he'd battled AIDS. Johnson's destruction—and his courage—refused to fade, and when it came time to dedicate *The Way to Cook,* she honored him with a tribute to his memory. Julia felt increasingly angry and confused—angry at her inability to make sense of what happened and confused by her attitudes toward homosexuality. Finally, she was forced to confront her own views and she recognized how narrow-minded they had been. Ironically, AIDS had helped bring them into focus.

"The whole culinary world was dealing with AIDS," recalls Clark

Wolf. "It was especially ravaging the restaurant industry, whose many chefs and waiters were gay and had been sleeping with one another for years." Wolf, who'd been instrumental in launching the New York chapter of AIWF, helped organize a two-day event at the Boston Garden called "Aid and Comfort," to raise awareness. It was a copycat version of a San Francisco rally at which fourteen local restaurants had donated food and Linda Ronstadt entertained. In Boston, there were similar celebrities, but one whose appearance provided an especially galvanizing charge. When the emcee introduced Julia Child, a thunderous roar rocked the arena.

"Last year, my husband and I stood by helplessly, while a dear and beloved friend went through months of slow and frightening agony," she said, her trademark hooting held to a measured grace. "But what of those lonely ones—the ones with no friends or family to ease the slow pain of dying? Those are the people we're concerned about this evening."

Afterward, as Julia walked backstage, she paused and let her eyes sweep across the indistinct crowd. How many sitting there in the dark were Bob Johnson, she wondered, silently fighting for their very lives? It distressed her to think of their burden. For all her efforts, for all the elegantly spilled words and the outpouring of support from the food world, there was little hope of stanching this plague. "This is how meaningless we are in the scope of things," she realized. For all her resources, Julia Child couldn't make a dent.

CIRCUMSTANCES CONSPIRED TO induce Julia's reflective mood. With her eightieth birthday fast approaching, there were so many transitions for her to absorb, some of them painful, all of them life-changing.

Paul, she realized, was slipping further from her grasp. After he was admitted to Fairlawn, his stretches of lucidity were fewer and farther between. Now, when Julia visited him—every day, without fail, when she was at home, in Cambridge—he often didn't recognize her or was stranded in the past. Despite his unresponsiveness, she would climb in bed next to him and rub his head lovingly, filling him in on everything she'd been doing. Then at night she would call him, just before going to bed. "They were always very affectionate conversations," recalls David McWilliams, Julia's nephew, a frequent visitor during his graduate-school days in Boston. "One night I overheard him go on and on about how 'we've got to go to the football game tomorrow, you can bring a lunch.' " Julia would play along with the story. "Dearie, how about I make your favorite BLTs? We shouldn't forget to pack blankets, just in case." Other times, he would get frustrated with his inability to come up with the right word. One night, trying to describe a meal they had, he said, "We had . . . we had . . . *Godammit, Julia, what was it?*" She'd calmly say, "Lettuce, Paul." "*Oui, laitue,*" he'd respond, switching to fluent French for the rest of the night.

After those calls, the house always felt emptier, her heart more tender and melancholy than before. The solitariness humbled her and touched off other regrets. A family, perhaps, someone close to share her love. Simca would understand; that was something they had in common. In a letter to her dearest colleague, Julia expressed the uncharacteristic emotions she was wrestling with. "That's something we lack, you and I, *ma chérie*—no children and grandchildren, and we ultimately take care of ourselves," she wrote. "But I realize at our time of life the great difference between ourselves and those who have produced!"

Thoughts of the past, of loss and regret, intertwined with present-day loss and regret. What other reason did she have for digging out an old scrapbook and tracing the faces of the dear ones she clung to—her brother-in-law, Ivan Cousins, who died of cancer in 1989, followed the next year by Avis DeVoto, who'd finally "slipped off the raft"?

Perhaps it was these memories, remnants of the past, that made Julia respond so keenly to an invitation from a Norwegian advisory board. "How would she like to go back to Oslo?" they wondered. They would lay out an itinerary of all her old haunts, as well as make it possible for her to experience Norway's hidden treasures. Money was no object. They would pick up the tab for the entire trip as well as underwrite a travelogue, which Russ Morash would produce.

Oslo: the city touched off a kaleidoscopic blur of faces and places. Julia loved the years she'd spent there and thought often—perhaps more so now—of the friends she'd made, the meaningful customs she'd encountered. What a thrill it would be to revisit that part of her past. "She said *yes* right away," Morash recalls. "WGBH agreed to put it on the air, and we left in July 1991 for a complicated two-week shoot."

Their biggest snag, he figured, was Julia's delicate age. "She was quite old at the time—just weeks shy of her seventy-ninth birthday—and the itinerary we'd laid out would have given a fifty-year-old pause." Julia dismissed his concerns with a wave of her hand. She was nothing if not a gamer and barreled through the locations without uttering a complaint.

They began nostalgically, walking through the home that she and Paul had rented, Julia running her gnarled hand over the kitchen counters where *Mastering* was completed. Tears tided into her eyes. There was a party in her honor at the American embassy, whose food hadn't improved any since that dreadful shredded chicken and Jell-O salad luncheon in 1959. And longtime Norwegian friends turned out for dinners that stretched long into the night.

The days were crammed with rugged sightseeing excursions. She visited an aquavit refinery and put away a stunning amount of the high-octane fuel; the Olympic village, on whose slopes she had skied as a young housewife; and a fishing camp, where you practically had to be royalty just to enter the gates. "We gave Julia an antique fly rod," recalls Morash, "and stood her in the middle of a river for several hours while we made shots of her fishing, which she loved." Later that day, they set out for a far-off mountain resort, where a chef doing indigenous food had popped up on Julia's radar. The only way to make it work was going by helicopter, so Morash arranged for a pair, in order that they could shoot Julia in flight.

"The guys who flew Julia were a couple of hot shots who wanted to show off what the helicopter could do," Morash recalls. "They started doing wheelies and banks, real scare-'em-out-of-their-wits moves. We almost barfed up our lunch trying to keep up with them, and I was furious for Julia, if for nothing but her age." Morash and the crew landed a few minutes ahead and waited for the second copter to come down alongside. The winds, when they finally arrived, were unusually strong. Morash checked his anger waiting for Julia to emerge, and after a few nerve-racking minutes decided to confront her pilot. "Just tell me, how is she?" he demanded, prepared for the worst. The pilot grinned and jerked a thumb inside. "She fell asleep," he said. So much for that.

"It had been a long sixteen-hour day, the likes of which I can't remember," Morash says. "My crew and I just hit the bed and crashed." Fifteen minutes later the phone rang in his room. It was eleven o'clock at night, although the sun was still high, and Morash was tempted not to pick up what was certain to be a business call from the States. He was wrong. It was Julia. "Where are we going to dinner?" she asked, ready to roll.

A LETTER HAD arrived for Julia when she returned from Norway. It was from Suzy Patterson, a writer for the Associated Press currently living in

Paris who was working on a manuscript with Simca for a recipe-filled memoir meant to summarize an illustrious career. Julia dreaded opening it. This book project of Simca's was something of an albatross. Simca had implored Julia to help her land a U.S. publishing deal while she was still hearty enough to do the legwork, but the response from editors had been underwhelming. Simca's first book, *Simca's Cuisine,* hadn't sold all that well and its disgruntled author had bad-mouthed those she felt were responsible. After that, few houses wanted to take her on. Even Judith Jones backed away faster than a car thrown into reverse. Julia knew better than most how "difficult" Simca could be. Already, an editor who saw a proposal thought "Simca's expectations were unreal," her ideas confusing and "sentimental." And she had taken up with a co-writer before Patterson, someone one editor felt not only couldn't "write, [but] hasn't the faintest idea how to put a book together." This was so typically Simca, Julia thought. Only someone as obstinate as Simca herself, and with an iron constitution, dared work with that harridan. And even then, you'd probably stomp a foot through the floor, like Rumpelstiltskin—take it from Julia Child. Still, Julia had graciously sent letters to a series of New York editors in support of Simca's project, which was pressing on, full steam ahead, in her Bramafam kitchen.

The back-and-forth had been ongoing for five long years, and Julia could only imagine what Suzy Patterson's letter might contain. When she finally opened it, however, she was immediately shaken. "Simca has been very, very ill, at death's door, so to speak," it said. "And there is nothing anybody can do about her." Apparently, Simca had fallen, and unable to move, had lain on the floor for "some time"—maybe days—before a friend eventually discovered her. In the meantime, she'd caught a chill and developed double pneumonia.

Poor Simca! Julia thought—isolated like that in an empty house at the age of eighty-six. Ever since Jean died there was no one to look after her. Julia had pleaded with her on occasion to consider consolidating her residences, perhaps selling Le Mas Vieux, and moving into a condominium in Cannes or Grasse. "It is never pleasant to contemplate our gradual degeneration and demise," Julia conceded, "but it makes sense that we do so before senility sets in, and it's then too late." Julia had what she called "a workable plan." She and Paul "put in at an attractive retirement complex," she told Simca, "where you have your own apartment with kitchen, and they take care of you until you 'slip off the raft.' " They were also members of the Neptune Society, which sponsored prearranged plans for their deaths, "and when we're gone, you just call them up and they pick you up and cremate you."

Simca, she knew, was unprepared for such an event, as were most older friends with whom she discussed death. "Death didn't faze Julia," says her nephew, Alex Prud'homme. "She regarded it as part of the process, the end, over-and-done-with." But, oh, how the deaths of close friends touched the heart! Only days after the letter about Simca's situation, Julia learned that her good friend Liz Bishop, who had stage-managed all of the cooking demos and organized Julia's schedule, had died of a brain aneurysm while on vacation in Canada. Worried that time seemed to be closing in around her, she immediately wrote Simca, promising to visit in January.

Friends—it was so crucial to be surrounded by friends. Young friends especially kept one feeling young. Julia's approach to old age was *deny, deny, deny,* and its repudiation was validated by those with whom she associated. For so long Julia's posse had been filled with her contemporaries, but gradually the group composite began to change. Socially, she began spending more time with Nancy Barr and Rebecca Alssid, both of whom were young enough to be her daughters. And she hired Stephanie Hersh, a young woman just out of cooking and secretarial school, to be her full-time personal assistant.

"It was very important for Julia to have an active social life," says Alssid, "to be always on the go, always keeping herself occupied. I can't tell you how many times she called and said, 'Let's go out, dearie.' To the movies or to dinner, anything to get out of the house." Julia and Barr made a pact to spend their Saturday nights together, and often wound up at a table at Jasper's, in the North End of Boston. A young, handsome chef surrounded by a young, handsome crowd—it was catnip for Julia. Jasper always kept a table reserved for when she dropped in—table one, the best seat in the house. On nights when Julia didn't appear, that table was taken by two regulars from the predominantly Italian neighborhood, Champagne Dennis and his sidekick, Tommy, two of the most feared heavy-duty North End gangsters.

One night the boys came in and their table wasn't ready. When they confronted Chef White, he said, "Sorry, fellas, but Julia's here and she gets table one." Did they go ballistic or threaten to heave her out by the ankles? *Au contraire.* "They were beside themselves, like little kids," White remembers. "These were guys who would stick their hands through your chest and rip your heart out, but when it came to Julia they were playful as kittens." Men like them didn't normally work during the day and spent afternoons in front of television sets—often watching reruns of *The French Chef.* If Julia Child was occupying their table, they'd be pleased, just *pleased,* to take other seats.

Halfway through the meal Dennis waved Jasper over to his table. "We want to send champagne to Julia," he said. "Send her the best bottle in the house."

White didn't know what to say. The last thing he wanted was to get her mixed up with these gentlemen, but he also was careful not to offend them *at any cost.* "Let me check with Julia, to see if she's drinking tonight," he said, which, of course, he knew she was, but wanted an easy out.

Furtively, Jasper bent over Julia and whispered that some customers wanted to buy her a bottle of champagne. "But between you and me," he said, "they are ruthless North End gangsters."

Julia looked at him curiously and said, "Oh, really? What *kind* of champagne?" When he explained it would be a three-hundred-dollar bottle of Dom Ruinart rosé, she said, "That would be fabulous, dearie."

"Okay," he said, "but you're going to have to talk to them afterward."

"No problem, dearie. You bring us that champagne."

After dessert plates were cleared, Jasper gave both tables the signal and everyone moved over to a vacant table in the corner. "They were probably the two single most frightening men I've ever met in my life," White says, "but for ten or fifteen minutes they sat there talking about food, looking up at Julia with big rheumy puppy-dog eyes, thrilled out of their skulls to be in her company."

Most Saturday nights were far less exciting. Julia and her coterie of young, attractive women hit the social circuit on a regular basis. But there was one thing sorely missing from the equation: men. "She just adored men, and having them around," says Rebecca Alssid. "The conversation always revolved around which men were the most handsome."

"Men, men, men—she was obsessed with them," says Nancy Barr. "Her relationship with Paul had been the most satisfying part of her life, and it was clear, even at her age, she still craved male company."

Her desire grew stronger as the year pressed on. "I don't think it's good for us to always be seen out with women," Julia complained to Barr toward the end of 1991. "I think we need to find some nice men to go out with."

Easier said than done, Barr thought. Available men were scarce enough to a middle-aged divorcée, let alone a six-three woman approaching eighty. There weren't any available prospects, as far as she knew. A few days later, however, Julia phoned Barr, apologizing that she'd be unavailable for their Saturday-night outing. "I've found a man," she said, with great significance.

It had happened so suddenly: a phone call out of the blue. The voice wasn't familiar, but the name, John McJennett, rang a bell. His wife had been a friend of Paul's in the very early days, in Paris during the late 1920s and at Avon Old Farms, where he taught. Julia had vaguely known the McJennetts—there had been a scattering of social occasions; she remembered liking them immensely. She even recalled that a painting of Charlie Child's, a Cezanne-like bushel of apples, hung prominently over the couple's hearth. McJennett explained that he'd recently become a widower and had heard about Paul. They commiserated over their circumstances, one thing led to another, and he invited Julia to dinner in Mason, New Hampshire, the little village where he was living.

The man Julia discovered was a splendid physical specimen. He was tall, somewhat taller than Julia, and powerfully built, "a big, strapping Scots-Irishman," slightly balding, with a kind of "domineering, old-fashioned masculinity," much like her father's, that she found wildly attractive. He had an unself-conscious, athletic way of carrying himself and the noticeably strong legs of the ex-Marine and baseball player he once had been. Known as "the big right-hander" in a series of newspaper clippings, he'd been a pitcher of some promise in the Red Sox farm system before a medical issue ended his chances at making the big league. Since then, he'd led a career that closely mirrored Paul's, as a foreign service officer in the Philippines and East Pakistan, before it became Bangladesh. Even long after retirement, McJennett was "interesting, dashingly handsome." Julia Child recognized a real he-man when she saw one.

Julia and McJennett hit it off from the get-go. Both were lonesome, both full of life, both unwilling to surrender to old age. She invited him to visit in Cambridge, and shortly thereafter he sold his house and moved around the corner from her, to a place on Day Street. Both seemed to think this was "a dandy arrangement," despite Julia's faithful continuing visits with Paul at Fairlawn. McJennett knew the score, he wasn't jealous. "It wasn't an issue for my dad," says his daughter, Linda, "and Julia was practical—Paul was pretty much out of it, suffering from dementia." A man, a *handsome* man, was a nice thing to have around.

"Julia never thought of it as dating," says Stephanie Hersh. "She loved men, and she enjoyed having an escort for parties and events." It meant the resumption of an active social life that she had sorely missed, a man to sit at the head of the table and pour wine when guests came for dinner. To help entertain. John was an eager conversationalist "who told the most hilarious dirty limericks," which amused her no end. Her friends repeatedly heard the mantra: "It is nice to have a chap around." And Julia meant it. John was changing her life.

Invigorated by his company and enamored of his charm, Julia looked forward to spending Christmas with John. She had a lot to be thankful for. It had been a weighty, exhausting year, a real emotional roller coaster, and finally there was promise of some joy as the holidays approached. Julia was even considering throwing her first party in some time, when news arrived that stopped everything in its tracks.

Simca was dead.

Julia felt as though "someone had slugged her." *Simca.* Dead. Impossible—*am-pah-seeb-luh*!

They had come through so much together. Simca, her *énorme chérie,* her *grande culinarieuse,* her *sœur,* all names Julia had called her over the years. Together, they had preserved the heritage of classic French food and introduced its wonders to American home cooks. Together they had collaborated—and battled. Together, they had invented the modern cookbook, perhaps the greatest cookbook of all time. Together, they had formed a sisterhood that defied the male hegemony of chefs in the kitchen. Together they had shared the remorse of childlessness, as well as secrets as intimate as any Julia would share. Together, they had changed the world.

Simca. It was the end of an era.

Julia and Paul, inseparable always, 1989

Twenty-five

No One Gets Out Alive

There was never any question about celebrating Julia's eightieth birthday, aside from where, when, who—and how often. The way people were making such a to-do about it, half of America wanted to take part. "I don't want a fuss," she told a Boston-based reporter. But from the outset, one thing was certain: her eightieth was going to be one hell of a bash.

Eighty! Julia could barely get the word out of her mouth. "I felt as young that day as I did my first week in France," she said. The magnitude of the number, the *audacity* of it, didn't signify. Sure, her knees were hobbled and her skin appeared pocked and pouchy; a bit of a widow's hump had bowed her once-ramrod back. But make no bones about it: she was young at heart.

Stephanie Hersh recalls her telling a group of friends: "I'm about to be in my eighties, and I think I should probably slow down a bit," after which the entire gathering broke out laughing. "No one believed a word of it," Hersh recalls. "And after about six months on the job, I laughed like everyone else."

Nothing, not even eighty, was going to slow Julia down. She had been breaking the speed limit from sixty to seventy-nine, and as the next decade loomed into view she cranked that old chassis into overdrive. Julia's datebooks for 1992 and 1993 were blocked in solidly with commitments. Charity work—for AIWF, Planned Parenthood, and a few other lucky benefactors—dominated the schedule, but her *Good Morning America* appearances continued unabated and plans were under way for a new TV series.

It had been almost ten years since Julia last had a show of her own, and for a while, at least, chances of a new one had looked dim. The channels were clogged with would-be cooking teachers mugging and mincing about, which seemed to trivialize the seriousness of cooking. Their collective culinary expertise was open to debate, but the general theme seemed to be youth, youth, youth. Julia Child at eighty was viewed as a somewhat prehistoric character. Even WGBH, which she'd put on the map, had balked at giving her a series commitment.

In late 1991, however, soon after she'd met John McJennett, Julia was introduced to a man named Geoffrey Drummond at a cocktail party at Rebecca Alssid's house. She had noticed him earlier that day, standing at the back of a cooking class she was giving with Jacques Pépin, at Boston University. He'd laughed particularly hard when she struggled with the spout of a kosher salt box; frustrated, she picked up a knife as big as a machete and just lopped off the top of the box, throwing it over her shoulder, to great cheers. Drummond was a TV producer. He'd done a PBS series called *New York's Master Chefs* and was behind the wonderful 1981 Louis Malle film *My Dinner with Andre*, both of which Julia had loved. Now, he was about to move on to another project involving new up-and-coming chefs, and was looking for a host, someone with street cred, the gravitas, to seal the deal. "You ought to talk to Julia," Jacques had told Drummond.

Julia listened intently as he made his pitch. Geof had a list of leading-edge restaurants that were attracting the new wave of uncompromising gastronomes, places where they naturally came for the food but were familiar with the chefs. "I want to take a look behind the doors of these restaurants and see what's going on," he explained. "Let's see what these chefs are cooking—and maybe what they are cooking in their homes." Some of the chefs he mentioned were friends of Julia's—André Soltner, Alice Waters, Jeremiah Tower, and, of course, Jacques Pépin. But others, like Emeril Lagasse, Nancy Silverton, Robert del Grande, and Patrick Clark were unknown quantities. She'd heard the buzz about Lidia Bastianich, but didn't know her. Drummond's idea was to shoot film with these chefs, then bring the rough cuts to Cambridge where Julia would create openings and closings, so she wouldn't have to travel that much. He intended to call the show *Masterpiece Cooking.* "And you," he said grinning, "can be Alistair Cookie."

Julia nearly jumped in his lap. "I think it's a terrific idea," she responded. It had always been her intention to have guests appear on *The French Chef,* but for one reason or another she couldn't convince the higher-ups. "I'd enjoy working on it with you. But if I'm going to be attached to this, I want to be there for the cooking."

The format was a cooking show she could sink her teeth into. Besides, Drummond was just her type—tall, young, and good-looking, with the kind of WASPish confident masculinity that turned her on. He reminded Julia of a young Russ Morash, a he-man with his let's-just-roll-our-sleeves-up-and-do-this attitude. He seemed like someone who knew how to call the shots.

The concept was a good one, but it was just a concept. There were still many details that needed to be pulled together. The chefs, for one thing. Julia was adamant they be good teachers, not just artisans who made good food. And the show had to be careful about choosing each of the participants. It was to be called *Cooking with Master Chefs,* so, in effect, they were deciding "who was a master chef—and who wasn't." She felt a great responsibility toward protecting her imprimatur. And what about Russ Morash? When it came to directors, he was Julia's first choice.

Julia and Geof took the show to Russ, who "was very gracious, but didn't want to go on the road with it." And then, to her great dismay, WGBH *passed.* "I'm not sure if they thought Julia was too old," Drummond says, "or if they were just gun shy from their experience with *Dinner at Julia's.* But it was clear WGBH wanted no part of it." Instead, Drummond took the show to a rival, Maryland Public TV, and they "jumped at being in business with her."

A new station was not the only sign of a new direction. Drummond had convinced Julia that the old how-to format was boring, outdated. It was futile to build a show around a single dish, especially a French classic. Restaurant food was the new culinary currency and their mission, it seemed to him, was determining how to bring that kind of cooking into home kitchens. Julia surprised him by having the answer at her fingertips. Rather than focus on a meal, she thought each show should examine a spectrum of ingredients and techniques. That way, they could underscore certain disciplines, certain information, in order to give people something valuable in terms of their cooking that they didn't have before.

"Nothing had prepared me for how insightful she was," Drummond says. "After thirty years plowing the same ground, I half-expected her to resist any change. But she was eager—excited—to reinvent the medium, even if it meant standing it on its head."

Julia couldn't wait to leap into the project, but first she needed to fulfill a previous obligation.

La Pitchoune. Legally, the house was the Childs' for as long as Julia and Paul were alive, but no life remained there for Julia to savor. It had been her and Paul's special getaway for twenty-five years. *Her and Paul's.* All her memories of it were invested in the good times they'd shared together. The meals on the porch with Jim Beard, the long walks to the village with Avis DeVoto, the day-to-day cooking with Simca. Without Paul—without all of them—it held no enchantment for her anymore. It was time, Julia knew, to give up the ghost.

In the summer of 1992, she returned there for a month, with her niece, Phila, and Susy Davidson. "We went to all her favorite places," Phila recalls, "a restaurant in Biot called Galerie des Arcades, the Gallery Maeght in Saint-Paul-de-Vence, the Forville Market in Cannes, her friends in Nice." Afterward, Julia began packing everything up: what she was taking back to Cambridge, giving to Phila, sending back to friends. "I'm ready," she said, looking over the sea of boxes. "It's time to move on." One last time, she walked across the lawn to Le Mas Vieux, to deliver the keys to Simca's heirs. Phila watched her aunt closely, hoping that she wouldn't be overcome. "We said our goodbyes," Phila recalls, "and Julia walked out, without looking back. There was no emotion whatsoever."

Unburdened, she was finally ready to face whatever the future held. A new romance, a new show, a new direction for food—she was ready for anything, any adventure or adversity that might come her way. *Eighty!* What did that have to do with anything? It was just another number, another step along the path. She could handle whatever got thrown at her.

Slow down? Julia Child? Not a chance.

BACK HOME IN Cambridge, Julia was poised to kick off a jam-packed year. The plans for her new show were rolling along in significant stages, and she'd agreed to attend a series of dinners honoring her eightieth birthday doubling as fund-raisers for AIWF. She was cookin', she was in demand. Any fears of obsolescence were fading fast.

Her enthusiasm was idling at an all-time high, when she learned that M. F. K. Fisher had died. Her D*e*a*r F*r*i*e*n*d, as she'd always addressed Mary Frances in letter upon letter, who had dignified the *art* of eating in whorls of sensuous prose, had just marked her eighty-fourth birthday, and the implication to Julia was loaded. Fisher had been full of piss and vinegar, writing right up until the end. Now she was gone, just like that. The same with her British friend Elizabeth David, who had died a few months earlier, as she approached the dire eighties. This watershed was some sort of abyss; it was like the Bermuda Triangle—and culinary writers disappeared into it. Julia thought often of Jim Beard, who was gone by his eighty-fifth year. The eighties were nigh. There was no time to waste.

Without delay, she set off with Geof Drummond to audition a few potential master chefs. They stopped in Houston to meet Robert del Grande, whose food was completely unpretentious, as was its architect. Del Grande, a former biochemist with a bluff, laid-back manner, made Julia's kind of bluff, laid-back food—rare steaks seared in southwestern spices like pasilla chiles and ground coffee, with plenty of bourbon to wash it down. There was no question that he would fit into their plans. The same with Emeril Lagasse, who threw Julia a bit of a curve.

"We hit it off the first time we laid eyes on each other," Emeril recalls. "She came in to eat at Commander's Palace and later, right after I'd opened Emeril's." He wanted to impress her, but only on his terms, so he did an étouffée and crab-and-crayfish boil in the backyard, like he'd do for friends. There were no flourishes—no kick-it-up-a-notch, no *bam.* This was pre-TV Emeril; "he was shy and quiet," all focus on the food. "He wasn't play-acting for her," Drummond recalls. "He was very much in the moment, and the moment was about his cooking and cooking for her."

Emeril treated food the way Julia did, by putting his hands right into it without any to-do. She loved how he put food on the table, actually *poured* it on the table, out of a huge vat. No pretenses, no excuses. And the way he said, "You see how we eat these crawfish, Julia? We suck the head and pinch the tail." He wasn't some Cajun yahoo, like the shrimpers and gator geeks she'd been reading about. He was serious about his approach and "he could really cook."

Julia trudged from city to city, "like an amazing trouper," Drummond marvels, carrying her own bags and rampaging through airports. She often disappeared before boarding a plane, foraging for hot dogs—or hot *dogs,* as she called them—so they could eat down-and-dirty while flying first-class.

The show started shooting before her eightieth birthday. It was filmed on location wherever the chefs worked—Los Angeles, New Orleans, Houston, Chicago, New York, Washington, Hawaii. Julia was on the move. She'd work with the chefs, helping to prep their recipes, then remain largely off-camera, while the episode played out. This was hard for her; she was used to being in control. And sometimes, things didn't work the way she'd intended.

The first show they did with Nancy Silverton was "a disaster," according to Drummond. Silverton, a master baker who owned Campanile with her husband, Mark, as well as the La Brea Bakery, decided to make sourdough bread from scratch using a grape starter. It was an ambitious recipe that progressed over eight separate stages, but nothing beyond Silverton's professional reach, and the setting was ideal: a private home in the hills above Sunset Plaza with a first-class kitchen that gave a sweeping view of Los Angeles. Everything was perfect until the cameras started to roll. "Nancy was totally locked up," Drummond says. "I could see it developing. She had stage fright. She could not speak; she'd stand in front of the oven for ninety seconds without saying anything."

Stage fright? This had never happened to Julia Child. She seemed mystified, watching from her position behind the scenes. It didn't occur to Julia that all chefs weren't naturals in front of a camera, so she jumped in to help, talking Nancy through the recipe. They worked from six in the morning until nine at night to get a single twenty-eight-minute show, something she and Russ used to do in two or three hours. Still, no problem: Julia would do anything that was asked of her. She cared only about the integrity of the cooking itself, and in the end, the Nancy Silverton segment was the most popular show in the series.

"You couldn't ask Julia to do enough," Drummond says of his star. In addition to her on-air duties, he'd negotiated a new book deal for her, a companion to *Cooking with Master Chefs*. And because it was sold on the air at the end of each show, she had to write copy in real time, as the segments were being filmed. This was no easy assignment for Julia. Her typewriting was famously sloppy; the publisher often needed a cryptographer to decipher her manuscripts. And the recipes needed to be tested.

Julia had heard about a new device called a laptop, something that was still being beta tested by several computer companies. Through a friend, she managed to get her hands on one, and it went on location with her wherever she went. When she wasn't needed on camera, she sat bent over that mini-computer, pounding away at it every chance she got. She wrote the book as she traveled, staying up late at night to polish copy, feeding it to Judith Jones the next day for immediate editing. "She was as efficient as that machine on her lap," Drummond remembers. "It was remarkable, considering her age."

Eighty. Who was he kidding? She'd stare that damn number into the ground.

Even so, the big day finally crept up on her and she could do nothing about it. Rather than make a big scene, she decided to spend August 15, 1992, quietly, out of the public eye. There was a party in her honor at her brother John's house, in Vermont, not the low-key affair she was hoping for, but something better: the entire family turned out—Dort and Phila and the entire McWilliams clan, nieces and nephews galore, several Childs, cats and dogs, and one new sweetie, John McJennett, who clutched Julia's hand throughout the day. It was a fine old celebration, exactly the way it was meant to be, save for one dear member who was sorely missed.

Later that night, Julia stole off by herself to call Paul. There was plenty she wanted to tell him, how much he was in everyone's hearts, how he was there *in spirit,* followed by a blow-by-blow description of the day's events. It took awhile until he came on the phone, but he had no idea who she was.

THE PUBLIC CELEBRATIONS were a horse of a different color. There was everything but fireworks to commemorate the occasion.

It began in Washington, D.C., at the Hay Adams Hotel in July 1992, where seven local chefs, including Jean-Louis Palladin and Bob Kinkead, prepared a feast fit for 170 guests and one culinary queen: smoked black cod cakes, spicy lobster taquitos, broiled clams, corn cake with smoked salmon, and risotto with porcini mushrooms, as well as three birthday cakes, one decorated with edible reproductions of Julia's cookbooks. The gala was a raucous, impassioned affair, while outside, on the pavement, a dozen animal-rights activists paraded with signs that read ANIMALS BEWARE, JULIA'S HUNGRY. The protest didn't faze her one bit. Waving cheerfully to the demonstrators, she proclaimed, "I'm a card-carrying carnivore." Didn't they know she was eighty? "I've got to keep up my strength."

No sooner had she digested her Washington feast than a trio of others followed suit, only larger and more copious, if that were possible. On November 2, six hundred fans paid $250 a head as a fund-raiser for

WGBH and AIWF, at the Copley Plaza in Boston, and on January 24, fourteen New York chefs prepared a menu of *French Chef* classics, including sweetbread *vol-au-vent,* quail egg in aspic, and duck with turnips for a packed house at the Rainbow Room on the sixty-fifth floor of 30 Rockefeller Plaza.

The largest and most over-the-top event was held on February 7, 1993, in Los Angeles, where spectacles are routinely produced by showbiz masters. This one, entitled "*Merci,* Julia," was of the *Ben-Hur* and *Spartacus* variety, with a cast of five hundred crammed into a dining room at the Ritz-Carlton. The star-studded lineup of chefs might have been assembled by Cecil B. DeMille: Paul Bocuse, Michel Rostang, Alain Ducasse, Roger Vergé, André Soltner, Michel Guérard, Daniel Boulud, Jacques Pépin, Jean-Georges Vongerichten, and David Bouley—forty-four chefs in all, who worked the line while guests watched the kitchen action on two overhead screens.

The stockpile of food on display was almost obscene. Each of the chefs had his or her own booth, where appetizers were staged like glitzy warm-up acts. There were leek tarts, hush puppies stuffed with shrimp, lobster sausage, venison in puff pastry, crab croquettes, braised rabbit, curried duck, smoked salmon rillettes, tuna tartare, foie gras stuffed in prunes that had been soaked in Armagnac for two weeks, eight pounds of caviar, and unlimited bottles of champagne. Anyone who had room left for dinner feasted on a menu of artichoke-fennel soup with black-olive quenelles, *marinière de coquille* Saint-Jacques, and roast saddle of veal, before a cheese course and dessert. In all, "*Merci,* Julia" cost somewhere between $350,000 and $450,000 to produce, about the same as a budget for an independent film.

Julia soaked up the spotlight like a Hollywood supernova. It was her night to bask in the splendorous glare, and she did it with gusto (and the minimum of indigestion), but the evening was not without controversy. French food had been feeling the pinch of late, thanks to the meteoric rise of New American cooking. "Our love affair with French food is over," *Newsweek* had declared, calling the stodgy French restaurant "almost extinct." "The fickle public had turned against the mother cuisine in favor of A.B.F., Anything But French," Marian Burros wrote in *The New York Times.* Even Italian food had staged its own culinary coup, and the atmosphere at the Ritz-Carlton was thick with regret. That night there was "a lot of hand-wringing about the state of French food in this country," according to Burros.

Julia, of course, wasn't having any of it. She rallied the troops, proselytizing for butter-and-cream sauces and well-marbled meats. "If we ate the way nutritionists want us to eat," she said, "our hair would be falling out, our teeth would be falling out, and our skin would be drying up." *Vive la France.*

At least the feminine *la* served to modify France, but that was the only thing feminine that served to elevate the gala. Its organizers took heat for the "paucity of women in the kitchen"—only two were listed on the official program and one, Maguy Le Coze of Le Bernardin, didn't cook. The flap was kicked up further in the press by Julia's old nemesis Madeleine Kamman, who complained that the event was nothing more than a testament to male chauvinism. "The mere fact that I haven't been invited is grotesque," she protested, a statement that cast doubt on the state of her mind. But the issue about women was no delusional matter. Why hadn't Alice Waters been invited to cook? Or Lydia Shire, whom Julia promoted every chance she got? Or Marian Morash, a dear and trusted friend? Wouldn't it have been prudent to ask Nancy Silverton to bake bread?

Asked to comment on the exclusion of women, Julia took umbrage. "This has nothing to do with women at all," she replied. "It's about French food and about friends." Her response sounded evasive and glib to some. She clearly intended that such evenings be exempt from disputes. But then she got downright insensitive. "I think women are getting tiresome."

I think women are getting tiresome! It was a rare misstep in a repertoire of sure-footed performances. Maybe after too many helpings of *foie de canard rôti* Julia had gotten a little cranky. Or maybe she wanted to lob a grenade into the bouillabaisse.

Be that as it may, Julia's eightieth birthday was an otherwise good excuse to shower love and affection on a woman now described variously as "the Queen of Cuisine" and "a national treasure." The celebrations were so gratifying—and addictive. Once Julia developed a taste for them, she added scores of similar events to her already crowded schedule. "Literally, there were birthday parties going on every week," recalls David McWilliams. It seemed that every community group vied to mark her anniversary. As long as they agreed to donate the proceeds to AIWF, Julia served gratefully as guest of honor. But the endless meals wreaked havoc on her eighty-year-old waistline.

A ladies' auxiliary in Natchez, Mississippi, for example, had prepared for Julia's appearance for months. When the day finally arrived, she and her assistant, Stephanie, walked into an enormous town hall, down the middle of which ran parallel rows of buffet tables piled with platters of down-home Southern fare. Each of about fifty women stood proudly by the dish she had prepared, each placing a generous helping on Julia's plate as she passed. "When we sat down, there was a mound of food on Julia's plate, and mine had only grits on it," Stephanie recalls. "She took one look at me and said, 'Oh, dearie, you must be hungrier than that,' and promptly slid her entire pile of food onto my plate." At other functions, when Julia found the food inedible, it either wound up on Stephanie's plate or in one of the small plastic Baggies she carried, which eventually disappeared into Stephanie's handbag.

She was determined to keep her figure for a multitude of reasons. Health, of course, was always a primary focus. That bum knee of Julia's, despite countless procedures, was unforgiving when it came to weight. The endless travel and constant activity was physically punishing enough, but excess poundage caused excruciating pain. Another concern was her television persona. "Nobody wants to see a fat Julia Child," she insisted, ever mindful of her brand. The new series, *Cooking with Master Chefs,* was incentive to watch what she ate, as was her continuing appearance on *Good Morning America.* But when push came to shove, Julia minded her figure to please her new beau, John McJennett.

"She really enjoyed having him around," says Marian Morash, "and his presence lifted her spirit enormously." With John by her side, Julia felt comfortable returning to a heavy entertaining mode, throwing dinner parties every chance she got for a parade of culinary dignitaries. "Everyone who came to town was invited for dinner," recalls David McWilliams, now living with his aunt Julia while attending graduate school in Boston. "She would have Stephanie call ahead and advise them: 'We're having lamb tonight,' which meant whoever showed up better be prepared to make something with lamb." Julia never cooked dinner ahead of time. *Never.* The meals were left up to whoever walked in the door, whether it be Marcella Hazan, or Jacques Pépin, or the renowned pastry chef Jim Dodge. Everyone pitched in to make dinner at Julia's. She loved watching other people cook in her house, and she *supervised,* however gingerly, suggesting subtle improvements and offering advice.

John McJennett was the exception. Not only didn't he cook, he knew very little about cuisine, *haute* or otherwise. "He was a man of a different era," recalls his daughter, Linda. "He didn't want his green beans *al dente* or his fish cooked rare. As for wine, forget it. Give him bourbon and a good rare steak."

McJennett presided at the head of Julia's table, amused by all the prep work that swirled around him. Feigning helplessness in the kitchen and having a plain-vanilla palate, this he-man still managed to charm Julia. More than that. "He made her *happy*," observed Corby Kummer. "He was like an old shoe that fit her style. She always looked very indulgently at him, delighted to have a Real Man around."

David McWilliams enjoyed watching their relationship develop. "It was very sweet, like come-a-courting," he recalls. "It reminded me of a schoolkid romance." Occasionally, David would hear their car pull into the driveway after an evening out, and he'd steal onto the second-floor balcony to watch them. "John was just like a young boy, trying to give her a kiss, and Julia would make it difficult, but always give in."

"He was crazy about her, and got progressively more serious," says Rebecca Alssid. "Before long, John suggested it would be easier for both of them if he lived with her, at 103 Irving." To friends, Julia would say, "I don't want to be with another man like that." Cooking and cleaning for someone new was too much to ask of her. "I've already taken care of one old man; I'm not going to take care of another one." Teasingly, her nephew, David, proposed they consider getting married. He must have forgotten: Julia already was married.

With John on the scene, Paul's presence in the house faded, but in his few lucid moments he'd call from his room at Fairlawn. If Julia answered the phone, he might ask her "Why am I here? I should be home. When are you coming to get me?" "It would just *kill* her," says Stephanie Hersh, who overheard the conversations. "No, Paul," Julia would respond patiently, "that's where you live now." Other days, he had no clue about what was going on. If he called and got the answering machine, the message left on it was often heartbreaking. "Julia, I hear your voice. *Why won't you talk to me?*" By the end of 1993, however, "he didn't know what a phone was or how to use it."

Julia tried hard to keep his condition in perspective. "Luckily, he doesn't know anything, whether I'm away or not, so that I can travel and can press on with my work," she said. Nevertheless, she continued to visit Paul whenever possible, every day when she was at home in Cambridge. Otherwise she had the visiting nurses spend time with him or sent George, their gardener, in her place. Physically, Paul was in decent shape, but his mind had deteriorated more rapidly of late. He spent most of his waking hours paging through *Time* magazine, just staring, unable to grasp what he was reading. Even when Julia appeared in its pages, there was no recognition.

In fact, Julia had been ever more newsworthy for issues that had nothing to do with French cuisine. Food in America was becoming an increasingly political hot potato, from the use of pesticides to diet to how McDonald's cooked their fries. Neither pro nor anti anything, Julia was a traditionalist. She believed in food that was classical and delicious, regardless of its source. "Eat everything. Have fun," was the motto she lived by. Moderation, moderation, moderation—she couldn't say it enough. Nutritionists, with their campaign against butter and fat, became the enemy to her. "They are ruining our food," she protested every chance she got. They were "scareheads" or "emotional cultists" who spread "an awful lot of romantic hogwash." Romantics were another species high on Julia's hit list. "Romantics feel we should eat wild instead of farmed salmon, even though you don't know the condition of the salmon on the line," she fumed. Romantics were against cooking with modern machinery, like the Cuisinart, which was "just crazy," according to Julia. And speaking of crazy, she had choice words for anti-veal activists, Rachel Carson's aversion to synthetic pesticides, cholesterol alarmists, organic gardeners, and Meryl Streep.

The actress crusaded against the chemical Alar, used as a growth regulator on apples. In interviews, she claimed that Alar contaminated apples, putting children at risk of cancer and other diseases. "She's not a scientist!" Julia complained. "Why take her word for anything?" It infuriated Julia that Streep was not only in league with the media but with the Natural Resources Defense Council, a nonprofit environmental group. Julia had enough run-ins with them on issues like irradiation and fertilizers. (She was in favor of both—"in moderation," of course.)*

More recently, she'd begun fencing with an anti-alcohol group that condemned the drinking of wine with meals. "Some people just can't be sensible," Julia bristled with indignation. "I feel we must attack these people and their silly ideas."

With all these battlefronts raging, along with a lingering trickle of birthday blowouts, Julia struggled to focus on *Cooking with Master Chefs*. The series had gone off swimmingly, considering the groundwork

---

* In the end, the Environmental Protection Agency (EPA) determined that "long-term exposure to Alar poses unacceptable risks to public health."

involved. Since each of the shows was shot on location, in the cities where the chefs cooked, the travel took its toll. New York, New Orleans, Washington, Houston, San Francisco, Hawaii—"The travel was beating her up," recalls Geof Drummond. Fortunately, as scripted, Julia was off-camera for much of the cooking, but her role was demanding nonetheless. She was always involved in the content, noting exactly what each chef did and testing their recipes, but as the series progressed she got more involved in the action. There was no holding her back, Drummond recalls. She worried constantly that *Master Chefs* wouldn't be perceived as a Julia Child show and took every opportunity to wade into the cooking.

Thankfully, she didn't have to worry about prep. The *mise en place* was handled by no less than Thomas Keller, who was between restaurants and happy to help. Some chefs, Julia felt, needed extra assistance. Julia liked what Susan Feniger and Mary Sue Milliken brought to the kitchen, their provenance and French-based training, but their food completely mystified her. Dal and curries were not her cup of tea. The same with Amy Ferguson-Ota, whose Polynesian-influenced menus were beyond Julia's grasp. Throughout the series, she still preferred French food to anything else. She was in heaven when Jean-Louis Palladin poached foie gras in an apple reduction and roasted duck breast in the fireplace. Jeremiah Tower's spectacle with chicken was right up her alley. Julia showed somewhat more enthusiasm for Lidia Bastianich's craft—she was particularly taken by the sauces that accompanied each dish—but she still had reservations about Italian cooking. "It really isn't my kind of food," she was overheard to say after the episode.

Perhaps the audience sensed her reservations—or maybe the restaurant fare didn't excite—but the series wasn't a ratings sensation. Apparently, the hosting job didn't satisfy; viewers wanted to see Julia Child *cooking* or, at the very least, infusing the show with her inimitable personality.

Despite the soft response, Maryland Public TV ordered a second series, this time longer, with more of Julia's involvement. The main difference, however, was location. This show would have a set—Julia's own kitchen at 103 Irving Street. "It was getting to be too much for Julia to traipse around the country," says Geof Drummond. "This would make the show easier for her and more personal, and for the chefs, coming to Julia's house was like visiting the Vatican."

In Julia's Kitchen with Master Chefs was a collaborative experience. Twenty-six of America's most inventive cooks brought their best recipes to Julia's table, where she questioned and analyzed everything that went into each dish. The old-guard French chefs were spurned in favor of mostly younger candidates, the country's brightest rising stars responsible for sharply redefining restaurant cooking: Charlie Trotter, Jean-Georges Vongerichten, Daniel Boulud, Alfred Portale, Dean Fearing, Rick Bayless, and Monique Barbeau, among others, who were taking ingredients and twisting them. The result was a series of dishes of furious, explosive flavor—a smoked salmon napoleon, jalapeño Caesar salad dressing, foie gras ravioli, white peppercorn ice cream—in which the order of ingredients was often changed, while keeping the integrity of the dish.

It had taken Julia a long time to accept these changes. They flew in the face of all her classic French training. But there was so much innovation going on, especially in Boston. The local chefs she mentored and promoted—Jasper White, Gordon Hamersley, and Jody Adams, now included in this TV series—had moved well beyond their French training, and she began to understand and embrace what they were doing.

Once again, Julia Child was at the forefront of American food.

BUT SHE WAS at the backside of exhaustion. The production had turned her home into a makeshift TV studio: the kitchen served as the set, with monitors and equipment clogging the dining room, and a full-scale prep kitchen spread throughout the basement, crawling with cooks and assistants. "The work was nonstop," recalls Stephanie Hersh. "Julia would get up at five in the morning, do hair and makeup, start filming at six, break twenty minutes for lunch, finish filming around four, work on the book for an hour, have dinner with the crew, work on the book for another two hours, sleep for five hours—then do it all over again. It was go go go go go!"

Often, after they broke for lunch, Julia would announce, "I'm going to take a nap," and Drummond would shut down production until she was rested. In the past, her stamina would have carried her through the day, but she was running out of steam. "I'm fine, dearie," she insisted to anyone voicing concern. She refused to let anyone see the fatigue. There were too many people involved in this enterprise who depended on her. Physically, the work was draining, but the excitement recharged her battery.

The cooking was exhilarating. She marveled at how Jean-Georges Vongerichten merged Asian ingredients with Alsatian cuisine. All those layers of flavor—lemongrass, coconut milk, and curries—lay outside her expertise. What sounded exotic and overwrought was anything *but* in his hands. Everything he made was simply prepared. Jody Adams's stuffed veal breast played right to Julia's sympathies, with its elaborately conceived braise in wine and aromatic vegetables. Nothing pleased her more than watching Daniel Boulud, whose technique was "as good as any chef [she'd] ever laid eyes on."

Julia insisted that Jasper White make his pan-roasted lobster. It was his signature dish, steeped in cognac and butter, and a perennial favorite of hers, perfect for the home cook, but there were problems before filming even began. Weeks before, during a cooking demonstration on *Today*, Katie Couric shrieked when a chef killed a lobster. It brought media attention to the process of killing lobsters and PETA jumped on it right away. The organization's power made Geof Drummond nervous. "He prefers we don't kill it on television," Julia explained to White, sitting in her garden during a break.

"That's fine," White said. "We can kill it before we start filming."

Julia shook her head. "Then we're not teaching them anything." She got up and walked around the yard.

"Julia, there are other lobster dishes to be made. I could do lobster quenelles that start with cooked meat."

A decision had to be made in the next couple of minutes. Finally, she said, "Fuck 'em! We're going to teach people the right way to do it. Fuck PETA, fuck the animal-rights people!"

Together, they concocted a way to sidestep a possible outcry. As the lesson began, Julia stood gazing at White and his lobster. "So, dearie, how do we start the dish?" she asked.

"First we cut up the lobster," he said.

Everything had to do with the expression on Julia's face. She kept it glassy-eyed, completely impassive. For all anyone knew, she might have been watching a mother diapering a newborn, as White dispatched the crustacean. He had a Chinese cleaver the size of a scimitar and he wielded it like a cartoon character. His hands were a blur—*swoosh, swoosh, swoosh!* Presto: the lobster lay in pieces on the cutting board.

No one uttered so much as a sigh.

BY MAY 1994, Julia needed a break. The unbroken stretches and incidents like the one with Jasper White had convinced her that a month off would help to conserve her energy for the rest of production.

She'd wrapped the last show with the chefs from Al Forno in Providence and heaved a sigh of relief as the crew broke down the set. It had been a long haul, perhaps harder than her other series. There were so many stages to the cooking, multiple cameras, much more *editing—twenty-six shows!* The book was behind schedule, as usual. But the month off would give her time to catch up.

That day, May 12, after filming had ended, she went to see Paul, changed her clothes, and went out to dinner. She took Geof Drummond, Nancy Barr, her lawyer Bill Truslow, and her nephew David to Jasper's, for—what else?—pan-roasted lobster. It was a double celebration—the start of her vacation and David's graduation, which was two weeks off. They'd already had a pitcher of Julia's reverse martinis and handfuls of Goldfish; everybody was in a festive mood.

At 9:45, Drummond got called to the maître d's station. Stephanie Hersh was on the telephone. "Has Julia eaten dinner yet?" she asked him. Drummond demanded to know why. She said, "Because she won't finish eating, and I need to make sure she has food in her stomach." Drummond told her they were working on dessert. Stephanie took a deep breath and said, "Paul has died."

Geof broke the news to Julia as gently as possible. "We have to go," she said to her nephew. "Now."

David McWilliams drove her out to Lexington. "In the car, we talked a bit about Paul, and Julia was very matter-of-fact," he recalled. "She didn't cry and wasn't deeply emotional. I sensed she knew this was coming." She told David that when she had visited Paul earlier that afternoon, he hadn't recognized her. It wasn't her Paul anymore. He was somewhere else, but mostly in her memory.

She remembered a letter he had written to Charlie about death, how he feared being recycled "to the common microbial and atomic pool." He was vehement, defiant. "I am *P. Child,* painter, photographer, lover boy, poet, judo-man, wine-guzzler, and Old Sour Ball, and it's taken me 70 mortal years to sculpt this masterpiece." Dust to dust, Julia thought; no one gets out alive.

"We got to Fairlawn and walked quickly into the room," David remembers. He was spooked. Julia had never let him visit Paul, and he had never seen a dead person before. "She stood very quietly over the bed and was very businesslike about what needed to be done. For her, Paul had died a long time ago."

Twenty-six

The Beginning of the End

The flowers started arriving at Irving Street by noon the next day. Word had spread of Paul's death, and the community of friends and fans rallied to express their sympathy. Great bouquets of chrysanthemums, daisies, and lilies filled every inch of the living room and most of the library. "I could open an FTD outlet," Julia told Sally Jackson, a publicist who worked the Boston restaurant scene and had come to help with getting an obituary ready.

"How are you doing, dearie?" Jackson asked, co-opting Julia's trademark pet name.

"Well, I've gotten over the Kleenex phase," she replied.

The evidence was unmistakable on Julia's face. She looked haggard, her eyes red-rimmed and sunken. Stephanie Hersh, who hadn't left Julia's side since she'd arrived back from Fairlawn, was alarmed by what she perceived as her lack of emotion. "She didn't cry," Hersh recalled. "I couldn't believe it—*she didn't cry*! More than anything I wanted her to release that pent-up grief." But it was clear that Julia had shed plenty of tears, but only in private, as had always been her way.

Thoughts of the past, of Paul, sardonic yet supportive, must have collided with the artifacts he had left behind. Everywhere she looked there were lovingly framed canvases he'd painted in Paris and Maine, the dark, brooding cityscapes and street scenes, the seaside vistas with blue-black waves breaking over the surf. Moody photos he'd taken lined the mantel

Julia and Jacques Pépin, cooking in concert, 1999

and bookshelves: the checkerboard of rooftops seen from out the back of Roo de Loo, the horseshoe harbor in Marseille, his nieces at play on the rocks in Lopaus, various markets in French villages, Julia piloting an ancient gas range. Paul's presence was everywhere and the memories collapsed around her. It was unthinkable that Julia Child could have been the person she was had Paul not been by her side. He had shaped her—an empty vessel, a *social butterfly*, adrift—given her purpose and strength and encouragement and *love*. My God, they had had love in spades! When it came to he-men, Paul was top of her list, in a class by himself. There was no one like him.

There were arrangements to be made, all kinds of matters to be settled. Sally Jackson was scheduled to chair an AIWF reception at Julia's house the next Monday. "We'll just cancel it," Jackson said, slashing across a memo on her punch list. Julia, tapping into some secret reserve of energy, bolted upright. "Absolutely not!" she said. "It's $150 per person for AIWF. Business as usual."

Jackson thought Julia was being unrealistic, but the night of the event, Julia greeted a crowd as they arrived at her door, then slipped out the back with Nancy Barr and went to a movie.

WITH PAUL'S DEATH, Julia began thinking about how to make use of the time that was left to her—what was important, what wasn't, what took precedence in her life. As always, she chose not to wind down, not to live in her memories but to charge full-steam ahead.

The remainder of shows for *In Julia's Kitchen* would help to take her mind off her loss, with plenty of appearances mixed in to keep her face in circulation. *Good Morning America* was a constant source of pleasure and relief. She looked forward to those trips to New York, which, since 1987, had become ever more meaningful. That February, Charlie Gibson had taken over the show's anchor from David Hartman, and from day one of his tenure Julia was smitten. "She was a great flirt," Gibson recalled. "I was the new guy, an unknown, and extremely nervous. But when I walked on the set, she took me by the hand and said, 'I've been looking forward to this, dearie. And let me tell you, *we're going to have so much fun!*'" She was right. Julia and Gibson formed a mutual admiration society, chatting endlessly between guest spots, enjoying the occasional dinner in a favorite New York haunt where conversation invariably turned to politics. "Reagan was president," Gibson recalls. "Julia hated him. She couldn't wait to tee off on him."

After Paul died, Gibson went out of his way to console Julia any chance he got. "We went out to dinner one evening soon afterward, and all she wanted to do was talk about the kitchens Paul had set up for her," he recalled, "all the design elements he'd brought to them, and how he'd taken such good care of her over the years." She confessed that, from the beginning, Paul had been much more interested in television than she was. He'd encouraged her to pursue it, and once she agreed to appear on TV, he had coached her, got her to relax, convinced her to just be herself. There it was in a nutshell, Gibson thought. That was the secret of Julia's success—allowing the idiosyncratic part of her character to come through. Most television personalities, in Gibson's experience, were what he called "cookie cutters"—bland, nondescript, indistinguishable from one another. "There was nothing average or ordinary about Julia Child," he says. "Her enthusiasm and humor made her instantly attractive and memorable; there was nothing unapproachable about her. All the qualities that made you think that she was *not* going to be good on television are what made her very *very* good on television."

Occasionally, Gibson found he needed to cover for her. "Julia's age began to catch up with her," he recalls. "There were days, when she arrived to do her segment, that she was not up to it. She'd forget ingredients or where she was in the recipe." Sara Moulton would cue Charlie that Julia was "off her game that day," and he'd conspire with the producer to cut her segment short.

But she'd have great days, too, when everything just clicked. No matter what, Julia refused to let up. In fact, she undertook more guest appearances during her visits to New York, turning up regularly to tangle with David Letterman, another he-man in her little black book. Talk shows showed off her wacky brand of humor, as long as the host was game.

Sometimes, however, Julia and her hosts were not *simpatico.* Stephanie Hersh recalled an appearance Julia made on *Live with Regis and Kathie Lee,* on behalf of *McCall's* magazine, which was celebrating an anniversary. Stephanie had prepped the segment the night before, making meringue disks and ganache for a special cake so that the *mise en place* was ready when she and Julia arrived. Regis Philbin and Kathie Lee Gifford would help assemble the dish on the air. But minutes before the spot, Kathie Lee balked. "She said she didn't want to get dirty," recalls Stephanie, "so she wasn't going to do it." Regis made it unanimous. "Then I won't either," he said. "We'll let Julia do it alone."

Julia was beside herself with fury. "Absolutely not, I refuse," she said intransigently. "You promised to do this so we could talk about *McCall's* anniversary recipe. I'm doing this with the two of you, and that's how it's going to work."

To Stephanie, under her breath, she said, "Make sure that the car is ready."

Come airtime, Julia was announced to great applause. She beckoned the hosts to the demo table, where three stations were decoratively arranged with the ingredients and enough ganache for each to do his or her own version of the recipe. A finished cake was waiting in the wings. But Kathie Lee, as promised, refused outright to cooperate. She simply stood by, not about to touch the food.

Julia turned a violent shade of red as she began putting the recipe together. Any trace of geniality drained from her face. "I'd never seen her that angry," Stephanie recalls.

Halfway through, the cameraman signaled for a commercial break. "Stay tuned to see how we finish this," Regis announced.

As soon as they were off the air, Julia said to Stephanie, "We're leaving now." Without a word, the two women scooped up their equipment, stormed out the stage door, and slipped into the waiting car. They had no idea how Regis finished the show.

Mostly, however, Julia's TV work was pure pleasure. In May 1995, she was invited to spend two weeks on location, gallivanting across Europe with the cast and crew of *Good Morning America*. "We went on live, from a different city every day," recalls Joan Lunden, "and travel was pretty difficult, by rail and bus." Because of her age—she was nearly eighty-three—Julia was offered a shortened schedule and lifts to each city by private plane. According to Lunden, she was having none of it. "She spent the entire time with us and handled her own baggage. Any special treatment was immediately refused."

By the time they reached Burgundy, Julia was as giddy as a schoolgirl. She was thrilled to be back in one of her favorite provinces of France and delighted to share some memories of earlier excursions there with Paul. The stories of gay picnics and life-changing meals flooded back with crystal clarity. Although "obviously wistful," Julia seemed particularly aroused. When the crew set up at Clos de Vougeot, a legendary vineyard along the Route des Grands Crus, something—the thought of Paul's romance with wine or just sentimentality—propelled her toward the *cave,* where the proprietors were pouring from their finest reserves. GMA went on the air back in the States at seven o'clock in the morning, Eastern time, which meant that they went live from France at 1 p.m. "We'd arrived at eight that morning, which is when Julia started sampling the wine," Gibson recalls, "and by the time we were ready to go she was just blotto."

Fortunately, the script called for Julia to make an omelet, her old standby, which she'd done hundreds of times; she could do it with her eyes closed, if necessary. Come air time, however, she was "just reeling" from the wine. She babbled gleefully through the introduction and fought the eggs for domination of the pan. "They just wouldn't congeal," recalls Joan Lunden, who stood by, wondering how to save the spot. Leave it to Julia, who pummeled those eggs unmercifully with her whisk. "And when they don't become omelets," she said, mugging comically into the camera, "you just make them *the best scrambled eggs ever.*" Simple as that.

There was nothing else for her to do until the end of the show. "We thought it would be nice, when we signed off, if Joan and I were on bicycles and rode off down a path through the vineyard," Gibson recalls. Someone handed Julia a burgundy-colored flag and suggested she wave it to start them on their way. The whole affair, from start to finish, would last fifteen seconds. Gibson could tell instantly that Julia was in an unusually merry mood. "She wore a glazed, almost deranged grin when she began waving us along," he says. She waved that damn flag like it was the last stand at the Alamo, continuing the entire time Lunden and Gibson were bumping along, still waving it when they walked the bikes back, long after the show had gone off the air. Gibson was unable to contain his laughter at the sight of Julia Child behaving like a coed on spring break. "I'm convinced she'd be waving it today if we hadn't taken it out of her hands."

WHEN JULIA GOT back to the States, John McJennett was waiting for her. He'd been looking forward to her return, having sorely missed her. Their relationship may not have reached a level of transcendent love, but it had sustained them both through personal upheavals and readjustments. John had good reason to be thankful; no one was more eager for fascinating company, even if Julia resisted something deeper. Her world captivated him: the creativity, the spotlight, "all those young women doing their thing!" He was an affectionate man; he enjoyed Julia's kisses, sisterly though they might be, and would take what he could get—more, if the situation availed. Dorothy Hamilton encountered him late one evening in the kitchen of 103 Irving. "Are you staying here tonight?" he asked her. "I am," she said. "So am I!" he replied, and winked lasciviously.

But by the fall of 1995, his health became an issue. "He suffered from heart failure," says his daughter, Linda. "He was on oxygen, toting a tank, when Julia returned from Europe. And he'd had various cancer operations, which left him with a colostomy bag."

"He's a sick man," Julia lamented the next time she saw Rebecca Alssid. She had cared for Paul through years of infirmity and that was enough, she seemed to be saying. The relationship with John had given her enormous pleasure. He was courtly, energetic, and attuned to her professional needs. But he couldn't be those things for her anymore. Despite these deterrents, Julia still clung to their relationship, but between John's health and her demanding schedule, the end was imminent. "I could tell she was prepared to move on," says Linda McJannet (she reverted to a more Scottish spelling of the family name). "Julia was, if anything, a very pragmatic person. Dad appreciated that quality in her. But pulling away from him would break his heart."

Julia tabled any decisions about John until she could sort out the business that had piled up while she was away. As usual, there was a book to promote. *In Julia's Kitchen with Master Chefs* was a popular success, more successful than its predecessor, and a tour was arranged in support of its publication. Knopf was eager to get her on the road. A TV series had a respectable effect on sales, but personal appearances by Julia always sent the figures soaring. Conflicting interests, however, created uncommon tensions.

Julia's connection with Geof Drummond, which had begun four years earlier, had isolated her from perhaps her greatest advocate. Judith Jones felt Drummond had become "quite possessive" of Julia, that he was manipulating her "for his own gain." Jones was unhappy with the two *Master Chef* books. "I don't think they were top Julia material," she says, voicing an editorial point of view. "There wasn't much of Julia in them. She didn't really have enough time to write them, so her voice was missing. And because the books had to get out so quickly, recipes were developed without proper care."

Jones worked on both manuscripts, but she did so begrudgingly. Because of a co-writer (Nancy Barr was responsible for much of the book's material), and what she considered Drummond's "hold over

Julia," Jones no longer played the quotidian role that she had when Julia and Simca shared authorship. "Geof put the idea in her head that I didn't do as much as I could have for her, and there is always a certain truth," she admits. Jones also admits she was prejudiced from the beginning. "They were terrible programs, there was no role for Julia. I think it would have been better had she stayed off TV, rather than being an inessential component. I think her day was over on TV."

A similar sentiment resonated from *Good Morning America*. While Julia was in Europe on location with the show, Disney announced its purchase of Capital Cities/ABC, the parent company that broadcast *GMA*. Not long afterward, Julia got the news that her contract wasn't being renewed. "Julia was convinced it was because of her age," says Stephanie Hersh. "She told me, 'From now on, they're going to use younger chefs.' " No matter what the reason, it had to be a blow. Hersh maintains that Julia loved doing that show; it had kept her sharp, in front of a national audience. But if truth be told, she was busier than ever and ready to pursue something fresh.

A live one, in fact, was already on the hook. Geof Drummond offered Julia a TV special with her longtime sparring partner, Jacques Pépin. Their act originally grew out of their appearance with Tom Snyder in 1978, the same show on which Julia cut her hand and inspired Dan Aykroyd. Julia and Jacques were cooking lobster that night, and had a big argument over the tomalley, the digestive gland which turns green when it's cooked. It began off-camera, but they continued it, only louder and hotter, once they went on the air. *Why wasn't it changing color?* "Jack, don't do it that way," Julia pecked. At which point Jacques got his hackles up and became defensive. "Because, my lovely Julia, *this is the way it is done!*"

Jacques adored Julia, respected her more than anyone, but they had serious disagreements when it came to technique. Jacques was a restaurant chef, Julia a home cook, and they often worked at cross-purposes: a restaurant chef always thinks in terms of efficiency, whereas Julia's goal was the method behind the recipe. Combining these two charged particles created nuclear fusion. "I thought it was great television and interesting cooking," Drummond recalled. "In front of an audience, it would be cooking as theater."

They'd road tested the concept again, in March 1994, with a sold-out performance called *Cooking in Concert* at Boston University's Tsai Auditorium. The show was a huge success. It was filmed in front of five hundred students and underwritten by Cuisinart, an appropriate sponsor, inasmuch as Julia and Jacques more than anyone else were responsible for the popularity of its ubiquitous food processor. The two cooks squared off over a four-course meal, and from the beginning, they had more chemistry than an explosives lab.

During a recipe for salmon, they wrangled over how best to slice it. "It's too thick!" Jacques warned her. "Let's do it this way instead." Julia ignored him and cut it however she wished. "So we got into a stupid argument about slicing salmon," Pépin recalls. "It was like being in the kitchen with my *wife*."

Another time, while making dessert, Jacques added more lemon to a recipe when Julia turned her back. When he turned *his* back, she added more vanilla. Back and forth it went like that, like an episode of *The Honeymooners*. It was hilarious, and the audience ate it up.

The only hitch came halfway through the performance, when they were working up a recipe for *gremolata*. Julia started in on the Cuisinart, to let the sponsors know she wasn't their shill. "One of the problems is that the blade gets too dull to cut parsley," she complained. "So if you're having a problem with the way your Cuisinart cuts the parsley, speak to Madame Cuisinart out there in the audience." Geof Drummond, who was watching the action on a monitor in a remote truck, saw Julia point out their client, sitting in the crowd with five of her colleagues. "But if you talk to Cuisinart, I'm sure they'll be glad to get you a sharper blade."

Drummond began sweating bullets. Cuisinart had sunk a lot of money into the evening, and he was counting on them in case it ever became a series.

"The other problem with the Cuisinart is latching the top and the safety mechanism," Julia continued. "What I learned to do is take a little emery board and file it down, and that makes it so much easier." On the monitor, you could see the company reps begin to twitch in their seats. "That's nothing," Jacques said, grinning. "In the kitchen, what we do is just jam a knife in to short out the mechanism. Then you can run it without the safety catch."

Drummond, nearly apoplectic, had an assistant call Bill Truslow, Julia's lawyer, and get him into the truck, so he could watch what was going on.

The show got even rowdier and more enjoyable, but needless to say Cuisinart never came back for a Julia Child program of any kind.

Whatever Julia did, she did to promote cuisine, not for promotion or any personal gain. When she cloned *Cooking in Concert* in San Antonio, with Graham Kerr, the Galloping Gourmet, it was because she wanted to raise money for the International Association of Culinary Professionals. Unfortunately, the electricity had lost its charge. Over the years, Kerr had become a dedicated health freak, which meant that butter and salt were banned substances, and Julia, as might be expected, lost her enthusiasm. "It became diet food versus non diet-food," Drummond recalls, nothing she wanted to actively pursue.

Drummond's goal had been to sell the show to network TV. Julia and Graham Kerr still had plenty of name recognition, and CBS was listening to his pitch. But after several attempts to create a show with broad-based appeal—in other words, an act that combined tension and comedy like Julia's work with Pépin—the program collapsed in a puff of uninterest.

In the meantime, Drummond was trying to package Julia with another viable concept. Despite her age, he felt "she still had enormous energy" and the desire to work, to explore new modes of cooking. Russ Morash, who watched from afar, wasn't so sure. He thought "the later shows didn't measure up to her high standards" and that "she looked feeble" on TV and "ought to know when to get off." But Julia wasn't prepared to call it a day. "I have no intention of stopping," she said, in a reflective moment. "When I do, you'll know I've finally slipped off the raft."

One theme, in particular, interested Drummond: baking. It had been a preoccupation of his since Nancy Silverton's appearance on *Cooking with Master Chefs*. Despite Silverton's rocky stint in front of the camera, the response it had gotten was nothing short of sensational—almost ten-to-one greater than the next-highest-ranking segment with Emeril Lagasse. Drummond thought that a series devoted entirely to baking could feature Julia in a new and different light. It wasn't cooking, per se, at least not classic French cuisine, but still ranged within familiar territory. In *Mastering*, Julia had left most of the baking to Simca, but over the years she had developed her own nice repertoire. Could she sustain a baking show for twenty-six segments? Most likely, Drummond assured her, if they used the *Master Chefs* format, with celebrated bakers contributing recipes and performing on air. Julia would assist them in her capacity as host—and as Julia Child, which was the icing on the cake.

Julia was sold the minute she heard it, and Maryland Public Television once again leaped at the opportunity to broadcast one of her series. The only stumbling block was what to do about a book. Drummond wanted something that was more than a companion piece. In his opinion, companion books were mostly rushed, slapdash affairs, with little long-term appeal. He felt that, with Julia's imprimatur, they could produce a handsome book that could become the baking bible, in the way that *Mastering* was the gold standard when it came to French food.

Far more important to Drummond's thinking was the advance the publisher was willing to pay. Except for the short time when Bob Johnson represented her, Julia took whatever Knopf had offered her—a fair sum, but nothing in the superstar category. Both Julia and Judith Jones engaged in an old-school publishing relationship in which money was rarely mentioned. "Ultimately," says Drummond, "neither of them believed in the new big advance structure of the book business or in flash in any way." Nor did he believe the company put their resources fully behind the *Master Chefs* books. He wanted to do the book on *his* terms, not theirs, and that meant more money.

According to Judith Jones, she received a letter written on Drummond's company stationery, advising her they were making multiple submissions of the book proposal to other publishers. "It was an outrageous thing to do," she says, hurt and offended. She and Julia had a relationship that went back thirty years—more than a relationship, a *friendship* that was deep and meaningful. Jones had nurtured Julia's career with loving care. They had been there for each other at key personal moments. "Geof didn't even have the decency to send me a personal letter," Judith said. It was addressed to her and contained the terms of the book he was offering, but ended: "Call me, Maria, if you have any questions." *A form letter!* She deserved more than that. "I thought, I won't even dignify this with an answer. I don't want to publish it. Let Julia go."

Drummond already had a relationship with William Morrow, which published Lidia Bastianich and the Frugal Gourmet under his stewardship. Morrow paid a million-dollar advance in 1988 for a baking book by Rose Levy Beranbaum. That was more in line with Drummond's thinking. "They offered Julia a fortune up front," he says, "and she jumped at it, she never looked back."

JULIA MIGHT HAVE cut her ties with Knopf, but it would be harder, much harder, with John McJennett. Ever since her return from Europe, he'd been in a fast decline, the heart failure a debilitating burden. In the winter of 1995, he moved out of his apartment near Julia's into an assisted-living facility in Westwood, a half hour away, where it was much harder for Julia to visit. There were so many drawbacks—time and distance, of course, but John's condition tapped into emotions for her, not just of Paul's decline, but her own dread of old age. She'd never been afraid to talk about death or how she'd face it—when it had been well in the future. But lately, in her mid-eighties, it had crept up on her. "She talked about death quite a bit," says Rebecca Alssid, "and I think she was trying to process it for herself, trying to confront it, what it would mean."

According to Judith Jones, Julia pooh-poohed the subject. It came up often in their conversations, especially after Paul had passed away. "I'm not sentimental," she told Jones defiantly. "Death is death. It's just another episode."

John's death, however, was suddenly staring her in the face. On one visit, she discovered he'd developed a form of bone cancer that was already quite well advanced. Through no fault of his own, his arm just spontaneously broke. "He was quite ill," according to his daughter, Linda. "When it was clear he wouldn't take a turn for the better, Julia said to me, 'I think I won't be coming down anymore.' "

A few weeks later, John was gone. "It had happened so fast," says Alssid, "Julia didn't know what had hit her. She wasn't prepared. It seemed like he'd been in her kitchen only the week before." There was a memorial service for him at Harvard, where he'd studied and played baseball in 1933. Julia went with Alssid, who'd spent many evenings socializing with the couple. They talked about what a lovely, old-fashioned guy John had been, how funny and smart and handsome he was, how he knew *nothing* about food. How he'd adored Julia—she had always felt his affection and generous warm heart. She'd been so lucky to meet him after Paul got sick, lucky to have another nice man in her life. All those memories; suddenly she was overcome. "It was the only time," says Alssid, "that I'd ever seen Julia cry."

There was hardly enough time for her to cope with her grief. A week or two later, she was tethered to another appearance at BU with Jacques Pépin, *More Cooking in Concert,* which was filmed for PBS. Again, it was strictly a sold-out affair, and again she teed off on a faithful sponsor—not Cuisinart, which had headed for the hills after the last contretemps, but Land O'Lakes Butter, a longtime ally. Land O'Lakes loved Julia's devotion to rich, creamy butter. Who else used such obscene quantities of it in their recipes? Who else scorned the hated *other* spread and refused all substitutes to make food so utterly delicious? Who else regarded butter the way Donald Trump regarded cash? And yet, it was necessary to remind them she couldn't be bought. She might have used thousands, *tens* of thousands of pounds of their butter over the years, but no matter—in the end she wasn't there to sell somebody's product.

"I remember Julia putting a stick of butter into a recipe we were doing," Pépin recalls, "and then another stick went into whatever it was." His eyes narrowed. "Julia, it's too much butter," he cautioned. She put a finger right in his face and said, "Okay, Jack, but you'll regret it." Her scorn was palpable. The president of Land O'Lakes was in the audience with a half-dozen reps, and the scene couldn't have played better for them. Jacques was preparing a flaky dough that he used for chicken potpie, which Julia thought sounded like a fine recipe. But three minutes before curtain, she announced a new plan. "I want to do my own dough," she said, "a sweet dough, with a dessert." "Fine, terrific," Jacques said, "whatever you want to do." He was used to her last-minute whims, which often signaled a different recipe than the one they'd rehearsed. "She was such a character," he says. "I never knew what was coming."

On stage, to the crowd's great pleasure, Jacques rolled out his dough with the fluency of a master baker. "Now," he announced, "Julia is going to do a dough."

"Actually," she said, "Jack is going to do it for me."

"I am?" Here we go again, he thought.

"And I want you to do it in the food processor."

He breathed a sigh of relief. That sounded like a good idea. He'd done his dough demo by hand; this would teach the audience a different, modern method. Who knew?—perhaps Julia was atoning for bashing Cuisinart last time around. Obediently, Jacques filled the machine with the ingredients Julia handed him—flour, salt, sugar, the appropriate measurements for each. "How much butter do you want?" he asked.

"We're doing it with Crisco," she said expressionlessly.

Crisco! They'd never used Crisco in any recipe before. He could only imagine the Land O'Lakes reps' discomfort as they watched this debacle. Well, he could head this off at the pass. "We don't have Crisco," Jacques said.

"*I* have Crisco." Julia reached underneath the counter, where she'd hidden a can of the shortening.

Of all the damnable tricks! She'd planned this switch all along. They ended up using half Crisco and half butter, which produced a perfect dough, but Jacques swore "that confounding woman" would never show him up like that again.

———

THE SPECIALS WITH Jacques galvanized Julia and her public. View-ers tuned in in droves once again for *Baking with Julia,* which ran for thirty-nine weeks in 1996 and 1997. As with the *Master Chefs* series, her participation was minimal; Julia more or less hosted the program as a cavalcade of twenty-six bakers turned out a tremendous range of baked goods, from muffins to madeleines, pies to pizza.

During the taping, which was done at 103 Irving, an erratic noise in the kitchen kept interfering with the recorded sound. The culprit, it turned out, was Julia's Westinghouse refrigerator, so cranky and old that when she opened its big door guests gaped at the *inside* freezer located down in the corner. It had broken down repeatedly over the years, but because it was under a service agreement, the company continued fixing the infernal beast. Now they had to find a way to silence its phlegmatic motor.

The repairman who showed up stared at the refrigerator as if he were looking at an exhibit in the Museum of Ancient History. "Sorry, but this is so old we don't make the parts anymore," he explained. "We're going to replace your refrigerator free of charge."

He must not have known Julia's aversion to free goods. She knew the trade-off: if she accepted free equipment, companies would invari-ably ask her do product endorsements. Her stock response was enough to forestall those offers: "If you give it to me and I don't like it, I will say that I don't like it in a public way." Meanwhile, Julia did not want a replacement Westinghouse. Cornering the repairman, she said, "Young man"—he was well into his seventies—"it says right here: *lifetime warranty.* And as you can well see, *I am still living.* Find a way to make this thing work."

If it had only been that easy when it came to her knee. The old append-age demanded constant care. For Julia, mobility was more than just a convenience, it was a vital necessity. With the bumper crop of appear-ances remaining on her schedule, she valued the importance of main-taining her stride. She prided herself on good fitness in general, staying active and vigorous even if it meant, at her age, working through a little pain. During those long book tours when she was always on the move, she would pop a few anti-inflammatories to keep her on the go. All told, it was a small price to pay.

But wear and tear was always a concern. In August 1997, on her eighty-fifth birthday, Julia was hopping between various events in Wash-ington, D.C., scrabbling around like a teenager, when her knee suddenly gave way. It swelled up like a cantaloupe and an infection developed. Despite excruciating pain, she attended a book signing, but the pain became too great; she was afraid she'd pass out. "We need to go," she told Stephanie Hersh, who took her straight to the airport.

In Boston, the doctor gave her antibiotics and advised her to stay off her feet. "It should clear up in a few days," he said. But it didn't—it got worse instead.

A few weeks later, Julia flew out to Santa Barbara, where she had recently settled in at the Casa Dorinda, a lovely retirement villa she and Paul had purchased years earlier. It had always been her intention to spend her golden years out West, although in Julia's mind the golden years weren't due until sometime well into the next century. Now, with *Baking* behind her, she planned to live at the Casa most of the year, with frequent visits to Cambridge and New York. The clinic at the Casa was a first-class establishment, and the doctors there recognized her persistent infection the moment they saw it. They immediately admitted her to the hospital, put her on intravenous antibiotics, and attempted to replace the knee. After two weeks and repeated procedures, the infection persisted, which delayed the implant. Instead, an antibiotic packet was placed directly in the wound, which Julia referred to as her Bouquet Gar-Knee.

But it was no laughing matter. It took several months for the infection to clear. The doctors were eventually able to replace the knee, but after the surgery, when Julia awoke, she seemed logy, almost aphasic: different. Stephanie Hersh, who hadn't left her side since Washington, sensed that something was horribly wrong. "It's the anesthesia," the doctors assured her. "It'll wear off soon." "No," she insisted, "something's not right, I can tell."

But a few days later, Julia was her old self again. There were some lingering symptoms, such as inflammation and pain. Julia had been immobile for so long that her muscles had atrophied and she could not walk. But her coordination would come back with some physical therapy. Nevertheless, Stephanie convinced her to have a CT scan. When the radiologist read the report, he confirmed her fears. "Yes, she's had a small stroke," he said.

"And that," says Stephanie, "was the beginning of the end."

In Santa Barbara, with Minou

Twenty-seven

The Raft

Creatively, intellectually, and emotionally, Julia was solid as a rock. She had often said that her work kept her vital. "As long as I am able to continue doing what I love, there's no stopping me," she had told her friend Pat Pratt, who admired that dauntless pioneer spirit. "My work gives me purpose; my purpose is my work," she explained to Stephanie Hersh after her operation, exercising like a demon to demonstrate her determination. On the threshold of her eighty-sixth birthday, she seemed hell-bent on defying it. "Her schedule never quieted down," Stephanie said. "Julia was still doing every interview that came her way, as well as book-related things and traveling for different causes."

Throughout the spring of 1998, 103 Irving teemed with enterprise and energy. The house "was a zoo," but wonderfully wild, with people coming and going all day long; the usual menagerie: neighbors, friends, chefs, consultants, fund-raisers, writers, scholars, anyone at any time could walk right through the open kitchen door—and did, inviting themselves inside. Most mornings Julia was squirreled away in the upstairs office, writing articles for *Food & Wine* or catching up with correspondence. Occasionally, she made notes for a memoir many begged her to write, but wound up tossing them out afterward. The accounts she conjured lacked the power of the great diarists whose work she'd devoured over the years. "I don't have it in me," she conceded, but the idea continued to intrigue. It was a good exercise nonetheless, keeping her mind alert, her writing skills sharp.

There was always someone waiting when she finally made her way down to the kitchen. Julia looked forward to routine visits from one of the young Boston chefs, especially the men, "the *boys*," whose attention she craved. Gordon Hamersley and Jasper White remained her all-time favorites. They were smart, serious chefs who observed the culinary strictures, but more important, perhaps, they were virile and tough-minded, her idea of he-men. And instead of food, they brought her news from the grapevine. "Julia loved gossip," White says. "She always wanted the latest scuttlebutt, who was doing what, and to whom and how. She was a live wire; the electricity turned her on."

Sara Moulton turned up from time to time to give her the behind-the-scenes poop at *Good Morning America,* or simply to ask some professional advice. Moulton, more than any of Julia's protégés, had made the most of her apprenticeship and training. Not only was she thriving at *GMA,* but also at the fledgling Food Network, where she had her own how-to show that attracted a wide audience. Recently, she'd also signed on at *Gourmet,* where she developed recipes for each monthly issue.

"I've done this terrible thing," she confessed to Julia one day that spring. Anguished, Moulton explained how they were working on an article about *gratins* for an upcoming issue of *Gourmet.* She and a few associates were testing the recipes that were credited to Madeleine Kamman, and they didn't work. Moulton recognized the problem: the ingredients were hazy; Kamman hadn't provided exact measurements. The editor wanted to kill the article, but Sara demurred. She thought, if nothing else, Kamman was a "great teacher" who deserved the space and acclaim. "So I called her up," she explained to Julia, "and before I could get the problem out of my mouth, she said, 'How *dare* you call me! You ripped off my recipe.' "

As it turned out, cooking teachers had longer memories than elephants. Years earlier, Moulton and Julia attended a demo Kamman did at which she boned out a salmon, and then put it back together with a smoked salmon-and-sour cream sauce. It was a nifty technique that impressed both women. A year or two afterward, Moulton did an article for *Cook's* magazine with a similar recipe and technique, but without crediting Kamman. She "felt weird about it at the time," but ran the story anyway.

"You're right," Moulton admitted. "I was wrong. Believe me, I'll never do it again. I've learned my lesson."

Kamman wasn't satisfied. She continued to berate Moulton, unwilling to cooperate or discuss the faulty *gratin* recipes. As a result, the editor killed the piece.

Julia listened to Moulton through narrowing eyes. "Dearie, she didn't invent that method of boning out fish," Julia said. "She learned it in France, just like all of us. If you want to get anywhere in this profession, you need to follow my advice. Just call her up, and say, 'Madeleine, *fuck you!*' " She made Moulton repeat it three times until she was satisfied with her delivery.

"Julia liked to swear," Moulton says, "and she did it like a sailor, but much of it was targeted at Madeleine, whom she loathed."

That Woman from Newton remained planted on Julia's enemies list—a short one, Julia liked to remind people, that aside from Madeleine included only Madame Brassart and the two Joes: McCarthy and Stalin. Friends had tried everything to reconcile their differences, without success. Kamman continued to bad-mouth Julia every chance she got, and Julia continued to swear at every mention of Madeleine's name.

Cooking teachers have longer memories than elephants.

Another visitor that spring was Geoffrey Drummond, who seemed eager to entice Julia with forbidden fruit, which in her case was work. Drummond had her number. She loved being on TV; she couldn't say no, and he devised new, exciting concepts that played right into her weakness. This one was irresistible: a series with Jacques Pépin, a spin-off of their *Cooking in Concert* shows.

Julia's health, for the first time, was a determining factor. Her knee was healed—*somewhat*—but still a source of lingering pain. She hobbled around on it as best she could, often leaning on a chair or a helping hand to get her balance. Knowing that she'd be on her feet for an ongoing production, she used every trick and dodge she could to downplay her condition, but Drummond could see she was in a fragile state. Yet she was stubborn, fearless, determined to do the show. Jacques discussed it with Julia and saw that "there was plenty of fire left in her." "She was an elderly woman," Drummond says, "but she made me forget she was old."

He wanted to make it easy for her to say yes. The original plan was to film the series in New York, at the French Culinary Institute, in front of a live audience, but it became apparent that Julia didn't have the stamina. Instead, they'd shoot it in her house, with a full staff of assistants. There'd be no script, no rehearsal, nothing for her to prepare in advance. She and Jacques would decide on a number of recipes and just cook them on the air any way they wished. They could improvise, wing it, whatever they pleased. It didn't matter how they did it or how long they took—twenty minutes, sixty, a hundred and twenty, all day; it would be edited afterward to fit the hour-long time frame. All Julia had to do was show up and be herself.

Drummond knew the key was their engaging personalities. Julia and Jacques were both perfectionists, headstrong, convinced their way was the right way, masters of their own kitchen. There was also a male-female tension that promised to throw sparks. Julia had neither forgotten nor forgiven the harsh treatment of women by French chefs. All these years, she'd exhorted women to stand up to those tyrants, to demand respect and equal rights in the kitchen. Jacques's voice, that arch French accent, would push a few buttons. There would be plenty to feast on aside from the food.

What people loved about *Cooking in Concert* was the friendly rivalry. By bringing it into Julia's kitchen, it would take on an intimacy, something viewers might regard as kitchen therapy.

Once Julia agreed, Drummond pushed for a book to accompany the series. The last thing Julia wanted to do was to write on deadline, not in her condition, not at eighty-six. All those late nights, trying to pound out copy—it made sense at one time, but not anymore. Still, she said, "Why don't you run it by Judith," a delicate proposition considering their itchy experience with *Baking*.

Drummond, reluctantly, sent a proposal to Knopf. He wasn't optimistic about a favorable response, nor an advance that would be competitive with other houses. Publishers also had long memories, and hard feelings were hard to assuage. But Jones, who wasn't inclined to hold grudges, saw the blockbuster potential right away. "I thought this could be a terrific book," she recalls. "The idea of two voices was fabulous, and it taught something so essential: that there is no one way to cook." It would be a "break-out for Julia," working with Jacques, she thought. Jones *had* to have the book. She wouldn't let this one get away.

She practically ran the proposal into the office of her publisher, Sonny Mehta. "This is going to be a monster—they're going to be hilarious together," she told him. Unlike her degrading experience with Alfred Knopf thirty-seven years earlier, Jones got immediate satisfaction from Mehta, who decided to make a preemptive offer: a million dollars guaranteed. It was staggering, an offer even Drummond couldn't refuse. Besides, Julia wanted to work with Jones again. Judith knew her style;

she'd protect Julia, particularly with a manuscript that would be largely ghostwritten.

Everything came together almost as neatly. The series was underwritten by KQED in San Francisco, which had a long-standing relationship with Jacques. He'd also discussed the show with his friend Jess Jackson, who owned the Kendall-Jackson Winery and stepped up to sponsor *Julia and Jacques.*

The series began filming in the summer of 1998, and from the first day of production it was everything everyone expected. The fireworks started flying the moment Julia walked on the set. "I think we should use an electric stove," she said. Pépin looked at her, bewildered. "Why?" he asked. "You don't cook on an electric stove." The old gas range in her kitchen had never let her down. It was like a lover; she knew every inch of it, its touch, all of its quirks, its infidelities. Besides, they'd built a new counter especially for the show and had put a gas stovetop in it, ready to go. "No, I want an electric stove," she insisted. "Jack doesn't appreciate that sixty-nine percent of Americans use an electric stove."

"But I don't cook on an electric stove," he told her, pleading his case.

"Fine," Julia said. "You cook over *there.* I'll cook over here." She spread her arms out to define center stage, where the crew was already drawing plans for an electric range.

Appliances weren't the only issue they wrangled about. "We could never agree—on *anything*," Pépin recalls. "An hour before filming, Julia would change the menu. She would find the producer and decide on a dish we'd never discussed." Jacques had no choice but to cook her recipe. He knew the score: "No one says no to Julia."

He also knew his role—not just as Julia's foil, but to be the perfect assistant so that nothing slowed down.

Julia's role was much more provocative. "She loved getting into conflict with Jacques and challenging him," says Geof Drummond. That was part of her incentive to do the series. "She loved getting his goat," recalls Judith Jones, who was on the set for practically every show.

"We argued over every single dish," Jacques says. "Because we used no recipes there was no reason to follow a particular structure, and that meant we could do what we thought worked best. I respected Julia's palate; she had taste. But there were many times I thought she was flat-out wrong."

Like the Greeks, they almost went to war over turkey. Julia insisted on cutting up the bird before roasting it, which Jacques thought was ridiculous, a recipe for disaster. He demanded they do it his way for once. "It's going to work better," he said, defending his technique. "*It will not work!*" she fumed. Julia was "mad as hell," but gave in this one time—even madder when the recipe turned out perfectly. Other times she stood her ground and made her point, like when they collaborated on a roast of veal. Jacques wanted to add endive to the pot. "It won't be good," Julia warned him in an obsequious I-told-you-so voice. You could almost see smoke coming out of his nostrils. "The juice of the veal will braise the endive," he assured her through clenched teeth, but he was wrong; it made the endive bitter.

Judith Jones didn't help the situation. She stood off-camera, watching over her million-dollar investment, trying to motivate Julia to take a strong position. "You're not going to take that French macho stuff from him, are you?" she'd mutter between takes. That was usually enough to light Julia's wick. When production resumed, she'd come out swinging, like a battered boxer who'd been revived between rounds.

"Don't let him get away with that," Judith prompted.

From time to time, Jones would encounter Jacques on the porch, cooling off. "He'd ball up his fist and rattle off a stream of French expletives," she recalls. "Then they'd call 'Action!' and, in front of the camera, his whole demeanor would change."

"Ooooh, Julia, *ma chérie*, whatever you want. You don't think that would be good? Okay, let's do it your way."

"She really frustrated him," Jones says, "no question about it."

The work was frustrating, but also long and hard. They cooked and filmed, filmed and cooked, until ten or eleven every night for the better part of three months. "Julia was already pretty shaky on her feet," Drummond recalls. "I could see the physical strain was catching up with her." There were days she could barely stand through a ten-minute take. Instead, she leaned her body against the counter and propped as much weight as possible on her hands. "She was worn out physically," says Stephanie Hersh. "Her legs were bothering her—the knee, which had never really recovered—and she needed to frequently sit down in order to recharge." Intermittent naps were also slotted into the schedule. "She needed rest; otherwise, she'd never make it through to the end."

Each night, after work was officially over, the entire cast and crew tromped into the dining room, where they ate all the food that was prepared during the day. Julia began the feast the same way every night, by raising a glass of wine and saying, "Don't we have fun!" Often, the meal lasted well past midnight. She reached deep into her reserve tank to keep up the pace.

By October 1998, Julia and Jacques's cooking duet had lapsed into an endless round of fencing: thrust and parry, frustration and reprisal. Their disparate techniques seemed to draw them further and further apart. Jacques used kosher salt, Julia wouldn't touch it; Jacques used black pepper, Julia only white. "The prices for some of these 'gourmet'-type salts are ridiculous and I don't want to be bothered with three kinds," her co-writer transcribed from tapes for the book, when what she actually told him was: "Fuck 'em! Fuck 'em all!" Jacques made his own mayonnaise, Julia preferred Hellman's. Jacques baked potatoes in the oven, Julia used the microwave. Jacques put white wine in his onion soup, Julia red. Fuck 'em! Fuck 'em all!

If their differences brought out Julia's petulance, the sponsors brought out her guile. It was standard procedure to invite the sponsors to visit the set out of appreciation for their generosity. Kendall-Jackson had been nothing if not supportive of *Julia and Jacques*. Not only had they underwritten much of the costly production, they'd also sent cases of wine from their best artisan vineyards that were used throughout for the cooking. Out of courtesy, Drummond invited their Boston distributor to take in one of the shows and to bring along some rising-star chefs.

Julia approved of the tradition, but she wasn't happy. Her friends Richard and Thekla Sanford were up in arms about Kendall-Jackson's activity in the Santa Ynez Valley. According to Sanford, "They bulldozed nine hundred ancient oak trees to make way for a new vineyard." The Sanfords had appealed to the the Environmental Defense Center, hoping to win an ordinance to protect the woodlands, but in the meantime they appealed to an even higher authority: Julia. Wasn't there something she could do for them? Thekla wondered. Perhaps if she rejected Kendall's sponsorship, it would bring enough pressure to end the deforestation. Julia suggested that she call Geof Drummond.

"It's too late—way too late," Geof told Sanford. "We're on our second-to-last show. Besides, Jess Jackson and his wife are personal friends of Jacques'. I'd love to help you, but it's out of my hands."

Julia, whose hands were bigger, had other ideas.

The day of the sponsor visit, Julia and Jacques were preparing a Mediterranean seafood stew, a saffron-infused broth on the order of bouillabaisse, with a variety of shellfish and chunks of meaty halibut and swordfish. It was a bold, flavorful dish sure to entice the onlookers, who were clustered in Julia's dining room watching the action on video monitors. When it was finished, Jacques placed the steamy tureen prominently on the counter, while Julia set out bowls and spoons. The soup was ladled out, after which Jacques uncorked two bottles of Jess Jackson's best wine, which he had been saving for the occasion.

"Julia, this lunch would be perfect with a nice chilled *sauvignon blanc* from the Santa Maria Valley," he said into the camera, careful to follow PBS rules not to mention Kendall-Jackson by name.

"No, Jack," she said, "we're not having wine. Today we're having beer."

Whaaaat? No one had ever seen Julia drink a beer before; she loved wine, sipped it passionately at every meal. It was unlikely she'd even had beer in the house.

The dining room gang surged toward the monitor in disbelief as Julia reached under the counter, where she had stashed two bottles of Sam Adams beer.

Jacques's face became visibly panicked. "Can't we have beer *and* wine?" he asked, a note of desperation in his deep, French-accented voice.

She looked at him as if he were her fourteen-year-old son. "No, Jack—we're having *beer*." End of story.

No opportunity to humble the powers-that-be went unturned. Even when Julia felt drained and depleted, she was willing to take on any comers. "Rules—she didn't like rules," says Eric Spivey, a fan who had befriended her in Santa Barbara.

But by the end of production on *Julia and Jacques,* she was ready to play by a whole new set.

IN THE SUMMER of 2001, just weeks before her birthday, Julia stunned Stephanie Hersh with an announcement. "I'm going to be shifting to California permanently," she said. "I'll be eighty-nine. I should start thinking about my future."

Julia later said that she decided to make the move many years before, when she was still in her seventies, with a stretch of time ahead of her. It was a typical Julia Child decision: brusque, pragmatic, irreversible, and utterly lacking in sentimentality. Her reasons were fairly uncomplicated, stemming from her Pasadena upbringing. "In her heart, Julia was always a California girl," say her niece, Phila Cousins. "She loved Santa Barbara, and had great memories of it as a kid. All along it was the place she knew she'd eventually end up." She had a close circle of friends there, from her childhood as well as the culinary world. There was family nearby, just miles from the Casa Dorinda, and the move offered her a chance to live close to Dort, who was not well. California was also an escape from the past, a place where she could go and leave ghosts behind. "Paul was gone," says Hersh. "There was no longer anything holding her back."

Once the decision was made, Julia put the plan immediately into motion. There were many loose ends that needed tying up, preparations she'd laid the groundwork for long in advance. It had always been Julia's intention to give her belongings away to deserving institutions and finally she did it, clearing everything out at once. Her house, 103 Irving, was being donated to Smith College; all of her private papers and vast cookbook collection went to the Schlesinger Library at Radcliffe, on the Harvard campus. Even that famous sanctuary, her kitchen, had a destination; she'd promised it to Copia, the American Center for Wine, Food, and the Arts in downtown Napa.

Robert Mondavi had started Copia with $20 million of his own money and a promise from Julia for similar funds. It was housed in a gorgeous modern facility surrounded by incredible gardens, with a restaurant, Julia's Kitchen, where the public would dine. "It was the only time Julia ever put her name on anything commercial," says Clark Wolf. "But its downfall was that they didn't cook her food." Be that as it may, Julia loved the concept: a cultural foundation to promote everything she held dear that would mirror and complement the Beard Foundation back East. "She was so impressed with the architecture and the building," says Richard Sanford, who took her to Napa for a groundbreaking tour. "On the spot, she decided to give her working kitchen to Copia, whenever the time came to move out of Cambridge."

Stephanie Hersh called Copia to give them a heads-up. "How do you want to handle the transfer?" she asked. They told her to pack everything up and send it west. "No, you don't understand; this is *Julia Child's kitchen*. You need to preserve it. Come up with a better plan." In the meantime, Hersh called her friend at the Smithsonian in Washington, D.C., and said, "The kitchen belongs with you. Do you want it?" Indeed they did, but so did Copia, which intended to hold Julia to her original promise. It took some fancy footwork to untangle the mess. In the end, Copia had neither the space nor the manpower to handle the transfer. As a compromise, they'd get Julia's copper pot collection; everything else would go to the Smithsonian's Museum of American History, where it would be part of the permanent exhibit.

Plans continued to close up the house. Julia instructed Stephanie to send a letter to her closest relatives asking if there was anything special of hers they'd like to have; otherwise, all her personal belongings would go to various charities. She intended to hold an auction and split the proceeds between the American Institute of Wine and Food and the International Association of Culinary Professionals for fellowships in her name, with the rest destined for Planned Parenthood. "Instead, all the relatives wrote back asking for details," Hersh recalls, "like how many pieces of silver were available, or if the artwork was valuable." Together, Julia and Stephanie inventoried the house. The relatives could have it all, Julia decided. "You handle it," she instructed Stephanie. "I don't want anything to do with it. Just make sure nothing leaves the house before I'm settled in California."

In a matter of weeks, mostly everything had been arranged, with the house in the final, topsy-turvy stages of moving. Julia was expressly focused on relocating out West—she couldn't wait to get out there—and she had decided to take Stephanie along with her. They already had their plane tickets, an American Airlines flight to Los Angeles, leaving from Boston's Logan Airport on Tuesday, September 11, 2001.

LEAVE IT TO Geof Drummond to bollix up the plans. Drummond had agreed to shoot a short video of Julia in her kitchen that would play as a loop at the Smithsonian exhibit. It required only the smallest possible crew, but the only day everyone could make it was that Tuesday. Julia instructed Stephanie to reschedule their tickets for the end of the week.

That morning the house was in chaos. Before any filming could begin, the moving boxes had to be dragged out of the kitchen so it would resemble the room as it looked on people's television screens. Julia, who had been doing makeup upstairs, asked Tommy Hamilton, the gaffer, if he could help her get HBO on her bedroom set. She wanted to be able to watch a rerun of *The Sopranos* and was having trouble with the cable connection. "Tommy flipped a switch on the back of the TV," Drummond recalls, "and that's when we saw the planes hit the Trade Center."

Julia watched with a familiar sense of horror. "This is just like Pearl Harbor!" she exclaimed. She was convinced the attack was only the first spark; all hell would break loose in the coming hours. Drummond wasn't sure whether to continue their session. "Let's get this done now," Julia advised him. "We may not have another chance."

Stephanie helped bring Julia down to the set. There was so much to do amid so much uncertainty. No one remembered whether or not they were aware that the tragic flights had originated in Boston. "In the confusion," Stephanie said, "I forgot to tell my parents we'd changed our travel plans. They were sure Julia and I were on that plane."

SANTA BARBARA GAVE Julia everything she wanted: peace and quiet—no tension, no TV crews, no deadlines, no harsh weather, no Woman from Newton, no unwanted guests barging into the kitchen all hours of the day. There was an immediate sense of serenity—of *relief*—of starting over, in a charming and manageable place. Santa Barbara "was always magical" for Julia. It was provincial and coastal, with wonderful palm trees and nectar-filled flowers, a fusion of her childhood with an inflection of France. Casa Dorinda added to the overall charm. It was a perfect hideaway—small but perfect: she had a sun-filled one-bedroom corner apartment, with a view of the mountains, off a private garden where she planned to raise herbs among the riot of flowers. She put in an apple and a pear tree. The Sanfords brought her a birdfeeder; within days, a stray cat showed up, which she named Minou and took in. The only real drawback was the galley kitchen, a cubbyhole so minuscule that barely two people could stand in it at the same time. *Tant pis:* so be it, Julia thought. Her splashiest cooking days were comfortably behind her. Besides, retirement brought with it a retiring way to eat. She'd make simple meals from now on, a kind of French classic lite, to complement a sensible eighty-nine-year-old's diet. Julia was open-minded, flexible, unopposed to change. One key adjustment had already occurred since moving west: grudgingly, she'd begun walking with a cane.

Her knee was acting up again. The old infection kicked up from time to time, but it was nothing that would keep her from getting out and about. Julia had an agenda. "She was going to take it easy, enjoy herself," Stephanie says, "go to the movies a lot and have dinner with friends." In her spare time, she might even tinker with a memoir. Her nephew Alex Prud'homme had spoken to her about collaborating on something to honor Paul, and Julia was intrigued. But at a slow and comfortable pace, not on any kind of a deadline.

"There wasn't a day when I didn't see her get up and do something," said Eric Spivey. Mostly, she connected with childhood friends. "She was very concerned about getting involved with the wrong social crowd," says

Richard Sanford. "The wealthy Pasadena transplants irritated her—the *robber barons*. She thought they were boring; she didn't like their politics."

"But she loved going out," says Thekla Sanford. "She wanted to be around people, wherever the excitement was."

Julia still championed liberal causes and also, to her credit, revised some of her earlier opinions. She came to appreciate movements she'd rejected in the past. "She supported the organic farmers in Santa Barbara," says Eric Spivey, who took her religiously every Saturday morning to the local open-air market, where she commiserated with the organic zealots. Vegetarians? They remained a work-in-progress, although Julia condescended to hear their appeals. Afterward, she always spent a few minutes talking to Tab Hunter, "a real he-man," who lived in the area and never failed to look for her. Then, for a treat, she'd head to Costco for two hot dogs, with mustard and kraut.

For the first year or so, Santa Barbara was pure bliss. A rotation of visitors showed up from the East, but sporadically—just enough to provide a needed lift. Julia loved hearing the latest gossip. There was still plenty to glean from the go-go culinary world, which had grown more competitive and contentious since she'd stood at its nucleus. And revolutionary! Food—cuisine—had developed into something strange and extraordinary, something exotic, something *else*. These days, everything that appeared on her plate in a restaurant was sculptural, innovative: unrecognizable. The young chefs had taken her beloved Escoffier and attached wires and electrodes to his balls. Scallops came to the table clouded in foams and gels, chiles rellenos were stuffed with goat cheese, pork loin was dressed with oysters and kimchi. And bacon-and-egg ice cream—imagine that! How far food had come since her first bite of *sole meunière*. But was it better? Her taste memory could still access each flavor of that life-affirming dish: fish, butter, and lemon as pure and unadulterated as they were meant to be savored. She still considered that lunch in Rouen "the most exciting meal of my life."

But the rest of it—the experimentation, the home-cooking sensation, the public's obsession with food—was simply thrilling. Everything she'd worked toward and hoped for had come true. Beyond her dreams! Wherever she went to dinner, whether in an ordinary restaurant or someone's home, the food was made with so much care. Even at McDonald's, where she put away the occasional cheeseburger. "It's tremendously impressive what we have to eat at our disposal," she said. "You just can't argue with *real food*. It's remarkably satisfying."

The restaurant scene in Santa Barbara was interesting enough to indulge her. The food wasn't fancy, but good, solid fare. "There were five or six restaurants that she frequented on a regular rotation," says Eric Spivey. Her favorite, Lucky's, was an old-fashioned steakhouse on the site of the original Montecito bungalows, where she could have her rib-eye rare, her asparagus well-cooked, her corn creamed, and her cheesecake extra dense. The Paradise Café was her burger joint of choice, and for Italian she headed to Olio e Limone. Any of those places would do nicely—or not at all. But the one meal she never missed was breakfast at the Casa Dorinda.

For Julia, it was a daily trip back in time, back to early mornings in "the Res" at the Katharine Branson School where, at a long wooden table, the girls would gossip and argue over steamy plates heaped with pancakes or eggs. Like the schoolgirls, a group of women at the Casa had formed a breakfast club at a sun-streaked corner table of the dining room, where they bantered about their doctors or other, often feeble, residents who wound up in "the Ga-Ga House," as Julia called the Casa's infirmary. Julia's buddies were a feisty gang of octogenarians—Dorothy Heightman, Betty Kelmer, Peg Wright, all Smith grads, and Jo Duff, who had lived around the corner from Julia in Pasadena. "We were all very copasetic," says Duff, "even though our opinions were occasionally at odds." Julia never missed an opportunity to provoke one or another of the women, who were fairly religious and vehemently Republican. "Go ahead—explain the war in Iraq," she'd sneer, or swipe at her favorite punching bag, George W. Bush. Some mornings, it looked as though an attendant might have to separate those women, no thanks to Julia, who fed the fire with liberal rhetoric.

Periodically Julia disappeared from their huddle each morning to scan the buffet table just minutes before closing. It was a ritual. "When no one was looking she'd stuff dozens of pieces of bacon into her purse," says Richard Sanford, who came often with his wife. "It would reappear magically at lunch, when she made us bacon, lettuce, and tomato sandwiches." This happened practically every day. "She lived off that bacon," recalls Eric Spivey, "until Stephanie eventually banned it from her diet."

More and more, Stephanie had to keep an eye on Julia, who was beginning to feel the weight of her years. Age was catching up with her. She had turned ninety in 2002, and with it came the breakdowns and repairs that bedevil an old chassis. In November, she developed another knee infection that put her in the hospital, this time with grave concern.

"It was worse than the last time," Stephanie said, "and at her age it was almost too much to bear."

"Julia was in horrible pain," recalls Thekla Sanford, who came to help out during the crisis. "The infection was deep; they couldn't get rid of it. We all worried that she wouldn't make it through." Julia stopped responding to the medication and refused extreme procedures. Eventually, the doctors took her kneecap out and let the knee drain before putting everything back together again, and gradually she began to come around, her old self. "I knew Julia was going to recover when she got interested in eating," says Thekla Sanford. "The problem was, she was living off the Casa's crappy food. So I brought her an egg salad sandwich and vanilla malt, and she sucked that malt down like there was no tomorrow. Then she made me promise to take her to Lucky's."

Getting there, however, wasn't going to be easy. Her legs were riddled with pain that had confined her to a wheelchair and her diet was being drastically restricted. No more rich foods, no tomatoes, no wine—they were out, along with a half-dozen goodies on a list Stephanie kept. "It was a thankless task policing Julia's eating habits," Stephanie recalls, "not that Julia ever helped the situation."

Rebellious as ever, Julia convinced friends to take her out for dinner every chance she could. "She liked to go where she wasn't supposed to," says Eric Spivey, one of her frequent companions. "And getting past Stephanie was no easy doing." Against Stephanie's wishes, Julia would plead with Spivey to pick her up at the Casa, where Julia would wheel past her jailer, announcing: "We'll be going! Don't wait up!"

Stephanie, unable to intervene, watched murderously from the porch as Julia, with much difficulty, was folded into a car by her accomplice. "And don't let her have any alcohol!" she demanded.

Most nights, they made a beeline for Lucky's, where Julia was friendly with the sommelier. Richard Sanford remembers meeting her there one night, as she was uncorking a split of champagne. "I knew Julia wasn't supposed to drink," he admits, "though I was more worried what Stephanie would do to us if she found out." He'd already told the maître d' not to send over the wine list, but somehow a bottle of pinot noir appeared. "She can't have it!" Sanford objected. But he wasn't about to try taking wine out of Julia Child's hands. "She was already pouring, so I just said, 'Screw it!' That's how it went on any given night."

It was clear, however, that her indulgence was taking a toll. One night that winter, toward the end of 2002, Julia showed up for a dinner party at Eric Spivey's house. She looked exhausted. Her face was puffy and her breath came in short, labored gasps. Spivey asked casually how her day had gone. Julia looked at him for some time before answering. "Not well," she said, her eyes distant, baleful. "This is really hard, and I'm not sure where it's going to go." It was a moment of vulnerability that she hadn't intended to share, a momentary lapse. "But how was *your* day, dearie?" she asked, using a tactic that always served to deflect attention from her personal life.

For the first time in Julia's life she was surrendering to physical limitations. The wheelchair and diet restrictions were visible encumbrances, but other underlying resistance was impossible to deny. Most days, she felt run-down, depressed. Worse, perhaps, was a rising boredom. It was the first time in fifty years that she wasn't immersed in a project, something that kept her mind engaged. More and more, Julia wanted to work again. As a way of keeping occupied, she began making notes—about her cooking, her marriage, her life in France.

It was time, she decided, to start that memoir.

On and off during 2003, Julia discussed such a book with her editor, Judith Jones. It seemed like a perfect idea to Jones, since both she and Julia had been roundly disappointed by a biographer's efforts some years earlier. A contract was no problem; they could work out the terms based on performance in the past. As for a deadline, Jones said, "we can just leave that open." Whenever the manuscript came in, she'd be happy to publish it.

Julia's nephew Alex was eager to be involved. "All right, dearie, maybe we *should* work on it together," she told him. There were several preconditions, however, that he needed to accept. Long, ponderous interviews were out of the question. She just wasn't up to it, her attention span short. And limiting the subject to France would narrow the focus. It would be therapeutic for her to reflect on Paul and those beautiful days, when all the pieces just seemed to fall into place.

That July, she learned from her lawyer that she would be receiving the Presidential Medal of Freedom, a prestigious award given to those who have made "an especially meritorious contribution" to the cultural or public interests of the United States. Past recipients had included Irving Berlin, Carl Sandburg, Mother Teresa, Norman Rockwell, and Nelson Mandela, all great, distinguished company. It was much deserved, considering Julia's huge gift. Yet, it was uncertain that she would accept the award. After all, it was coming from George W. Bush, a *Republican,* her longtime whipping boy. If only Bill Clinton had stepped up during his term! "Julia loved Clinton," says Rebecca Alssid, "She thought he was brilliant, 'a real he-man.' But for some reason, his administration didn't respond." George Bush: it was almost ironic. Nevertheless, he *was* her president. In the end, she found it impossible to say no.

On the morning of July 23, 2003, the phone rang at the Casa Dorinda. Julia picked it up on the second ring. "Julia, I wish you were here," the president said in that familiar folksy twang. It was almost surreal, George Bush come-to-life—the Decider himself—telling her how much he appreciated her, how as a kid he'd watched her on TV, as had his mother, Barbara. They'd made her recipes, bought her books. He giggled fondly at the memory. No doubt he'd seen Dan Aykroyd's sketch, but if he had he wasn't saying. The call didn't last more than four or five minutes, but left her feeling conflicted, off her liberal guard. "I hate to admit it," Julia said afterward, "but he was a very charming man." Not that she'd ever go as far as voting for him. When Rebecca Alssid came to visit that summer, Arnold Schwarzenegger was running for governor, a bit of a political wild card to the folks back East. "I think I'm going to vote for him," Julia told her matter-of-factly. "But, Julia, you're a Democrat," Alssid reminded her. "I know, dearie," Julia said, "but I'm finding him *very* attractive." Even at ninety-one, she'd cross the aisle for a hunky man.

Men, hunky or otherwise, still figured prominently in her world. When her niece Phila took her to see *Troy* at a local movie theater that May, Julia almost leaped out of her seat. "My *God,* that Brad Pitt is certainly handsome," she gasped, wondering what might lie under that tunic. The thought still excited her. Then, in September, Jasper White called on his way to a charity cook-off in Los Angeles. He hadn't seen Julia since Boston and wanted to pay his respects. "Oh, that would be great, dearie," she told him. There was only one hitch. He said, "I have my *sous* chefs with me." There was a two- or three-second delay until she responded.

"Boys?!"

"Yeah, boys."

"Well, bring 'em along, dearie!"

If old friends rarely stopped by these days, it was out of respect for her age and privacy. Julia seemed happy to live out of the limelight, but there were those who worried that she might be unwell. White couldn't have been more relieved at what he found. "Mentally, she was a hundred percent," he said. "She was wheelchair-bound and embarrassed about it, refusing to sit in that damn contraption a moment longer than necessary." But others encountered a Julia who was weak and disoriented. Clark Wolf dropped by one afternoon that fall and was startled by her condition. "She seemed half-asleep on her feet," he said, "completely lost in the conversation."

"It was clear that her health was failing," says Alex Prud'homme, "although she was mentally acute." To maintain the progress on the memoir, he tried to engage Julia regularly in reminiscing about the favorite years of her life. Throughout the early winter, between knee treatments and setbacks, they went over and over fond, familiar territory: her initiation at Le Cordon Bleu, meeting Simca and Louisette, writing *Mastering*. Paul. She lost herself in the romance of those stories, reliving some, unburdening herself of others. According to Prud'homme, "she would never complain. But the nurses told me later that she was in a lot of pain and sleeping hour upon hour."

That May 2004, during a stretch of two weeks, everything seemed to cave in around her. "She was in and out of the hospital *a lot*," says her internist, William Koonce. "She was really losing her quality of life." Julia developed congestive heart failure on top of another knee infection. If that weren't bad enough, her kidneys started to fail. A regimen of serious medications was knocking her for a loop. Her doctor at the Casa called various family members. "We really don't have much time left," he advised.

Alex and Phila helped Julia write a health-care proxy that clearly stated: "I don't want any extraordinary measures." They also made sure that everyone dear to her would be in Santa Barbara for Julia's ninety-second birthday in August, fearing that it might be her last. They'd planned a bash to end all bashes at a local restaurant, and so far, more than a hundred friends had promised to attend.

Later that May, Rebecca Alssid came to visit. "Julia was really getting disgusted with all the infirmary visits and I worried that she was just giving up," Alssid says. "The worst part was that she had lost her sense of taste." Julia blamed the medications, and her spirit swung between anger and despair. Her *taste*—it seemed like too cruel a joke. Without taste, she might as well be dead. Despite her condition, Julia sent Rebecca to the greenmarket to collect groceries for dinner that night. Julia remained behind, working with Alex, and afterward took a late-afternoon nap. When she awoke, she craved an artichoke and asked Rebecca to make a hollandaise sauce.

"I'd never done that before," Rebecca recalls. So she opened a copy of

Mark Bittman's *How to Cook Everything* and gave hollandaise a test run, for better or worse.

"Let me taste it, dearie," Julia called from the bedroom. Rebecca was anxious; this was Julia Child, after all. Julia's face loosened gratefully as she licked at the leaves. "Umm, good. But it needs more salt."

That's odd, Rebecca thought. She shouldn't be able to taste that. At dinner, Julia devoured a half rack of lamb chops, cooing with pleasure after each bite. "That was so delicious, dearie—so wonderful. I enjoyed every bite of it."

That's when Rebecca knew Julia had gone off her meds.

"I don't care," she said when Alex confronted her. "I have to taste the food, otherwise there's no use sticking around."

And Julia seemed in no great rush to slip off the raft. A nephrologist promised her two good years, minimum, if she consented to dialysis three days a week. It was a brutal treatment that left her withered and nauseated. For all her expectations, there were few good days. More often than not, she was overcome with depression. Her family was outraged; she'd said no to extraordinary measures; the dialysis seemed to be pushing that to extremes.

Dr. Koonce warned her about staying fit and healthy. Following a mild heart attack, he and Julia's cardiologist visited her in the hospital. "You have to clean up your diet," Koonce told her, "and you especially have to stop eating butter."

Julia struggled up on her side to look her doctors in the face. "Oh, such silly boys!" she said.

"The cardiologist and I just looked at each other and laughed," Koonce recalls. "We had fulfilled our responsibility as doctors to tell Julia Child to stop eating butter. And we really felt like such silly boys."

On her own she was able to enjoy a good meal. On August 11, two days before her ninety-second birthday, Julia decided to reach into the past. What she wanted, what she *craved*, was a good onion soup. "You must let the onions cook slowly and long, browning them in lots of butter," she'd told her audience on an early episode of *The French Chef*. Following her own advice, she made a fragrant pot of soup and ate two bowls with abundant pleasure. "That's a wonderful smell and a very appetizing one," she declared in 1965; thirty-nine years later she couldn't improve on that. She'd given American cooks a damn good recipe—a lifetime of recipes—that *worked* and satisfied.

The next morning, however, she was sick—very sick. A visit to Dr.

Koonce in the Casa's infirmary confirmed the worst. The port for her dialysis had become infected; as a result she'd developed sepsis. "If it isn't treated immediately," he said, "you will die within forty-eight hours."

"You mean: kick the bucket?" she asked.

Koonce nodded.

Julia took the verdict stone-faced. "If we treat this and get rid of the infection, can you promise me that I'm going to get the energy level I had before this started?"

"No," the doctor said, without equivocation.

"Then don't treat it," Julia said.

Stephanie cried all the way back to the apartment. Throughout the long circuitry of corridors in the Casa Dorinda, Julia stared straight ahead, wordless, lost in thought.

"I'm not ready for you to go," Stephanie whimpered through her tears.

Julia patted her hand stoically. "It's time, dearie," she said, her voice quavering. "If I can't live the way I want to live, I'd rather not live at all. Now, if you don't mind, I'm just going to take a little nap."

After Julia crawled into bed, Minou curled near her side, Stephanie picked up the phone and called everyone who mattered—Alex, Phila, David McWilliams, the Sanfords, the Spiveys, dozens more—and gave them the terrible news. They came from everywhere to say their goodbyes while Julia slept, peaceful, painless, at last. Even her friends at the Casa, the Breakfast Club gals, came through her room, held her hand, wept, said a few private words. Goodbye, Julia.

EARLY THE NEXT evening, the phone rang in the kitchen at Olio e Limone. There was a full house in the dining room, mostly regulars who had just sat down, and it was hard for Elaine Morello, the chef's wife, to hear above the din. She turned away from the crowd and cupped a hand over her ear, listening as best she could through the clatter and static.

A few minutes later, she went to the front of the house and clanked a knife against a wineglass to get everyone's attention.

"Our dear friend and mentor Julia Child passed away today," she said. A chorus of gasps and cries sifted through the room. "So we invite all of you to raise a glass in her honor." With great vivacity, she sang out: "*Cin cin! Salute,* Julia."

Someone had the good sense to shout, "And *bon appétit!*"

Sources and Acknowledgments

The genesis of this book sprang from my amazing luck, traveling with Julia Child in Sicily in 1992. For several weeks, we crisscrossed the island, eating, of course, but talking every chance we got. She was already a beloved icon, larger than life in so many different ways, but perhaps the most down-to-earth celebrity I'd ever encountered. Inasmuch as I was writing about her for several magazines, we were on the record throughout the trip, but she never held back from speaking her mind, never shied from a tough opinion, never pulled her punches, never blinked. She was *exactly* like her TV persona: warm, funny, outgoing, whip-smart, incorrigible, and, most of all, *real.* If I have to admit to one prejudice confronting this book, it is that I had a powerful crush on her. Sorry. Deal with it.

We began discussing a biography almost from the moment we got back, but in the intervening months I became involved with the Beatles. Work on that book ballooned from two to almost nine years, a span that included Julia's death. The chance to collaborate had sadly eluded me. Yet the minute I finished my Beatles opus, I always knew what the next biography would be. There was no escaping her powerful hold, and if I were about to commit another ridiculous chunk of my life to a subject, it was going to be to a person whose life was a bottomless source of inspiration.

Julia Child was that—and more. In the four years that went into this project, I was humbled by her contribution to our culture and our lives. The gift that she left us with is invaluable and undeniable.

Crushes, inspiration, and humility are quickly dispatched, however, once the work begins.

No matter how an author perseveres during years of research, a biography is wholly dependent upon outside sources: libraries, archives, foundations, and people who are generous with their time when it comes to sharing memories. Thankfully, my work was sustained by Julia Child herself. Before she moved out of Cambridge, Julia donated her entire vast archive to the Schlesinger Library on the Harvard campus, where it is catalogued in more than eighty-five boxes. Simca's letters are also there, as are Paul Child's papers—thousands of gorgeously evocative handwritten letters, including those to his brother Charlie that began in 1942 and continued on an almost daily basis until his health prohibited in 1974. Julia always intended her papers to be in one place, and the Schlesinger was an inspired choice. It is a scholar's dream, the perfect place to work, and I owe a great debt to its staff, especially Ellen Shea and Diana Carey. I am indebted also to Mark DeVoto, who shared not only his mother, Avis's, letters to Julia (similarly housed at the Schlesinger Library) but also an unpublished memoir she'd written in 1988 about their remarkable relationship.

The Julia Child Foundation and the James Beard Foundation provided constant support. I wish also to thank the Smith College library, which yielded a trove of wonderful information stretching all the way back to Caro Weston, and its archivist, Nancy A. Young, for providing assistance. I am indebted, as well, to the Vassar College Alumnae Office, the Shorenstein Center on the Press, Politics and Public Policy (Edie Holway), the Pasadena Museum of History (Laura Verlaque, Bill Trimble, and Bob Bennett), the OSS Society (Charles Pinck and Betty McIntosh), and Cindy Eisenmenger at *Gastronome*.

I am grateful to everyone in Pasadena, Cambridge, and Santa Barbara who opened up their doors to me and shared countless stories about Julia's remarkable life. Those who agreed to be interviewed are cited in the notes. There are several, however, who deserve special mention. Russ and Marian Morash provided a fascinating behind-the-scenes tour of *The French Chef* set and the pioneering days of educational TV. In addition, they withstood enough queries and calls to have my number blocked by the phone company, but never failed to make themselves available. Only Russ, the Ayatollah, could stand up to Julia's relentless drive; his stealth contribution to the rise of public broadcasting is incalculable. Judith Jones's recollections of the early days at Knopf may force my publisher to take their name off the spine of this book; nevertheless, her insights and extremely frank conversations with me were instrumental in understanding Julia's ambitions. Another individual who deserves special mention is Geof Drummond, Julia's indefatigable producer for the latter part of her TV career, who was more than generous with his time and tidings. Geof has been criticized for "dragging an old lady across the TV screen," yet he not only saw beyond age, he gave Julia a second act, which she deserved and loved (as did we).

I received encouragement and assistance from several Julia Child scholars, who made my work on this biography so much easier. Laura Shapiro's wonderful portrait of Julia for the Penguin Lives series is as incisive as it is irresistible. Her writing in general about the incestuous *pas de deux* between food and culture is a valuable resource to any author. Alex Prud'homme's lovely memoir, *My Life in France,* written in collaboration with his aunt, was extremely helpful in capturing Julia's entrée into the world of cuisine, and his discussions with me were equally effective.

My deepest gratitude, as always, goes to my dear friend Sandy D'Amato, one of America's most distinguished chefs, who answered every question I had about food and cooking with his usual perceptive wisdom. William Grimes, the former food critic for *The New York Times* as well as one of my editors at the paper, came to my rescue at several culinary impasses. I also tapped into the collective brilliance of Rozanne Gold and Michael Whiteman, in addition to Fuchsia Dunlop, Marion Nestle, Joan Nathan, Nancy Silverton, Anne Willan, Jane and Michael Stern, and the late Michael Batterberry, all of whom contributed their food-related expertise. I would also be remiss if I didn't thank Henri Cointreau and Catherine Baschet for their hospitality at Le Cordon Bleu in Paris. The school has come a long way since Madame Brassart's reign of terror, and counts Julia among its emissaries in its more modern existence.

The McWilliams, Child, and Weston families were immensely supportive of this book, every step of the way. I'd especially like to express my appreciation to Phila Cousins, David and Rachel McWilliams, Saba McWilliams, Patti McWilliams, Carol McWilliams Gibson, Josephine McWilliams, James Alexander McWilliams, Erica Child Prud'homme, Rachel Child, Jon Child, David Brownell, Chris Crane, John Kittredge, Josie Green, and Alicia Crane Williams, the archivist for the Weston and Crane families. Duncan Kennedy, whose father, Robert Woods Kennedy, was almost like family to Julia and Paul, filled in special information about his grandmother, Edith, and the intellectual life of Cambridge in the 1930s.

Others who made a significant contribution to my work but, for one reason or another, weren't quoted in the text are: Kathi Alex at La Pitchoune, Fern Berman, Martha Coigny, Woody Fraser, Alexis Gelber, Tosca Giamatti, Gael Greene, Dorie Greenspan, Lauren Groveman, Barbara Haber, Susie Heller, Dick Holden, Sally Jackson, Jim Johnston, Kristyn Keene at ICM, Christopher Kimball, William Koonce, Jennifer Krauss, Lindsay Krauss, Susan Lewinnek, Dennis McDougal, Marilyn Mellowes at WGBH, Susan Patricola, Ken Schneider at Knopf, Chris Styler, Teri Taylor, Bern Terry, and, of course, William Truslow, Julia's lawyer.

I am grateful to Willa B. Brown, who assisted in all of my research at Harvard, and to Roberta Martinez for her intelligence-gathering in Pasadena. Lindsay Maracotta and Peter Graves provided me with a home away from home in California, not to mention their long and enduring friendship. Fred Plotkin and Jim Falsey weighed in regularly with encouragement and advice, and Neal Gabler, good friend and biographer extraordinaire, helped me to keep everything in perspective.

I have long depended on the sage advice and muscle of my literary agent, Sloan Harris, and the men and women at Knopf, who have worked hard on my book. I am especially indebted to my editor, Peter Gethers, for his prodigious efforts in shaping this manuscript, and to his long-suffering assistant, Christina Malach, as well as their new protégé, Jade Noik. Lastly, I would like to thank Carol Carson for a lovely jacket and Sara Eagle for getting out the word.

If a writer's work is only as valuable as those who encourage, sustain, and defend him, to that extent I am a wealthy man. My daughter Lily made every day precious and inspiring. And my parents—especially my mother, to whom this book is gratefully dedicated—motivated me always to follow my dream. Even so, I owe everything to my wife, Becky: my perspective, my well-being, my appreciation for everything that is right in life, to say nothing of her ability to come up with a better adjective when the situation demands it. This is her book as well as mine (and I hope she responds in kind when her book is published). Together, we're one hell of a team.

Few words can express adequately the satisfaction for such bounty, so I'll borrow Julia's most heartfelt expression of best wishes. Simply put— *bon appétit.*

Author's Note

It was originally my intention to include a selected bibliography as well as a complete set of notes so that the reader could identify the source of all factual material used in the book, and so that I could provide additional relevant information about Julia Child. Unfortunately, due to the extremely large volume of notes that ran more than seventy pages, the length of the book became unwieldy and unmanageable. As a compromise it was decided to separate the bibliography and notes from the text and put them online. This solution allows readers to browse freely through the material or to go directly to the notes for a particular page in the book. It is my hope that you'll find the notes to be an informative aid, but also an entertaining annotation to the text.

To access them, please go to: www.bobspitz.com/dearienotes.

Index

Page numbers in *italics* refer to illustrations.